POWER OF...

DR DOS

THROUGH VERSION

6.0

First edition—1991

ISBN 1-55828-182-7

Printed in the United States of America

10 9 8 7 6 5 4 3

MIS:Press books are available at special discounts for sales promotions, premiums, fund-raising, or educational use. Special editions or book excerpts can also be created to specification.

For details contact: Special Sales Director
MIS:Press
a subsidiary of Henry Holt and Company, Inc.
115 West 18th Street
New York, NY 10011

Dedication

For Julia Claire

Acknowledgments

I would like to thank the following people for their help and support during the preparation of this book:

My wife, Barbara, and daughters, Sarah and Julia, who arranged their days and nights around my writing schedule; Lily Lasker, who worked long evenings and weekends preparing the manuscript; the staff of MIS:PRESS, who, as always, provided expert advice and direction; and, the clients of *Integrated Knowledge Systems, Inc.*, who continue to present me with interesting and challenging problems.

Table of Contents

Introduction

The DOS operating system for personal computers was developed by the Microsoft Corporation for the first IBM-compatible PC, and has been the standard operating system for these PCs ever since. Microsoft has continued to evolve their releases of DOS, but in spite of their efforts, Digital Research has recognized many areas that could be improved. They have therefore developed and evolved their own version of the DOS Operating System for personal computers, known as DR DOS to distinguish it from MS DOS. This book will use the terms DR DOS, DR DOS 6.0, and DOS interchangeably—all three refer to DR DOS 6.0, the most recent release of DR DOS.

Since MS DOS set the standard for PC operating systems, DR DOS is carefully designed to be compatible with it in all significant ways. Any software that runs under MS DOS should run under DR DOS, and will sometimes run better because of the superior memory management and disk management capabilities of DR DOS.

There are three ways in which DR DOS differs from MS DOS: there are minor syntax differences in some of the commands; there are major extensions to many commands; and there are several powerful commands and utilities that are not provided with MS DOS. DR DOS 6.0 is a major step in the evolution of the DOS operating system for IBM-compatible personal computers. It adds numerous features and commands that permit far more control over the computer's use of memory and disks than any previous version. A few examples are: the MOVE command for moving files from one directory to another; the TOUCH command for changing the date and time stamp on files; the Diskopt utility, which is a disk optimization program for optimizing the organization of information on your hard disk; a complete on-line DOS reference manual; a superior task swapper for running multiple applications at once; and extensive password protection for locking your entire PC against intruders and for protecting individual files and directories. There are numerous other enhancements as well.

With this expanded power comes a price, however. In order to make full use of it, PC users will have to understand their computers better than ever before. This book is written with that need in mind.

The *Power of... DR DOS 6.0* is intended for all users of DR DOS 6.0 who know at least the basics of how to use their computer. The material is presented 'from the ground up,' assuming little or no familiarity with how personal computers work on the inside. Only after establishing a clear understanding of the basics are the advanced topics covered. Novice users will want to start with the fundamental material at the beginning of each chapter, and some may never find it necessary to go any further. Advanced users may want to skip some of the introductory material and go right to the advanced topics.

While each chapter can stand alone, the sequence of the chapters within the book provides a logical structure for learning DR DOS 6.0. If your goal in reading this book is to move from a novice to an advanced stage of understanding, then you may want to read the chapters in order.

Briefly, the chapters cover the following material:

Chapter One provides an introduction to the fundamentals of personal computers, explaining the various parts of the computer and the role that DOS plays in making them all work together.

Chapter Two discusses ViewMAX, which provides easy, intuitive access to DR DOS and to the programs installed on your computer. ViewMAX is menu driven, so it alleviates the need to memorize DOS commands, and makes it much easier to manage the disks and files in your computer. You may also run TaskMAX from within ViewMAX; TaskMAX lets you run more than one program at once, and switch back and forth between them. This chapter covers ViewMAX, and how to customize it to fit your own particular set of programs and work habits. Since ViewMAX provides access to many of the features of DR DOS 6.0 that are discussed in greater detail in subsequent chapters, this section also serves as an introduction to those features.

Chapter Three discusses TaskMAX, which is a utility that comes with DR DOS 6.0 that allows you to run multiple programs at the same time. For example, by using TaskMAX you could have your word processor, spreadsheet, and database applications all running at once, and switch between them at the touch of a key. TaskMAX makes use of whatever memory and hard disk resources your computer has, to make task switching as efficient and fast as possible. TaskMAX also provides the ability to cut information out of a screen in one program, and paste it into another program. This chapter covers TaskMAX from the ground up, explaining the basics of how to use it as well as advanced features and customization options.

Chapter Four provides a detailed explanation of the DOS command line, which is where you can enter DOS commands and run programs. Working at the command line gives you a finer level of control over your computer than ViewMAX provides.

Chapter Five explains the functioning and management of the one of the most important resources available to a computer: electronic memory. How DR DOS 6.0 controls these resources, and how you can fine tune that control, is also explained.

Chapter Six discusses files, directories, and their management. Files are the repositories of all of the programs and data that your computer uses. Directories provide the structure for keeping them organized on your disks. DR DOS 6.0 provides numerous commands to facilitate the creation and management of these structures.

Chapter Seven explains the functioning and management of another major resource in the computer: disk storage. Disk storage is often treated as part of the subject of files and directories, but this tends to obscure the fact that there are distinct issues surrounding each of these topics, and distinct DOS commands for dealing with them. This chapter provides a thorough presentation of the inner workings of disks and disk drives, and of the DOS commands used to maximize their performance.

Chapter Eight teaches you how to use EDITOR, the text editor that comes with DR DOS 6.0.

Chapter Nine explains BATCH files, which permit you to write programs using DOS commands. The creation and use of BATCH files is discussed in depth.

Chapter Ten discusses commands used to configure DOS to closely match your own working needs. As you use your computer and install new software and hardware on it, you will find that some programs and devices require special commands to be executed to configure the DOS environment properly. The kinds of settings you are likely to encounter and how they are installed is explained. DOS is configured using the CONFIG.SYS and AUTOEXEC.BAT file, both of which are discussed in this chapter.

Chapter Eleven provides a command dictionary for quickly identifying the syntax and usage of the most common DOS commands. While many of these commands are discussed in more detail elsewhere, this chapter provides the most convenient reference summary for them. The complete syntax of each command, a brief description of what it does, and a listing of parameters and switches, are given here. If you are familiar with the basics of a command, this chapter may contain all the information you need.

Each chapter is designed to lead you gradually from basic concepts to advanced material. Some chapters end with an *Advanced Topics* section, which discusses material that goes into more technical detail than is generally required for using DOS, but provides interesting background information.

While the material in each chapter is inevitably related to the rest of the book, the chapters are designed to stand on their own as much as possible. The book does not have to be read in sequence—you may want to jump from one place to another, learning the various aspects of DR DOS 6.0 as the need arises. For example, if all you want to do is to use ViewMAX to run programs and manipulate files, then you can refer directly to Chapter Two. However, if you are relatively new to personal computers, then you should read Chapter One, which presents the basic material essential to understanding the rest of the book.

DR DOS 6.0 is an exciting product. It provides better memory management, better file and disk management, and more commands and utility programs, than any previously released version of DOS. There is no other version of DOS that will let you get as much performance and efficiency out of your PC. This book is presented in the spirit of helping you get the most out of DR DOS 6.0 with the least amount of effort.

Chapter 1

Understanding Personal Computers and DR DOS 6.0

Computers are usually thought of as machines—collections of electronic and mechanical devices that interact with each other. This view only considers the hardware—the physical devices that make up the machine. A computer cannot accomplish anything without instructions, however, and there are even instructions that are built into the hardware. Most of the instructions that tell a computer what to do are referred to as software, because they come on disks and can be erased or changed without modifying the hardware. The instructions that are built into the hardware are called firmware, because they cannot be changed without modifying the hardware. It is most useful to think of a computer as the combination of hardware, software, and firmware. This chapter reviews the fundamentals of how a personal computer is organized, how it works, and what DR DOS 6.0 is and does. Readers who have a basic understanding of how Personal Computers work, and are familiar with other versions of DOS, may want to skim this chapter.

The words bits, bytes, kilobytes, and megabytes are used in many contexts when talking about computers, so it is important to have a clear understanding of what these mean. A computer is really just a huge collection of switches, each of which can either be off or on. The states of off and on correspond to the numbers 0 and 1. Consequently, all of the information in a computer is comprised of sequences of 0s and 1s. In other words, binary, or base two numbers. When operating on alphabetic characters, the computer represents the letter A by the number 65, which in base two is 01000001. So when an A appears on your screen, somewhere inside your computer is a set of switches in the following sequence: OFF ON OFF OFF OFF OFF OFF ON.

A single switch, or binary digit, is called a *bit*. Since a single bit is such a small amount of information, bits are organized into groups of eight (notice that eight bits were used to represent the letter A above, even though the left most one was a zero and therefore not numerically relevant). A collection of eight bits is called a *byte*. Bytes are sometimes also grouped together, into sets of two or four. These groups are called *words*. A word of two bytes is called a 16-bit word, while a word of four bytes is called a 32-bit word. Information is represented inside the computer as one or more bytes. All alphabetic characters require a single byte. The largest number that can be represented by a single byte is 255, so to store numbers larger than 255, and for *real* numbers, two or more bytes are used.

Since computers work in base two numbers, their storage capacities are measured in powers of the number two. That is why we commonly see the numbers eight (23), sixteen (24), thirty-two (25), sixty-four (26), etc. Two to the tenth is 1024. This number is pretty close to 1,000, so the term *kilobyte*, which literally means "1,000 bytes," is used to refer to 1024 bytes of information. Likewise, the term *megabyte* refers to 1024 squared, which is 1,048,576, or about one million bytes. Rather than spell out kilobyte and megabyte, the terms K and M, or KB and Meg, are commonly used. Thus, 640K or 640 KB refer to 640 kilobytes; and 4M, or 4 Meg, refer to 4 megabytes.

How Personal Computers are Organized

The hardware that defines a Personal Computer is organized into five primary parts, or groups of parts: (1) the CPU, or Central Processing Unit, and related circuits; (2) a monitor, or screen; (3) a keyboard; (4) one or more disk drives; and (5) electronic memory. There can be other hardware devices attached to the computer as well, such as printers, mice, and modems. These are referred to as *peripheral devices*.

Integral to the organization of the Personal Computer is the concept of *expansion slots*. In order to make the Personal Computer flexible and adaptable, it was designed to allow various parts to be replaced and upgraded without having to replace the entire computer. The core elements of the machine—the CPU, electronic memory, and other vital circuits that are not likely candidates for upgrading are placed on a single board, called the *motherboard*, that is permanently installed in the computer case. The rest of the circuits go on cards that plug into the *expansion slots*. Expansion slots are sockets on the motherboard, with space above them to accommodate circuit boards that plug into the sockets. When you hear reference to the *number of slots* a machine has, it means the number of expansion slots.

Expansion slots are used for a variety of purposes. If you want more electronic memory than can be stored on the computer's motherboard, you can install a card with additional memory in one of the expansion slots. The computer's disk drives and monitor both require special circuits to control them. These are placed on cards that plug into the expansion slots, making it easy to upgrade the disk drives and monitor without having to buy a new computer or replace the motherboard. You can even buy expansion cards that contain complete modems and hard drives.

Expansion slots come in different lengths, referred to as full length, three-quarters length, and half length. Often the internal design of a computer case does not leave room for a full length slot, but rather than waste that space, a shorter slot is provided. Not all expansion cards come in different lengths; some are only available in full-length versions.

The Central Processing Unit (CPU)

The CPU is the "brains" of the computer. Everything the computer does is directed by this chip (the word *chip* refers to integrated circuits, which are the devices that store electronic information and execute electronic instructions). There are two primary functions that the CPU carries out: (1) it directs information flow and coordinates the actions of other devices in the computer; and (2) it performs the actual computing steps involved in running software programs.

Since the CPU is the brains of the computer, it makes sense that it is the single most important hardware component—it defines the ultimate limits of what the computer can do. References to different types of IBM-compatible personal computers invariably make reference to the type of chip used for the CPU. The original IBM PC was introduced in 1981 and used a chip known as the 8088, manufactured by the Intel Corporation. The 8088 had a "big brother" named the 8086. Both chips were capable of 16-bit processing, which means that they could operate on information in chunks of 16 bits, or two bytes, at a time. These two chips were identical in all respects except one: the 8088 communicated with the rest of the computer in 8-bit, or 1-byte, chunks of information, while the 8086 communicated in 16-bit, or 2-byte, chunks. The 8088 was chosen for the first PC because it was less expensive to build a computer around an 8-bit communication path, or *bus*, than a 16-bit bus. Since the first PC was built, there have been a number of generations in this family of chips, each providing more power and sophistication than the previous one. In subsequent redesigns, the 8086 evolved into the 80286 (16-bit), 80386 (32-bit), 80486 (32-bit), etc.

The first chip to follow the 8088/8086 was the 80286. The 80286 was used to build the IBM-AT Personal Computer. This chip, which increased the amount of memory the computer could use, also performed computing and internal communication operations at much faster speeds than the original PC. The next chip to come along was the 80386. The 80386 not only provided dramatically higher operating speeds, but also vastly increased the amount of memory the computer could address. It provided the ability to operate on 32-bit chunks of information, and went from a 16-bit bus to a 32-bit bus, effectively doubling the speed with which it could communicate with other parts of the computer. The 80486 provided yet another leap in processing speed and also had specialized circuitry built into it for very high-speed mathematical processing—an ability that previously required purchasing a special add-on chip (the 80x87). The 80586 is currently in development, and Intel has drawn up the first plans for the 80686. This family of chips will continue to evolve, providing more and more computing power at lower and lower prices. Since the names of all these chips begins with 80, they are usually referred to simply by the last three digits—hence the common references to a "286 computer" or a "386 computer."

One of the significant features of the 80x86 line of chips is that they are all backward compatible. This means that all software that runs on 8088 machines will run on any PC that has one of these chips as its CPU.

In other words, each chip in the line can run software designed for earlier chips. The chips are *not* forward compatible—software written to take advantage of the special features of the 80386 chip will not run on 8088 or 80286 machines. Most software is still designed to run on the entire line of chips, but it is becoming more common for software to be designed to only run on the 80386 or later CPUs. In many cases, software developers will release two versions of their software—one which runs on any machine, and one which runs only on the higher-end machines.

Computer manufacturers and dealers typically refer to two aspects of the CPU when describing computers: the chip that the computer is built around, as discussed above, and the *clock speed* of that chip. Every computer has an internal clock—actually a specialized chip that creates electronic "ticks" at precise intervals. With each tick of the clock, the CPU moves forward one step in the sequence of instructions that it is executing. Consequently, the faster the clock, the faster the computer can carry out a given task. You cannot arbitrarily increase the clock speed of a computer, however, because every CPU has a maximum clock speed that it can handle.

The original IBM PC had a clock speed of 4.7 Megahertz (MHZ), or 4.7 million ticks per second. This seems like a lot, but the basic operations a CPU carries out are very simple. The commands we enter into the computer, and those that our software packages execute, are much more complex and are often broken down into hundreds or thousands of CPU operations. For much of today's sophisticated software, a 4.7 MHZ machine is agonizingly slow. As Intel developed new generations of chips in the 80x86 family, they also developed different versions of each generation. In most cases the difference between two versions of a chip is simply in the clock speed. The 80386 chip is available in 16 MHZ, 25 MHZ, and 33 MHZ versions. The 80486 is available in 25 MHZ, 33 MHZ, and 50 MHZ versions, with faster versions in development.

As the 80386 chip caught on and software was developed to take advantage of it, Intel recognized an undeveloped market—users who wanted to run software designed for 32-bit processing, but who could not afford the cost of a 32-bit computer built around the 80386. Remember that the 80386 chip uses a 32-bit bus, or communication path. The larger the bus width, the more expensive the computer. So Intel developed another version of the 80386, named the 80386SX. The relationship between the 80386SX and the 80386DX (as the original version came to be called) is the same as that between the 8088 and the 8086—the 80386SX uses a 16-bit bus, allowing manufacturers to build less expensive computers and still provide the 32-bit processing power of the 80386 chip.

The Monitor

There are really two hardware components to consider when discussing a monitor: the monitor itself, and the video card that drives it. There is usually nothing built into the computer itself that directly provides the output necessary to display an image on a monitor. That capability is provided by a video card. There is a good reason for this design: it allows you to upgrade your display without having to buy a new computer. As new and better monitor technologies have appeared, all that has been necessary to take advantage of them is to replace the video card and the monitor. When buying a video card and monitor, it is important to make sure they are well suited to each other—there is no point in buying a monitor that can display higher resolutions than the card can deliver, unless you intend to buy a better card later.

Monitor resolutions are described in terms of picture elements, or *pixels* for short. A pixel is the smallest area of the screen that the computer can display. Images, both text and graphics, are created as groups of pixels. The maximum resolution of a monitor is defined by the number of horizontal and vertical pixels that the monitor/video card combination is capable of displaying.

The original IBM PC had two options for the monitor: the MDA, or Monochrome Display Adapter, and the CGA, or Color Graphics Adapter. The MDA allowed only the display of text characters, which included a limited set of line-drawing characters. Its resolution was 720 pixels horizontally and 350 pixels vertically.

The CGA monitor allowed both text and graphics to be displayed, but the text was much lower resolution (320 x 200) than the Monochrome monitor provided and was therefore harder on the eyes. By today's standards the graphics capabilities were crude. As is typical of graphics cards and monitors, it has several modes, each of which offers a specific resolution combined with a maximum number of colors that can be displayed at once. There is a trade-off between resolution and number of colors, because there is only a certain amount of memory that is available to store all of the information necessary to display an image. If more of that memory is used for pixels—which means higher resolution—then less is available for color information.

The MDA and CGA were the first video standards for IBM-compatible personal computers. Since that time there have been a total of seven additional standards developed, each one offering more resolution and/or more colors than the previous one. The history of PC video standards, and their capabilities, is shown in Table 1.1.

Table 1.1 Evolution Of Video Displays

Name	***Year***	***Resolution***	***Modes***	***Colors***
MDA (Monochrome Display Adapter)	1981	720x350	Text	1
CGA (Color Graphics Adapter)	1981	640x200	Text	16
		320x200	Text	16
		160x200	Graphics	16
		320x200	Graphics	4
		640x200	Graphics	2
MGA (Hercules Mono. G.A.)	1982	720x350	Text	1
		720x348	Graphics	1
EGA (Enhanced Graphics Adapter)	1984	640x350	Text	16
		720x350	Text	4
		640x350	Graphics	16
		320x200	Graphics	16
		640x200	Graphics	16
		640x350	Graphics	16

Table 1.1 continued ...

Name	***Year***	***Resolution***	***Modes***	***Colors***
MCGA (Memory Controller Gate Array)	1987	320x400	Text	4
		640x400	Text	2
		640x480	Graphics	2
		320x200	Graphics	256
VGA (Video Graphics Array)	1987	720x400	Text	16
		360x400	Text	16
		640x480	Graphics	16
		640x480	Graphics	2
		320x200	Graphics	256
8514/A	1987	1024x768	Graphics	16
		640x480	Graphics	256
		1024x768	Graphics	256
Super VGA	1989	800x600	Graphics	16
XGA (Extended Graphics Array)	1990	1056x400	Text	16
		640x480	Graphics	256
		1024x768	Graphics	256
		640x480	Graphics	65,536

When reviewing VGA and Super VGA monitors, you will often hear reference to *dot pitch*. This is the size of the dots the monitor uses to display pixels. The smaller the dot pitch, the sharper the image.

As Table 1.1 shows, most video cards support a variety of modes. You can use DOS to shift the cards into their various modes, using the MODE command, which is discussed in Chapter 10.

The Keyboard

The keyboard is the most common device used to communicate with personal computers. The functioning of the keyboard is straightforward, but perhaps not quite as obvious as you might guess.

When you press a key on the keyboard, the corresponding character shows up on the screen, so it is natural to assume that, for example, the "A" key always means the letter "A." But in the spirit of keeping the computer flexible and adaptable, an additional step was inserted in the communication between the computer and the keyboard.

Every key on the keyboard has a *scan code*. The scan codes are just numbers, starting with one and ending with the number of keys on the keyboard. When a key is pressed, the scan code for that key is sent to the computer, where DOS reads it and interprets the code to have a particular meaning—for example, the letter "A." Some keys are designed to be used in combination with other keys. These are referred to as Shift keys—they shift the keyboard to have a different set of meanings. For example, the "A" key can mean either upper or lower case A, depending on the state of the case-shifting key, [symbol]. So when the keyboard sends a scan code to the computer, it also sends the shift states of each of the Shift keys. DOS interprets each key differently depending on the state of the Shift keys.

The keyboard also sends a key-released code to the computer when a key is released. In this way DOS can tell when a key is being held down, and repeat it - this is how the typematic action is accomplished on PC's. Since the repeat rate, and the amount of time you must hold down a key before repeating starts, is controlled by DOS and not the keyboard, it follows that this rate should be adjustable. And indeed it is, using the DOS MODE command.

Since it is the operating system that determines the meaning of the scan codes, it is easy to modify this meaning so that the same keyboard can be used for different languages. This can be accomplished with the DOS KEYB command.

The KEYB and MODE commands are discussed in Chapter 10.

There is a large variety of keyboard layouts today, particularly among laptop computers. But at least for desktop machines, nearly all are identical or very similar to the layout shown in Figure 1.1, which is known as the Enhanced Keyboard Layout.

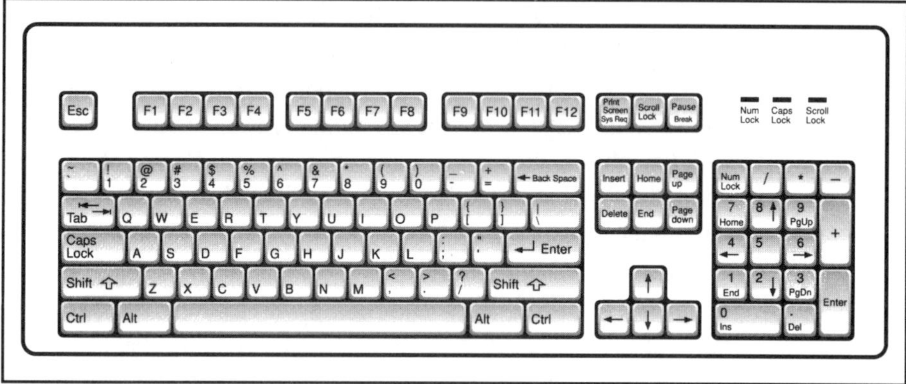

Figure 1.1 Enhanced Keyboard Layout.

While keyboards remain the predominant method of communicating with the computer, a number of other technologies have appeared that are becoming increasingly important. The most common of these is the mouse, which is essential for running graphics programs, such as computer-aided design (CAD) packages, and graphical environments such as Microsoft Windows. For situations in which desk space is very limited, an alternative to the mouse is the trackball. A trackball is like an upside down mouse; the ball is on top, and instead of moving the device around the desk, you roll the ball under your palm. It is not as convenient or easy to use as a mouse, but in tight spots it is an acceptable alternative.

Disk Drives

Disk drives are used for permanent storage of information. For example, when you save a file in your word processor, it is saved on a magnetic disk. There are three main reasons that disk drives are used: they provide *nonvolatile* storage, which means that the information on them is not lost when you turn off your computer; they provide the capability to store large quantities of information at low cost; and they provide a convenient way of transporting information between computers. For example, when you purchase a new software program, it comes on a magnetic disk.

Computers can accomplish only two tasks with disk drives: they can read information from the disk into memory, and they can write information onto the disk from memory. Anything else the computer does with the information stored on a disk must be done with a copy that is read into memory.

Disk capacity is measured in kilobytes and megabytes. Because electronic memory is also measured in kilobytes and megabytes, and because both disks and memory store information, people sometimes confuse the two. The essential difference between them is that disks are used for permanent storage of information, whereas memory is used to temporarily store information while the computer acts on it. Everything in the computer's memory is lost when you turn the power off. Everything on the disks remains.

There are two types of disks: floppy disks and hard disks. Floppy disks are inserted into disk drives on the front or side of your computer. There are two physical sizes of floppy disks: $3^1/_2$ inch and $5^1/_4$ inch. For $5^1/_4$ inch disks there are five different capacities supported by DR DOS 6.0, depending on the number of sides that can be used and the density of the magnetic particles. For $3^1/_2$ inch disks there are three different capacities supported. Both sides of $3^1/_2$ inch disks are always usable. The different sizes and capacities are shown in Table 1.2.

Table 1.2 Floppy Disk Capacities

Disk Size	***No. of Sides***	***Capacity***
$5^1/_4$ inch	1	160K
$5^1/_4$ inch	1	180K
$5^1/_4$ inch	2	320K
$5^1/_4$ inch	2	360K
$5^1/_4$ inch	2	1.2M
$3^1/_2$ inch	2	720K
$3^1/_2$ inch	2	1.44M
$3^1/_2$ inch	2	2.88M

The 160K, 180K, 320K, and 360K $5^1/_4$ inch disks, and the 720K $3^1/_2$ inch disk, all have a low density of magnetic particles, and are therefore used with low density drives. The 1.2M $5^1/_4$ inch and 1.44M $3^1/_2$ inch disks both have a high density of magnetic particles and therefore require high density drives. The 2.88M $3^1/_2$ inch disk requires yet another type of drive, specially made to handle its very high capacity. High density disk drives can read and write both low and high density disks, but low density drives can only read and write low density disks.

Unlike floppy disks, which can be easily removed from a computer, hard disks are permanently installed. They have two main advantages over floppy disks: they can store much more information; and they can move information to and from electronic memory much faster. Recall that the computer can only operate on information that has been copied from a disk into memory. Since the computer operates at electronic speeds, the mechanical processes of reading from and writing to disks is the slowest operation the computer performs. Because hard disks are extremely fast at reading and writing, compared to floppy disks, this speed increase alone is enough to justify their existence.

Hard disks come in many sizes. The smallest is 10 megabytes, but you rarely encounter hard disks that small anymore. Sizes today range from 20 up to 650 megabytes and more.

Disk drives are referred to by letters of the alphabet. If a computer contains two floppy drives, they are probably referred to as drive A and drive B. If a computer contains a hard drive, that drive is almost always referred to as drive C. If a computer contains only one floppy drive and a hard drive, the floppy drive is generally designated to be both A and B, while the hard drive is drive C. Additional drives are referred to as D, E, F, etc. When specifying a drive, the letter is followed by a colon. Thus, you type A: to reference drive A.

Information on disk drives is stored in structures called *files*. There are essentially two types of files: executable files and data files. An executable file instructs the computer to do something. A data file contains information that an executable file can manipulate. An example of an executable file is a word processor program; an example of a data file is a letter you write in your word processor.

DOS refers to files by their file names, which consist of two parts: a name and an extension, separated by a period. The name can include up to eight characters. The extension, which is optional, can contain up to three characters. The extension is commonly used to indicate the type of information stored in a file—you may use the extension LET for all of the files that contain letters you have written. Examples of file names are WP.EXE and JIMSMITH.LET.

Several extensions have special meaning to DOS, and therefore should not be used for other purposes. These special extensions are EXE, COM, BAT, and SYS. All of these refer to files that DOS can execute. In fact, DOS cannot execute a file whose name does not end with one of these extensions. All software programs—word processors, spreadsheets, database managers, etc.—are executable files with extensions of either EXE or COM. Files with BAT extensions are *batch* files, which consist of batches of one or more DOS commands that are executed in sequence. It is a simple task to create your own batch files, and they are discussed in detail in Chapter 9. The fourth extension, SYS, refers to files that contain special commands used by DOS when you start your computer. These are discussed in Chapter 10.

On hard disks, where the number of files can be quite large, files are organized into tree structures called directories. Files and directories are discussed in detail in Chapter 6.

Electronic Memory

Memory refers to electronic storage locations inside the computer. Memory is measured in bytes, kilobytes, and megabytes. The computer keeps track of what is in memory, and where it is located, by assigning an *address* to each byte in the computer. The amount of memory the computer can make direct use of is determined by the CPU and the operating system. The determining factor in how much memory the computer can use is the size of the address the CPU and operating system are capable of referencing.

The 8088 CPU chip used by the original IBM PC could reference a 20-bit address. This meant the largest address the computer could use was at the one megabyte position (2^{20} is 1 megabyte). Because the original version of DOS for personal computers was intended for this PC, DOS was also designed to use a 20-bit address. This limited DOS to addressing a maximum of 1 megabyte of memory. In fact, DOS was actually designed to be able to use only the first 640K of memory for programs and data—the rest was reserved for special system functions, such as video memory. At the time, 640K seemed like a ridiculously large amount of memory for a personal computer - most PCs were shipped with 128K or 256K of memory, and required expansion boards to add more than that.

The 80286 chip has a 24-bit address bus. This allows the chip to recognize up to 16 Megabytes of memory. The 80386 and 80486 chips have 32-bit address busses, which means they can address up to 4,294,967,296 bytes, or 4 gigabytes, of memory. Unfortunately, it is much easier to change the design of the computer than the design of the operating system, so even DR DOS 6.0 must still struggle with fitting all of its program instructions and data into the one-megabyte address space. A number of schemes have developed, and become industry standards, for helping programs exceed this limit while still using DOS as the operating system. DR DOS 6.0 has been designed to facilitate these schemes, which are discussed in detail in Chapter 5.

There are two types of information that can be stored in memory: instructions that the computer executes, and data that the computer operates on. Regardless of the nature of the information, it must be read into electronic memory before the computer can do anything with it. One of the interesting things about the design of computers is that the same memory is used for both programs and data. Memory is treated as one large pool, to be divided up as needed. When you run a program, the instructions for the program are read into memory, and whatever is left over is used for data. Since there is frequently not enough room in memory for all of the data a program needs, software has ways of moving information between the disk and memory as it is needed. There are ways of configuring DR DOS 6.0 to increase the efficiency of this process. How all of this is managed is discussed in later chapters.

DOS

As stated earlier, the CPU is the hardware component that controls and coordinates all of the other parts of the computer. But if the CPU is the brains of the computer, then the Disk Operating System (DOS) is its mind—the knowledge, rules, and quirks that collectively define how the computer will behave all reside in DOS. DOS is the software that tells the CPU how to control and coordinate all the various tasks the computer carries out.

DOS is referred to as a *disk* operating system because it is permanently stored on disk, rather than in the computer. This is one of the design features of the IBM PC that make it so flexible—if you want a different operating system, or a new version of DOS, you simply start the computer with the appropriate disk (a process known as *booting*).

When you boot your computer, one of the first things it does is load some of the DOS programs from disk into memory. Until these programs are loaded this is all the computer knows how to do. Control of the computer is then transferred to one of these programs. From then on, everything the computer does is controlled by DOS. If you enter a command to run your word processor, it is a DOS program that interprets your request, loads the program, and tells the computer how to execute it. While the word processor is running, it makes use of a number of services that DOS provides, such as displaying things on the screen, receiving commands from the keyboard, and sending output to the printer. When the word processor is finished, control is returned to DOS, which then waits for another command from the keyboard. DOS can therefore be thought of as a master program which controls everything else the computer does.

DOS actually consists of a large number of programs, which fall into two broad categories. The first category consists of the programs that are essential for the computer's operation—the ones that receive keyboard input, read and write disks, etc. These programs are used by other programs; they are not invoked by typing commands in directly from the keyboard. The second category is a set of programs that can be thought of as utilities, which are provided to make your life easier by automating a lot of tasks. Examples of these are the DIR program, which displays a list of the files that are on a disk, and the DR DOS Editor, a mini-word processor that comes with DR DOS 6.0.

The DOS programs that are loaded into memory when the computer boots remain in memory until the computer is turned off. Other DOS programs remain on the disk, and are only loaded when you run them, just like any other software. The programs that are stored in memory are the ones that provide the essential operations necessary for your computer to function, and the utility programs that are used most often, such as the DIR program. The programs that are left on the disk are generally used less often.

The reason for not loading all of the DOS programs into memory is that they take up space. Recall that DOS can only make use of a maximum of 640K of memory for programs and data. When DOS is loaded, it takes some of that memory for itself. So the more DOS programs there are in memory, the less space there is for other programs to run. DR DOS 6.0 is one of the few versions of DOS that can actually load most of itself into memory that lies outside of the conventional 640K, leaving more of the 640K available for your programs and data.

DOS is not the only operating system that will run on IBM-compatible personal computers, but it is far and away the most common. Examples of other operating systems that can run on personal computers are Unix and OS/2. If a different operating system is used, then all of the commands you learn for DOS will be useless and none of your software will work, unless the operating system is specifically designed to mimic DOS. Unix is quite different from DOS; OS/2 has been designed as an evolution from DOS and therefore has some similar commands. It also includes a *DOS window* which behaves just like DOS and allows you to run DOS programs.

DOS was originally designed as a *command line* operating system, which means that you had to type in a command to make the computer do anything. This meant memorizing a great many commands, and keeping a good mental picture of how your files were organized on your hard disk. DR DOS 6.0 includes a program named ViewMAX, which provides a graphical user interface to DOS. This means that you can carry out most tasks without entering commands. Instead, graphic symbols on the screen indicate the various tasks you can perform, and show how files are organized on your disks. You can select tasks and files using a mouse. Consequently, there are now two quite different ways of accessing the many features of DOS: via the command line, and via ViewMAX. Each has its own place in the world of computing; both are covered in detail in the following chapters.

Chapter 2

Using ViewMAX

For many users of personal computers, ViewMAX may be the single most important facility provided by DR DOS 6.0. ViewMAX does away with the necessity of memorizing DOS commands, and remembering the details of how a hard disk is organized. It provides menu-driven screens, with on-line help, for running programs and managing disks. This chapter will explore ViewMAX in detail, discussing all of its features and explaining how to customize it to fit your own particular needs. In order to understand how ViewMAX works, it is necessary to have a basic understanding of DOS directories and files. This subject is briefly covered below, in the section *Managing Files And Directories*, and is discussed in detail in Chapter 6.

The best way to learn about ViewMAX is to experiment with it. As you read through this chapter, you are encouraged to take the time to try out the various features. ViewMAX requires a graphics adapter and monitor in order to work. If your system has a text-only monitor, you will have to upgrade in order to use ViewMAX.

Overview of ViewMAX

ViewMAX provides a graphical view of your disk drives, files, and directories. The screen is divided into different areas that can be used to display the drives installed on your PC, the directory structures of those drives, and the files and sub-directories present in a directory. If, during installation of DR DOS 6.0, you indicated that ViewMAX should come up automatically when the computer starts, then when the computer is booted, the first screen to appear will be the ViewMAX screen. If ViewMAX does not automatically appear when you boot your computer, it can be brought up by entering the following command at the C:> prompt:

```
VIEWMAX
```

When ViewMAX first starts, the screen is divided into two halves, the top and the bottom. In either half of the screen, there may be one or two windows present. For each window there are several distinct areas. The ViewMAX screen that appears the first time ViewMAX is started appears in Figure 2.1.

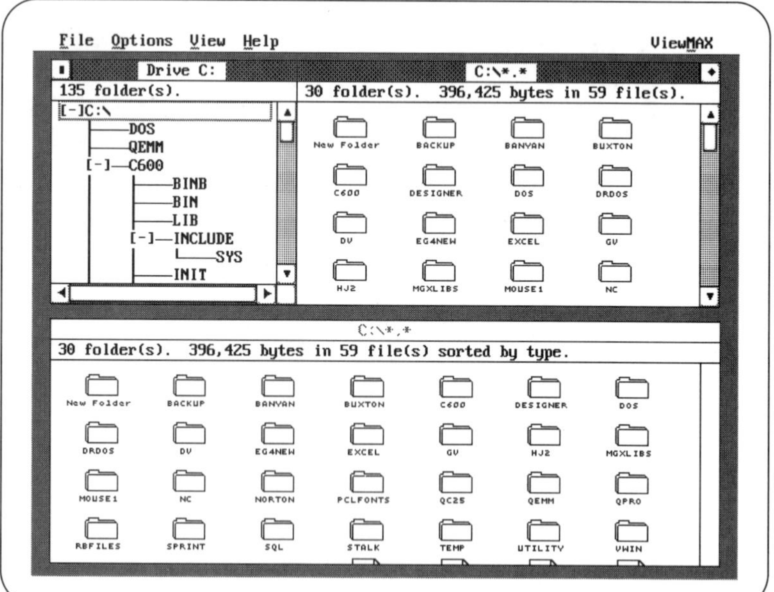

Figure 2.1 ViewMAX Screen

In order to be as intuitive as possible, ViewMAX refers to DOS directories as *folders* and uses graphical icons to represent them. Different types of files may also be given different icons, in order to see quickly what their purpose is. Assigning icons to files is discussed later in this chapter, in the section *Setting The Icons For Applications And Documents*. The icon for folders can be seen in the upper right window of Figure 2.1, where 16 folders are displayed.

The names of the folders and files that appear on the ViewMAX screen will be different on each PC, but the windows that make up the screen will be the same. When ViewMAX starts, as shown in Figure 2.1, the screen contains the following areas:

- The Menu Bar, which appears along the top line of the screen and is like a master control center for ViewMAX. It provides access to a variety of features available for manipulating folders and files, running programs, and customizing ViewMAX.
- The upper left window, which shows a tree representation of the folders (directories) on the currently selected disk drive.
- The upper right window, which shows the folders and files that are contained in the folder that is selected in the left window.
- The bottom window, which in Figure 2.1 displays the same information as appears in the upper right window.

For each window there is a title bar which indicates the nature of the contents of the window. In Figure 2.1, the title bar for the upper left window says "Drive C:", indicating that the tree structure which appears in that window is on drive C. The title bar for the right window shows the complete path name of the folder whose contents are displayed in the window.

For each window there is an information line, which provides summary information about the contents of the window. In Figure 2.1, the information line for the upper left window says "135 folder(s).", indicating that there are 135 folders, or directories, in the tree structure in the upper left window. The information line for the upper right window informs you that there are 30 folders and 59 files in the displayed folder, and that the files occupy a total of 396,425 bytes of disk space.

The screen shown in Figure 2.1 is the default ViewMAX startup screen. The two windows in the top half of the screen work together—the right window displays the contents of the folder selected in the left window. The bottom window initially has the same contents as the upper right window. However, the bottom window can be also split into two windows, and different drives and/or folders can be displayed on each half of the screen. The top and/or bottom halves of the screen can also be changed to show the different disk drives that are present. Thus, the bottom window and the top window can display information about different parts of your system at the same time.

When you modify ViewMAX, as discussed throughout this chapter, you may save the modifications in a special file named VIEWMAX.INI. This file is read each time ViewMAX is started, so you always come back to the last configuration you saved. If your screen does not appear as shown in Figure 2.1, it is because the last time the ViewMAX configuration was saved, the screen layout was different from the default startup screen. Saving your configuration in VIEWMAX.INI is discussed in the section *Managing The ViewMAX Environment*.

When ViewMAX starts, it reads the entire directory structure on the disk. While it is doing this, it displays a dialog box in the middle of the screen, showing its progress. This may take a little time, depending on the type of PC and its configuration. You have to wait for ViewMAX to finish reading the disk before you can use any of the ViewMAX features.

Navigating in ViewMAX

There are several ways of getting around in ViewMAX and using its various features. All of them rely on one of two tools: the keyboard and the mouse. You can make good use of ViewMAX even if you do not have a mouse, and some tasks are more easily carried out by the keyboard even if you do have a mouse. However, there are some tasks that are definitely easier with a mouse, and some require a mouse, so if you anticipate using ViewMAX a lot, and you don't have a mouse, it is worth getting one.

Using ViewMAX Menus and Dialog Boxes

The top of the ViewMAX screen always displays the Menu Bar. The menu bar consists of several options, each of which has a drop-down menu that contains choices that can be selected. The menu bar is circled in Figure 2.2.

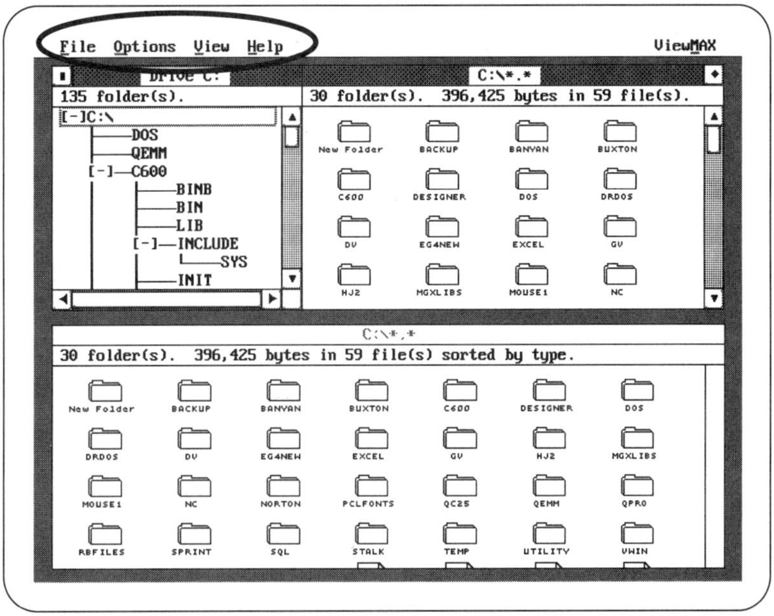

Figure 2.2 ViewMAX Menu Bar

The menu bar is activated in either of two ways: simply moving the mouse pointer over one of the options causes the corresponding drop-down menu to appear; and with the keyboard, holding down the Alt key and pressing the letter that is underlined on one of the options causes the drop-down menu for that option to appear. For example, pressing the Alt+F key combination will display the File menu. Once a drop-down menu is displayed, the left and right arrow keys can be used to display the other drop-down menus. The ViewMAX menu bar with the File menu displayed is shown in Figure 2.3.

There are several variations on how items may appear on a menu:

1. Some of the menu options may be followed by an ellipsis (...). This means that a dialog box will appear when the option is selected. The dialog box will prompt you for some type of information. In Figure 2.3, the Open/Run, Find, and Copy options are a few examples of menu options that bring up dialog boxes.

2. Some of the options on a menu may not be available. This is dependent on what window is active when the menu is pulled down. If an option is currently unavailable, it will be appear in light gray.

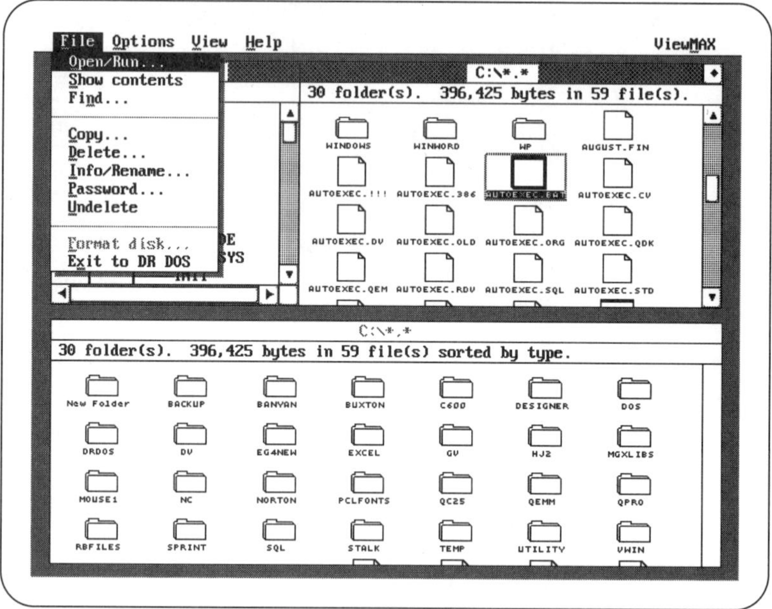

Figure 2.3 File Menu On ViewMAX Screen

In Figure 2.3, the *Format disk ...* option is not available. Attempting to select it will have no effect.

3. Some menu options are switches—they turn a feature on or off. When one of these menu options is turned on, a right-pointing arrowhead appears to the left of it.

There are three ways to select items on a menu:

1. You may use the up and down arrow keys to move the highlight bar from one option to the next. From the top of the menu, the Up arrow key causes the highlight to jump to the last menu item. From the bottom of the menu, the Down arrow key causes the highlight to jump to the first menu item. When you have highlighted a menu option in this way, press the Enter key to select it.

2. Each menu item has one letter highlighted. This letter is the *hot key* for that item and pressing it causes the highlight to jump immediately to that item and execute it.
3. If you are using a mouse, you may position the mouse cursor on a menu item. Clicking once on the item will cause the highlight bar to jump to it and execute it.

When ViewMAX requires some input from you in order to carry out a task, it uses a dialog box. There are five devices used within dialog boxes to capture your input: data entry fields, check boxes, scroll bars, exit buttons, and option buttons. A dialog box always has at least one exit button. In addition, it may also have any combination of the other four devices. For example, consider the "File Information/Rename" dialog box, shown in Figure 2.4.

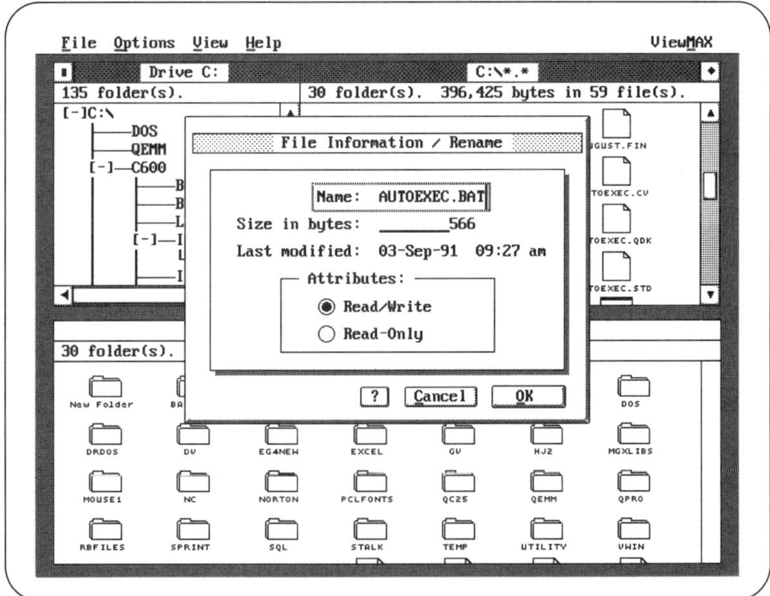

Figure 2.4 File Information/Rename Dialog Box

This dialog box is used to rename a file, or to change its attributes (file attributes are discussed below, in the section *Managing Files In ViewMAX*, and in Chapter 6). It contains a data entry field labeled "Name:", two option buttons labelled "Read/Write" and "Read-Only", and three exit buttons labelled "?", "Cancel", and "OK". The selection frame can be moved from one item to the next using the Tab, Shift+Tab, up arrow, and down arrow, keys.

When the "File Information/Rename" dialog box appears, the "Name:" field is selected. This field is where you can type a new filename. The cursor may be moved through the text with the right and left arrow keys. Text in dialog box data entry fields is always entered in Insert mode—if you position the cursor in the middle of existing text, whatever you type will not overwrite what is already there, but will be inserted into the existing text. The delete key and the backspace key can be used to delete individual characters in a data entry field. To delete the entire line of text, press the Ctrl+Backspace key combination.

The option buttons in Figure 2.4 appear as small round buttons, which indicates that they are mutually exclusive - selecting one deselects the other. In Figure 2.4, the "Read/Write" button is selected. The "Read-Only" button may be selected by moving the selection frame to it and pressing the Space bar, or by clicking the mouse pointer on it. This will automatically deselect the "Read/Write" button.

Exit buttons are used to leave a dialog box. Like option buttons, exit buttons can be selected by moving the highlight to them and pressing the Spacebar, or by clicking the mouse pointer on them. When the name of an exit button includes an underlined character, holding down the Alt key and pressing the underlined character selects that button. For example, in Figure 2.4, the Cancel button has the C underlined, so holding down the Alt key and pressing the C key selects the Cancel button.

The "?" button provides context-sensitive help: it pops up an information box that tells you what the dialog box is used for. The Cancel button closes the dialog box and ignores any changes you made in it, and the OK button closes the dialog box and carries out any changes you made. For example, if you changed the name of a file and selected Cancel, the file would not be renamed; if you selected OK it would be renamed.

The "TaskMAX Preferences" dialog box, in Figure 2.5, shows the last two devices used in dialog boxes: check boxes and scroll bars.

The check box in Figure 2.5 is labelled "ViewMAX controls TaskMAX?". The box is blank, indicating that the corresponding function is turned off. To turn it on, press the spacebar, or click on the box with the mouse pointer. An X will appear in the box, indicating that the function has been turned on.

The scroll bar at the bottom of the screen is labelled "Maximum Allowed LIM Memory Use". Scroll bars are used in several ways in ViewMAX screens, so they are discussed in the following section.

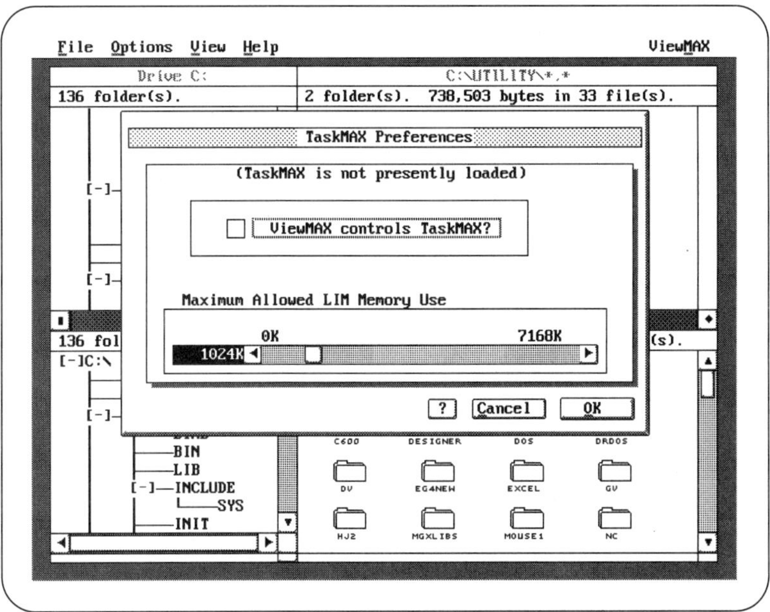

Figure 2.5 TaskMAX Preferences Dialog Box

Using Scroll Bars

There is a vertical scroll bar along the right edge of each ViewMAX window. When two windows are displayed in either the upper or lower half of the screen, there is also a horizontal scroll bar along the bottom edge of the left-hand window. In Figure 2.1, the vertical scroll bars appear in a hatch pattern. Near the top of the vertical scroll bars is a small rectangular box. On a color monitor the scroll bar and the small box may appear either gray or in color, depending on the color scheme you select. The small box is called the slider, because it can be slid along the scroll bar to display items that don't fit in the window. When the slider is smaller than the scroll bar, as in Figure 2.1, the list of items in the window is too long to fit on one screen. The size of the slider indicates the percentage of the entire list that is visible on the screen, and the position of the slider indicates the section of the list that is visible. For example, the scroll bar for the upper left window in Figure 2.1 indicates that about one-eighth of the directory tree is visible, and that the portion that is displayed is the top of the list. If the entire list is visible, the slider will fill the scroll bar.

When a slider is shown, a mouse can be used to scroll up and down through the list. There are three ways to do this:

1. Position the mouse pointer on the slider, and hold down the left mouse button. The slider can now be dragged up and down (or left and right in a horizontal scroll bar) with the mouse. When the mouse button is released, the display changes to show the section of the list represented by the new position of the slider.
2. Position the mouse on one of the arrows at the ends of a scroll bar. Clicking the left button once will scroll the list in the direction indicated by the arrow. On vertical scroll bars, the list will move one line. On horizontal scroll bars, the list will move one character. Holding the button down while the pointer is on an arrow will scroll the list continuously.
3. Position the pointer anywhere on the scroll bar above or below the slider. Briefly clicking the button will scroll the list one full window toward the mouse pointer. Holding he button down will scroll the list continuously, one window at a time, until the slider meets the pointer.

There are four ways of using the keyboard for scrolling:

1. The Up arrow key and the Down arrow key scroll the Selection Frame up and down through the list one item at a time. When the frame is at the top or bottom of the window, the contents of the window scroll.
2. The right and left arrow keys scroll the Selection Frame right and left one item at a time. When the frame is at the left or right edge of the window, the contents of the window scroll.
3. PgUp and PgDn scroll through the list one full window at a time.

4. Ctrl+PgUp and Ctrl+PgDn scroll the list left and right one full window at a time.

Moving Around the ViewMAX Screen

At any given time, either the top half or the bottom half of the screen may be active. You can tell which half is active because the Title Bar for the windows in that half of the screen will be highlighted. Within the active half of the screen, one window will be the active window. This is the window in which you may select items, and to which menu choices will apply.

Within the active window, there is a currently selected item—the program you are going to run, or the folder or file you are going to display or manipulate. A Selection Frame indicates the currently selected item. The Selection Frame appears as an outline around the selected item. In Figure 2.1, the Selection Frame is on the first folder (C:\) in the tree.

If you are using a mouse, the mouse pointer appears in addition to the Selection Frame. The mouse pointer is represented by an arrow that points toward the upper left corner of the screen. It is the Selection Frame, not the mouse pointer, that indicates a currently active window. The mouse pointer can be anywhere on the screen, but it has no effect until you click the mouse button, which moves the Selection Frame to the window that contains the mouse pointer. When you use the mouse to move the selection frame to a new window, the frame moves to the item in the upper left corner of that window, regardless of what item the mouse pointer was clicked on. Once the window with the mouse pointer is current, the mouse can be used to select a new item.

As an alternative to using the mouse, the Tab and Shift+Tab keys can be used to move between windows. When ViewMAX starts, the upper left window is active, and the top folder of the current drive is selected. Pressing the Tab key moves the Selection Frame to the upper right window, making that the active window. The currently selected item will be the first folder (labelled "New Folder") in that window. Pressing the Tab key again moves the Selection Frame to the bottom window.

Within the active window, the arrow keys are used to move between items. If you have a mouse, then you can jump directly from one item to another, by positioning the mouse pointer on the new item and clicking the left mouse button.

Changing and Updating the Window Display

When ViewMAX starts, the display looks similar to Figure 2.1. This screen provides a particular view of some of the information available within ViewMAX. However, there may be times when this is not the most convenient view. For example, to work on file management it would be helpful to see more of the tree structure and file list than this view affords. There are several different ways in which the display can be adjusted, allowing you to change the size and contents of the different windows. Any of these changes may be selected from the View menu, shown in Figure 2.6.

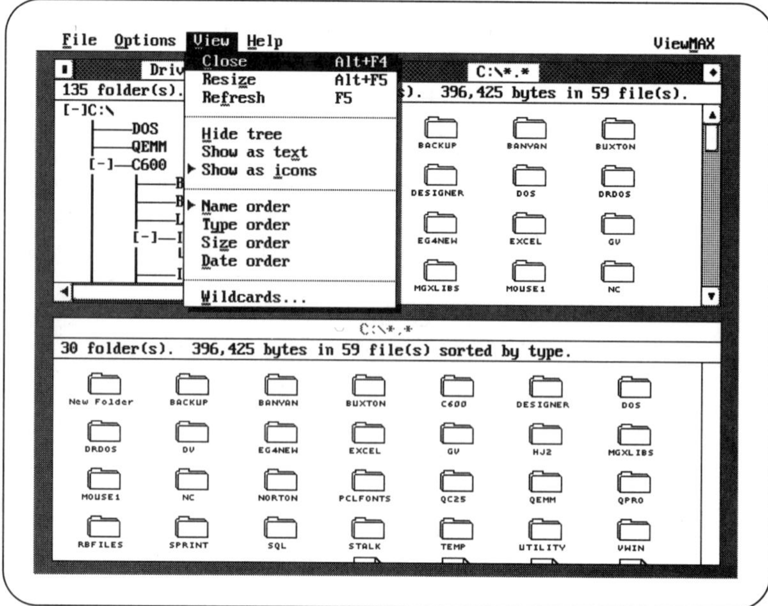

Figure 2.6 ViewMAX View Menu

The View menu is divided into four boxes. The top box contains three options that affect the physical characteristics of the active half of the screen. The second box contains three options that affect the appearance of the active half of the screen. The third box contains four options that determine how the names of files and folders in the right hand window are sorted. And the bottom box contains one option which allows you to limit the folders and files that appear in the right hand window, based on their names.

Depending on which window is active, some of the options on the View menu may not be available. If they are not available, they will appear in light gray, rather than black, letters. All of the options are available when the upper right window is selected, so that window will be used for the following discussion.

To change the view, highlight your choice on the View menu and press the Enter key, or double click on the choice with the mouse pointer.

Options on the View Menu

The Close option closes the currently active area of the screen—either the upper half or the lower half. Closing an area of the screen changes the display of the current folder to the display of the previously selected folder. When the display is closed on the last folder that ViewMAX remembers, it is replaced by a display of all the disk drives on the computer. The last folder remembered by ViewMAX will depend on how many folders you have displayed, and on what operations you have carried out between changes to the display. ViewMAX stores as many folders as it can in memory, but some actions require it to release that memory to carry them out.

To close the lower half of the screen, move the Selection Frame to a window in that area and select Close from the View menu. When the disk drives are displayed, the screen will appear similar to that in Figure 2.7.

There are two shortcut options for closing the current area of the screen: the Alt+F4 key combination can be used, or you may click the mouse pointer on the small box at the left end of the title bar. This box is called a *close box*, and acts as a button to close the corresponding half of the screen.

To restore the file list, or to display a list from another drive, select the drive that contains the files to be displayed and press the Enter key. Alternatively, you may select the drive and choose the Show Tree option on the View menu.

The Resize option on the View menu acts as a *toggle switch* for the inactive half of the screen. For example, if the upper half is active, selecting the Resize option will cause the lower half to disappear, thus providing a full screen for the display of the tree and file list in the upper half. Choosing Resize again will restore the lower half of the screen. Shortcuts for Resizing the screen are the Alt+F5 key combination, and clicking the mouse pointer on the small diamond in the upper right corner of the right-hand window.

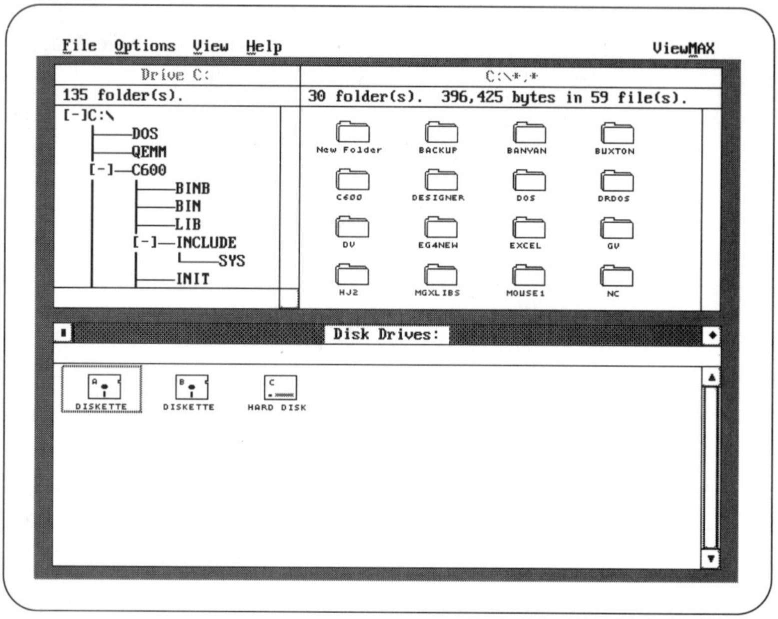

Figure 2.7 ViewMAX Screen with Disk Drive List Displayed

When ViewMAX starts, it reads all of the directory and file names on the disk and constructs the tree and file list that appear in the upper left and right windows. If you replace the diskette in a floppy drive, the change will not be reflected in the tree and/or file list windows, since it happened after the contents of those windows were constructed. To bring these windows up to date, you must force ViewMAX to reread the drive. This can be done either by choosing the Refresh option from the View menu, or by pressing F5.

The Hide Tree option on the View menu changes the current half of the screen to remove the tree display, thereby providing more space for the file list display. When the tree is hidden, this option on the View menu changes to "Show tree".

The "Show as text" and "Show as icons" options on the View menu are mutually exclusive: selecting one deselects the other. The currently selected option has a small arrowhead next to it; in Figure 2.6, "Show as icons" is selected. Icons are small pictures that indicate the type of object, as well as its name. They can only be used to indicate files and folders, so these options are not available when the tree window is active—folders in the tree must always be displayed as text. Switching to "Show as text" changes the display to that shown in Figure 2.8.

When the file list is displayed as text, there is some additional information provided which is not shown when icons are used. In Figure 2.8, the date of last modification for each folder and file can be seen. If you hide the tree as well, there is room for even more information to be displayed. Figure 2.9 was created by choosing the Resize option to use the entire screen to display the upper windows, then the Hide Tree option to hide the tree, and the "Show as text" option to display the folders and files in text form.

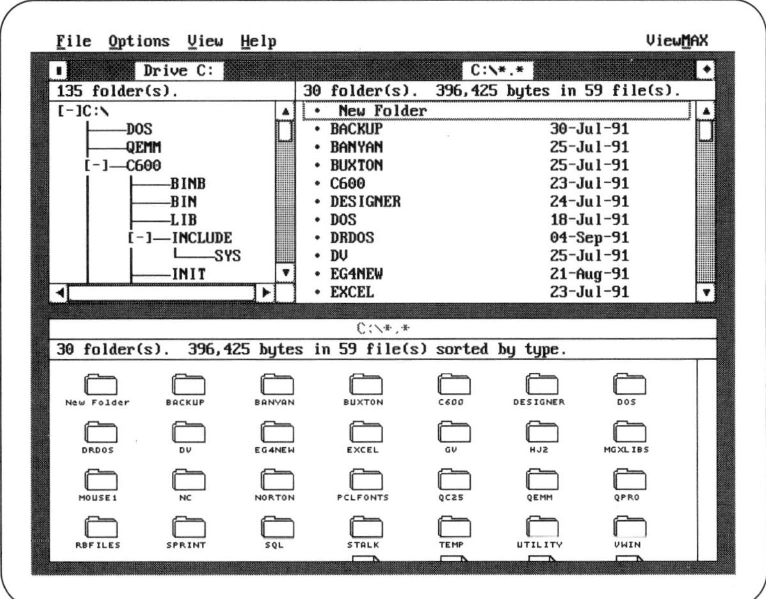

Figure 2.8 ViewMAX Screen in Text Mode

In addition to the date of last modification, the time of last modification and the attributes for the folder or file are also shown. Folders are identified in two ways: the "Directory" attribute is set, as indicated by the "d" in the right-hand column, and there is a small diamond to the left of the folder's name.

The four items in the third section of the View menu represent different ways in which the folders and files in the right hand window will be sorted. These four options are mutually exclusive—only one can be selected at at a time. When ViewMAX is first started, the "Name order" option is selected, which sorts the folders and files according to their names. The Type option sorts the files according to their extensions, because the file extension normally indicates the type of file. For example, a BAT extension is used to indicate a batch file. When the Size option is selected, folders are grouped together and appear first, but are not sorted by size. Files appear after the folders, and are sorted by size. When the Date option is selected, folders are also grouped together and appear first, but in this case they are sorted by date, followed by the files, which are also sorted by date.

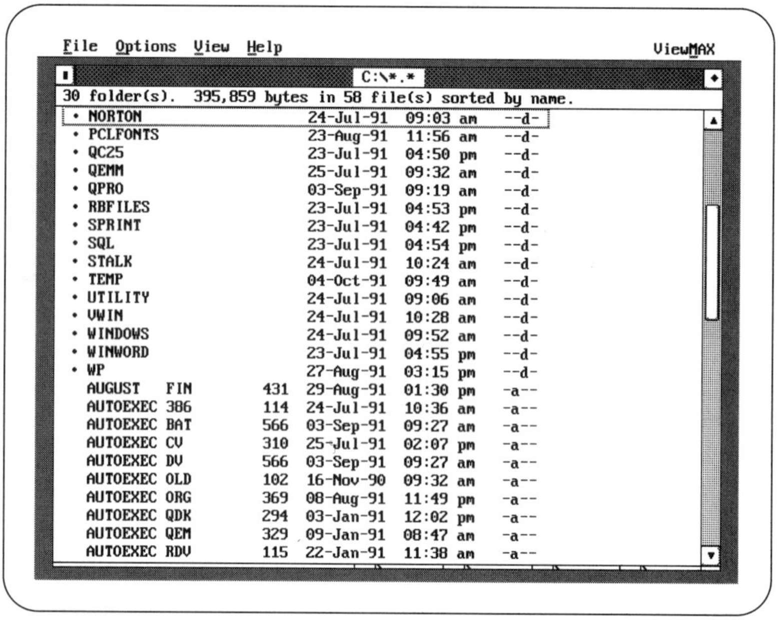

```
File  Options  View  Help                                          ViewMAX
                              C:\*.*
30 folder(s).  395,859 bytes in 58 file(s) sorted by name.
 • NORTON                    24-Jul-91  09:03 am   --d-
 • PCLFONTS                  23-Aug-91  11:56 am   --d-
 • QC25                      23-Jul-91  04:50 pm   --d-
 • QEMM                      25-Jul-91  09:32 am   --d-
 • QPRO                      03-Sep-91  09:19 am   --d-
 • RBFILES                   23-Jul-91  04:53 pm   --d-
 • SPRINT                    23-Jul-91  04:42 pm   --d-
 • SQL                       23-Jul-91  04:54 pm   --d-
 • STALK                     24-Jul-91  10:24 am   --d-
 • TEMP                      04-Oct-91  09:49 am   --d-
 • UTILITY                   24-Jul-91  09:06 am   --d-
 • VWIN                      24-Jul-91  10:28 am   --d-
 • WINDOWS                   24-Jul-91  09:52 am   --d-
 • WINWORD                   23-Jul-91  04:55 pm   --d-
 • WP                        27-Aug-91  03:15 pm   --d-
   AUGUST   FIN        431   29-Aug-91  01:30 pm   -a--
   AUTOEXEC 386        114   24-Jul-91  10:36 am   -a--
   AUTOEXEC BAT        566   03-Sep-91  09:27 am   -a--
   AUTOEXEC CV         310   25-Jul-91  02:07 pm   -a--
   AUTOEXEC DV         566   03-Sep-91  09:27 am   -a--
   AUTOEXEC OLD        102   16-Nov-90  09:32 am   -a--
   AUTOEXEC ORG        369   08-Aug-91  11:49 pm   -a--
   AUTOEXEC QDK        294   03-Jan-91  12:02 pm   -a--
   AUTOEXEC QEM        329   09-Jan-91  08:47 am   -a--
   AUTOEXEC RDV        115   22-Jan-91  11:38 am   -a--
```

Figure 2.9 Full File List in Text Mode

The last option on the View menu, "Wildcards...", is used to restrict the files that are shown in the right-hand window to those whose names match a certain pattern. Patterns are defined using the DOS *wildcards*—an asterisk (*) and a question mark (?). Folders are not affected by the wildcards setting—all folders appear regardless of their name. When the wildcards option is selected, the dialog box in Figure 2.10 appears.

The * is referred to as the "many" wildcard and it means: any set of characters can go here. For example, to indicate all files that have an extension of LET you would enter *.LET. This means: select files that have any name, as long as the extension is LET. Files named R.LET, R10.LET, and ROBERT.LET would all appear in the right-hand window. You could also select all files that begin with the letter R and have any extension by specifying R*.*, or files that begin with R and have an extension of LET by specifying R*.LET. You cannot, however, specify *R.* because DOS won't know where in the name the R should occur. Consequently, when this setting is used, DOS ignores all files and displays only folders.

The ? is referred to as the "single" wildcard and it means: any single character can go here. For example, specifying R?.LET would select R1.LET and RA.LET, but not ROB.LET. Unlike the *, the ? can be both preceded and followed by other letters. Question mark and asterisk wildcards can also be mixed in a single file specification.

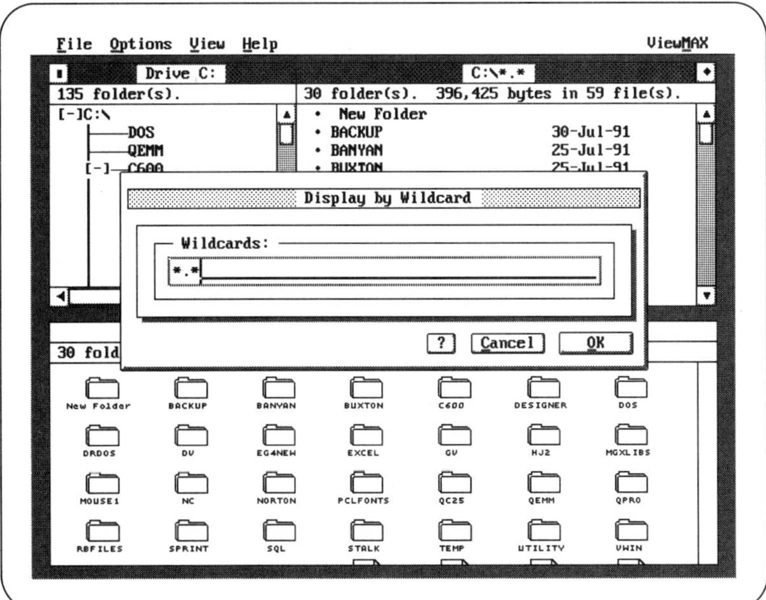

Figure 2.10 ViewMAX Wildcard Dialog Box

Figure 2.11 shows several legal file specifiers, and some sample file names that would be selected by them.

File Specifiers	*Sample Files Selected*		
?OB.LET	BOB.LET	DOB.LET	FOB.LET
*.DBF	A.DBF	BOOK.DBF	XYZ.DBF
R?B.*	RAB.	RIB.X	ROB.LET
B??K*.*	BEAK.FY	BOOK.LET	BOOK12.DBF
B*.?ET	BAR.BET	B.GET	BOOK.LET

Figure 2.11 Examples of Filename Wildcards

As shown in Figure 2.10, the default value for the Wildcards setting is *.*, which means that all files will be shown.

Selecting Disks

To display the contents of a different drive than the one currently displayed, you must repeatedly close the active half of the screen until the list of disk drives appears. The active half of the screen may be closed by pressing Alt+F4, selecting the Close option on the View menu, or clicking on the Close box in the upper left corner of the active area. Each time you "close" the display, it changes to show the previously selected folder. When you get back to the first folder displayed, closing the display brings up the list of disk drives.

The display will change to show a list of all the drives installed on the PC, as in Figure 2.7. The contents of the selected drive can be displayed using one of the following techniques:

1. Double clicking the mouse pointer on the drive icon.
2. Selecting the drive icon and pressing the Enter key.
3. Selecting the drive icon and choosing the Tree option on the View menu.

When ViewMAX reads the contents of a disk, it attempts to store the entire list of folders and the files they contain in memory. (If you have a large hard disk with a lot of folders and files, or a small amount of available memory, a message will be displayed indicating that there is not enough memory to display all of the folders and files). Since there are two areas on the screen (the upper and lower halves) for displaying the contents of disks, ViewMAX can display the contents of up to two disks at once. When ViewMAX starts, it places the contents of the current drive in both areas. You may change either or both of these areas to store the contents of a different drive. ViewMAX will attempt to remember the contents of previous drives that were displayed, but depending on the number and size of drives you have, it may not always be able to do so. If ViewMAX does not have enough free memory available to store an additional drive, it will release the memory for a drive that is no longer displayed. The next time you display that drive, ViewMAX will have to re-read it. Because it can be time-consuming to read an entire hard disk, it is important to keep this in mind when displaying different drives—it may not always be worth the wait to change.

Since keeping track of the folders and files occupies memory, when you perform operations in ViewMAX that require memory to be available, the list of folders and files is released. For example, running a program or executing a DOS command from within ViewMAX will release the memory so that the program or command will have as much memory as possible. This means that when the program or command is finished, ViewMAX must re-read the contents of the disk. This can take time, particularly on a slower computer with a large hard disk, but there is no way to avoid it.

Exiting ViewMAX

You may exit ViewMAX to work at the command prompt in either of two ways: permanently or temporarily. There are several reasons for wanting to work at the command prompt: you may find it faster to type in specific commands than to navigate through menus; you may want to free up the memory that ViewMAX occupies, to provide more memory for a program; or you may want to use DOS commands that are not available within ViewMAX.

When you exit ViewMAX temporarily, part of it remains in memory, allowing you to return to it very quickly. This is convenient if you have just a few tasks to do at the command prompt and want to come back to ViewMAX. The disadvantage is that leaving part of ViewMAX in memory uses up about 17.5K of memory that would otherwise be available for programs.

To temporarily exit ViewMAX, drop down the Options menu and choose the "Enter DR DOS commands" choice at the bottom of the menu. After a moment ViewMAX will disappear and the traditional command prompt will be displayed. To return to ViewMAX from the command prompt, type

```
EXIT
```

and press the Enter key. ViewMAX will return to the screen.

It is worth understanding how this works. The principle is the same for any program that has the ability to temporarily exit to the command prompt. There is a DOS program named COMMAND.COM that is loaded into the computer's memory at boot time. COMMAND.COM interprets the commands that are sent to the computer. This includes commands that come from programs, so when a program is running, COMMAND.COM is needed to manage the program's execution. ViewMAX is a program, so it requires the attention of COMMAND.COM. When you exit ViewMAX temporarily, ViewMAX is still in memory and therefore continues to require COMMAND.COM's attention. But the reason for exiting to the command prompt is to type in more commands. Since the copy of COMMAND.COM that was loaded when the computer was started is tied up monitoring ViewMAX, another copy of COMMAND.COM must be loaded into memory.

This second copy of COMMAND.COM is unaware that ViewMAX is in memory, and is therefore free to monitor the commands typed in at the keyboard. COMMAND.COM takes up about 2.5K of memory, and ViewMAX takes up about 14.7K. So when you temporarily exit ViewMAX, the total memory required is about 17.2K. Because of minor inefficiencies in the way in which these various programs load into memory, there are a few extra tenths of a K used up, and almost exactly 17.5K is lost to ViewMAX.

In most cases you can afford to sacrifice 17.5K because it is not a tremendous amount of memory. But if you don't intend to return to ViewMAX, or if that 17.5K is important, then you can permanently exit ViewMAX. This removes ViewMAX entirely from memory. To get back to ViewMAX requires running it again, by entering the ViewMAX command at the command prompt. To permanently exit from ViewMAX, drop down the File menu by holding down the Alt key and pressing the F key, then choose the "Exit to DR DOS" option at the bottom of the menu.

Getting On-line Help in ViewMAX

There is on-line Help available within ViewMAX, and there are two ways to get to this Help: choosing the Help option on the Menu Bar; or selecting the ? option in a dialog box. The first option is like opening a book to its table of contents; the drop-down Help menu shown in Figure 2.12 is displayed.

There are four options on this menu: Menus, Dialogs, Windows, and Trees. Choosing any one of these will bring up a Help screen that has information on the keys used to work with the selected subject.

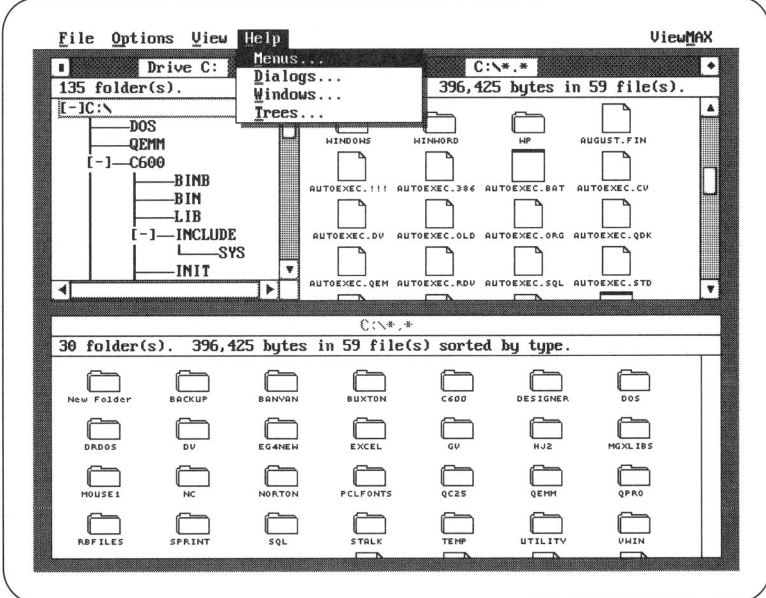

Figure 2.12 ViewMAX Help Menu

More detailed help can be obtained by using the second option for on-line help—selecting the ? option in a dialog box. This displays a context-sensitive Help box, which means that the Help box that appears pertains to the dialog box that is currently displayed. For example, if the "File Information/Rename" dialog box (Figure 2.4) is displayed, and the ? exit button is selected, the Help box in Figure 2.13 appears.

All Help boxes contain an exit button labelled "OK". This button is used to close the help box and return to the dialog box.

Selecting Items on the ViewMAX Screen

Items that may appear in the various ViewMAX windows are disk drives, folders, and files. You must select an item before you can work with it. When an item is selected, the box defined by the Selection Frame reverses colors, to display white letters against a black background. There are two ways to select an item: use the Up and Down arrow keys to move the Selection Frame to the desired folder and press the Spacebar, or move the mouse pointer to the item and click the left mouse button. Once an item has been selected it can be worked with. For example, after a folder in the left-hand window is selected, pressing the Enter key changes the right-hand window to display the contents of the selected folder. (If you are using a mouse, double clicking on an item has the effect of selecting the item and pressing the Enter key).

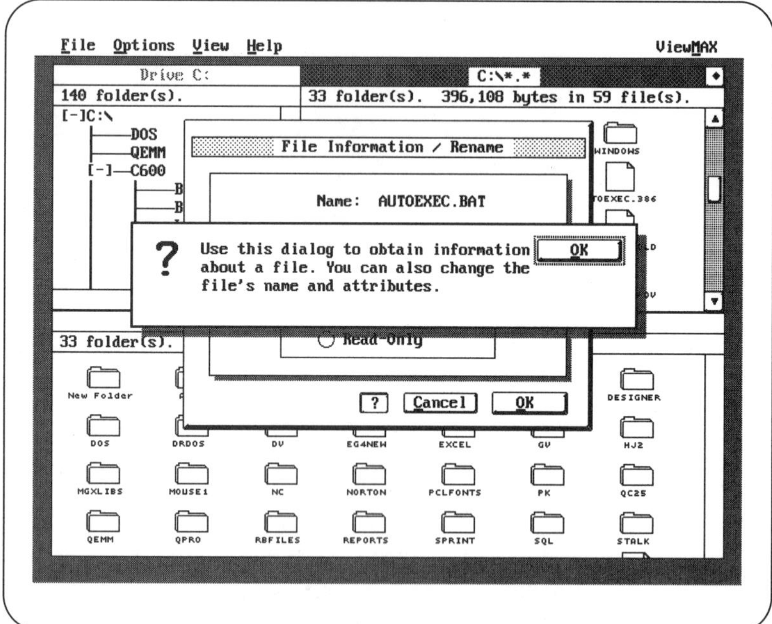

Figure 2.13 Help Box for File Information/Rename Dialog

Some actions can affect several items at once. For example, you may want to delete a number of folders and/or files. Rather than having to select and delete each one separately, you may select all of the items that you want to delete, then choose the Delete option on the File menu to delete all of them in one step.

The mouse and the Spacebar function a little differently when selecting multiple items. If you are using the Spacebar, you may simply move the Selection Frame to each item that you want to select and press the Spacebar - the previously selected items will remain selected. With the mouse, however, selecting one item deselects the previous item. There are two ways to get around this: the first is to hold down the Shift key while selecting items with the mouse. This prevents previously selected items from being deselected. The other is use to a feature known as *rubber banding*. If you position the mouse pointer between items and hold down the left button, a tiny rectangle will appear at the tip of the pointer. Moving the mouse down, and/or to the right, will enlarge the rectangle, as though it is made of a stretchy rubber band, which is where the term *rubber banding* comes from. The rectangle can only be enlarged down and to the right; moving the mouse pointer to the left or above the starting point will not enlarge the rectangle. You may stretch the rectangle to touch one or several items; when you release the mouse button, each item that was touched will be selected. Note that you do not have to completely enclose an item in the rectangle - it merely has to be touched by it to be selected.

When drawing a rubber band rectangle, ViewMAX pays no attention to window boundaries—it is actually possible to draw a rectangle that extends outside the current window, but only items within the current window will be selected—items outside of the current window are ignored, even if they appear inside the rectangle.

The mouse+shift key and keyboard techniques for selecting items may be used in combination. Some items may be selected with the mouse+shift key, and others with the Spacebar. To use the rubber band technique in combination with the others it must be used first, followed by whatever other technique(s) you want to use. This is because the instant you click the mouse pointer on a space between items, as you must do to draw a rubber band rectangle, all selected items are deselected—even if the shift key is held down. Consequently, you can only use the rubber band rectangle to select an initial group of items.

Scrolling the window immediately deselects any selected items, so you may only select items that all appear in the window at once. Consequently, if you want to select a lot of items, it is wise to resize the window (using the Resize option on the View menu, or by pressing the Alt+F5 key combination, or double clicking the mouse pointer on the small diamond in the upper right corner of the right-hand window), to use the whole screen for a single list. Also, if you are selecting items in the right-hand window, you should make sure they are displayed as icons, rather than as text, because more items fit on the screen as icons than as text. (The View menu contains the "Show as text" and "Show as icons" options).

Changing the current window also deselects all selected items, so you must perform any desired actions on selected items before moving to another window.

Managing Folders (Directories) in ViewMAX

The commands on the File menu are used for managing directories and files. Although directories and files are discussed in detail in Chapter 6, a brief introduction is necessary here in order to understand the file management features of ViewMAX.

All of the software programs used on Personal Computers, and all of the data stored on Personal Computers, are kept in files on magnetic disks. If you write a letter in your word processor, the letter will be stored in a disk file. The word processor itself consists of one or more files that contain instructions for the computer to execute. When Personal Computers first appeared, few of them had hard disks. Organizing and keeping track of files was relatively easy, because a single disk generally had only a handful of files on it. All of the files on a particular disk were usually related in some way, and the label stuck to the front of the disk was sufficient for indicating what the disk held.

With the increasing use of hard disks, however, things changed. To begin with, a hard disk is permanently installed inside your computer, so there is no way to attach a physical label to it. Furthermore, hard disks can contain more than a thousand files, and the files will not all be related. Some will be for a word processor, some for a spreadsheet, some for the DOS programs, and so on. It therefore became necessary to provide some means of managing all this.

DOS has the ability to group the files on a disk into directories. A directory can contain files and subdirectories. The subdirectories in turn can contain files and subdirectories of their own. This creates a branching structure of directories. You give the directories their names, and you decide what files will go into them, so you can create whatever file organization works best for you. Directories may be created on any kind of disk, floppy or hard, regardless of its size. Since a directory contains files, it is somewhat analogous to a file folder, so ViewMAX refers to directories as *folders*.

In order to manage a directory structure, DOS must be able to locate it and make sense of it. Before a disk can be used with DOS, the disk must be formatted. During the formatting process DOS creates something known as the *root directory* on the disk. The root directory always occupies a particular location on the disk so DOS can always find it. The size of the root directory depends on the type of disk; with a 360K floppy disk, the root directory can contain a total of 112 files and subdirectories. Most hard disks have root directories that contain 512 files and subdirectories. Root directories are always named by the letter of the drive, followed by a colon and a backslash. For example, C:\ is the root directory of drive C.

A directory is really just a kind of file—it stores the names and locations of the files that belong to it, and the names and locations of its subdirectories. The root directory is the only one that has a limit placed on how many files and subdirectories it can contain. There is no limit to the number of files and subdirectories that can be stored in any other directory. This provides a very flexible structure for organizing the files on a hard disk.

The terms directory and subdirectory are somewhat interchangeable: a subdirectory can be thought of as the directory of the files and subdirectories that it contains, and as the subdirectory of its parent directory. The root directory cannot be a subdirectory because it has no parent. In ViewMAX, the word *folder* is used in place of the words *directory* and *subdirectory*, and the term *main folder* is used in place of the term *root directory*.

The left-hand windows of the ViewMAX screen show a graphical representation of the folder structure of a disk. Figure 2.14 shows the ViewMAX screen with the entire screen used to display the tree and file list for a typical hard disk.

The tree structure of the folders can be seen here: C:\ is the main folder. It contains numerous other folders: DOS, QEMM, C600, etc. Some of these folders also contain folders. For example, the C600 folder contains nine folders: BINB, BIN, LIB, INCLUDE, INIT, HELP, SOURCE, PG, and TEMP. Some of these, in turn, contain folders of their own. The right-hand screen shows the contents of the currently selected folder.

Creating Folders

The right-hand window displays the items in the folder that is selected in the left-hand window. The first item in the right-hand window is always labelled "New Folder". It does not represent a real folder, but rather is used to create new folders. To add a new folder, select "New Folder" and press the Enter key, or double click on it with the mouse pointer. The "New Folder" dialog box shown in Figure 2.15 appears.

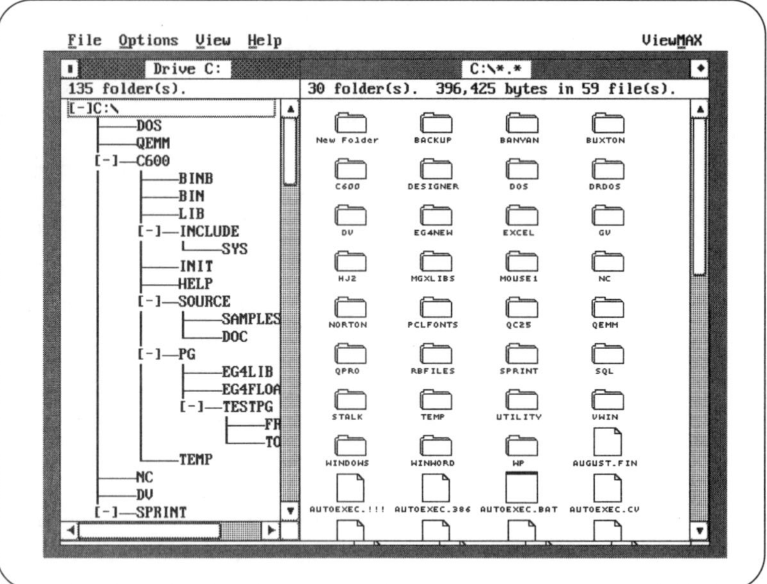

Figure 2.14 Tree and File List of Typical Hard Disk

Folders are named according to the same rules as files: a name consisting of one to eight characters, followed by a period and an optional extension of one to three characters. When entering the name in the "New Folder" dialog box, the cursor jumps to the extension area when eight characters have been entered for the name, or when a period is typed. While extensions are allowed for folder names, the industry standard is to leave them off. Folder names with extensions are practically never seen.

Folder names must be unique, within the folder in which they occur. For example, in Figure 2.15, there is a folder named BACKUP. You cannot create another folder named BACKUP in the current folder, because DOS would have no way of keeping track of them. A folder named BACKUP could be created in another folder, say the one named BANYAN which appears next to the BACKUP folder, as long as BANYAN didn't already have a folder named BACKUP in it.

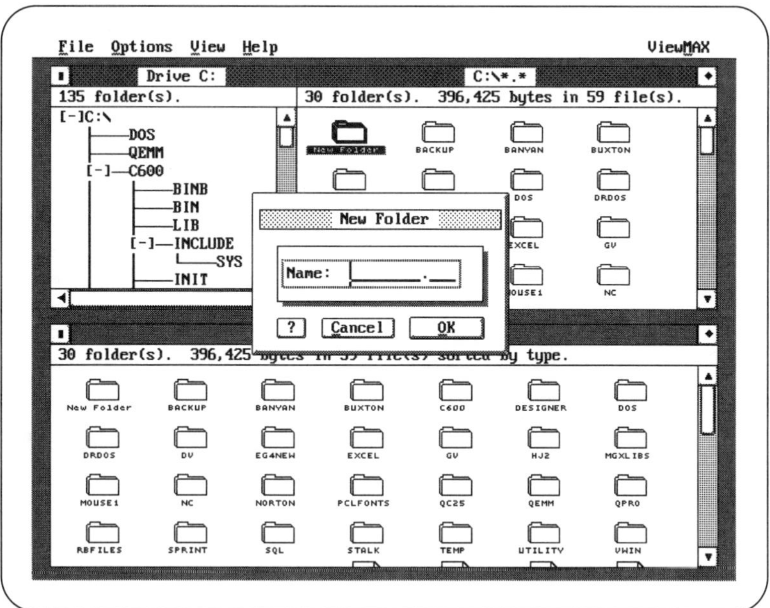

Figure 2.15 New Folder Dialog Box

Besides the problem of duplicate names, there is one other problem that may arise when creating a new folder: the disk may be full. Folders occupy disk space, even if they are empty, so there must be some disk space available before you can create a new folder. If either of these problems occurs when you attempt to create a new folder, the warning dialog box in Figure 2.16 appears.

It is easy to tell if the folder name is a duplicate—simply check the folders that appear in the right-hand window. If the name is not a duplicate, then the problem is that there is no free disk space, and you will have to delete one or more files or folders before you can create new ones.

It is possible, though rare, that the warning box in Figure 2.16 will appear because of an error that occurred when DOS checked the disk. Such errors can occur for a variety of reasons—there may be a hardware problem developing, or there may have simply been a random electronic event that caused a momentary miscalculation. While such events are statistically improbable, they do occur once in a great while. Consequently, you may choose the Retry option in the dialog box, to make sure the problem is real and not the result of such an event. If you frequently get this warning box, and the Retry option works, you should have your computer checked out, because it is likely that a problem is developing with the disk.

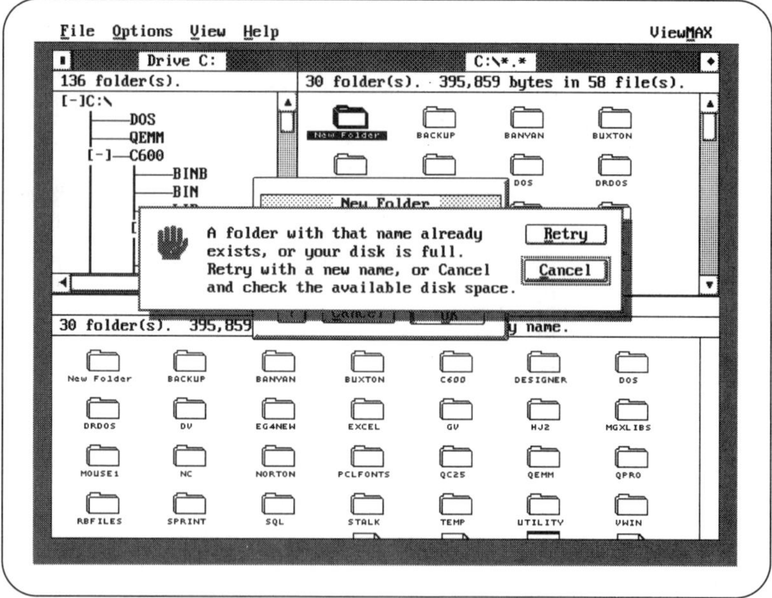

Figure 2.16 Duplicate Name/Disk Space Warning

Deleting Folders

The Delete option on the File menu is used for deleting folders. Folders to be deleted may be selected in either the left-hand or right-hand window. To delete one or more folders, select them and choose the

Delete option on the File menu. The Delete option acts on all selected items.

Note that the Delete option on the File menu is disabled if the main folder is selected. DOS depends on the presence of the main folder for disk management functions, so the main folder must always exist. If you have selected several items and the Delete option is not available, check to make sure that the main folder s not one of the selected items.

The steps for deleting a folder are:

1. Select the folder(s) to be deleted, either with the keyboard or the mouse.
2. Press Alt+F, or move the mouse pointer to the word File in the menu bar, to drop down the File menu.
3. Press D, or click the mouse pointer on the Delete option. This will pop up the "Delete Folders/Files" dialog box (Figure 2.17), unless you have turned off the Confirm Deletes option (discussed later in this chapter in Managing The ViewMAX Environment). If Confirm Deletes is off, the folder will be deleted without showing the dialog box.
4. If the "Delete Folders/Files" dialog box appears, press the Enter key, or select the Yes button to delete the folder and update the display.

When a folder is deleted, everything in it is deleted as well. Consequently, the "Delete Folders/Files" dialog box shows the total number of folders and files that will be deleted. In Figure 2.17, there are two folders (the one being deleted, plus one that it contains) being deleted, plus three files, which reside in one or the other of the two folders.

You should be cautious when deleting folders, since it is possible to delete a tremendous amount of information if the folder contains many folders and/or files. It is particularly important to make sure the Confirm Deletes option is turned on when deleting folders, so you get a chance to catch a mistake. In general, this option should be left on, and only turned off for specific delete operations that you are certain you don't want confirmed.

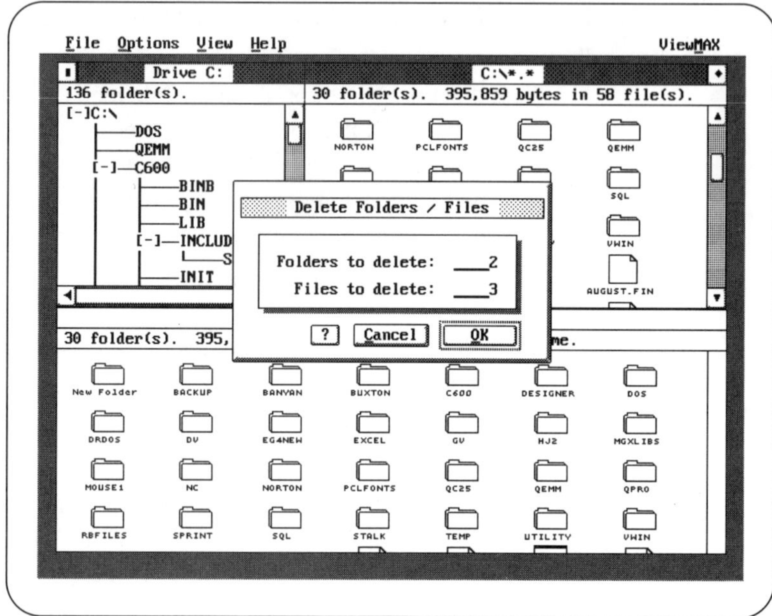

Figure 2.17 Delete Folders/Files Dialog Box

Renaming Folders

Folders may be renamed using the Rename option on the File menu. Selecting Rename pops up the "Folder Information/Rename" dialog box, shown in Figure 2.18.

This dialog box displays the current name, the date the folder was created, the numbers of folders and files it contains, and the total number of bytes in its folders and files. There is a data entry field for entering a new name. The steps for renaming a folder are:

1. Select the folder to be renamed, either with the keyboard or the mouse.
2. Press Alt+F, or click the mouse pointer on the word File in the menu bar, to drop down the File menu.
3. Press I, or click the mouse pointer on the Info/Rename menu option to pop up the "Information/Rename Folder" dialog box.
4. Enter the new name for the folder in the Folder name: data entry field.

5. Press the Enter key, or select the OK button. The folder will be renamed and the windows will be updated to reflect the change.

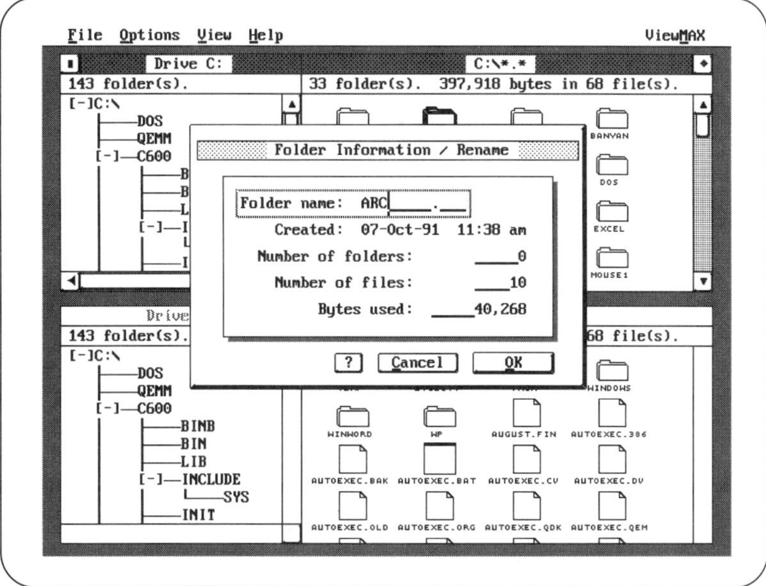

Figure 2.18 Rename Folder Dialog Box

Expanding and Collapsing Folders

In Figure 2.14, the left window is displaying the top section of the folder tree, so the first folder shown is the main folder, C:\ . Beneath this there are folders contained within the main folder: DOS, QEMM, C600, and so on. Scrolling down will reveal more folders.

When you start ViewMAX, the tree is fully expanded, which means that all folders are shown. In Figure 2.14, seven of the folders in the tree have a minus sign (-) in the square brackets next to them: C:\ , C600, INCLUDE, SOURCE, PG, TESTPG, and SPRINT. The minus sign indicates that they contain folders, and that the folders are displayed on the screen. If a folder contains other folders, but they do not appear on the screen, then a plus sign (+) appears instead of the minus sign. The tree can be collapsed, to show only folders that are nested to a certain level beneath the main level, or to show only the main folder and those folders that are nested beneath a particular folder. In order to expand

and collapse the tree, the left window must be active. Expanding and collapsing the tree can be accomplished with either the keyboard or the mouse.

There are basically three states of expansion that can exist for a folder:

1. It can be completely collapsed, so that none of the folders it contains appear in the tree.
2. It can be expanded to one level, so that those folders that it contains appear in the tree, but the folders contained within those folders do not appear.
3. It can be fully expanded, so that all folders that stem from it appear in the tree.

Any of these states can be set with one or two keystrokes or mouse clicks. The Selection Frame must first be moved to the folder on which you want to operate. You don't have to actually select the folder—i.e., you don't have to press the Enter key after it has been selected, but you do have to move the Selection Frame to it.

If the tree beneath the selected folder is completely collapsed, so that a plus sign appears next to the folder name, clicking once on the plus sign, or pressing the plus key, will expand the tree to show one level of folders. The plus sign will turn into a minus sign. Alternatively, you can click twice on the plus sign, or press the Alt+plus key combination, and the tree beneath the folder will be fully expanded.

If the tree beneath the selected folder is completely expanded, it can be collapsed to one level by either clicking once on the minus sign that appears to its left, or pressing the minus key. Alternatively, it can be completely collapsed by double clicking on the minus sign to the left of the folder, or by pressing the Alt+minus key combination. When completely collapsed, the minus sign next to the folder will turn into a plus sign, and none of the folders that branch out from it will be displayed.

If the tree beneath the selected folder is expanded to one level, a minus sign will appear next to the folder. Pressing the plus key will expand the tree fully beneath the selected folder, and pressing the minus key will completely collapse the tree beneath the folder. Clicking once with the mouse pointer on the minus sign next to the folder will also completely collapse the tree. There is no way to expand the tree completely using the mouse when a minus sign appears next to the selected folder—you must first collapse the tree, so that the plus sign reappears.

Table 2.1 summarizes these options.

Table 2.1 Actions for Expanding and Collapsing the Tree

Current State	***Desired State***	***Required Action***
Fully collapsed	Expanded one level	Plus key or single click mouse on plus sign
Fully collapsed	Fully expanded	Plus key twice or double click mouse on plus sign
Expanded one level	Fully expanded	Plus key
Expanded one level	Fully collapsed	Minus key or single click mouse on minus sign
Fully expanded	Expanded one level	Minus key or single click mouse on minus sign
Fully expanded	Fully collapsed	Minus key twice or double click mouse on minus sign

Since all folders stem from the main folder, you can expand and collapse the entire tree by using these operations on the main folder. It is worth spending a little time experimenting with these techniques to develop a feel for how they work.

Configuring Applications in ViewMAX

There are two broad categories of files that exist on a PC: executable files, which are the programs, or software, that you run; and data files, which contain the information that the executable files work with. In ViewMAX, executable files are referred to as applications. For example, a word processor is an application. Data files are referred to as documents. Almost all applications use document files to store the information they work with.

Many applications allow you to enter parameters that affect how they will behave. ViewMAX allows you to configure applications in three ways: (1) to prompt for parameters when they are run; (2) to associate particular file extensions with the application, so that the application program can be run by selecting a document file; and (3) to assign meaningful icons to the application file, and to the associated document files.

ViewMAX can store up to about fifty application configurations at once.

To configure an application, the "Configure Application" dialog box must be called up for the executable file that contains the program. To accomplish this, follow these steps:

1. Select the folder in the left-hand window that contains the executable file, and press the Enter key to display the contents of that folder in the right-hand window.
2. Select the executable file for the application in the right-hand window. The file must have one of the following extensions: BAT, COM, EXE, or APP. These are the only file types that DR DOS can execute.
3. Hold down the Alt key and press the O, to drop down the Options menu.
4. Press the letter C, to select the "Configure application" option.

The "Configure Application" dialog box shown in Figure 2.19 will appear.

It is within this box that all of the configuration settings are made for an application.

Setting Up a Parameters Dialog Box for an Application

Parameters are specifications that are entered on the command line, following the name of the program. Parameters are generally used to modify the way the application functions. For example, a word processor that is started with the command WP may accept a parameter which specifies that it should run in black and white mode, rather than in color. If the parameter were specified with the symbol /BW then the following command line would start the word processor in black and white mode:

```
WP /BW
```

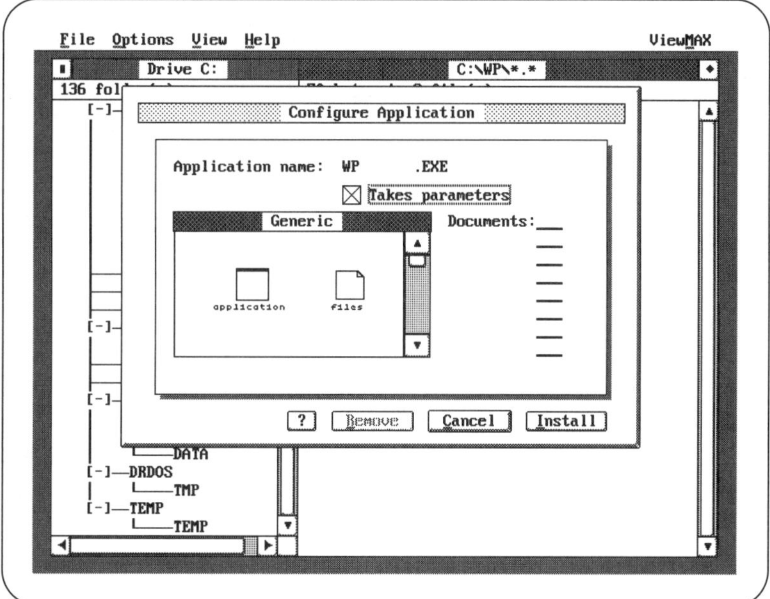

Figure 2.19 Configure Application Dialog Box

Parameter dialog boxes are used within ViewMAX to prompt the user for any parameters that should be passed to an application. Some applications do not accept parameters, so you have the option of turning off the parameters dialog box. In Figure 2.19, the selection frame is around the words "Takes parameters", and the box next to these words is checked. When this box is checked, the "Open Application" dialog box shown in Figure 2.20 will appear whenever the application is run.

Any parameters that would normally be entered on the command line can be entered in this dialog box. Selecting the Cancel button will return you to ViewMAX, cancelling the command to run the application.

If you do not want the "Open Application" dialog box to appear when you start the application, press the Spacebar to erase the check mark in the "Takes parameter" box. You may select the Install button in the lower right corner of the dialog box to save your setting, or move to another area of the dialog box to make other changes to the configuration.

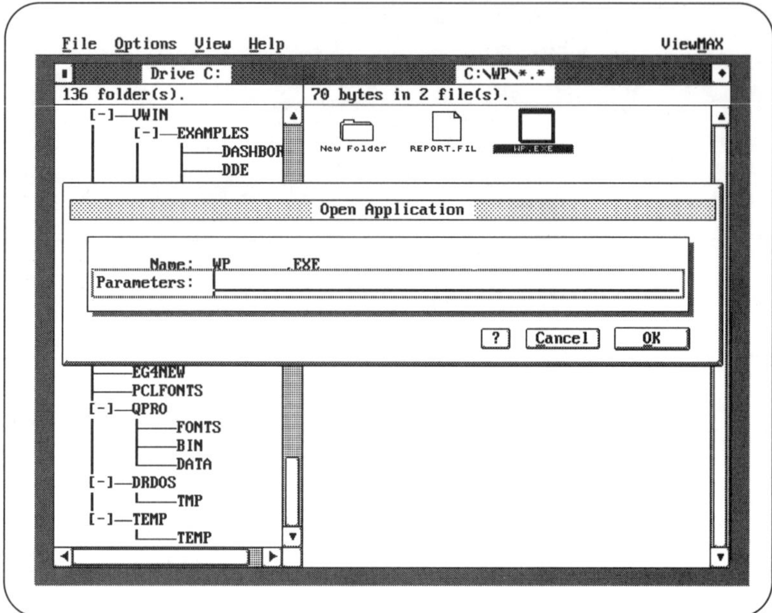

Figure 2.20 Open Application Dialog Box

Associating Document Files with an Application

Many programs accept the name of a document file as a parameter. This causes the document file to be loaded automatically when the program starts. This is very common with word processors, and spreadsheets. For example, if the WP command starts your word processor, then entering

```
WP BOBSMITH.LET
```

at the command prompt will bring up the word processor with the file BOBSMITH.LET loaded and ready for editing. This saves several steps over starting the word processor, then loading the file.

You can streamline this process even more within ViewMAX, by using the Configure Application feature on the Options menu. ViewMAX uses the extension part of a filename to determine the file type. For example, if you name the files that contain your correspondence with the extension LET, you can configure your word processor program to recognize that extension as indicating a type of file that your word processor can use. You can then select and open any file that has the LET extension, which will automatically run the word processor, passing the selected file as a parameter.

A program may be configured to have more than one file type, or extension, associated with it. For example, if the extension LET is used for correspondence files, and the extension RPT for reports written with a word processor, then both of these extensions could be associated with the word processor. On the other hand, any given extension can be associated only with a single program. The LET extension could not be associated with a word processor and a database program at the same time. If you associate a particular file extension with two different applications, ViewMAX will remove the association with the first application when the second association is created. Therefore, only the last association defined for a particular file type will be in effect.

To associate file extensions with an application, bring up the "Configure Application" dialog box for the application as discussed above (Figure 2.19). Press the Tab key once, to move the Selection Frame from the "Takes parameters" check box to the "Documents" data entry fields. Enter the first file extension to be associated with this application, then press the Tab key to move to the next line, where you can add another file extension. You may associate up to eight file extensions with a single application.

There are three ways to open a file, whether it is an application file or a document file that is associated with an application:

1. Double click on it with the mouse.
2. Highlight it with the Selection Frame and press the Enter key.
3. Highlight it with the Selection Frame and select Open/Run from the File menu.

There are two main advantages gained by configuring applications to recognize their document file types: running the application by selecting the document is faster than running the application and then opening the document file; and it allows you to run the application from whatever folder a data file is in, with a single keystroke or mouse click. If the document file types for an application are not associated with it, then you must go to the folder that contains the application file and run it from there. Once within the application, you will have to change to the folder that contains the document files.

When all of the associated document types have been entered, you may select the Install button in the lower right corner to save the configuration, or move to another area of the dialog box to make other changes to the configuration.

Setting the Icons for Applications and Documents

ViewMAX includes a set of 20 pairs of icons that can be assigned to applications and their associated documents. Each pair consists of an application icon and a document icon; all document files associated with a particular application will have the same icon.

To assign an icon pair to an application, bring up the "Configure Application" dialog box for the application as discussed earlier (Figure 2.19). Move the Selection Frame to the scroll bar, or use the mouse pointer, to scroll through the available icon pairs until the one you want to use appears.

You may select the Install button in the lower right corner of the Dialog Box to save your setting, or move to another area of the dialog box to make other changes to the configuration.

Managing Files in ViewMAX

When you select a folder in the upper left window, the files contained in that folder are displayed in the right-hand window. When ViewMAX first appears, the right-hand window displays all the folders and files in the main folder. The folders appear first, sorted by name, followed by the files, sorted by name. However, it is possible to change the right-hand window to more closely meet your own particular needs. For example, you may only want to see files with the extension of .BAT, and you may want them to appear in date order. Techniques for fine-tuning the display of ViewMAX windows are discussed above, in the section "Changing and Updating the Window Display".

In order to understand file management, you must have a basic understanding of how folder and filenames are specified. The backslash character (\ ) is used to separate the names of folders and files. Since the main folder is always named by a single backslash, you can specify the full path from the main folder to any file by starting with the drive specifier and a backslash, then naming all of the folders that lead to the file—separated by backslashes—and finally specifying the file itself. For example, this is the full path name for a file named BOBSMITH.LET in a folder named LETTERS, which is contained in a folder named WP, which in turn is contained in the main folder of the C: drive:

```
C:\WP\LETTERS\BOBSMITH.LET
```

On the ViewMAX screen, the title for the right-hand window always shows the full path and file specifier used to select files. In Figure 2.14, this is C:*.*. Thus, the current drive is C:, the folder is the main folder, and the file specifier is *.* (all files).

Setting the Read/Write Status of a File

Figure 2.21 shows the "File Information/Rename" dialog box for a file named SUMMARY1.FIL.

Beneath the Name: data entry field are two option buttons. The first is labelled Read/Write, and the second is labelled Read-only. These buttons determine whether or not a file can be modified. Most files are marked Read/Write, which means it is possible to both read them and modify them. However, it is sometimes desirable to restrict access to a file, so that it can only be read, but not modified. For example, you may want to grant access to some users to view the contents of a file, but not allow them to change those contents. Executable files, which are files that contain the software progams you use, can be set to read-only status to prevent them from being erased. To set a file to read-only status, select the second button in the "File Information/Rename" dialog box. It will now be impossible to delete or modify the file, but it will still be possible to read it.

Displaying Technical Information About a File

Technical information about the files in the right-hand window may be displayed by choosing the "Hide tree", "Resize", and "Show as text" options on the View menu. This produces a display like that in Figure 2.22.

The information displayed for each item is: a small diamond to the left of the name, if the item is a folder; the name of the item; the number of bytes it occupies on the disk, if it is a file; the date it was last modified; the time it was last modified; and a list of its attributes. File attributes are discussed in greater detail in Chapter 6. The attributes can be:

- **r** for read-only
- **a** for archive
- **d** for directory
- **p** for password protected

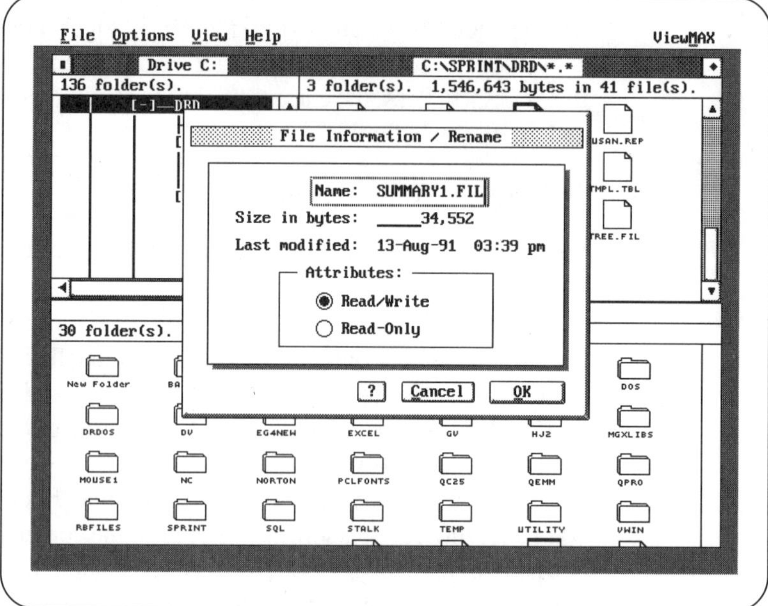

Figure 2.21 File Information/Rename Dialog Box

Any combination of these attributes may be set for a file or folder. In Figure 2.22, all of the files named AUTOEXEC.386 have their Archive attributes set. The names that have a small diamond to their left, at the top of the list, are folders. These also have the "d" attribute set, since folders are directories.

Working with the File Menu

There are a lot of things you might want to do with files on your disk: delete them, copy them from one folder to another, run them (if they are program files), and so on. ViewMAX provides easy access to all of these actions through the File menu. Figure 2.23 provides a quick reference to the options that are available when the right-hand window

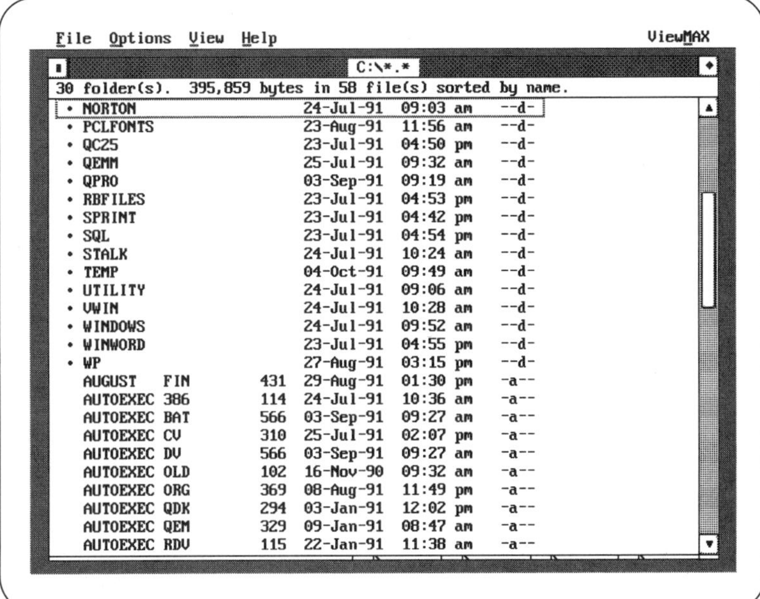
File Options View Help ViewMAX
C:*.*
30 folder(s). 395,859 bytes in 58 file(s) sorted by name.
• NORTON 24-Jul-91 09:03 am --d-
• PCLFONTS 23-Aug-91 11:56 am --d-
• QC25 23-Jul-91 04:50 pm --d-
• QEMM 25-Jul-91 09:32 am --d-
• QPRO 03-Sep-91 09:19 am --d-
• RBFILES 23-Jul-91 04:53 pm --d-
• SPRINT 23-Jul-91 04:42 pm --d-
• SQL 23-Jul-91 04:54 pm --d-
• STALK 24-Jul-91 10:24 am --d-
• TEMP 04-Oct-91 09:49 am --d-
• UTILITY 24-Jul-91 09:06 am --d-
• VWIN 24-Jul-91 10:28 am --d-
• WINDOWS 24-Jul-91 09:52 am --d-
• WINWORD 23-Jul-91 04:55 pm --d-
• WP 27-Aug-91 03:15 pm --d-
AUGUST FIN 431 29-Aug-91 01:30 pm -a--
AUTOEXEC 386 114 24-Jul-91 10:36 am -a--
AUTOEXEC BAT 566 03-Sep-91 09:27 am -a--
AUTOEXEC CV 310 25-Jul-91 02:07 pm -a--
AUTOEXEC DV 566 03-Sep-91 09:27 am -a--
AUTOEXEC OLD 102 16-Nov-90 09:32 am -a--
AUTOEXEC ORG 369 08-Aug-91 11:49 pm -a--
AUTOEXEC QDK 294 03-Jan-91 12:02 pm -a--
AUTOEXEC QEM 329 09-Jan-91 08:47 am -a--
AUTOEXEC RDV 115 22-Jan-91 11:38 am -a--

Figure 2.22 File List in Text Mode

is active. Some of these options have already been discussed; the rest are described in detail in the sections that follow.

Figure 2.23 Summary of File Menu Options

File Menu Option	*Effect*
Open/Run	If an executable file is selected, this option runs it. If a non-executable file is selected, and its type is configured to run an application, then this option runs the executable application file, with the selected file passed as a parameter.
Show Contents	Displays the contents of a file. Permits switching between ASCII and hex displays.
Find	Searches the current drive for a specified file name.
Copy	Copies selected files from one disk and/or folder to another.
Delete	Deletes selected files and/or folders from the disk.

Figure 2.23 continued ...

File Menu Option	*Effect*
Info/Rename	If a folder is selected, displays the name, date and time created, the number of folders contained in it, the number of files contained in it, and the total bytes occupied by its contents. Allows you to rename the folder. If a file is selected, displays the name, size in bytes, date and time of last modification, and the current setting of the Read/Write status. Allows you to rename the file, and change its Read/Write status. Info/Rename can only act on a single item; you cannot select multiple items and rename all of them.
Password	If a file is selected, allows you to assign or remove a password for the file, and set the level of protection (Delete, Delete/Write, or Delete/Write/Read). If a folder is selected, allows you to assign or remove a password for the folder. Passwords on folders automatically provide read, write, and delete protection. Passwords can only be assigned to a single item at a time; you cannot select multiple items and assign a password to all of them.
Undelete	Allows you to recover files and folders that have been deleted.
Format disk	Formats a diskette. Cannot be used to format a hard drive.
Exit	Exits ViewMAX permanently, returning you to the DR DOS command prompt.

Opening Files

The Open option on the Files menu is used to open, or start, the currently selected file in the right-hand window. If the currently selected file is an executable file (i.e., if it has an extension of BAT, COM, EXE, or APP) then the file itself is started. If the file is not executable, but has been associated with an application file in the "Configure Application" dialog box, then the associated program file is run with the selected file passed as a parameter.

If the selected file is neither executable nor associated with an executable file, then Open causes the "Open a file" dialog box to appear, as shown in Figure 2.24.

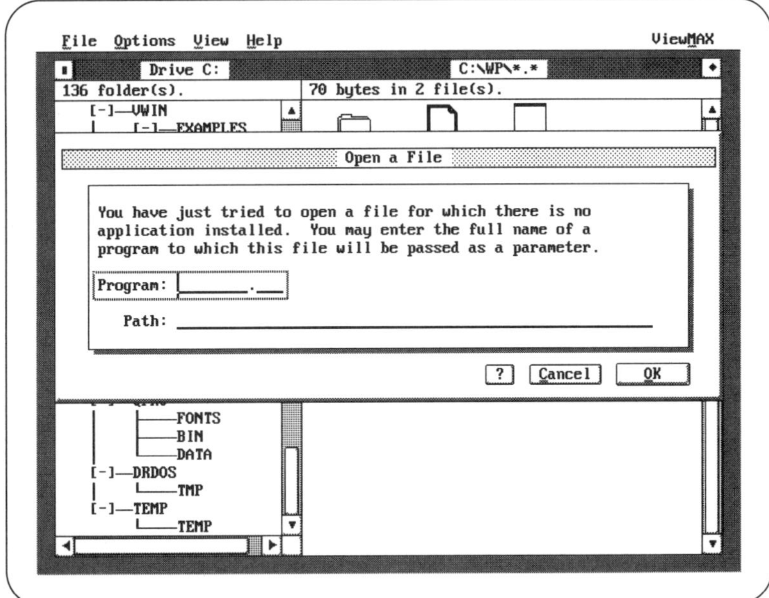

Figure 2.24 "Open a file" Dialog Box

This dialog box allows you to enter the name of an application file and the path which contains the file. When these have been filled in, pressing the Enter key will run the application, and the file that was selected before this box appeared will be passed to it as a parameter.

Application files, and their associated document files, may also be run simply by selecting them and pressing the Enter key.

The Show Contents Option

The "Show contents" option on the File menu is used to examine the contents of a file. It is intended to give you a quick way of checking a file's contents; it is not meant to be used for reading or reviewing files. You may want to make such a quick check before deleting a file, or to identify a file that you want to copy. You will normally only want to view text files—ones that only contain ASCII characters.

An example of an ASCII file is the AUTOEXEC.BAT file in the main folder of your hard drive. To see the contents of AUTOEXEC.BAT, select it in the right-hand window, then select the "Show contents" option on the File menu. A screen similar to that in Figure 2.25 will be displayed.

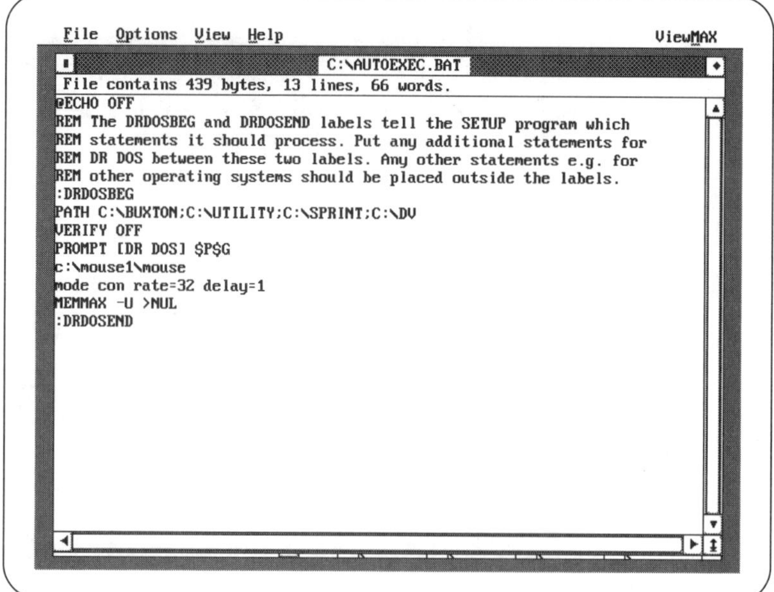

Figure 2.25 AUTOEXEC.BAT file in Show Contents Screen

If the file contains more information than will fit on the screen, you may scroll through it in any of the following ways:

1. Press PgUp and PgDn to scroll one screen at a time.
2. Press Ctrl+PgDn to scroll the screen to the left, and Ctrl+PgUp to scroll the screen to the right.
3. Use the techniques discussed above, in the section "Navigating in ViewMAX", for scrolling with the mouse pointer.

There is no way to scroll one line at a time from the keyboard; this can only be done with a mouse.

There is a menu bar at the top of the screen with three options: Display, View, and Help. This menu bar is activated in the same way as the ViewMAX menu bar; by pressing Alt or pointing with the mouse. The Help drop-down menu provides the same options discussed earlier in this chapter, in the section titled, *Getting On-line Help*.

There are three options available on the View menu when displaying the contents of a file: Close, Resize, and Show as text. These function in the following ways:

- ***Close*** is used to stop viewing the contents of the file. It returns you to the previous screen display. Alt+F4 is the shortcut for this option.
- ***Resize*** is used to shift the display into split-screen mode, displaying the contents of the selected file in the top half of the screen and the usual right and left hand windows in the bottom half. Alt+F5 is the shortcut for this option.
- ***Show*** as text is used to switch the display of the file contents between text and hex modes. This option is discussed in the following paragraphs. Ctrl+T is the shortcut for this option.

To understand text and hex modes, you must know a little about how information is stored in files.

All files contain sequences of numbers, nothing more. When you look at the contents of a letter in your word processor, the characters and punctuation marks you see on the screen are interpretations of the numbers contained in the letter file. These interpretations are carried out using a set of 128 numeric codes defined by ASCII (the American Standard Code For Information Interchange). These codes start with the number 0 and end with 127. For example, in ASCII, the number 84 corresponds to an uppercase T. When ViewMAX displays a file in text mode, it interprets all of the numbers in the file as ASCII codes. If the file contains numbers that were not intended to be interpreted as ASCII codes, then the display contains odd symbols because ViewMAX cannot interpret them correctly.

There are several reasons files may have non-ASCII codes:

- They may have been produced by a word processor or other software that inserts special formatting codes into its files.
- They may have been created by a program that encodes data before storing it.
- They may not be data files at all.

Executable program files—those that have COM and EXE extensions in their names—do not use ASCII codes. Instead they use numeric codes that the computer interprets as instructions to perform specific tasks.

Whatever the reason for the non-ASCII codes, it is more useful to see their numeric representation than the symbols they produce on the screen. A knowledgeable programmer can interpret these numbers and learn something about the file being viewed. The Show as text option on the View menu switches the display of the file contents to the numeric codes instead of their ASCII interpretation. They are not, however, displayed in the base ten, or decimal, number system. They are displayed in the base 16, or Hexadecimal, number system. This is closer to the way the computer actually represents these numbers internally, and consequently it is easier for programmers to interpret. The Hex version of the AUTOEXEC.BAT file in Figure 2.25 is shown in Figure 2.26.

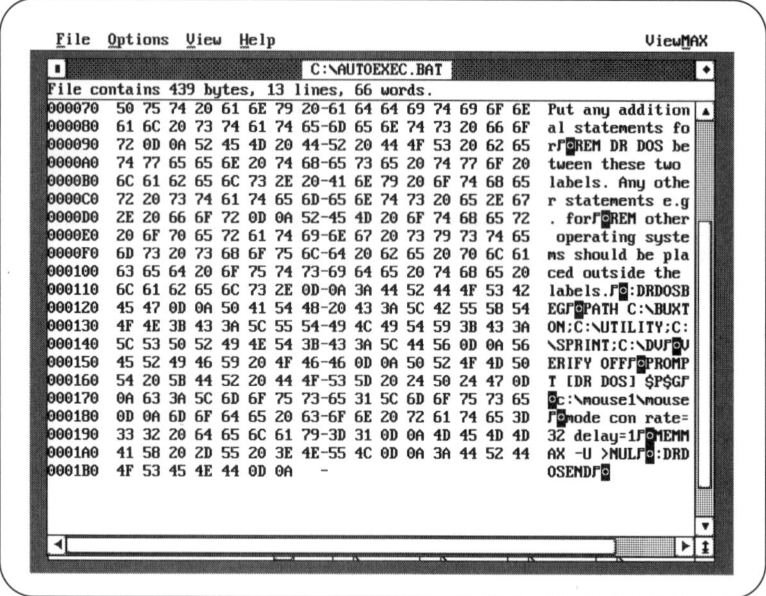

Figure 2.26 AUTOEXEC.BAT Contents Displayed in Hex Mode

Even when Hex mode is selected, the ASCII interpretation of the codes will still be displayed in a vertical column at the right side of the screen. This is useful because executable programs will often have strings of ASCII codes embedded in them. These strings may contain messages the program displays on the screen. This can be demonstrated by Viewing the file COMMAND.COM that comes with DR DOS 6.0. If you scroll through a few screens of this file, you will see that there are meaningful messages interspersed with apparently meaningless symbols.

The numbers in the vertical box at the left of the Hex mode screen represent the physical location of each line in the file—how many bytes there are between the beginning of the file and the beginning of the line.

When you use the "Show contents" option to display the contents of a file, ViewMAX automatically determines the initial mode. If ViewMAX interprets the file as containing 100 percent ASCII symbols, then it displays the file in ASCII format. If it interprets any part of the file as non-ASCII code, it displays the file in Hex format. Ctrl+T, or the "Show as text" option on the View menu, may be used to switch back and forth between these two modes.

Finding Files with the Find Option

The Find option on the File menu is used to locate a file on the disk. When there are a lot of files on a hard disk it is easy to forget which folder a particular file is in. The Find option provides an easy way to find files. When Find is selected, the dialog box in Figure 2.27 is displayed.

The "File to find" data entry field is used to enter the name of the file or files to search for. You may enter either a single file name here, or use the file name wildcards, asterisk (*) and question mark (?), to indicate groups of files to search for. If you want ViewMAX to search a drive other than the one indicated below the "File to find" data entry field, you may press the Tab key to move the "Drive to search" data entry field and change the drive specifier. After the correct drive and file specifiers have been entered, select the Find option button or press the Enter key to start the search process. As ViewMAX scans the folders on the disk it will display the full path name to any files that match the specification in the "Files Found" area of the dialog box. Figure 2.28 shows the results of a search for all files with a BAT extension.

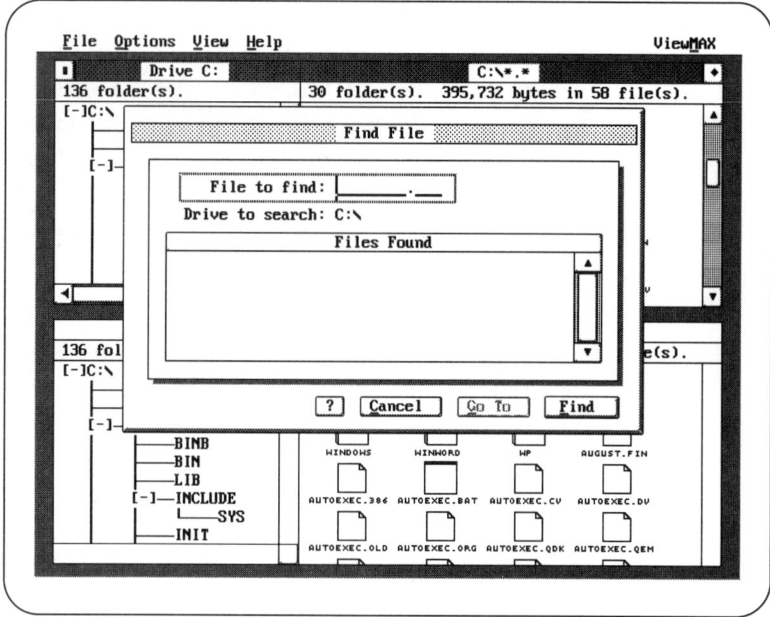

Figure 2.27 Find File Dialog Box

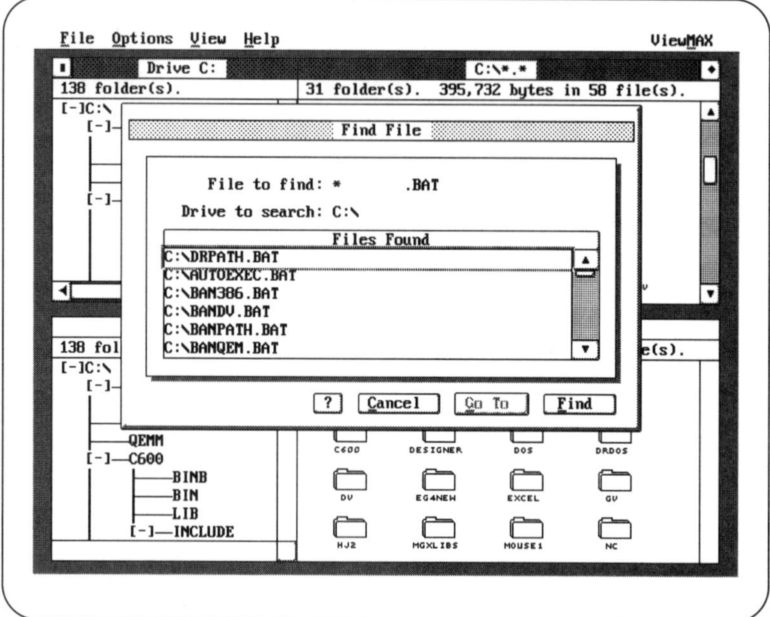

Figure 2.28 Results of Find Operation

The third option button from the left at the bottom of the screen is labelled "Go To". You may notice that this button appears shaded when you are entering the file specification, and when the search operation is being carried out. After the search is completed and a list of files appears in the Files Found area, you may move the Selection Frame into the list of files. You may select a file by moving the Selection Frame to a file and pressing the Enter key. The Go To button will lose its shading and become active. Selecting this button closes the dialog box, changes the contents of the windows to the folder that contains the selected file, and selects that file in the right-hand window.

The Cancel button can be used instead of the Find and Go To buttons, to cancel the Find operation and return to the previous screen.

Copying Folders and Files

Folders and files may be easily copied between the folders and disks on your PC. Folders and files to be copied are referred to as *source folders* and *source files*, and the folders and files that they will be copied to are referred to as the *target folders* and *target files*. For this discussion, the term *files* refers to both folders and files. Copying can be accomplished with either the mouse or the keyboard, but is considerably easier with the mouse.

If you are using a mouse, files may be copied directly to a folder that appears in the same window as the source files. If you are using the keyboard, or if the target folder does not appear in the same window as the source files, then the target folder must be displayed in the other half of the screen. The target folder in the other half of the screen may be on the same or a different disk as the source files.

To copy files from one folder to another using the mouse, follow these steps:

1. Display the contents of the folder with the source files in the upper right window. If the target folder is not visible in this window, display it in the other half of the screen. (Techniques for changing the display in the different parts of the ViewMAX screen are discussed above, in the section titled *Changing and Updating the Window Display*).
2. Select the folder(s) and/or file(s) to be copied. All but the last one may be selected using either the spacebar or the mouse,

but the last one must be selected with the mouse. When selecting the last item to be copied, do not release the mouse button. Holding down the mouse button will cause the mouse pointer to turn into a hand symbol.

3. While continuing to hold down the mouse button, move the hand symbol to the target folder.
4. Release the mouse button.

A dialog box like that in Figure 2.29 will appear.

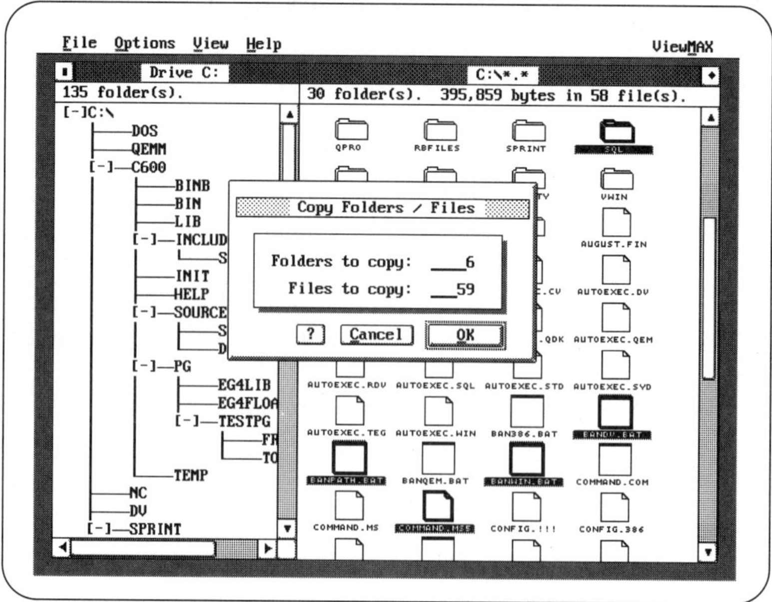

Figure 2.29 Copy Folders/Files Dialog Box

Selecting the OK button will begin the copy operation. The Cancel button can be used to terminate the copy operation.

To copy files from one folder to another using the keyboard,follow these steps:

1. Display the contents of the folder with the source files in the upper right window, and the contents of the target folder in the lower right window. (Techniques for changing the display in the different parts of the ViewMAX screen are discussed above, in the section titled *Changing and Updating the Window Display*).

2. Select the folders and/or files to be copied.
3. Hold down the Alt key and press the F, to drop down the File menu. Then press the C for the Copy option. This will pop up the "Copy Folder/Files" dialog box, shown in Figure 2.29.

Selecting the OK button will begin the copy operation. The Cancel button can be used to terminate the copy operation.

Regardless of whether you are using the keyboard or the mouse, once the Copy operation begins, the numbers in the "Copy Folder/Files" dialog box will count down as the folders and files are copied. If there is a file of the same name in the target folder, a "Name Conflict" dialog box appears, like that shown in Figure 2.30.

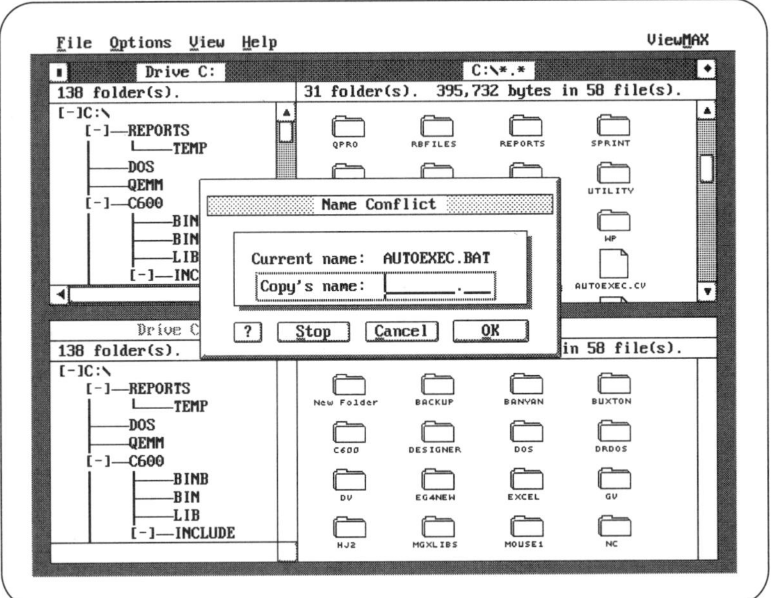

Figure 2.30 Name Conflict Dialog Box

Pressing the Enter key, or selecting the OK button, will accept the specified name, causing ViewMAX to overwrite the file of the same name in the target folder. Alternatively, you may enter a new name for the target file. Selecting the Stop button stops the entire copy operation and returns you to the previous display. Selecting the Cancel button cancels copying the specified file, but continues attempting to copy any other files that were selected.

You can copy folders and files to the same folder they are already in, by selecting them and moving the mouse hand into a blank area of the window in which they appear. When you release the mouse button, the "Copy Folders/Files" dialog box will appear, and when you select the OK button, the "Name Conflict" dialog box will appear for each file. If you are using the keyboard, you must have the same folder displayed in both halves of the screen to duplicate files in it.

The confirmation dialog boxes for confirming the copying and overwriting of files may be turned off, using the techniques discussed later in this chapter, in the section *Managing The ViewMAX Environment.*

Deleting Files

The Delete option on the File menu is used to remove files from a disk. To delete files, first select them in the right-hand window, then either select the Delete option on the menu or press the Delete key. The "Delete Folders/Files" dialog box in Figure 2.31 is displayed.

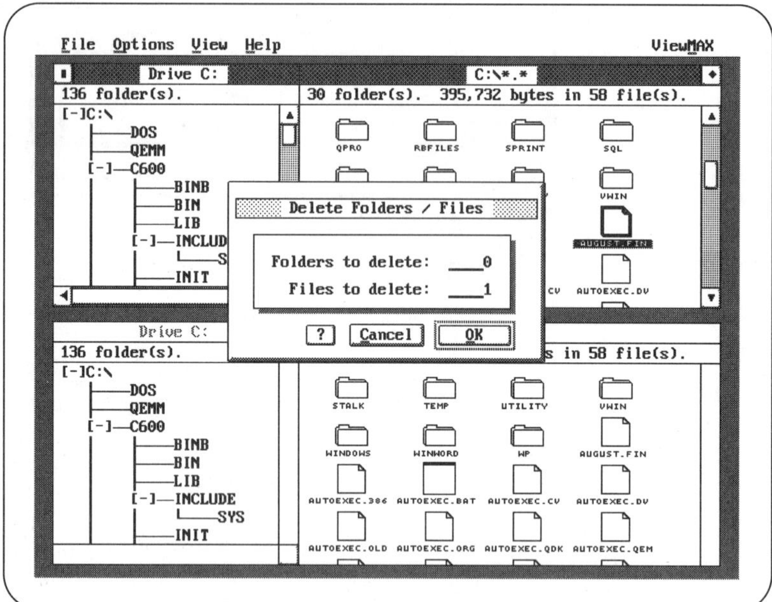

Figure 2.31 Delete Folders/Files Dialog Box

Pressing the Enter key or selecting the OK button will delete the selected folders and/or files.

Confirmation dialog boxes can be turned off, so that files are deleted without requiring your review. Turning off confirmation dialog boxes is discussed later in this chapter, in the section titled, *Managing the ViewMAX Environment*.

It is sometimes possible to recover a file that has been accidentally deleted. See *Undeleting Files* later in this chapter and Chapter 6, for directions on undeleting files. For the best chance of success, undeletion should be attempted as soon as possible after the deletion.

Renaming Files

To rename a file, select the file, then choose the Info/Rename option on the File menu. The "File Information/Rename" dialog box, shown in Figure 2.32 will appear.

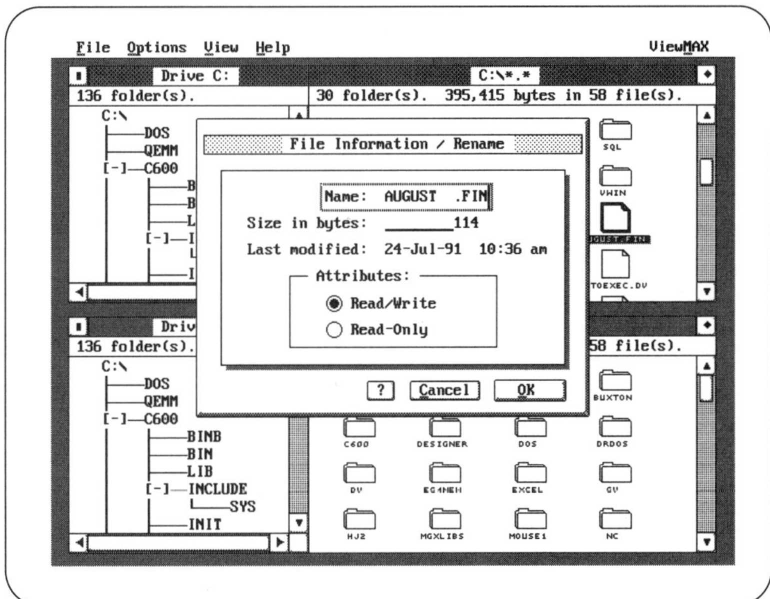

Figure 2.32 File Information/Rename Dialog Box

To rename the file, simply type in the new file name in the "Name:" data entry field. The date and time on which the file was last modified, and the size of the file in bytes, are also shown. The "Attributes" area of this screen are discussed in the section *Setting The Read/Write Status Of A File*, earlier in this chapter.

You can only rename a single file at a time. If more than one file is selected, the Info/Rename option on the File menu will not be available.

When a file is renamed, the file itself is not touched. The name is stored in the folder, so the only change that occurs in a Rename operation is that the file's name in the folder is changed.

Assigning and Removing Passwords

Files can be protected by passwords. The ability to include a password for a program allows you to provide security on your system. If the program permits access to confidential data then a password is a good idea. Passwords can be used to prevent anyone but yourself and other authorized individuals from viewing data or using programs. Passwords are discussed in greater detail in Chapter 6.

To assign a password to a file, select the file and choose the Password option on the File menu. The "Assign/Remove File Password" dialog box shown in Figure 2.33 will appear.

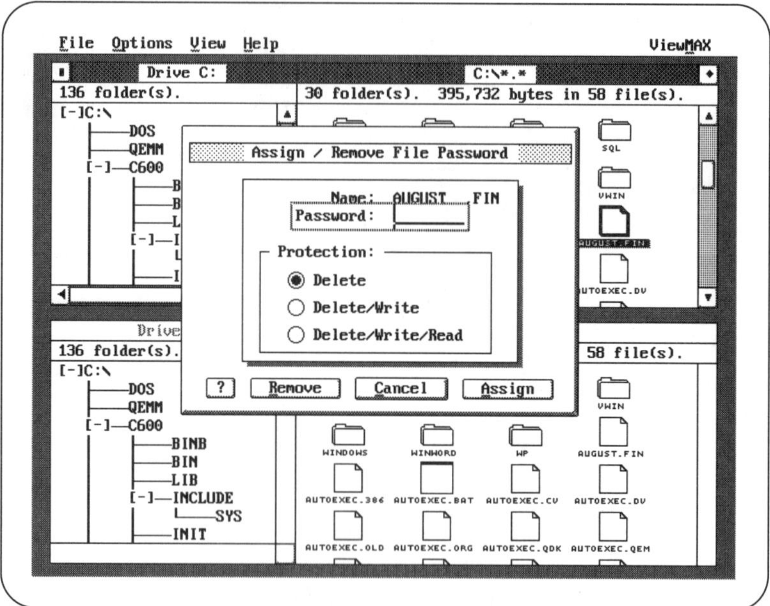

Figure 2.33 Assign/Remove File Password Dialog Box

This dialog box contains one data entry field and three mutually exclusive option buttons. (The three option buttons do not appear if you are assigning a password to a folder. Folder passwords are discussed at the end of this section; see Figure 2.35). The data entry field, labelled "Password:", is where you can type the password that will be assigned to the file. Passwords may be up to eight characters long and may include any alphabetic or numeric character. Passwords are not case sensitive; when you type the password into the Password data entry field, it appears in upper case, regardless of how you enter it. After you have typed in the password, selecting the Assign button will assign the password to the file. It is important to know that the Cancel button is selected if you press the Enter key before moving the frame to the Assign button, so that entering a password and pressing the Enter key has no effect—the operation is cancelled. You must first move the selection frame to the Assign button, then press the Enter key. Alternatively, you can simply press the Alt+A combination, or click the mouse pointer on the Assign button, regardless of where the selection frame is.

When using ViewMAX, you may include blank spaces as part of the password. However, blank spaces are not permitted in passwords entered at the command prompt, and you will not be able to access a file from the command prompt if the file's password contains blanks. Consequently, it is best not to use blank spaces in your passwords.

Passwords are entirely optional and it is generally not a good idea to use them unless they are really necessary. They slow down the opening of a file, since ViewMAX must pause and request that you type in the password each time the file is opened. There is also the risk that the password will be forgotten, and there is no simple way to retrieve a lost password.

If a password is defined for a file, you will be asked to enter the password not only for accessing the file, but also for changing or removing the password. If you forget the password it will be impossible to change it, so you must be sure to use passwords you will remember, or write them down somewhere they can be looked up.

When a file is password protected, whenever the file is accessed the "Password Protected File" dialog box in Figure 2.34 is displayed. As shown there, when the password is typed in, it does not appear in the data entry field. Instead, a series of black boxes appear, one for each character typed. This allows you to see how many characters you have typed, but does not permit prying eyes to see your password. This feature is one of the advantages of working in ViewMAX rather than at the command prompt, since passwords entered at the command prompt do appear on the screen, exactly as you type them, under most circumstances. If the wrong password is entered, the message "Wrong Password" appears above the "Password" data entry field, and the field is cleared so you can try again. If the correct password is entered, you are granted access to the file.

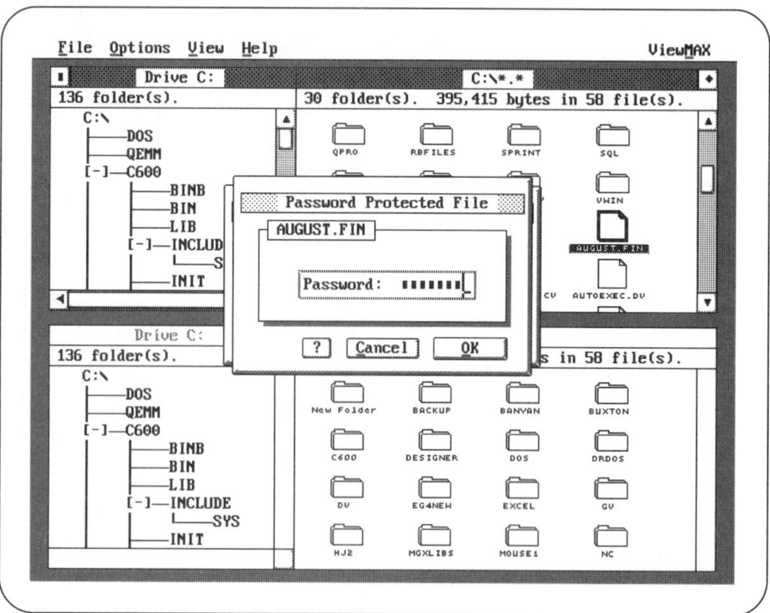

Figure 2.34 File Password Entry Dialog Box

The three option buttons in Figure 2.33 are in the rectangle labelled "Protection:". There are three levels of protection which can be assigned to a file. The lowest level of protection is labelled Delete, and prevents unauthorized users from deleting the file. However, anyone can read or modify the file. The second level of protection is labelled Delete/Write, and prevents unauthorized users from either deleting or modifying the file. However, anyone can read the file. The third level of protection is labelled Delete/Write/Read, and prevents unauthorized users from deleting, modifying, or even reading the file. If the file contains a program, this level will prevent unauthorized users from running it.

If you assign a password to a folder, the "Assign/Remove Folder" dialog box in Figure 2.35 appears.

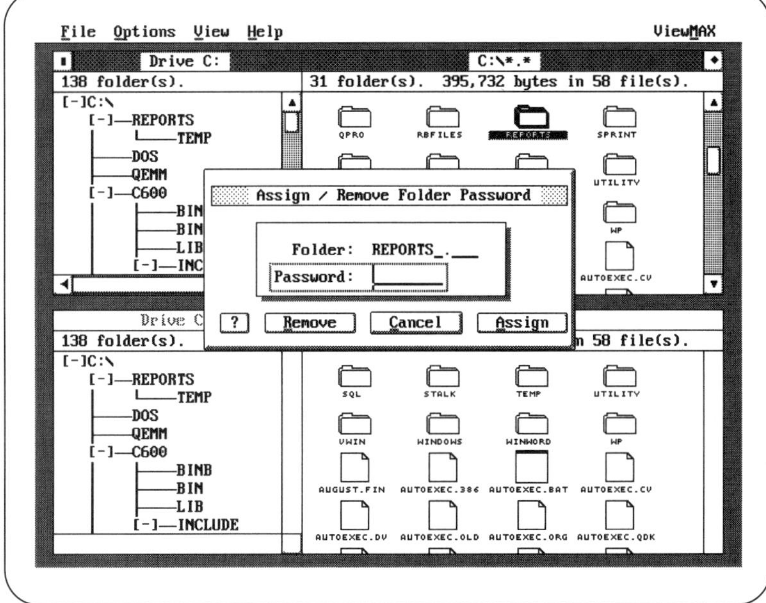

Figure 2.35 Assign/Remove Folder Password Dialog Box

This dialog box is simpler than that in Figure 2.33, in that it does not have the three "Protection" option buttons. When passwords are assigned to folders, the highest level of protection—*Delete/Read/Write*—is always assigned. If a folder has a password assigned to it, you will be prompted to enter the password when ViewMAX reads the disk at startup time. However, pressing Cancel instead of entering the password is perfectly acceptable—ViewMAX will display the full folder tree. Even if you enter the password when ViewMAX is reading the tree, you will still have to enter it again when you attempt to open that folder.

It is important to keep in mind that passwords assigned in ViewMAX are in effect at all times, whether you are working in ViewMAX or at the command prompt. Passwords assigned from the command prompt are in effect at all times as well.

Undeleting Files

The Undelete option on the File menu is used for recovering files that have been accidentally erased. This option runs the UNDELETE program, which can also be run from the command prompt.

Undeleting files is discussed in detail in Chapter 6. For now, there are a few points that are important to know:

1. A deleted file should be recovered as soon as possible after it has been deleted. The more activity the computer carries out after a file is deleted, the less likely it is to be recoverable.
2. As an extra measure of safety, it is advisable that Undelete not be used when TaskMAX is active. TaskMAX is discussed in Chapter 3.
3. You should not attempt to undelete a file on a full, or nearly full disk.
4. Once a folder is deleted, the files that were in it can only be undeleted after the folder itself is undeleted.
5. There are two other DR DOS programs, discussed in Chapter 6, named DELWATCH and DISKMAP. If DELWATCH was run at the start of the session, before deleting the file, the file can almost certainly be recovered. If DELWATCH was not run before deleting the file, but DISKMAP had been run recently, chances are lower, but still good, that the file can be recovered. If neither of these programs has been used, it is still possible that Undelete will be able to recover the file, but the chances are not as good.

Once you start the Undelete program, you can move from one directory to another. Consequently, you do not have to select or display the folder containing the deleted files before starting Undelete. However, the initial Undelete screen does display the folder from which Undelete was started, so if you know what folder contains the files to be recovered, starting from that folder will save you some keystrokes in Undelete.

The Undelete screen appears in Figure 2.36, where the folders within the C:\UTILITY folder are displayed. There are two of them: PK and REPORTS. REPORTS is a folder that has been deleted; this is indicated by the word Delwatch to the right of the folder information. Delwatch indicates that the recovery technique used by UNDELETE will be to find out where the deleted folder exists from information stored by the DELWATCH program. If DELWATCH had not recorded information about this folder, then to the right of the folder name would be one of the following terms:

Diskmap
Unaided
Cannot recover

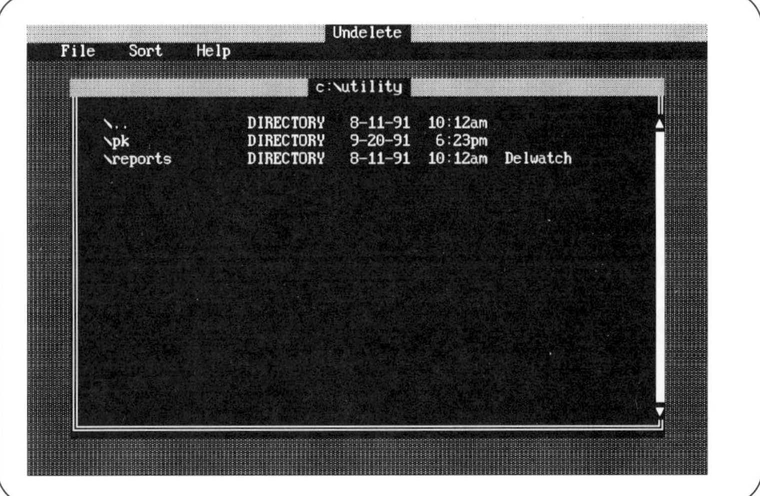

Figure 2.36 Undelete Screen

Since there is no term to the right of the name of the PK folder, we know that this folder has not been deleted. If there were other deleted files in the C:\UTILITY folder, they would also appear here. The UNDELETE screen displays all folders, whether they have been deleted or not, since you may need to go into a folder in order to undelete files in it. However, UNDELETE only displays deleted files, not ones that have not been deleted. This makes sense: there is no reason to see files that have not been deleted, and displaying them would only take up space and make it harder to locate deleted files.

There are two ways to undelete folders and files that appear on the UNDELETE screen: the first is to move the selection frame to the item you want to undelete and press the Enter key; the second is to select items in the list by moving the selection frame to them and pressing the Spacebar. This will cause a small diamond to appear to the left of the selected item—this technique permits you to select multiple items before starting the undelete operation. After selecting all of the items you want to undelete, pressing the Alt+U key combination will start the Undelete operation.

A dialog box will be displayed before Undelete starts to recover folders and files, informing you of what it is about to do and giving you the option of continuing or cancelling the operation. If you select the OK button on this dialog box, Undelete will go ahead and recover the files you have marked. As files are recovered, the word RECOVERED will appear where the undeletion technique was identified.

After a folder has been undeleted, the files that it contained may also be recoverable. To change folders on the UNDELETE screen, move the selection frame to the folder name and press the Enter key. The folder MUST exist; if it was deleted and not recovered, this will cause the folder to be recovered. If it exists, the screen will change to display folders and deleted files that reside in the selected folder. You can then go ahead and select folders and files to undelete.

Note that, when selecting multiple items to undelete, you can only select items in the same folder. If you want to undelete items in different folders, you will have to do each folder separately.

When entered on the command line, there are several optional parameters that may be used with the Undelete command. Using parameters bypasses the UNDELETE screen and performs only the specific operations specified on the command line. If you want to use parameters for UNDELETE from within ViewMAX, you can run it by selecting the UNDELETE.EXE file in the DRDOS folder and choosing the Open/Run option on the File menu. This will bring up the "Open Application" dialog box (Figure 2.20), which can be used to enter the parameters. Using this technique is equivalent to entering the UNDELETE command on the command line.

The DR DOS 6.0 UNDELETE program is a powerful tool; to get the most out of it, you should understand thoroughly how it works, how to use its menus, and what the various options are for running it from the command line. These are all discussed in Chapter 6.

Under the best of circumstances—when a file is relatively small, the disk is relatively unfragmented, and no disk activity has occurred since the file was deleted—recovering a file is straightforward and safe. However, if these circumstances are not all met, undeletion can become a complex task with many hidden dangers. It is important to have a good understanding of how files are managed in order to make the best use of the Undelete program. There are circumstances under which Undelete cannot recover a file, but other more sophisticated programs may be able to. These programs are specialized utilities that have been developed for disk repair and file recovery; some of them seem almost capable of miracles. If the deleted or damaged file is very important, it may be worth the time and money to purchase one of these programs and to learn how to use it. Some good examples are Mace Utilities, Norton Utilities, and PC Tools.

Formatting a Diskette from ViewMAX

The ninth option on the File menu is "Format a diskette". Formatting disks is discussed in detail in Chapter 7.

The "Format a diskette" option can only be used for formatting diskettes; ViewMAX will not allow you to format a hard disk. Consequently, in order for this option to be available a diskette drive must be selected in the active window. You do not have to display the contents of the drive, but the drive icon must be highlighted. When you have selected a diskette drive, this option will be available on the File menu. Choosing this option displays the dialog box shown in Figure 2.37.

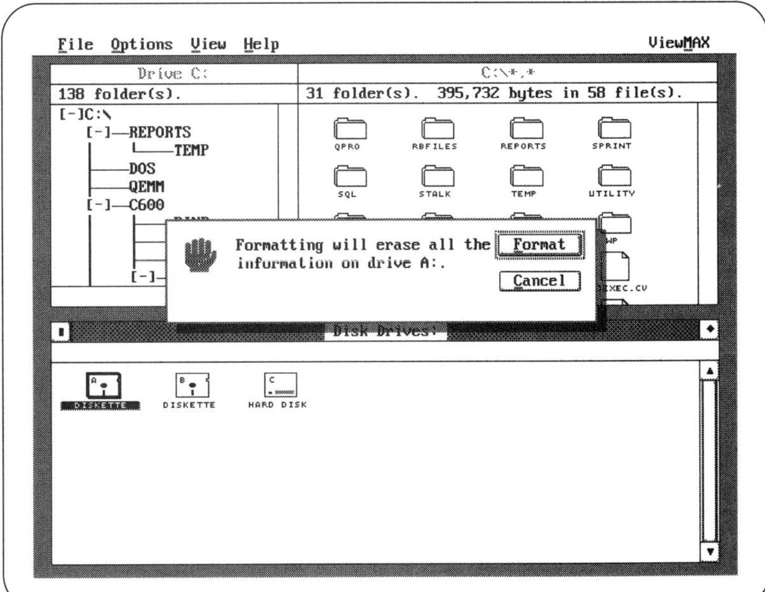

Figure 2.37 Format Diskette Dialog Box

The progress of the format operation will be displayed, and when it is done you will be asked whether you want to format another disk.

Running Programs in ViewMAX

There are two ways to run programs within ViewMAX. The choice of which one to use is based on what view is presently displayed, how you want to use the program, and what else you want to do in addition to running the program. The two ways of running programs are:

1. When a program file, or a file associated with a program, has been selected in the right-hand window, the program may be run by pressing the Enter key, by clicking twice with the mouse pointer on the file name, or by choosing Open/Run from the File menu.
2. Programs may be run from the command prompt. To go to the command prompt, select "Enter DR DOS commands" from the Options menu. The advantages of this option are that a little more memory is available for the programs, and that it is not necessary to select this option for each command you want to enter.

From the Right-Hand Window

Program file names must have one of the following four extensions: BAT, COM, EXE, or APP. (The first three of these are traditional DOS file extensions for executable programs; the fourth extension is used by Digital Research graphics applications). It is these extensions that tell DOS that a file is an executable program. Each extension represents a different kind of executable file, and when DOS runs a program it does so in a way determined by the extension. The extensions are not interchangeable—you cannot rename a .COM file to an .EXE file, for example. Files with any one of these four extensions may be run from the right-hand window.

There are three ways to run a program from the right-hand window: clicking twice on the file name with the mouse pointer; selecting the file name and pressing the Enter key; and selecting the file name and choosing the Open/Run option from the File menu.

Files that do not have an executable extension may be run if they are associated with an executable file. Any one of these techniques can be used on this non-executable file, which will call up the associated executable file and pass the selected file as a parameter. File associations, and techniques for creating and removing them, are discussed in an earlier section of this chapter titled, *Associating Document Files With An Application.*

From the Command Prompt

Choosing the "Enter DR DOS commands" option on the Options menu takes you to the command prompt, where you can enter commands and run programs just as you would if you had never entered ViewMAX. When you are done, typing the command EXIT and pressing the Enter key will return you to ViewMAX.

Using TaskMAX to Run More Than One Program at Once

One of the most significant limitations of most versions of DOS has been their inability to run more than one program at one time. When the IBM PC was first developed, it was not imagined that it would ever develop into a machine powerful enough to run multiple programs at once (a process known as multi-tasking), so DOS was designed to be a single-tasking operating system. However, recent versions of the Personal Computer provide more than enough power to run multiple programs. DR DOS 6.0 provides a utility named TaskMAX that allows you to run several programs at once, and switch back and forth between them at the touch of a key. TaskMAX is not a part of ViewMAX, and must be started from the command prompt before entering ViewMAX. Once TaskMAX has been started you can start ViewMAX, and control TaskMAX from within ViewMAX.

TaskMAX is a sophisticated utility, and is discussed in full detail in Chapter 3. If you are not familiar with TaskMAX, you may want to review that chapter now. A complete understanding of TaskMAX also requires some knowledge of the types of memory on a personal computer and how they are used; memory is discussed in Chapter 5. The present discussion is limited to how TaskMAX can be accessed and controlled from within ViewMAX.

Since a single program can occupy most or all of the available memory in the computer, TaskMAX is faced with the problem of providing that memory to whichever program you want to have active, while still remembering the status of the other programs that are open. It solves this problem by using three resources to store programs that are not currently active: the hard disk, expanded memory, and extended memory. TaskMAX will automatically choose the best resource, depending on what is available in your computer.

As you switch between programs, you may notice that the computer will pause, and the light flash on your disk drive. What TaskMAX is doing is taking a snapshot of the computer's memory, with the current program active, and writing a copy of the memory to a temporary disk file. The program being switched to is then loaded into memory. If there is sufficient expanded or extended memory available, then TaskMAX will store its copies of program memory for the different programs there, and not use the disk at all. In this case, switching will be almost instantaneous and the disk drive light will not flash.

For example, suppose you wanted to run two programs under TaskMAX—Lotus 1-2-3 and WordPerfect—and each of them needed all of the available conventional memory in the computer. Under TaskMAX, the first program (say Lotus) would be loaded into memory and run. Then, when TaskMAX received the command to run WordPerfect, the current contents of the memory (with Lotus 1-2-3 loaded) would be copied to a temporary file before WordPerfect was loaded into memory. This file would be stored in expanded memory, extended memory, or on the disk. Now WordPerfect is running. When you ask TaskMAX to switch back to Lotus 1-2-3, the contents of memory with WordPerfect loaded are saved in a file, and the file that contains the memory contents for Lotus 1-2-3 is read back into conventional memory. In this way TaskMAX can permit many programs to share the memory.

This approach to Task Swapping is effective and universal. It will work on any IBM-compatible personal computer with a reasonable amount of memory, since ViewMAX and TaskMAX themselves do not require too much memory to manage the programs. However, since this approach may require intensive use of the hard disk to switch between programs, switching will be slow on computers that have neither expanded nor extended memory, as discussed in Chapter 3.

To use TaskMAX, you must start it from the command prompt by entering the command

```
TASKMAX
```

You will see a screen like that in Figure 2.38.

```
[DR DOS] C:\>taskmax
TaskMAX R1.00 Application switcher
Copyright (c) 1989,1991 Digital Research Inc. All rights
reserved.
The DR DOS application switcher is now loaded.
Use Ctrl+Esc to display the TaskMAX menu,
or Ctrl+number to switch between existing tasks.
[DR DOS] C:\>
```

Figure 2.38 TaskMAX Startup Message

Once this screen appears, you can go ahead and start ViewMAX by entering the command

```
VIEWMAX
```

When ViewMAX starts, it is a task running under TaskMAX. However, using the techniques described in the following section, ViewMAX can act as the control center for TaskMAX, so that other tasks can be started and switched to from within ViewMAX. This provides a graphical ViewMAX screen for controlling TaskMAX, which displays more information than the TaskMAX menu, and which is similar to other ViewMAX screens.

Configuring ViewMAX to Control TaskMAX

To control TaskMAX from within ViewMAX, drop down the Options menu by pressing the Alt+O keys, and select the TaskMAX

Preferences option to display the "TaskMAX Preferences" dialog box, shown in Figure 2.39.

When this dialog box appears, the "ViewMAX controls TaskMAX?" check box is selected, but the box is not checked, indicating that ViewMAX is not presently controlling TaskMAX. Pressing the Spacebar will place an X in the box, which causes ViewMAX to take over control of TaskMAX. From now on, until you exit ViewMAX or turn this option off, the Ctrl+Esc keys will not pop up the TaskMAX menu when you are in ViewMAX. To switch tasks or access TaskMAX within ViewMAX, you will use the steps outlined below. When the active task is a program other than ViewMAX, Ctrl+Esc is used to get back to ViewMAX, from where you can switch to another task.

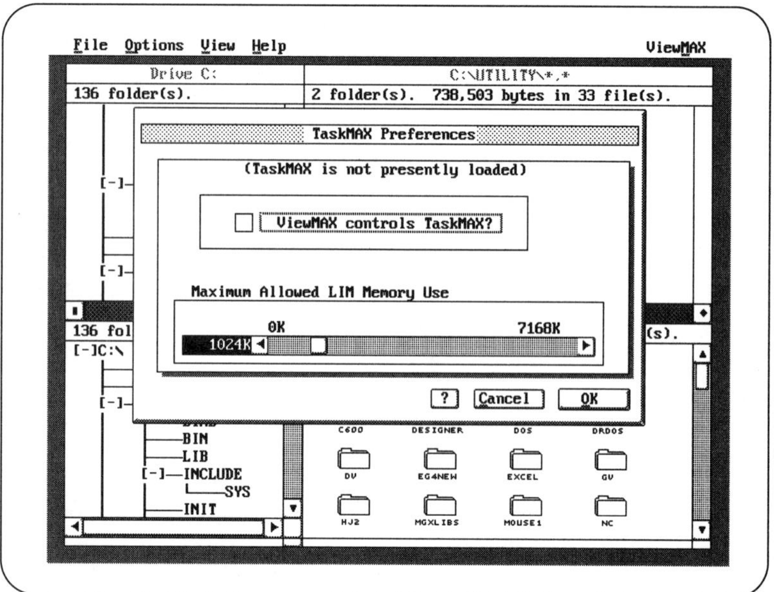

Figure 2.39 TaskMAX Preferences Dialog Box

At the bottom of the "TaskMAX Preferences" dialog box is a horizontal scroll bar labelled "Maximum Allowed LIM Memory Use". The meaning and use of this box is discussed briefly here; for a full explanation of LIM memory, refer to Chapter 5.

The term LIM memory refers to expanded memory. There are several ways in which expanded memory can be used by a computer, and TaskMAX can permit some of it to be used in one way and some in others. One way in which expanded memory can be used by TaskMAX is to store tasks that are not active. Another way TaskMAX can use expanded memory is to make it available to programs that are designed to use it for their operation. For example, many spreadsheet programs can use expanded memory to store spreadsheets larger than the available conventional memory. Often such programs will grab all of the expanded memory that is available, leaving none of it for other programs. The scroll bar at the bottom of the "TaskMAX Preferences" dialog box (Figure 2.39) is used to limit the amount of expanded memory that TaskMAX will let any one program use. In Figure 2.39, it is set to 1024K, or 1 megabyte, of expanded memory. Thus, if the computer has 7168K of expanded memory, as shown, seven different applications could each get 1 megabyte. Alternatively, if only one application is using 1 megabyte of expanded memory, the rest can be used by TaskMAX to store background tasks.

After you have checked the check box and set the amount of LIM memory to be assigned to applications, pressing the Enter key or selecting the OK button will leave ViewMAX in control of TaskMAX. If you drop down the Options menu again, you will see that the choice beneath "TaskMAX preferences", labeled "TaskMAX interface", which was previously shaded and therefore not available, can now be accessed. Choosing it brings up the dialog box in Figure 2.40.

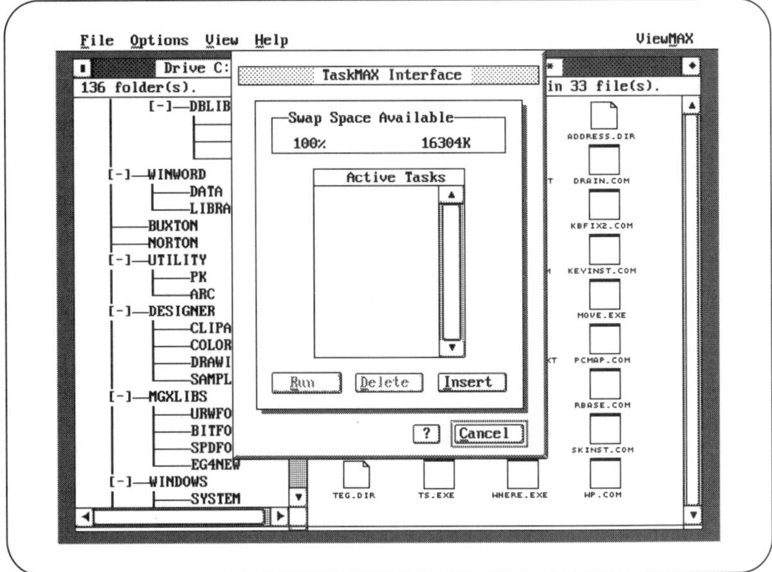

Figure 2.40 TaskMAX Interface Dialog Box

This is the dialog box that will be used to control TaskMAX.

Adding Programs to the Active Tasks List

The main body of the "TaskMAX Interface" dialog box, seen in Figure 2.40, contains the Active Tasks list. In Figure 2.40 the Active Tasks list is empty, because ViewMAX is the only program running under TaskMAX. (If you had added tasks other than ViewMAX before setting ViewMAX to control TaskMAX, then those tasks would also appear here.) Of the the three exit buttons that appear beneath the Active Tasks list, only the Insert button is available. The other two buttons, Run and Delete, will be available as soon as there are tasks in the list.

There are two ways to add a program to the Active Tasks list. The first is to select the Insert button from the "TaskMAX Interface" dialog box. The ViewMAX screen will then be replaced with a command prompt similar to that seen when you start the computer. From here you can start a program as you normally do. For example, if you normally start your word processor by switching to the C:\WP\DATA directory and entering the command WP, then following those same steps now will take you to your word processor. It will appear that your computer is functioning the way it normally does, without ViewMAX or TaskMAX running. However, if you now press the Ctrl+Esc keys, you will be returned to the ViewMAX screen in Figure 2.40, with the WP program added to the Active Tasks list. Figure 2.41 shows the Active Tasks list with three tasks running: WP, LOTUS, and RBASE.

The second way to add a task to the Active Tasks list is to run a program from within ViewMAX. This can be done by selecting the file name and pressing the Enter key, or by selecting the file and choosing the Open option on the File menu. These options are discussed earlier in this chapter, in the section *Opening Files*. When a program is run from within ViewMAX, and ViewMAX is controlling TaskMAX, then the program is automatically added to the Active Tasks list.

Note that the task name that appears in the Active Tasks list may be different than the command you typed in. This is because some commands actually call another program file that contains the program you want to run. The name that appears in the Active Tasks list is the name of the program file that is actually executing. This can be seen by creating a simple batch file that calls a program file. When you execute the batch file, by entering its name at the command prompt, the name that will appear in the Active Tasks list is the name of the program called by the batch file, not the batch file name itself. Batch files are not the only files that can cause this problem: some software is designed to use a file with a COM extension to load a program file with an EXE extension. In this case, the COM file name is what you type in, but the EXE file name is what will appear in the Active Tasks list. If the COM file and EXE file have the same name, you won't notice this, but if they are different, you will.

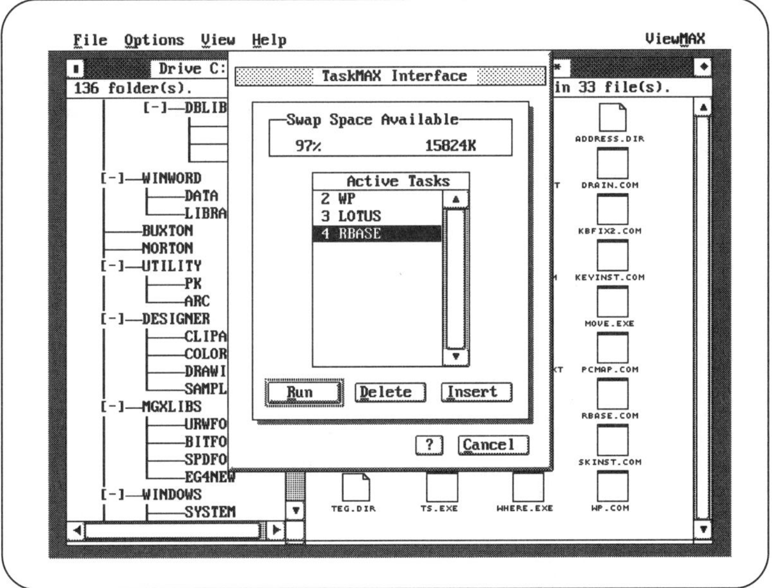

Figure 2.41 TaskMAX Interface Dialog Box with Three Tasks Running

Removing Tasks from the Active Tasks List

There are three ways to remove tasks from the Active Tasks list:

1. Exit from the program in the normal way. This will return you to the command prompt. From there, enter the command EXIT. This returns you to the "TaskMAX Interface" dialog box in ViewMAX, with the program you just ended deleted from the Active Tasks list.

2. Exit from the program in the normal way. This will return you to the command prompt. From there, pressing Ctrl+Esc returns you to the "TaskMAX Interface" dialog box in ViewMAX. The name of the task is now "Command". You can select it, then choose the Delete button. The task will be removed from the list.
3. Without exiting the program in the normal way, return to the "TaskMAX Interface" dialog box by pressing Ctrl+Esc. Now select the program to be deleted, and choose the Delete button. One of two things will happen: either the task will be deleted, or a dialog box similar to that in Figure 2.42 will appear. This option for deleting tasks should only be used if a task has locked up; the reasons for this are explained in the following paragraphs.

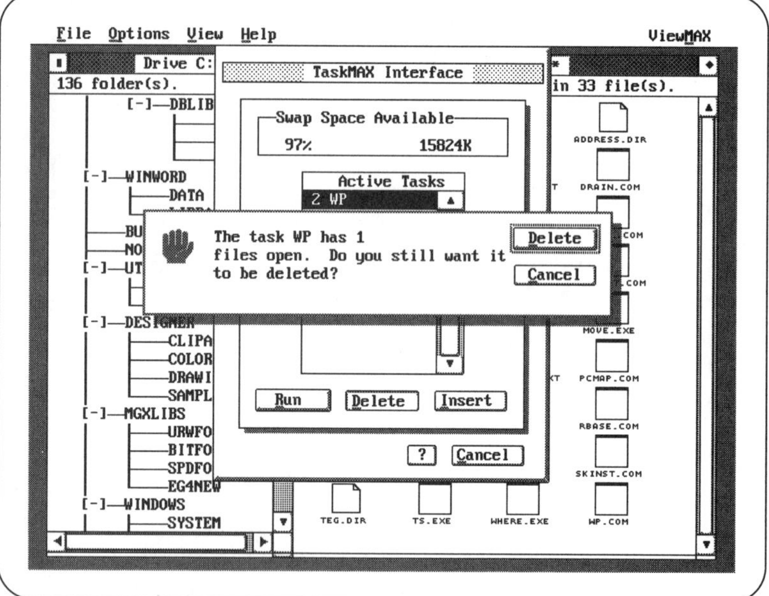

Figure 2.42 Warning Message When Deleting a Task with Open Files

This dialog box is telling you that the task you want to delete has a data file that it has been working with, and that is still open in the program. If you have not saved the data file, any changes to it will be lost if you delete the task. In general, you do not want to delete a task if there are data files open. In some programs, such as databases and speadsheets, this may actually damage the file so that it is no longer useful. Consequently, you should select the Cancel button, close the data file from within the application, then return to ViewMAX to delete the task.

Many programs go through some "house cleaning" routines when they are terminated normally. These include not only closing data files, but also deleting temporary files from the hard disk and other operations. If you delete the program from the Active Tasks list without terminating it normally, the program does not have a chance to go through these house cleaning routines. This can have anything from a minimal to a serious impact on your computer system, depending on the program and the conditions under which it was terminated. Consequently, you should not normally use the Delete option to delete a program from the Active Tasks list. Instead, you should exit the program normally, which returns you to a command prompt. From there, you can delete the task either by typing the Exit command, or by pressing Ctrl+Esc to return to the "TaskMAX Interface" dialog box and deleting the Command task.

There is one circumstance under which you will have to use the Delete option on a program in the Active Tasks list, and that is when the program has "locked up"—the keyboard does not respond and it is not possible to terminate the program. When this happens, it may still be possible to switch back to ViewMAX by holding down Ctrl and pressing Esc. If this works, the program can be terminated by going to the Active Tasks list, selecting the program, and choosing the Delete option.

This option should only be used when there is no other way to terminate the program. After deleting the offending program, you should immediately quit all other programs, exit ViewMAX and TaskMAX, and reboot your computer. A program that has locked up may have corrupted parts of DOS or other programs that are stored in memory. Continuing to run your applications may result in lost data or damaged files.

It may not be possible to return to ViewMAX when a program has locked up. In this case, you will have to reboot your computer without returning to ViewMAX. Rebooting can be accomplished by simultaneously pressing Ctrl-Alt+the Delete key. If the computer does not reboot, you must press the Reset button, (if your computer has one), or turn off the power switch, wait about fifteen seconds, then turn it back on. If you have to reboot your computer while programs are running, you should check any files that were open at the time the machine locked up, in case they were damaged. Examples of files that might have been open are documents being edited in a word processor, a worksheet being used in a spreadsheet, or files that store data for a database.

Navigating in TaskMAX

When multiple applications are running under TaskMAX, and TaskMAX is controlled by ViewMAX, there are several ways of moving between the applications, and moving to and from ViewMAX.

To move from ViewMAX to an application, there are three techniques that can be used:

1. If the TaskMAX interface is not already displayed, hold down the Alt+O keys to drop down the Options menu, then press the T key for the "TaskMAX Interface" dialog box. Now use the arrow keys or the mouse to select the task you want to switch to. If using the keyboard, press the Spacebar to highlight it, then press the Enter key. If using a mouse, double click on the task. The screen will switch to display the selected task, and you can go ahead and work in that program.
2. If you know the number that corresponds to the application on the "TaskMAX Interface" dialog box, you do not have to display the dialog box to switch to the application. Instead, regardless of what ViewMAX screen is displayed, holding down the Ctrl key and pressing the appropriate task number on the numeric keypad will automatically take you to that application. For example, Figure 2.41 shows three tasks, numbered 2, 3, and 4. From any ViewMAX screen, pressing the Ctrl+2 keys would take you to the WP application; Ctrl+3 would take you to Lotus, and Ctrl+4 would take you to RBase. You must be sure to use the numeric keypad numbers; the number keys across the top of the keyboard will not work.
3. From any ViewMAX screen, you may hold down the Ctrl key and press the Plus (+) key on the numeric keypad. This will cycle through the tasks, in the order they appear in the Active Tasks list of the "TaskMAX Interface" dialog box.

There are three corresponding ways to move from an application to ViewMAX:

1. Hold down the Ctrl+Esc keys. This will take you directly to the "TaskMAX Interface" dialog box in ViewMAX.
2. If you know the number that corresponds to ViewMAX, you may hold down the Ctrl key and press that number ON THE NUMERIC KEYPAD to switch directly to ViewMAX. Whatever ViewMAX screen was displayed when you switched away from the ViewMAX task will be displayed again. Normally, if you are going to control TaskMAX from ViewMAX, then ViewMAX is the first task you run after starting TaskMAX, so the number for ViewMAX will be 1. However, as discussed at the end of this section, it is possible to start other tasks before and after ViewMAX, in which case ViewMAX will not be assigned the number 1.
3. Holding down the Ctrl key and pressing the Plus (+) key ON THE NUMERIC KEYPAD will cycle through the tasks. Since ViewMAX is one of the tasks running, this will eventually get you to the ViewMAX screen.

There are two ways to switch directly between applications, without first going to ViewMAX:

1. Hold down the Ctrl key and press the number ON THE NUMERIC KEYPAD that corresponds to the application you want to switch to.
2. Hold down the Ctrl key and press the Plus (+) key ON THE NUMERIC KEYPAD repeatedly until the application you want to switch to appears.

The order in which tasks are numbered in TaskMAX is the order in which they are started. Notice in Figure 2.41 that the numbers for the three programs are 2, 3, and 4. This is because ViewMAX was started first, so it has the number 1. If you start tasks before ViewMAX, then ViewMAX will not be assigned the number 1. For example, suppose you started the WP program and the LOTUS program, then started ViewMAX. In the "TaskMAX Interface" dialog box, WP would have the number 1 and LOTUS would have the number 2. ViewMAX would have the number 3, though this doesn't show up in the "TaskMAX Interface" dialog box. In this case, you would hold down the Ctrl+3 key to switch to ViewMAX, rather than the Ctrl+1 key.

It is even possible to have ViewMAX have a number that falls between those of other tasks. To see this, start TaskMAX and run a program as the first task. Now run ViewMAX as a second task, but don't set ViewMAX to control TaskMAX. Instead, hold down the Ctrl+Esc keys to pop up the TaskMAX menu and add a third task. Now go back to ViewMAX and set ViewMAX to control TaskMAX (by selecting the "TaskMAX preferences" option on the Options menu and checking the "ViewMAX controls TaskMAX?" check box, as discussed above). Now, when you choose the "TaskMAX interface" option on the Options menu, you will see that the first task you started has the number 1, there is no number 2, and the last task you started has the number 3. There is no number 2 because ViewMAX was the second task you started, so the number 2 is assigned to ViewMAX, which does not appear in the Active Tasks list of the "TaskMAX Interface" dialog box.

If ViewMAX is not number 1, as tasks with numbers less than ViewMAX are deleted, the number for ViewMAX decreases until it becomes number 1.

Using the Calculator and Alarm Clock Utilities

In the upper right corner of the ViewMAX main menu is the ViewMAX option. Selecting this option by double clicking with the mouse pointer, or pressing the Alt+M keys, pulls down the menu shown in Figure 2.43.

There are three options on this menu: Information, Calculator, and Clock. The Information option pops up an information-only dialog box that identifies the Digital Research name and copyright dates for ViewMAX. The other two options select the Calculator and Clock, which are discussed in the following sections.

The calculator and clock do not turn off the rest of the ViewMAX screen, which means you can leave them displayed while using ViewMAX. Once they have been displayed, they are treated like additional windows on the screen. Consequently, the tab key or the mouse pointer can be used to move to and from these utilities and other windows on the screen. If they get in the way visually, they can be moved by making them active, then moving the mouse pointer into the title bar, holding down the left mouse button, and dragging the calculator or clock to the position you want it in. (They can be made active with the tab key or the mouse. As with other windows on the screen, when one of them is active its title bar will be highlighted.)

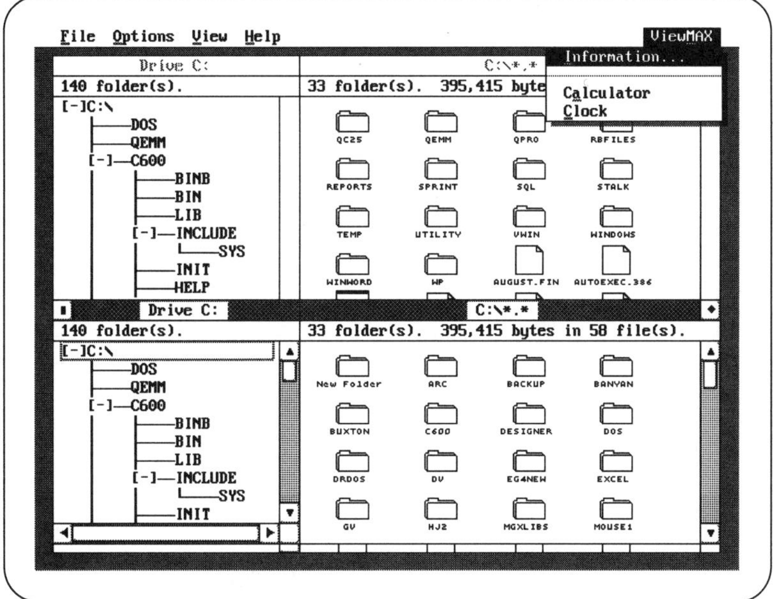

Figure 2.43 ViewMAX Menu

The ViewMAX Calculator

The Calculator option on the ViewMAX menu can be selected by pressing the A key, or clicking on the option with the mouse, when the menu is displayed. This pops up the ViewMAX calculator shown in Figure 2.44.

The ViewMAX calculator is a standard four-function calculator with memory. To enter numbers, you may either use the numbers across the top of the keyboard or the numeric keypad; if you use the numeric keypad, the NumLock key must be on. You can also click on numbers with the mouse. As numbers are entered they will appear in the display part of the calculator.

Any keys that are not part of the computer's numeric keypad can be entered either by clicking on them or entering the corresponding letters. For example, to clear the display, you can click on the C button or type the letter C. You do not have to press the Enter key—as soon as the appropriate letters are pressed, the corresponding action will occur. Pressing the Enter key is equivalent to press the equal sign on the calcultor.

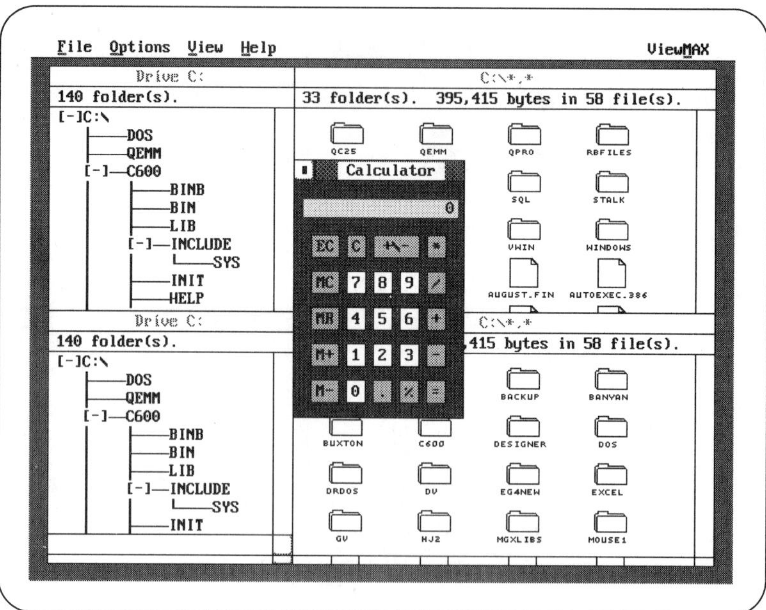

Figure 2.44 The ViewMAX Calculator

Table 2.2 summarizes the functions of the calculator keys.

Table 2.2 Summary Of ViewMAX Calculator Keys

Calculator Key	***Function***
*	multiplies the numbers entered before and after the *
/	divides the numbered entered before the / by the number entered after the /
+	adds the numbers entered before and after the +
-	subtracts the number entered after the - from the number entered before the -

Table 2.2 continued ...

Calculator Key	***Function***
=	completes the last operation
%	entering the number 200, then any of the four arithmetic functions (*, /, +, -), then the number 25 followed by the % key, produces the number 50 (25% of 200 is 50)
M-	subtracts the displayed number from the amount in memory
M+	adds the displayed amount to the amount in memory
MR	displays the amount in memory, but doesn't change the contents of memory
MC	clears the memory
EC	clears the currently displayed number, but does not affect the previous number
C	clears the currently displayed number and the previous amount
+/-	reverses the sign of the displayed number; pressing the backslash (\) key has the same effect

When a number is stored in memory, a small "M" appears at the left cnd of thc calculator display.

When you are done using the calculator, clicking on the small square in the upper left corner, or pressing the Alt+F4 keys, will close it. When the calculator is closed, all numbers are cleared from the display and from memory.

The ViewMAX Alarm Clock

The Clock option on the ViewMAX menu can be selected by pressing the C key, or clicking on the option with the mouse, when the menu is displayed. This pops up the ViewMAX clock shown in Figure 2.45.

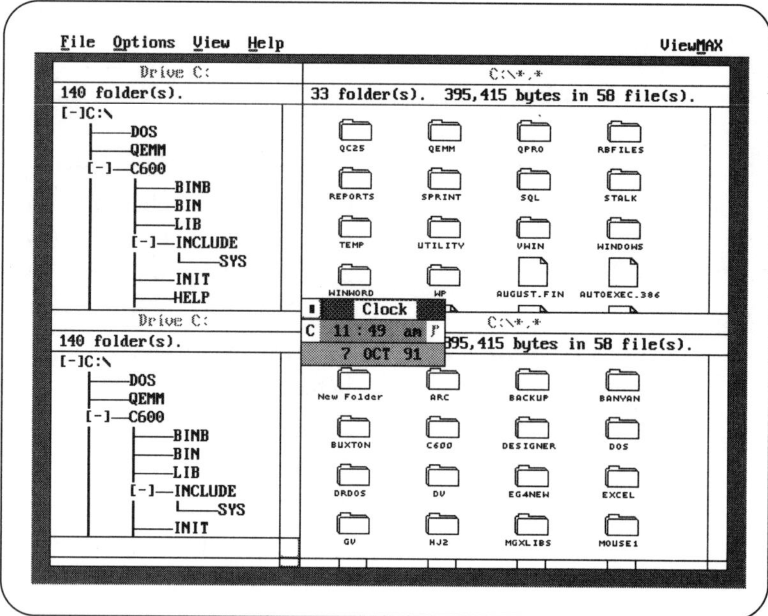

Figure 2.45 The ViewMAX Alarm Clock

Changing the time on the clock actually changes the time in your computer's system clock. This is a useful feature, since it lets you change the system date and time from within ViewMAX. The change to the system takes effect when you close the clock display, either by pressing Alt+F4 or clicking on the Close button in the upper left corner of the clock display.

When the clock first appears, it displays the letter C in the left-hand corner, next to the time. This indicates that it is in Clock mode, displaying the time, rather than Alarm mode, displaying the time the alarm is set to go off. To change the time, press the right arrow key or select the hour with the mouse pointer. This will highlight the hour number of the time. The number can be changed with the up and down arrow keys, or by typing in a new number. Pressing the right arrow moves the highlight to the minutes number, where you can use the same techniques to set the minutes. From the minutes, the right arrow takes you to the am/pm indicator. The up and down arrows are used to change this indicator; you cannot type am or pm directly.

From the minutes setting, the right arrow can be used to move the highlight to each part of the date, which can be set one at a time. The day and year can be set with either the number keys or the up and down arrows; the month can only be set with the arrow keys. From the year, the right arrow key turns off the highlight, leaving the clock displayed and active but with nothing highlighted.

The clock will not permit you to enter an invalid date or time; if you try, it will beep at you.

To set the alarm, press the Enter key or click on the C next to the time. This will change the C to an A, and the time will switch 12:00 to am (the default setting for the alarm). The keys now work the same as for setting the clock time. The alarm can be turned on by pressing the Spacebar or by clicking the mouse pointer on the musical note to the right of the time. The note will change from gray to black, indicating that the alarm has been turned on.

After the alarm time has been set, the clock can be restored by pressing the Enter key or clicking the mouse pointer on the letter “A”.

The alarm will go off as long as you are in ViewMAX when the set time arrives, and have not exited ViewMAX since setting the alarm. If you leave ViewMAX before that time, or run an application from within ViewMAX, the alarm is turned off and the alarm time is reset to 12:00 am. However, if you are using TaskMAX, the alarm is not reset when you switch between applications. If you are in an application when the set time comes the alarm will not go off, even if you switch back to ViewMAX afterwards, but if you switch to ViewMAX before the set time, the alarm will go off.

Managing the ViewMAX Environment

So far this chapter has focused on how to manipulate the various areas of the ViewMAX screen, and how to use the specific features available in ViewMAX. There are some additional features that do not apply to a single area of the screen or a specific feature, but rather affect the overall appearance and performance of ViewMAX.

Updating the Screen

When ViewMAX starts, it reads all of the folder and file names on the current disk in the PC and constructs the tree and file list for it. If a floppy disk is replaced, the change will not be reflected in the

ViewMAX windows, since it happened after their contents were constructed. To bring the windows up to date, you must force ViewMAX to reread the contents of the disk. This can be done either by choosing the Refresh option from the View menu, or by pressing the F5 key.

Changing Screen Colors

ViewMAX provides a number of different color schemes for the screen. Schemes are complete color sets that define colors for all areas of the screen. While it is easy to switch schemes, ViewMAX does not provide a direct way of manipulating the colors of individual screen areas (the menu bar, or the window titles, for example). To change colors, select the "Color schemes" option on the Options menu. The "Color Schemes" dialog box, shown in Figure 2.46 will be displayed.

When this screen appears, the current color scheme is selected. The Up arrow key and the Down arrow key, or the mouse pointer and scroll bar, can be used to scroll up and down through the list of available schemes. If you want to see what a scheme is like before choosing it, select the scheme, either by moving the selection bar to it and pressing the Spacebar, or by clicking on it with the mouse. The color scheme for the dialog box will change to show the selected scheme, but the rest of the ViewMAX screen will be unchanged. If you like the new scheme, click on the OK button or press the Enter key. If you want to try another one, repeat this process. If, in the end, you decide you liked the original, you may choose the Cancel button and the original color scheme will be left unchanged.

Controlling the Display of Confirmation Dialog Boxes

Certain operations, such as deleting files and folders, cause confirmation dialog boxes to appear. Confirmation dialog boxes are safeguards that are built into ViewMAX to protect against accidentally deleting something that you need. When you are working on a long list of items, however, the confirmation boxes can be a nuisance, since you have to respond to them for each item. Consequently, ViewMAX provides a way to turn them off. This should always be done with caution, since it removes an important level of protection against mistakes. In general, it is wise to turn these off for a specific operation, then turn them back on again when you are finished. Changes to these options are only effective for a particular session; they will be reset the next time you start ViewMAX, unless you specifically tell ViewMAX to save your changes.

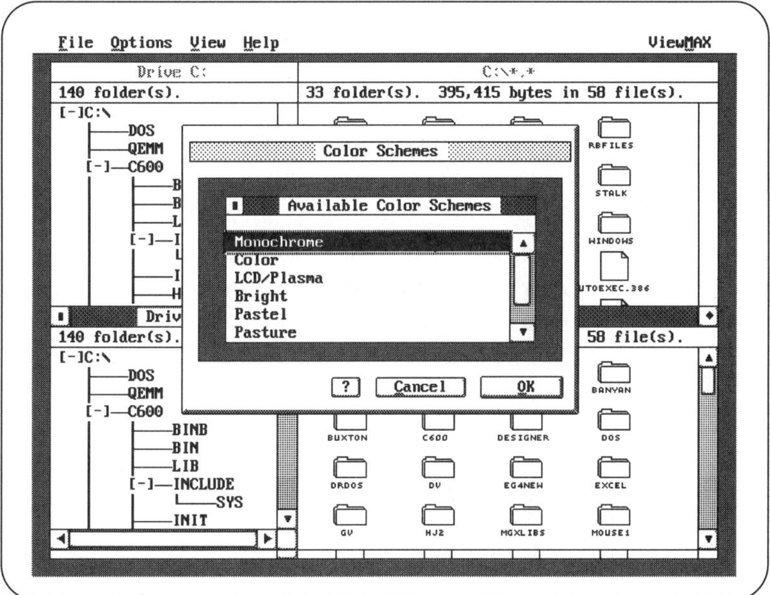

Figure 2.46 Color Schemes Dialog Box

To turn confirmation messages on or off, select Preferences from the Options menu. This brings up the "Set Preferences" dialog box shown in Figure 2.47.

The top half of this box is labelled "Safety", and is where these protections can be set. The default is for all of the confirmation options to be turned on, as indicated by the X's in the check boxes. Turning off an option is accomplished by selecting the option and pressing the Spacebar, or clicking once on the option with the mouse pointer. The X will disappear. The same steps are used to turn the options back on again. When you have each option the way you want it, select the OK button or press the Enter key to save your choices. Selecting the Cancel button or pressing Esc will cancel your choices.

Confirm deletes: Controls the "Delete Folders/Files" dialog box (see Figure 2.17). With this option turned off, files and folders are deleted automatically when they are selected and the Delete key is pressed, or when Delete is chosen from the File menu. You will not be prompted to confirm the deletion.

Confirm overwrites: Controls the "Name Conflict" dialog box (see Figure 2.30), which is displayed when you attempt to copy a file to a folder which already has a file with the same name in it. With this option turned off, the file in the target folder will automatically be replaced with the file in the source folder when the copy operation is carried out. You will not be prompted to confirm the replacement.

Confirm copies: Controls the "Copy Folders/Files" dialog box (see Figure 2.29), which is displayed whenever a copy operation is performed, regardless of whether or not the copy will overwrite another folder or file. When this option is turned off, ViewMAX will perform the copy without displaying this dialog box or waiting for your confirmation.

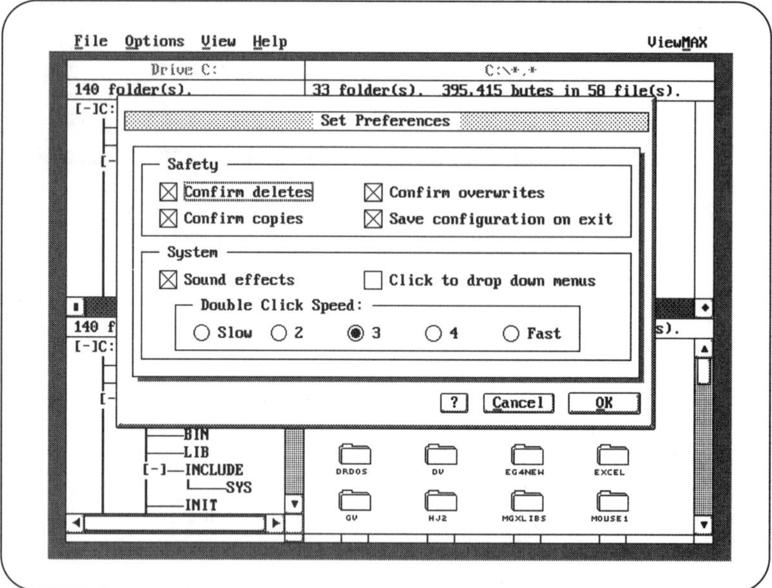

Figure 2.47 Set Preferences Dialog Box

Saving the Configuration Settings

ViewMAX saves all of the configuration settings in a file named VIEWMAX.INI. This file is read each time ViewMAX starts. If you change some of the options in the "Set Preferences" dialog box, those changes will only be in effect until you exit ViewMAX. The next ViewMAX starts, it will read the settings defined in VIEWMAX.INI and set the configuration accordingly. If you want to save your new settings, so that they are automatically in place whenever you start ViewMAX, you should check the "Save configuration on exit" check box. If this box is checked, when you exit ViewMAX the VIEWMAX.INI file will be updated with your new settings.

Saving your configuration saves more than just changes to the settings in the "Set Preferences" dialog box; it also saves the color scheme you have selected and the current window setup. The window setup includes the sizes of the windows and the current folders selected in the left-hand windows, and displayed in the right-hand windows.

Controlling Sound Effects in ViewMAX

Beneath the Safety box in the "Set Preferences" dialog box (Figure 2.47) is a box labelled "System". There are two check boxes and a set of option buttons in this area that affect the way ViewMAX behaves.

Normally, if you attempt to display a menu when a dialog box is displayed, or click the mouse pointer outside the dialog box, ViewMAX will cause the computer to beep, indicating those are not legal actions. The "Sound effects" check box is used to turn this feature on and off; it is on by default, as shown Figure 2.47.

Controlling the Mouse Behavior in ViewMAX

When you move the mouse pointer to touch an item on the ViewMAX Main Menu at the top of the screen, the drop down menu beneath that item automatically appears. This makes it very fast and easy to navigate through the menus, but it is different from the way most software behaves; most software requires you to click on the item before the menu drops down. The "Click to drop down menus" option on the "Set Preferences" dialog box is used to set ViewMAX to require a click of the mouse button to drop down a menu. The default setting is off (i.e., the box is not checked), which means that the menus drop down without a click. To change this setting, move the selection frame to this option and press the Spacebar, or click on it with the mouse pointer.

The three option buttons at the bottom of the "Set Preferences" dialog box are used to set the speed with which a double click of the mouse must occur for it to register as a double click, rather than two single clicks. The default setting is 3, which corresponds to the way most software is configured.

Chapter 3

Understanding and Using TaskMAX

When the IBM personal computer was first developed, it was expected to be a *single-tasking* computer, which meant that it would only run one program at a time. Given the limitations of computer chips and other hardware at that time, this made sense. The only computers capable of running several programs at once were mini-computers and mainframes, which were orders of magnitude more expensive than the PC. In order to multi-task, several requirements must be met: the computer must have the memory capacity to store all or most of the code and data for several programs at the same time; it must have the hard disk capacity to provide permanent storage of software and data, as well as extra space to act as virtual memory; and it must have a clock speed that is fast enough so that multi-tasking can occur at reasonable speeds. The first PCs met none of these requirements. Consequently, DOS itself was designed to be a single-tasking operating system.

Today, PCs have become vastly more powerful than anyone anticipated when they first appeared, and they have more than enough computing power to run multiple programs at once. However, PCs are still controlled by DOS, and DOS does not allow more than one program to run at once. DR DOS 6.0 includes a powerful utility named TaskMAX that overcomes this limitation of DOS and allows multiple programs to be loaded at once.

Understanding TaskMAX

The term *multi-tasking* is a little misleading, in that it implies that the computer is actually running more than one program at once. In fact, even on mainframe computers, this isn't usually the case. On mainframes, a technique known as timeslicing is used to divide the CPU resources between many programs. Thus, several people may be logged into the computer at the same time and appear to be working on it simultaneously. But what is actually happening is that every second is divided into thousands of slices. The computer is constantly cycling through all of the users that are logged on, giving each user one slice at a time. The computer operates at such high speeds that this is invisible to the users, so the illusion of simultaneity is created. There are multi-tasking operating systems for PCs, and multi-tasking programs that can be run under DOS, that use this technique as well, but TaskMAX takes a different, and simpler, approach.

TaskMAX allows you to load multiple programs—up to 20 of them—as separate "tasks". You can even load several copies of the same program as separate tasks. After programs are loaded as tasks, you can switch between them at will. However, only one task will be active at any given time; the computer is not actually providing time slices to each task in turn, but instead is providing all of the CPU resources to the active task. The others are frozen in the background, waiting to be activated.

TaskMAX also provides the ability to load tasks automatically when it starts, and to cut and paste between programs. For example, if you want the contents of a spreadsheet to appear in a letter you are typing in your word processor, you can start both of them under TaskMAX, then cut the material out of the spreadsheet screen and paste it into the word processor screen.

How TaskMAX Works

It is possible to use TaskMAX without understanding how it works at all, but knowing how something works always enhances your ability to use it to its best advantage. In order to really understand TaskMAX, you must know some of the technical details about the types of memory that can be installed on a personal computer, and how DOS controls the computer. These subjects are treated fully in other chapters, particularly Chapters 5 and 10. What follows is a brief discussion that will be sufficient for understanding TaskMAX.

There are three types of memory that are commonly referred to in PCs: conventional memory, expanded memory, and extended memory. The term *conventional memory* refers to the first 640K of memory, and is where programs and data are loaded. For example, if you are writing a letter in a word processor, the word processor program and the letter you are writing are stored in conventional memory.

In the early days of PCs, 256K of memory was more than enough for most programs and their data, but software today has gotten very sophisticated, and is often cramped even within 640K of memory. For this reason, a technology known as *expanded memory* was developed, which allowed a personal computer to use more than 640K of memory. Expanded memory could be installed on any IBM compatible PC, whether it had an 8088, 80286, or later chip. Expanded memory works by using a technique known as *paging*, in which program code and data that is not currently being used is stored in expanded memory. When that code or data is needed, some of the code and/or data in conventional memory is swapped out to expanded memory, and the needed code or data is loaded into the area of conventional memory that has been freed up. Software cannot automatically use expanded memory, but must be written specifically to take advantage of it.

As PC hardware developed, a second form of memory that went beyond 640K was designed. This memory is known as *extended memory*, and can only exist on 80286, 80386, and later, PCs. Extended memory has several advantages over expanded memory, but again software has to be specifically designed to take advantage of it.

Extended memory can be converted into expanded memory by certain software programs; the opposite is not true—memory that is designed as expanded memory cannot be converted into extended memory.

There is a third way in which software can exceed the 640Kbarrier of conventional memory: it can use disk space as virtual memory. When this technique is used, the software sets up a temporary file on the disk and treats this file as though it is electronic memory. This can be done because memory is simply storage locations that are referenced with certain types of addresses; it does not matter what physical form those storage locations take, as long as they meet the normal addressing requirements for memory. The software is set up to convert memory addresses to locations in the temporary file. There is a major drawback to this technique: it is very slow relative to electronic memory, because sending information to and from the disk requires several mechanical processes. These processes are thousands or millions of times slower than the process of transferring information electronically.

TaskMAX is a program that can make use of all of these techniques. If your computer has expanded memory, it can use that; if your computer has extended memory, it can use that; and if your computer has disk space that can be used as virtual memory, it can use that as well.

If you load several tasks into TaskMAX, one of them will be stored in conventional memory and will be active—i.e., the computer is actually executing that program. Any other tasks are stored in the other memory resources of the computer. When you switch tasks, the active task is swapped out to one of these resources, and the new task is copied into conventional memory from wherever it was stored.

TaskMAX will use any extended memory it has available before it uses expanded memory, and it will use all of the expanded memory it has available before it uses any of the disk space. This allows TaskMAX to maximize the efficiency of your computer, because extended memory is faster to access than expanded, and expanded memory is much faster to access than the hard disk. If TaskMAX runs out of all resources for swapping, when you attempt to add another task it will display a message box indicating you must first remove an existing task.

There is one other aspect of TaskMAX that should be understood, and that is its relationship to DOS. TaskMAX is a type of program known as a *TSR* (Terminate and Stay Resident). These programs load themselves into memory, then exit and return you to the command prompt. However, unlike most programs, which release the memory they occupy when they terminate, these programs remain in memory and continue to function in the background, usually monitoring the keyboard to see if their *hotkey* is pressed; when it is, they pop up. This is exactly what TaskMAX does. Right after you start TaskMAX, it returns control to DOS, but it remains in memory and monitors every keystroke that is typed. If the Ctrl+Esc key combination is pressed, TaskMAX pops up. If any other keys are pressed, TaskMAX passes them along to the program that is running. This happens so quickly that you are unaware that TaskMAX intercepted your keystrokes at all.

When you boot your computer, DOS loads a program named COMMAND.COM into memory. This program controls all the functions of the computer. When it is loaded, it creates an area of memory known as the "DOS environment". This is where the current path, the prompt definition, and some other system settings, are stored. The DOS environment is discussed in more detail in Chapter 10. What is important to understand here is that when TaskMAX is loaded, it creates a copy of the environment, which it stores in memory.

The COMMAND.COM program that DOS loads at boot time is required to control the computer, and every program that runs must have access to its own copy of COMMAND.COM, and its own copy of the DOS environment. Consequently, whenever a new task is created, another copy of COMMAND.COM is loaded, and the original DOS environment is duplicated for that task. As you work with TaskMAX, you will notice that changing the path or prompt in one task has no effect on the other tasks. This is because each task has its own copy of the DOS environment. In effect, TaskMAX is turning your PC into multiple "virtual PCs", each one running independently of the others.

You may want to use other TSR programs in addition to TaskMAX. For example, Sidekick is a popular TSR that provides a pop up calculator, notepad, phone dialer, and other utilities. If you load one of these TSRs after TaskMAX is started, then the TSR will only be available within that task. If you want such a TSR to be available to all tasks, then it should be loaded before TaskMAX. Anything loaded before TaskMAX becomes part of the global environment that TaskMAX stores; this is the environment that is reproduced for each task. Other TSRs that you would normally load before TaskMAX include your mouse driver, network software, and print spooler.

There is a disadvantage to loading TSRs globally. Since they are available to all tasks, they are reducing the available memory for all tasks. Consequently, if a TSR is only needed for a particular task, it is better to load it as part of that task, rather than globally.

To summarize, when TaskMAX is started it saves a copy of the DOS environment and returns control to DOS. However, it remains in memory and monitors the keyboard. When the Ctrl+Esc key combination is pressed, TaskMAX pops up its menu. When new tasks are added, each one is given its own copy of COMMAND.COM, and its own copy of the DOS environment. The active task is stored in conventional memory, which is where programs must reside in order to execute. When a task is not active, it is stored in one of the memory resources available to TaskMAX: extended memory; expanded memory; and hard disk space set up as virtual memory. When you switch between tasks, they are swapped in and out of conventional memory and these other resources. TSRs that are to be used by all tasks should be loaded before TaskMAX; TSRs that will be used by just a single task should be loaded after TaskMAX, within the desired task.

Using TaskMAX

Before TaskMAX can be loaded, you must run a program named SHARE. This program is in the DRDOS directory, and provides support for file locking, which allows multiple programs to access the same file. SHARE is normally used with networks, where file sharing is common, but since TaskMAX also allows multiple programs to access the same file, SHARE must be loaded before TaskMAX can be used. If you attempt to use TaskMAX without first loading SHARE, an error message will appear and TaskMAX will not load. Loading SHARE increases the amount of memory used by DR DOS. If there is room in either high or upper memory, SHARE will automatically load itself in one of these areas, but if there is not enough room there, it will load into conventional memory, thereby reducing the amount of space available for running programs. You can force SHARE to load into a specific type of memory using the command parameters discussed for the SHARE command in Chapter 11. A memory manager must be loaded that can support high or upper memory for SHARE to load itself in one of these. SHARE occupies about 787 bytes of memory.

Starting TaskMAX

Once SHARE is loaded, the following command loads TaskMAX:

```
TASKMAX
```

When TaskMAX loads, the screen in Figure 3.1 appears.

```
C:\>TASKMAX


TaskMAX R1.00 Application switcher
Copyright (c) 1989,1991 Digital Research Inc. All rights reserved.


The DR DOS application switcher is now loaded.
Use Ctrl+Esc to display the TaskMAX menu,
 or Ctrl+number to switch between existing tasks.


C:\>
```

Figure 3.1 TaskMAX Startup Screen

If you want TaskMAX to load automatically whenever you start your computer, you can put the SHARE and TASKMAX commands into your AUTOEXEC.BAT file. There is a number of variations on how you start TaskMAX. These are discussed below, in the section *The Full TASKMAX Command Syntax.*

As shown in Figure 3.1, once TaskMAX is loaded you are returned to the command prompt. This prompt actually represents the first task; you can go ahead and start a program from here, or you can press Ctrl+Esc to bring up the TaskMAX menu. If you start a program, Ctrl+Esc will bring up the TaskMAX menu from within the program. The TaskMAX menu appears in Figure 3.2.

The TaskMAX menu is divided into two parts: the Tasks menu and the Functions menu. Figure 3.2 shows three tasks running: WP, LOTUS, and COMMAND. The third task is named COMMAND because no program was started in that task, so task number 3 is still at the command prompt.

You cannot have more than one copy of TaskMAX running at once. If you attempt to start TaskMAX as a task, TaskMAX will display a message that it is already running, and will list the tasks that are loaded.

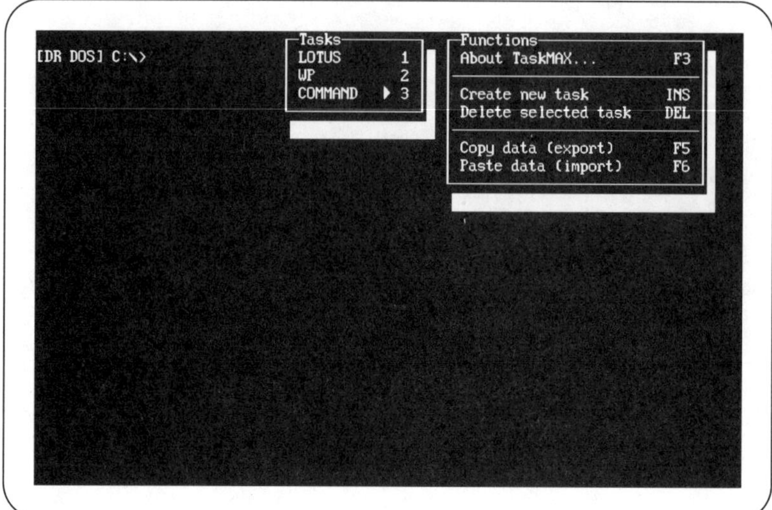

Figure 3.2 TaskMAX Menu

Adding and Deleting Tasks

New tasks are added by going to the TaskMAX menu and pressing the Insert key. After a moment, the screen will switch to display a command prompt. This prompt is a new task, in which you can enter DOS commands or run a program. When you are ready to add yet another task, or use some other TaskMAX feature, pressing the Ctrl+Esc keys pops up the TaskMAX menu again.

When you exit a program that is running as a task, you are returned to the command prompt. The task itself is still running, and it is still occupying system resources; it has simply changed from a program task to a command prompt task. To remove the task, press Ctrl+Esc to pop up the TaskMAX menu, use the up and down arrow keys to highlight the task to be deleted, and press the Delete key.

You should remove programs from the task list as soon as you are done using them. There are two reasons for doing this: the first is that there are only finite memory resources in your computer, and removing unneeded tasks will help to use those resources in the best possible way.

If you leave tasks that are not needed in memory, you may not have enough room to add tasks that are needed. The second reason for removing programs is to protect your data files. If the computer shuts down accidentally while a program is open, it is possible that the data file it was working on will be damaged, and you may not be able to retrieve the data that was in it. By removing tasks that are not needed you reduce the number of data files that could be damaged by a system failure.

It is possible to delete a task that has a program running. However, this is not recommended, because it could damage any open data files, and because it does not allow the program to do any "house cleaning" operations that it may go through with a normal termination. These include not only closing data files, but also deleting temporary files from the hard disk, and other operations. Terminating the program without letting it go through these operations can have anything from a minimal to a serious impact on your computer system, depending on the program and the conditions under which it was terminated. Consequently, you should not normally use the Delete option to delete a program from the Tasks list. Instead, you should exit the program normally, which returns you to a command prompt. From there, you can delete the task by pressing Ctrl+Esc to return to the TaskMAX menu, and selecting the delete option from there.

If you attempt to delete a program from the Tasks list, the dialog box in Figure 3.3 appears.

Normally you would respond with an N, which returns you to the program. You can then terminate the program normally, which returns you to the command prompt. Then go to the TaskMAX menu, and delete the task from thcrc.

There is one circumstance under which you will have to use the Delete option on a program running under TaskMAX, and that is when the program has *locked up*—the keyboard does not respond and it is not possible to terminate the program. This can happen if the program has a bug in it, or if it is not compatible with TaskMAX. It can also happen when a momentary failure occurs in the computer, or when one of the computer components is going bad. When a program locks up, it may still be possible to switch back to the TaskMAX menu by pressing the Ctrl+Esc keys. If this works, the program can be terminated by selecting the program in the Tasks list and choosing the Delete option.

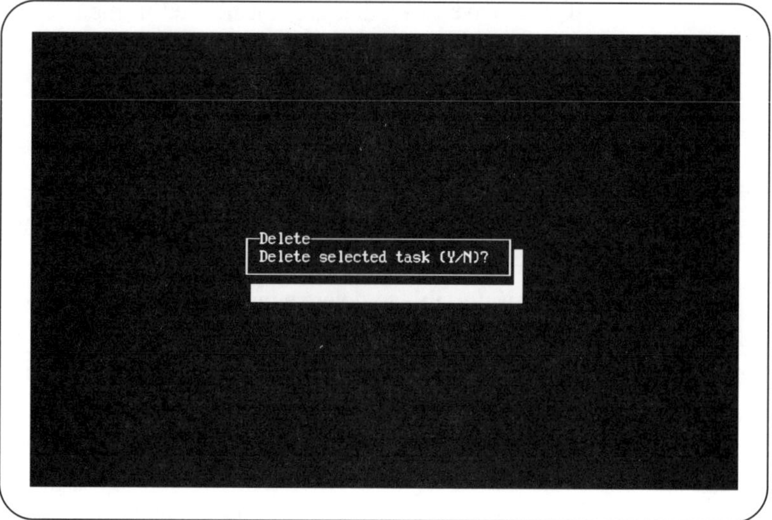

Figure 3.3 Confirmation Box When Deleting a Program Task

This should only be done when there is no other way to terminate the program. After deleting the offending program, you should immediately quit all other programs, exit TaskMAX, and reboot your computer. A program that has locked up may have corrupted some parts of DOS or other programs that are stored in memory. Continuing to run your applications may result in lost data, damaged files, or a corrupted disk.

It is not always possible to return to TaskMAX when a program has locked up—it may be that the entire computer is locked up and won't respond to any keystrokes. In this case, you will have to reboot your computer. Rebooting can usually be accomplished by simultaneously pressing Ctrl-Alt+the Delete key. If this does not reboot the computer, you must press the Reset button, (if your computer has one), or turn off the power switch, wait about fifteen seconds, then turn it back on.

If your computer locks up and you have to either terminate a program using the TaskMAX Delete key, or you have to reboot the computer while programs are running, you should check any files that were open at the time the machine locked up, in case they were damaged.

Examples of files that might have been open are documents being edited in a word processor, worksheets being used in a spreadsheet, or files that store data for a database program.

Checking the Available Memory Resources

While TaskMAX will use all of the memory and disk resources as efficiently as possible, there is still room for only a finite number of tasks. You can check the available resources by pressing the F3 key when the TaskMAX main menu is displayed; this selects the "About TaskMAX" option, and displays a message box similar to that in Figure 3.4.

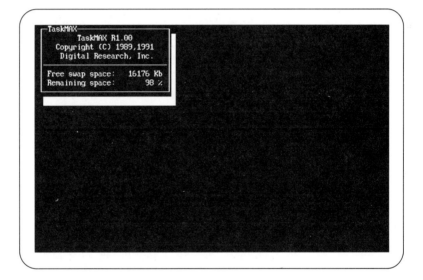

Figure 3.4 About TaskMAX Message Box

The top part of this box tells you the version number and copyright information for TaskMAX; the bottom half tells you what the total system resources are for storing applications, and the percentage of those resources that are still available. In Figure 3.4, the total resources available are 16,176 Kilobytes, or just under 16 megabytes. Taken together, the resources are referred to as *swap space* because programs are swapped back and forth between them and conventional memory.

The swap space includes any expanded or extended memory, and any swap file space set up on the hard disk. In this example, 98% of the total resources is available, indicating that there is room to add many more tasks.

Switching Between Tasks

There are three ways to switch between tasks:

1. From the active task, press the Ctrl+Esc keys to pop up theTaskMAX menu. Now select the task you want to switch to, either by typing the number shown to the right of the task or by using the up and down arrow keys. When the task is highlighted, press the Enter key. TaskMAX will switch to that task.
2. From the active task, press the Ctrl+Plus key ON THE NUMERIC KEYPAD—the plus key along the top of the keyboard will not work. Ctrl+Plus cycles through the tasks that are running under TaskMAX in the order they appear on the TaskMAX menu. The Ctrl+Minus key (again on the numeric keypad only) will cycle through the tasks in the reverse order.
3. From the active task, hold down the Ctrl key and press the number key (on the numeric keypad only) that corresponds to the task you want to switch to. This is the fastest way to switch tasks, since it jumps immediately to the desired task, but it also requires that you know the number of the task you want to switch to.

You may occasionally encounter a program that cannot be switched out of—you will be able to load it, and switch to it, but the only way you can get back to TaskMAX is to exit the program and switch to TaskMAX from the resulting command prompt. As discussed earlier, in the section *How TaskMAX Works*, TaskMAX constantly monitors every keystroke that is typed, waiting for one of the key combinations (Ctrl+Esc, Ctrl+Plus, etc.) that tell it to pop up its menu or switch tasks. Some programs interfere with this process. Once they are running, they intercept the keystrokes BEFORE TaskMAX sees them, and never pass them on to TaskMAX. Consequently, it is possible to switch into these programs, but once in them there is no way to switch out of them. There are three ways in which you can attempt to get around this. Which, if any, will work depends on the nature of the program.

1. You can use the DR DOS Setup program to change the hotkey from Ctrl+Esc to some other key combination. How to do this is discussed below, in the section *Configuring TaskMAX Using The SETUP Program*. The recommended alternative hot key, to try first, is Ctrl+Left Shift.
2. The program may have the ability to temporarily go to the command prompt, without exiting the program. This feature is often referred to as "Shelling to DOS", "DOS Shell", or "System". From the command prompt, the TaskMAX hot keys should work. Many spreadsheet, database, and word processor programs include this ability. Note that if you use this option, when you switch back to this task, you will be returned to the command prompt that you switched away from. In order to get back to the program itself, you should type EXIT at the command prompt and press the Enter key.
3. The program may provide the ability to selectively turn off its interception of specific keystrokes. The GrandView program, from Symantec, is an example. With its default installation, GrandView cannot be switched out of when it is running as a TaskMAX task. However, GrandView includes a utility named GVKEYMOD, which is run from the command prompt and allows you to selectively turn off GrandView's interception of specific keystrokes. Turning off the interception of Ctrl+Esc makes it possible to switch out of GrandView.

Copying Information Between Tasks

One of the biggest drawbacks to the single-tasking nature of PCs is the difficulty of transferring information between applications. For example, suppose you were writing a memo in your word processor, and wanted to include a portion of a spreadsheet in the memo. In single-tasking mode, you would have to exit your word processor, load the spreadsheet, save the part you want to use in a text file, exit the spreadsheet, restart your word processor, and import the text file created by the spreadsheet. TaskMAX gets around all this by allowing you to copy information from one task and paste it into another.

Transferring information between tasks is accomplished by copying a rectangular area on the screen of one task and pasting it into another task. This means that you can only copy as much information as can be displayed on the screen. If you need to copy more than that, you must repeat the copy and paste operations for each screenful of information.

To copy information from a task, make the task active, make sure the information you want to copy is displayed on the screen, and pop up the TaskMAX menu (Figure 3.2). The fourth option on the menu is "Copy data (export)", and the key that corresponds to it is F5. Pressing F5 while the TaskMAX menu is displayed brings up the Copy Dialog Box shown in Figure 3.5.

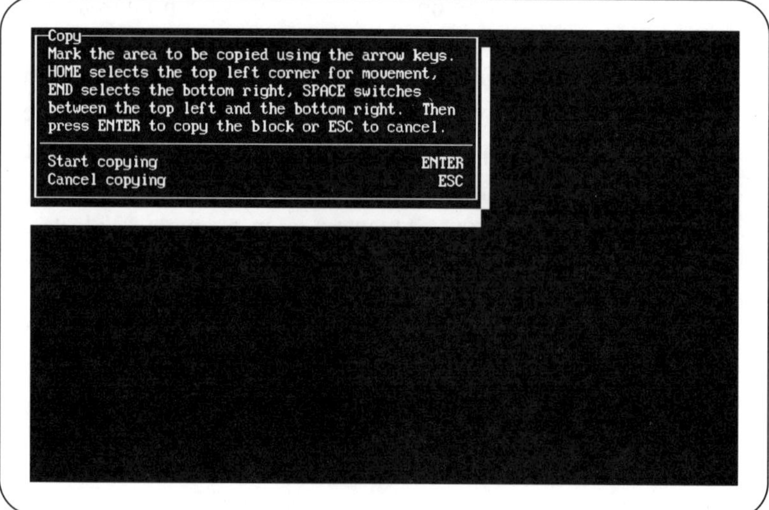

Figure 3.5 TaskMAX COPY Dialog Box

Copying is accomplished by first specifying the upper left corner of the rectangle to be copied, then specifying the lower right corner. These two positions define the rectangle to be copied. The Copy Dialog Box serves to remind you of the keystrokes required for copying, and to give you the opportunity to abort the copy operation by pressing the Esc key.

Pressing the Enter key when the Copy Dialog Box is displayed returns you to the screen that you are going to copy from. Whatever line the cursor was on in the program will be reverse highlighted. At this point, the upper left corner of the rectangle to be copied is the left end of this line, and the lower right corner is the right end of this line. You may use the arrow keys to change the upper left corner. When the upper left corner of the highlighted region is at the upper left corner of the rectangle you want to copy, you should press the End key to begin marking the lower right corner. Now the arrow keys will move the lower right corner of the rectangle. If you change your mind, or made a mistake, and want to change the upper left corner again, you may press either the Spacebar or the Home key. The Home key shifts the position being marked to the upper left corner and the End key shifts it to the lower right corner; the Spacebar toggles back and forth between these two. If you decide you don't want to perform a Copy operation after all, the Esc key cancels it and returns you to the program you were copying from.

You can also use a mouse to mark the rectangle to be copied. The mouse pointer appears as a small rectangle on the screen. Move it to the upper left corner and press the left mouse button. Now, while continuing to hold down the button, drag the mouse pointer to the lower right corner of the rectangle. You will see the area inside the rectangle become reverse highlighted as you drag the mouse pointer. If you change your mind about what area to copy, simply release the mouse button, move the pointer to the new upper left corner, and start over again.

One word of caution about using the mouse: pressing and releasing the left button without moving the pointer will abort the Copy operation and return you to the TaskMAX menu. You can begin again by pressing F5, but this is a nuisance, so you should be sure to hold the button down after you press it.

When the rectangle to be copied has been marked, pressing the Enter key completes the copy operation—an image of the highlighted rectangle is stored in memory. The next step is to paste the information into the target task.

To paste the rectangle, switch to the task that will receive it, and position the cursor at the desired location. Now press Ctrl+Esc to pop up the TaskMAX menu, and press F6 to begin pasting. The menu in Figure 3.6 will appear.

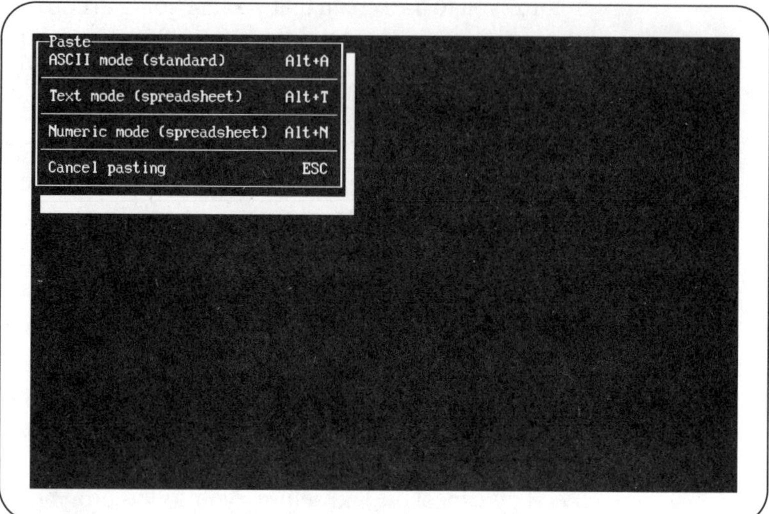

Figure 3.6 TaskMAX Paste Operation Menu

This menu offers three different *modes* for how the paste operation should be handled. The first is for use with most programs other than spreadsheets; the other two are for use with spreadsheets. To select an option with the keyboard, press the hot key combination shown to the right of the option, or use the up and down arrow keys to highlight the option and press the Enter key. To select an option with the mouse, click the mouse pointer on the option.

The "ASCII mode (standard)" option pastes the rectangle, character for character, exactly as it appeared in the source task. At the end of each line, a carriage return character is inserted. This gives the same results as typing the text into the target location, and pressing the Enter key after each line. This mode would be used with word processors, data base applications, and most other programs.

The "Text mode (spreadsheet)" option is used if the information being copied is text, rather than numeric, and you want to copy it into a column of cells in a spreadsheet. Each line of the rectangle will be preceded by a single quote (‘), which is the standard way of telling a spreadsheet to treat what follows as text. Each line will be followed by a down arrow character, which will paste the next line of text into the cell below the one just filled.

The “Numeric mode (spreadsheet)” option is used if the information being copied contains numbers, and you want only the numbers to be copied into a column of cells in a spreadsheet. When this mode is used, any characters that do not have numeric meaning in a spreadsheet are ignored, and each line is followed with a down arrow character, which will paste each line of numbers into the cell below the one just filled.

The characters that have numeric meaning in a spreadsheet are the number characters, the period (interpreted as a decimal point), the minus sign, and parentheses (interpreted to mean the enclosed number is a negative value).

This mode is useful if you want to copy numbers from a table in a word processor file, and the table contains text as well as numbers. However, it is important to be aware of how TaskMAX will interpret some of the symbols when they appear in lines that also contain text. If you do not pay close attention to where some of these characters appear, you will end up with mistakes in your data.

If a left parenthesis appears anywhere to the left of a number, the number will be interpreted as a negative value. For example, consider the following lines:

```
The value which (is 10 and no more
The value (which is 10 and no more)
```

If either of these lines is pasted using the “Numeric mode (spreadsheet)” option, the text will be stripped out and the number -10 will be inserted into the target location.

If two numbers appear in a line they will be joined into one number, even if they are separated by text. For example, the following line is transferred as the number 2002:

```
The number 200 is greater than 2.
```

Periods and minus signs anywhere in the line are taken as part of the number. Consider the following line:

```
The-number 10 is big. The number 01 is not so -big.
```

When this line is pasted, it comes out as "-10.01-.". Notice that both periods, and both minus signs, are transferred.

You must keep these peculiarities in mind when pasting numerically into a spreadsheet, and exercise care when marking the rectangle to be copied to be sure it does not contain symbols that will create invalid data.

You can paste the same rectangle into as many different areas of a task, and as many different tasks, as you like—it remains in the Copy memory until you replace it with another Copy operation.

The only restriction on what screens you can copy between is that the task you are copying from must be text based. If you attempt to copy from a screen that is in graphics mode, TaskMAX will display the message box in Figure 3.7.

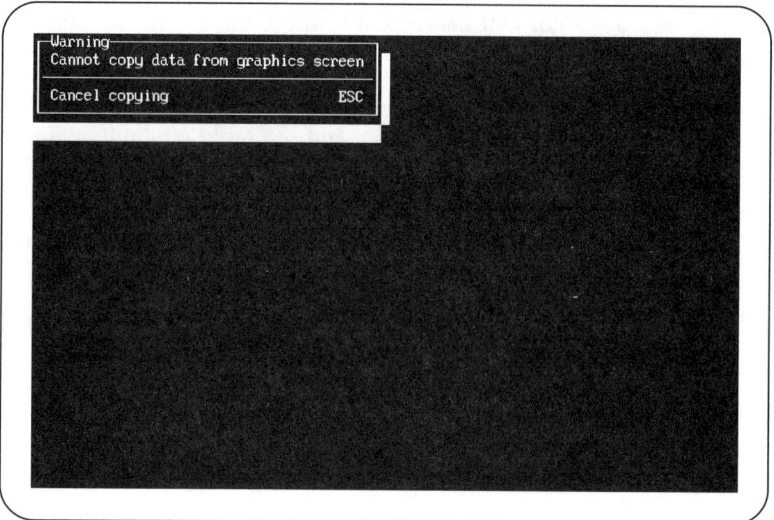

Figure 3.7 Warning Box When Attempting to Copy a Graphics Screen

You can, however, paste into a screen that is displayed in graphics mode.

Removing TaskMAX from Memory

TaskMAX is an excellent tool for running multiple programs simultaneously. However, there are two reasons you may want to remove it from memory: the first is that TaskMAX occupies some of the computer's memory resources. On a PC that has upper memory available, TaskMAX will load most of itself into the upper memory area. In this configuration, it takes up about 816 bytes of conventional memory, and about 5405 bytes of high memory. These are not huge amounts of memory, but they are enough to make a difference in the performance of some programs. If you are only running one program at a time, you may want to remove TaskMAX from memory in order to provide as much memory as possible to the program.

The second reason for wanting to remove TaskMAX from memory is that it is possible, though not likely, that you will come upon a program that will not run when TaskMAX is loaded. There are also programs, such as Disk Optimizers, that should not be run when TaskMAX is loaded because doing so may damage your disk. These programs are discussed in more detail below, in the section *Warnings, Error Messages, And Notes*.

To remove TaskMAX from memory, you must first remove all tasks. When one or more programs are running as tasks, the third item in the Functions part of the TaskMAX menu is "Delete selected task" (see Figure 3.2). When the last task has been removed, the TaskMAX menu will show a single task named COMMAND, and the third item on the Functions menu will have changed to "Remove TaskMAX". Pressing the Delete key will remove TaskMAX from memory, leaving your computer configured as though TaskMAX had never been loaded.

The Full TaskMAX Command Syntax

When TaskMAX is installed during the DR DOS installation and setup, several of its characteristics are defined. For example, the ways in which extended and expanded memory should be used by TaskMAX are defined during setup. So far, the discussion in this chapter has assumed that all of the settings for these characteristics are those that the SETUP program chooses automatically. It is possible to choose alternate settings, either during the initial installation of DR DOS or later, by running the SETUP program. This permanently alters the default configuration of TaskMAX, which means that whenever the TASKMAX command is entered without any switches specified, the settings defined during setup are in effect. Using the SETUP program to change these defaults is discussed below, in the section *Configuring TaskMAX Using The SETUP Program.*

The settings defined by the SETUP program are those that you normally want to use. However, you may find that occasionally you want to change one or more of these settings for a single TaskMAX session. Rather than require you to run the SETUP program to reconfigure TaskMAX every time you want a different setting, it is possible to specify alternate settings on the command line. These settings are defined with *switches* that follow the word TASKMAX. In addition to changing some of the default settings, switches for the TASKMAX command can also be used as shortcuts for some of the TaskMAX menu options. If you attempt to use an invalid switch, TaskMAX will display a help screen that shows the allowable switches. There are some settings, such as the specification of the hot key that pops up the TaskMAX menu, that can only be defined with the SETUP program.

Any TaskMAX switches that are used to override the default settings remain in effect only until TaskMAX is removed from memory. The next time you start TaskMAX, the default settings will again be in place, unless you specify different ones with command line switches.

Getting On-line Help for TaskMAX

There are two ways to get on-line help for TaskMAX: using the DOSBOOK command, and using the /? switch with the TASKMAX command.

The DOSBOOK command is discussed fully in Chapter 4. It provides extensive on-line documentation for all aspects of DR DOS 6.0. To use it for help on TaskMAX, enter the following command:

```
DOSBOOK TASKMAX
```

This brings up a series of screens that provide extensive descriptions of the TaskMAX command. The up and down arrow keys, and the PgUp and PgDn keys, can be used to scroll through the text.

If you are somewhat familiar with TaskMAX, and only want a summary of the TaskMAX syntax, the /? switch will display a single screen that shows all of the switch settings and a brief description of each.

Adding Tasks from the Command Line

Rather than returning to the TaskMAX menu every time you want to add a task, you may add them directly from the command line using the /C switch, followed by the name of the program you want to load. For example, the following command adds the WP program as a new task:

```
TASKMAX /C WP
```

When this command is executed, the WP program will be loaded and the screen will briefly display it before returning to the command prompt. If you then pop up the TaskMAX menu, you will see that the WP program has been added to the end of the TASKS list. You may switch to it in any of the usual ways.

You must have loaded TaskMAX into memory before using the /C switch; you cannot use it with the same TASKMAX command that starts TaskMAX. Thus, this switch may only be used from a COMMAND task.

The /N switch, discussed below, can be used in combination with /C, to simultaneously start a new task and specify an alternate name for it.

Removing a Task from the Command Line

Tasks may also be removed directly from the command line, using the /K switch. When tasks are removed using the "Delete selected task" option on the TaskMAX menu, a confirmation dialog box appears if the task has a program running. This is a safety precaution, since it is generally not wise to delete a task until the program running in it has been exited. However, when the /K switch is used to remove a task, you will not be prompted with a confirmation dialog box, even if the task has a program running in it.

The following command removes task number 2 in the Tasks list:

```
TASKMAX /K:2
```

When this command is entered, the screen for task number two is displayed briefly, then returns to the command screen from which the "TaskMAX /K:2" command was entered. If you then pop up the

TaskMAX menu, you will see that task number 2 has been removed. If there were more than two tasks running, those with numbers greater than two will all have been moved down in the list—i.e., the previous task number three will have become task number two, and so on.

In general, you should avoid removing tasks that have programs running in them, unless it is absolutely necessary. Tasks should only be removed when they are at the command prompt. A full discussion of the reasons for this were given earlier in this chapter, in the section *Adding And Deleting Tasks*. That section should be reviewed before using the /K switch to remove a task that has a program running.

Changing the Names of Tasks on the TaskMAX Menu

The task name that appears in the Tasks list may be different than the program name you entered at the command prompt. This is because some programs actually call another program file that contains the program you want to run. The name that appears in the Tasks list is the name of the program file that is actually executing. This can be seen by creating a simple batch file that calls a program file. When you execute the batch file, by entering its name at the command prompt, the name that will appear in the Tasks list is the name of the program called by the batch file, not the batch file name itself.

Batch files are not the only files that can cause this problem: some software is designed to use a file with a COM extension to load a program file with an EXE extension. In this case, the COM file name is what you type in, but the EXE file name is what will appear in the Tasks list. If the COM file and EXE file have the same name, you won't notice this, but if they are different, you will.

TaskMAX provides the ability to change the name that appears on the TaskMAX menu for any of the tasks. You may want to do this to make the name correspond to what you typed at the command prompt, or you may just want to give the task a more meaningful name.

To change the name of a task, you must be at a command prompt. If the task already has a program running, you can exit the program to get to the command prompt or, if the program allows you to temporarily exit to the command prompt, you may use that feature. Alternatively, you can switch to a task that is at the command prompt and rename the program.

If the task you want to rename is the active task, then at the command prompt enter the following:

```
TASKMAX /N newname
```

where "newname" is the new name of the task. The name may be up to eight characters long. When you switch back to the TaskMAX menu, you will see the new name in the Tasks list.

If the task you want to rename is not the active program, then you must specify the task number as well as the new name. For example, the following command will rename task number 2 to the name "REPORTS":

```
TASKMAX /N:2 REPORTS
```

You may also restore the original name of a task using the /N switch without a new name. The following command renames task number 2 to its original name:

```
TASKMAX /N:2
```

You may rename the current task by simply entering the /N switch, without a task number or name:

```
TASKMAX /N
```

Names on the TaskMAX menu always appear in upper case, regardless of how you enter them.

When you specify a name for a task using the /N switch, that name will continue to be used for the specified task number regardless of what program you run in that task. For example, suppose you start your word processor, then rename the task to be WRITE. If you now exit the word processor, which returns you to a command prompt, the task will still be named WRITE. Even if you then start your spreadsheet or another program at the command prompt, the task will retain the name WRITE.

Using Expanded Memory for Storing Tasks

If your computer has expanded memory available, the /X switch may be used to tell TaskMAX to use some or all of the expanded memory to store background tasks. To specify a certain amount of the expanded memory for storing tasks, the switch is followed with an equal sign and the number of kilobytes to use. For example, the following command tells TaskMAX to use 512K of expanded memory for storing background tasks:

```
TASKMAX /X=512
```

Using expanded memory to store tasks is much faster than using the disk, which is what TaskMAX will do when there is not enough memory to store all of the tasks. However, if one or more of your programs uses expanded memory, then you must be aware that any expanded memory allocated to TaskMAX for storing background tasks will not be available to those programs. Depending on what you are doing, and on how much expanded and extended memory your computer has, you may find that you get better overall performance by leaving the expanded memory for use by your programs and using other resources for storing background tasks.

You may disable the use of expanded memory by entering a 0 for the amount of expanded memory to use:

```
TASKMAX /X=0
```

You would want to do this if, during the SETUP program, you had specified that TaskMAX should use expanded memory for storing background tasks, and you want to temporarily override this and not allow TaskMAX to use expanded memory.

If you omit the kilobytes setting, or use a number larger than the total amount of expanded memory available, TaskMAX will use all of the expanded memory for storing background tasks. For example, on a PC that has 1024 Kilobytes (1 megabyte) of expanded memory, all three of the following commands will cause TaskMAX to use all of the expanded memory for storing background tasks:

```
TASKMAX /X
TASKMAX /X=1024
TASKMAX /X=2000
```

The /X switch can only be used when TaskMAX is started; it cannot be used to modify the use of expanded memory after TaskMAX is already loaded into memory.

Using Extended Memory for Storing Tasks

If your computer has extended memory available, the /E switch may be used to tell TaskMAX to use some or all of the extended memory to store background tasks. To specify a certain amount of the extended memory for storing tasks, the switch is followed with an equal sign and the number of kilobytes to use. For example, the following command tells TaskMAX to use 512K of extended memory for storing background tasks:

```
TASKMAX /E=512
```

Using extended memory to store tasks is much faster than using the disk, which is what TaskMAX will do when there is not enough memory to store all of the tasks. However, if one or more of your programs uses extended memory, then you must be aware that any extended memory allocated to TaskMAX for storing background tasks will not be available to those programs. Depending on what you are doing, and on how much extended and expanded memory your computer has, you may find that you get better overall performance by allocating the extended memory to your programs and using other resources for storing background tasks.

You may disable the use of extended memory by entering a 0 for the amount of extended memory to use:

```
TASKMAX /E=0
```

You would want to do this if, during the SETUP program, you had specified that TaskMAX should use extended memory for storing background tasks, and you want to temporarily override this and not allow TaskMAX to use extended memory for task swapping.

If you omit the kilobytes setting, or use a number larger than the total amount of extended memory available, TaskMAX will use all of the extended memory for storing background tasks. For example, on a PC that has 1024 Kilobytes (1 megabyte) of extended memory, all three of the following commands will cause TaskMAX to use all of the extended memory for storing background tasks:

```
TASKMAX /E
TASKMAX /E=1024
TASKMAX /E=2000
```

The /E switch can only be used when TaskMAX is started; it cannot be used to modify the use of extended memory after TaskMAX is already loaded into memory.

Limiting the Amount of Expanded Memory Per Task

Programs must be specifically designed to take advantage of expanded memory; if they are not so designed, expanded memory is useless to them. Most programs cannot use expanded memory, though the number that can is growing. If you do not run any programs that use expanded memory, then you should allocate all expanded memory for task swapping.

When a program that uses expanded memory is started, it usually reserves a certain amount of the expanded memory for itself. That memory will then be unavailable to other programs, until the first program is exited. Many programs that use expanded memory automatically reserve all of the expanded memory that is available. This is not unreasonable—since DOS is a single-tasking operating system, it makes sense to assume that no other program will need any expanded memory until the current program terminates. However, when TaskMAX is running it is possible to have several programs all wanting access to expanded memory at the same time. Consequently, TaskMAX includes the /L switch, which allows you to specify a maximum amount of expanded memory that can be reserved by any one task.

The following command tells TaskMAX to limit each task to a maximum of 256 Kilobytes of expanded memory:

```
TASKMAX /L=256
```

The /L switch can only be used after TaskMAX has been loaded; it cannot be used with the command that starts TaskMAX.

Specifying the Location of Swap Files on the Disk

When TaskMAX uses the hard disk for storing tasks, it stores them in a directory that was specified during setup. The default directory, if not changed during setup, is C:\DRDOS\TMP. There are two common reasons for overriding this default and telling TaskMAX to use a different directory:

1. The drive for the default directory may not have enough room to store all the tasks you want to run.
2. You may want to set up the swap file on a RAM disk, to speed up task switching. Techniques for setting up a RAM disk are discussed in Chapter 10. In most circumstances this is not recommended, since the RAM disk itself takes up memory that could be used for tasks. However, if there is not enough room on your hard disk it may be worth sacrificing the memory, since storing the swap file on floppy disks will make task switching extremely slow.

The /D switch is used to specify an alternate directory for the disk swap file. The following command tells TaskMAX to store the swap file on the D drive, in the \TMSWAP directory:

```
TASKMAX /D=D:\TMSWAP
```

Note that the specified directory must exist before you use it; TaskMAX will not automatically create a directory that does not exist.

To determine the amount of space required by the swap file, load all of the applications you want to have running simultaneously. Then, in a COMMAND task, enter the following two commands:

```
CD C:\DRDOS\TMP
XDIR /P
```

The first command changes the directory to the C:\DRDOS\TMP directory. If TaskMAX is set up to store the swap file in a different directory, then switch to that directory instead. The second command lists all files in that directory, pausing after each screenful until you press a key. One of the files listed should be named TASKMAX.SWP. This is the TaskMAX swap file, and its size in bytes will be displayed. This is how much disk space TaskMAX will require for the swap file when running this particular set of programs. The disk on which the swap file is stored should have a little more space available than the displayed size of the swap file. If you are creating a RAM disk specifically for the swap file, you should make the disk a little larger than the swap file size. Keep in mind that programs running under TaskMAX may require additional space on the disk.

The /D parameter can only be used when you start TaskMAX; you cannot change the directory specification while TaskMAX is loaded.

Configuring TaskMAX Using the SETUP Program

The settings that TaskMAX uses as defaults are determined by the SETUP program. This program is run during the DR DOS 6.0 installation, and can be run again at any time by entering the command:

```
SETUP
```

The TaskMAX settings specified during setup are stored in a file named TASKMAX.INI, which is read every time TaskMAX is started. The SETUP program is the only way in which this file should be modified.

The difference between settings defined used SETUP and settings defined on the command line is that SETUP settings are permanent—they are in effect whenever you start TaskMAX—while command line settings are temporary, taking effect only for a single TaskMAX session.

The first screen you see after entering the SETUP command is the DR DOS 6.0 SETUP screen. You should press the Enter key to accept the displayed settings, then wait while SETUP reads the various DR DOS intialization files—you will see their names appear as they are read. After reading the initialization files, SETUP displays another screen that gives you several options for how to balance functionality versus available application memory. The cursor will be in the option labelled "Continue without changing any current settings." You should press the Enter key to accept this option, which will take you to the screen shown in Figure 3.8.

The up and down arrow keys may be used to select one of the options on this screen. Choosing TaskMAX takes you to the screen shown in Figure 3.9.

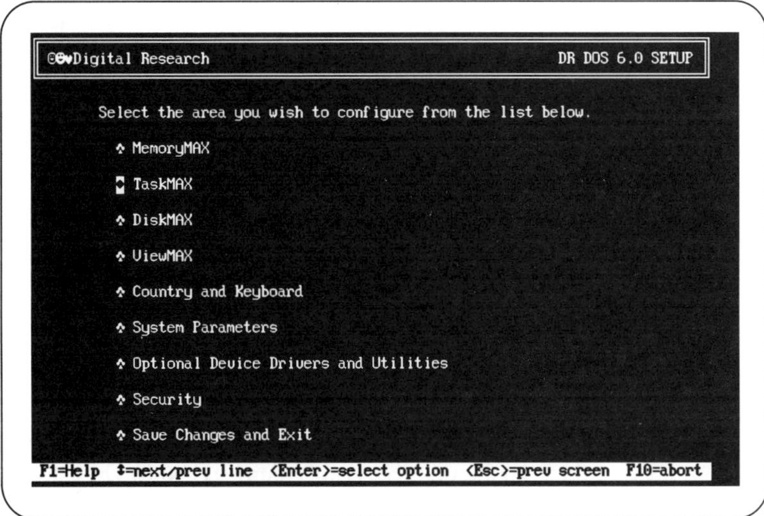

Figure 3.8 Options in the SETUP Program

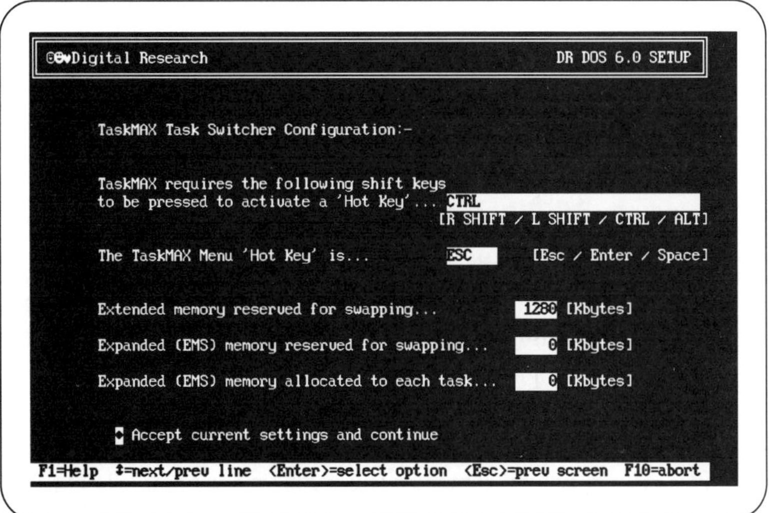

Figure 3.9 Screen One of TaskMAX Setup

Setting the TaskMAX Hot Key Combination

The first item on this screen that can be customized is the hot key combination. The hot key combination consists of one or more shift keys which must be held down while a non-shift key is pressed. The possible shift keys that can be used are:

R SHIFT	The Right shift key.
L SHIFT	The Left shift key.
Ctrl	The Ctrl key.
Alt	The Alt key.

To change the shift key part of the hot key combination, use the up or down arrow key to move the cursor into the data entry field for the shift key, and press the Spacebar or the right and left arrow keys, to cycle through the possible combinations of shift keys. In Figure 3.9, the shift key is Ctrl, which is the default setting.

The possible non-shift keys are:

Esc
Enter
Space

To change the non-shift key part of the hot key combination, use the up or down arrow key to move the cursor into the hot key data entry field on the screen, and press the Spacebar to cycle through the three possibilities. In Figure 3.9, the non-shift key is set to Esc, which is the default setting.

Setting the Use of Extended Memory for Swapping

If your PC has extended memory, it may be used for swapping background tasks, or it can be saved for use by applications. You may also divide it up, setting some aside for swapping, and reserving some for applications.

To specify how much, if any, extended memory should be used for swapping, use the up and down arrow keys to put the cursor in the "Extended memory reserved for swapping..." field of the first TaskMAX configuration screen (Figure 3.9), and enter the number of kilobytes you want to reserve. Remember that extended memory provides very fast task switching, but any extended memory reserved for this purpose will not be available to applications that may use extended memory. In Figure 3.9, 1280 KBytes are specified.

Setting the Use of Expanded Memory for Swapping

If your PC has expanded memory, it may be used for swapping background tasks, or it can be saved for use by applications. You may also divide it up, setting some aside for swapping, and reserving some for applications.

To specify how much, if any, expanded memory should be used for swapping, use the up and down arrow keys to put the cursor in the "Expanded (EMS) memory reserved for swapping..." field of the first TaskMAX configuration screen (Figure 3.9), and enter the number of kilobytes you want to reserve. Remember that expanded memory provides fast task switching, but any expanded memory reserved for this purpose will not be available to applications that may use expanded memory. In Figure 3.9, 0 KBytes are specified.

PCs that have 386 and later CPU chips usually come with some extended memory, which can be converted to expanded memory with software, such as the EMM386.SYS driver that comes with DR DOS 6.0. Extended memory is faster than expanded memory, so if you have a choice it is best to use the memory as extended, rather than expanded, memory. PCs based on 286 and earlier chips may have expanded memory installed in them, which cannot be converted to extended memory. In this case, the expanded memory must be used as is. The different types of memory are discussed in detail in Chapter 5.

Setting the Maximum Amount of Expanded Memory to be Given to a Task

Many programs that use expanded memory will attempt to grab all that is available. If you have two such programs, whichever is loaded as a task first will prevent the other from getting any expanded memory. To get around this problem, TaskMAX allows you to specify the maximum amount of expanded memory that can be assigned to any given task, leaving the rest to be provided to other tasks.

To set the maximum expanded memory per task, use the up and down arrow keys to move the cursor to the "Expanded (EMS) memory allocated to each task..." data entry field in the first TaskMAX configuration screen (Figure 3.9) and enter the desired number of kilobytes. For example, if your computer has 1024kilobytes (1 megabyte) of expanded memory, specifying 256 in this field will allow up to four applications to each use 256K of expanded memory. In Figure 3.9, the maximum expanded memory is set to 0 kilobytes, indicating that expanded memory is not to be made available to tasks.

When all of the specifications on this screen have been set to your satisfaction, move the cursor to the "Accept current settings and continue" field and press the Enter key. The screen in Figure 3.10 will appear.

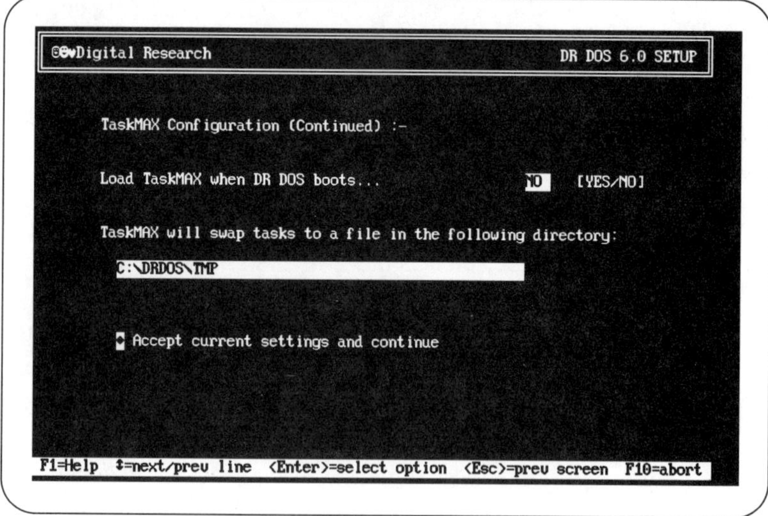

Figure 3.10 Screen Two of TaskMAX Setup Options

Setting TaskMAX to Load Automatically at Boot Time

If you will almost always use TaskMAX when you use your computer, you may want to set it up to automatically load when the computer is booted. This is done by selecting YES in the "Load TaskMAX when DR DOS boots..." field on the second TaskMAX configuration screen (Figure 3.10). The Y and N keys, or the spacebar, can be used to switch this setting.

Setting the Directory for Swap Files

The screen in Figure 3.10 is also used to determine the drive and directory in which the disk swap file will be stored. This file is temporary—it will be deleted as soon as TaskMAX is removed. The default directory, shown in Figure 3.10, is C:\DRDOS\TMP. To change this value, use the up and down arrow keys to move the cursor into the data entry field below the "TaskMAX will swap tasks to a file in the following directory:" line and type in the new drive and/or directory. You must make sure there is enough space on the drive you specify to store the swap file. The specified directory must already exist, or be created before you actually run TaskMAX. TaskMAX will not create the directory for you.

To determine the amount of space required by the swap file, first set the drive and directory to a location that you know has enough space—e.g. a hard drive that has one megabyte of free disk space for each program you will run simultaneously should be sufficient. Then load all of the applications you want to have running simultaneously. Next, in a COMMAND task, enter the following command:

```
XDIR C:\DRDOS\TMP TASKMAX.SWP
```

The name of the swap file is TASKMAX.SWP, and by default it will be in the C:\DRDOS\TMP directory. If you are using a different directory to store the swap file, specify that directory insteadof C:\DRDOS\TMP. The XDIR command should be used rather than the DIR command because the swap file is marked as both hidden and system, so the DIR command won't display it unless you enter special switches to do so. The XDIR command is easier.

Along with the name of the file, XDIR displays the size of the file. This will be the minimum amount of disk space you will want to have free for the swap file. Remember that any disk space required by applications will be in addition to this. For example, if you needed two megabytes for the swap file, and you were going to run a spreadsheet program and create a new worksheet that would be one megabyte in size, you must have three megabytes of disk space free. If you don't, when you attempt to save the worksheet, the spreadsheet program will give you an "out of disk space" error message.

If you specify a RAM drive for the swap file, the RAM drive must have been created before running the SETUP program, and it must always exist when running TaskMAX. For these reasons, it is not advisable to set TaskMAX to use a RAM drive by default. If you occasionally want to use a RAM drive, you may use the /D switch on the TaskMAX command line, as discussed above, in the section "The Full TaskMAX Command Syntax". The /D switch will temporarily specify a RAM drive for a single TaskMAX session.

When all the switches on this screen have been set to your satisfaction, move the cursor to the "Accept current settings and continue" field and press the Enter key. The screen in Figure 3.11 will appear.

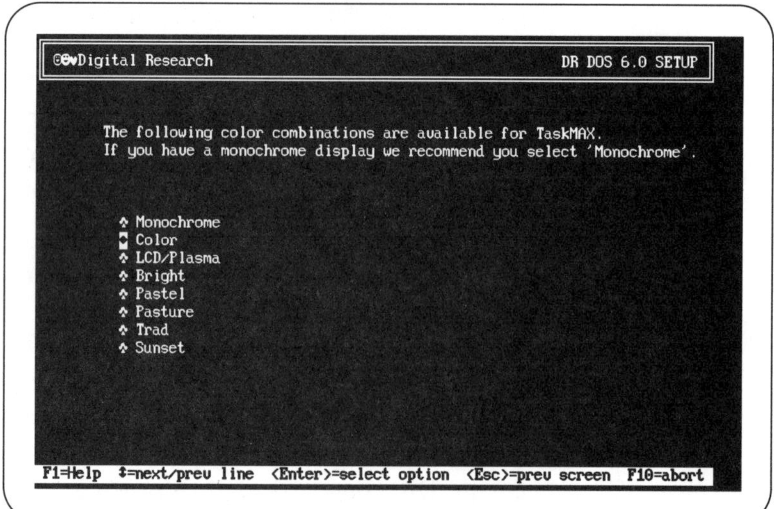

Figure 3.11 Screen Three of TaskMAX Setup Options

Setting the Screen Colors

The screen in Figure 3.11 allows you to select the color set that will be used by TaskMAX. It is worth experimenting with each setting to determine which one best suits your taste. If you are using a laptop computer that converts VGA colors to a gray scale, you should choose the LCD/Plasma option. If your computer does not have color capabilities, choose the Monochrome option.

Warnings, Error Messages, and Notes

TaskMAX is a complex program, and uses the PC in ways which were not intended in the original design of either the hardware or the operating system. There are certain types of programs that perform operations which may conflict with what TaskMAX is doing with swap files and memory. It is important to be aware of these programs, and to avoid using TaskMAX in ways that can interrupt their normal operation. It is also possible that environment settings will need to be modified to run all of the programs you want under TaskMAX, and some programs may not function properly when you attempt to run multiple copies of them.

Dangers of Disk Modification Tools with TaskMAX

As you work with your computer, files on the disk become fragmented—different sections of a file can get scattered around the disk, instead of being stored in adjacent areas of the disk. This leads to inefficient disk performance, so it is important to *optimize* the disk periodically, which places all of the sections of each file in contigous regions of the disk. It also places all of the free space on the disk in one large block, following the last file on the disk. Disk optimization is carried out with a "Disk Optimizer" program; the DISKOPT program which comes with DR DOS 6.0 is an example. Disk optimization and the DISKOPT program are discussed in detail in Chapter 7.

It is possible that using a disk optimizer while TaskMAX is running will cause either TaskMAX or the task programs to lose track of where their files are stored on the disk. This can result in a system crash, a corrupted hard disk, and lost data and programs.

There are also programs known as *Disk Editors* which permit you to manipulate the contents of disks directly, without regard to file boundaries or directory locations. These are very powerful tools that can change the contents of disks in ways that would be impossible without them. A disk editor can repair damaged disks, and recover information from disks that cannot be repaired. Disk editors should only be used by highly experienced users, because they can cause tremendous damage to a disk if not used properly.

Since these disk editors directly change the contents of the disk, they should never be run when TaskMAX is running. It is quite possible that they would change the contents of an area of the disk that TaskMAX or a program is using—either in the swap file or in a program or data file. As with disk optimizers, using these programs when TaskMAX is loaded can lead to serious system failures and loss of files.

Use of Communications Programs with TaskMAX

Communications programs are used to permit two computers to communicate with each other, usually through a modem attached to a telephone line. These programs permit the transfer of information between computers—one computer can transmit a file to the other.

Communications programs can be run as tasks in TaskMAX, but you must be sure to never switch to another task when there is data being transferred. To ensure that files are sent and received accurately, the two computers are continuously sending signals back and forth, the sender indicating what has just been sent and the receiver indicating what has just been received. If TaskMAX suspends this communication on one end of the connection, the other computer has no way of knowing that, and will attempt to continue with the transmission. This will disrupt the transfer of information. At the very least, the file transfer will have to be started over again. Switching tasks may be also break the connection between the computers entirely, requiring you to reconnect them before starting the transfer again. If the computer at the other end of the line doesn't automatically sense that the connection was broken and hang up, you will have to wait until someone notices and physically hangs up the line.

Error Messages in TaskMAX

Under some circumstances, you may find that attempting to run a program under TaskMAX will result in an error message. The message may be generated by either TaskMAX or the program. TaskMAX error messages appear in dialog boxes and are generally self-explanatory.

When you start your computer, a file named CONFIG.SYS is read by DOS. The information in CONFIG.SYS is used to configure the DOS operating environment. The CONFIG.SYS file and techniques for customizing the DOS environment are discussed in detail in Chapter 10. What is important to know here is that there is a FILES command in the CONFIG.SYS file that determines the maximum number of *file handles* that may be used at any one time. A file handle is required for a file to be accessed. The FILES command in CONFIG.SYS creates a pool of file handles. When a file is accessed by a program, a file handle is assigned to it. When the file is no longer being used by the program, the file handle is returned to the pool so it can be used again. Normally, DOS expects one application to run at a time, so the number of file handles that might be in use at any given time is relatively small—even complex database applications do not usually need more than 20 or 30 file handles.

However, when TaskMAX is running, you may have several such programs running, and the FILES command will have to create enough file handles to allow all of them to have their files open at once. If the FILES command in the CONFIG.SYS file does not specify a large enough number of file handles, when you attempt to load an application that exceeds the limit, the application will generate an error message. The message will be something like:

Not enough file handles available. Check the CONFIG.SYS file.

To determine the proper setting for the FILES command, examine the documentation for each application that you want to run simultaneously under TaskMAX. The documentation will tell you the minimum number of files that must be specified in CONFIG.SYS. Add up the numbers for each application; this total is the number that should be specified in CONFIG.SYS. For example, suppose you want to run your word processor and database at the same time. If your word processor requires 10 files, and your database requires 25, then you should put the following line in your CONFIG.SYS file:

```
FILES=35
```

When changing the FILES number, you want to provide as many file handles as your programs need, but you do not want to provide more than that. Each file handle occupies memory, and therefore reduces the total amount of memory resources available to your programs. It is worth going to the trouble of determining the correct number.

Another problem that may occur with TaskMAX is that some programs will not allow you to run multiple copies of themselves, or they will not function properly when you do. There are two common reasons for this: there may be overlay files that can only be used by one copy of the program at once; and the program may create temporary files with a fixed name, so that one copy of the program overwrites the temporary files created by another copy.

If the problem is with overlay files, you will probably see a message generated by the program that says something like:

```
Cannot open overlay file
```

Overlay files are used by programs to minimize the amount of memory required by the program. They contain parts of the program code that stay on the disk until they are needed. Then part of the program that is in memory is overwritten with the part that is in the overlay file. When the first part is needed again, it is read from its own overlay file. Some programs are designed to only permit the overlay files to be used by one copy of the program at a time, so when a second copy attempts to access the overlay file, an error message like that shown above is generated. Turning on the read-only file attribute of the EXE and overlay files for the program may solve this problem. If the EXE file is named WP.EXE, then the following command will do this:

```
ATTRIB +R WP.EXE
```

The names of the overlay files should be listed in the software documentation.

If problems are arising because of temporary files that are being created, it may be possible to provide your own name for the files, or specify the directory in which they should be stored. If this is possible, then you can customize each copy of the program to use a different name or location for its own temporary files, thereby eliminating the conflict. Again, the program's documentation should tell you if this is possible.

Other Multi-tasking Programs

TaskMAX is a useful tool for running multiple programs at once. However, if you find that you need more sophisticated multi-tasking capabilities than those provided by TaskMAX, there are other programs available from software dealers that provide more features. Two of the most common of these are DESQView from Quarterdeck Office Systems, and Windows 3.0 from Microsoft.

DESQView is a text-based program, like TaskMAX, which means that it runs in text mode rather than graphics mode. It is possible to run graphics programs as tasks, but the multi-tasking software itself runs as a text application. DESQView provides much more control over how tasks are set up and appear on the screen. DESQView also provides a faster cut-and-paste operation, permits you to create keyboard macros for each task, uses timeslicing techniques to allow background tasks to continue running, and includes a host of other advanced features. DESQView also has one of the best memory managers available. Virtually any program that will run on a PC using DR DOS will run as a task under DESQView.

Windows 3.0 is a graphics-based program, and therefore provides all the advantages of a graphical user interface. There is also a growing body of powerful software that will run only under Windows. Like DESQView, Windows uses time-slicing techniques to continue running programs in the background while you interact with another program in the foreground. However, these features come at a price: Windows requires substantially more powerful hardware to obtain the same operating speed as TaskMAX and DESQView, and some programs that are not designed specifically for the Windows environment will not run properly under Windows.

Chapter 4

DOS Command Line

To make the computer do something, you must give it a command. On computers that use DR DOS 6.0, there are two ways of giving commands: by using ViewMAX and its menus; and by typing commands on the DOS command line. When the computer is booted it will display either the ViewMAX screen or a command prompt, depending on how DR DOS 6.0 was configured during installation. Using the ViewMAX program was the topic of Chapter 2—this chapter will discuss working at the command prompt.

The command prompt is a symbol that indicates the computer is waiting for a command. The appearance of the command prompt can be modified. During installation, DR DOS 6.0 sets the prompt to display the name DR DOS and the current drive and directory, followed by a greater-than sign (>), followed by the blinking cursor. For example, the following command prompt indicates that the current drive is C: and the current directory is the root directory:

```
[DR DOS] C:\>_
```

A somewhat less common prompt is one that simply indicates the current drive, but does not indicate either the DR DOS name nor the directory:

```
C>_
```

Many other command prompts are possible—in fact, there is a DOS command that allows you to configure the prompt to be almost anything you like. The actual symbols used for the command prompt do not affect the behavior of the computer. Whatever its appearance, the command prompt simply indicates that the computer is waiting for a command. Customizing the appearance of the prompt is discussed later in this chapter.

The *DOS command line* is the rest of the line following the prompt. This is the space where you type in the commands. The phrases "Enter a command on the command line" and "Enter a command at the DOS prompt" are both commonly used and are synonymous. They mean that you should type the command on the command line, and press Enter. When a command is typed at the command prompt, it appears on the screen but nothing is done with it until you press Enter, at which time DOS sends the entire command to the CPU.

One of the simplest commands is the one that tells DOS to change the current drive. This command consists of the new drive letter, followed by a colon. For example, if a computer has two disk drives, A and C, and the current drive is C, then typing A: and pressing Enter will make A the current drive (the prompt will change from C:\> to A:\>).

There are two kinds of commands that can be entered on the command line: program commands, which run software programs that you have purchased or written yourself, and DOS commands. From the computer's point of view, there is no real distinction between these: DOS commands are simply programs that come with DOS. However, from a human perspective it is useful to distinguish between them because DOS commands are generally used for managing and maintaining computer resources (such as disks, files, and memory), while programs are used for accomplishing "real" work. For the purposes of this chapter, the terms *program name* and *command* are used interchangeably.

In order to use the command line effectively, it is necessary to have a basic understanding of how files are organized on disks. If you need more information, you can find a basic explanation of files and directories in Chapter 2, in the sections titled, *Managing Folders (Directories) in ViewMAX* and *Managing Files In ViewMAX*. Chapter 6 provides a detailed discussion of this topic in the section titled *Directories*.

When a command is entered on the command line, it instructs the computer to run a program. There are two places that programs might be stored: in the computer's memory, or on a disk. The only programs that are stored in memory are those for some of the most common DOS commands. These are contained in a file named COMMAND.COM, which is loaded into memory as part of the computer's boot sequence, and stays there until the computer is turned off. For example, the DIR command, which displays the files in a directory, is stored in memory. By storing these programs in memory, DOS can execute them very quickly. These are all small programs, so they don't occupy a lot of memory. Since they are used so frequently, it is worth giving up the memory they need to make them execute quickly. Furthermore, since they are in memory, they will always be available—they will not require a particular disk or directory to be available in order to run them—and they cannot be accidentally erased. DOS programs that are stored in memory are referred to as *internal commands*. Those that are stored on disk are called *external commands*.

Understanding the Path

In order for DOS to locate the file for an external command or program, it must know where to look. Hard disks can store thousands of files, so it could be quite time-consuming for DOS to search through all of the file names on a disk every time you wanted to run a program. On the other hand, it is a nuisance to always have to type in the names of all the directories that lead to the program file every time you want to run it. To make this easier, DOS provides a command called PATH. The PATH command allows you to generate a list of directories that DOS searches to locate programs. This enables you to run commonly used programs from anywhere in the system. PATH is an internal command, so it is stored in memory and is always available. For more information on using the PATH command, see Chapters 6 and 11.

When you enter a command, DOS first looks to see if it is one of the internal DOS commands stored in memory. If it isn't found there,

DOS next looks in the current directory of the current drive. If the program is not found there, DOS starts searching each directory in the path. If the program still cannot be found, DOS displays the message "Bad Command or file name not recognized." In this case, you must specify the full path name of the program. The term *full path name* refers to the name of a program file, prefixed with the complete drive and directory path leading to it. Let's take a program named WP.EXE located in the \WORDPROC directory, on the C: drive, for example. If the current directory is not C:\WORDPROC, you must enter C:\WORDPROC\WP to run the program (you can just enter \WORDPROC\WP if the current drive is C).

To see the current path, type the command PATH and press Enter. The list of directories that DOS will search is displayed, with each directory separated from the previous one by a semi-colon. Here is a typical path for a computer with a single hard drive:

```
C:\;C:\DRDOS;C:\WP;C:\123;C:\RBFILES
```

This path tells DOS to search the root directory (C:\), the C:\DRDOS directory, the C:\WP directory the C:\123 directory, and the C:\RBFILES directory, when it cannot locate a program file in the current directory. Note that for each directory, the letter of the drive that contains the directory is also included (in this example, the drive is always is C:). Floppy drives are not usually included on PATHs, for three reasons:

1. Access to floppy disk drives is very slow, so having DOS search the disk in a floppy drive is not efficient.
2. Floppy disks are frequently removed from their drives; if DOS attempts to search for a drive that has no disk in it, it will display an error message and wait for you to put a disk in.
3. Even if there is a disk in the floppy drive, there is no certainty that it will contain the directory and program that you want to run.

When DR DOS 6.0 is installed, it automatically puts a PATH command in the AUTOEXEC.BAT file. The AUTOEXEC.BAT file executes every time the computer is started, so the PATH command found there creates a Path that takes effect when the computer is booted. The contents of the Path command in AUTOEXEC.BAT will vary, depending on the configuration of your computer before installing DR DOS 6.0. The person who set up your computer may have further modified the Path.

Syntax of Commands

The syntax of commands is the same whether they are DOS commands or program commands. Commands may consist of more than just the command or program name. In fact, they may have up to four parts, in the following order:

Location Command Parameters Switches

Location: Identifies the specific drive and directory in which the program file is stored. The location is only required if the program is not in the current directory, or a directory specified in the path. When a location is specified, it must be joined directly to the command name—there must be no space between them. For example, to run a program named WP on a disk in the root directory of the A: drive, the following command would be entered:

```
A:\WP
```

Since the location identifier is joined directly to the command name, with no space separating them, it is sometimes considered part of the name. This is then referred to as the full path name for a command.

A location specifier is not required for internal DOS commands, because they are stored in memory. On computers with a hard disk, the DR DOS 6.0 installation program puts the programs for external DOS commands on the hard disk, in a directory named \DRDOS, which is part of thc Path. Consequently, unless the Path is modified to remove this directory, or these files are moved to a different directory, a location specifier is not required for DOS commands.

Command: The command name itself, which may be up to eight characters long, is the name of the command or program you want to run. File name extensions are not included when entering the command name—to run the program WP.EXE, simply type WP and press Enter. While it does not hurt to include the extension, the name is the only part of the command that is always required for all commands.

Parameters: Parameters indicate items that the command should operate on. For example, when starting a word processor you might enter

WP JIM.LET, where JIM.LET is a parameter that tells the WP program to load the file JIM.LET for editing. Parameters save time, since commands to load files into a program don't have to be entered after the program starts. Some commands take more than one parameter; an example is the DOS COPY command, which copies a file from one disk and/or directory to another. This command frequently takes two parameters: the first indicating the file to be copied, and the second indicating the location it should be copied to. For example, the following command copies the file named JIM.LET from the C:\WP\DATA directory to the A: drive:

```
COPY C:\WP\DATA\JIM.LET A:
```

COPY may actually take many parameters, since you can copy several files together into one large file. The details for the COPY command are discussed in Chapter 6.

For most commands, parameters are optional. However, some commands require them, and some don't use them at all. Parameters must be separated from the command name by a space.

Switches: Switches modify the way a program works, or how it interacts with the computer. Switches are usually entered as a forward slash (/), followed by the switch specifier. The switch specifier usually consists of a single letter or a number. Switches for most DOS commands are listed in Chapter 11.

Switches can have many different uses. Some examples are:

- to control how much memory a program uses
- to specify whether a program should use color or not
- to indicate whether a program should use a mouse
- to control how frequently a program should create backup files.

Not all programs or DOS commands use switches. Of those that do, each has its own unique set, so you must read the documentation for each program or command to determine what switches it uses and what they mean. When more than one switch is specified, they may all be run together, as in /W/A/S, or they may be separated with a space, as in /W /A /S. Since the slash tells DOS that what follows is a switch, a space is not required between the slash and the command name or parameters that precede it.

An example of a DOS command that accepts switches is the DIR command, which displays the names of files in a directory. /P causes the DIR command to pause and wait for a key to be pressed whenever the screen is full. This prevents file and directory names from scrolling off the top of the screen before you have a chance to see what they are.

An example of a command that may use all four parts is the DOSBOOK command, which starts the DR DOS on-line help system. This is an external command. On a computer with a hard drive, the program file for DOSBOOK is normally stored in the \DRDOS directory. If that directory has been removed from the path, then starting DOSBOOK requires specifying the location for the file. Assuming these conditions, here is a sample DOSBOOK command:

```
C:\DRDOS\DOSBOOK TASKMAX /B
```

The location specifier in this command is C:\DRDOS; the command name is DOSBOOK; the single parameter is TASKMAX, which tells the help system to display information about the TaskMAX program; and the switch is /B, which tells DOSBOOK to display its screen in black and white. DOSBOOK is discussed in detail in Chapter 4.

Using the DOS Command Line

The DOS command line is limited to 127 characters. If you attempt to type more than 127 characters for a single command, the computer will stop displaying characters after the 127th and beep whenever a key is pressed. Since the computer screen is only 80 characters wide, long commands will wrap to a second line. This happens automatically—the Enter key cannot be used to move to the next line because as soon as Enter is pressed, DOS assumes the full command has been entered and executes it. Just keep typing when you reach the end of the line, and DOS will jump down to the beginning of the next line and continue accepting your keystrokes. It doesn't matter if the break occurs in the middle of a word, it's all the same to DOS.

While 127 characters seems like a lot, complex programs sometimes involve a large number of parameters and switches. If data files specified in the parameter list are not in the current directory, then each one must have its full path name included in the parameter list. Consequently, 127 characters is not always sufficient for program commands. The SUBST command can be used to create abbreviations for long paths. SUBST is discussed in detail in Chapter 7.

DOS ignores leading blanks on the command line, so if you happen to hit the space bar before typing a command it doesn't matter. However, leading blanks do count as part of the 127 maximum.

Backspace is used to make corrections to the command line. Each time backspace is pressed, the cursor is moved back one space and the character that occupied that space is erased. There is a limitation to this, though: if a command wraps to a second line, backspace will not move the cursor back up to the first line. Consequently, when two-line commands are entered, the first line should be checked and corrected, if necessary, before the cursor moves to the second line. The left arrow key functions in the same way as backspace.

Shortcuts for Re-entering and Editing Commands

Backspace is of limited use, particularly when you need to make a number of corrections to a command, or when corrections are needed on the first line after the second line has been started. Furthermore, it is often useful to be able to repeat a command, with some minor modifications. DR DOS 6.0 has several features that make it easy to re-enter and edit commands that have already been typed.

When a command is entered, DOS stores it in an area of memory that has been reserved for just this purpose. This area is called the *template*. Keystrokes stored there can be played back and edited. The template is 127 bytes long, and always contains the most recently entered command. Whenever a new command is entered, the previous command is overwritten by the new one. A command is not stored in the template until Enter is pressed. For example, typing the letters AAA, then backspacing over them, will not put them into the template.

There are several keys on the keyboard which provide access to the template. All of these keys operate only on the template, and therefore only on the most recently entered command. As a result, it is not possible to use these keys to retrieve commands that were entered prior to the one in the template. These keys are discussed in detail in the following paragraphs, and are summarized in Table 4.1 at the end of this section. The History program, discussed later in this chapter, allows you to create a *command stack* that remembers multiple commands as they are entered, and lets you recall them for replaying or editing.

There are three ways in which the template can be played back. Note that playing back the template only displays the stored characters on the screen, it does not execute the command. The Enter key must be pressed for the command to be carried out.

The first, and simplest, means of replaying the template is the use of F1. Each time F1 is pressed, it plays back the next character in the template. The keyboard's typematic feature works with F1, so holding the key down will play back the characters in the template, until the end is reached or the key is released. This is convenient when you want to repeat only the beginning part of a command, either to use the first part by itself or to give it a different ending. For example, suppose you want to copy three files, named JIM.LET, FINANCE.DOC, and ACCOUNTS.WKS, from the C:\WP\DATA directory to the A: drive. The following command copies the first file:

```
COPY C:\WP\DATA\JIM.LET A:
```

Now, rather than retyping the first part of the command, you can press F1 or right arrow 16 times to repeat the first part of the command:

```
COPY C:\WP\DATA\
```

The command can be finished by typing in the next filename:

```
FINANCE.DOC A:
```

You may insert something into the middle of a command by playing back the first part of it, then pressing the Insert key and typing the characters to be inserted, then using F1 to finish the command. For example, suppose you intended to perform the above COPY command, but you left out the \DATA subdirectory by mistake. The template would contain this command:

```
COPY C:\WP\JIM.LET
```

When DOS attempts to execute this command, it will not be able to find the file and will display the following message:

```
File not found
0 File(s) copied
```

To fix the problem without retyping the entire command, use F1 to replay the first part of the command:

```
COPY C:\WP\
```

Press the Insert key, type the missing information DATA\ then use F1 to finish the command. Insert mode can be turned off by pressing the Insert key a second time. It is automatically turned off when Enter is pressed.

In a similar way, characters can be deleted from the middle of a command. To accomplish this, press F1 to replay the command up to the part to be deleted, then press the Delete key once for each character to be deleted. Finally, F1 is used to replay the rest of the command.

The second technique for playing back the template is to use F2. Pressing F2, followed by a single character, plays back the characters in the template, up to but not including the first occurrence of the character typed. Again using the above example, pressing F2, then D, would put the following command on the screen:

```
COPY C:\WP\
```

Now the command may be finished in whatever way you like.

F2 may be used repeatedly to get to the second, third, or later occurrence of a particular key. For example, if the command DIR C:\WP\DATA\LETS were entered, the files in the LETS directory would be listed. Now, to list the files in the C:\WP directory, press F2, then \, then F2 and \ again. This would display the command:

```
DIR C:\WP
```

The third technique for playing back the template is to use F3. When you start to type in a new command, you overwrite the template, one character at a time. F3 plays back the template from the current cursor position. For example, suppose you wanted to copy the file C:\WP\DATA\JIM.LET to the A: drive, then wanted to use the COMP command to make sure the copy was successful. After the COPY command, the template looks like this:

```
COPY C:\WP\DATA\JIM.LET A:
```

To execute the COMP command, all you have to do is type the word COMP, then press F3. The following command would appear on your screen:

```
COMP C:\WP\DATA\JIM.LET A:
```

If all you want to change in a command is the very end of it, use F3 to replay the entire command, then use backspace to delete the end. Also, if you have used F1 and the Insert key to insert something into a command, using F3 to play back the rest of the command is faster than holding down F1 while it plays back each character individually.

There are four more keys used for affecting the template, although they do not play it back directly. These are F4, F5, F6, and Esc.

F4, like F2, is used in conjunction with a character key. However, where F2 plays back everything up to but not including the character, F4 deletes everything up to but not including the character, starting with the current position. For example, if you play back the first three characters using F1, then press F4, then the character that appears in the sixth position, the fourth and fifth characters are deleted from the template. Pressing F3 after F4 plays back what is left. Alternatively, you may use the Insert key to insert a new beginning for the command before pressing F3, as in the following example.

If the template contains the command, COPY C:\WP\DATA\JIM.LET A:, then pressing F4, then J, then F3, will display the following:

```
JIM.LET A:
```

If, after pressing F4 and J, the Insert key was pressed, followed by the characters, COPY A:, then pressing F3 would cause the following to appear on the screen:

```
COPY A:JIM.LET A:
```

Now, the final A: could be changed to whatever drive the file should be copied to, using backspace, and the new command would be ready.

As mentioned above, a new command is only stored in the template after Enter is pressed to execute the command. This is usually acceptable, but there are times when it is desirable to store a command in the template without executing it. For example, if a command has extended to a second line before an error is spotted on the first, you don't want to attempt to execute the command before the error is corrected. However, there is no direct way to get back to the first line.

F5 can be used to store a command in the template without executing it. F1 can then be used to replay and correct the first part of the command,

and F3 used to replay the rest. In fact, F5 is useful for any long command with an error near the beginning, even if the entire command fits on one line. It is quicker to press F5 to store the command, use F1 to correct the error, then F3 to replay the rest, than it is to backspace over the entire command, fix the error, then retype it.

F6 can be used to place a control-Z symbol (^Z) in the command line. ^Z is a special symbol that means *end of file*. It is used to indicate to DOS, or to any other program, that the end of the file has been reached. Even though it occupies two spaces on the screen, ^Z is really just one symbol. Pressing F6, or holding down Ctrl and pressing Z, will create a ^Z symbol. It is not common for F6 to be used on command lines, but a few programs expect a ^Z symbol to appear as part of a parameter.

Esc is used to cancel a command, without executing it and without affecting the template. Pressing Esc moves the cursor to the next line, but no command prompt appears there. Nonetheless, you may go ahead and enter a new command at that point.

Table 4.1 summarizes the keys that may be used for editing the command line.

Table 4.1 Keys Used for Replaying and Editing Commands

Key	***Effect***
F1 or right arrow	Plays back one character at a time from the template.
F2 + Character	Plays back the template, up to but not including the first instance of Character.
F3	Plays back the template, from the current position to the end.
F4 + Character	Deletes characters from the template, starting at the current position and continuing up to but not including Character.
F5	Copies the current command line to the template, but then terminates the command without executing it, as though Esc had been pressed.
F6	Places a control-Z (^Z) character into the command line.
Backspace or ←	Deletes the character to the left of the cursor on the command line, without affecting the template.

Table 4.1 continued ...

Key	*Effect*
the Delete key	Deletes the character in the template that appears in the current position.
the Insert key	Turns on Insert mode, causing characters typed to be inserted into the template at the current position. When Insert mode is on, pressing Insert again turns Insert mode off.
Esc	Cancels the current command line, without affecting the template.

These keys can be used in many ways, and in many combinations, to provide very efficient control over the replaying of commands. For example, the command

```
COPY C:\WP\DATA\JIM.LET A:
```

can be converted to

```
COPY A:\DATA\JIM.LET C:
```

with the following steps:

1. Press F2, then C, which brings up COPY.
2. Press F4, then D, to delete C:\WP\ .
3. Press the Insert key and type A:\ , to insert the new drive identifier.
4. Press F2, then : — the command line now contains COPY A:JIM.LET A.
5. Press Backspace, then type C: and press Enter to execute the command.

In these steps, the 23 keystrokes that would have been required to type the new command from scratch have been replaced with 14 keystrokes. If you work at the command prompt a lot, it is worth becoming proficient with the command line editing keys. You should also learn to use the History program, discussed later in this chapter.

Pausing and Stopping DOS Commands

Many DOS commands produce some form of output—information that is displayed on the screen. For example, the DIR command displays a list of all the files in a directory. The information displayed does not always fit on one screen, but DOS does not automatically pause the display after the screen is full. Instead, it simply continues displaying more information, letting the previous information scroll off the top of the screen. There are two ways to temporarily suspend the execution of the program. This allows you to review the screen before anything scrolls off of it.

The first way to do this is by using the Ctrl-S key combination, or the Pause key. When information is scrolling up the screen, holding down Ctrl and pressing S will stop the display from scrolling. Pressing any key on the keyboard (except Shift, Ctrl, Alt, or Pause) will restart the display. This can be repeated as often as you like for any command. The Pause key has the same effect as Ctrl+S.

A more effective way of controlling the display is to use the MORE command along with the Pipe symbol (|). The Pipe symbol is discussed in detail in the next section of this chapter. To use the MORE command, simply follow any command with a space, followed by the pipe symbol, another space, and then the word MORE. (The spaces are optional, but they make the command more readable.) The output from the command will now appear as usual, but when the screen is full the display will stop scrolling and display the message "Strike any key when ready . ." at the bottom of the screen. Pressing any key (except Shift, Ctrl, Alt, or Pause) will display the next screen.

The MORE command is useful when you know you want to pause the display after each screen. The Ctrl-S (Pause) option is more useful if there are many screens, and you only want to pause the display once or twice while they scroll by. MORE can be used with any program that displays information directly onto the DOS screen. Programs that take control of the screen, like word processors, cannot be used with MORE.

DOS commands may be stopped in the midst of execution by holding down Ctrl and pressing either C or Break. Other programs may or may not respond to these keystrokes, depending on how they were written. Occasionally, a program will not respond to Ctrl-C, but will respond to Ctrl-Break. On the other hand, all programs that respond to

Ctrl-C will also respond to Ctrl-Break, so it is a good idea to rely on Ctrl-Break for this purpose.

You may want to terminate a command that you no longer want to execute, but that will take awhile to complete. For example, you may start a directory listing of a very long directory, then decide you don't want to see it after all. Ctrl-Break will end it for you. However, if part of a command has already been carried out, that part will not be undone by Ctrl-Break. For example, if the command DEL *.* was entered, instructing DOS to delete all files in the current directory, then pressing Ctrl-Break would only save the files that had not been deleted. Any files that were deleted before you pressed Ctrl-Break would be gone.

Redirecting Command Line Input and Output

DOS commands receive their input from the keyboard, and send their output to the screen. This is what is usually wanted, but sometimes it is useful to be able to use some other source for the input, and to send the output to some destination other than the screen. For example, it might be useful to store a DIR listing in a file.

Changing the source of input, or destination of output, for a command is known as *redirection*, and is accomplished with the greater-than (>) and less-than (<) symbols. The greater-than symbol is used to redirect output, while the less-than symbol is used to redirect input. These can be remembered by thinking of them as arrowheads that point to the object they are redirecting. The < symbol points to the left, which is where input comes from, and the > symbol points to the right, which is where output goes. To store a listing of the current directory in a file named LIST.DIR, the following command could be used:

```
DIR > LIST.DIR
```

If this command is executed when a file named LIST.DIR already exists, the existing file will be overwritten with the new one. Be careful with this command—there is no safety net. If you would prefer to append the new listing to the old one, use two greater-than symbols (>>). The above command would then appear as:

```
DIR >> LIST.DIR
```

If LIST.DIR does not exist, it is created by >>, just as it would have been with a >. But if the file already exists, the output will be appended to the end of the existing file.

When there is an error in the way a DOS command is entered, DOS displays an error message. Some of these messages are the result of the command itself diagnosing the error, while other messages are the result of DOS diagnosing the error. Error messages diagnosed by the command are affected by the output redirection symbol, the others are not. For example, when the command DIR XXX is entered, if there is no file named XXX, the following messages appear on the screen:

```
  Volume in drive C is DRDOS6
  Directory of  C:\
File not found
        0 File(s)   4110336 bytes free
```

The "File not found" part of the message is produced by DOS, so it cannot be redirected. The rest of the message is produced by the DIR program, so it can be redirected. Consequently, when the command

```
DIR XXX > ERROR.FIL
```

is executed, the first part of the message (File not found) is displayed on the screen, while the rest of the message is written to the ERROR.FIL file.

Output redirection is useful when you want the output of a command to be sent to some destination other than the screen. For example, it can be used to send output to a printer. In most cases, your printer is connected to a port on the computer which is referred to as either LPT1 or PRT1 (the two names are synonymous). Consequently, entering the command DIR > LPT1 will print a directory listing. If the LPT1 port is used for some other device, or if you have two printers, the LPT2 (or PRT2) port may be used.

You can also redirect the output of a command to be used as the input to one of the filter commands. In much the same way, input redirection can specify that a disk file be used as input to a command. However, you cannot use the < or > redirection symbols to specify that the output of one command is to be used as the input to another. To connect input and output using these requires two command sequences and an intermediate file. For example, to apply the MORE filter to the results of the DIR command, the following two commands could be used:

```
DIR > TEMP.FIL
MORE < TEMP.FIL
```

The Pipe symbol (|) can be used to simplify this process. It is called a Pipe because of the way it connects the two commands, sending the output of the first command into the input of the second. Using Pipe, the two commands listed above can be replaced with the single command:

```
DIR | MORE
```

The Pipe not only reduces two commands to one, but also eliminates the need for an intermediate file. Note that the blank spaces before and after the Pipe symbol are not required, but they make the command more readable.

The DOS Filter Commands—MORE, FIND, and SORT

Filter commands are used to divide, rearrange, or extract parts of their input. They are external commands. There are three filter commands:

- MORE accepts input, then displays it on the screen, pausing after each screen until a key is pressed.
- FIND is used to search through its input to locate a particular text string.
- SORT sorts its input alphabetically.

By using filters in conjunction with the redirection symbols, the input can come from a file or another command, and the output can go to a file, a printer, or another command. The filter commands and their switches are summarized in Table 4.2.

Table 4.2 The DOS Filter Commands and Their Switch Settings

Filter	*Switch*	*Effect*
MORE	None	Displays the input on the screen, pausing for a key to be pressed after each screen.
FIND	None	Searches for a specified string in a specified file. Displays all lines in which the string appears.
	/B	Displays the underlined name of each file searched above the matching lines.

Table 4.2 continued ...

Filter	***Switch***	***Effect***
	/C	Produces a count of the lines in which the search string occurs. The lines themselves are not displayed.
	/F	Shows only the names of files that contain matching lines.
	/N	Displays line numbers at the beginning of each displayed line.
	/S	Searches files in subdirectories of the current directory, as well as the current directory.
	/U	Makes the search case-sensitive, so that F is considered different from f.
	/V	Displays all lines in which the search string does not appear.
SORT	None	Reads its input, sorts it in alphabetic order, and sends the sorted data to the output.
	/+N	Bases the sort on column N of each line.
	/R	Reverses the sort order.

Filter commands are best used with plain ASCII files—files that do not contain any special formatting characters. If you see non-alphanumeric symbols on the screen when a file is displayed with one of the filters, then the file contains non-ASCII symbols. Most word processor, spreadsheet and database files contain non-ASCII formatting symbols. This makes them difficult, if not impossible, to interpret. The filters cannot be used with executable files—files with .COM or .EXE extensions—because they consist of computer instructions, rather than data that is stored in ASCII codes.

MORE allows you to view the contents of a file, one screen at a time. It does this by redirecting the input (the file), through the filter

(MORE), to the screen (the output). MORE allows data to scroll onto the screen, until the screen is full. It then adds the message "Strike a key when ready . . ." at the bottom of the screen and waits for an input from the keyboard. Pressing any key causes the next screen to be displayed.

To examine a file named MYFILE.TXT, enter the command MORE < MYFILE.TXT. If the file to be displayed is not in the current directory, a complete pathname must be specified:

```
MORE < C:\WP\LETTERS\MYFILE.TXT.
```

FIND is used to determine whether an input source contains a particular string of characters. Unless the /U switch is specified, FIND is not case-sensitive—i.e., it treats F the same as f. For the following examples, the FIND filter will be applied to a file named GREEN.LET, shown in Figure 4.1.

```
June 1, 1991


Mr. William Green, President
Green Industries, Incorporated
1900 Industrial Boulevard
Minneapolis, Minnesota 55411
Dear Mr. Green,
I am writing to thank you for having the sample products sent
to me last week.  My staff has begun reviewing and testing the
products, and should have recommendations on some of them by the
end of next week.   Our impression so far has been quite
favorable, and I am sure we will be able to work out a mutually
satisfying relationship.
Please let us know when your new product line is available, as
there are several items we are interested in.
Sincerely,


Susan Anderson
Vice President, Automation

P.S. The "Ultra" products are especially exciting.
```

Figure 4.1   Sample Input File For The FIND Filter

The following command searches the file in Figure 4.1 for the word *Green*:

```
FIND "Green" GREEN.LET
```

The result of this command is:

```
c:green.let:  Mr.  William  Green,  President
c:green.let:  Green  Industries,  Incorporated
c:green.let: Dear Mr. Green,
```

When using the FIND filter, the character string to be searched for is required, and must be enclosed in double quotes. The file name to search is not required, but if you do not enter one, FIND will display a blank command line and accept whatever you type as its input. To break out of the FIND command under these circumstances, press F6 followed by Enter. F6 inserts a ^Z character, which is the symbol used to indicate the end of a file. When FIND sees the ^Z it assumes the input has ended and returns you to the command prompt.

If you want to search for a string that contains double quotes ("), you must enter the quotes twice in the search string. The following command successfully searches the sample file for the string, The "Ultra" products:

```
FIND "The ""Ultra"" products" GREEN.LET
```

If the file to be searched is not in the current directory, its full path must be specified. The DOS wild cards (* and ?) may be used with FIND to search multiple files. For example, the following command searches all files with the extension LET for the string "Green":

```
FIND "Green" *.let
```

FIND does not recognize strings broken by carriage returns—symbols that indicate where one line ends and the next begins. Most text files include carriage return symbols at the end of each line, but some do not, in which case they consist of one or more long stream(s) of words. FIND will not locate a string that is broken by a carriage return. For example, the first full line of the letter shown in Figure 4.1 ends with the word "sent." The second line begins with the word "to." It is not possible to use the FIND filter to locate the string "sent to" in this file.

The output of the FIND command can be piped to the input of the MORE command, to prevent the FIND output from scrolling off the screen. For example, to search a file named SALES.MEM for the string "Midwest sales percentages," and prevent the output from scrolling off the screen, the following command could be used:

FIND "Midwest sales percentages" SALES.MEM | MORE

There are seven switches that can be used with FIND: /B /C, /F, /N, /S, /U, and /V. The /B switch is used to display a header above the matching lines in the files. For example, using the sample file in Figure 4.1, the command FIND /B "GREEN" GREEN.LET produces the following output:

```
FILE: c:green.let

________

Mr. William Green, President
Green Industries, Incorporated
Dear Mr. Green,
```

The /C switch is used to display just a count of the lines that contain the specified string. The command FIND /C "Green" GREEN.LET displays the following line:

```
3  c:green.let
```

You may want to simply determine which files contain the search string, and not care to see the actual occurrences. This can be accomplished with the /F switch, which displays only the names of files that contain the string. Consider two files, GREEN.LET and BLACK.LET, both of which contain letters written on June 1, 1991. The command FIND /F "June 1, 1991" *.LET would produce the following output:

```
c:green.let
c:black.let
```

Sometimes displaying the lines that contain the search string is not sufficient, particularly in a large file. It may be important not only to see the line, but to know where it is in the file. The /N switch precedes each displayed line with its line number in the file. The command

```
FIND /N "Green" GREEN.LET
```

produces the following output:

```
c:green.let(5): Mr. William Green, President
c:green.let(6): Green Industries,Incorporated
c:green.let(10): Dear Mr. Green,
```

By default, the FIND command searches only files in the current directory. You may use the /S switch to direct FIND to also search subdirectories of the current directory. Suppose the current directory is C:\WP\DATA, and it contains the file GREEN.LET. Further suppose that the file BLACK.LET is in the C:\WP\DATA\TEMP, and that both files were written on June 1, 1991. The command

```
FIND /S "June 1, 1991" *.LET
```

produces this output:

```
c:\wp\data\green.let: June 1, 1991
c:\wp\data\temp\black.let: June 1, 1991
```

By default, the FIND filter is not case-sensitive. Using the file in Figure 4.1, the command FIND "green" GREEN.LET will locate the same lines as FIND "GREEN" GREEN.LET. The /U switch is used to indicate that the search should be sensitive to case. The command

```
FIND "green" GREEN.LET/U
```

would not locate any lines in the file.

FIND normally displays all of the lines in the input that contain the specified string. Sometimes the opposite effect is desired—you want to see all lines that do not contain the search string. The /V switch is used to accomplish this. Using the file in Figure 4.1, the command

```
FIND /V "Green" GREEN.LET
```

produces this output:

```
c:green.let: June 1, 1991
c:green.let:
c:green.let:
c:green.let:
c:green.let: 1900 Industrial Boulevard
c:green.let: Minneapolis, Minnesota 55411
c:green.let:
c:green.let:
c:green.let: I am writing to thank you for having the sample products sent
c:green.let: to me last week.  My staff has begun reviewing and testing the
c:green.let: products, and should have recommendations on some of them by the
c:green.let: end of next week.  Our impression so far has been quite
c:green.let: favorable, and I am sure we will be able to work out a mutually
c:green.let: satisfying relationship.
c:green.let:
c:green.let: Please let us know when your new product line is available, as
c:green.let: there are several items we are interested in.
c:green.let:
c:green.let: Sincerely,
c:green.let:
c:green.let:
c:green.let:
c:green.let: Susan Anderson
c:green.let: Vice President, Automation
c:green.let:
c:green.let: P.S. The "Ultra" products are especially exciting.
```

Many of the switches may be combined. For example, using the /C switch with the /V switch results in a count of all the lines that do not contain the search string. Some of the combinations do not make sense, in which case one switch will override the other. For example, if /C and /N are both used, /N is ignored.

SORT is used to sort an input source, usually a file. The output can be the screen, a new file, or a device, such as a printer. SORT can handle files up to 64K bytes in size. The examples here will be based on a file named ADDRESS.LST, shown in Table 4.3.

Table 4.3 Sample File for Use with the SORT Command

Williams, Frank	1011 Zenith Ave. So.	Minneapolis, MN	55401
Andrews, Bill	14 North Snelling	St. Paul, MN	55408
Banks, Susan	2022 Hacienda Blvd.	San Diego, CA	91020
Yeoman, Mary	134 North Summit	Silver Spring, MD	32976
Hoffman, Andy	132 E. Franklin	Seattle, WA	80971
Manchester, Chris	9501 Drew Ave. So.	Bloomington, MN	55321

Unless the /+N switch is used, the SORT filter determines the sorted order based on the character in the first column of each line. If the first character of two lines match, it sorts on the second character, and so on. When considering what criteria SORT will use to determine the new order for a file, it is usually sufficient to expect it to sort according to the ASCII table, without distinguishing between upper and lower case letters—lower case letters are treated as upper case. A complete ASCII table appears in the Appendix. Since the blank space symbol appears before numbers and letters in the ASCII table, all the blank lines come out first.

> ***Note:*** For the technically minded, SORT actually uses the collating sequence table that corresponds to the country code and code page setting for which your computer is configured. For characters that have ASCII codes greater than 127, SORT uses information supplied in the COUNTRY.SYS file, which is in the DOS directory, or in an alternate file that you may have specified using the COUNTRY command in your CONFIG.SYS file.

The input redirection symbol must be used to sort a file. Otherwise, SORT operates on keyboard input until F6 is pressed, followed by Enter. The following command sorts the file in Table 4.3 by the first character in each line:

```
SORT < ADDRESS.LST
```

The results of this command appear on the screen, as follows:

Andrews, Bill	14 North Snelling	St. Paul, MN	55408
Banks, Susan	2022 Hacienda Blvd.	San Diego, CA	91020
Hoffman, Andy	132 E. Franklin	Seattle, WA	80971
Manchester, Chris	9501 Drew Ave. So.	Bloomington, MN	55321
Williams, Frank	1011 Zenith Ave. So.	Minneapolis, MN	55401
Yeoman, Mary	134 North Summit	Silver Spring, MD	32976

There are two switches that can be used to modify the way SORT works: /R and /+N. /R is used to reverse the sort order. In the above example, the command

```
SORT < ADDRESS.LST /R
```

would put the Mary Yeoman line at the beginning of the list, and the Bill Andrews line at the end.

/+N enables you to sort your data based on the characters occurring in a column other than the first column of each line (where N represents the column in which to start the sort). For example, to sort the ADDRESS.LST file in Table 4.3 by zip code, which begins in column 60, and save the output to a file named ADDRSORT.ZIP, the following command would be used:

```
SORT /+60 < ADDRESS.LST > ADDRSORT.ZIP
```

If sort decisions need to be made beyond the end of a data line, SORT will wrap back to the beginning of the line.

If you want to see the output of a SORT command on the screen, and there will be more than one screen of information, the output may be piped through the MORE filter. The following command sorts a file named NAMES.FIL based on the characters in position 10 of each line, and uses the MORE command to pause the display after each screen of information:

```
SORT /+10 < NAMES.FIL | MORE
```

Obtaining On-line Help for DR DOS

DR DOS 6.0 provides on-line help for all of the DOS commands. The /? switch may be appended to any command to obtain a single screen that summarizes the command syntax, and the DOSBOOK command can be used to obtain detailed help.

The /? Switch

You may obtain brief help for a command by typing the command name followed by the question mark switch (/?). For example, typing DIR /? will display the screen shown in Figure 4.2.

	DIR	Displays the files in a directory.
Syntax:	DIR	/H
	DIR	[wildspec] [/L|/2|/W] [/P|/N] [/A|/D|/S] [/C|/R]
	/H	gives this screen
	wildspec	files to be displayed (wildcards allowed)
	/A	displays all files
	/C or /R	make other switches default for next time
	/D	displays files without system attribute set (default)
	/L	long format. Include size, date and time (default)
	/2	as above except files are displayed in two columns
	/N	return to default paging switch
	/P	pause at end of full page. Default is no paging
	/S	displays files with system attribute set
	/W	wide format. Displays file and directory names only
	none	no parameters displays all files using current default switches
Example:		
	DIR /C /W	

Figure 4.2 DOS On-line Help Screen for DIR Command

The DOSBook Program

You may obtain extensive help for all of the DR DOS 6.0 commands and utilities using the DOSBook program. DOSBook is a complete on-line reference manual for DR DOS. There are two ways of starting DOSBook:

1. Enter either the command DOSBOOK or HELP at the command prompt.
2. Enter the command DOSBOOK or HELP followed by a command name. This takes you directly to the section of DOSBook that contains the information for the specified command.

When the DOSBOOK or HELP command is entered by itself, the DOSBook Welcome screen shown in Figure 4.3 appears.

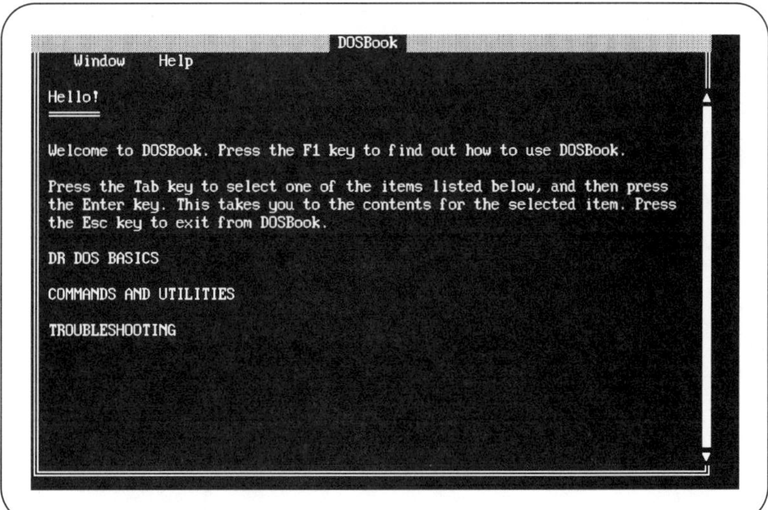

Figure 4.3 DOSBook Welcome Screen

As seen in Figure 4.3, DOSBook is divided into three topic sections: ***DR DOS Basics***, ***Commands And Utilities***, and ***Troubleshooting***. Each of these sections consists of a list of key words and phrases. Once you have entered one of these sections, you may select any of the key words to display detailed help screens for the specified topic. Pressing the F1 key from the Welcome screen takes you to a set of screens that explain what DOSBook is and how it works.

The ***DR DOS Basics*** section is used to learn the fundamental concepts required for working with DR DOS, such as disk drives, filenames, and DOS commands. The ***Commands And Utilities*** section is used for obtaining help with specific DOS commands and programs. Topics include the basics of working at the command prompt, the DR DOS commands, and the various utilities that come with DR DOS 6.0, such as TaskMAX and SStor. The ***Troubleshooting*** section is used to diagnose problems that may arise when working with DR DOS. The list of topics includes all the error messages that may be generated by DR DOS.

Navigating in DOSBook

DOSBook contains a tremendous amount of information. In order to easily find the information you need, there is a variety of means for quickly moving to the topic of choice and displaying the help screens for it.

When a screen contains words or phrases that have help screens behind them, those words or phrases appear in reverse highlight. The Tab key can be used to move from one key word to the next; the Shift+Tab keys move to the previous key word.

When there is more information than can fit on one screen, the scroll bar on the right edge of the screen indicates the percentage of the total information that is displayed, and which section of the information is displayed. The up and down arrow keys can be used to move the cursor through the screen, and to scroll it one line at a time. The PageUp and PageDown keys can be used to move through the information one screen at a time. The Home key moves the cursor to the top of the screen, and the End key moves it to the bottom of the screen. The Ctrl+Home and Ctrl+End move the cursor to the top and bottom of the total information. Alternatively, pressing the first letter of a key word jumps directly to the first key word that begins with that letter.

For example, if Commands And Utilities is selected from the Welcome Screen (Figure 4.3), the screen in Figure 4.4 appears.

In this figure, the scroll bar at the right side of the screen indicates that about 1/6 of the total list is displayed, and that the portion that is displayed is the top of the list. The first topic is reverse highlighted. You may move the highlight bar through the list one item at a time by pressing the Tab key or the down arrow key; you may move backwards through the list using Shift+Tab and the up arrow keys. Alternatively, pressing any alphabetic character jumps the highlight immediately to the first topic that begins with that letter. Pressing T takes you directly to the TASKMAX topic. Pressing Enter when TASKMAX is selected displays the screen in Figure 4.5.

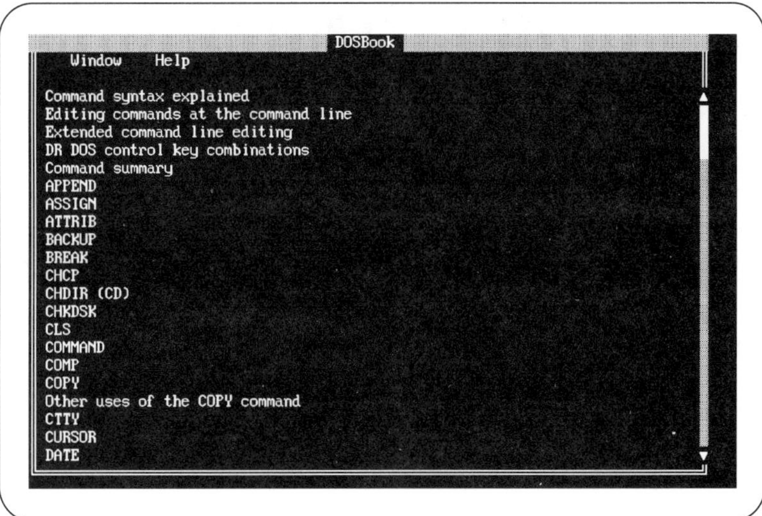

Figure 4.4 First Screen of the DOSBook Commands and Utilities Topics

In Figure 4.5, the cursor appears near the top of the display. There are several key words highlighted: *Format*, *utility*, *applications*, and so on. Pressing the Tab key takes you from one key word to the next, and pressing the Enter key when one of them is selected pops up the help screen for that topic. For example, highlighting the word "Format" and pressing Enter brings up a help screen that explains the syntax of the Format command. There are additional key words on this screen that lead to further help screens.

When exploring a specific topic, it is possible that you will move through a variety of help screens as you choose key words to learn about. You can move back through the screens you have visited by pressing Alt+B; each time you press these keys, you move back one screen, until you return to the DOSBook Welcome Screen.

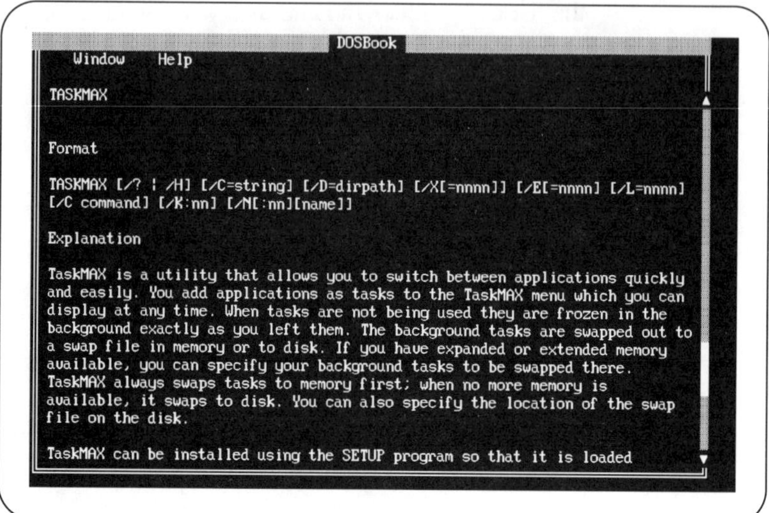

Figure 4.5 DOSBook Help Screen for TaskMAX

The Esc key may be pressed at any time within DOSBook to return directly to the Welcome screen, without having to revisit the previous screens you have seen.

There are several ways of getting to lists of topics and topic sections in addition to moving from the Welcome screen into one of the three topic groups. The Help menu has options for using any of these alternate ways of accessing DOSBook topics. To see the Help menu, press the Alt+H keys from any DOSBook screen. The Help menu is shown in Figure 4.6.

As you can see in Figure 4.6, each of the alternate methods for accessing DOSBook information has a hot key associated with it. The hot key can be used at any time within DOSBook to use the associated Help menu option.

The Contents option displays a table of contents for DOSBook, with related topics grouped together. Selecting a topic and pressing the Enter key displays the help screens for that topic.

The Glossary option displays a list of DR DOS terms. Selecting one of them and pressing the Enter key displays a definition of the selected term.

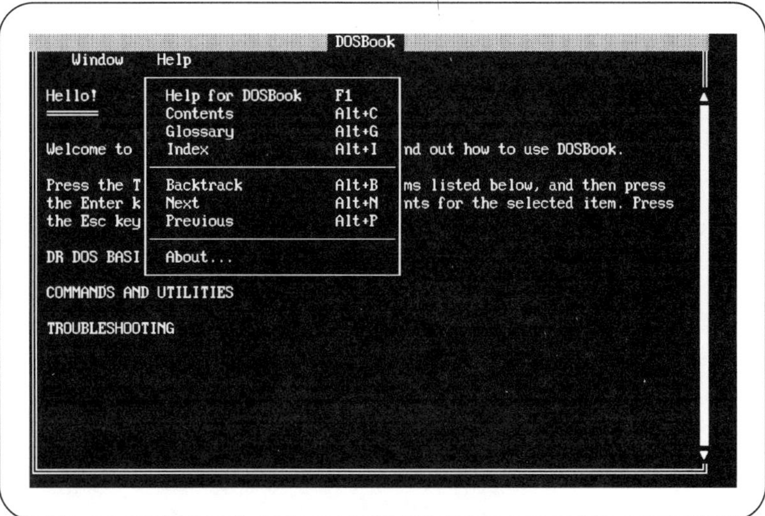

Figure 4.6 DOSBook Help Menu

The Index option displays an index for DOSBook. Key words and phrases appear as headings, with related sub-headings. For example, beneath ANSI.SYS is a sub-heading for *escape sequences*. Selecting a heading or sub-heading takes you to the appropriate help screen.

The Backtrack option returns you to the last section you reviewed. The Next option takes you to the DOSBook section following the one currently displayed, and the Previous option takes you to the preceding one.

Changing the DOSBook Window Size

You may prefer to see part of the computer screen that was displayed before calling up DOSBook, rather than having DOSBook occupy the entire screen. The DOSBook screen can be toggled between full screen and an alternate, smaller size in either of two ways:

1. Holding down the Alt key and pressing the F5 key.
2. Selecting the "Resize window" option on the DOSBook Window menu. The Window menu is displayed by holding

down the Alt key and pressing W from any DOSBook screen. Figure 4.7 shows the Welcome screen with the Window menu displayed.

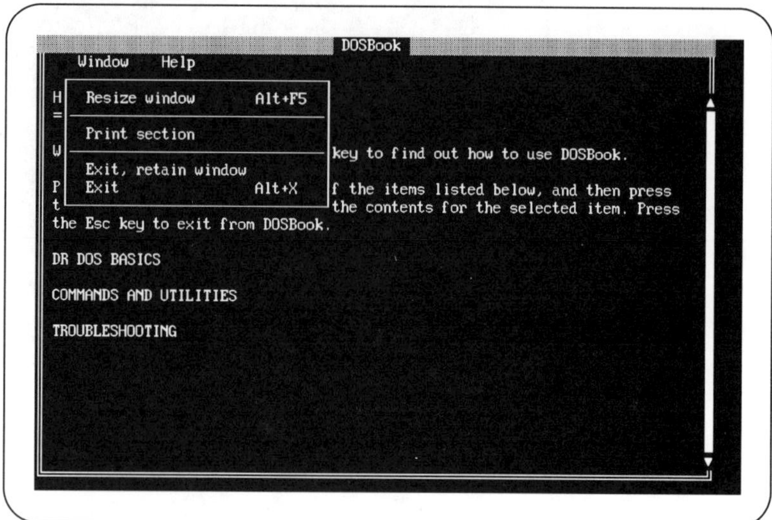

Figure 4.7 DOSBook Window Menu

The Resize option on the Window menu, and the Alt+F5 key combination, act as toggle switches—they switch the display between its two sizes.

Printing a DOSBook Section

You can print any section of DOSBook by displaying part of the desired section, then choosing the "Print section" option on the Window menu (Figure 4.7). For example, to print the complete text of the help screens for the TaskMAX program, select TaskMAX on the Commands And Utilities topics list and press the Enter key, then drop down the Window menu by pressing Alt+W and choose the "Print section" option. Make sure your printer is connected and turned on.

Exiting DOSBook

There are two ways to exit DOSBook. The first is to press the Esc key when the Welcome screen is displayed. This will return you to the command prompt, and restore the screen to the way it appeared before starting DOSBook. Sometimes, however, it is useful to leave the DOSBook information displayed when you return to the command prompt, so that you may refer to it as you enter a command. To accomplish this, make sure the text you will want to see is displayed, then hold down Alt+W to display the Window menu and select the "Exit, retain window" option. You may want to combine this option with the "Resize window" option discussed above, to leave the smaller window displayed when you return to the command prompt.

Obtaining Help with DOSBook

There is a series of screens available within DOSBook that explain how DOSBook works. There are two ways to access these screens: pressing F1, or choosing the "Help for DOSBook" option on the Help menu. The Help menu is accessed by pressing the Alt+H keys. Either of these techniques may be used from any DOSBook screen.

The About option on the Help menu shows you the version number and copyright notice for DOSBook.

Frequently Used DOS Commands

This section provides an introduction to some of the most frequently used DOS commands. This introduction is sufficient for most uses of the commands, but Chapter 11 provides detailed syntax diagrams and full explanations of how the commands work, and what parameters and switches they accept. Many of these commands are also discussed in the appropriate sections of this book. For example, the DEL, DIR, RENAME, and TYPE commands are used for file management, so they are covered thoroughly in Chapter 6. In addition to the commands discussed here, FIND, HELP, MORE, and PROMPT are frequently used commands that are discussed in detail in other sections of this chapter. The commands presented here appear in alphabetical order.

CLS

The CLS command clears the screen, and positions the cursor at the top left corner of the screen. CLS is useful for eliminating clutter from the screen, and for providing a clear screen for messages and command output during batch file execution.

DEL

The DEL command is used to delete one or more files from a directory. The simplest version of the command is:

```
DEL filename.ext
```

This deletes the specified file from the current directory. Paths may be specified to delete files in other directories, and DOS wild cards may be used to delete sets of files.

DIR

The DIR command is used to display a list of the files in a directory. Entering the command by itself, with no switches or parameters, displays all files in the current directory, except those whose Hidden attribute is set to ON. File names are displayed in all upper case letters. The size of each file, as well as the date and time of its last modification, are shown.

If you want to see information about just one file, then a file name may be specified, as in:

```
DIR JIMSMITH.LET
```

To see a group of files whose names match a pattern, the DOS wild cards (* and ?) may be used. The following command displays all of the files with a BAT extension:

```
DIR *.BAT
```

You may also specify a different directory than the current one. The following command specifies all files in the C:\WP\LETTER directory:

```
DIR C:\WP\LETTER
```

Switches can be used with the DIR command to cause the output to

- pause after each screen is displayed
- display in several columns across the screen, instead of one long column down the left side of the screen
- show all files, regardless of attribute settings
- show only files whose system attribute is set
- display files from sub-directories

All of these options are discussed in detail in Chapter 6. The XDIR command, discussed below and in Chapter 6, provides extended DIR options.

FORMAT

Floppy disks usually need to be formatted before they can be used. Formatting organizes a disk so that DOS will know how to use it. Hard disks also need formatting, but this is usually done by the computer manufacturer or dealer before the computer is sold, so the FORMAT command is normally used only with floppy disks. To format a disk in drive A: enter the following command:

```
FORMAT A:
```

DOS will prompt you to insert a disk in the A: drive and press Enter when ready. It will then format the disk, display information about the size of the disk, and display messages regarding the results of the FORMAT operation. There are several switches that may be used with FORMAT, which provide control over certain aspects of how a disk is formatted. When FORMAT is done, it asks if you want to Format another disk. You may either choose Y, for Yes, in which it case you are prompted to put another disk in the drive; or N, for No, in which case you are returned to the command prompt. FORMAT is discussed in detail in Chapter 7.

MOVE

The MOVE command is used to move one or more files from one directory to another, on the same or a different drive. MOVE may also be used to move an entire subdirectory from one directory to another.

The MOVE command provides a very fast and efficient means of moving files, because all it has to do is copy the directory entry for a file from one directory to another. It does not have to copy the file itself. This is especially valuable with large files. However, if you are moving a file from one disk to another, then MOVE is functionally identical to a COPY and DEL command.

The syntax of the MOVE command is:

```
MOVE filespec directory
```

where filespec is the file specifier of the file(s) to be moved, and directory is the name of the directory the file(s) should be moved to. To move an entire subdirectory, filespec should be the name of the subdirectory being moved. When moving a subdirectory, the /T switch must also be used. The following command moves the file WP.BAT to the \WP directory:

```
MOVE WP.BAT \WP
```

To move the entire \WP\DATA subdirectory to the \TEMP\DATA directory, use the following command:

```
MOVE \WP\DATA \TEMP\DATA /T
```

After this command has executed, there will no longer be a DATA subdirectory under \WP, and there will be one under \TEMP.

The MOVE command is discussed in detail in Chapter 6.

RENAME

The RENAME command is used to rename a file. It may also be used to move a file from one directory to another on the same disk. The syntax is:

```
RENAME name1 name2
```

where name1 is the current name of the file, including the extension, and name2 is the new name of the file, also including the extension. A path may be specified for name1, name2, or both. If a file with the name2 name already exists in the specified directory, the message "File already exists" will be displayed and the file will be left unchanged.

To move a file from one directory to another, use the following syntax:

```
RENAME name1 path2
```

where path2 is the new location for the file. For example, to move a file named WP.BAT from the current directory to the \WP directory, enter the following command:

```
RENAME wp.bat \wp
```

After this command executes, the WP.BAT file will exist in the \WP directory, but not in the current directory. This is a very fast way to move a file, because the only thing that needs to be copied is the directory entry, not the file itself.

TYPE

TYPE is used to type the contents of one or more text files to the screen. If a file contains anything other than plain text characters, the non-text characters will appear as odd symbols on the screen. These non-text characters are typically used by word processors to indicate special formatting commands—to print text in boldface or underlined, for example. To display a text file named SAMPLE.TXT on the screen, the following command is used:

```
TYPE SAMPLE.TXT
```

Wildcards may be used in the filename to specify a set of files, rather than a single file. For example, the following command displays the contents of all files with a BAT extension:

```
TYPE *.BAT
```

When a wildcard specificier is used to type multiple files, the name of each file is displayed right before its contents.

You may append the /P switch to the TYPE command, in order to pause the display after each screenful:

```
TYPE AUTOEXEC.BAT/P
```

VER

The VER command displays the version number and copyright notice for DR DOS that is being used. If you are using DR DOS 6.0 and enter the VER command, the following message will display on your screen:

```
DR DOS Release 6.0
Copyright (c) 1976,1982,1988,1990,1991
Digital Research Inc.
All rights reserved.
```

XDIR

XDIR is an extended directory command; it provides all the functionality of DIR, but includes numerous additional options. Using XDIR, you may display only files that have specified attributes set, you may omit the size, date, and time information from the display, and you may sort the file listing in a variety of ways. XDIR is discussed in detail in Chapter 6.

Customizing the Command Prompt

The default command prompt, which appears when you boot your computer if no PROMPT command appears in the AUTOEXEC.BAT file, is simply the drive letter followed by a greater-than sign. For example, if the current drive is C, then the default command prompt is:

```
C>_
```

This prompt provides a minimal amount of information: it tells you what the current drive is, but no more. The PROMPT command is used to modify the command prompt, to provide more useful information than just the drive letter. It is common practice to place a PROMPT PG command in the AUTOEXEC.BAT file, to define a prompt that indicates the current directory as well as the current drive. If the current drive is C, and the current directory is \WP\LETTERS, then this prompt will appear as:

```
C:\WP\LETTERS>_
```

For an experienced user, this is a meaningful prompt. However, for people who are not familiar with DOS, this prompt is fairly cryptic. The PROMPT command allows you to design a prompt that will be suitable for almost any circumstances. Among other things, you may use a text message for the prompt, and you may embed the current date, time, drive, directory, and other information, in the prompt. For example, to create a prompt that says "Enter your command here: ", the following command is used:

```
PROMPT Enter your command here:
```

There are fourteen parameters that may be used with the PROMPT command (a complete list can be found in Chapter 11). Each parameter is preceded by a dollar sign ($). The dollar sign is used to tell DOS that the character which follows it should be interpreted as a parameter, rather than a text character. The parameters allow you to embed a variety of items in the prompt. Examples in this book always use upper case letters for the Prompt parameters, but lowercase letters work just as well. You may intersperse text before, between, and after parameters. If you want to reset the DOS Prompt to its default value (the current drive letter followed by a greater-than sign), you may do so by entering the PROMPT command without parameters.

Including a Dollar Sign in the Prompt

Since a single dollar sign is used to indicate that the following character should be interpreted as a parameter, it cannot be used to simply display a dollar sign in the prompt. To include the dollar sign character in a prompt, two dollar signs are used. For example, to change the prompt to "Enter your command $ ", the following command is used:

```
PROMPT Enter your command $$
```

Changing the DOS Prompt to a Text Message

You may change the prompt to a message, without any drive or directory designators, by entering the PROMPT command followed by the text you want to use. If you enter the following command:

```
PROMPT Type your DOS command here:
```

The DOS prompt will look like this:

```
Type your DOS command here:_
```

If you want a space to appear at the end of the prompt, before the cursor position, then you should leave a space at the end of the prompt message when you enter the PROMPT command.

Including a Greater-than Sign (>) in the DOS Prompt

It has been a standard convention since the first version of DOS to end the prompt with a greater-than sign. However, since the greater-than sign is the DOS output redirection symbol, you may not use it directly in a text message. If you include it in the text of your prompt, you will get the error message "Invalid drive specified" because DOS will think you are trying to redirect the output of the PROMPT command to a file on one of the disk drives. The $G parameter is therefore used to include a greater-than sign in the prompt. To replace the colon with a greater-than sign in the prompt described above, the following command would be used:

```
PROMPT Type your DOS command here$G
```

This will result in the following prompt:

```
Type your DOS command here>_
```

Including a Less-than Sign (<) in the DOS Prompt

The less-than sign is the DOS input redirection symbol, so it too requires a parameter to be included in a prompt message. The $L parameter is used to place a less-than sign in a prompt. To embed text between less-than and greater-than signs you enter the text between the $L and $G parameters. To make the prompt appear like this:

```
Type your < DOS > command here:_
```

the following command would be used:

```
PROMPT Type your $L DOS $G command here:
```

Including the Current Drive Letter in the DOS Prompt

The current drive letter can be included in the prompt with the $N parameter, as in the following PROMPT command:

```
PROMPT The current drive is: $N
```

If your current drive is C this will result in the following prompt:

```
The current drive is: C_
```

It is helpful to terminate any prompt message with a symbol, so that it is clear where the prompt ends and a command that has been entered begins. This is why the greater-than sign developed as a standard terminator for DOS command prompts. The above prompt command is improved by adding the $G parameter:

```
PROMPT The current drive is: $N$G
```

This produces the following prompt:

```
The current drive is: C>_
```

Including the Current Directory Path in the DOS Prompt

The $P parameter is used to insert the path from the root directory to the current directory into the DOS prompt, as in the following command:

```
PROMPT The current directory is $P:
```

If you are in the C:\DRDOS directory this will produce the following prompt:

```
The current directory is C:\DRDOS:_
```

Notice that the path includes the drive letter so there is no need to combine the $N and $P parameters. In fact, if you used NP in a prompt you would have the drive letter duplicated at the beginning of the prompt.

One of the most common PROMPT commands is simply:

```
PROMPT $P$G
```

This prompt is usually installed in the AUTOEXEC.BAT file, making it the prompt that automatically appears when the computer is booted. If you are in the DRDOS subdirectory this prompt will look like this:

```
C:\DRDOS>_
```

Note: When the $P parameter is used, it causes DOS to read the directory of the disk in the current drive after each command. This is necessary because some commands change the current directory. Since $P displays the current directory name, it must check after each command to see which directory is current. With floppy drives, reading the directory after each command significantly slows down DOS's response time. Furthermore, floppy disks frequently do not have subdirectories because of their relatively low capacities. Consequently, if you frequently use a floppy drive as the current drive, you may want to set a prompt that does not use the $P parameter.

An additional problem can arise when using $P with a floppy drive. In order for DOS to read the directory of a floppy drive, there must be a formatted disk in the drive. Consequently, if you are going to use a floppy drive as the current drive with the $P parameter, you must be sure the drive has a formatted disk in it. If it doesn't, DOS will display the following message:

```
Not ready error reading drive A
Abort, Retry, Fail?
```

There are two ways of responding to this message: the first is to put in a formatted floppy disk and select either A (Abort) or R (Retry). Either one will result in the drive being read and the correct prompt appearing. The other option is to select F (Fail). Depending on what command caused this prompt to appear, this will result in either the prompt appearing with the previous directory displayed, even though no disk is in the drive, or in the following message:

```
Physical Media Error
```

Under these circumstances you do not need to worry about this message—there is nothing wrong with the disk, but DOS thinks there is since it has failed to read it properly. After displaying this message, DOS will return to the last displayed prompt. Possible actions are:

1. Insert a formatted disk in the floppy drive and enter a DOS command, to force DOS to re-read the disk and display the current directory in the prompt.
2. Change the current drive to one that has a valid disk in it—either another floppy drive or a fixed disk drive. To change to your C: (fixed) drive, enter C:. This will result in drive C becoming the current drive and the DOS prompt will display the current directory on drive C.

Including the Date in the DOS Prompt

The $D parameter is used to insert the system date into the DOS prompt. The following command demonstrates the use of the $D parameter:

```
PROMPT Today's date is $D. Enter your command$G
```

This produces the following prompt:

```
Today's date is Thu  9-19-1991. Enter your command>_
```

Since DOS stores the date of last modification with each file name, it is important to have the system date set properly. Most computers today have battery powered clocks that maintain the system date and time even when the computer is turned off, but under some circumstances these clocks can lose their setting. Including the date in the prompt is one way of being sure you know what the system date is. It also provides a useful way of checking today's date—simply look at your computer screen.

Including the Time in the DOS Prompt

The system time may be inserted into the DOS prompt using the $T parameter. When the time appears in the command prompt, it will always be displayed in 24 hour format. The following command demonstrates the use of the $T parameter:

```
PROMPT The time is $T. Enter your command$G
```

This results in the following prompt (assuming it's 2:06:17.35 PM):

```
The time is 14:06:17.35. Enter your command>_
```

You may not want the entire time displayed, out to hundredths of a second. The $H parameter, discussed below in the section *Using a Backspace in the DOS Prompt*, can be used to truncate numbers off the time.

Including the DOS Version Number in the DOS Prompt

If you are running different versions of DOS on your computer, or have more than one computer with different versions of DOS, it can be useful to know what version of DOS is running. This can be shown with the $V parameter. The version number, the manufacturer, and the copyright notice, are shown. The following command demonstrates this:

```
PROMPT $V
```

If you are running DR DOS 6.0, this produces the following prompt:

```
DR DOS Release 6.0
Copyright(c)1976,1982,1988,1990,1991
Digital Research Inc.
All rights reserved.
```

Including a Vertical Bar (Pipe) Symbol in the DOS Prompt

Like the greater-than and less-than signs, the vertical bar is a DOS redirection symbol, and therefore cannot be used directly in a prompt message. To include a vertical bar in the DOS prompt, the $B parameter is used. The following command demonstrates the use of the $B parameter:

```
PROMPT Enter your command here$B
```

This will produce the following prompt:

```
Enter your command here|_
```

Including an Equal Sign in the DOS Prompt

In some versions of DOS, there have been circumstances in which the equal sign (=) could not be used directly in a prompt message. It was therefore necessary to define a special parameter to specify an equal sign. The equal sign parameter is $Q. The following command demonstrates this:

```
PROMPT Today's date $Q $D$G
```

This produces the following prompt:

```
Today's date = Thu  9-19-91>_
```

In DR DOS 6.0, the following PROMPT command works just as well:

```
PROMPT Today's date = $D$G
```

Using a Backspace in the DOS Prompt

You may include a backspace character in your PROMPT command with the $H parameter. The effect of this is to erase the character immediately preceding the $H. For example, if you used the following command:

```
PROMPT This demonstrates the use of a b$Hackspace.
```

the prompt would look like this:

```
This demonstrates the use of a ackspace._
```

At first sight, this seems to be a useless parameter—why display a character you're just going to erase? But remember that some of the other parameters display whole strings of characters as part of the prompt. For example, the $T (time) parameter displays the time as hh:mm:ss.hs. You may prefer to have the time displayed only as hours and minutes. The last six characters of the time can be erased using the $H parameter, as in the following command:

```
PROMPT The time is $T$H$H$H$H$H$H$G
```

If the system time is 10:04:02.01, the prompt will appear as:

```
The time is 10:04>_
```

Displaying More than One Line in the DOS Prompt

As the DOS prompt gets longer, it gets harder to distinguish the different pieces of information, and there is less room for you to type in your commands and keep them on one line. DOS will allow you to wrap your commands to subsequent lines, but they are harder to read. The $_ parameter allows you to break your prompt into separate lines. Take, for example, the following command:

```
PROMPT The current directory is $P. The date is $D. The time is $T.
```

This results in a prompt that is so long it actually wraps to the next line:

```
The current directory is C:\. The date is Thu  9-19-1991. The
time is 14:24:38.48.
```

You can make this prompt more readable by using the $_ parameter to separate the three statements, as follows:

```
PROMPT The current directory is $P.$_The date is $D.$_The time is $T.
```

This will produce the following prompt:

```
The current directory is C:\DRDOS.
The date is Thu  9-19-1991.
The time is 14:24:38.48._
```

Changing the Color of the Prompt

The PROMPT command can be used to provide extensive control over the colors and positioning of text on the screen. This use of the PROMPT command is discussed in detail in Chapter 10. A limited application of these techniques, to change the color of the prompt itself, is presented here.

In order for this technique to work, the following command must appear in your CONFIG.SYS file:

```
DEVICE=ANSI.SYS
```

If the ANSI.SYS file is not in the root directory of the boot disk, then the path to the file must also be specified. The most common version of the command is:

```
DEVICE=C:\DRDOS\ANSI.SYS
```

If this command does not appear in the CONFIG.SYS file, you may add it, using a text editor. For this command to take effect, you must reboot your computer after adding it to the CONFIG.SYS file. Once you have rebooted with the ANSI.SYS driver loaded, the following command will create the standard command prompt, but it will appear in reverse video:

```
PROMPT $E[7M$P$G$E[0M
```

There are three parts to this prompt:

- a command to the ANSI.SYS driver $E[7M
- the normal PROMPT parameters PG
- the second command to ANSI.SYS $E[0M.

The first ANSI.SYS command tells DOS to start using a reverse video display, the PG displays the current directory and the greater-than sign, and the final ANSI.SYS command tells DOS to stop using the reverse video display.

Any of the standard prompt parameters can be used in addition to, or in place of, the PG shown above. There are many different commands that can be sent to ANSI.SYS, allowing you to position text in various areas of the screen, display text and prompt messages in different colors, and affect the way the keyboard works. All of these are discussed in detail in Chapter 10.

Using CURSOR to Change the Cursor Blink Rate

Some computers, primarily laptops and portables, use monitors that cannot keep up with a rapidly changing screen. This is often noticed when the cursor appears as a dim blur which is difficult to locate on the screen, because the monitor cannot keep up with the normal blink rate of the cursor. The small size of the normal cursor also makes it difficult to find on these screens. DR DOS 6.0 includes a program named CURSOR that allows you to change the cursor shape from a thin underscore to a large block, and to change the blink rate of the cursor. The syntax of the CURSOR command is:

```
CURSOR /Sxx /C OFF
```

The first switch setting, /Sxx, is used to set the speed of the cursor blink rate. The xx represents a number from 1 to 20, and the interval between blinks is set to xx/20. For example, the following command sets the cursor to flash every half second:

```
CURSOR /S10
```

The second switch, /C, is used to make the CURSOR program compatible with CGA monitors. Software that affects the display often generates interference that appears as "snow" on CGA monitors. The /C switch will prevent this from happening.

The third setting, OFF, is used to disable the CURSOR program after you have started it.

When you run the CURSOR program, it installs itself in memory and controls the shape and blink rate of the cursor. To do this, it must occupy some memory—a little over 1K. This memory is taken from conventional memory, regardless of whether you have upper memory available or not. Furthermore, the memory used by CURSOR is not reclaimed when you enter the CURSOR OFF command; the only way to reclaim it is to reboot the computer and not load the CURSOR program. 1K of memory is not a lot, and in most cases would be unnoticeable, but it is worth being aware of the memory lost to CURSOR. There are occassional situations in which 1K of available memory can make the difference between a program being able to run and not being able to run.

Using LOCK to Prevent Access to Your Computer

DR DOS 6.0 provides a variety of security features for protecting your computer from unauthorized use, and for protecting individual files and directories from being accessed by unauthorized users. The password security system is discussed in Chapter 6, since it is used in conjunction with file management. However, there is an additional command, LOCK, which is used to lock your computer and prevent anyone from using it who does not know the password.

To lock your computer, enter the following command:

```
LOCK password
```

where “password” is the password you want to use to unlock your computer. Upon entering this command, the screen in Figure 4.8 will appear.

Upon entering the correct password, the screen will be restored to the display that appeared before LOCK was invoked.

For the LOCK screen in Figure 4.8 to appear properly on your screen, the following command must be included in your CONFIG.SYS file:

```
DEVICE=C:\DRDOS\ANSI.SYS
```

If the ANSI.SYS file is not in the C:\DRDOS directory, you should adjust the above command accordingly. ANSI.SYS is a program known as a *device driver*; it provides the ability to manipulate the screen display in certain ways that are needed for displaying the LOCK screen. Alternatively, you can edit the LOCK.TXT file, which contains the LOCK screen definition, to remove the ANSI.SYS commands. LOCK.TXT is a text file in the DRDOS directory; it can be edited using any text editor, such as the EDITOR program that comes with DR DOS. The contents of LOCK.TXT appear in Figure 4.9.

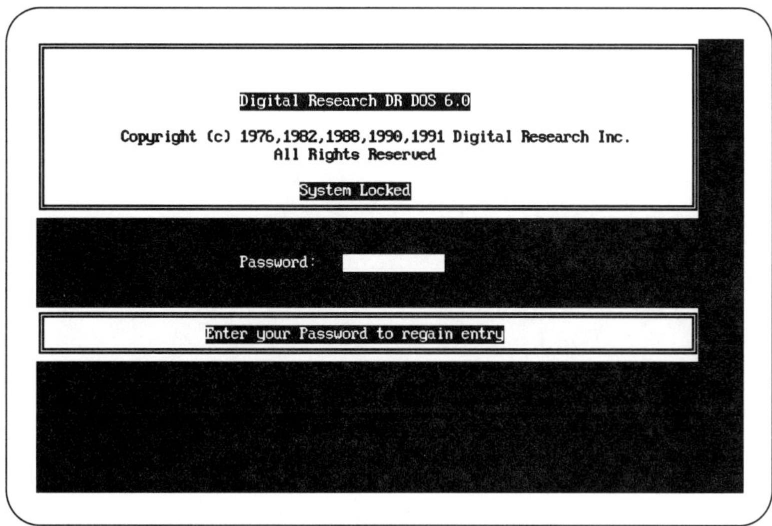

Figure 4.8 Password Entry Screen when LOCK Command is in Effect

As you can see, LOCK.TXT does not appear to be a normal text file. All of the character strings that begin with a caret (^) are ANSI.SYS commands. The LOCK.TXT file with these commands edited out appears in Figure 4.10.

As you may have guessed, it is possible to edit any other aspect of LOCK.TXT as well. If you like, you can change the LOCK screen to contain your own logo, name, or whatever else you like. The LOCK program itself generates the "Please enter your password:" message, so you do not need to include it in your screen.

```
q[2J[41;36m


[4;1H                      [1mDigital Research DR DOS 6.0[0;41;36m

        Copyright (c) 1976,1982,1988,1990,1991 Digital Research Inc.
                           All Rights Reserved

                          [1mSystem Locked[0;41;36m

[40m




[41m
                [1mEnter your Password to regain entry[0;41;36m

[0m
[13;25H              [7m              [0m
[13;25HPassword:   [7m<PASSWORD>[0m
[20;1H
```

Figure 4.9 Contents of LOCK.TXT File

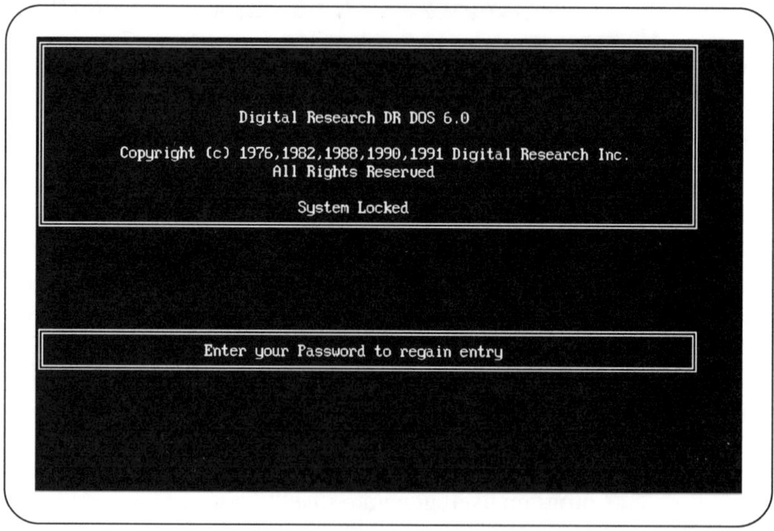

Figure 4.10 LOCK.TXT File without ANSI.SYS Escape Sequences

If you installed TaskMAX and the System Security features during DR DOS installation, or later using the Setup program, then the LOCK program will have been automatically loaded as a TaskMAX task. If you did not install both of these systems during installation, you may load LOCK as a TaskMAX task using the /C switch:

```
TASKMAX /C LOCK password
```

The LOCK program will now appear as a task under TaskMAX; switching to it will lock your computer and prevent anyone from using it until the password has been entered. Using LOCK while running TaskMAX is especially handy, since you can lock your computer without having to exit any of the programs you are working on. When you return to your computer, simply enter the password and you are returned to the TaskMAX menu. When you want to lock the computer again, choose the LOCK task from the TaskMAX menu again.

If you installed System Security during the DR DOS installation, or later using the Setup program, then you do not have to include a password when you enter the LOCK command—the existing log-in password will be used. If you do specify a different password than the system log-in one, you will not be able to use the system log-in password until you reboot the computer. The System Security features of DR DOS are discussed in detail in Chapter 10.

Installing and Using the History Command Stack

The HISTORY command is used to load the History program into memory, and to use the program after it is loaded. History is a program that provides two features for streamlining your work at the command prompt. The first feature is a *command stack*, which remembers previous commands that have been entered. The second feature provides extended editing capabilities for the command line.

History is known as a Terminate and Stay Resident (TSR) program. When you include the History program in your CONFIG.SYS file, it loads itself into memory, then allows you to go about using the computer for your usual tasks. However, it is always there in the background, memorizing everything you enter at the command line. Because it is a TSR, and therefore resident in the computer's memory, History takes a small amount of memory away from your other programs. The amount of memory used by History, as well as other variations on how History works, can be controlled with switches when History is started. These switches are discussed later in this chapter, in the section titled, *The HISTORY Command Syntax*. For now, simply start History by including the following command in your CONFIG.SYS file:

```
HISTORY=ON
```

Recalling Previous Commands

When History is loaded, it remembers all commands entered at the command prompt by placing them in the command stack. The command stack can be thought of as a stack of DOS command lines. The first command line entered is placed on the bottom of the stack. The next command line is then pushed onto the stack beneath the first one, in effect pushing the first one up. This continues until the command stack is filled up. When the stack is full, and another command line is entered, the command line at the top of the stack, which is the oldest command, is removed and the new one is pushed onto the bottom.

By default, History will reserve 512 bytes of memory for holding the command stack and macros. This amount can be changed, as discussed below in the section *Controlling HISTORY Memory Usage*. Each character in a command occupies one byte, so 512 bytes permits a total of 512 characters to be stored. If the average command is eight characters, then History can store 64 commands.

There are several keys used for recalling previous commands from the stack, making it easy to quickly find the command you want. These keys and others used with the History program are summarized in Table 4.4.

For the examples that follow, the command stack shown in Figure 4.11 will be used.

The blank command line on which you enter new commands can be thought of as a blank space beneath the stack (line 10 in this example). As new commands are entered, they are pushed into the bottom of the stack. The Up Arrow is used to recall the previous command from the stack. For example, after the last command in Figure 4.11 has been executed (DIR), a blank command line will be displayed. Pressing the

Up Arrow, or Ctrl+E, once displays the DIR command (number 9 in the stack). The DIR command is not executed, it is only displayed. To execute it, press Enter, or Ctrl+M. If you do not press Enter, then pressing the Up Arrow again will display the CD \ command (number 8 in the stack), and so on. The Down Arrow, or Ctrl+X, is used to move down the stack (towards the newest command). The Up Arrow is used to move up the stack (towards the oldest command). When Down Arrow is pressed at the bottom of the stack, it moves to the top of the stack. Thus, in Figure 4.11, when either the DIR command at the bottom of the stack is displayed, or the blank command line beneath the stack, pressing the Down Arrow key moves to the the CD \WP\LETTERS command. Likewise, from the top of the stack ,the Up Arrow moves to the last command in the stack.

```
1: CD \WP\LETTERS
2: FIND "Southern Region Sales" *.LET
3: DIR A*.LET
4: COPY A*.LET C:\BACKUP\LETTERS
5: DEL A*.LET
6: CD C:\BACKUP\LETTERS
7: DIR A*.LET
8: CD \
9: DIR
```

Figure 4.11 Sample History Command Stack

Ctrl+R is used to cycle through a subset of the commands in the stack. The subset is defined as those commands that begin with specified characters. For example, if the blank command line beneath the bottom of the stack in Figure 4.11 is displayed, pressing C, then pressing Ctrl+R, would display line 8, CD \ . Pressing Ctrl+R again would display line 6, CD C:\BACKUP\LETTERS. Pressing Ctrl+R again would display line 4, and so on. Ctrl+R treats the stack as a circular queue, so that when the specified command at the top of the stack is reached, pressing Ctrl+R again returns to the bottom of the stack, where the letters to search for were entered. In this example, starting at the bottom of the stack with the letter C and pressing Ctrl+R four times would display line one in the stack, CD \WP\LETTERS. Pressing Ctrl+R again would display the line with the letter C on it.

When Ctrl+R is pressed following a search string, the cursor stays in the same position when matching commands are displayed. Using the command stack in Figure 4.11, if the letter C were the search string and the currently displayed command were:

```
COPY A*.LET C:\BACKUP\LETTERS,
```

the cursor would be beneath the O in COPY. Ctrl+R uses everything prior to the cursor as the search string. It can therefore be used for increasingly selective searches. For example, pressing C and Ctrl+R once displays the command CD \, with the cursor blinking beneath the D. Pressing the End key moves the cursor to the end of the command line. Pressing Ctrl+R again will display line 1, CD \WP\LETTERS, which is the next previous command that begins with CD \.

By pressing Ctrl+hyphen (-), you can turn on a more powerful search facility. After Ctrl+hyphen is pressed, entering any letter recalls the previous command that started with that letter. This search moves backwards from the current position in the command stack. Thus, if the extended search feature was turned on and you were at line five in Figure 4.11, deleting the line and pressing the pressing the C key would replay line 4. Pressing Ctrl+hyphen again turns off the extended search feature.

When a particular command from the stack is displayed, you are positioned at that line in the stack. In other words, you may use Ctrl+R to jump to a location in the stack, then use the arrow keys to move away from that point one command at a time.

When a line from the stack is displayed and Enter is pressed, History does not execute the original copy of the command. Instead, it moves to the bottom of the stack and inserts a new copy there, which it then executes. Consequently, the commands in the stack are always left unchanged, and whenever a command is executed you are again placed at the bottom of the stack. If you want to replay two or three lines from the same part of the stack, you will have to return to that part of the stack for each command.

Esc clears a command from the screen, without changing your location in the stack or affecting the command in the stack. For example, with the stack shown in Figure 4.11, if the currently displayed command were line 3, DIR A*.LET, pressing Esc would display a blank command line. Pressing Up Arrow would display line 2, and pressing Down Arrow would display line 3 again. If you typed a new command and pressed Enter, that command would be placed at the bottom of the stack.

Keys Used for Editing the Displayed Command

History implements several keys to provide editing capabilities on displayed commands. Many of these keys match the original Wordstar cursor movement keys. The function of these keys is listed in Table 4.4.

Table 4.4 Keys Used for Working with the History Command Stack

Key	*Effect*
Left arrow or Ctrl+S	Moves the cursor one character to the left.
Right arrow or Ctrl+D	Moves the cursor one character to the right.
Ctrl+A	Moves the cursor one word to the left.
Ctrl+F	Moves the cursor one word to the right.
Home or Ctrl+Q	Moves the cursor to the beginning of the line.
End or Ctrl+W	Moves the cursor to the end of the line.
Backspace or Ctrl+H	Deletes the character to the left of the cursor.
Del or Ctrl+G	Deletes the character at the cursor.
Ctrl+B	Deletes all characters from the beginning of the line up to but not including the cursor.
Ctrl+K	Deletes all characters from the cursor to the end of the line. The character at the cursor is deleted.
Ctrl+T	Delete from the cursor to the end of the word.
Ctrl+Y	Delete the entire line.
Ins or Ctrl+V	Toggles between Insert mode and Overstrike mode.
Esc	Clears the displayed line from the screen.
Enter or Ctrl+M	Executes the command line.
Up Arrow or Ctrl+X	Plays back the next command in the stack.

Table 4.4 continued ...

Key	*Effect*
Down Arrow or Ctrl+E	Plays back the previous command in the stack.
Ctrl+R	Plays back the previous command that matches the characters on the command line.
Ctrl+hyphen	Toggle the extended search feature on and off.
Ctrl+P	Toggle switch for sending screen output to the printer.
Pause or Ctrl+S	Pauses the scrolling of the screen until a key is pressed.
Ctrl+Break or Ctrl+C	Interrupts the execution of a command and returns to the command prompt.

There are six keys used for moving the cursor around on the command line: Left Arrow, Right Arrow, Ctrl+A, Ctrl+F, Home, and End. All of these affect the cursor position only—moving them does not change the command line itself. For the Ctrl+A and Ctrl+F keys, a word is defined as whatever appears between any two symbol delimiters. Symbol delimiters include blank spaces, periods, and slashes.

Six keys are provided for deleting all or part of a command: Backspace, Delete, Ctrl+B, Ctrl+K, Ctrl+T, and Ctrl+Y. When Ctrl+K is used, the character at the cursor is included in those deleted. When Ctrl+B is used, the character at the cursor is not deleted.

The Insert key is used to toggle between Insert mode and Overstrike. Insert mode means that anything that is typed is inserted into the line, moving everything following the cursor position to the right. Overstrike mode means that anything that is typed replaces what is at the cursor. By default, History is in Overstrike mode, unless History is started with the insert switch turned on.

Esc clears the displayed command from the screen. It does not, however, remove the command from the command stack. If a line from the stack is displayed, then Esc is used to clear it from the screen. Pressing Up Arrow, then Down Arrow, will restore it to the screen because it still exists in the stack.

The Ctrl+S and Pause keys are used to temporarily suspend the scrolling of information. For example, if you enter the DIR command for a directory with a large number of entries, you can press Ctrl+S to pause the scrolling of the directory listing while you examine the part that is on the screen. Pressing any key restarts it, until you press Ctrl+S or Pause again.

There are three additional keys that are shown in Table 4.4 that affect the handling of the output from DOS commands. The Ctrl+C and Ctrl+Break keys are used to interrupt the execution of a command and return you to the command prompt. For example, if you entered a TYPE command that was displaying a long text file to the screen, you could press Ctrl+C to stop the command and return immediately to a command prompt.

The Ctrl+P keys are used to route screen output to the printer. For example, if you want to print a directory listing, you could press Ctrl+P, then enter the DIR command. Be sure to press Ctrl+P again when you are done, to avoid printing the output of subsequent commands.

Controlling HISTORY Memory Usage

Since History remains in memory while other programs run, it reduces the amount of memory available to those programs. While some TSRs use a lot of memory, History is relatively small—with its default command stack of 512 bytes, it occupies about 1K of memory. If there is upper memory available, History will automatically install itself there, leaving conventional memory for running programs.

You can change the amount of memory History reserves for the command stack on the CONFIG.SYS line that contains the HISTORY command. The simplest form of the History command is:

```
HISTORY=ON
```

The amount of memory to use for the command stack may be specified following the word ON. The following command specifies a stack of 256 bytes:

```
HISTORY=ON,256
```

The minimum amount of memory that can be reserved by History is 128 bytes; the maximum amount is 4096 bytes. If no size is specified, History reserves 512 bytes.

Changing the amount of memory reserved for the command stack will also change the total amount of memory used by History. Consequently, you want to determine the smallest size that will meet your needs, and set the History command accordingly.

The HISTORY Command Syntax

The full syntax of the HISTORY command is:

```
HISTORY=ON or OFF,memory size,ON or OFF
```

The first setting—ON or OFF—determines whether or not History will be installed in the computer's memory. The OFF setting is provided so that you may leave the command in your CONFIG.SYS file at times when you don't want History installed.

The second setting, discussed in the previous section, is used to adjust the size of the command stack.

The third setting, another ON or OFF switch, is used to set the insert mode. By default, the OFF setting is in effect. When insert mode is OFF, characters typed in the middle of a command line overwrite the characters that are already there. When insert mode is ON, characters are inserted, pushing all the characters following the cursor position to the right.

Using the SCRIPT Command to Create PostScript Output

PostScript printers can only be used with programs that produce PostScript output. This frequently means that two printers must be maintained—one for PostScript programs, and one for programs that produce non-PostScript output. DR DOS includes the SCRIPT command to convert non-PostScript output to PostScript commands. Thus, any program can be used with DR DOS to produce output on a PostScript printer.

There are two different ways in which the SCRIPT command can be used: as a TSR, in which case it intercepts all printer output and converts it to PostScript commands; and as a stand-alone program, to convert a particular file or characters typed at the keyboard. Any text files can be converted, including those conforming to the Hewlett-Packard LaserJet II standard.

Converting a Single File

When converting a file, the following syntax should be used:

```
SCRIPT source target
```

where "source" is the name of the file being converted, and "target" is the destination of the PostScript commands. The target may be a device, such as a printer, or it may be another filename. If no target is specified, LPT1 is assumed. Thus, to print a text file named MYFILE.LET on a PostScript printer attached to the LPT1 port, the following command would be sufficient:

```
SCRIPT MYFILE.LET
```

If you want to take input from the keyboard and send it to the standard output device (normally LPT1), enter the SCRIPT command with neither source nor target.

Using SCRIPT As A TSR

To load SCRIPT as a TSR, specify an output device as the source and do not specify a target. SCRIPT will then intercept all output directed to the specified device and convert it to PostScript commands.

There are several switches which may be used with SCRIPT, to control the orientation, pointsize, and timeout period, for the printer. To set the orientation, the /O switch is used:

```
SCRIPT LPT1 /ORIENTATION=PORTRAIT or LANDSCAPE
```

You may abbreviate each of the words in the switch setting to their first letter. For example, to set LPT1 to have an orientation of LANDSCAPE, the following command could be used:

```
SCRIPT LPT1 /O=L
```

The point size can be adjusted using the /POINTSIZE switch:

```
SCRIPT LPT1 /POINTSIZE=xx
```

where xx is the pointsize. The default point size is 11. Again, the switch may be abbreviated to a single letter. The following example sets the orientation to LANDSCAPE, and the pointsize to 16.5:

```
SCRIPT LPT1 /O=L /P=16.5
```

The TIMEOUT switch is used to override the normal spooler or printer timeout and force anything remaining in the spool or printer to print immediately, before the printer times itself out. This switch should be used when the spool or printer is timing itself out too quickly. The default timeout is 10 seconds; the following command sets the timeout to 5 seconds:

```
SCRIPT LPT1 /TIMEOUT=5
```

/TIMEOUT may be abbreviated to /T.

The last switch available for the SCRIPT command is /RESET, or /R for short. This sends a software reset to the printer before any data is processed. This can be useful if the printer is continuing to hold settings from a previous print job that are interfering with what you are trying to print.

After SCRIPT has been loaded as a TSR, the SCRIPT command can be used to change any of these settings.

SCRIPT can be uninstalled by using the /U switch. This will remove it from memory and restore your system to its normal functioning:

SCRIPT /U

Chapter 5

Understanding and Managing Memory

While disk files are used for permanent storage of information—both software programs and data—information must be transferred from the disk to electronic memory before it can be used by the computer. The CPU (Central Processor Unit) then accesses the information from memory as it is needed. There are no physical laws that require this. You could design a computer in which there was no electronic memory, where all information was transferred directly between the CPU and disk files. However, reading and writing to disks is agonizingly slow in comparison to reading and writing to electronic memory. A computer designed to use disk files instead of electronic memory would be useless for today's applications because it would take too long to do anything.

When the computer needs to run a program, it reads the entire program into memory at once. This is referred to as *loading* the program. After the program is loaded, the CPU starts executing the instructions in the program, reading them one at a time from their memory locations. When the program needs to access data—say from a file to be edited in a word processor—the computer copies that data into memory. The CPU then retrieves the data from memory as it is needed. Consequently, the computer must have enough memory to store both the program and the data it uses.

The memory capacity of personal computers has grown tremendously since PCs first appeared. The original PCs were designed to have a maximum of 640K of memory, which at that time seemed like more than anyone would ever need on a PC. Personal computers were typically purchased with 256K installed, and more memory was added if and when it was needed. As software evolved, PCs were used for more and more complex tasks—tasks that previously had been tackled only by expensive mainframe computers. To manage these tasks efficiently, more and more memory was required on PCs. It became increasingly difficult, and in some cases impossible, to fit all of the program code and data into 640K of memory.

Today, machines with two megabytes of memory are common, and it is possible to purchase personal computers that have over 100 megabytes of memory. However, because the original design of PCs embodied the philosophy that 640K was more memory than anyone would ever need, the operating system for PCs was designed to use only 640K. Since the machines themselves could only manage this much memory, there was no point in writing an operating system that could handle more. No one anticipated that the PC would rapidly evolve into a machine that could handle over a thousand times that much memory. This limitation of 640K of memory is so deeply embedded in the design of DOS that it is almost impossible to change. Consequently, making use of memory above the 640K limit is not straightforward. There are many ways n which memory can be configured, depending on what type of PC you have, how much memory the PC has, and how the memory is installed in the PC. This chapter discusses all of these aspects of computer memory, as well as the DR DOS 6.0 commands that can be used to control how memory is configured, and how it is used by the software.

Throughout this chapter, mention is made of the different types of CPU chips. The term 8088/8086 refers to all personal computers that use either the 8088 or 8086 CPU chip. The terms 286 and 80286 are used to refer to PCs that use the 80286 chip, and the term 386 and 80386 are used to refer to PCs that use the 80386 and later chips.

Understanding Memory Resources

Physically, there are two kinds of memory in PCs: *RAM* and *ROM*. RAM stands for Random Access Memory. RAM is so called because it can be accessed in a random sequence—the computer can instantly retrieve information that is stored anywhere in RAM, without having first to retrieve everything that appears ahead of the desired information. This is the memory that is usually referred to when just the term *memory* is used. For example, a machine that is said to have "640K of memory" has 640K of RAM.

For the purposes of this chapter, the terms "RAM" and "memory" will be used interchangeably. Where it is necessary to mention ROM, it will be referred to explicitly.

ROM stands for Read Only Memory. ROM also allows random access, but as its name implies, the computer cannot write information into ROM, but only retrieve it. ROM contains information that should never be changed, and this information is built into the ROM before it is installed in the computer. For example, there are some fundamental routines the computer uses for accessing peripheral devices, such as disk drives and printers. These routines are known as the Basic Input Output System or BIOS. These routines are also referred to as ROM-BIOS. When DOS needs to access a device, it sends a request to the BIOS, which then handles the actual communication with the device. Since the BIOS handles the very low-level communications between the computer and its devices, the BIOS routines should never be changed. Most software programs are designed to communicate with the BIOS in a well-defined ways, so if the BIOS were changed, the various programs designed to run on the PC may not be able to function properly. Consequently, the BIOS is written into ROM.

There are two advantages to having something stored in ROM. First, ROM is non-volatile memory, which means that it does not lose its contents when the computer is turned off. Consequently, information stored in ROM is always available as soon as the computer is booted; it does not have to first be read in from a disk. In fact, the initial instructions that tell the computer what to do when you boot it are stored in ROM. The second advantage to having something in ROM is that it cannot be inadvertently changed by a program. The only way to change the contents of ROM is to replace the ROM chips with ones that contain different information.

Some ROM is installed on the system board when you buy your computer, and some may be on add-on boards that are installed in the computer's expansion slots. The BIOS routines are in ROM that is installed on the system board.

When you buy a personal computer, it comes with a certain amount of RAM installed. You may add more later, up to some maximum amount that the computer is capable of managing. This maximum amount varies from one manufacturer and model to another. There are two places on the computer where RAM can be stored: on the system board (also known as the mother board), and on expansion cards that plug into expansion slots on the system board. Most computers are capable of using more memory than will fit on their system board and when the system board is filled to capacity, it is necessary to install expansion boards to add more memory.

Bits and Bytes

In order to talk about memory, it is necessary to know some terms that are used to describe it. Electronic memory consists of millions of tiny switches, which can either be on or off. These switches are referred to as *bits* and a bit is the smallest amount of information a computer can store. A bit can be set to "on," which is interpreted by the computer as a one, or "off," which is interpreted by the computer as a zero. Since a single bit can only mean one of two things, in order to represent complex information, computers work with groups of eight bits. A group of eight bits is called a *byte*. Software that runs on IBM-compatible personal computers most often works with one byte at a time, but some software uses groups of two or four bytes. These groups are known as *words*. A two-byte word is called a 16-bit word, and a four-byte word is called a 32-bit word.

It takes a large number of bytes for the computer to be able to do anything useful, so memory is measured in terms of kilobytes and megabytes. A kilobyte is 1,024 bytes, and a megabyte is 1,048,576 bytes. The term *kilobyte* literally means 1,000 bytes, but the computer does everything in multiples of two, since it is operates on the base two number system. 1,024 is 2^{10}. Since this is approximately 1,000, 1,024 bytes is referred to as a kilobyte. Similar reasoning leads to the term *megabyte*, which is approximately one million bytes. Thus, when you hear of a computer having 640K, this means the computer has 640 x 1,024, or 655,360 bytes of memory.

How does a computer manage to perform all the complex tasks it does, if everything it works with consists only of a series of 0s and 1s? The computer distinguishes between two different interpretations of the contents of a byte: one interpretation is as an instruction to the CPU, and the other is as data that the CPU can work with. When a byte contains part of a program the computer is running, the CPU interprets the contents of the byte as containing an instruction. There are several hundred instructions the CPU understands, and all of the computer's actions ultimately are reduced to sequences of these instructions. An example of an instruction that the CPU understands is:

```
ADD AL 13
```

This instruction adds 13 to the value stored in a part of the CPU known as the AL register. The number of bytes required to store an instruction varies with the instruction. Internally, the ADD AL 13 instruction would occupy three bytes; the 13 would be represented as 00001101—the binary version of the number 13. The ADD and AL would be represented by binary codes that are interpreted by the CPU as ADD to the AL register.

When a byte contains data, rather than an instruction for the CPU, then the computer interprets the byte as having a numeric or text meaning. For example, the binary number 00101101 could represent an instruction to the CPU that tells it perform some operation on a number, or it could represent the number 45.

By having two different ways of interpreting the same binary codes, the computer can store instructions to the CPU in the same memory as it stores data. By differentiating between the two, and accurately interpreting the meaning of each byte in its memory, the computer carries out all of the various tasks that it performs.

How Memory is Organized

Since 640K of memory is 655,360 bytes, and a byte is the basic unit of information storage, there are 655,360 places in which an item of information might be found in a 640K PC. In order to keep track of all these locations, and to make it easy to access any particular location quickly, the computer assigns an address to each byte, starting with 0 and proceeding up to the last byte of memory the computer contains.

The limiting factor in determining how much memory a computer can have is the size of the address. Computers use binary addresses—numbers consisting only of ones and zeros. DOS is designed to use addresses that are 20 bits long, so the largest address it can reference is 11111111111111111111, which is 1,048,575 in decimal notation. Since the first address is 0 and the last address is 1,048,575, DOS can reference up to 1,048,576 bytes of information—exactly one megabyte.

While DOS is capable of addressing up to one megabyte of memory, only the first 640K of that memory is available for programs and data. This is because the PC reserves the memory addresses from 640K to 1 megabyte for special purposes. The memory area from zero to 640K is termed *conventional memory*, because it is the area that is conventionally used for running programs. The memory from 640K to 1 megabyte is referred to by several names, including *reserved memory*, *upper memory area*, or *high memory*. The region from 640K to 1 megabyte contains the addresses for 384K of memory. To see where the number 384 comes from, consider what the terms *640K* and *1 megabyte* mean: 640K is 640 x 1,024, or 655,360 bytes, since there are actually 1024 bytes in 1K. Likewise, 1 megabyte is 1,024 x 1,024, or 1,048,576 bytes. Subtracting 640K from 1 megabyte leaves 393,216 bytes left in the upper memory area. 393,216 divided by 1,024 is 384; thus, there is 384K of memory addresses in the upper memory area.

There is a variety of ways in which the computer makes use of the upper memory area. For example, images displayed on the screen must be stored in memory, so a part of this upper memory area is reserved for the contents of the screen. The area of memory reserved for the screen is also known as video memory. The computer is constantly monitoring the video memory, and updating the screen whenever the contents of video memory change. Read Only Memory (ROM) was mentioned earlier in this chapter. All ROM addresses are in the region from 640K to 1 megabyte. The ROM BIOS routines are stored in addresses at the very top of this region. If a network adapter card is installed in your computer, there is ROM on that card whose addresses appear in the upper memory area. Any other expansion cards that contain ROM will use addresses in the upper memory area as well.

A typical configuration of the memory in a 640K Personal Computer is shown in Figure 5.1.

```
     ADDRESS RANGE
=================================   Approx.
Hexadecimal      Decimal            Size   Description
-----------      -------            ----   -----------
00000 - 003FF    0000 - 1023        1K     Interrupt Area
00400 - 004FF    1024 - 1279        0.3K   BIOS Data Area
00500 - 006FF    1280 - 1791        0.5K   System Data
00700 - 0DFBF    1792 - 57279       54K    DOS
0DFC0 - 0F28F    57280 - 62095      4.7K   Command.com
0F290 - 9FBFF    62096 - 654335     578K   Available for
                                             programs
9FC00 - 9FFFF    654336 - 655359    1K     UMB
A0000 - AFFFF    655360 - 720895    64K    VGA Graphics
B0000 - B7FFF    720896 - 753663    32K    UMB
B8000 - BFFFF    753664 - 786431    32K    VGA Text
C0000 - C7FFF    786432 - 819199    32K    Video ROM
C8000 - EFFFF    819200 - 983039    160K   UMB
F0000 - FFFFF    983040 - 1048575   64K    System ROM
```

Figure 5.1 Memory Layout of a 640K Personal Computer

As you can see in Figure 5.1, a 640K computer actually has more than 640K of memory. The 640K refers to the RAM available for running programs—the RAM from address 0 to address 655,359. How much more memory the computer has depends on what additional devices are attached to it. A monochrome text video adapter will not have as much video memory as a color graphics adapter. Some PCs will have adapter cards, such as those used for connecting to local area networks, that have ROM on them.

If all of the reserved memory were filled—either with reserved RAM, such as the video memory contains, or with ROM—then a 640K PC would actually have 1 megabyte of memory. However, this is never the case. There are always gaps in the reserved memory area. Where those gaps lay, and how big they are, varies from one PC to the next, depending on the exact hardware devices the computer has. These gaps are known as *Upper Memory Blocks*, or UMBs for short. Several UMBs are shown in Figure 5.1.

If the first megabyte of memory is accounted for on a computer that is said to have 640K of memory, then a question arises: how much memory does a computer have if it is referred to as having 1 megabyte of memory? The answer is that it has exactly what a 640K computer has, plus an additional 384K. However, the addresses for this additional 384K lay above the one megabyte address, and therefore cannot be referenced directly by DOS, since the largest address DOS can store is 1 megabyte. This 384K of additional memory is called *extended memory*, since it extends the addresses of the computer beyond the traditional 1 megabyte limit. A computer that is said to have two megabytes of memory would have 1408K of extended memory: 384K, plus 1024K (which is one megabyte), equals 1408K. Extended memory is discussed in greater detail later in this chapter.

How DOS Uses the First 640K of Memory

DOS itself consists of two parts: an internal part and an *external* part. The internal part is in a program named COMMAND.COM, which is loaded into memory when the computer is booted. All of the internal DOS commands are stored in COMMAND.COM. The external part is a set of programs that are run from the disk, just like any other program. The TaskMAX program is an example of the external part of DOS. The Command Dictionary (Chapter 11) indicates for each command whether it is stored internally or externally.

Since COMMAND.COM is loaded permanently into memory when the computer is booted, it uses up some of the first 640K of memory. In addition to loading COMMAND.COM into memory, DOS sets up an area of memory for the DOS environment. The DOS environment contains information that DOS needs to have as it goes about directing the computer's operation. For example, the current Path, as defined by the PATH command, is stored in the environment, as is the current PROMPT definition. If there are environment variables defined, these are also stored in the DOS environment. The amount of memory reserved for the environment is 512 bytes by default, but this can be varied using the SHELL command. The SHELL command is discussed in Chapter 10.

All programs and all data are stored in files. For the computer to run a program or access the data in a file, DOS must first *open* that file. For example, when a word processor is used, the word processor program is stored in one or more files, and each of these must be opened before DOS can load the program. Each time you edit a document in a word processor, the file that stores the document must also be opened. Many word processors allow you to have many document files open at once. When you execute one of the DOS external commands, such as FORMAT, the command is a program that is stored in a file. Database programs typically require numerous files to be open in order to manage all the data in a database.

Opening a file requires that DOS identify the file name, locate it on the disk, load it into memory, and remember where it is stored on the disk. A number, called a *file handle*, is associated with each open file. When a program opens a file, DOS assigns a file handle to it and tells the program what that number is. The application then refers to the file handle, rather than the file name itself.

For example, when you want to edit a file called "MYFILE.LET" with a word processor, you first identify the file name. The word processor then passes that name to DOS, where the file handle is assigned and passed back to the word processor. If DOS assigns the file handle 8 to the file, the word processor then refers to "file 8" when it reads or writes that file.

Memory is required to keep track of the file handles. This memory must be allocated when the computer is booted; DOS cannot increase or decrease the amount of memory available for file handles after the computer is in use. Allocating memory for file handles is done with the FILES command in the CONFIG.SYS file. The following command specifies that DOS should reserve memory for having up to 16 files open at the same time:

```
FILES=16
```

The maximum number of files that may be specified with the FILES command is 255. If there is no FILES command in the CONFIG.SYS file, the default value of 20 is used, which is the minimum number that may be specified. DOS requires 64 bytes of memory for each file handle, so if 25 file handles are specified in the CONFIG.SYS file, DOS will reserve 1600 bytes of memory for them. For most applications, the default value of 20 file handles is sufficient. However, if you ever see an error message that indicates there are not enough file handles available, you must increase the number of files specified in CONFIG.SYS.

Applications that require more than the minimum number of file handles usually point this out in their installation documentation. Some programs will automatically adjust the CONFIG.SYS file when they are installed, if the number of file handles is too low. Note that the computer must be rebooted for any changes to the CONFIG.SYS file to become effective.

Another command that appears in the CONFIG.SYS file, and that affects available memory, is the BUFFERS command. BUFFERS sets up memory buffers that increase the efficiency with which data can be transferred between disks and memory. The BUFFERS command is discussed in Chapter 7, but for now it is important to understand that each buffer occupies 532 bytes of memory. If your CONFIG.SYS file contains a BUFFERS=20 command, then 10,640 bytes of memory will be taken for buffers. You may specify anywhere from 3 to 99 buffers. The default depends on how much memory is installed on your PC; on a 640K PC, the default is 15.

The CONFIG.SYS file may also contain one or more DEVICE commands. These commands take the following form:

```
DEVICE=filename
```

Where *filename* is the name of a file that contains the device driver. For example, if you use a mouse with your computer, then a device driver for the mouse is loaded, communicating between the mouse and the computer. The DEVICE command loads the device into memory, where it stays until the computer is turned off. The amount of memory taken up by device drivers varies widely, from less than a hundred bytes to thousands.

Besides COMMAND.COM, file handles, buffers, and device drivers, there are programs known as *TSRs* (Terminate and Stay Resident). A TSR program remains in memory after it returns control to DOS. From memory, it can be recalled by pressing a special key combination. A program named *Sidekick* is probably the most well-known TSR. After Sidekick is loaded into memory and control is returned to DOS, Sidekick can be recalled by pressing both Shift keys at the same time. Sidekick then provides you with a note pad, a calculator, a phone dialer, and other utilities. Pressing both Shift keys again makes Sidekick disappear until you call it up again. The HISTORY program, discussed in Chapter 4, is another example of a TSR.

TSRs are very useful—they provide handy utility and time-saving features that can be used while you are using the computer for your work.

However, they require memory. Programs like Sidekick can occupy anywhere from 30K or 40K to over 100K, depending on the particular configuration you choose. HISTORY takes up about 1K.

There are, then, the following five different ways in which DOS uses the first 640K of memory, each of which reduces the amount of memory available for programs:

- COMMAND.COM
- File handles
- Disk buffers
- Device drivers
- Terminate and Stay Resident programs

On some computers, after all of the required configuration commands and device drivers are loaded, there is less than 450K of available memory left to run programs. TSRs can reduce this even further. There are several features built in to DR DOS 6.0 to help reduce the amount of memory used by these resources; these features are discussed later in this chapter.

Expanded Memory

As personal computers evolved, it became evident that some means would have to be found for getting past the 640K barrier. Software was appearing that, in some cases, was capable of performing tasks that were more complex than could be accomplished in the available memory. In other cases, the lack of memory slowed down the processing to unacceptable rates because disk space had to be used in lieu of additional memory.

In understanding how this problem was addressed, it is important to keep in mind that there are two aspects to the 640K barrier: the first is the 20-bit addressing limitation of the 8088 chip—the CPU used in the first IBM Personal Computers. This is a hardware problem and there is nothing that can be done that will allow that chip to directly address more than one megabyte of memory. The second aspect of the problem is the addressing capability of DOS. This is a software problem; no matter how much memory the hardware in a particular PC is capable of addressing, as long as that PC is running DOS it will only be able to directly address one megabyte of memory. CPUs that were developed after the 8088 chip—the 80286, 80386, and so on—are capable of addressing more memory than the 8088. The 80286 can address up to 16 megabytes of memory, and the 80386 and subsequent chips can address up to four gigabytes of memory. They do this by having more than the 20 address bits available to the 8088 chip. However, since DOS uses the same 20-bit address as the 8088, these chips were designed to run in different *modes*. When they are running on PCs that use DOS, they run in what is called *Real mode*. Real mode makes them emulate the 8088 chip, dropping their address size down to 20 bits and limiting them to one megabyte of memory. To access memory beyond the one megabyte barrier, these chips use a mode called *Protected mode*.

There were, then, really two problems to address: the first was the hardware limitation of PCs running in Real mode—whether they were 8088-based machines or had a more advanced chip in them; and the second was how to make the greater addressing capability of the later chips available to DOS. The hardware problem was dealt with first, by developing a technology known as *expanded memory*. The term expanded memory was used because the technology effectively expanded the existing memory, without requiring either the hardware or DOS to use any new addresses.

Expanded memory technology was developed as a joint venture between three companies: Lotus, Intel, and Microsoft, and is therefore known as LIM EMS, for Lotus Intel Microsoft Expanded Memory Specification. The first version was dubbed Version 3.2; the recent version is 4.0. From a technical perspective, implementing EMS is quite complex. However, conceptually it is not too difficult to understand.

Expanded memory technology uses a technique known as *mapping*. Mapping allows the computer to use a large amount of memory by examining it in small pieces. To visualize this, imagine that you have a very large sheet of paper, covered with numbers, but you are only able to look at this sheet through a small, immovable frame, which shows only a tiny part of the sheet. Now imagine that you can cut the sheet of paper, into pieces just the size of your frame, and can put whatever piece of paper you want behind the frame. It is now possible to view the entire sheet of paper, albeit one small frame at a time. This process, of moving different parts of the sheet of paper behind the frame, is referred to as mapping.

On the computer, mapping is accomplished by setting up a 64K region of memory known as the *page frame*. The page frame lies somewhere within the first megabyte of memory, so it can be read from and written to by DOS. The page frame itself is divided into four 16K pages. Special memory management software is run that creates the page frame and manages its use.

An expanded memory board is then added to the computer, which can contain up to 32 megabytes of memory (under LIM EMS Version 4.0). This board must be specifically designed to have its memory used as expanded memory. This memory is not addressable by normal DOS. Instead, it is addressed using a technique that is built into the memory management software that created the page frame. Now, when a program wants to use memory beyond one megabyte, it uses the address of the page frame, which DOS recognizes. The program then informs the memory management software what part of the expanded memory it wants to use. The memory management software then maps that area of EMS into one of the pages in the page frame. If the area of EMS that is wanted is larger than a single page, multiple pages are used. If it is larger than the entire page frame, it is broken into segments that are mapped in one at a time. Figure 5.2 shows a 64K page frame mapped into memory, beginning at address 917,506.

```
          ADDRESS RANGE
=================================   Approx.
Hexadecimal       Decimal           Size   Description
-----------       -------           ----   -----------
00000 - 003FF     0000 - 1023       1K     Interrupt Area
00400 - 004FF     1024 - 1279       0.3K   BIOS Data Area
00500 - 006FF     1280 - 1791       0.5K   System Data
00700 - 0DFBF     1792 - 57279      54K    DOS
0DFC0 - 0F28F     57280 - 62095     4.7K   Command.com
0F290 - 9FBFF     62096 - 654335    578K   Available for
                                             programs
9FC00 - 9FFFF     654336 - 655359   1K     UMB
A0000 - AFFFF     655360 - 720895   64K    VGA Graphics
B0000 - B7FFF     720896 - 753663   32K    UMB
B8000 - BFFFF     753664 - 786431   32K    VGA Text
C0000 - C7FFF     786432 - 819199   32K    Video ROM
C8000 - DFFFF     819200 - 917503   96K    UMB
E0000 - EFFFF     917506 - 983039   64K    Page Frame
F0000 - FFFFF     983040 - 1048575  64K    System ROM
```

Figure 5.2 Memory Layout Showing EMS Page Frame

The advantage of using EMS memory is that it provides more memory than DOS allows, without interfering in any way with DOS or with programs written to run under DOS. On the other hand, in order to use EMS memory, a program must be written specifically to take advantage of it, since the program must make calls to the expanded memory manager. Furthermore, it is slower to use EMS memory than conventional memory because there is an extra step involved—calling the expanded memory manager—and because the memory must be mapped back and forth between the page frame and EMS memory in relatively small chunks.

Computers built around the 80386 or later CPU do not require a special expanded memory board to use expanded memory—all they require is memory management software that can manage the page frame and EMS. This is because the expanded memory hardware capabilities are built into the chips.

DR DOS 6.0 includes two expanded memory managers, EMM386.SYS and EMMXMA.SYS. EMM386.SYS can be used to convert extended memory to expanded memory on 386 and later machines. 8088 and 286 PCs that have expanded memory boards must use the expanded memory manager that came with the board, because each board manufacturer provides their own unique expanded memory manager. EMMXMA.SYS can be used with IBM-brand PCs that have XMA boards in them.

Extended Memory

Extended memory is simply memory that has addresses above one megabyte. A computer that has an 80286 or later chip, and that is described as having more than 640K of RAM, has extended memory. Thus, as described above, a computer that is said to have one megabyte of RAM has 640K of conventional RAM and 384K of extended RAM. However, because of the one megabyte address limitation of DOS, this memory is non-existent as far as DOS is concerned. Extended memory cannot exist on a computer based on the 8088 chip, since that chip itself can only recognize one megabyte of memory.

If your CPU can directly address its extended memory, then the only problem that needs to be overcome is that DOS is unable to address it. There are three ways of doing this.

The first way is to purchase software that is designed to use it directly. Such software uses a technology known as a *DOS Extender*, which shifts the CPU into protected mode, where it can directly address extended memory. The DOS extender then interfaces between DOS and the software, essentially making DOS capable of using extended memory for the particular program.

DOS extenders are costly for software developers and can create conflicts when they are used in conjunction with other programs. Consequently, four companies—Lotus, Intel, Microsoft, and AST—jointly developed a second solution to the extended memory problem—the *Extended Memory Specification* (XMS). DR DOS 6.0 has features that are compatible with version 2.0 of XMS. XMS provides a standard technique for software programs to use when accessing extended memory, without employing a DOS extender. In order for the programs to do this, XMS memory manager software must be installed. The EMM386.SYS driver that comes with DR DOS 6.0 provides XMS memory management. For machines based on the 286 chip, the HIDOS.SYS device driver is provided to load DOS into high memory, provided the computer has extended memory installed.

The third way to use extended memory is to convert it to expanded memory, then run software that can make use of expanded memory. This is currently the most common use of extended memory, since much more software has been developed to use expanded memory than extended. However, this can only be done on PCs using the 386 and later chips, because these chips have the hardware requirements for EMS 4.0 built in to them. On 286 machines, expanded memory must be installed on a special expanded memory board that requires its own unique expanded memory manager. The EMM386.SYS driver provided with DR DOS 6.0 can be used to convert extended memory to expanded on 386 machines.

Expanded memory is a short-term solution to a long-term problem. As DOS extenders become more commonplace, extended memory will become the standard and the use of expanded memory will probably disappear. Eventually DOS itself may evolve into an operating system that can make direct use of extended memory by using larger addresses. Consequently, when planning for the long term, equipment should be purchased with extended memory. If, on the other hand, you have an older or lower-end machine and all you want to do is extend the life of that machine, expanded memory is the cheapest way to do this.

Managing Memory Resources

As seen in the preceding section, there are three types of memory resources that may be available on a computer: conventional memory, which is all memory up to one megabyte; extended memory, which is memory beyond one megabyte on an 80286 or later PC; and expanded memory, which provides additional memory that does not fit into the normal addressing scheme of DOS and the 80x86 family. DR DOS 6.0 provides features for maximizing the use of all three types of memory.

Maximizing the Use of Conventional Memory

Figure 5.3 shows the layout of the first megabyte of memory in a typical PC.

```
      ADDRESS RANGE
=================================    Approx.
Hexadecimal       Decimal            Size   Description
-----------       -------            ----   -----------
00000 - 003FF     0000 - 1023        1K     Interrupt Area
00400 - 004FF     1024 - 1279        0.3K   BIOS Data Area
00500 - 006FF     1280 - 1791        0.5K   System Data
00700 - 0DFBF     1792 - 57279       54K    DOS
0DFC0 - 0F28F     57280 - 62095      4.7K   Command.com
0F290 - 0F500     62096 - 62720      0.6K   File handles
0F501 - 11D01     62721 - 72961      10K    Buffers
11D02 - 12D62     72962 - 77154      4.1K   Ansi.sys device
                                              driver
12D63 - 13D63     77155 - 81251      4K     Doskey
13D64 - 9FBFF     81252 - 654335     560K   Available for
                                              programs
9FC00 - 9FFFF     654336 - 655359    1K     UMB
A0000 - AFFFF     655360 - 720895    64K    VGA Graphics
B0000 - B7FFF     720896 - 753663    32K    UMB
B8000 - BFFFF     753664 - 786431    32K    VGA Text
C0000 - C7FFF     786432 - 819199    32K    Video ROM
C8000 - DFFFF     819200 - 917503    96K    UMB
E0000 - EFFFF     917506 - 983039    64K    Page Frame
F0000 - FFFFF     983040 - 1048575   64K    System ROM
```

Figure 5.3 Memory Layout of a 640K Personal Computer

About 87K of memory is occupied by DOS, file handles, buffers, the ANSI.SYS device driver, and the Delwatch TSR program. If yours is a standard 640K machine, then that leaves about 552K for user memory and there is nothing more you can do about it. However, if your PC has one megabyte or more of memory, then there is at least 384K of extended memory. Looking back at Figure 5.3, there is about 129K of unused memory address space in the UMBs. Since the UMBs represent only empty ROM addresses (there are no memory chips in the sockets, and on some machines, no sockets), it is possible to *back-fill* your extended memory into this area. On PCs using 386 and 286 chips, DR DOS 6.0 has the capability of backfilling the UMBs with parts of this 384K, thereby making the UMBs available for normal use. In the example shown in Figure 5.3, there is a 96K UMB beginning at address 819,200, and 384K of extended memory beginning at address 1,048,576. DR DOS 6.0 can change the address for the top 96K of the extended memory to be 819,200. Now, if DOS or another program references address 819,200, the physical memory that was addressed at the top of the extended area would be used. This reduces the amount of extended memory by 96K, but conventional memory is generally more useful than extended memory.

On machines using 8088/8086 chips, the DR DOS 6.0 memory managers cannot be used to back-fill UMBs, so a separate memory manager must be purchased in order to make use of this technique. On machines that have an 80286 chip, the HIDOS.SYS driver may be used to backfill the UMBs. The following examples assume that you have an 80386 PC. The HIDOS.SYS driver for 80286 machines is discussed below, in the section *Managing Memory On 80286 PCs*. If you have an 8088/8086 with an expanded memory board in it, the memory manager that came with the board may provide the ability to utilize the UMBs; you will have to refer to the instructions for the software that came with the board to see how this is done.

Any item that occupies memory—whether it is the file handle memory space, a device driver, a program, or some other item—requires contiguous memory. Contiguous memory has an unbroken sequence of addresses. Thus, three stretches of memory, each of which is 80K large, can only be used individually for programs that require 80K or less; they cannot be used collectively for a program that requires 240K. This is why, in Figure 5.3, all of the memory that is occupied by DOS, file handles, and so on, is at the bottom of the memory. By putting each new item at the bottom of available memory, all memory above the last item loaded is left unbroken, thereby leaving the largest amount of contiguous memory possible for running programs and storing data.

UMBs are relatively small, and they are scattered around the upper memory area. Consequently, they cannot be used to directly increase the memory available for large programs and data files. However, items that tend to reduce the available memory—like file handles and TSR programs—tend to be small, so they are candidates for relocation into UMBs.

In order to back-fill UMBs, two things must be accomplished: the memory above one megabyte must be made available as XMS 2.0 memory (there must be a memory manager installed that can access this memory according to the XMS Version 2.0 specification); and a memory manager must be installed that can back-fill UMBs with extended memory. In DR DOS 6.0, the EMM386.SYS provides these capabilities. To set up backfilling, the following command must be added to the CONFIG.SYS file:

```
DEVICE=C:\DRDOS\EMM386.SYS /FRAME=NONE
```

There is a variety of ways in which EMM386.SYS can be used; backfilling UMBs is only one of them. The /FRAME=NONE setting tells EMM386 not to convert extended memory to expanded. This provides the maximum amount of memory possible in UMBs. When EMM386.SYS is used to convert extended memory to expanded memory, part of the UMB memory is used for a page frame. Setting up EMM386.SYS to convert extended memory to expanded memory is discussed in the next section, *Managing Expanded Memory.*

DOS does not automatically use UMBs for whatever it can, even after they have been set up. Therefore, the last step in using UMBs is telling DOS what to put in them, and what to leave in the usual, low memory area. This is done with the HIBUFFERS, HIDEVICE, HIDOS, HILOAD, and HIINSTALL commands.

The HIBUFFERS command causes the disk buffers to be loaded into the High Memory Area if enough memory is available there (the High Memory Area is the first 64K of extended memory, as discussed below, in the section *Managing Extended Memory*); if there is insufficient memory in the HMA, then HIBUFFERS will attempt to load the buffers into upper memory. If there is also insufficient memory in upper memory, HIBUFFERS will load the buffers into conventional memory. The following command will set up 30 disk buffers, and will load them into the highest memory possible:

```
HIBUFFERS=30
```

HIDEVICE loads device drivers into UMBs. It is used in exactly the same way as the DEVICE command, which loads device drivers into low memory. The following command loads a driver named ANSI.SYS into a UMB:

```
HIDEVICE=C:\DRDOS\ANSI.SYS
```

There is one variation on the HIDEVICE command that does not apply to the DEVICE command: the *size* parameter. Since the number and size of UMBs varies with different hardware configurations, there is no way for DOS to predict how many UMBs there will be, or how large they will be. Therefore, there is the possibility that there will not be a UMB large enough for any particular device driver. If you attempt to load a device driver using HIDEVICE, and there is no UMB large enough for it, one of two things will happen: HIDEVICE will act like DEVICE, and load the driver in low memory; or your PC may lock up, forcing you to reboot. The reason the PC may lock up is that HIDEVICE may believe the device driver will require less memory than it does. Therefore, HIDEVICE goes ahead and tries to load the driver into a UMB too small for it. This can cause the computer to lock up. Obviously, loading the driver low is preferable to locking up the computer, but given the tremendous variety of device drivers in existence, it is not possible to insure that HIDEVICE will always accurately perceive the memory requirements of a particular driver.

Since the HIDEVICE command is in the CONFIG.SYS file, if it locks up the computer there is no way to boot from the disk that contains the CONFIG.SYS file. Usually this is a hard disk, which cannot easily be replaced. Therefore, it is important to make sure you have a floppy disk from which you can boot your PC. After booting with the floppy disk, you can edit the CONFIG.SYS file on the hard disk to remove the HIDEVICE command. A bootable floppy disk may be created simply by putting a floppy disk in a drive and entering the command FORMAT A:/S (assuming that the floppy drive is the A drive).

To avoid the problem of HIDEVICE locking up the PC, HIDEVICE can accept a parameter, telling it the minimum amount of space that must be available in a UMB for it to load the driver in high memory. This parameter uses hexadecimal (hex), or base 16, numbers. The following command tells HIDEVICE to load the ANSI.SYS driver into a UMB, if there is a UMB with at least 4128 bytes free (the decimal number 4128 is represented as 1020 in hex):

```
HIDEVICE SIZE=1020 C:\DRDOS\ANSI.SYS
```

To determine the number of bytes required by a device driver, the driver should be loaded into low memory with a DEVICE command, then the following command entered at the command prompt:

```
MEM /D | MORE
```

This command displays a list of the device drivers currently in memory. A number of device drivers that are built in to your computer will be shown, as well as any loadable device drivers which were installed with the DEVICE or HIDEVICE commands. For each loadable device driver, the following information is shown:

- the hexadecimal address at which the driver is located
- the driver's "owner"; this is usually the name of the device driver
- the item's size in bytes, in hexadecimal format, followed by the size in decimal format
- the item's *type*—this will usually be either *loadable* or *Built-in device driver*

Figure 5.4 shows a sample screen of the MEM command output, with the /D and /B switches set to show all device drivers and programs loaded into memory.

The ANSI.SYS device driver appears at address 24F:0000, and it's owner is identified as "CON". Since its name does not appear in the MEM output, the only way to identify it is to run the MEM command with and without the driver loaded and see what changes. The ANSI.SYS driver is designated as requiring 4128 bytes, or 1020 bytes in hexadecimal format.

After determining the size of the device driver with the MEM command, use this value with the SIZE parameter on the HIDEVICE command. For example, to specify the size for ANSI.SYS, the following HIDEVICE command is used:

```
HIDEVICE SIZE=1020 C:\DRDOS\ANSI.SYS
```

Address	Owner	Size		Type
0:0000	--------	400h,	1,024	Interrupt vectors
40:0000	--------	100h,	256	ROM BIOS data area
50:0000	DR DOS	200h,	512	DOS data area
70:0000	DR BIOS	B20h,	2,848	Device drivers
70:050B	PRN			Built-in device driver
70:051D	LPT1			Built-in device driver
70:052F	LPT2			Built-in device driver
70:0541	LPT3			Built-in device driver
70:0553	AUX			Built-in device driver
70:0565	COM1			Built-in device driver
70:0577	COM2			Built-in device driver
70:0589	COM3			Built-in device driver
70:059B	COM4			Built-in device driver
70:0602	CLOCK$			Built-in device driver
70:0645	CON			Built-in device driver
70:0671	A:-C:			Built-in device driver
122:0000	DR DOS	11B0h,	4,528	System
122:0048	NUL			Built-in device driver
23D:0000	DR DOS	10920h,	67,872	System
24F:0000	CON	1020h,	4,128	Loadable device driver
3B2:0000	DR DOS	3C00h,	15,360	30 Disk buffers
760:15C0	DR DOS	DE0h,	3,552	DR DOS BIOS code
69A:3000	DR DOS	9440h,	37,952	DR DOS kernel code
12CF:0000	COMMAND	1590h,	5,520	Program
1428:0000	COMMAND	210h,	528	Environment
1449:0000	MEM	B0h,	176	Environment
1454:0000	--------	10h,	16	FREE
1455:0000	DELWATCH	13D0h,	5,072	Data
1592:0000	MEM	13AD0h,	80,592	Program
293F:0000	--------	76810h,	485,392	FREE
9FC0:0000	--------	400h,	1,024	Extended ROM BIOS data area

Figure 5.4 MEM /D /B Command Output

This technique will work for most device drivers. However, some drivers use extra memory during the loading process, then cut back to their final size. In this case, the size shown with the MEM command will not provide enough memory to load the driver, resulting in either the driver being loaded into low memory or the PC locking up. In this case, you must either find out from the manufacturer of the driver how much memory is required to load the driver, or incrementally increase the size allotment until HIDEVICE loads the driver into high memory.

Most device drivers will run successfully in a UMB, if there is a large enough UMB available. However, some are not designed to correctly use the addresses in the upper memory area, in which case they will not function when loaded high, and may cause the PC to lock up. While EMM386.SYS must be loaded before the UMBs can be used to load devices, it will relocate most of itself into upper memory after loading, so that it only takes up about 1K of conventional memory. The VDISK.SYS, PRINTER.SYS, DISPLAY.SYS, and ANSI.SYS drivers, all work properly when loaded into a UMB. Most mouse drivers will also work properly.

The HILOAD command is used to place TSRs and other programs into the UMBs. HILOAD is a command that may be entered at the command prompt, and it can therefore be run at any time. It does not have to be specified in the CONFIG.SYS file, which executes only when the computer is booted. If there are programs that you always want to have loaded into high memory, you may include HILOAD commands in the AUTOEXEC.BAT file, to avoid having to type the commands every time you boot your computer.

To load a program into high memory, you type the command HILOAD, then follow it with the program command you would normally enter at the command prompt. For example, to load the DELWATCH program into a UMB, the following command can be used:

```
HILOAD DELWATCH C:
```

Any parameters or switches the command uses may be included, just as they would on the command line. If there is no UMB large enough for the program, HILOAD will load the program in low memory. Unfortunately, HILOAD does not indicate which memory area is used, so it is necessary to use the MEM command before and after loading the program, to see whether the program went into a UMB or into low memory.

To see the effects of the HIBUFFERS, HIDEVICE and HILOAD commands, compare Figure 5.4 with Figure 5.5.

Both figures were produced on a 486 PC with eight megabytes of RAM. Both have one device driver (ANSI.SYS), and one TSR (DELWATCH) loaded. In Figure 5.4, the disk buffers appear in low memory, EMM386.SYS is not loaded, and the upper memory area is not used. In Figure 5.5, EMM386.SYS is loaded and the upper memory area is used.

There are several significant differences in these two figures. To begin with, in Figure 5.4, where EMM386.SYS is not loaded, there are 566,160 bytes free for running programs in conventional memory (this

Address	Owner	Size	Type
0:0000	--------	400h, 1,024	Interrupt vectors
40:0000	--------	100h, 256	ROM BIOS data area
50:0000	DR DOS	200h, 512	DOS data area
70:0000	DR BIOS	B20h, 2,848	Device drivers
70:050B	PRN		Built-in device driver
70:051D	LPT1		Built-in device driver
70:052F	LPT2		Built-in device driver
70:0541	LPT3		Built-in device driver
70:0553	AUX		Built-in device driver
70:0565	COM1		Built-in device driver
70:0577	COM2		Built-in device driver
70:0589	COM3		Built-in device driver
70:059B	COM4		Built-in device driver
70:0602	CLOCK$		Built-in device driver
70:0645	CON		Built-in device driver
70:0671	A:-C:		Built-in device driver
122:0000	DR DOS	11B0h, 4,528	System
122:0048	NUL		Built-in device driver
23D:0000	DR DOS	C360h, 50,016	System
24F:0000	EMMXXXX0	640h, 1,600	Loadable device driver
304:15C0	DR DOS	DE0h, 3,552	DR DOS BIOS code
23E:3000	DR DOS	9440h, 37,952	DR DOS kernel code
E73:0000	COMMAND	210h, 528	Program
E94:0000	COMMAND	210h, 528	Environment
EB5:0000	MEM	B0h, 176	Environment
EC0:0000	MEM	13AD0h, 80,592	Program
226D:0000	--------	7D520h, 513,312	FREE
9FBF:0000	EXCLUDED	28410h, 164,880	Upper system memory
9FC0:0000	--------	400h, 1,024	Extended ROM BIOS data area
C800:0000	--------	FF0h, 4,080	FREE
C8FF:0000	EXCLUDED	13010h, 77,840	Upper system memory
DC00:0000	DR DOS	1040h, 4,160	System
DC02:0000	CON	1020h, 4,128	Loadable device driver
DD04:0000	--------	2FB0h, 12,208	FREE
DFFF:0000	EXCLUDED	D010h, 53,264	Upper system memory
E600:0000	EMM386	7000h, 28,672	EMM386 device driver code
ED00:0000	--------	2FF0h, 12,272	FREE
EFFF:0000	EXCLUDED	6010h, 24,592	Upper system memory
F600:0000	DELWATCH	12D0h, 4,816	XMS Upper Memory Block
F72D:0000	DELWATCH	C0h, 192	XMS Upper Memory Block
F739:0000	--------	C70h, 3,184	FREE
FFFF:00E0	COMMAND	1380h, 4,992	Program
FFFF:1470	--------	ADB0h, 44,464	FREE
FFFF:C220	DR DOS	3C00h, 15,360	30 Disk buffers

Figure 5.5 MEM Command Output with Disk Buffers, ANSI.SYS and Delwatch Loaded High

figure is determined by adding up the bytes free at address 293F:0000, and the bytes occupied by the MEM program immediately preceding this address—80,592 bytes at address 1592:0000). Some of the low memory is occupied by DOS, disk buffers, ANSI.SYS, COMMAND.COM, DELWATCH, and built-in device drivers. In Figure 5.5, where EMM386.SYS is loaded, there are 594,080 bytes free for running programs. Besides loading the DELWATCH program and ANSI.SYS driver into UMBs, the disk buffers have been loaded into high memory, at address FFFF:C220. Thus, by using UMBs for the ANSI.SYS device driver and the DELWATCH TSR, and the high memory area for disk buffers, 27,920 bytes of memory have been reclaimed for running programs. Notice that, while EMM386.SYS uses 30,272 bytes of memory, almost all of this has been placed in a UMB, at address E600:0000. Only 1600 bytes of conventional memory are used by EMM386.SYS.

In Figure 5.4, the only address shown above the free conventional memory is that for the Extended ROM BIOS data area. In Figure 5.5, on the other hand, there are many addresses above conventional memory. These addresses show that the ANSI.SYS device driver and DELWATCH TSR have successfully been loaded into UMBs, and that there are still some UMBs available for loading additional device drivers and/or TSRs.

The HIINSTALL command can be used in the CONFIG.SYS file in place of the HILOAD command, which is used in a batch file or at the command prompt. The following two commands have the same effect, but the first goes in CONFIG.SYS while the second is executed at the command prompt:

```
HIINSTALL=C:\DRDOS\CURSOR.EXE
HILOAD=CURSOR
```

The full pathname to the program being loaded is required for the HIINSTALL command, while the HILOAD command will work as long as the program resides in a directory included in the current path. Also, the HIINSTALL command requires that the extension be used for the program being loaded, while the extension is optional and usually ignored with the HILOAD command.

In summary, to maximize the use of conventional memory on a 386 PC that has at least one megabyte of RAM, perform the following steps:

1. Place the `DEVICE=C:\DRDOS\EMM386.SYS /FRAME=NONE` command in the CONFIG.SYS file.
2. Replace the BUFFERS command with the HIBUFFERS command in CONFIG.SYS.
3. Use HIDEVICE rather than DEVICE in CONFIG.SYS to load device drivers. Be sure the HIDEVICE commands come after the command in step (1).
4. Use the HILOAD or HIINSTALL command to place any TSRs in UMBs.
5. If one or more of the device drivers does not work, or the computer locks up, then use the DEVICE command to load

the problem driver(s) into low memory, and the MEM command to determine their size requirements. Then try using the HIDEVICE command again, this time with the SIZE parameter.

If you have applications that need expanded memory, you should use the /FRAME=AUTO switch instead of /FRAME=NONE on the EMM386.SYS line. This sets up the page frame required for expanded memory; the price you pay is that the page frame takes up 64K of memory that could be used for UMBs.

When you have more device drivers and/or TSR programs than will fit into the available UMBs, there are usually several possible configurations. For example, suppose that you have three TSRs you want to put into high memory, one which is 20K, one 30K, and one 40K. Now suppose that there is one 80K UMB available. You cannot fit all three into the UMB, since they total 90K, but any two of them will fit. Since the one that's left will have to go into conventional memory, it is to your advantage to make that one the smallest. Therefore, you should put the 30K and 40K TSRs into high memory, and the 20K TSR into low memory. This is a simple example, but it illustrates the point that it is worth examining carefully what is going into high memory and what is going into low memory, when you cannot put all of your device drivers and TSRs into high memory.

If you have a 286 PC with one megabyte or more of memory, it is still possible to make use of the UMBs. You may do so by using the HIDOS.SYS memory manager instead of EMM386.SYS. HIDOS.SYS is discussed below, in the section *Managing Memory On 80286 PCs*.

Managing Expanded Memory

If you plan on using expanded memory, there are two things to remember:

- On 8088 and 80286 PCs, expanded memory requires a special add-on board, and software that comes with the board.
- Expanded memory can only be used with software that has been specifically designed to use it. Other software will ignore expanded memory.

PCs based on the 80386 and later chips have the hardware that is required to use expanded memory built in. Consequently, all they need is the proper software to convert extended memory to expanded memory. Therefore, it is not necessary to buy add-on boards to put expanded memory on an 80386 or later PC. Furthermore, since the hardware portion of expanded memory management is built in to the CPU, and all 80386 PCs use the same CPU chip, regardless of the PC manufacturer, the same expanded memory management software will work on all 80386 PCs. For this reason, DR DOS 6.0 includes an expanded memory manager for 80386 PCs: EMM386.SYS.

EMM386.SYS is what is known as an *expanded memory emulator* because it uses extended memory to emulate expanded memory. In other words, EMM386.SYS can be used to trick the computer into thinking that its extended memory is actually expanded memory. If you are using another expanded memory manager, you should not use EMM386.SYS. You should decide which suits your needs better, and eliminate the other one.

In order to use expanded memory, a 64K page frame must be set up to map the expanded memory into conventional memory, and an expanded memory manager must then handle the mapping. These two tasks are provided by EMM386.SYS. There are numerous switches that can be used with EMM386.SYS to specify the precise location in memory of where the page frame is located, and how EMM386.SYS behaves. These switches are rarely needed, and their use is quite technical. They are therefore discussed in the *Advanced Topics* section of this chapter. In general, allowing EMM386.SYS to use the default settings defined by the INSTALL or SETUP program for these switches works best. However, there are some other switches that are more commonly used, and they will be discussed here.

EMM386.SYS is loaded with a DEVICE command in the CONFIG.SYS file. If the /FRAME switch is not specified, then EMM386.SYS will go ahead and set up a 64K page frame in upper memory, at whatever location it determines to be best. If you do not need expanded memory, then use the following command:

```
DEVICE=C:\DRDOS\EMM386.SYS /FRAME=NONE
```

This will leave all of your extended memory configured as extended, rather than expanded, memory. Since no page frame is set up in upper memory, there will be 64K of upper memory saved for UMBs.

You may also use the /FRAME switch to specify a specific address at which the page frame should be installed. Since the page frame is 64K, the address you specify must have at least 64K of available contiguous memory following it. The following command tells EMM386.SYS to install the page frame starting at address C000:

```
DEVICE=C:\DRDOS\EMM386.SYS /FRAME=C000
```

If 64K of contiguous memory is not available starting at the specified address, EMM386.SYS will generate a warning message. you may also specify the word AUTO for the address, in which case EMM386.SYS will search for a suitable 64K of available upper memory in which to install the page frame. Excluding the /FRAME switch has the same effect as using /FRAME=AUTO.

The amount of extended memory to be converted to expanded memory can be specified in the CONFIG.SYS file, by including the desired number of kilobytes as a parameter on the DEVICE command line. For example, to set up 512K of expanded memory, the following command should be included in the CONFIG.SYS file:

```
DEVICE=C:\DRDOS\EMM386.SYS /KB=512
```

The amount of memory specified may be anywhere from 0K to 32,768K. The KB amount is specified in decimal; this is different from most of the other EMM386.SYS switches, which use hexadecimal numbers. Memory should be specified in multiples of 16. If the number used is not a multiple of 16, then EMM386.SYS will automatically round the number down to the nearest multiple of 16. For example, if you specified 520, EMM386.SYS would round it down to 512. If no value is specified, EMM386.SYS uses 256. It is a good idea to make sure you use a multiple of 16 when specifying the amount of expanded memory, because it is then obvious how much expanded memory is actually available.

To convert all extended memory to expanded memory, use either a 0 or the word AUTO. Both of the following commands will automatically convert all extended memory to expanded memory:

```
DEVICE=C:\DRDOS\EMM386.SYS /KB=0
DEVICE=C:\DRDOS\EMM386.SYS /KB=AUTO
```

EMM386.SYS is a fairly intelligent device driver—it has the ability to determine whether an application requires expanded memory, and leaves the memory configured as extended when expanded is not needed. Consequently, you may convert all of the extended memory to expanded, and still have it available for programs that only use extended memory. However, if you will be using a multi-tasking program, such as TaskMAX, then beware that a program that uses expanded memory may cause EMM386.SYS to convert all extended memory to expanded, leaving none for programs that want extended memory and that are running at the same time.

If you want to use EMM386.SYS to provide access to UMBs, but don't need it as an expanded memory manager, then use the /FRAME=NONE switch on the DEVICE=EMM386.SYS line in the CONFIG.SYS file.

EMM386.SYS also supports the Virtual Control Program Interface (VCPI), which is a programming interface that some programs use to access advanced features of the 80386 and later chips. Such programs will run successfully while you are using EMM386.SYS.

Using EMMXMA.SYS To Convert Extended Memory To Expanded Memory On IBM PS/2 Computers

IBM PS/2 PCs often have extended memory installed on special memory cards referred to as IBM XMA cards. You may use the EMMXMA.SYS device driver to convert this extended memory to expanded memory, so it can be used with programs that require expanded memory. To use this driver, include the following line in your CONFIG.SYS file:

```
DEVICE=C:\DRDOS\EMMXMA.SYS
```

There are two optional switches that may be set with the EMMXMA.SYS driver. Recall that use of expanded memory requires a 64K page frame. The /FRAME switch allows you to specify the address at which the page frame will be installed. For example,the following command specifies that the page frame be installed at address C000:

```
DEVICE=C:\DRDOS\EMMXMA.SYS /FRAME=C000
```

Note that the address must be entered in hexadecimal format. If the /FRAME switch is excluded, EMMXMA.SYS searches the upper memory region (from address C000 to DFFF) for a 64K stretch of available memory.

The second switch, /KB, allows you to specify how much of the extended memory should be converted to expanded. This is useful if you have some programs that use extended memory and some that use expanded memory. The following command converts 512K of the extended memory on an IBM PS/2 with an IBM XMA card installed:

```
DEVICE=C:\DRDOS\EMMXMA.SYS /KB=512
```

Note that the amount of memory to be converted is entered as a decimal, rather than hexadecimal, value. If the /KB switch is omitted, all of the extended memory is converted to expanded memory.

Managing Extended Memory

If you want to make use of extended memory, your software must be designed to use it. Software that is not designed to use extended memory will ignore it. Extended memory can only exist on PCs that use 286, 386, and more advanced chips. There are two techniques that software developers can use to design software that takes advantage of extended memory. The first is to build a *DOS extender* into the software, in which case nothing needs to be done to the system to make the extended memory available.

The second approach is to design the software to conform to the XMS Version 2.0 protocol. If the computer has an extended memory manager installed that also conforms to this protocol, the extended memory will be available to the program. As for expanded memory management, the EMM386.SYS device driver handles this function. Install EMM386.SYS is discussed above, in the section *Managing Expanded Memory*. There are several switches that can be used with EMM386.SYS. These switches are highly technical, however, and are usually best left to their default values. A few are discussed above, and the rest are discussed in the *Advanced Topics* section of this chapter.

In addition to providing extended memory management, DR DOS 6.0 has two features that make use of a special 64K area of extended memory, as though it were conventional memory. This area is known as the HMA, or High Memory Area. This terminology is a little confusing, since the region from 640K to 1 megabyte is referred to as the Upper Memory Area, or High Memory. The HMA is not part of the Upper Memory Area. Rather, it is the first 64K of extended memory—the memory that extends from address 1,048,576 (1 megabyte) to address 1,114,112 (64K past 1 megabyte). It is possible to put a substantial portion of DOS itself into the HMA, thereby freeing up additional conventional memory. To load the DOS kernel into the HMA, include the /BDOS switch on the EMM386.SYS line in your CONFIG.SYS file:

```
DEVICE=C:\DRDOS\EMM386.SYS /BDOS=FFFF
```

FFFF is the starting address for the HMA. The DOS kernel consists of two hidden system files, IBMBIO.COM and IBMDOS.COM. When these are loaded into the HMA, conventional memory and the UMB memory are conserved for other uses. You may use an address in upper memory, rather than FFFF, providing there is sufficient memory available at the specified address. However, this will reduce the memory available for UMBs.

There are two other settings you may use in place of FFFF with the /BDOS switch: AUTO, which is the default and tells EMM386.SYS to use an area of upper memory (not the HMA), if there is one large enough available. If there is no area in upper memory that is large enough, then FFFF is used. You may use /NONE to tell EMM386.SYS not to relocate the DOS kernel. This loads the kernel into conventional memory, thereby reducing the amount of memory that will be available to programs.

Besides loading the DOS kernel into the HMA, it is possible to load some of the DOS data structures there as well. This is done with the HIDOS command, which also goes into the CONFIG.SYS file, as follows:

```
HIDOS=ON
```

You may specify OFF instead of ON. If the HIDOS command is omitted from CONFIG.SYS, the effect is the same as specifying OFF—the DOS data structures are loaded into conventional memory.

This command may be used on any PC that runs on a 286 or later chip, and that has extended memory available. This includes all PCs having one or more megabytes of RAM.

To see the effect of loading DOS high, compare Figure 5.6 with Figure 5.5. Figure 5.6 was generated with the MEM /B /D command after the /BDOS=FFFF switch was added to the EMM386.SYS line in the CONFIG.SYS file, and the HIDOS=ON command was added to CONFIG.SYS.

Address	Owner	Size		Type
0:0000	---------	400h,	1,024	Interrupt vectors
40:0000	---------	100h,	256	ROM BIOS data area
50:0000	DR DOS	200h,	512	DOS data area
70:0000	DR BIOS	B20h,	2,848	Device drivers
70:050B	PRN			Built-in device driver
70:051D	LPT1			Built-in device driver
70:052F	LPT2			Built-in device driver
70:0541	LPT3			Built-in device driver
70:0553	AUX			Built-in device driver
70:0565	COM1			Built-in device driver
70:0577	COM2			Built-in device driver
70:0589	COM3			Built-in device driver
70:059B	COM4			Built-in device driver
70:0602	CLOCK$			Built-in device driver
70:0645	CON			Built-in device driver
70:0671	A: -C:			Built-in device driver
122:0000	DR DOS	11B0h,	4,528	System
122:0048	NUL			Built-in device driver
23D:0000	DR DOS	D70h,	3,440	System
24F:0000	EMMXXXX0	640h,	1,600	Loadable device driver
314:0000	COMMAND	210h,	528	Program
335:0000	COMMAND	210h,	528	Environment
356:0000	MEM	B0h,	176	Environment
361:0000	MEM	13AD0h,	80,592	Program
170E:0000	---------	88B10h,	559,888	FREE
9FBF:0000	EXCLUDED	28410h,	164,880	Upper system memory
9FC0:0000	---------	400h,	1,024	Extended ROM BIOS data area
C800:0000	DR DOS	FF0h,	4,080	System
C8FF:0000	EXCLUDED	13010h,	77,840	Upper system memory
DC00:0000	DR DOS	1040h,	4,160	System
DC02:0000	CON	1020h,	4,128	Loadable device driver
DD04:0000	DELWATCH	C0h,	192	XMS Upper Memory Block
DD10:0000	---------	2EF0h,	12,016	FREE
DFFF:0000	EXCLUDED	D010h,	53,264	Upper system memory
E600:0000	EMM386	7000h,	28,672	EMM386 device driver code
ED00:0000	---------	2FF0h,	12,272	FREE
EFFF:0000	EXCLUDED	6010h,	24,592	Upper system memory
F600:0000	DR DOS	CD0h,	3,280	System
F6CD:0000	DELWATCH	12D0h,	4,816	XMS Upper Memory Block
F7FA:0000	---------	60h,	96	FREE
FFFF:00E0	COMMAND	1380h,	4,992	Program
FFFF:1470	---------	120h,	288	FREE
FFFF:1590	DR DOS	DE0h,	3,552	DR DOS BIOS code
FFFF:2370	DR DOS	9440h,	37,952	DR DOS kernel code
FFFF:B7B0	---------	A70h,	2,672	FREE
FFFF:C220	DR DOS	3C00h,	15,360	30 Disk buffers

Figure 5.6 MEM Command Output with ANSI.SYS, DELWATCH and DOS Kernel And Data Structures Loaded High

In Figure 5.6, the DR DOS BIOS code and DR DOS kernel code can be seen in the HMA, at addresses FFFF:1590 and FFF:2370. This frees up 41,504 bytes of memory that previously was occupied in conventional memory (at addresses 304:15C0 and 23E:3000 in Figure 5.5). The result, seen in Figure 5.6, is a total of 640,656 bytes of conventional memory free for running programs.

In some circumstances, a commercial memory manager such as QEMM-386 may provide even more efficient use of the UMBs and HMA than EMM386.SYS does. In particular, EMM386.SYS uses the HMA to load part of DOS, but this leaves part of the 64K HMA unused and unavailable. QEMM-386, on the other hand, allows you to fully utilize the HMA. Consequently, when running QEMM-386 it may be better to load DOS into low memory and use QEMM-386 to manage the HMA.

Comparing Figures 5.4 and 5.6, 74,496 bytes have been added to available conventional memory by utilizing UMBs to load the ANSI.SYS device driver and the DELWATCH program, and by loading much of DOS into the HMA. There are still some UMBs available, so if you use more TSRs or device drivers than shown here you may save even more space.

Managing Memory On 80286 PCs

So far, all of the memory management techniques have focussed on 386 or later PCs, which permit the use of the EMM386.SYS device driver for memory management. However, if you have a 286-based PC with 1 meg or more of memory, you can still take advantage of many of these techniques, using the HIDOS.SYS device driver instead of EMM386.SYS.

HIDOS.SYS can be used to load DOS into the HMA, and to make the UMBs available for loading TSRs and device drivers. However, it does not set up an expanded memory page frame and therefore cannot emulate expanded memory with extended memory. This limitation is due to the fact that 286 chips, unlike 386 chips, do not have the hardware capability built in for managing expanded memory. Consequently, to have expanded memory on a 286 machine, you must install an expanded memory board and use the software that comes with it to create the page frame and to manage the expanded memory.

To use HIDOS.SYS, include the following line in your CONFIG.SYS file:

```
DEVICE=C:\DRDOS\HIDOS.SYS
```

There are numerous switches that can be set for the HIDOS.SYS device driver. The most commonly used one is /BDOS, which works exactly the same as the /BDOS switch for the EMM386.SYS driver, as discussed above. The other switches are fairly technical in nature, so discussion of them is reserved for the Advanced Topics section.

The HIBUFFERS command can also be used with the HIDOS.SYS driver.

If your computer is based on the Chips and Technologies LeaAPSet, LeAPSetsx ChipSET, Neat, Neatsx ChipSET, or SCAT chip set, then after the HIDOS.SYS driver is loaded, you may use the HIDEVICE, HILOAD, HIINSTALL, and HIDOS commands in the same way you can with the EMM386.SYS driver. Discussions of these drivers are in the sections *Managing Expanded Memory* and *Managing Extended Memory*, above.

Using The MemMAX Command

DR DOS 6.0 provides three device drivers (EMM386.SYS, HIDOS.SYS, and EMMXMA.SYS) and five commands (HIBUFFERS, HIDEVICE, HIDOS, HIINSTALL, and HILOAD) for managing the memory on your PC. Taken together, these drivers and commands are referred to as MemoryMAX. When used properly they can provide you with extremely efficient use of the memory in any IBM-compatible personal computer.

One additional command is provided, MEMMAX, in order to allow you to control some of the MemoryMAX features from the command line, even though they are set up in the CONFIG.SYS file. This is useful because some of the memory settings that EMM386.SYS and HIDOS.SYS are capable of may conflict with some programs. With the MEMMAX command, you can turn them on and off at will. MEMMAX can also be used to examine the status of different portions of memory.

Under normal circumstances, the DOS kernel and data structures are loaded into memory at the very bottom of conventional memory. Since this is the traditional location for DOS, programs normally do not expect to be loaded into this area. Most programs don't care, and will work fine when they are loaded here, but occasionally a program may fail to operate properly when it is loaded into these very low memory addresses. When this happens there will usually be an error message that says something like "!Packed file is corrupt". In order to get around this problem, the -L switch may be used to disable access to low memory. When -L is in effect, programs are loaded as if DOS still occupied the low memory locations. The +L switch can be used to re-establish use of these low memory locations. The following two commands turn off and on access to low memory:

```
MEMMAX -L
MEMMAX +L
```

Remember that the L switch only works if the DOS kernel is loaded into high or upper memory.

Just as some programs will not work properly when they are loaded into the very low addresses normally used by DOS, some will also not work properly when loaded into the upper memory regions that can be made available by EMM386.SYS. The -U switch can be used to temporarily disable use of upper memory, and the +U switch can be used to re-enable it. The following two commands turn off and on the use of upper memory that has been made available via EMM386.SYS:

```
MEMMAX -U
MEMMAX +U
```

As discussed in the *Advanced Topics* section, HIDOS.SYS can be used to increase the available conventional memory by using the graphics portion of video memory for running applications. When this is done, the graphics portion of video memory is not available to the video adaptor, and therefore you cannot run graphics programs. The +V and -V switches are used to switch this memory between use for applications and use for graphics. When EMM386.SYS or HIDOS.SYS reserves the video graphics memory for use by applications, it does not actually put it into use. Instead, this memory continues to be used by the video adaptor, until you transfer it to conventional memory with the following command:

```
MEMMAX +V
```

If, after entering this command, you want to run a graphics program, you must first return the graphics memory to the video adaptor with the following command:

```
MEMMAX -V
```

To examine the status of lower memory, the /L switch is used. To examine the status of upper memory, the /U switch is used. And to examine the status of video memory, the /V switch is used. The following command displays the status of video memory:

```
MEMMAX /V
```

The nine switches that may be used with MEMMAX are summarized in Table 5.1.

Table 5.1 MEMMAX Switch Settings

Switch	***Effect***
+L	Enables access to lower memory.
-L	Disables access to lower memory.
+U	Enables access to upper memory.
-U	Disables access to upper memory.
+V	Enables memory reserved by the /VIDEO option.
-V	Disables memory reserved by the /VIDEO option.
/L	Displays the status of lower memory.
/U	Displays the status of upper memory.
/V	Displays the status of VIDEO memory.

Memory Management Summary

While all memory on personal computers is physically the same, there are three ways in which that memory can be configured, depending on the type of hardware (CPU and memory boards) installed: conventional memory, which all PCs have; expanded memory, which can be added to any type of PC; and extended memory, which can only exist on PCs that use an 80286 or later CPU.

The advantage of providing as much conventional memory as possible is that all programs can make use of conventional memory, and in general it is the fastest memory for a program to use, since no additional overhead is involved in managing it. DR DOS 6.0 provides the EMM386.SYS and HIDOS.SYS device drivers, and the HIDOS command, to provide the largest possible amount of conventional memory for programs.

The advantage of expanded memory is that it can be added to any type of PC, and that there is a fairly large number of software programs that can take advantage of it. The disadvantage is that it is slower to access than either conventional memory or extended memory, because of the complex paging mechanism by which it is implemented. Furthermore, computers and software are evolving away from the use of expanded memory, toward the use of extended memory, so that expanded memory must be seen as a short-term investment. To use expanded memory on an 80286 PC, expanded memory management software must be installed. This software is specific to the particular brand of expanded memory board you purchased. To use expanded memory on an 80386 PC, the EMM386.SYS device driver can be used to convert extended memory to expanded.

The advantages of having extended memory are that it is very fast (for programs that can make use of it) and that it is a good long-term investment, since the industry is evolving towards extended memory as the standard way of using memory over 1 megabyte. The disadvantages are that it cannot be added to 8088 PCs, and that most programs cannot make use of it.

Extended memory can also be used to increase the amount of conventional memory available to programs, by loading DOS into the HMA. Extended memory may also be used to back-fill the UMBs, which can then be used to load device drivers and TSRs. This makes even more conventional memory available to programs. Extended memory on PCs using the 80386 and later chips is made available by including the line DEVICE=C:\DRDOS\EMM386.SYS in the CONFIG.SYS file. Loading DOS into the HMA and backfilling UMBs are both accomplished on 386 PCs by also including the line DEVICE=EMM386.SYS /FRAME=NONE /BDOS=FFFF.

On 80286 PCs, DOS may be loaded into the HMA by including the lines DEVICE=C:\HIDOS.SYS and HIDOS=ON in the CONFIG.SYS file. The HIBUFFERS command may also be used with HIDOS.SYS, to load disk buffers into the HMA. If your computer contains one of the specified chip sets, the HIDOS.SYS device driver also makes it possible to use the HIDEVICE, HIINSTALL, and HILOAD commands to load TSRs and device drivers into upper memory.

The MEMMAX command can be used to turn on and off some of the features defined with the EMM386.SYS device driver in the CONFIG.SYS file. It can also be used to examine the status of lower memory, upper memory, and video memory.

Advanced Topics

There are several topics related to computer memory that are quite technical in nature, and that do not need to be understood by most personal computer users. However, for highly technical users this knowledge can help you to fine-tune the configuration of a PC. You must understand the information presented earlier in this chapter in order to follow this material.

Understanding Memory Addresses

So far, addresses have simply been referred to as numbers that tell DOS where a piece of information lies. However, the internal workings are not quite that simple because the original PCs were only capable of manipulating 16 bits at a time. Consequently, they could only directly manage a 16-bit address. However, that would have limited the PCs to 2 to the 16th, or 65,536 bytes (64K) of memory. In order to achieve a 20 bit address, a scheme known as *segmented addressing* was used. As its name implies, segmented addressing breaks the entire memory area down into segments. A specific address then consists of two numbers: the 4-bit segment address, also known as the base address, and a 16- bit offset address, which indicates how far into the specified segment a particular address lies.

To envision this, think of having 10,000 boxes, each of which must be assigned a unique numeric code. But you are limited to using codes that are no more than two digits long. That means each box can only have an *address* that falls between 0 and 99. So to get around the problem, you arrange the boxes into groups. Since you are capable of managing two-digit codes, you can have up to 100 groups, labeled 0 through 99. These *group addresses* are the segment, or base, addresses. After arranging the boxes into these groups, each box within a group is assigned its own two-digit code. Again, up to 100 boxes can be in each group, with *offset addresses* ranging from 0 to 99. Now, to specify a particular box, you provide two numbers: the base address, and the offset address.

When actually referencing a particular box, you must use the offset and base addresses, but for thinking about what you want to put into and remove from the boxes, and how much they can hold, you can imagine that they have one long sequence of 10,000 addresses, ranging from 0 through 9,999. The first box in group 0 has an offset address of 0, but it can be thought of as having an *absolute address* of 1. The first box in group 1 can be thought of as having an "absolute" address of 101, even though the two- digit numbering scheme cannot directly represent the number 101. This is what has been done up to now in this chapter—

memory locations have been referred to with their *absolute address*, rather than their segment plus an offset address.

The segment part of the address in an IBM PC uses 4 bits, so there are 16 segments (2 to the 4th power) in the memory space of a PC. Since the segment address uses up only four bits, and the total address is 20 bits, the offset address uses 16 bits. This means that each segment is 65,536 bytes long. The result of 16 segments, each of which contains 65,536 bytes, is the total address space of a PC: 16 times 65,536 equals 1,048,576, which is one megabyte.

Switch Settings for the EMM386.SYS Device Driver

The commonly used switches for EMM386.SYS are discussed earlier in this chapter. The switches discussed in the following paragraphs provide a fine level of control over precisely how EMM386.SYS sets up the page frame, as well as other aspects of its behavior. None of these switches are required to be specified—they all have default values that are used if they are not specified. In most cases the default values are acceptable. Except where noted otherwise, any of the EMM386.SYS switches may be used with any of the other switches.

Caution should be exercised when using these switches. Valid settings not only depend on the values specified for the switch, but in some cases on the particular hardware configuration. Setting them improperly may cause the PC to lock up. You should have a very good understanding of the various types of memory before adjusting these switches.

Any of the EMM386.SYS switches may be abbreviated to their first letter. For example, the following two commands are equivalent:

```
DEVICE=C:\DRDOS\EMM386.SYS /FRAME=C000
DEVICE=C:\DRDOS\EMM386.SYS /F=C000
```

You may notice that the hexadecimal addresses are all four digits, which does not translate to the large decimal numbers they should correspond to. This is because all of the addresses must lie on a 16K boundary, which means that the final digit is always zero. Consequently, the final zero is assumed and therefore not entered.

In order to understand what some of these switches do, it is necessary to understand some of what EMM386.SYS does when it is loaded. The following steps are part of the EMM386.SYS load process:

1. Since EMM386.SYS sets up the UMBs, none are available when it is loaded. Consequently, it is initially loaded into conventional memory. It then scans upper memory for an unused space that is large enough to store most of itself, and if it finds one, it relocates most of the EMM386.SYS code into that space, leaving conventional memory for applications.
2. If EMM386.SYS is establishing a page frame for expanded memory management, then it must locate a 64K stretch of available memory.
3. Since EMM386.SYS backfills memory into the UMBs, it must locate unused memory addresses in the upper memory area (between 640K and 1 megabyte) which can be used as UMBs. Consequently, when EMM386.SYS is loaded, it automatically scans all memory between 640K and 1 megabyte, 4K at a time, to see where there are free addresses.
4. If EMM386.SYS is relocating the DR DOS kernel, it must locate an appropriate address at which to store it.

Many of the EMM386.SYS switches discussed below are used to control precisely how these startup operations are carried out.

When EMM386.SYS is used to manage expanded memory, it creates a 64K page frame in the upper memory area. It is no coincidence that 64K is also the size of a memory segment. By making the page frame 64K, a single address can be stored as the segment address of the page frame, and any other address reference to the page frame is seen as the offset. This means that only 16 bits are needed to specify an address within the page frame, since the offset never changes.

The page frame is the area that expanded memory pages are mapped into as they are needed. Each page is 16K, so there are four of them in the page frame. If left to itself, EMM386.SYS will determine an appropriate location within the upper memory area for the page frame to be located. However, there are three settings for the /FRAME switch that can be used to tell EMM386.SYS precisely where to put the page frame. Since EMM386.SYS can only create one page frame, these settings are mutually exclusive—you may use only one of them. Addresses for the page frame must start on a 16K (16,384 byte) boundary—they must be a multiple of 16,384. In the discussion that follows, you will see that all valid values for the page frame address meet this condition.

The first of these settings is AUTO, which tells EMM386.SYS to automatically scan upper memory for a free 64K block. The second setting is NONE, which tells EMM386.SYS not to create a page frame, and therefore not to make expanded memory available to your programs. The third setting is a hexadecimal number which identifies a specific address at which to place the page frame.

Normally, EMM386.SYS senses what addresses are already in use and avoids them when setting up the page frame or UMBs. However, there may be circumstances under which you want to fine-tune how EMM386.SYS scans upper memory. The /AUTOSCAN switch tells EMM386.SYS to automatically scan 4K blocks of the specified range of upper memory to see if they are free. The following command tells EMM386.SYS to autoscan all addresses from D000 to E000.

```
DEVICE=C:\DRDOS\EMM386S.SYS /AUTOSCAN=D000-E000
```

/AUTOSCAN uses a very sensitive test to determine whether an area of memory is free, so it is the switch that is most likely to incorrectly mark an area as in use. The /INCLUDE switch, discussed below, uses a less sensitive test. If /AUTOSCAN is not used, EMM386.SYS autoscans all memory between 640K and 1 megabyte.

The /INCLUDE switch can be used to specify a range of addresses that should be tested, but not as strictly as with /AUTOESCAN, for use in an EMS page frame or UMB. The syntax of this switch is:

```
DEVICE=EMM386.SYS /INCLUDE=start-end
```

The addresses are specified in hexadecimal, and may be in the range from A000 (655,360, or 640K) through FFFF (1,047,552, or 1023K). The addresses should be multiples of 4k (4,096). If they are not, they are rounded down to the nearest multiple of 4k. This switch is useful when AUTOSCAN identifies an area of upper memory as being used, when in fact it is not.

The /EXCLUDE switch is the opposite of /INCLUDE, and has the following syntax:

```
DEVICE=C:\DRDOS\EMM386.SYS /EXCLUDE=start-end
```

This switch is useful if EMM386.SYS is detecting an area of memory that it believes is available, but which in fact is in use. This situation most commonly arises when special cards are installed, such as network cards, which use some of the upper memory addresses for ROM that is installed on the card. The start and end addresses are specified in the same way as for /INCLUDE.

There is a considerable amount of memory reserved in the upper memory area for video options. Unlike UMBs, which must be backfilled from extended memory, video memory is memory that actually exists—it is installed on your video card. If you have an MDA, Hercules, EGA, or VGA video card, then the memory on that card is divided into two sections: one for text, and an additional one for the extra memory requirements of graphics applications. If you use your computer in text mode only, then the video memory for graphics applications is wasted. The /VIDEO switch can be used to reclaim the graphics memory and add it to the pool of conventional memory. This memory is contiguous with conventional memory, and therefore increases the amount of memory available to an application. The following command reserves the graphics portion of video memory for use as part of conventional memory:

```
DEVICE=C:\DRDOS\EMM386.SYS /VIDEO
```

Normally, EMM386.SYS will determine the type of card you have and set the addresses correctly. However, you may override the default addresses and specify your own start and/or end address with the following syntax:

```
DEVICE=C:\DRDOS\EMM386.SYS /VIDEO=start-end
```

You may omit the start address, and just specify the end address (including the hyphen in front of it). If the start address is specified, it must always be A000. Both addresses are entered as hexadecimal numbers.

If your computer has an MDA or Hercules video adaptor, /VIDEO will increase conventional memory by 64K; if your computer has an EGA or VGA adpator, /VIDEO will increase conventional memory by 96K.

The /VIDEO switch does not, by itself, automatically add the memory to conventional memory. Rather, it sets up the internal structures necessary for doing so. To actually add the video memory to conventional memory, you must enter the MEMMAX +V command on the command line. The reason that /VIDEO is implemented in this manner is to allow you to switch the use of the video memory back and forth between conventional memory and the video adaptor.

Note that you may ***not*** use graphics applications on your PC while the additional memory is added to conventional memory. To restore the memory for use with the video card, use the MEMMAX -V command on the command line.

At the top of conventional memory, just before the video memory, is an area known as the extended BIOS data area. In order to make the video memory contiguous with conventional memory, the extended BIOS data area must be moved. EMM386.SYS does this by relocating it to the bottom of conventional memory. (The extended BIOS data area is moved regardless of whether the /VIDEO switch is used). The effect of this relocation is to leave the same amount of conventional memory available, but to have it start and end at higher addresses. Now, when the video memory is added in, it lies directly at the top of conventional memory, thereby increasing the conventional memory available to programs.

Relocating the extended BIOS data area does not normally create any problems, but occasionally you may encounter a program that requires the extended BIOS data area to be in its usual location, at the top of conventional memory. You can prevent the relocation from occurring by using the /XBDA switch:

```
DEVICE=C:\DRDOS\EMM386.SYS /XBDA
```

When this switch is used, the extended BIOS data area is left at the top of conventional memory. This will prevent the /VIDEO switch from adding the video memory to conventional memory.

The /USE switch forces EMM386.SYS to use the specified area of upper memory, regardless of whether it thinks that area is in use. This switch overrides all of the EMM386.SYS memory tests that are normally used to determine availability for a region of memory. This switch should only be used if you are very confident of what you are doing, as it can easily create a memory conflict that will lock up your computer. Be sure to have a bootable floppy disk available, in case your computer does lock up. The syntax of the switch is:

```
DEVICE=C:\DRDOS\EMM386.SYS /USE=start-end
```

Start and *end* must be entered as hexadecimal numbers.

As discussed earlier, many of the upper memory addresses are used by ROM rather than RAM. ROM chips are considerably slower to access than RAM chips, so EMM386.SYS provides the ability to map the ROM code into RAM. It does this by reading the contents of the ROM, then writing those contents into an area of RAM and changing the RAM address to replace that of the ROM. Thus, when programs reference the ROM address, they actually connect with the RAM, which is much faster. This can significantly speed up the operation of your computer. To map ROM into RAM, the /ROM switch is used:

```
DEVICE=C:\DRDOS\EMM386.SYS /ROM=xxxx
```

The xxxx can be any of the following three settings:

1. ***AUTO***, which means that all ROMs in upper memory will be mapped into RAM.
2. ***NONE***, which means that no ROM is mapped into RAM. This is the default, if the /ROM switch is not specified.
3. ***start-end***, specifying the start and end addresses of the ROM you want to map.

Compaq 386 and 486 computers that have more than 1 megabyte of RAM can be reconfigured to add an extra 256K of extended memory. This is done with the /COMPAQ switch:

```
DEVICE=C:\DRDOS\EMM386.SYS /COMPAQ
```

As discussed earlier, EMM386.SYS will relocate most of itself into upper memory, leaving only about 1600 bytes of itself in conventional memory. If you are limited in the amount of available upper memory, and want to reserve it for other uses such as network cards or a page frame, you can force EMM386.SYS to keep all of itself in low memory, with the /LOWEMM switch:

```
DEVICE=C:\DRDOS\EMM386.SYS /LOWEMM
```

If you are running Windows 3.0, and want to use it in Standard mode, you must use the /WINSTD switch. This switch disables the use of upper memory, and therefore reduces the amount of conventional memory available to applications. Standard mode is the normal operating mode for Windows 3.0 on a 286 or later PC with at least one megabyte of memory. It allows access to extended memory and lets you switch among non-Windows applications. The following command installs EMM386.SYS for use with Windows 3.0 standard mode:

```
DEVICE=C:\DRDOS\EMM386.SYS /WINSTD
```

Switch Settings For The HIDOS.SYS Device Driver

The HIDOS.SYS device driver, used on PCs that have an 80286 CPU chip, uses the following switches:

```
/AUTOSCAN=start-end
/INCLUDE=start-end
/EXCLUDE=start-end
/VIDEO=start-end
/BDOS=xxxx
/ROM=xxxx
/XBDA
/USE=start-end
/CHIPSET=chipset
```

The use of each of these switches except the last is identical with its use for EMM386.SYS, discussed above.

As mentioned earlier, the HIDOS.SYS driver provides extended features on computers that use one of the Chips and Technologies chip sets that provide Shadow RAM. These chip sets are: LeAPSet, LeAPSetsx, NEAT, NEATsx, and SCAT. On computers that use these chip sets, the Shadow RAM can be mapped back into the upper memory, providing UMBs for installing device drivers and TSRs. Normally, HIDOS.SYS will correctly identify the chip and make the appropriate adjustments. However, if HIDOS.SYS is not correctly identifying the chip set, or if your computer has EMS 4.0 or EEMS memory and the corresponding device driver has been loaded, then the /CHIPSET switch can be used. The syntax for using this switch is:

```
DEVICE=C:\DRDOS\HIDOS.SYS /CHIPSET=xxxx
```

The xxxx can be any one of the following:

- ***AUTO***, which tells HIDOS.SYS to automatically detect the chip set being used. This is the default if the /CHIPSET switch is not used.
- ***NEAT***, which tells HIDOS.SYS to configure itself for the Chips and Technologies NEAT, NEATsx, LeAPSet, or LeAPSetsx CHIPSet.

- ***SCAT***, which tells HIDOS.SYS to configure itself for the Chips and Technologies SCAT chip set.
- ***EMSUMB***, which tells HIDOS.SYS that EMS 4.0 or EEMS memory is available. This switch enables HIDOS.SYS to set up UMBs and enable the use of the HIDEVICE, HIINSTALL, HIDOS, and HILOAD commands.
- ***EMSALL***, which tells HIDOS.SYS to use all EMS upper memory, including the page frame. This disables the use of EMS for programs.
- ***RAM***, which tells HIDOS.SYS to enable permanent upper RAM. This switch can only be used in conjunction with the /USE switch, which tells HIDOS.SYS where the upper RAM is.
- ***NONE***, which tells HIDOS.SYS that it should not attempt to use any mappable Shadow RAM.

More on RAM

For most purposes it is sufficient to consider all RAM as being created equal. However, there are some differences among various RAM chips. The most commonly discussed difference is the access time—how long it takes to read or write information to and from a chip. Access times are typically measured in nanoseconds. A nanosecond is 10^9 seconds, or one billionth of a second. When the first PCs appeared, access time wasn't much of an issue. Access times of memory chips was around 150 nanoseconds, which was plenty fast for the CPUs in use at that time. However, these memory chips were unable to keep up with the faster CPUs that developed, so faster memory chips were designed. This evolutionary process will continue as CPUs get faster and faster.

In addition to different access times, there are two physically different types of RAM chips that may be installed in a computer: *SRAM* and *DRAM*. These terms stand for Static RAM and Dynamic RAM. DRAM is the most common form; it utilizes the charge stored on a capacitor to maintain its contents. Capacitors inevitably have some leakage, so DRAM must be continually refreshed. That is why Dynamic RAM is so named—its contents are dynamically changing. DRAM is less expensive to manufacture, but also has a longer access time, than SRAM. SRAM does not need to be refreshed, and has a faster access time, but is more expensive to produce.

Real, Protected, and Enhanced Chip Modes

When the first PCs were made, and there was only one kind of CPU that a PC could have, the term *mode* was not used. When the 80286 chip was developed, it had capabilities that went far beyond the original 8088/8086 chips. These capabilities included a larger address bus (24-bit, rather than 20-bits) which allowed it to recognize up to 16 megabytes of memory. However, all of the software up to that time had been designed to use the 20-bit address found on the 8088/8086 chips. To permit the 80286 chip to run the existing software, it was designed to operate in two *modes*. The first mode, called *real mode*, emulates the 8088/8086 addressing scheme. This permits the 80286 to run 8088/8086 software, but also gives it the same 1 megabyte limitation of addressable memory. Real mode is so named because the address generated by software is translated directly into the real address of a memory location.

In order to make it possible for future software to utilize the larger memory capacity of the 80286, a second mode was implemented, termed *protected mode*. In protected mode, the chip uses the full 24-bit address.

The 80286 can be shifted back and forth between real and protected mode under software control. Consequently, as software developed that made use of protected mode, all it had to do was send a signal to the chip to tell it which mode was desired.

In protected mode, software does not generate a real address. The offset part of the address is real—it refers to a specific offset within the specified segment—but the segment address is actually a reference to a lookup table, where the real segment address is stored. This scheme is not simple, but it provides an extremely flexible means for efficiently managing memory under very complex software requirements. In protected mode, different areas of memory may be set up for different programs, all of which are running at the same time. These areas of memory must be protected from each other—one program must not be allowed to intrude on the memory assigned to another program. Protected mode is also referred to as "standard" mode. Further discussion is beyond the scope of this book, but it is interesting to see where the terms real and protected come from.

The 80386 and 80486 chips also support real and protected mode operations. As with the 80286, real mode permits them to run all of the software developed for the IBM PC. However, in protected mode, these chips use their full 32-bit address. This permits them to address up to 4 gigabytes of memory. These chips also support a third mode, known as *386 enhanced mode*. 386 enhanced mode uses essentially the same addressing scheme as protected mode. However, at the point at which protected mode has retrieved its segment address from the lookup table and is ready to produce a physical memory address, 386 enhanced mode references into yet another lookup table.

This lookup table may contain addresses for as much as four times the RAM that actually exists in the computer. The table keeps track of which addresses correspond to actual RAM, and which do not. Those that do not are assigned to a swap file on the computer's hard disk. This swap file is used as virtual memory, so when a piece of data is read from or written to one of these addresses, it actually goes to and from the disk.

Swap files are vastly slower than electronic memory, but they do provide the ability to perform operations on computers that do not have the necessary RAM. For example, if a computer has four megabytes of RAM, then programs requiring up to 16 megabytes of memory could be run in 386 enhanced mode. Of course, this assumes that there is enough free disk space to create a 12 megabyte swap file.

Windows version 3.0 and later uses all of these techniques to maximize the performance of each computer it runs on.

Chapter 6

Understanding and Managing Files and Directories

All of the information a computer uses, whether it is programs that the computer runs or data that the computer works on, is stored in disk files. The files on a disk may be organized into groups, called *directories*. Directories are groupings that you can create and modify at will, allowing you to organize your files into a structure that reflects the way you work, and the ways in which you are likely to use your files. This chapter explores the file and directory features of DR DOS 6.0, and explains the commands used for managing them.

Files

A file is a physical structure stored on a magnetic disk. It contains information that the computer can read and manipulate. In order to keep track of files, each one is assigned a name. When you purchase a new software program, that program will have one or more files whose names were assigned by the software manufacturer. When you save information that you have entered into the computer—say, a letter in a word processor—you provide a name for the file in which it will be saved. That name is then stored on the disk, along with the information contained in the file. When you want to retrieve that information, you specify the name of the file and the computer knows where to look for it.

Since files are storage places for information that will be loaded into memory, where the computer can work with it, the information in files should be stored in a way that reflects the structure of electronic memory. As discussed in Chapter 5, electronic memory consists of millions of tiny switches, which can be either on or off. These switches are referred to as *bits*. A bit is the smallest amount of information that a computer can store.

A bit that is on is interpreted by the computer as a one. A bit that is off is interpreted by the computer as a zero. Since a single bit can only mean one of two things, computers work with groups of eight bits in order to represent complex information. This group of eight bits is called a *byte*. Since electronic memory uses information stored as a series of bytes, a computer file also stores information as a series of bytes. Each byte represents a binary number. Depending on the type of information that is stored, the computer can interpret those numbers literally, as numbers, or as characters. If the file contains characters, then the numbers are translated into their corresponding characters according to a table known as the ASCII (or extended ASCII) table. For example, the letter *A* is represented by the number 65, which in binary (base two) is 01000001. Consequently, when you retrieve a file that shows the letter A on your screen, there is a corresponding location in the file that stores the binary number 01000001.

File sizes are measured in the numbers of bytes they contain. It takes a large number of bytes to store useful information, so file sizes are frequently referred to in terms of kilobytes and megabytes. A kilobyte is 1,024 bytes; a megabyte is 1,048,576 bytes. The term *kilobyte* literally means 1,000 bytes, but the computer does everything in multiples of two (since it operates on the base two number system). 1,024 is two raised to the tenth power (2^{10}) and since this is approximately 1,000, 1,024 bytes is referred to as a *kilobyte*. Similar reasoning leads to the term *megabyte*, which is approximately one million bytes. Thus, when you hear of a file being "100K," it means 100 kilobytes (100 X 1,024, or 102,400 bytes).

File Names

A DOS file name consists of two parts: a name part, and an extension part. Together, they are referred to as the file name or filespec. The name may contain up to eight alphanumeric characters, and it is required for saving files. The extension may contain up to three alphanumeric characters, and is not required. The legal alphanumeric characters that may appear in a file name are shown in Table 6.1.

Table 6.1 Legal Characters for Use in File Names

Symbol	***Name***
A to Z	Letters of the alphabet (not case sensitive)
0 to 9	Numbers
_	Underscore
^	Caret
$	Dollar sign
#	Number sign
%	Percent sign
&	Ampersand
-	Hyphen
{	Left curly bracket
}	Right curly bracket

DOS ignores the case of an alphabetic character in a file name, so that *A* and *a* are treated as the same letter. Only the symbols shown in Table 6.1 can be used in file names. File names may not contain commas or slashes. If an extension is specified, the name part and the extension part are separated by a period. This is the only place a period may be used in a file name. There are also a few special names reserved by DOS, which cannot be used for file names. These are: CLOCK$, CON, AUX, COMx (where x is 1, 2, 3, or 4), LPTx (where x is 1, 2, 3, or 4), NUL, and PRN.

With a few exceptions, any file can be assigned any combination of name plus extension, as long as the complete file name is unique within its directory. An example of a complete file name is:

```
ROBERT.LET
```

In this example, the name is ROBERT and the extension is LET.

File name extensions are generally used to indicate the type of information stored in the file. For example, all word processing files that contain letters could be given the extension LET, and all files that contain memos could have the extension MEM. In most cases, there are no rules about this, so you may make up whatever extensions make sense to you. Developing and using a set of conventions for naming files makes it much easier to manage your files, particularly when you want to perform operations on whole groups of files. Table 6.2 shows a list of commonly used file extensions.

There are a few types of files that are required to have particular extensions in order for them to be usable by the computer. These fall into two categories: extensions required by DOS, and extensions required by software.

The extensions required by DOS arise from the fact that there are only two types of files that can exist in the computer: program files and data files. A program file contains instructions that the computer executes, while a data file contains information that a program can work with. DOS interprets the contents of each of these file types differently. If a file contains a program, then DOS loads the entire program into memory, then tells the CPU to start executing the instructions in the program. The CPU then reads the first byte in the file, interprets it as an instruction, and carries it out. It then goes back to the file (in memory), reads the next item, interprets that as an instruction, and carries it out. This continues until the last instruction in the program is carried out, at which time the program returns control of the CPU to DOS.

Data files, on the other hand, do not contain program instructions. They contain information that programs can manipulate. For example, the file ROBERT.LET could contain a letter written to someone named Robert, created with a word processor. When the word processor edits that file, it tells the CPU to interpret the contents of the file as data rather than as instructions. By distinguishing between program files and data files, the same set of binary numbers can be used to mean two different things to the CPU. This is necessary because the computer is limited to only 256 different codes that it can use. (The number 256 is 2^8—since a byte contains eight bits, 255 is the largest number that can be represented in a single byte. A zero is also a code, and this results in 256 possible codes.)

In order to distinguish between program files and data files, DOS reserves three file extensions to identify the three types of program files it knows how to execute. These extensions are BAT, COM, and EXE. If you want to run a program with any one of these extensions, you simply type the name of the file on the command line (the extension may be entered, but it is not required and is generally left off), and press Enter. DOS then goes to the disk and searches for a file that has that name, followed by one of these three extensions. If DOS finds one, it executes the program in the file. If DOS does not find one, it displays the message "Command or file name not recognized."

The reason there are three different extensions for executable files is that each one represents a different technique for creating an executable file. Each type requires DOS to load it and interpret its contents in a different way, so by checking the file extension, DOS automatically knows how to load and interpret the file.

The first extension, BAT, indicates that the file is a BATCH file. A BATCH file consists of a list of DOS commands that are executed in sequence, as though they were typed on the DOS command line. These are discussed in detail in Chapter 9.

The COM extension represents an executable file that contains a relatively simple program. Files with a COM extension are limited in size and complexity. Many of the early PC programs were COM files, but as the capabilities of PCs grew, it became necessary to create programs that were more complex than could be produced in the COM format.

The EXE extension represents an executable file that usually contains a more complex program than what you find in COM files. Most software today is distributed as EXE files. The primary difference is that COM files are limited to a maximum of 64K of program space, while EXE files have no such limitation.

You can have three executable files with the same name, but each of the different executable extensions, in the same directory. For example, you could have files named WP.BAT, WP.COM, and WP.EXE.

When DOS locates two or three executable files with the same name, and in the same directory, it chooses to run the COM file over either the BAT or EXE file, and it chooses the EXE over the BAT. If you have such a situation, and want to run, say, the BAT file, you must type in the extension as well. DOS will then execute the correct file.

While the above extensions are intended for use only with executable files, there is nothing in DOS or in the computer that enforces this convention. You could, for example, name a file that contains a word processing document ROBERT.EXE. DOS would permit this, but it is dangerous, since entering the command ROBERT would cause DOS to attempt to load and execute the file. This would cause the computer to lock up, requiring you to reboot. These naming conventions are universally respected.

DOS imposes no conventions on either the name or the extension for data files. However, many software programs automatically assign an extension, and therefore only permit you to assign the name. In some cases, you have the option of changing the extension, while in other cases you are required to accept the assigned extension. For example, the Microsoft Excel spreadsheet automatically assigns an extension of XLS to spreadsheet files, unless you include one when you name the file. If you do include an extension, Excel accepts it. In general, it is a good idea to let the programs assign the extensions when they are designed to do so. Commonly used extensions, their typical uses, and what types of programs or software vendors use them, are shown in Table 6.2. Extensions which are listed as ubiquitous, in the last column, are commonly used in a large number of settings.

Table 6.2 Commonly Used File Extensions

Extension	***Typical Use***	***Where Used***
$$$	Temporary files	Ubiquitous
BAK	Backup copies of files	Ubiquitous
BAS	BASIC language programs	BASIC language
BAT	Batch files	DOS batch files
BIN	Binary object files	Computer languages
C	C language programs	C language

Table 6.2 continued ...

Extension	***Typical Use***	***Where Used***
COM	Simple executable programs	Computer programs
CPI	Code Page Information file	DOS
DAT	Data files	Ubiquitous
DBF	Database files	dBASE and clones
DOC	Word processing documents	Word processors
DRV	Device driver files	Device driver vendors
DTA	Data files	Ubiquitous
EXE	Large executable programs	Computer programs
LIB	Libraries of language	Computer languages functions
NDX	Database index files	dBASE and clones
OBJ	Object files	Computer languages
OVR	Overlay files	Large computer programs
PAS	Pascal language programs	Pascal language
PRG	dBASE program files	dBASE and clones
RBF	R:BASE database files	R:BASE
SYS	Device drivers	DOS
TXT	Plain ASCII text files	Ubiquitous
WK1	Spreadsheet files	Some spreadsheet programs
WKS	Spreadsheet files	Some spreadsheet programs
XLS	Excel Spreadsheet files	Microsoft Excel
XLM	Excel macro files	Microsoft Excel

It is best to avoid using these common extensions for other purposes.

File names are frequently used as parameters for DOS commands. For example, the DIR command is used to list the files in a directory. If a file name is passed as a parameter, then only the directory listing for that file is shown. For example, the following command shows the directory listing of the AUTOEXEC.BAT file:

```
DIR AUTOEXEC.BAT
```

Using Wild Cards and Filelists

Sometimes it is useful to refer to a group of files, rather than a single file. This can be done using the DOS *wild card* symbols. The asterisk (*) is referred to as the *many wild card.* It means "any set of characters can go here." For example, to indicate all files that have an extension of LET you would enter *.LET. This means "select files that have any name, as long as the extension is LET." Files named R.LET, R10.LET, and ROBERT.LET would all be selected. You could also select all files that begin with the letter R and have any extension by specifying R*.*, or files that begin with R and have an extension of LET by specifying R*.LET. You cannot, however, specify *R.*. Anything that appears between the asterisk wild card and the period is ignored, so *R.* selects all files.

The question mark (?) is referred to as the *single wild card.* It means "any single character can go here." For example, specifying R?.LET would select R1.LET and RA.LET, but not ROB.LET. Unlike the asterisk, the question mark wild card can be both preceded and followed by other letters. Question mark and asterisk wild cards can be mixed in a single file specification.

Figure 6.1 shows several legal file specifiers, and some sample file names that would be selected by them.

File Specifications		***Sample Files Selected***	
?OB.LET	BOB.LET	DOB.LET	FOB.LET
*.DBF	A.DBF	BOOK.DBF	XYZ.DBF
R?B.*	RAB.	RIB.X	ROB.LET
B??K*.*	BEAK.FY	BOOK.LET	BOOK12.DBF
B*.?ET	BAR.BET	B.GET	BOOK.LET

Figure 6.1 Examples of Wild Cards in File Specifications

The use of wildcards is convenient when all the files you want to work with have a common pattern in their names. However, sometimes it is convenient to group files together that have no such pattern. To facilitate this, DR DOS 6.0 provides the ability to create *filelists*. A filelist is a text file that contains the names of the files you want to work with. The names can include wildcards and directory paths. Some of the DR DOS commands can be applied to a filelist file, and will then automatically be executed against each file named in the filelist. Suppose the following list of file names is stored in a file named NAMES.FIL:

```
*.LET
SUSAN.REP
C:\WP\DATA\MARY.NOT
```

To use NAMES.FIL as a filelist, precede its name with an @ symbol. For example, the following command will search each file for the string "August report":

```
FIND "August report" @NAMES.FIL
```

The DOS commands that will work with filelists are shown in Table 6.3.

Table 6.3 DR DOS Commands that Work with Filelists

```
ATTRIB
FC
FILELINK
FIND
MOVE
PASSWORD
REPLACE
SCRIPT
TOUCH
XCOPY
XDEL
```

To create a filelist, use any text editor that can create plain ASCII files—the EDITOR program that comes with DR DOS works well for this purpose. If you are using a word processor, make sure you specify that the file should be saved as a DOS text file, or ASCII file. Within the file, each filename must be on a separate line, or be separated from others on the same line by a space, a tab, or a comma.

Directories

When the first PCs appeared, most of them only had floppy disk drives. A floppy disk cannot hold very many files, so files were kept organized simply by organizing the floppy disks they were stored on. For example, one floppy disk might contain all of the correspondence you have had with a particular company. However, today most computers have hard disks capable of storing a very large number of files. Trying to keep track of a large number of files by their names alone is unwieldy, so DOS allows you to organize the files into groups called *directories*. Directories are similar to file cabinets—each one can hold many files, and you can add and remove them as you need. However, unlike file cabinets, a directory can contain subdirectories as well as files.

In order to manage this system, every disk is given a single directory, called the *root directory*, when the disk is formatted. (Floppy disks usually have to be formatted before you can use them, while hard disks are usually formatted for you by the manufacturer or dealer.) The root directory is capable of storing two types of structures: file names and subdirectories. Subdirectories, in turn, are also capable of storing file names, as well as more subdirectories. This leads to a tree-like structure of directories, each of which may contain files and/or subdirectories. The term *directory* is used to refer to any type of directory: the root directory, and/or any subdirectory, or sub-subdirectory. Part of the directory structure for a hard drive is shown in Figure 6.2.

The root directory for a disk is specified by a backslash (\ ). It is often preceded by the drive letter, followed by a colon. Thus, in Figure 6.2, the root directory, shown at the top, is C:\ .

All directories other than the root are assigned names. Directory names must meet the same criteria as file names: they consist of a required name, up to eight characters long, followed by an optional extension, up to three characters long. If an extension is given, it is separated from the name by a period. However, it is an almost universal convention to not use extensions for directory names. The legal characters for directory names are the same as those for file names (see Table 6.1).

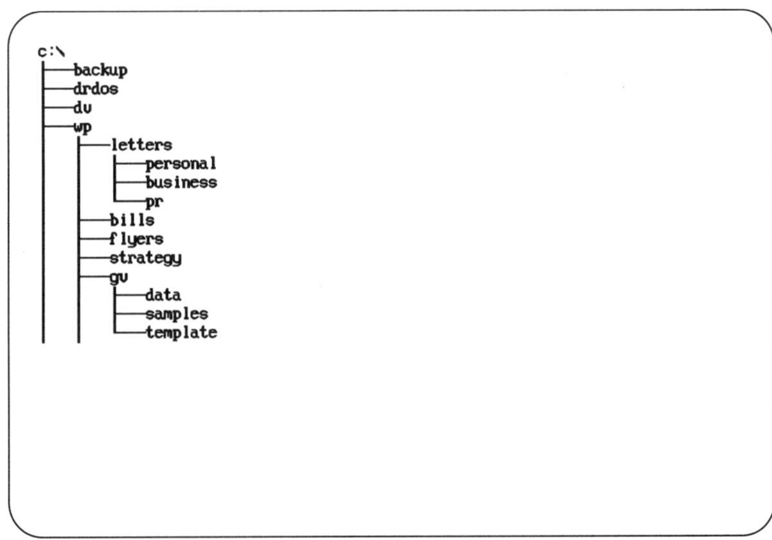

Figure 6.2 Portion of the Directory Tree on a Hard Disk

In Figure 6.2, the root directory contains five subdirectories: BACKUP, DRDOS, DV, and WP. The WP directory in turn contains five subdirectories of its own: LETTERS, BILLS, FLYERS, STRATEGY, and GV. The LETTERS directory is divided into three subdirectories, as is the GV directory.

Each disk drive in your computer has a current directory. When the computer starts, all current directories are initialized to be the root directory. You can change to a different directory with the CHDIR (or CD) command. The directory you change to then becomes the current directory for that drive. DOS keeps track of the current directory for each disk drive in your computer. Thus, if you have a single floppy drive designated A:, and a single hard drive designated C:, DOS will remember the last directory you changed to for each of those drives. When the drive letter is referred to with no directory specification, DOS automatically goes to the current directory on that drive.

All of the files within a directory must have unique names, otherwise DOS would have no way of telling them apart. However, many files may have the same name, as long as each one is in a separate directory.

The TREE Command

While ViewMAX provides a graphical representation of the directory tree, it is also possible to examine the directory tree from the command line, using the TREE command. When entered by itself, with no parameters or switches, the TREE command displays the directory structure that begins with the current directory. Figure 6.2 was created with the TREE command.

The root directory shown in Figure 6.2 is symbolized by a backslash. The single period (.) is also used by DOS to refer to the current directory, and a double period (..) is used to refer to the current subdirectory. Thus, when you list the contents of a subdirectory, the first two items shown are a single period and a double period, marked as directories.

The TREE command displays the complete tree for the current drive, regardless of what directory is current. Thus, had the TREE command in Figure 6.2 been entered when the WP directory was current, the display would be the same.

There are four switches that may be used with the TREE command: /B, /F, /G, and /P. When no switches are specified, TREE displays a text listing of all directories and subdirectories on the current drive, and shows the number of bytes and number of files in each directory. A summary of the total bytes and files on the disk is also shown. The same directory tree shown in Figure 6.2 appears in Figure 6.3, but in Figure 6.3 no switches were used.

The use of the four switches for the TREE command is described in Table 6.4.

Table 6.4 Switches for Use with the TREE Command

Switch	***Effect***
/B	Produces a brief listing of directory names only, without the bytes or file counts.
/F	Displays files in each directory, as well as subdirectories.
/G	Displays a graphical structure, with lines to shown the tree structure. Figure 6.2 was produced with the /B and /G switches.
/P	Pauses after each screenful until you press a key.

bytes	*files*	*path*
5,761,498	67	c:\
303,909	23	c:\backup
1,982,334	106	c:\drdos
348,830	80	c:\dv
177,776	16	c:\wp
42,933	26	c:\wp\letters
90,588	11	c:\wp\letters\personal
118,847	5	c:\wp\letters\business
4,327	5	c:\wp\letters\pr
12,257	3	c:\wp\bills
63,059	9	c:\wp\flyers
10,980	6	c:\wp\strategy
1,144,912	16	c:\wp\gv
1,124	4	c:\gv\data
83,802	2	c:\gv\samples
127,166	5	c:\gv\template
total bytes 10,274,342		
total files	384	

Figure 6.3 Output of TREE Command with No Switches

Note that when using the /G switch, you may not be able to route the output to your printer, unless it is capable of printing the graphical characters used to create the image of the tree structure.

The /F parameter is particularly useful for performing cleanup operations on a disk. Using the /F switch, you can print the entire contents of the disk, then go through it and see which files can be deleted. This helps to eliminate old and unnecessary files that have been forgotten, particularly on PCs that are shared by several people or that have been passed from one person to another.

It is a good idea to use the MORE filter with the TREE command, since the directory tree is usually larger than one screen. The MORE filter causes the display to pause, and wait for a key to be pressed, after each screen. The following syntax pipes the output of the TREE command through the MORE filter:

```
TREE | MORE
```

Any of the TREE parameters and switches may be used with the MORE filter; simply place them after the TREE command, as you would without the filter, then append | MORE to the end of the command.

The TREE command can also be used to locate a file on a disk. To do this, specify the filename following the word TREE. The filename may contain DOS wild cards. For example, to locate all files that have a LET extension, the following command could be entered:

```
TREE *.LET
```

This produces the same results as the XDIR filename /S command, discussed below.

The DIR Command

The TREE command is useful when you want to get an overall picture of how the directory structure of a disk is laid out, but it is a clumsy way to see the files that are stored in a particular directory. For this purpose, the DIR command may be used. When entered by itself, with no parameters or switches, DIR displays all of the files and subdirectories in the current directory. However, unlike the TREE command, it does not show the subdirectories of subdirectories; it only shows the contents of the current directory. The DIR command displays file and directory names in upper case. Using the same disk as in the earlier figures, the DIR command executed from the root directory will display the output shown in Figure 6.4.

In addition to displaying the file and directory names that exist in a directory, the DIR command provides several other pieces of useful information.

Every disk can be given a *label*—a name that identifies it. The FORMAT and LABEL commands are used to assign labels to disks; these commands are fully discussed in Chapter 7. In Figure 6.4, the label is DRDOS6.

When a file or subdirectory is created, the date and time are recorded along with the name. Each time a file is modified, the date and time are updated to reflect the time of modification. For each file, the date and time of last modification is shown. For each subdirectory, the date and time of creation is shown. Because of its general usefulness for displaying the location and vital statistics about a directory or file, DIR is probably the most frequently used of all DOS commands.

```
  Volume in drive C is DRDOS6
  Directory of  C:\
BACKUP      <DIR>     10-03-91   4:17p
DRDOS       <DIR>     10-03-91   4:17p
DV          <DIR>     10-03-91   4:17p
WP          <DIR>     10-03-91   4:17p
COMMAND   COM     50456  8-23-91   6:00a
AUTOEXEC BAT     566     9-03-91   9:27a
CONFIG    SYS     191     8-05-91  10:18a
    8 File(s) 165478400 bytes free
```

Figure 6.4 Sample Output of DIR Command

Within the directory listing generated by the DIR command, subdirectories are identified with the symbol <DIR>.

DIR accepts a single, optional parameter: a drive, directory, and/or file name specifier. This parameter may be used to specify a directory other than the current one, or to limit the files that are displayed to some subset of the entire directory. The following two commands demonstrate this. The first lists all files in the current directory that begin with the letter A, while the second lists all files on drive B: that have an extension of BAT:

```
DIR A*.*
DIR B:*.BAT
```

There is a shorthand technique for using the .* wild card specification with the DIR command: simply type the name part of the specifier, then press Enter. DIR then assumes .* for the extension specifier. Thus, if the current directory contains the files REPORTS, REPORTS.JAN, REPORTS.FEB, REPORTS.MAR, and REPORTS.APR, the following command would list all of them:

```
DIR REPORTS
```

The only time this does not work is when there is a subdirectory named REPORTS. In this case, the above command would display the contents of that directory, rather than those files that have a name of REPORTS.

In addition to the file name parameter, the DIR command accepts a number of switches (/A, /C, /D, /L, /2, /N, /P, /R, /S, /W).

These switches and their functions are shown in Table 6.5.

Table 6.5 Switches for the DIR Command

Switch	***Effect***
/A	Displays all files and subdirectories in the current directory, except those with the Hidden attribute set.
/C	Sets default switches for use with subsequent DIR commands.
/D	Displays those files for which the system attribute is off. This switch is on by default.
/L	Displays the file size, and the date and time of last modification. This switch is on by default.
/2	Produces the same display as /L, except it produces two columns side by side, instead of one.
/N	If you have changed the default DIR switch using /C or /R, /N returns you to the default switches for the current DIR command.
/P	Causes the display to pause after each screenful of information.
/R	Should be specified as the last switch in a series; executes the DIR command with the preceding switches, and remembers them for future DIR commands.
/S	Displays files that have the System attribute set.
/W	Displays just the names of files and directories in five columns across the screen. Sub-directories are indicated by a backslash (\) in front of the name.

The following explanations are in the order in which these switches are normally used.

The /P switch causes the display to pause after each screen, and wait for a key to be pressed. The message "Strike a key when ready . . ." will be shown at the bottom of the screen when there is more output to come. This has the same effect as the MORE filter, but is easier to type.

The /W switch causes the list of file names to appear in "wide" format: the names appear in five columns across the screen. Only the names are shown—the time, date, and file size are not shown. Directory names are preceded by a backslash (\). This switch is useful for seeing a large number of file names on one screen. A listing of the root directory of a hard disk, using the /W switch, is shown in Figure 6.5.

```
Volume in drive C is DRDOS6
Directory of  C:\
C:\DOS          :\QEMM          :\C600          :\NC            :\DV
C:\SPRINT       :\EXCEL         :\GV            :\QC25          :\RBFILES
C:\SQL          :\WINWORD       :\BUXTON        :\NORTON        :\UTILITY
C:\DESIGNER     :\MGXLIBS       :\WINDOWS       :\MOUSE1        :\STALK
C:\VWIN         :\BANYAN        :\WP            :\BACKUP        :\HJ2
C: DRPATH   BAT : AUTOEXEC  BAT :\EG4NEW        : AUGUST   FIN  :AUTOEXEC SYD
C: CONFIG   OLD : WINA20    386 : AUTOEXEC 386  : AUTOEXEC CV   : AUTOEXEC
DV
C: AUTOEXEC OLD : AUTOEXEC  QDK : AUTOEXEC QEM  : AUTOEXEC RDV  : AUTOEXEC
SQL
C: AUTOEXEC TEG : AUTOEXEC  WIN : BAN386   BAT  : BANDV    BAT  : BANPATH BAT
C: BANQEM   BAT : BANWIN    BAT : CONFIG   386  : CONFIG   BAT  : CONFIG  CV
C: CONFIG   DV  : CONFIG    EXP : CONFIG   EXT  : CONFIG   QDK  : CONFIG  QEM
C: CONFIG   RDV : CONFIG    SQL : CONFIG   TEG  : CONFIG   WIN  : DV      BAT
C: PIPES    BAT : SD        INI : SET386   BAT  : SETCV    BAT  : SETDV   BAT
C: SETQEM   BAT : SETSQL    BAT : SETWIN   BAT  : CONFIG   BAK  : MIRROR  FIL
C: MIRROR   BAK : AUTOEXEC  STD : CONFIG   STD  : SETPCL   BAT  : EDPATH  BAT
C: COMMAND  MS5 : CONFIG    SYS :\REPORTS       : MOUSE    SYS  :AUTOEXEC ORG
C:\PCLFONTS     : SFINSTAL  DIR :\PK            : CONFIG   !!!  :\ARC
C:\QPRO         :\DRDOS         : SETPATH  BAT  : COMMAND  MS   : COMMAND COM
C:\TEMP
       91 File(s) 166576128 bytes free
System files exist
```

Figure 6.5 Directory Listing Created with the /W Switch

The /L switch causes the DIR command to include the size, date, and time in the listing. If /L is used with /W, /W is ignored since there is not room to display the size, date, and time in wide format. /L is on by default, so you need only use it if the default setting has changed as a result of the /C or /R switches, discussed below.

The /2 switch produces the same result as /L, except it creates a 2-column display, allowing you to see twice as many files on the screen.

The /S switch is used to display only those files that have the System attribute set. Keep in mind, however, that many files that have the System attribute also have the Hidden attribute set, and the /S switch will not display files with the Hidden attribute set. The XDIR command, discussed below, must be used to display hidden files. File attributes are discussed in the section titled "How Files Are Stored" in the *Advanced Topics* section of this chapter.

The /A switch displays all files in the current or specified directory, including files with the System attribute set. The DIR command by itself will ignore files that have the System attribute set. /A does not, however, cause DIR to display files that have the Hidden attribute set. The XDIR command, discussed below, must be used to display hidden files. File attributes are discussed in the section titled "How Files Are Stored" in the *Advanced Topics* section of this chapter.

When the /C switch is used, the DIR command is not executed but any other switches specified are remembered and put into effect as the default DIR switches. For example, /2 /C would cause /2 to be in effect for subsequent DIR commands. Since the DIR command is not executed when /C is specified, a DIR /C command can be included in the AUTOEXEC.BAT file to set whatever default switches you like whenever the computer is booted. Entering DIR /C by itself will cancel the effect of the command and restore the standard default switches.

The /R switch is similar to the /C switch, except the DIR command is executed. In other words, if DIR /2 /R is entered, the directory listing will be displayed in two columns. Subsequent DIR commands will continue to be in two columns. /R should be the last switch on the command line. Entering /R by itself will cancel the effect of the command and restore the standard default switches.

The effects of /R and /C are mutually exclusive; that is, entering a DIR command with the /R switch will remove any switches set with /C, and vice versa.

The /N switch is used to restore the standard default switch settings for a single use of the DIR command. For example, if DIR /2 /C were entered, you could execute the DIR command in the normal single column mode by entering DIR /N. The next time DIR is entered, the /2 will be in effect again.

The /D switch is used to display those files that have the system attribute turned off. This is the default for the DIR command, so this switch is only used if it has been overridden by the /C or /R switches.

It has become conventional among software developers, as well as PC users, to include extensions in the names of all files, but to never use extensions in the names of directories. Consequently, you can usually see the names of all subdirectories in a directory with the following command:

```
DIR *.
```

This command tells DIR to display all those items in the current directory that have nothing after the period—those files with no extensions, which generally consists of just the subdirectories.

The DIR command can also be used to show the file and subdirectory contents of a directory other than the current one, using the conventions discussed in the section *Specifying Subdirectories* below.

The XDIR Command

The XDIR command is an enhanced version of the DIR command. It provides the ability to sort the directory listing in various ways, and to select files based on their attribute settings. XDIR may also be used to look for files in the current directory and all of its subdirectories. XDIR displays file and directory names in lower case, while DIR displays them in upper case.

When entered by itself, the XDIR command displays the names of all files and subdirectories in the current directory. The listing is sorted alphabetically, and includes the drive on which the file resides, the attribute settings, the size, and the date and time of last modification, for all files and directories. Using the same directory as that shown in Figure 6.4, the XDIR command produces the listing shown in Figure 6.6.

When XDIR sorts files, either alphabetically or using a criteria specified by one of the switches discussed below, it does so in memory. If there is a large number of files to sort, XDIR may not have enough memory available to sort all of them. In this case the following message will be displayed:

```
Too many files to sort (>xxxx)
```

```
DIRECTORY             10-03-91     4:17p   c:backup
DIRECTORY             10-03-91     4:17p   c:drdos
DIRECTORY             10-03-91     4:17p   c:dv
DIRECTORY             10-03-91     4:17p   c:wp
-a--          50456    8-23-91     6:00a   command.com
-a--            566    9-03-91     9:27a   autoexec.bat
-a--            191    8-05-91    10:18a   config.sys
total files 3 total bytes 51,213 disk free space 165,478,400
```

Figure 6.6 Sample Output of XDIR Command

where xxxx is the number of files that XDIR was able to sort. In this case XDIR will go ahead and display the directory listing, but it will not be sorted.

The attribute settings are listed in the left-hand column of the XDIR display; in Figure 6.6 all three of the files have only the Archive attribute set.

As with the DIR command, XDIR accepts a single, optional, parameter: a drive, directory, and/or file name specifier. This allows you to show an XDIR listing of a directory other than the current one, and to limit the files displayed to a subset of those in the directory. Wild cards may be used in this specification. You may want to refer to the previous section, on the DIR command, for a review of the use of file specifiers and wild cards.

In addition to the file name parameter, XDIR accepts a variety of switches. These are summarized in Table 6.6.

Table 6.6 Switches for the XDIR Command

Switch	***Effect***
+/-A	Selects/excludes files with the Archive attribute set.
+/-D	Selects/excludes files with the Directory attribute set.
+/-H	Selects/excludes files with the Hidden attribute set.
+/-R	Selects/excludes files with the Read-only attribute set.
+/-S	Selects/excludes files with the System attribute set.

Table 6.6 continued ...

Switch	***Effect***
/B	Displays a brief listing, showing only the drive and file names.
/C	Calculates a checksum for each file; used to verify that two files are identical.
/L	Produces the default display.
/N	Does not sort the directory alphabetically.
/P	Causes the display to pause after each screenful.
/R	Reverses the sort order, whether sorting is the default (alphabetical) or specified by a switch.
/S	Displays files in subdirectories as well as in the current directory.
/T	Sorts the directory listing by date and time.
/W	Displays just the names of files and directories in five columns across the screen. Subdirectories are indicated by a backslash (\) in front of the name.
/X	Sorts the listing by filename extension.
/Y	Sorts the directory according to its SuperStor file compression ratio. This switch only works on a drive set up as a SuperStor compressed drive.
/Z	Sorts the listing by file size.

The first four switches are used to select or exclude files that have only certain attributes set. The attribute letters are:

A for Archive
D for Directory
H for Hidden
R for Read-only
S for System

For example, the following command will display all files for which the Hidden attribute is set:

```
XDIR +H
```

If you wanted to see all files that have the Hidden attribute set, but do not have the Archive attribute set, you would use this command:

```
XDIR +H -A
```

File attributes are discussed in detail in the section titled "How Files Are Stored" in the *Advanced Topics* section of this chapter.

The /B switch is used to get a brief directory listing. A brief listing shows only drive identifiers, file names and directory names. There is no heading for the disk label or directory name. Neither are the file sizes, or dates and times of creation for files and directories displayed. Directories do not have any distinguishing symbols in this list, so there is no way to tell whether a name in the list applies to a file or a directory. The /B switch is useful when you want to save a set of file names in a file, for use with a program. For example, there are programs used to transfer files between different computers. Typically, these programs require just the file name to be specified; if there is extraneous information, they won't know how to handle it. To save a list of file names in a file, use the DOS output redirection symbol (>). The following command sends all of the file names in the current directory that have a BAT extension to a file named BATCH.FIL:

```
XDIR *.BAT > BATCH.FIL /B
```

The /C switch is used to display a *checksum* for each file. A checksum is a number calculated from the contents of a file. It is generally a unique number, so this switch can be used to check whether the contents of two files are the same—if they are, the checksum for the two files will be the same as well. The checksum value is displayed as a four-digit hexadecimal number. A sample of the XDIR output using the /C switch appears in Figure 6.7.

The checksum value appears between the time and the filename. The master checksum is calculated from all of the selected files.

The /L switch is used to display a "long" format, which is the default shown in Figure 6.6.

The /N switch produces a list which is not sorted alphabetically. The result is that files and directories appear in the order in which they are stored in the directory.

The /P switch causes the display to pause after each screenful.

The /R switch reverses the sorting order. For example, the command XDIR /R will list files and directories in reverse alphabetical order, and

XDIR /R /T will list files and directories in reverse time order—that is, the most recent files will be listed first, and the oldest files last.

```
—a—    566   9-03-91    9:27a   00FE   c:autoexec.bat
—a—     94   8-03-90   11:29a   265C   c:ban386.bat
—a—     35   7-01-91   11:24a   C1F6   c:bandv.bat
—a—    108   7-30-91    1:02p   0258   c:banpath.bat
—a—     76   7-25-91   12:07p   C1FB   c:banqem.bat
—a—     24   8-09-90   10:17a   BE3C   c:banwin.bat
—a—    134   1-22-91   11:41a   F068   c:config.bat
—a—     88   9-06-91   11:46a   7434   c:drpath.bat
—a—     59   3-25-91   11:49a   667F   c:dv.bat
—a—     77   8-03-91   12:52p   4F48   c:edpath.bat
—a—    108   5-14-91   10:13a   62BA   c:pipes.bat
—a—     59   1-02-91    4:11p   0FF9   c:set386.bat
—a—     57   1-02-91    4:14p   90B1   c:setcv.bat
—a—     59   1-02-91    4:15p   DC60   c:setdv.bat
—a—     89   9-05-91   10:21a   62C4   c:setpath.bat
—a—     41   8-01-91    2:32p   82F7   c:setpcl.bat
—a—     61   1-09-91    8:47a   E0CD   c:setqem.bat
—a—     60   5-30-91    9:52a   A056   c:setsql.bat
—a—     59   1-02-91    4:11p   A03B   c:setwin.bat
total files 19  total bytes 1,854  disk free space 166,354,944
master checksum 6D1F (hex)
```

Figure 6.7   Sample Output of XDIR /C Command

/S is used to tell XDIR to list the contents of subdirectories of the specified directory. When /S is used, the complete path for each file and directory appears at the beginning of the filename, rather than just the drive letter. A segment of a directory listing produced with the /S switch is shown in Figure 6.8.

The /T switch is used to sort the directory listing by date and time.

The /W switch is the same as that for the DIR command—it displays the directory listing in five columns across the screen, with only the filenames shown. Directories are identified by a backslash (\) that appears in front of the name.

The /X switch is used to sort the directory listing by filename extension.

```
-a--   41,904    8-09-91  12:59p  c:\wp\clip\clip1.gv
-a--    1,236   10-07-91   1:33p  c:\wp\clip\bill.not
-a--    4,552    8-13-91   3:39p  c:\wp\letters\mary1.let
-a--   13,616    9-05-91  11:15a  c:\wp\letters\roger1.let
-a--   23,510    9-05-91  11:04a  c:\wp\letters\roger2.let
-a--    5,156    9-05-91  11:07a  c:\wp\letters\mary2.let
-a--   19,752    9-05-91  11:45a  c:\wp\letters\mary3.let
-a--    1,616    9-05-91  11:46a  c:\wp\invoices\acme1.inv
-a--    1,130    9-05-91  11:59a  c:\wp\invoices\disco1.inv
-a--    6,287    9-16-91   9:47a  c:\wp\invoices\disco2.inv
-a--    4,565    9-23-91   3:14p  c:\wp\invoices\acme2.inv
-a--    9,457   10-02-91   4:01p  c:\wp\invoices\fast1.inv
-a--    9,321   10-02-91   4:07p  c:\wp\invoices\fast2.inv
```

Figure 6.8 Partial Directory Listing Using /S Switch on XDIR Command

The /Y switch is used to sort the directory listing by the *SuperStor* compression ratio of the files. *SuperStor* is a program that comes with DR DOS 6.0, and is used to effectively increase the capacity of a disk by compressing the way information is stored on the disk. The *SuperStor* compression ratio is a number that indicates the amount of space saved by compressing a file. SuperStor is discussed in detail in Chapter 7.

The /Z switch is used to sort files by size.

XDIR will accept multiple sorting switches, providing you with the ability to group and sub-group files. For example, the following command will sort all files by extension (/X), and within the groups of extensions, files will be sorted by date and time (/T):

```
XDIR /X/T
```

Note that when specifying two sort switches, the order in which the switches appear is important. If the above command were entered as XDIR /T/X, files would be sorted first by date and time, then, within matching dates and times, they would be sorted by extension.

Specifying Subdirectories

DOS keeps track of whatever directory you are currently working in (the *current directory*). When a file name is used as a parameter to a command, DOS looks only in the current directory to locate it. If the file cannot be found there, DOS displays an error message. However, since it is often necessary to refer to files that are not in the current directory, DOS provides several convenient symbols for specifying the directory in which a file is located along with the file name.

Since the root directory does not have a name, the backslash character is used to identify it. Thus, to see the directory listing for a file named ROBERT.LET that is stored in the root directory, the following command could be used:

```
DIR \ROBERT.LET
```

If the root directory were the current directory, the backslash would not be necessary, but if any other directory were current, then this command would still display the directory listing of the ROBERT.LET file in the root directory.

The backslash is also used to separate subdirectory names and file names when specifying the location of a subdirectory or file. For example, to display all of the files in the LETTERS subdirectory of the WP directory, on the C: drive, the following command is used:

```
DIR C:\WP\LETTERS
```

In addition to the backslash, there are two more special symbols used in specifying directories: the single period (.) and the double period (..). These two symbols are used by DOS to keep track of the directory tree. The single period refers to the current directory. Thus, the command

```
DIR .
```

is the same as the command

```
DIR
```

The double period refers to the *parent directory*—the directory for which the current directory is a subdirectory. All directories have a parent directory, except for the root directory. The double period makes it easy to specify directories that are nearby. For example, referring to the directory tree in Figure 6.2, if the current directory is C: \ WP \ LETTERS \ BUSINESS, then the following command will display a listing of all files in the C: \ WP \ LETTERS directory:

```
DIR ..
```

Again, if the current directory is C: \ WP \ LETTERS \ BUSINESS, then the following command displays a listing of all files with the extension LET, in the PR directory:

```
DIR ..\ PR\*.LET
```

These abbreviations are much shorter and easier to type than the full path name for the specified directories.

Printing and Saving Directory Listings

You may send a directory listing to the printer by using the output redirection symbol (>) with the PRN specifier, as follows:

```
DIR > PRN
```

You may also use the output redirection symbol to store a directory listing in a file. Simply replace the word PRN above with the name of a file. For example, to store a listing of all files in the C: \ WP \ LETTERS directory in a file named LIST.DIR, in the C: \ GV \ DATA directory, the following command would be used:

```
DIR C:\WP\LETTERS > C:\GV\DATA\LIST.DIR
```

Organizing Directories

The DOS directory system provides an excellent means of organizing and arranging your files. However, if there is no method as to how it is used, you could end up with more chaos than if you simply put all of your files into the root directory. How your directories should be organized is, therefore, worth some careful thought.

There are basically two approaches to organizing directories. One is to have one set of directories for programs, and another for data files. For example, suppose you have three programs you want to use on your computer: WordPerfect for word processing; Excel for spreadsheet work; and R:BASE for database management. You could create one subdirectory beneath the root for each of these programs, and another subdirectory beneath the root for the data files that are used with each program. The data file subdirectories could be further divided into more subdirectories, if you had a variety of categories for the data files for each program.

The second approach is to create a subdirectory for each program, then create subdirectories beneath it for the data files that go with the program. In this scheme, following the example above, you would have three subdirectories beneath the root—one each for: WordPerfect, Excel, and R:BASE. Beneath each of these would be one or more subdirectories for the data files that go with the program.

Either system works well. What is important is to decide on an approach, and stick to it. You should understand where in your system a particular file or directory should fit, before you create it. Creating directories without having an overall plan for your directory structure will lead to a cluttered disk and files that are difficult to locate.

DOS Commands for File and Directory Management

Nearly one-third of all DOS commands are used for file and directory management. This reflects the central role that files and directories play in using a personal computer, and the importance of having commands to facilitate managing them. This section arranges these commands into logical groups. Within groups, they are presented alphabetically, except where two related commands should logically follow each other. Each command is identified as being either an internal or external command. Internal commands are commands that DOS stores in memory at the time the computer is booted. Therefore, they do not have to be read from the disk before they can be used. External commands, on the other hand, are commands that DOS does not store in memory. Consequently, they must be read from the disk, just like any other program, before they can be used.

Commands for Comparing, Copying, and Deleting Files

The COMP command compares the contents of two files. The files are compared on a byte-by-byte basis. Since a byte is the smallest unit that can be stored in a file, COMP performs a precise comparison of the two files. The files can be in the same or different drives and directories. The syntax for the COMP command is:

```
COMP filespec1 filespec2 switches
```

The file specifiers may include drive and/or directory references, as well as file names. Wild cards are permitted, so groups of files may be compared. For example, the following command compares all batch files in the A: \ directory with batch files of the same names in the C: \ directory:

```
COMP A:\*.BAT C:\*.BAT
```

You do not have to provide a complete file specifier for either filespec1 or filespec2. If you enter the command COMP with no file specifier, then you are prompted for the first file specifier, then for the second file specifier. If you enter only a drive specifier, or only a directory specifier, for filespec1, then COMP assumes that the file specifier is *.*. If filespec2 contains only a drive or directory specifier, then COMP assumes the file name in that drive or directory will be the same as that in filespec1. Thus, the following command takes each file in the A: drive root directory, and looks for a file of the same name in the C: drive root directory. If a matching file name is found, the files are compared:

```
COMP A:\ C:\
```

If no matching file name is found in the second directory, COMP displays the message "Comparing filespec1 with filespec2 - File not found," where filespec1 and filespec2 are the file names for the files to compare. It then goes on to the next file in filespec1.

When COMP compares two files, it displays the message "Files compare OK" if they match. If they do not match, COMP displays a message indicating the exact location in each file at which the mismatch occurred. To demonstrate, the following two files were compared:

```
filespec1 (named TEST1.FIL):
This is line one.
Line two is here.
filespec2 (named TEST2.FIL):
This is line one.
Fine two is here.
```

The difference between these files is that the first character of the second line is the letter L in the first file, and the letter F in the second file. The COMP command displays these results:

```
Comparing    TEST1.FIL with    TEST2.FIL - Compare failure.
Offset 13h  Source = 4ch  Destination = 46h
1 Mismatches - Ending comparison.
```

The position of the error is shown in hexadecimal; the hex value 13 is the decimal number 19. Hence, there is a mismatch in the two files at position number 19. There is a carriage return symbol at the end of the first line, which is why the first character of line two is at position 19, rather than 18. COMP also says what the difference is—the first file contains the number 4C (hex), and the second file contains the number 46 (hex). These numbers, when translated through the ASCII table, correspond to the letters L and F.

There are two switches that COMP accepts, both of which are optional. The /A switch causes COMP to display the actual lines on which the mismatch occurs, and to point to the mismatched characters. When the above two files are compared with the /A switch, the following output appears:

```
Comparing    TEST1.FIL with    TEST2.FIL - Compare failure.
Offset 13h
Line two is here.
Fine two is here.
^
Missing End Of File character
1 Mismatches - Ending comparison.
```

The small caret symbol (^) beneath the F points out the mismatch. When /A is used, the message "Missing End Of File character" also appears. Text files generally have a Ctrl+Z (^Z) symbol to mark the end of the file. Even though it takes up two characters to display it, ^Z is stored as a single character. When COMP is used with the /A switch, and encounters a text file that does not end with a ^Z character, it reports this as well.

The comparison that COMP makes is case sensitive: it will detect a mismatch if one file contains, say, a lowercase *a* in theposition where the other file has an uppercase *A*.

The second switch that COMP accepts is the /M:x switch, where x is a number that specifies the maximum number of mismatches that COMP should permit before stopping the comparison. The default value of x is 10. 0 is used to specify no limit, in which case COMP continues comparing the files until it reaches the end, regardless of how many mismatches it encounters.

You may also want to review the FC command, discussed below, for comparing files.

COMP is an external command.

The COPY command copies a file from one location to another. The second location may be anywhere that a file could reside—another disk, another directory on the same disk, or even the same directory on the same disk, if the name of the source file and target file are different. The simplest form of the COPY command is:

```
COPY file1 file2
```

This command copies a file named file1, in the current directory, to a file named file2, also in the current directory. In this case, file2 cannot have the same name as file1, since you cannot have two files with the same name in the same directory. If you attempt to copy a file to the same name in the same directory, DOS will display the following message:

```
Source and Destination cannot be the same file
        0 File(s) copied
```

However, if you include a drive and/or directory specifier for either or both files, then the second file may have the same name as the first, as long as the drive and/or directory is different. In fact, you do not even have to specify a file name for the second file. If no file name is specified for file2, the COPY command assumes it should have the same name as file1. For example, assuming that the current drive and directory are C: \ WP \ LETTERS, the following four commands all perform exactly the same function:

```
COPY A:\ROBERT.LET C:\WP\LETTERS\ROBERT.LET
COPY A:\ROBERT.LET C:\WP\LETTERS
COPY A:\ROBERT.LET C:
COPY A:\ROBERT.LET
```

Each of these commands copies a file named ROBERT.LET from the root directory of the A: drive to a file named ROBERT.LET in the current directory, which is C: \ WP \ LETTERS. The first command provides a complete specification for both source and target files. The second provides a drive and directory specification for the target file, but leaves it up to the COPY command to use the same target file name as the source. The third command lets COPY retrieve the current directory on the C: drive from DOS. As long as only the drive letter is specified, with no directory symbols or names, then the current directory for that drive is assumed. The fourth command lets COPY assume the entire current drive and directory from DOS. If you want to use a different name for the target, then that name must be specified. However, you may still let COPY assume a current drive and/or directory.

DOS wild card symbols may be used to copy sets of files. For example, to copy all files with an extension of BAT from the root directory into a directory named \BATCH, enter the following command:

```
COPY \*.BAT \BATCH
```

When the COPY command is used to duplicate files, the new files have the same date and time stamps as the original files, since they have not been modified since that date and time. However, the COPY command may also be used to combine files, by using a plus sign between the names of the files to be combined. When a combination is performed, the target file is modified, and so the date and time stamp of the target are set to the current date and time. The following command combines two files, named TEST1.FIL and TEST2.FIL, into a third file, named TEST3.FIL:

```
COPY TEST1.FIL + TEST2.FIL TEST3.FIL
```

If no target file is specified when combining files, the first file named is assumed to be the target. For example, the following command combines TEST1.FIL and TEST2.FIL, and stores the result back in TEST1.FIL:

```
COPY TEST1.FIL + TEST2.FIL
```

You may also use wild cards to combine files. For example, the following command combines all batch files into a single file named BATCH.ALL:

```
COPY *.BAT BATCH.ALL
```

Wild cards may be used to selectively combine one set of files with another set, resulting in a third set. For example, the following command combines all files with the extension LET, with all the corresponding files of the same name but with the extension ENV, producing files with the same name but the extension FIN:

```
COPY *.LET + *.ENV *.FIN
```

Thus, the file ROBERT.LET is combined with the file ROBERT.ENV, producing the file ROBERT.FIN. Likewise, SUSAN.LET and SUSAN.ENV are combined to produce SUSAN.FIN, and so on. On the other hand, if you wanted to combine all of the LET and ENV files into one big file named ALL.FIN, the following command could be used:

```
COPY *.LET + *.ENV ALL.FIN
```

Caution: When combining files, if the name of the target file is the same as the name of one of the source files other than the first, then the file identified as the target is overwritten before its original contents are read. In this case, the contents of that file are not copied into the target, and DOS displays the following message when the copy operation is complete:

```
Destination file contents lost before copy
```

As an example, consider the following command:

```
COPY TEST1.FIL + TEST2.FIL + TEST3.FIL TEST2.FIL
```

This command attempts to link TEST2.FIL with TEST1.FIL and TEST3.FIL, and store the result in TEST2.FIL. Here is what the output of the command looks like:

```
TEST1.FIL
TEST2.FIL
Destination file contents lost before copy
TEST3.FIL
       1 File(s) copied
```

The result of this command is that TEST2.FIL contains the combined contents of TEST1.FIL and TEST3.FIL, but the original contents of TEST2.FIL are lost.

The COPY command accepts six optional switches: /A, /B, /V, /S, /C, and /Z. The /V is used to verify a copy—it performs a test during a copy operation to make sure that the new file is written correctly. Copying with the /V switch takes considerably longer than copying without it, because DOS must double check everything that is written into the target file. In general, the /V switch is not needed because the

COPY command is quite accurate. However, when copying critical data under circumstances where a bad copy would create severe problems, it is worth using /V to make sure the copy is completed successfully.

DOS distinguishes between two types of files: ASCII text files, and binary files. An ASCII text file contains only ASCII codes, while a binary file contains information that is not interpreted according to the ASCII table. Some word processing files are ASCII text files, while program files and most spreadsheet and database files are binary files. For the purposes of the COPY command, the significant difference is in how the two types of files indicate where the file ends. ASCII text files indicate the end of file with a control-Z character, which is known as the *end of file marker.* The control-Z character is displayed as a caret followed by the letter Z like this: ^Z. Even though it is displayed as two characters, control-Z is actually stored as a single character (ASCII code 26 hex).

To determine the end of a binary file, on the other hand, the COPY command uses the file size as specified in the directory. For example, if a file's directory listing shows it as containing 1,537 bytes, then COPY will copy exactly 1,537 bytes, starting from the beginning of the file.

The /A switch tells COPY to interpret the file as an ASCII text file, and therefore to determine the end of the file by looking for a control-Z. It is possible for a file to contain more than one control-Z, but with the /A switch, COPY only copies the file up to, but not including, the first control-Z. However, when the entire COPY is finished, if /A was specified then COPY places a final control-Z at the end of the target file.

The /B switch, on the other hand, tells COPY to interpret the file as a binary file, and to determine the length of the file from its directory entry. Everything in the file is copied, including any control-Z characters. No control-Z is automatically added to the end of the target file when /B is specified.

When files are not being combined, but simply copied, then /B is the default because this technique for determining the end of the file works for either file type. If the source file has a control-Z at the end of it, the control-Z is copied. If it does not, then none is added. However, when combining files, the /A switch is the default because with this switch, ASCII files are correctly combined, with only a single control-Z ending up in the target directory. Since it is rare to combine binary files, but relatively common to combine ASCII text files, it makes sense to use /A as the default for combining files. However, if you are combining binary files, you must be sure to specify the /B switch. Otherwise, a control-Z will be added to the end of the target file, probably making it unusable.

The /A and /B switches may be combined in a single command to treat different files in different ways. When either switch precedes all of the file names, then it applies to all file names up to but not including the one that precedes the appearance of the other switch. The other switch then applies to all file names up to but not including the one that precedes the reappearance of the first switch, and so on. For example, in the following command, the initial /A applies to FILE1 and FILE2. The /B applies to FILE3 and FILE4, and the second /A applies to FILE5, FILE6, and FILE7:

```
COPY /A FILE1 + FILE2 + FILE3 /B + FILE4 + FILE5 /A + FILE6 FILE7
```

The COPY command can also be used to trick DOS into changing the date and time stamp of a file to the current date and time. The command to accomplish this is:

```
COPY /B TEST.FIL+,,
```

This command looks strange, but it has meaning. The /B tells the COPY command not to append a control-Z to the end of the file. This is important because the file should be left unchanged, and /A (the default for combining files) will add the control-Z at the end of the file. The file name is TEST.FIL, and the + sign following it says "this is a combining operation." However, the first comma says "omit the second source file," and the second comma says "omit the target file." The result is that the file is left unchanged, but since this is a file combination operation, the date and time stamp are updated. The TOUCH command achieves the same result.

The COPY command can also be used to copy to or from a device, such as the printer or the keyboard. As far as DOS is concerned, devices are no different from files—they are either sources or targets for transferring information. The term CON is a reserved word that DOS uses to refer to the *console* (the keyboard and the screen). When the word CON appears in a place where a source file would be specified, then input is taken from the keyboard. When the word CON appears in a place where a target file would be expected, then output goes to the screen. Consequently, the COPY command can be used to create a file using the following command:

```
COPY CON TEST.FIL
```

This command will take the keyboard as the source file, and create a file named TEST.FIL that contains whatever is typed at the keyboard. This will be an ASCII file, since only ASCII characters can be generated by the keyboard. Recall that ASCII files are terminated with a control-Z character. To tell DOS when to stop copying from the keyboard, a control-Z character is entered by holding down Ctrl and pressing Z. A shortcut is to press F6, which generates a control-Z. Enter must be pressed after the control-Z. In the same manner, the contents of a file may be displayed on the screen with the following command:

```
COPY TEST.FIL CON
```

This will display the contents of the file TEST.FIL on the screen. To see how these two commands work, enter the following:

```
COPY CON TEST.FIL [Enter]
Hello. This is a test file [Enter]
being created with the COPY command. [Enter]
This is the last line of the file. [Enter]
^Z [Enter]
COPY TEST.FIL CON [Enter]
```

The first five lines create the file TEST.FIL, and the last line displays it back on the screen.

The word PRN is another reserved word. DOS uses it to refer to a printer port. If you have a printer connected to your computer, then you can use the COPY command to print out an ASCII text file, as follows:

```
COPY TEST.FIL PRN
```

There are two types of copying operation that COPY does not perform: it cannot copy files that have a file size of 0 bytes, and it cannot copy files from more than one directory at once. Both of these operations can be accomplished with the XCOPY command, discussed below.

COPY is an internal command.

The DEL command deletes files from a disk. There are actually two identical commands supplied for this purpose: DEL (for DELete) and ERASE (which can be abbreviated to ERA). These commands behave identically. The DEL command accepts wild cards as well as individual file names, and a drive and/or directory may be specified. To delete one or more files, enter the following command:

```
DEL filespec
```

For example, to delete all files with a BAK extension in the root directory of the C: drive, enter the following command:

```
DEL C:\*.BAK
```

DEL accepts two optional switches: /C and /S. The /C switch tells DEL to prompt you for confirmation before each file it deletes. For example, if there were files named AUTOEXEC.BAK, CONFIG.BAK, and WP.BAK in the current directory, then entering the above command with the /C switch would cause DEL to display the following message:

```
AUTOEXEC.BAK (Y/N) ?
```

Pressing Y deletes the file, while pressing N leaves the file intact. You do not need to press Enter after pressing the Y or N—the keystroke is accepted as soon as you press it. The message then will be repeated for each of the other files. If you press any key other than Y or N, it will be taken as an N and the file will not be deleted.

The DEL command does not delete files that have the Hidden, System, or Read-only attribute set. However, if you specify the /S switch, then DEL will work on system files.

Be careful when you use the DEL command, particularly when using wild cards, since this can delete a large number of files at once. If you accidentally erase one or more files, they may be recoverable using the UNDELETE command, discussed later in this chapter in the section titled *File Protection and Recovery Commands*. However, this is time-consuming and only works under certain circumstances. When using wild cards, it is particularly important to specify the /C switch to make sure you do not delete a file you want to keep. An alternative is to first use the DIR command with the same wild card specification, to review all of the file names at once.

There are two ways to delete all the files in a directory: using the *many wild card* (*) for both the name and the extension specifier, and using just the directory name, with no file specifier. Thus, both of the following commands accomplish the same thing—deleting all files in the C: \ WP \ LETTERS directory:

```
DEL C:\WP\LETTERS\*.*
DEL C:\WP\LETTERS
```

Deleting all the files in a directory is a fairly drastic move, so DEL has built-in protection to prevent mistakes. When a request is made to delete all the files in a directory, DEL displays the following message:

```
Are you sure (Y/N) ?
```

In this case, you must type either a Y or an N, and then Enter. Enter is required in case the wrong key is accidentally pressed.

The DEL command is normally sufficient for removing files from a disk—it frees up the space occupied by the file, for use by another file. However, such a file can be undeleted because the information stored in the file is not actually removed from the disk until another file overwrites the same area of the disk. If you want to make sure that the information is completely removed from the disk, the XDEL command, discussed below, can be used. XDEL can also be used to delete files from multiple directories.

DEL is an internal command.

There is a variation on the DEL and ERASE commands: DELQ and ERAQ. Like DEL and ERASE, these two commands are identical. These commands are functionally equivalent to the DEL /C command: they pause after each file and ask for confirmation.

The DISKCOPY command creates an exact duplicate of a disk. When DISKCOPY is used, the source disk is duplicated byte for byte on the target disk. Since every byte on the target disk is copied from the source disk, any information that may be stored on the target is destroyed by the DISKCOPY command. To understand how DISKCOPY is different from using the COPY or XCOPY command to copy all of the files on a disk, it is necessary to understand a little about how files are stored on disk.

When files are created on a disk, space is not allocated to them on a byte-by-byte basis. Instead, space is allocated in units called *clusters*. The size of a cluster varies with different types of disks; a cluster of 2048 bytes is common for hard disks, and clusters of 512 and 1024 bytes are common for floppy disks. So when a file is created on a typical hard disk, DOS will reserve a minimum of 2048 bytes for it. If the file size is 2049 bytes, then two clusters (4096 bytes) will be reserved for it, and so on.

As files are created and deleted, the available clusters on the disk become noncontiguous, or fragmented. Imagine creating four files on a new disk: file1, which occupies one cluster; file2, which occupies three clusters; file3, which occupies two clusters; and file4, which occupies one cluster. Thus, the arrangement on the disk will be:

```
< file1 >    < file2 >    < file3 >    < file4 >
1 cluster   3 clusters   2 clusters   1 cluster
```

Beyond file4 is a large amount of empty disk space. Now suppose file3 is deleted. That leaves a two-cluster hole in the file sequence. The free disk space is now fragmented into two pieces: the two-cluster hole between file2 and file4, and the large space beyond file4. If file5 is now created, and requires four clusters, where will it be placed? It won't fit into the two-cluster hole, but if files could only be put into contiguous clusters, eventually the disk would become so fragmented that much of it would be unusable. So DOS puts the first two clusters of file5 into the hole where file3 used to exist, and the rest of it into the space following file4. This allows all disk space to be used, regardless of the degree of fragmentation. Fragmentation is discussed in detail in Chapter 7.

Now that you understand how files are stored on the disk, you can understand the main difference between DISKCOPY and COPY. When a file is copied from one disk to another with the COPY command, the copy of the file is placed into whatever clusters are free on the target disk. Thus, the two copies of the file may be in totally different areas of the two disks. When DISKCOPY is used, the second disk is an exact byte-for-byte duplicate of the first—every file occupies exactly the same clusters on both disks.

Since DISKCOPY must make an exact duplicate of a disk, it makes sense that only disks that are the same size and format can be used with DISKCOPY. Furthermore, DISKCOPY only works with floppy disks. Even if your computer has two hard disks of the same size, DISKCOPY cannot be used to duplicate one on the other. The XCOPY command was designed for this purpose. You rarely need to make an exact duplicate of a hard drive, but it is sometimes necessary to duplicate floppies. DISKCOPY provides a convenient mechanism for accomplishing this. Since DISKCOPY copies every byte on a disk, hidden files and system files are also copied, and their attributes are left unchanged. Consequently, if the source disk is a startup disk, the target disk will be as well.

> ***Note:*** Some original program disks contain data stored before or after the normal recording tracks to prevent duplication (on track -1, or track 41, on a 40-track floppy, for example). DISKCOPY will not copy this extra data.

If the target disk has not been formatted, or has a different format than the source disk, then DISKCOPY will automatically format the target disk as it goes, and will display the message "Formatting while copying," to let you know what it is doing. This will take longer than copying to a formatted disk. If you want to copy files between disks that have different formats, the COPY or XCOPY command should be used.

If the source and/or target drive is not specified, DISKCOPY will use the current drive for the missing drive specifier(s). Thus, DISKCOPY can be used with computers that have a single drive. When the same drive is used as the source and target, DISKCOPY alternately prompts you to place the source or target disk in the drive.

There are three optional switches that may be used with the DISKCOPY command: /1, /A, and /M. Floppy disks can be either single-sided or double-sided, though single-sided disks are rarely seen anymore. Normally, DISKCOPY determines the number of sides based on the type of disk drive that DOS senses. However, you can force DISKCOPY to copy only the first side of a disk with the /1 parameter (it's the numeral one, not the letter L).

The /A switch tells DISKCOPY to sound a beep on the computer's speaker when the copy operation is complete, or when you need to change disks on a single-floppy computer.

DISKCOPY can also accept a file name as the target. This will create a type of file referred to as an *image file*, because it contains an exact image of the source disk's contents. The following command will make an image file named IMAGE.DSK in the C:\IMAGE directory; the image file will contain a copy of the disk in drive A:

```
DISKCOPY A: C:\IMAGE\IMAGE.DSK
```

This image file can now be used as the source for creating a copy of the original A: drive disk. If you are making multiple copies of a disk, this will be faster than having to read the disk from a floppy drive many times.

The /M switch is used to make multiple copies of a disk. /M is commonly used with an image file. When /M is specified, each time a copy is complete you are asked if you want to make another copy. If you respond with a Y (for Yes), you are prompted to put in another target disk. This will repeat until you respond with an N (for No).

There is frequently not enough available conventional memory to store the entire contents of a floppy disk. To avoid having to perform multiple reads, DISKCOPY will use expanded memory, extended memory, and a temporary swap file on the hard disk (in that order), to store the entire contents of a floppy disk. This considerably speeds up the copying process, particularly if expanded or extended memory is available. In order for DISKCOPY to use expanded or extended memory, an appropriate device driver must be loaded, such as EMM386.SYS. Memory types and their device drivers are discussed in detail in Chapter 5.

DISKCOPY is an external command.

The FC command compares two files and displays the differences between them. The difference between the COMP and FC commands is that COMP is designed primarily for determining that two files are identical, while FC is designed primarily for helping you see the differences between two files. COMP is typically used after copying a file, to see if the copy was successful. FC, on the other hand, is typically used to compare two files that are known to be different, in order to decide which one to keep.

Unless you specify otherwise with the optional switches, FC determines the type of file (ASCII or binary) from the filename extension, and performs the appropriate type of comparison. Files are assumed to binary if they have one of the following extensions: BIN, CMD, COM, EXE, LIB, OBJ, and SYS. All other files are assumed to be ASCII.

The syntax of the FC command is:

```
FC file1 file2
```

When FC encounters a mismatch in an ASCII file, it displays the complete lines that do not match in each file, and tells you to replace the lines in file1 with the lines in file2. In order to demonstrate the FC command, the following two files will be used:

```
TEST1.FIL
This is line one of the test file.
This is line two of test file1.
a
b
c
d
e
f
g
h
This is line three.
This is line four.
This is line five of test file1.
This is line six of the test file.
This is line seven of the test file.
This is line eight.
```

```
TEST2.FIL
This is line one of the test file.
This is line two of test file2.
a
b
c
d
e
f
g
i
This is line three.
This is line four.
This is line five of test file2.
This is line six of the test file.
This is line seven of the test file.
This is line eight.
```

The command FC TEST1.FIL TEST2.FIL produces the following output:

```
Replace line 2 in c:\sprint\drd\TEST1.FIL
< This is line two of test file1.
with line 2 from c:\sprint\drd\TEST2.FIL
> This is line two of test file2.
Replace lines 10-13 in
c:\sprint\drd\TEST1.FIL
< h
< This is line three.
< This is line four.
< This is line five of test file1.
with lines 10-13 from c:\sprint\drd\TEST2.FIL
> i
> This is line three.
> This is line four.
> This is line five of test file2.
```

When FC encounters a line that does not match, it tells you to replace that line in the first file with the corresponding line in the second file. In the example above, a mismatch occurs in line two, so FC advises you to replace line two in the first file with line two in the second file.

When comparing ASCII files, FC is careful to keep the two files synchronized. This means that if one file has an extra line it, FC will figure that out, and continue to compare the appropriate lines. When FC encounters a mismatch, it waits until it finds five lines in a row that match before it considers the files resynchronized. Thus, when there are two mismatched lines near each other, FC advises you to replace both of them, as well as all lines in between. In the example, lines 10 and 13 have mismatches, so FC considers lines 10 through 13 all to be mismatched and advises you to replace all of them.

Note that FC always tells you what changes are required to make the first file match the second file, not vice versa.

When FC compares binary files, it compares the files byte for byte, rather than line for line, and displays the differences in hexadeximal format. The command FC TEST1.FIL TEST2.FIL /B instructs FC to compare the files in binary mode; it produces the following output:

```
Offset  Hex ASCII   Hex ASCII
000042  31    1     32    2
00005C  68    h     69    i
0000A8  31    1     32    2
```

For each mismatch, the *offset* is given first. The offset is the number of bytes in from the start of the file at which the mismatch occurred. Following the offset, the hexadeximal and ASCII codes for the mismatched byte in each file is given. Note that FC does not attempt to resynchronize binary files after a mismatch.

The number of lines that must match for FC to consider the files resynchronized may be adjusted with the /G switch. To set the number of lines to 3 when comparing TEST1.FIL and TEST2.FIL, the following command would be used:

```
FC TEST1.FIL TEST2.FIL /G3
```

The default number of lines required for resynchronization is five.

The /A switch is used to abbreviate the output when comparing in ASCII mode. This switch is convenient if there is going to be a large number of lines displayed by FC. With /A, only the first and last lines of a group are displayed, with an ellipsis in between. For example, the command FC TEST1.FIL TEST2.FIL /A results in the following output:

```
Replace line 2 in c:\sprint\drd\TEST1.FIL
< This is line two of test file1.
with line 2 from c:\sprint\drd\TEST2.FIL
> This is line two of test file2.
Replace lines 10-13 in
c:\sprint\drd\TEST1.FIL
< h
< (...)
< This is line five of test file1.
with lines 10-13 from c:\sprint\drd\TEST2.FIL
> i
> (...)
> This is line five of test file2.
```

The /B switch is used to compare binary, rather than ASCII, files. The difference between these two file types was previously discussed in the COPY command section. When the files being compared have a BIN,

CMD, COM, EXE, LIB, OBJ, or SYS extension, this setting is assumed unless the /L switch is used. For all other file extensions, the /B switch is off by default. When /B is in effect, FC does not attempt to resynchronize the files after finding a mismatch, and mismatches are reported in the following format:

```
File1   File2
Offset  Hex ASCII   Hex ASCII
```

Offset is a hexadecimal number representing the byte position within the file of the mismatch, File1 Hex ASCII is the hexadecimal and ASCII representations of the mismatched byte in file1, and File2 Hex ASCII is the hexadecimal and ASCII representations of the mismatched byte in file2.

The maximum number of mismatches that may occur in a binary comparison is 20 by default. If this number of mismatches occurs, FC terminates with the message "Comparison stopped after 20 mismatches." This number can be changed with the /M switch. To specify 10 mismatches as the maximum, the following command would be used:

```
FC FILE1.EXE FILE2.EXE /M10
```

To tell FC to continue with the comparison no matter how many mismatches appear, the /M0 setting should be used.

Normally, FC comparisons are case sensitive, so that *a* and *A* are seen as different. Case sensitivity is turned off with the /C switch. Thus, without /C the following lines would be considered mismatched, and with /C they would be considered identical:

```
LINE ONE
line one
```

The /L switch forces the comparison into ASCII mode. For files that have any extension other than BIN, CMD, COM, EXE, LIB, OBJ, and SYS, ASCII mode is the default and /L has no effect. For files that have one of these extensions, binary mode is the default and the /L switch is needed for an ASCII comparison.

When FC encounters *white space* (blank spaces and tab stops) in a file, it compares them just as it would any other characters. This can be turned off with the /W switch. When /W is specified, white space is ignored. Consequently, the following lines would match when /W was specified:

```
This is line one.
Thisisline   one.
```

Wild cards may be used with the FC command to compare multiple files against a single file, or to compare multiple files against similarly named files. If a wild card is used in the first file name, all of the specified files are compared to the second file. If a wild card is used in the second file name, all of the files specified in the first file name are compared with all of the files specified in the second file name. The following commands demonstrate the wild card substitution:

```
FC *.BAT BATCHFIL.BAK
```

The above command compares all files with a BAT extension to the file named BATCHFIL.BAK.

```
FC AUTOEXEC.BAT *.BAK
```

The above command compares the AUTOEXEC.BAT file with all of the files with a BAK extension.

```
FC *.BAT *.BAK
```

The above command compares all files with an extension of BAT, with all files that have a matching name and an extension of BAK.

The use of wild cards makes it very easy to compare all the files on two disks. The following command compares all files on drive A: with all files on drive B:

```
FC A:*.* B:*.*
```

Besides wild cards, the FC command can make use of a filelist to comparc filcs in thc list with files of the same name in a different directory. For example, the following command compares the files identified in the file NAMES.LST with files of matching names in the C:\WP\DATA directory:

```
FC @NAMES.LST C:\WP\DATA
```

If NAMES.LST contains the file names MARY.LET, BILL.LET, and JOHN.LET, then this FC command will compare MARY.LET in the current directory with MARY.LET in the C:\WP\DATA directory, and so on. Filelists are discussed in detail above, in the section *Using Wildcards and Filelists*.

If no differences are found between two files, FC displays the following message:

```
ASCII differences between c:\MARY.LET and c:\MARY.BAK
Files match.
```

The first line, "ASCII differences between file1 and file2" does not mean that differences were found; it merely means that the statements that follow this line will describe any differences that were found.

The use of the MORE filter and the output redirection symbol (>) can make the FC command much easier to use. The MORE filter pauses the screen and waits for a key to be pressed whenever the screen is full, and the output redirection symbol redirects the information that would appear on the screen, to a file or printer. The following three commands demonstrate this: the first uses the MORE filter to pause the display, the second sends the output to a file named FC.OUT, and the third sends the output to the printer:

```
FC TEST1.FIL TEST2.FIL | MORE
FC TEST1.FIL TEST2.FIL > FC.OUT
FC TEST1.FIL TEST2.FIL > PRN
```

FC is an external command.

MOVE is a command that is used to move files from one disk and/or directory to another. When files are moved from one directory to another on the same disk, all that MOVE has to do is copy the directory entry to the target directory and delete it from the source directory. The file itself stays in the same place on the disk. This is much faster than actually copying and deleting the file. If you are moving a file that is marked *Read-only*, it is actually copied and the source file left unchanged. Also, if you are moving an entire subdirectory, the empty directory is not deleted after the files in it are moved, unless the /T switch is specified. /T is discussed below. When moving files from one disk to another, MOVE must actually copy the file to the target and delete the file from the source. In this case, the command is essentially the same as performing a COPY and DEL, and takes about as much time.

The syntax of the MOVE command is:

```
MOVE source target switches
```

Source refers to the files being moved, *target* refers to the destination they will be moved to, and *switches* can be any of the optional switches discussed below and summarized in Table 6.7. The source specifier may include wild cards or a filelist; the target specifier must be a specific path with an optional drive identifier. Wild cards cannot be used in the target.

To move all of the files with the extension BAK from the \WP\LETTERS directory to the \WP\BACKUP directory, the following command would be used:

```
MOVE \WP\LETTERS\*.BAK \WP\BACKUP
```

If the drive for either source or target is different from the current drive, then the drive must be specified as well.

The /A switch is used to tell MOVE to move only those files that have their Archive attribute set. If theArchive attribute is set, it means the file has changed since the last BACKUP was performed on it. When the BACKUP command is used, it turns off the Archive attribute; as soon as the file is modified in any way, DOS turns the Archive attribute back on. Consequently, by using the /A switch with MOVE, you can move only those files that have changed since the last backup.

If you want MOVE to turn off the Archive attribute, the /M switch should be used instead of the /A switch. For example, the following two commands move all files in the current directory that have their Archive attribute on. However, the first command leaves the Archive attribute on, while the second turns it off:

```
MOVE *.* \WP\LETTERS /A
MOVE *.* \WP\LETTERS /M
```

The /D:date switch is used to move only those files that were changed on or after the specified date. The following command moves only those files in the current directory that have an extension of LET, and that were modified on or after 8/1/91:

```
MOVE *.LET *.BAK /D:8/1/91
```

The /S switch moves files in subdirectories as well as files duplicating the source subdirectory structure on the target. However, the source subdirectory structure is not deleted after the files are moved. If a subdirectory on the source does not exist on the target, the /S switch will cause it to be created on the target, even if the source subdirectory is empty. The target may be another disk or another directory on the source disk. For example, consider the partial directory structure shown in Figure 6.9.

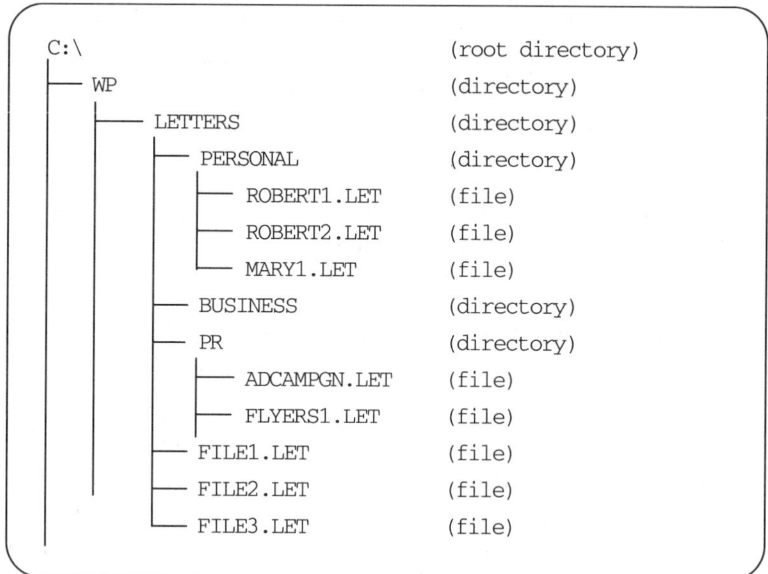

```
C:\                                  (root directory)
├── WP                               (directory)
│   ├── LETTERS                      (directory)
│   │   ├── PERSONAL                 (directory)
│   │   │   ├── ROBERT1.LET          (file)
│   │   │   ├── ROBERT2.LET          (file)
│   │   │   └── MARY1.LET            (file)
│   │   ├── BUSINESS                 (directory)
│   │   ├── PR                       (directory)
│   │   │   ├── ADCAMPGN.LET         (file)
│   │   │   └── FLYERS1.LET          (file)
│   │   ├── FILE1.LET                (file)
│   │   ├── FILE2.LET                (file)
│   │   └── FILE3.LET                (file)
```

Figure 6.9 Partial File and Directory Structure

The C: \ WP \ LETTERS directory contains three files: FILE1.LET, FILE2.LET, and FILE3.LET; and three subdirectories: PERSONAL, BUSINESS, and PR. The PERSONAL subdirectory contains three files of its own: ROBERT1.LET, ROBERT2.LET, and MARY1.LET, while the BUSINESS subdirectory is empty, and the PR subdirectory contains two files: ADCAMPGN.LET and FLYERS1.LET.

MOVE can be used with the /S switch to move the files and copy the subdirectory of the C: \ WP \ LETTERS directory to the A: drive with the following command:

```
MOVE C:\WP\LETTERS A:\ /S
```

The backslash on the target tells MOVE to move files from C: \ WP \ LETTERS into the root directory on the A: drive, and create subdirectories of C: \ WP \ LETTERS in the A: root directory. If the target disk was empty when this command was entered, it would end up with the structure shown in Figure 6.10.

Note that the /S switch for the MOVE command behaves differently with respect to empty subdirectories than the /S switch for the XCOPY command, discussed below. /S for XCOPY does not recreate empty subdirectories, while /S for MOVE does.

If you want to delete the source directory structure after the files have been moved, the /T switch should be used. If the above command were entered as MOVE C:\WP\LETTERS A:\ /T, then after moving all of the files to the A: drive the C:\WP\LETTERS directory, and all directories beneath it, would be removed.

```
A:\                         (root directory)
   LETTERS                  (directory)
       PERSONAL             (directory)
           ROBERT1.LET      (file)
           ROBERT2.LET      (file)
           MARY1.LET        (file)
       BUSINESS             (directory)
   PR                       (directory)
       ADCAMPGN.LET         (file)
       FLYERS1.LET          (file)
   FILE1.LET                (file)
   FILE2.LET                (file)
   FILE3.LET                (file)
```

Figure 6.10 File Structure for the Target Drive

When /S is used, MOVE displays the name of each file as it is moved; when /T is used, MOVE does not display the file names.

MOVE does not normally move files that have the Hidden or System attribute set. However, the /H switch can be used to tell MOVE that it should move hidden and system files.

The /P and /C switches are identical—they tell MOVE to prompt you before moving each file. This is useful when you want to move a lot of files, but they do not have enough common features in their names to use wild cards to specify them as a group. For example, you may have 20 files with a BAT extension, but only want to move 12 of them. Rather than typing in 12 file names, the following command could by used:

```
MOVE \WP\LETTERS\*.LET \WP\ARCHIVE /P
```

When this command is entered, MOVE will display each file name that has an extension of LET, followed by a (Y/N)? prompt. Pressing Y causes MOVE to move the file, while pressing N causes the file to be skipped.

Instead of prompting you for each file, it is sometimes helpful to have MOVE prompt you once before beginning the entire MOVE operation. This can be accomplished with the /W switch, which causes MOVE to display the following prompt, then wait for you to press a key:

```
Strike a key to start moving
```

This is useful if you need to put a disk in a floppy drive before letting the MOVE operation continue. The /W switch is commonly used in batch files that include the MOVE command for a floppy drive. It can also be used to load MOVE from a floppy disk that is in the same drive you want to use for the source and/or target disk. When the above message appears, you may abort the MOVE operation by the Control + C or Control + Break keys.

If a file already exists that has the same name as the target file, it is overwritten, just as it is with the COPY command. However, if the Read-only attribute is set, then the file is not copied. If MOVE encounters a file that has the same name as the target and the Read-only attribute set, it displays the following message:

```
FILESPEC ...access denied
```

To override this, and cause MOVE to overwrite files in the target directory that have the Read-only attribute set, the /R switch is used. The following command moves all files in the \WP\LETTERS directory to the \WP\ARCHIVE directory, and tells MOVE to overwrite any matching target filenames, even if the Read-only attribute is set:

```
MOVE \WP\LETTERS \WP\ARCHIVE /R
```

As with the COPY command, it is rare that MOVE does not accurately duplicate a file. However, with very important information, or under circumstances in which a bad move would create serious problems, you may want to use the /V switch to cause MOVE to verify each file moved. This will slow down the performance of MOVE, but decreases the likelihood of a bad move.

Table 6.7 Switches for Use with the MOVE Command

Switch	***Effect***
/A	Only moves files that have the Archive attribute set, and leaves the Archive attribute set after moving the file.
/D:date	Only moves files whose date is on or after the one specified. The format of the date is determined by the current country code.

Table 6.7 continued ...

Switch	***Effect***
/H	Includes hidden and system files in the move operation.
/M	Turns off the Archive attribute after moving the file.
/P or /C	Pauses for confirmation before moving each file.
/R	Causes MOVE to overwrite files with the same name as the source, even if they have the Read-only attribute set.
/S	Duplicates source subdirectories on the target, but does not delete the source subdirectories after moving their files.
/T	Duplicates source subdirectories on the target, and deletes the source subdirectories after moving their files.
/V	Performs a verification of the moved file. This slows down the process but increases reliability.
/W	Pauses after the MOVE command is entered and waits for a disk to be inserted. You may interrupt the command at this point by pressing Ctrl+C or Ctrl+Break.

MOVE is an external command.

The XCOPY command, which is similar to the COPY command, adds the ability to copy subdirectories and the files they contain. The syntax of the XCOPY command is:

```
XCOPY source target switches
```

If no switches are specified, XCOPY copies only the files in the directory specified by source. If the source contains only a file name specifier, with no directory, XCOPY uses the current directory as the source.

When XCOPY is used without switches it functions similarly to the COPY command, in that it copies files from the source directory only, not its subdirectories. However, because of its sensitivity to directory structures, XCOPY is more careful than COPY about determining whether the target specifier is a file name or a directory name. For example, consider the following COPY command:

```
COPY TEST1.FIL TEMP
```

If the current directory does not contain a subdirectory named TEMP, this command copies the file TEST1.FIL to a file named TEMP in the current directory. If there is a subdirectory named TEMP, TEST1.FIL file is copied to that directory, and the name TEST1.FIL is preserved in the copy. However, if the same command is entered with XCOPY instead of COPY, and no subdirectory named TEMP exists, the effect is different; XCOPY prompts you with the following message:

```
Is "temp" a File (F) or Directory (D) on the destination ? (F/D)
```

If you press F, the file is copied to a file named TEMP in the current directory. If you press D, a directory named TEMP is created as a subdirectory of the current directory, and TEST.FIL is copied into that directory. This feature is effective for any file specifier that does not end with a backslash. For example, if no there is no directory named \ WP \ LETTERS \ NEWFILES, then the following command will cause the File or Directory prompt to appear:

```
XCOPY TEST1.FIL \WP\LETTERS\NEWFILES
```

To override this prompt, and force the creation of a new directory if the specified directory does not exist, a backslash is appended to the final directory name. The following command will copy TEST1.FIL into the \ WP \ LETTERS \ NEWFILES directory, creating the directory if it does not exist, without a prompt:

```
XCOPY TEST1.FIL \WP\LETTERS\NEWFILES\
```

The reason this works is that the final backslash clearly defines NEWFILES as a directory, since file names cannot end with a backslash. Without the backslash, there is some ambiguity as to whether the word NEWFILES represents a file name or a directory name, and the only way to resolve this ambiguity is for XCOPY to ask what you mean.

XCOPY can be used to back up files. The /A switch is used to tell XCOPY to copy only those files that have their Archive attribute set. If the Archive attribute is set, it means the file has changed since the last BACKUP was performed on it. When the BACKUP command is used, it turns off the Archive attribute. As soon as the file is modified in any way, DOS turns the Archive Attribute back on. Consequently, by using the /A switch with XCOPY, you can copy only those files that have changed since the last backup. XCOPY automatically turns on the Archive attribute on the target file, but it leaves the source file Archive attribute unchanged.

If you want XCOPY to turn off the Archive attribute on source files, the /M switch should be used instead of the /A switch. For example, the following two commands copy all files in the current directory that have their Archive attribute on. However, the first command leaves the source file Archive attribute on, while the second turns it off:

```
XCOPY *.* A: /A
XCOPY *.* A: /M
```

The reason for providing the ability to turn off the Archive Attribute after copying a file is to allow you to use the XCOPY command as a backup utility. By copying only those files that have the archive attribute on, and turning it off when they are copied, you can repeatedly execute the XCOPY command to copy only files that have changed since the last time XCOPY was used.

The /D:date switch is used to copy only those files that were changed on or after the specified date. The following command copies only those files in the current directory that have an extension of LET, and that were modified on or after 8/1/91:

```
XCOPY *.LET *.BAK /D:8/1/91
```

The /S switch copies subdirectories as well as files. If a subdirectory on the source does not exist on the target, the /S switch will cause it to be created on the target. However, only subdirectories that have files in them are created. If the subdirectory on the source is empty, then it will not be created on the target. The target may be another disk or another directory on the source disk. For example, consider the partial directory structure shown in Figure 6.9.

The C: \ WP \ LETTERS directory contains three files: FILE1.LET, FILE2.LET, and FILE3.LET; and three subdirectories: PERSONAL, BUSINESS, and PR. The PERSONAL subdirectory contains three files of its own: ROBERT1.LET, ROBERT2.LET, and MARY1.LET, while the BUSINESS subdirectory is empty, and the PR subdirectory contains two files: ADCAMPGN.LET and FLYERS1.LET.

XCOPY can be used with the /S switch to duplicate the files and non-empty subdirectories of the C: \ WP \ LETTERS directory to the A: drive with the following command:

```
XCOPY C:\WP\LETTERS A:\ /S
```

The backslash on the target tells XCOPY to copy files from C: \ WP \ LETTERS into the root directory on the A: drive, and create subdirectories of C: \ WP \ LETTERS in the A: root directory. If the target disk was empty when this command was entered, it would end up with the structure shown in Figure 6.11:

```
A:\                             (root directory)
    LETTERS                     (directory)
        PERSONAL                (directory)
            ROBERT1.LET         (file)
            ROBERT2.LET         (file)
            MARY1.LET (file)
    PR                          (directory)
        ADCAMPGN.LET            (file)
        FLYERS1.LET             (file)
    FILE1.LET                   (file)
    FILE2.LET                   (file)
    FILE3.LET                   (file)
```

Figure 6.11 File Structure for the Target Drive

Note that the /S switch for the XCOPY command behaves differently with respect to empty subdirectories than the /S switch for the MOVE command, discussed above. /S for XCOPY does not recreate empty subdirectories, while /S for MOVE does.

If you wanted to copy the empty BUSINESS directory as well, the /E switch could be used in conjunction with the /S switch. /E tells XCOPY to copy all subdirectories, regardless of whether or not they are empty. The above command would be modified as follows:

```
XCOPY C:\WP\LETTERS A:\ /S/E
```

The /E switch cannot be used unless the /S switch is also specified.

XCOPY does not normally copy files that have the Hidden or System attribute set. However, the /H switch can be used to tell XCOPY that it should copy hidden and system files.

XCOPY copies only files and directories, but does not affect the volume label of a disk. The /L switch can be used to copy the volume label from the source disk to the target disk.

The /P and /C switches are identical. They tell XCOPY to prompt you before copying each file. This is useful when you want to copy a lot of files, but they do not have enough common features in their names to use wild cards to specify them as a group. For example, you may have 20 files with a BAT extension, but only want to copy 12 of them. Rather than typing in 12 file names, the following command could by used:

```
XCOPY *.BAT *.BAK /P
```

When this command is entered, XCOPY will display each file name that has an extension of BAT, followed by a (Y/N)? prompt. Pressing Y causes XCOPY to copy the file, while pressing N causes the file to be skipped.

Instead of prompting you for each file, it is sometimes helpful to have XCOPY prompt you once before beginning the entire XCOPY operation. This can be accomplished with the /W switch, which causes XCOPY to display the following prompt, and wait for you to press a key:

```
Strike a key to start copying
```

This is useful if you need to put a disk in a floppy drive before letting the XCOPY operation continue. The /W switch is commonly used in batch files that include the XCOPY command for a floppy drive. It can also be used to load XCOPY from a floppy disk that is in the same drive you want to use for the source and/or target disk. When the above message appears, you may abort the MOVE operation with the Control + C or Control + Break keys.

If a file already exists that has the same name as the target file, it is overwritten, just as it is with the COPY command. However, if the Read-only attribute is set, then the file is not copied. If XCOPY encounters a file that has the same name as the target, it displays the following message:

```
FILESPEC ...access denied
```

To override this, and cause XCOPY to overwrite files that have the Read-only attribute set, the /R switch is used. The following command copies all files with a BAT extension to files of the same name with a BAK extension, and tells XCOPY to overwrite any matching target filenames, even if the Read-only attribute is set:

```
XCOPY *.BAT *.BAK /R
```

As with the COPY command, it is rare that XCOPY does not accurately duplicate a file. However, with very important information, or under circumstances in which a bad copy would create serious problems, you may want to use the /V switch to cause XCOPY to verify each file copied. This will slow down the performance of XCOPY, but decreases the likelihood of a bad copy.

As with the DISKCOPY command, XCOPY sets the ERRORLEVEL environment variable when it terminates. There are four possible numbers to which XCOPY may set the ERRORLEVEL variable. Their values and meanings are shown in Table 6.8.

Table 6.8 Values of ERRORLEVEL Set by XCOPY Command

Value	*Meaning*
0	XCOPYwas successful; no errors occurred.
1	There were no files that matched the source specifier, so no files were copied.
2	XCOPY was terminated by the user pressing Ctrl-C or Ctrl-Break.
4	An initialization error occurred. This is caused by one of the following problems: insufficient memory; insufficient disk space; and invalid drive specifier; or a syntax error in the XCOPY command.
5	A disk write error occurred.

The ERRORLEVEL variable can be referenced on the IF line of a batch file to take an appropriate action if XCOPY returns a value other than 0. Batch files are discussed in Chapter 9.

For copying the entire contents of a disk, XCOPY is generally preferred over DISKCOPY for two reasons: XCOPY unfragments the files as it copies them, while DISKCOPY duplicates fragmentation; and XCOPY does not require that the disks be in the same format, while DISKCOPY does. When XCOPY has finished copying a file, it turns on the Archive attribute in the target file, even if that attribute is not set in the source file. DISKCOPY leaves the Archive Attribute unchanged in the target. File attributes and the ATTRIB command are discussed in the *Advanced Topics* section of this chapter.

Either DISKCOPY or XCOPY can be used to copy a disk that has hidden and/or system files on it. Software installation disks are common examples of disks that will have hidden and system files on them. DISKCOPY does this automatically, while XCOPY requires the use of switches. The following command will make a complete copy of a disk that has a volume label, system files, hidden files, and subdirectories with and without files in them:

```
XCOPY A:\*.* B: /L/H/S/E
```

This command would be useful for copying a software installation disk from 5.25 inch media to 3.5 inch media.

XCOPY can be used with a filelist, as well as with wild cards. Filelists are discussed in detail above, in the section *Using Wildcards and Filelists*. If a file named NAMES.FIL in the C:\WP\LETTERS directory, contains a list of file names that are in the same directory, then the following command will copy all of them to the A: drive:

```
XCOPY @C:\WP\LETTERS\NAMES.FIL A:
```

The switches for XCOPY are summarized in Table 6.9.

Table 6.9 Switches for Use with the XCOPY Command

Switch	***Effect***
/A	Only copies files that have the Archive attribute set, and leaves the Archive attribute unchanged on the source file.
/D:date	Only copies files whose date is on or after the one specified. The format of the date is determined by the current country code.

Table 6.9 continued ...

Switch	*Effect*
/E	Creates subdirectories at the target, even if they are empty. This switch only works if /S is also specified.
/H	Includes hidden and system files in the copy operation.
/L	Copies the volume label of the source disk on the target disk.
/M	Resets the Archive attribute of the source file after copying it.
/P or /C	Pauses for confirmation before copying each file.
/R	Causes XCOPY to overwrite files with the same name as the target, even if they have the Read-only attribute set.
/S	Copies subdirectories of the source directory. Empty subdirectories are not copied.
/V	Performs a verification of the copy after it is made. This slows down the process but increases reliability.
/W	Pauses after the XCOPY command is entered and waits for a disk to be inserted. You may interrupt the command at this point by pressing Ctrl+C or Ctrl+Break.

XCOPY is an external command.

The XDEL command is an extended DEL command that can be used to delete files in subdirectories of the source, to remove empty directories, and to completely remove the contents of a deleted file from the disk, so that it cannot be unerased or its contents examined. When used without switches, XDEL is the same as DEL.

To delete files in subdirectories of the source, the /S switch is used. All subdirectories that stem from the source, including sub-sub-directories, are affected. Consider the directory tree in Figure 6.9. If the WP directory is the current directory, then the following command will delete all files with an LET extension from the WP, WP\LETTERS, WP\LETTERS\PERSONAL, and WP/LETTERS/PR directories:

```
XDEL *.LET /S
```

(Figure 6.9 does not show any files with a LET extension in the WP directory, but if there are any below the tree fragment shown, they will be deleted.)

It is often convenient to be able to remove empty directories as well as files with a single command. This is accomplished with the /D switch. The following command will delete all files with a BAK extension from the current directory, and will also remove any empty subdirectories in the current directory:

```
XDEL *.BAK /D
```

Because XDEL has the ability to remove large numbers of files and directories in one step, it needs to be used with caution. To provide an extra measure of safety, XDEL prompts you to confirm your request before it continues. For example, the command XDEL *.BAK produces the following message:

```
        path:  c:\
        file:  *.bak
Is this what you wish to do (Y/N)?
```

You can override this message and have XDEL immediately carry out your request without prompting you for confirmation by using the /N switch. The following command deletes all files with an LET extension in the current directory, and will not pause for confirmation:

```
XDEL *.LET /N
```

You may also direct XDEL to exercise extra caution, with the /P or /C switch. These switches are identical; they tell XDEL to prompt you before deleting each file. This is useful when you want to delete a lot of files, but they do not have enough common features in their names to use wild cards to specify them as a group. For example, you may have 20 files with a BAT extension, but only want to delete 12 of them. Rather than typing in 12 file names, the following command could by used:

```
XDEL *.BAT *.BAK /P
```

When this command is entered, XDEL will display each file name that has an extension of BAT, followed by a (Y/N)? prompt. Pressing Y causes XDEL to delete the file, while pressing N causes the file to be left unchanged.

Like the DEL command, XDEL does not delete files that have the Read-only attribute set. However, you can override this with the /R switch. The following command deletes all files with a BAK extension in the current directory, even if the Read-only attribute is set:

```
XDEL *.BAK /R
```

When a file is deleted, whether with the DEL or XDEL command, the contents of the file itself are left untouched—only the directory and File Allocation Table entries for the file are changed, to indicate that the disk space occupied by the file can now be used for other files. (The structure of the directory and File Allocation Table are discussed below, in the section *File Protection and Recovery Commands.*) Since the contents of the file itself are not changed until they are overwritten by a new file, it is possible to examine their contents after they have been deleted, and even to undelete them. Normally this is all right—it is even desirable when a file is accidentally deleted. However, if your file contains sensitive information, you may not want to run the risk of having someone come along and undelete it. The /O switch can be used to overwrite a file before deleting it. When /O is specified, XDEL displays the following warning message:

```
WARNING:  file contents will be PERMANENTLY LOST
Is this what you wish to do (Y/N)?
```

If you respond with a Y, XDEL replaces the entire contents of the file with the following message:

```
Overwritten & deleted by XDEL. Copyright (c) 1987,1988,1990 Digital
Research Inc

. Overwritten & deleted by XDEL. Copyright (c) 1987,1988,1990 Digital
ResearchIn

c. Overwritten & deleted by XDEL. Copyright (c) 1987,1988,1990 Digital
Research

I
```

The message will be repeated as many times as necessary to fill the contents of the file. After overwriting the file with this message, the file is deleted. This switch should only be used with great caution, because it totally destroys the contents of a file, making it impossible to recover any part of it.

Filelists may be used with the XDEL command to specify the files to delete. Filelists are discussed above, in the section *Using Wild Cards and Filelists*.

XDEL is an external command.

Renaming Files and Directories

The RENAME command renames files. A drive and path specifier may used for the source file, but the target specifier must contain only a file name. The file is being renamed, not copied, so it must remain in the same directory. The RENAME command has the following syntax:

```
RENAME source target
```

Wild cards may be used with RENAME. For example, the following command uses the *many wild card* (*) to rename all files that have a BAT extension to a BAK extension:

```
RENAME *.BAT *.BAK
```

The target file name cannot already exist. RENAME will not overwrite an existing file, as COPY does. Instead, when RENAME encounters a target file name that already exists, it displays the following message:

```
File already exists
```

If the source file does not exist the message "File not found" appears.

The *single character wild card* (?) may also be used with the RENAME command, but it only works if the source and target file names have the same number of characters in them. For example, suppose there were three files named TEST1.FIL, TEST2.FIL, and TEST3.FIL, in the current directory. These three files could be renamed to TEMP1.FIL, TEMP2.FIL, and TEMP3.FIL with the following command:

```
RENAME TEST?.FIL TEMP?.FIL
```

However, consider the following command:

```
RENAME TEST?.FIL TST?.FIL
```

RENAME will rename the first file, TEST1.FIL, to TSTT.FIL. It copies the first three letters from the first file name, then takes the next letter (T) to match the wild card in the target, ending up with TSTT.FIL. Now RENAME will attempt to copy the second file,

TEST2.FIL, but the same thing happens. This time TSTT.FIL already exists, so RENAME displays the message "File already exists" and terminates the operation.

A similar problem arises if the target file name has more characters than the source file name. Consider this command:

```
RENAME TEST?.FIL TESTER?.FIL
```

RENAME renames the first file, TEST1.FIL, to TESTER.FIL. It replaces the first four characters of the source file with the first four characters of the target file, then matches the wild card specifier in the source file name with the next character in the target file name (an E). It then continues to use the rest of the target file name (an R), and adds on the extension, resulting in TESTER.FIL. Now, RENAME will attempt to copy the second file, TEST2.FIL, but the same thing happens. This time TESTER.FIL already exists, so again the error message is displayed and RENAME terminates. Consequently, when using the single wild card with RENAME, you must make certain the number of characters in the source and target names are identical.

The RENAME command can also be used to move files from one directory to another, just as MOVE can. The following command moves all of the files that have a LET extension from the \WP\LETTERS directory to the \WP\ARCHIVE directory:

```
RENAME \WP\LETTERS\*.LET \WP\ARCHIVE
```

This use of RENAME works in exactly the same way as MOVE—if the files are being moved from one directory to another on the same disk, only the directory entry is changed. This is much faster than copying and deleting the files, and is also easier on your hard disk.

RENAME is an internal command.

The RENDIR command is used to rename subdirectories. The syntax of the command is:

```
RENDIR oldname newname
```

Oldname is the current name of the subdirectory to be renamed, and *newname* is the new name for it. If the subdirectory is not in the current directory, then the path to it must be specified in both oldname and newname. If it is not on the current drive, then the drive must also be specified. If the current directory is C:\WP, then the following command renames the C:\WP\LETTERS directory to C:\WP\LETS:

```
RENDIR LETTERS LETS
```

If the current directory is C:\, then the following command would be required to accomplish the same result:

```
RENDIR WP\LETTERS WP\LETS
```

In this case, if the directory is specified only for the old name, but not the new name, then RENDIR does not rename the directory, and displays the following message:

```
This utility only changes the NAME of a directory
- it cannot be used to make a directory a child
of another directory or move it to a different
disk
```

If you attempt to rename a subdirectory to a name that already exists, the following error message is displayed:

```
The new name of your directory is the same as an
already-existing file or directory
```

You may use RENDIR to rename the current directory by specifying the path to it from its parent. For example, if the current directory is \WP\LETTERS, then the following command will rename it to \WP\LETS:

```
RENDIR ..\LETTERS ..\LETS
```

Note that the path specifier is required on both the old name and the new name.

RENDIR is an external command.

Resetting Date And Time Stamps With The TOUCH Command

The TOUCH command is used to change the date and/or time stamp of a file, without actually changing the file itself. If a new date and time is not specified, the current date and time are used. The following command resets the date and time of a file named MARY.LET to the current date and time:

```
TOUCH MARY.LET
```

The /D switch is used to specify a new date. The following command resets the date for MARY.LET to 12-1-91, and the time to the current time:

```
TOUCH MARY.LET /D:12-1-91
```

The date format is that defined by the current COUNTRY setting. This may be overridden with the /F switch, discussed below.

The time is set with the /T switch. Time is always specified using a 24-hour clock, with midnight being 00:00. You must specify hours and minutes, and may specify seconds if you like. The following command resets the time for MARY.LET to 2:14:30 PM (fourteen minutes and 30 seconds after 2:00 in the afternoon):

```
TOUCH MARY.LET /T:14:14:30
```

If you want to specify the date in a format other than the one defined by the current COUNTRY setting in the CONFIG.SYS file, the /F switch is used. Acceptable country formats are E for European, J for Japanese, and U for USA. The following command resets the date for MARY.LET to 12-1-91, and uses the Japanese format (yy-mm-dd):

```
TOUCH MARY.LET /D:91-12-1 /F:J
```

In this example the date is given in Japanese format, regardless of what the current country setting is.

You may want to have TOUCH prompt you before it touches each file specified. This is useful if you want to change a lot of files using a wild card specifier, but there are a few that match the specifier that should not be changed. This is accomplished with the /P switch.

Normally, TOUCH will not change the date and/or time of files that have the Read-only attribute set. The /R switch tells TOUCH to ignore Read-only attributes, and to change the date and/or time on all files that match the file specifier.

TOUCH works on files in the current or specified directory, but does not touch files in subdirectories. The /S switch tells TOUCH to search all subdirectories of the specified directory, and to change any files found that match the file specifier. The following command changes the date and time of all files in the \WP\LETTERS directory, and any subdirectories that stem from it, to 12-1-91:

```
TOUCH \WP\LETTERS\*.* /D:12-1-91 /S
```

You may also use a filelist with the TOUCH command. For example, suppose the file FILES.LST contained the following filenames:

```
*.LET
MARY.NOT
JAMES.WKS
REPORTS\*.RPT
```

The following command would change the date and time of all files that match these specifiers to the current date and time:

```
TOUCH @FILES.LST
```

Note that paths may be specified as part of the file specifier in file lists.

TOUCH is an external command.

Commands for Locating and Displaying Files

The DIR and XDIR commands display all of the file names and subdirectories in a directory. These commands have a variety of switches for selecting the particular files that will be shown, and can also be used to search through subdirectories for one or more files. DIR and XDIR were discussed in detail earlier in this chapter.

The FIND command is used to locate one or more files that contain a particular text string, and to display the lines in the files that contain the string. There are several switches that can be used to adjust the case sensitivity of the command, to add line numbers to the displayed lines, and to display only lines that contain the specified string, only lines that do not contain it, or only a count of the lines that contain it. FIND is discussed in detail in Chapter 4 in the section titled, *The DOS Filter Commands—FIND, MORE, and SORT.*

The MORE command can be used as a filter for other commands, or as a command in its own right. When used as a command, it requires the input redirection symbol (<) to send it a file name. This displays the contents of the file on the screen, pausing after each screen until you press a key. This is the same effect achieved by the TYPE command combined with the MORE filter. TYPE is discussed next.

There are no switches for the MORE command. MORE is discussed in detail in Chapter 4 in the section titled *The DOS Filter Commands—FIND, MORE, and SORT.*

The TYPE command displays the contents of an ASCII (or extended ASCII) text file on the screen. It has one required parameter, and one optional switch. The parameter is the name of the file to display. The following command displays the contents of the AUTOEXEC.BAT file:

```
TYPE AUTOEXEC.BAT
```

ASCII text files are files that contain only the standard ASCII codes—those numbered from one to 127. If the file contains extended codes (those numbered from 128 through 255), strange characters may appear on the screen. Furthermore, if the file is produced with a word processor or other software package that provides special formatting codes, it will also display these as strange characters, and line breaks may not be shown at the appropriate places. Files created with the DR DOS EDITOR utility will be properly displayed with the TYPE command. The only difficulty that could arise with these files is that they may contain lines that are more than 80 characters wide. Since there are only 80 characters on the screen, the longer lines will wrap at the right edge of the screen.

Attempting to display binary files—those that have extensions of BIN, COM, EXE, LIB, or OBJ—will not damage them, but the display will not be readable.

Since most files contain more information than will fit on one screen, the /P switch is provided to cause the display to pause after each screenful until a key is pressed. Alternatively, TYPE may be combined with the MORE filter:

```
TYPE REPORT.FIL | MORE
```

This will cause the display to pause and wait for you to press a key, whenever the screen is full.

The TYPE command can also be used to send the contents of a file to the printer, using the output redirection symbol (>) and the standard device name for the printer (PRN). The following command will print the contents of the AUTOEXEC.BAT file:

```
TYPE AUTOEXEC.BAT > PRN
```

TYPE is an internal command.

File Protection and Recovery Commands

It is inevitable that sooner or later you will have a problem with an important file—you will accidentally erase it and be unable to recover it with the UNDELETE command, or something will go wrong with your computer that damages the disk that contains the file, or your computer will be stolen, and the disk along with it, or some other such unforeseen event. Recognizing the inevitability of such events, the designers of DR DOS built a number of commands into DR DOS 6.0 for protecting yourself against such happenings.

Commands used to protect against accidental loss are all based on the same principle: they create a copy of the file to be protected, so that if the file is lost or damaged the copy can be used to restore it. There are a variety of ways to manage the creation of such copies, and each command takes a somewhat different approach. In addition to the commands discussed below, the simple COPY and XCOPY commands discussed earlier are effective for small numbers of files, if the target disk has sufficient space to hold them.

The BACKUP command is useful for backing up large numbers of files and subdirectories all at once. BACKUP uses a special data compression technique to efficiently pack the files onto the target disk. BACKUP is used to back files up from one drive to another. When the target is a floppy drive and is not big enough to contain all of the source files, BACKUP will use multiple floppy disks. The simplest form of the BACKUP command is:

```
BACKUP source target
```

The source specifier may contain a drive and/or a directory specifier, as well as a file name specifier. The target, however, can consist only of a drive specifier. For example, the following command backs up everything in the root directory of the C: drive to floppy disks in the A: drive:

```
BACKUP C:\*.* A:
```

When this command is entered, BACKUP displays the following message:

```
Backing-up from C:\ to A:\
Insert disk number 001 in drive A:
All files in the root directory of the destination disk will be deleted.
Strike a key when ready.
```

After you have placed a disk in the target drive and pressed a key,

BACKUP displays the following message:

```
Backing up to disk 001
```

BACKUP then proceeds to list the names of the files it is backing up, as they are added to the backup disk. If the disk fills up, BACKUP prompts you for Disk 2, and continues.

BACKUP does not simply copy files from the source to the target. Instead, it combines the files, using a file compression technique that reduces the amount of space required by the files. When BACKUP runs out of space on one disk, it stops compressing the files and prompts you to put another disk in the drive. It then begins compressing again. It can interrupt the compression process even in the middle of a file. This assures that every byte of space on the target disk will be used. If you use the DIR command to examine the contents of Disk 1, you will see that it contains just two files: BACKUP.001 and CONTROL.001. Disk 2 will have files named BACKUP.002 and CONTROL.002, and so on. The BACKUP.XXX file contains the actual file contents, while CONTROL.XXX contains information used by the RESTORE command to correctly decipher the information in BACKUP.XXX, and restore it to the correct files and directories.

BACKUP continues prompting you for more disks until all of the specified files have been backed up. It is important to number the disks as you go, so that you will know what order to restore them in.

When BACKUP is used without switches, it simply backs up all of the files in the specified directory. It is often desirable to back up subdirectories, as well. This can be done with the /S switch. The following two commands demonstrate this: the first backs up all files in all directories on the C: drive, while the second backs up all files in the C: \ WP \ LETTERS directory, as well as all files in any subdirectories of C: \ WP \ LETTERS.

```
BACKUP C:\*.* A: /S
BACKUP C:\WP\LETTERS\*.* /S
```

When BACKUP backs up a file, it turns off the archive attribute for that file. If the file is modified in the future, DOS will automatically turn the Archive attribute back on. Thus, the Archive attribute always indicates whether or not a file has been modified since it was last backed up. The /M switch uses the archive bit to only back up files that have changed since the last backup. With large hard disks this makes it easy to develop an efficient means of maintaining backups without wasting a lot of time repeatedly backing up files that have already been backed up, since only a handful of files out of thousands may have changed. The following command backs up all files on drive C: that have changed since the last backup:

```
BACKUP C:\*.* A: /S/M
```

The /D switch is used to back up only files that were changed on or after a specified date. The following command backs up all files in the root directory of the C: drive that were changed on or after 12/1/91:

```
BACKUP C:\*.* A: /D:12/1/91
```

In addition to specifying the date, you may also specify the time. The following command specifies that all files modified at or later than 2:00 pm be backed up:

```
BACKUP C:\*.* A: /T:14:00
```

Normally the time switch is used in conjunction with the date switch, but it may be used by itself if you like.

The BACKUP command provides the ability to create a *log file* whenever a backup is performed. The log file is a listing of each file that was backed up, the date and time at which they were backed up, and the disk number that the file was stored on. To create a log file, the /L switch is used. The following command backs up all files in the C: \ WP \ LETTERS directory onto the A: drive, and creates a log file:

```
BACKUP C:\WP\LETTERS\ /L:filename
```

The name of the log file is specified by *filename* in the example above. If no filename is specified, then the log file is named BACKUP.LOG. In either case, the log file is placed in the root directory of the source disk. In this example, it is in the C: \ directory. If the specified log file already exists, BACKUP adds the new information to it. The log file can be very useful if, in the future, you need to remember which files were backed up.

BACKUP normally deletes any files that already exist in the root directory of the target disk. Files in subdirectories are not affected. However, sometimes it is desirable to backup files to a floppy disk without deleting files in the root directory. There are typically two reasons for doing this: to create a disk that contains copies of files in both backup and standard formats, and to add files to a backup file that already exists on a disk. The former is commonly done in order to provide a simple batch file that someone can use to restore the files on the disk, without having to know the RESTORE command. The latter is done when a lot of files have already been backed up, and you want to continue with the same set of disks, rather than have two different sets of backup disks.

The /A switch is used to accomplish both of these tasks—it leaves files in the root directory unchanged, and it adds files to an existing backup file. The following command backs up the files with a LET extension in the C:\WP\LETTERS directory and subdirectories, and adds them to an existing set of backup disks:

```
BACKUP C:\WP\LETTERS\*.LET /S /A
```

When this command is entered, BACKUP will display the following prompt:

```
Backing-up from C:TEMP to A:\
Adding to files already backed-up on A:\
Insert last backup disk in drive A:
Strike a key when ready.
```

The last backup diskette used in the previous sequence must be inserted in the A: drive. If a diskette that does not contain BACKUP files on it is used, BACKUP will display the message "No backup files present on destination disk," and terminate.

> ***Note:*** Since BACKUP requires that a disk have backup files on it before the /A switch can be used, the only way to save a non-backup file in the root directory is to first create a small backup file on the disk, leaving enough space for the non-backup file. Then copy the non-backup file to the root directory of the backup disk, and use the BACKUP command with the /A switch to put the rest of the files into the backup file.

If the target disk is not formatted, BACKUP automatically formats it before attempting to write information to it. However, there are different capacities, or densities, that a disk can be formatted to, and BACKUP assumes the highest possible capacity that the backup drive can handle. This is not always desirable because you may need to restore your disks on a computer that has a lower capacity drive. In this case, the /F:XXX switch may be used to specify a particular density to which the disk should be formatted. Table 6.10 shows the various disk sizes and capacities, and the possible values that may be used for XXX in the /F switch.

Table 6.10 Formatting Values of /F Switch for BACKUP Command

Disk Size	*No. of Sides*	*Capacity*	*XXX Value*
5.25"	1	160K	160
5.25"	1	180K	180
5.25"	2	320K	320
5.25"	2	360K	360
5.25"	2	1.2M	1.20
3.5"	2	720K	720
3.5"	2	1.44M	1.44
3.5"	2	2.88M	2.88

To specify that a disk be formatted to 720K, the following command would be used:

```
BACKUP C:\*.* A:\ /F:720
```

If /F is used without a colon and an XXX value, BACKUP uses the default value for the target drive. For BACKUP to format a disk, the DOS FORMAT.COM program must either be in the current directory, or in a directory specified in the PATH.

It is important to develop a plan for periodic backups. This should include occasional complete backups of your entire hard disk, as well as more frequent partial backups of files that have changed. In general, the following scheme works well, though the exact time periods may need to be adjusted to reflect the frequency with which you use your computer.

Once a month, perform a complete backup of the entire hard disk. Store this in a safe place, preferably in a different building from the computer, in case of a fire or other catastrophic disaster.

Once a week, perform an incremental backup, backing up only those files that have changed since the last backup.

Keep two generations of each set of disks: at the end of the first month, use a new set of disks for the complete backup. At the end of the second month, re-use the first month's disks, and so on. Follow a similar pattern for the weekly backups.

There are a few points of caution to keep in mind with the BACKUP command. It cannot back up the system files, IO.SYS, MSDOS.SYS, and COMMAND.COM. However, these files can be transferred to a floppy disk with the SYS command. The BACKUP command provided with DR DOS 6.0 cannot be used with a RESTORE command from DOS 3.2 or earlier. The format of the backup files changed with DOS 3.3. It has remained consistent since then, so a RESTORE command from DOS 3.3 or later will be consistent with DR DOS 6.0.

Since BACKUP encodes files, there is an increased likelihood of a backed up file having problems—each time an additional step is added to the copying process, the likelihood of errors increases. Consequently, for small numbers of files it is best to maintain your backups as normal copies of files. The COPY or XCOPY commands can be used for this purpose, but the REPLACE command, discussed later in this chapter, is usually better. When using COPY or XCOPY to back up files, you can use the /V switch.

> ***Note:*** If you have used the ASSIGN, JOIN, or SUBST commands to redirect a drive, you should not use the BACKUP command with that drive. It should be restored to its original configuration before BACKUP is used with it. Otherwise, the RESTORE command may not be able to restore the files.

BACKUP leaves a return code in the DOS environment variable ERRORLEVEL. Table 6.11 shows the return code values and their meanings for the BACKUP command.

Table 6.11 Values of ERRORLEVEL Set by BACKUP Command

Value	***Meaning***
0	BACKUP was successful; no errors occurred.
1	There were no files that matched the source specifier, so no files were backed up.
2	File-sharing conflicts on a network prevented some files from being backed up.

Table 6.11 continued ...

Value	***Meaning***
3	BACKUP wes terminated by the user pressing Ctrl-C or Ctrl-break.
4	BACKUP terminated because of an error.

The BACKUP command is an external command.

The RESTORE command restores files from disks created with the BACKUP command. The syntax is therefore the reverse of that for BACKUP; the source specifier can only be a drive letter, while the target may contain drive, path, and file name specifiers:

```
RESTORE source target
```

Source is the drive on which the backup files are stored, and target is the drive to which those files should be restored. It can be a little confusing at first to understand why the target should have drive and file name specifiers, since the files exist on the source drive. Recall that when BACKUP backs up files, all of the files are compressed into one single backup file in the root directory of the backup disk. Consequently, there is no directory name to specify for the RESTORE source disk. In fact, there isn't even a file name, since the file names are all encoded along with the directory names. Furthermore, if a file was in a directory named \ WP \ LETTERS \ BUSINESS on the drive that was backed up, then RESTORE can only place it into a directory named \ WP \ LETTERS \ BUSINESS on the target drive. For these reasons, the directory and file name specifiers are always applied to the target drive in the RESTORE command.

You may use file names and wild cards to restore only selected files from a backup disk. For example, the following command restores the file ROBERT1.LET in the \ WP \ LETTERS \ PERSONAL directory:

```
RESTORE A: C:\WP\LETTERS\PERSONAL\ROBERT1.LET
```

By default, the RESTORE command restores files only to the specified directory. The following command restores all files that were backed up from the root directory of drive C:, but does not restore subdirectories:

```
RESTORE A: C:\*.*
```

To restore subdirectories of the specified directory, use the /S switch. The following command restores all of the files that were backed up from any directory in drive C:

```
RESTORE A: C:\*.* /S
```

RESTORE can be used to list the files that are backed up on a backup disk. This is particularly useful if no log file exists for the backup disks. To display a list of the files on a backup disk, enter the following command:

```
RESTORE A: C: /R
```

The /R switch disables the actual restoration of files, so that the file names are simply listed on the screen. Nonetheless, the command still requires that a target drive be specified. The listing of files can also be routed to a file or printer, instead of the screen. The following command prints the list of files:

```
RESTORE A: C: /R > PRN
```

When this command is entered, RESTORE responds with the message "Strike a key to continue." Pressing a key causes RESTORE to print the files on the printer.

If RESTORE encounters a file on the target disk that has the same name as one being restored, the file on the target disk is replaced with the one from the backup disk. This can create problems—the one on the target disk may in fact be the preferred version of the file. Consequently, RESTORE includes switches that let you set a level of protection against accidental replacements.

If a file exists on the target disk that has the same name as one being restored, the /P switch will cause RESTORE to check the Read-only and Archive attribute settings for the file on the target disk. If the file's Read-only attribute is on (which means the file cannot be modified by most commands or programs), or if the Archive attribute is on (indicating that the file has been changed since its last backup), then this switch causes RESTORE to pause and prompt you for confirmation before replacing these files.

You can avoid overwriting any files at all by using the /N switch,

The /B:DATE switch is similar to the /D:DATE switch on the BACKUP command. However, where /D:DATE tells BACKUP to back up files modified on or *after* the specified date, /B:DATE tells RESTORE to restore only those files that were modified on or *before* the specified date. The date on the /B switch applies to the dates of files on the target disk, not the backup disk.

The /A:DATE switch tells RESTORE to restore only those files whose date on the target disk was modified on or after the specified date.

The /E:TIME switch tells RESTORE to restore only those files whose time of last modification was at or earlier than the specified time.

The /L:TIME switch tells RESTORE to restore only those files whose of last modification was at or later than the specified time. As with the date specifiers, the time refers to the time stamp of the file on the target disk, not the backup disk.

The /M switch restores only those files modified since the last backup (those whose Archive attribute is on).

The RESTORE command leaves a return code in the DOS environment variable, ERRORLEVEL. Table 6.12 shows the return code values and their meanings for the RESTORE command.

Table 6.12 Values of ERRORLEVEL Set by RESTORE Command

Value	***Meaning***
0	RESTORE was successful; no errors occurred.
1	There were no files that matched the target specifier, so no files were restored.
3	RESTORE was terminated by the user pressing Ctrl-C or Ctrl-break.
4	RESTORE terminated because of an error.

RESTORE is an external command.

The DISKMAP command provides an automatic measure of protection for recovery of accidentally deleted files, or an accidentally formatted disk that has valuable files on it. To understand how DISKMAP works, it is necessary to understand a little about how directories keep track of files. This material is covered in detail in Chapter 7, so the discussion here will be brief.

Keeping track of directories actually involves two types of structures created by DOS. The first is a table known as the *File Allocation Table*, or *FAT* for short. The second is the directory structure. As mentioned earlier in this chapter, when a file is stored on a disk, it may not be stored in consecutive clusters, but instead could be stored on clusters that are scattered all around the disk. The problem for DOS, then, is how to keep track of which clusters belong to which files. This information is stored in the FAT.

The FAT contains information about every cluster on the disk. Among other things, each cluster entry contains a number that indicates the next cluster in the sequence for a particular file. For example, if a file occupies clusters 9, 12, and 27, then the FAT entry for cluster 9 would contain the number 12 as the next cluster in the sequence, and the entry for cluster 12 would contain the number 27. The last cluster for the file, 27 in this example, has a special symbol that says, "This is where the file ends." Thus, by starting at the first cluster for a file and following the sequence of next cluster numbers, it is possible to determine all of the clusters assigned to a file, and the sequence in which those clusters should be read. The only problem that remains is knowing which cluster marks the beginning of a particular file. This information is recorded in the directory. For example, a file named ROBERT1.LET, in the C: \ WP \ LETTERS directory, was stored on clusters 9, 12, and 27. The C: \ WP \ LETTERS directory stores the name of the file, information about the file's attribute settings, and the starting cluster for the file. When the file is accessed, DOS gets the starting cluster from the directory, then goes to the FAT to locate the rest of the clusters.

When a file is deleted, the information in the file is not really removed from the disk. This would take a long time, particularly for large files, and it would make file recovery impossible. Instead, two things happen when a file is deleted: the first letter of the file name in the directory is changed to ASCII code 229 (E5h) which is the Greek Sigma character (σ). This tells DOS that that space in the directory can be used for a new file, but until it actually is used, all of the information about the old file is preserved (except for the first letter of the file name). The second thing that happens when a file is deleted is that the FAT entries for that file—the cluster map for the file—are changed to indicate that the clusters are available for use. This eliminates the information that linked the clusters together for the file that was deleted. Now, when DOS wants to create a new file on the disk, it sees those clusters as available for storing the new file. However, until new information is actually written into those clusters, the old information is still there.

File recovery, then, may be fairly simple. If the file is small enough to fit in a single cluster, and neither the directory entry nor the FAT entries that the file used have been overwritten, all that is required is to change the first letter of the file name back to its original value, and change the cluster marker in the FAT back to the value that indicated the cluster was in use. Since the starting cluster number is stored in the directory, there is no problem locating it.

If the file occupied several clusters, file recovery is a little more difficult, because only the starting cluster is recorded in the directory, and the FAT pointer to subsequent clusters has been lost. If the file was not too badly fragmented—if it was stored on consecutive or nearly consecutive clusters—then it is often possible to determine which clusters belonged to it by examining the pattern of used and unused clusters in the immediate vicinity. If the file was highly fragmented, however, or if the directory entry and/or the FAT entries for the file have been overwritten, then recovery becomes more difficult.

The UNDELETE command can do a pretty good job of recovering simple files, since the information is still mostly available, and what's missing can be easily deduced. But as the task becomes more complex, UNDELETE by itself becomes less and less effective. This is where the DISKMAP command comes in.

DISKMAP creates a special file named DISKMAP.DAT. DISKMAP.DAT contains a copy of the FAT. Recall that the FAT contains the locations on the disk where each file is stored. When a file is deleted, that information is lost. Creating a copy of the FAT before deleting a file saves that information in the copy. If, after deleting a file, the space the file occupies on the disk is overwritten by another file, then the deleted file will not be recoverable, but until it is overwritten, it can be recovered using the information in DISKMAP.DAT.

Information on the locations of files that were deleted before DISKMAP.DAT was created, however, is not saved, because that information was deleted from the FAT before the FAT was copied into DISKMAP.DAT. Furthermore, information on files that are created after DISKMAP.DAT is created is not stored either, because that information does not exist when DISKMAP.DAT is created. Consequently, it is a good idea to run DISKMAP frequently. Each time DISKMAP is run for a particular drive, the DISKMAP.DAT file on that drive is updated.

This means that information already in the DISKMAP.DAT file is left there, but information added to the FAT since DISKMAP.DAT was created is added to DISKMAP.DAT.

The DISKMAP command requires a drive letter to identify the drive on which the DISKMAP.DAT file should be created. To create a DISKMAP.DAT file for the C: drive, enter the following command:

```
DISKMAP C:
```

After the DISKMAP command is entered, the computer will pause for a moment while it creates the DISKMAP.DAT file. You can see this file by executing a DIR command. DISKMAP.DAT is a read-only file, which means it cannot be modified or deleted unless you use the ATTRIB command to change its Read-only attribute.

The drive identifier is required for DISKMAP, even if you want to run it for the current drive. You may specify more than one drive with a single DISKMAP command. For example, the following command creates DISKMAP.DAT files on both the C: and the A: drives:

```
DISKMAP C: A:
```

It does not matter which drive you specify first. Once a DISKMAP.DAT file has been created on a disk, it can be used by the UNDELETE program to recover deleted files.

Since the FAT changes every time you add or delete a file, and frequently when files are modified, you may want to put the DISKMAP command in your AUTOEXEC.BAT file, to update the DISKMAP.DAT file every time you start your computer.

Periodically it is a good idea to delete the DISKMAP.DAT file and create a new one, since over time there will be old information in the file that you no longer want to keep. To delete the current DISKMAP.DAT file and create an entirely new one, the /D switch is used:

```
DISKMAP C: /D
```

It is important to recover a file as soon as possible after it has been deleted. Anything you do that causes information to be written to the disk can overwrite clusters that contain some or all of the file that you want to recover. Some commands and programs create temporary files on the disk that are unknown to you. For example, the MORE command sometimes creates a temporary file to store information that will be displayed on the screen, and the DISKCOPY program sometimes creates a temporary file to store information from the disk being copied. It is often difficult to tell whether or not a program will create such temporary files, so after discovering that a file needs to be undeleted, no programs or commands other than UNDELETE should be used.

Because file recovery becomes more complex, and less likely to be successful, on highly fragmented disks, it is worthwhile to use the DR DOS DISKOPT program periodically. DISKOPT is a program that rearranges the files on a disk, so that all of the clusters for each file are consecutive. This not only makes file recovery simpler, it also reduces the amount of time the computer spends retrieving information from files, and reduces wear and tear on the disk drive. Beware, however, that once you have optimized your disk, it will probably be impossible to recover files that were deleted before the optimization process.

DISKMAP should not be used with drives affected by a SUBST or JOIN command, and if you want to use the ASSIGN command, it must be done before loading DISKMAP.

To provide even more protection than DISKMAP offers against accidental deletion, the DELWATCH program may be used. If information from DELWATCH is available, UNDELETE uses that information. If DELWATCH was not used to protect the file, but DISKMAP was, then UNDELETE uses the DISKMAP information. If neither DELWATCH nor DISKMAP were used, then UNDELETE will attempt to recover the file without help. DELWATCH and UNDELETE are discussed below.

DISKMAP is an external command.

The DELWATCH command offers a greater level of protection against accidental deletions than DISKMAP. DELWATCH is a *TSR* (*Terminate and Stay Resident*) program, which means that once you run it, it remains in memory and monitors all file deletions until you turn off your PC.

Normally, when a file is deleted, the first character of its name is replaced with ASCII 229, which is the Greek Sigma character (σ). When DOS encounters a file whose name begins with this character, DOS knows that the file has been deleted and can therefore be overwritten. However, when DELWATCH is installed, deleting a file causes the first character to be replaced with a cloverleaf (ASCII 5). When DOS encounters this character, it treats the file as though it has been deleted—

it does not show up in DIR or XDIR listings, or in programs that can show directory listings. However, the FAT entries for the file are not deleted and the disk space occupied by the file is not reused. Consequently, the file is not actually deleted, but instead is marked as a *pending delete*, until the DELPURGE command is used to actually delete it. DELPURGE is discussed below.

DR DOS takes one additional precaution when a file is deleted, regardless of whether or not DELWATCH is installed: before changing the first character of the filename to either a Sigma or cloverleaf, it stores that first character in the third byte of the directory following the filename. That way, if you decide to undelete the file, DR DOS will know what the first character should be.

Besides changing the first character of a deleted filename to a cloverleaf, DELWATCH does one more thing: the first time a file is deleted after DELWATCH is started for a particular drive, a file named @DLWATCH.DAT is created in the root directory of the drive. @DLWATCH.DAT has the Read-only,System, and Hidden attributes set, so it is not seen with the DIR command. To see the @DLWATCH.DAT file, the XDIR command must be used. @DLWATCH.DAT stores the full paths and names of deleted files, so that UNDELETE will be able to determine the location of the file on the disk. Using the information in @DLWATCH.DAT, it is possible to have several deleted files with the same name in the same directory, and to selectively undelete the ones of choice. This requires use of the /B switch, discussed below.

To start DELWATCH, enter the command followed by the drive letters for the drives you want to monitor. For example, to start DELWATCH for the C: drive, the following command should be used:

```
DELWATCH C:
```

After DELWATCH has been started, the following message appears:

```
DELWATCH TSR successfully installed.
Logging in all enabled drives.
Enabling DELWATCH on drive C:
Checking directories on drive C:
```

There are two drawbacks to using DELWATCH. The first is that disk space for deleted files is not actually released for use by other files, so it is possible to fill up a disk with deleted files. To deal with this, the

DELPURGE command must be used on a regular basis. DELPURGE is used to actually delete files that have been marked as pending deletes. The second drawback to using DELWATCH is that, since it is a TSR, it occupies memory (about 5K) that would otherwise be available for other uses. If there is upper memory available, DELWATCH will automatically load itself there—you don't have to use a HILOAD command to place DELWATCH in upper memory. However, if sufficient upper memory is not available, then DELWATCH will load into conventional memory, thereby reducing the amount of memory available to applications.

There are several switches available with DELWATCH to provide fine control over how it behaves, and how much disk space it will allow pending deletes to occupy, as well as to review the status of DELWATCH. These settings are discussed below, and are summarized in Table 6.13. Note that the switch settings are particular for each drive, so that drive A:, for example, may have a totally different DELWATCH configuration than drive C:.

Under some circumstances, you may want to disable DELWATCH. For example, if you are going to do some general "house cleaning" on your hard drive, and know that you won't want to recover a lot of files that you are going to delete, it is easier to disable DELWATCH than to run DELPURGE on all of those files after deleting them. The /D switch is used to disable DELWATCH. You may selectively disable a specific drive, and leave other drives enabled. For example, if DELWATCH was enabled for both drives A: and C:, the following command would disable it for drive C: but leave it enabled for drive A:

```
DELWATCH C: /D
```

You may not use any other switch in combination with /D.

Rather than entirely disable DELWATCH, you may specify that it should only monitor files that have certain extensions. All other files will be deleted by the DEL command, just as though DELWATCH were not installed. To specify extensions to be protected by DELWATCH, the /O switch is used. The following command tells DELWATCH to mark any files on the C: drive with a LET extension as pending deletes, but to allow all others to be deleted:

```
DELWATCH C:/O:LET
```

You may specify up to ten extensions with the /O switch, by concatenating them with the plus sign (+). The following command specifies that files with LET or RPT extensions should be protected:

```
DELWATCH C:/O:LET+RPT
```

Each use of the /O switch overrides any previous uses. Consequently, if the above command were followed by the command DELWATCH C:/O:BAT, then only files with a BAT extension would be marked as pending deletes.

Wild card characters can also be used with the /O switch. The following command protects all files whose extension begins with **L** and ends with **T**, and all files whose extension ends with **R**:

```
DELWATCH C: /O:L?T+*R
```

Once /O has been used, its effect can be removed with the /E: switch, discussed next. The following command will turn off the effect of the /O switch:

```
DELWATCH C:/E:
```

The /E switch has the opposite effect of /O—it specifies file extensions that will not be protected, while all others will. /O can be thought of as *Only*, while /E can be thought of as *Except*. The following command tells DELWATCH to protect all files except those with an LET extension:

```
DELWATCH C: /E:LET
```

As with /O, up to ten extensions can be linked together with plus signs (+), and wildcard symbols may be used. To turn off the effect of /E, the /O switch is used. The following command eliminates the effects of /E and restores DELWATCH to monitoring all file deletions, regardless of extension:

```
DELWATCH C: /O:
```

It is possible to have several deleted files with the same name in the same directory, since once a file has been deleted its name can be reused. Normally, DELWATCH keeps track of only the most recently deleted such file. When UNDELETE is used on a directory that has two or more deleted files with the same name, it will use the DELWATCH information on the first one and attempt to recover any others without assistance. However, you may want to have DELWATCH keep track of multiple files with the same name in the same directory. This is done with the /B switch. /B can be used to specify that DELWATCH should track anywhere from one to 65,535 files with the same name in the same directory. The following command tells DELWATCH to track up to five deleted files that have the same name in the same directory on the C: drive:

```
DELWATCH C: /B:5
```

Note that this tracks up to five deleted files with the same name in each directory on drive C:. If the /B switch is not used, the default value is one. Even if /B is not used, you may be able to recover multiple files with the same name, depending on how much disk activity there has been since the earlier deletions occurred.

To avoid having the disk fill up with deleted files, and to place a reasonable limit on how long pending deleted files will be kept on the disk, the /F switch is used to specify the maximum number of files that will be saved as pending deletes. When this maximum is reached, DELWATCH deletes the oldest pending delete file when another file is deleted. The following command instructs DELWATCH to save up to 100 pending delete files on drive C:

```
DELWATCH C: /F:100
```

You may specify anywhere from one to 65,534. Specifying 65,535 tells DELWATCH to save all pending delete files until the disk is full. When the disk becomes full, DELWATCH will then start deleting the oldest pending delete files to make room for new ones. If you want DELWATCH to save all pending delete files, and not make room for new ones even if the disk becomes full, then the word ALL should be used in place of a number. When ALL is specified, the /B switch is ignored (if it was used).

The /F command behaves a little differently for files in the root directory than in other directories. This is because the root directory has a limit to the number of files that can be stored in it, unlike other directories. Most hard disks have root directories that can store up to 512 files. Consequently, if the root directory becomes full, pending delete files will be removed from it even if the limit specified by /F has not been reached. The only exception to this is when /F:ALL has been used.

In this case, pending delete files are never removed, even from the root directory, except by the DELPURGE command.

If /F is not specified, the default value is 200 for a hard disk and 20 for a floppy disk.

As mentioned earlier, DELWATCH will automatically install itself in upper memory if possible. Otherwise, it installs itself in lower memory. When DELWATCH goes into lower memory it reduces the amount of memory available for running programs by about 5K. It may be more desirable not to use DELWATCH than to have it take memory away from applications. Consequently, The /MU switch is used to tell DELWATCH to load itself only if upper memory is available. If no upper memory is available, then DELWATCH does not load. You must be sure a device driver that supports upper memory, such as EMM386.SYS, is loaded before attempting to use the /MU switch.

The opposite of /MU is /ML. Under some circumstances it may be more desirable to load DELWATCH into low memory. For example, you may have another program that will make better use of upper memory than DELWATCH, and there may not be enough upper memory available for both of them. In this case, the /ML switch forces DELWATCH to load itself into lower memory, even if upper memory is available.

The /S switch is used to review the status of DELWATCH. Entering the command DELWATCH /S when it is installed for drive C: will display a message similar to the following:

```
DELWATCH installed.
Drive C: enabled
0 clusters occupied by pending delete files
20323 unused clusters
```

This tells you that DELWATCH is currently installed in memory, that it is tracking deletions on drive C:, that there is currently no space occupied by pending delete files, and that there are 20323 clusters available on drive C:. If DELWATCH were disabled (using the /D switch), then DELWATCH /S would simply produce the message "DELWATCH installed,"but would not give any statistics.

Table 6.13 Switches Used with DELWATCH Command

Switch	***Effect***
/B:nnn	Sets the number of files with the same name in the same directory to save as pending delete files. The default value is 1.
/D	Disables DELWATCH for the specified drive(s). No other switches can be used with /D.
/E:ext[+ext...]	Tells DELWATCH to save all deleted files as pending deletes, except for those specified by the extensions. Up to 10 extensions may be specified.
F:nnn|ALL	Determines the maximum number of files that DELWATCH will save as pending delete files. nnn may be anywhere from 1 to 65,534. 65,535 specifies that the disk capacity is the limit at which to start removing pending deletes to make room for new ones. ALL specifies no limit, and pending deletes are never removed, even if the disk becomes full.
/ML	Forces DELWATCH to load into low memory, even if high memory is available.
/MU	Forces DELWATCH to load into high memory. If insufficient high memory is available, DELWATCH does not load.
/O:ext[+ext...]	Tells DELWATCH to save only deleted files that have the specified extensions. All other files are deleted as though DELWATCH were not loaded. Up to ten extensions may be specified.
/S	Displays the current status of DELWATCH.

DELWATCH is an external command.

The DELPURGE command is used to actually delete files that have been marked as pending deletes by DELWATCH. When the DELPURGE command is entered, it searches the current or specified directory for pending delete files and displays their directory information and the date and time of deletion, and asks whether you want to remove them. Answering Y causes them to be removed.

When DELPURGE removes a file, it does two things to the directory entry for the file: it changes the cloverleaf symbol in the first character to a Greek Sigma, which tells DOS that the file has been deleted, and it also changes the third byte following the filename in the directory to a Greek Sigma, which tells the UNDELETE program that this file has been removed by DELPURGE and therefore cannot be undeleted. Recall that DR DOS changes the third byte following the filename to the first character of the file when deleting the file. If you need to recover a file that has been removed by DELPURGE, you may be able to do so using a third-party file recovery program, such as the one that comes with the *Norton Utilities*, since these programs work only with the filename itself in the directory, and do not rely on the third byte following the name for the first letter. Instead, they prompt you to provide the first letter of the filename.

To remove all pending delete files in the current directory, enter the command DELPURGE by itself. This will cause DELPURGE to search the directory for pending delete files. For each one, you will be prompted as to whether or not you want the file removed. When DELPURGE is done, it will display statistics regarding the total number of files removed, and the total number of bytes occupied by those files. The display will be similar to that in Figure 6.12.

```
Pending Delete Directory entries matching: a:\*.*
mary1.let   -a-    566 9-03-91 9:27a ( Deleted 10-15-91 12:19p )
  ...Removed
mary2.let   -a-    191 8-05-91 10:18a ( Deleted 10-15-91 12:19p )
  ...Removed
total entries removed 2 (2 found)   total bytes removed 757
```

Figure 6.12 Sample Results of DELPURGE Command

There are several switches that can be used with DELPURGE to make it easier to use. These are summarized in Table 6.14.

Table 6.14 Switches Used with DELPURGE Command

Switch	***Effect***
/A	Removes pending delete files that match the file specifier, without prompting first.

Table 6.14 continued ...

Switch	**Effect**
/D:date	Removes files before the specified date.
/D:-nn	Removes files deleted before the last nn days. nn is an integer number.
/L	Lists pending delete files that match the file specifier, but does not remove them.
/P	Causes the display to pause after each screenful of information, until a key is pressed.
/S	Removes files in subdirectories of the specified directory.
/T:time	Removes files deleted before the specified time. This is normally used in conjunction with the /D:date or /D:nn switch.

The UNDELETE command recovers files that have been deleted with the DELETE command or by a program such as a word processor. If you are unfamiliar with the DISKMAP, DELWATCH, and DELPURGE commands, and with the mechanics of how files are deleted, you should review the preceding material on those commands. The discussion that follows assumes you are familiar with that material.

There are three sources of information that UNDELETE can use to recover a deleted file. In order of usefulness, they are: information from the DELWATCH program, information from the DISKMAP program, and information from the directory and FAT on the disk. If DELWATCH was loaded when the file was deleted, and DELPURGE was not used to remove the file, then recovery is certain because the file is still intact on the disk. If DELWATCH was not loaded, but DISKMAP was run prior to deleting the file, then there is a good chance the file can be recovered. Success will depend on how much disk activity has occurred since the file was deleted. If the space occupied by the file on the disk has not been overwritten by another file, recovery will be successful, otherwise it will not.

If no DISKMAP file is present, UNDELETE uses the information in the current directory to attempt to identify and recover deleted files.

If little or no disk activity has occurred since the file was deleted, and it is small and is stored in one cluster on the disk, or if it is stored in contiguous clusters, then prospects are good that UNDELETE will be able to recover it. On the other hand, if the file is large and the disk is highly fragmented, recovery may not be possible.

To recover a single file, enter the UNDELETE command, with the file name passed as a parameter. A drive and/or directory specifier may precede the file name. The following command tells UNDELETE to recover all files with a LET extension in the root directory of the current drive:

```
UNDELETE \*.LET
```

What happens after this command is entered depends on whether or not DELWATCH or DISKMAP information is available. Suppose there are three files that have LET extensions: MARY1.LET, MARY2.LET, and MARY3.LET. If DELWATCH information is available for MARY1.LET, only DISKMAP information is available for MARY2.LET, and neither is available for MARY3.LET, then a separate message will appear for each file. After the three files are recovered, the screen will appear similar to that in Figure 6.13.

```
Directory entries matching: a:\*.let

The following files can definitely be recovered using Delwatch.

mary1.let       -a-         566 9-03-91 9:27a
...Recovered

The following files will be recovered using Diskmap. However you
should check the files contents after they have been recovered to
ensure they are correct.

mary2.let       -a-         191 8-05-91 10:18a
...Recovered

WARNING: The following files will be recovered unaided, without
assistance from either Delwatch or Diskmap. You should therefore
check the file contents after they have been recovered.

mary3.let       -a-         59 3-25-91 11:49a
...Recovered (check file)

total entries undeleted 3 (3 found)   total bytes recovered 816

A:\>
```

Figure 6.13 UNDELETE Message for the Three Types of File Recovery

If there is already a file in the specified directory with the name of the one being recovered, UNDELETE prompts you to enter a new name.

If you do not want to be prompted for confirmation before a file is undeleted, the /A switch may be used. In this case, UNDELETE recovers all files that match the filename specification, without prompting you for confirmation.

If you are using UNDELETE in interactive mode, as discussed below, then the /B switch may be used to force it to display in monochrome. Otherwise, colors are used.

You may also use the UNDELETE command to list files that would be undeleted, without actually undeleting them. This is done with the /L switch. The directory entries are displayed for each file that would be undeleted, but the method that would be used for undeleting is not indicated.

The /D:date switch can be used to recover or list all files that were marked as pending deletes by DELWATCH, and whose date stamp is on or after the specified date. For example, to list all deleted files for which there is DELWATCH information is available, and whose date stamp is on or after 10-1-91, the following command would be used:

```
UNDELETE *.* /L/D:10-1-91
```

You may also request UNDELETE to list or recover all files for which DELWATCH information is available, and whose date stamp is within a certain number of days of the current date. For example, the following command tells UNDELETE to recover all files that were deleted while DELWATCH was active, and whose date stamps are within 100 days of the current date:

```
UNDELETE *.* /D:-100
```

You may also specify a time stamp for the files to be recovered, providing the files were deleted when DELWATCH was active. The following command instructs UNDELETE to recover all files for which DELWATCH information is available, providing their date stamp is on or after 10-1-91, and their time stamp is later than 14:30:30 (30 seconds past 2:30 PM):

```
UNDELETE *.* /D:10-1-91/T:14:30:30
```

The /P switch may be combined with any of the other switches to pause the display after each screenful.

By default, the UNDELETE command recovers files using whatever information is available. However, it is sometimes desirable to undelete only files that have a certain type of information available. For example, perhaps you know that there is DISKMAP information for the file you want to recover, but that DELWATCH information is not available. The /R switch is used to specify a recovery method. The syntax for the /R switch is:

```
UNDELETE filespec /R:method
```

The method may be any one of the following: DELWATCH, DISKMAP, or UNAIDED.

Normally, UNDELETE only looks in the current or specified directory for deleted files. However, you may want to tell it to search subdirectories of the specified directory as well. This is done with the /S switch.

The UNDELETE switches are summarized in Table 6.15.

Table 6.15 Switches Used with UNDELETE Command

Switch	***Effect***
/A	Causes UNDELETE to recover files without first prompting for confirmation.
/B	When UNDELETE is run in interactive mode, this switch forces it to display in monochrome rather than color.
/D:date	Recovers all pending delete files saved by DELWATCH whose date stamp is on or after the date specified.
/D:-nn	Recovers all pending delete files saved by DELWATCH whose date stamp falls within nn days of the current date.
/L	Lists the specified deleted files but does not recover them.
/P	Pauses the display after each screenful.

Table 6.15 continued ...

Switch	***Effect***
/R:method	Only recovers files using the indicated method, where the method is DELWATCH, DISKMAP, or UNAIDED.
/S	Recovers files from subdirectories of the specified directory, as well as from the specified directory.
/T:hh:mm:ss	Recovers all pending delete files saved by DELWATCH whose time stamp is on or after the time specified.

UNDELETE may also be used in interactive mode, using menus to select and recover files. To start UNDELETE in interactive mode, enter the command UNDELETE without any filenames or switches (the /B switch may be used to force black and white mode; no other switches may be used with UNDELETE in interactive mode). A screen similar to that in Figure 6.14 will appear.

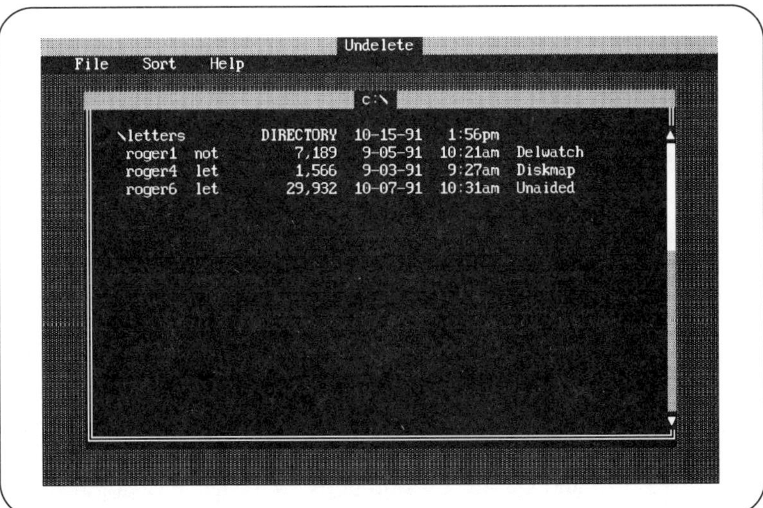

Figure 6.14 UNDELETE Screen in Interactive Mode

As seen in Figure 6.14, each deleted file in the current directory is shown, along with its directory information and the technique that

UNDELETE will use to recover it. You may undelete a file by highlighting it and pressing the Enter key. A dialog box will pop up to confirm that you want to recover the file—you may choose to cancel or to proceed with file recovery. You may also navigate through other directories on the disk by highlighting the directory names and pressing the Enter key. There are several menus on the UNDELETE screen that can assist in locating files and selecting them for recovery.

Holding down the Alt key and pressing the F key will pull down the File menu, shown in Figure 6.15.

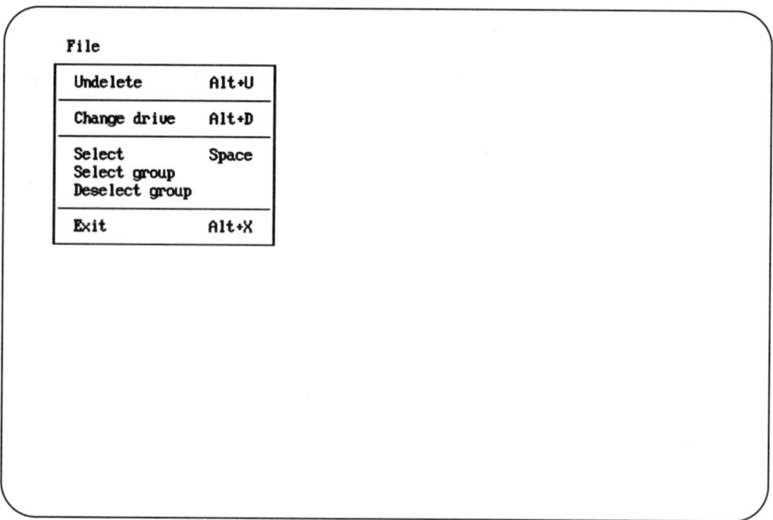

Figure 6.15 File Menu for UNDELETE Screen

The Undelete option, or Alt+U keys, is used to start the Undeletion process on selected files. Change drive, or Alt+D, allows you to switch to a different disk. The Select option, or Spacebar, is used to select the currently highlighted file. Select group pops up a dialog box that prompts you for the wild card file specifier to select a group of files, and Deselect group pops up the same dialog box for deselecting files. In this way you can quickly select a subset of the existing files. For example, to select all files except those with a LET extension, first use Select group to select all files, then use Deselect group to deselect those with a LET extension.

The Exit command is used to exit the UNDELETE program.

Holding down the Alt+S keys pulls down the Sort menu. This menu contains options for sorting the files that are displayed on the UNDELETE screen. The Sort menu appears in Figure 6.16.

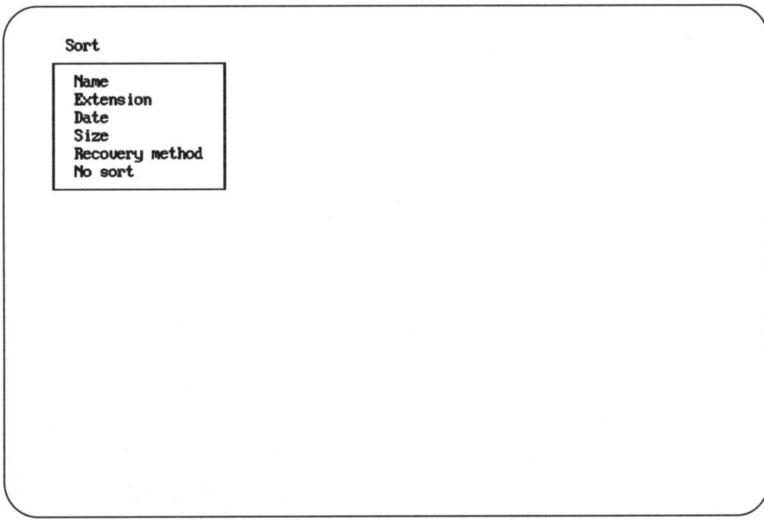

Figure 6.16 Sort Menu for UNDELETE Screen

Using the options on this menu you can rearrange the screen to have the files sorted by name, extension, date, size, or recovery method, or to display them in unsorted order.

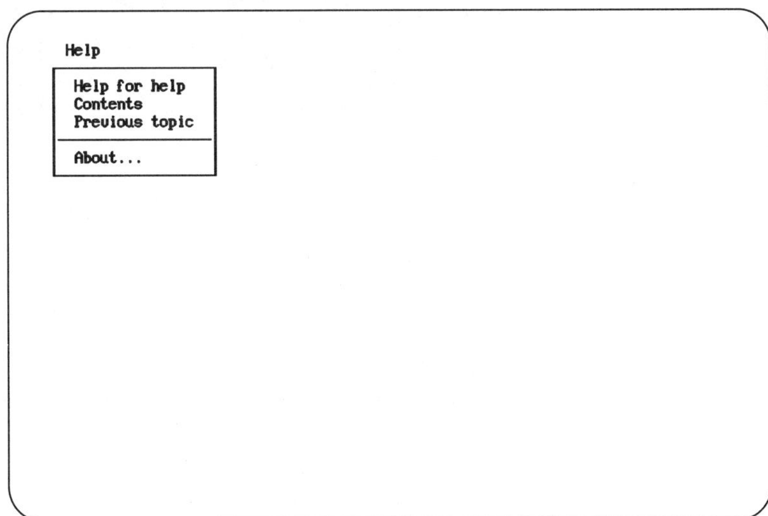

Figure 6.17 Help Menu for UNDELETE Screen

Holding down the Alt+H key will pull down the Help menu, shown in Figure 6.17.

The options on the Help menu provide on-line help for using UNDELETE interactively. The Help for Help option provides instructions on how to use the online help system. The Contents option provides a table of contents that can be used to select topics such as dialog box titles and menu titles. The Previous topic option takes you to the previously displayed Help screen.

When a Help screen is displayed, it appears as a window within the larger UNDELETE screen. The UNDELETE screen with the top portion of the help system table of contents displayed is shown in Figure 6.18.

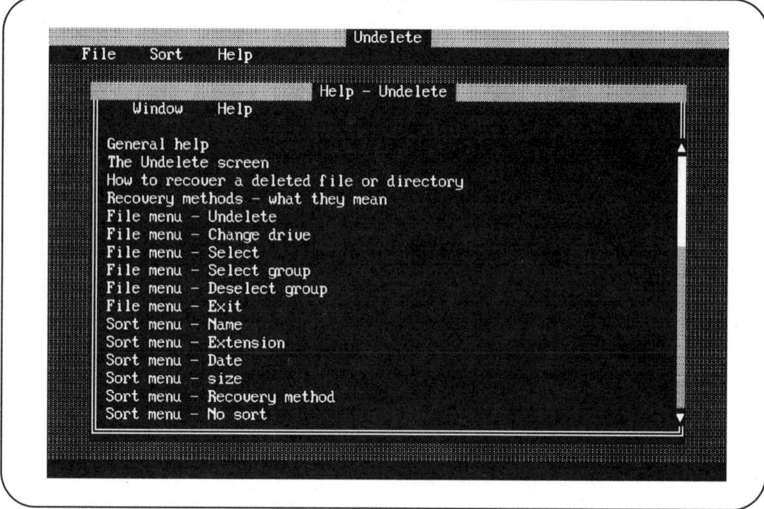

Figure 6.18 Table of Contents for UNDELETE Help System

When this screen is displayed, the Alt+W keys pull down the Window menu, shown in Figure 6.19.

The Resize option switches the HELP screen between being a window inside the UNDELETE screen to filling the entire screen, and vice versa. The Close Help window option returns you to the UNDELETE screen, as do the Alt+X and Esc keys.

The Help menu available from a Help screen is shown in Figure 6.20.

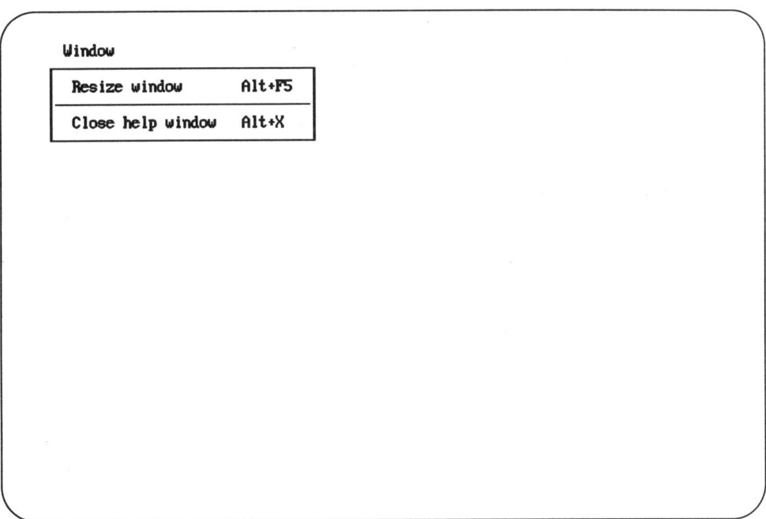

Figure 6.19 Window Menu for UNDELETE Help Screens

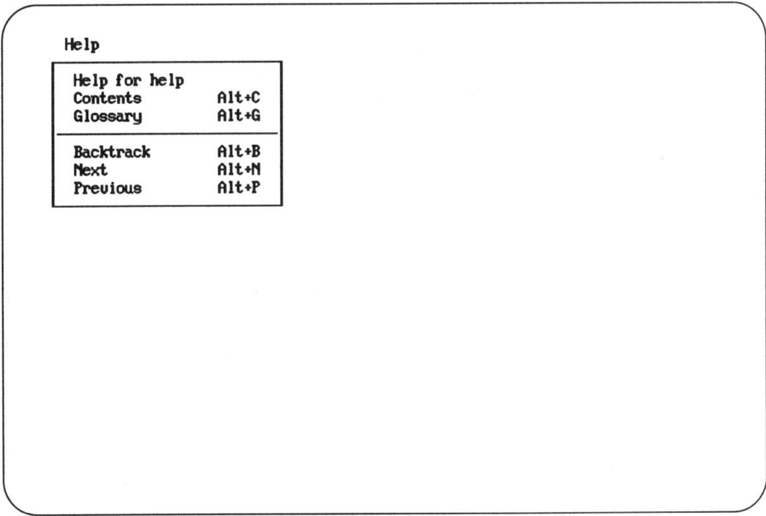

Figure 6.20 Help Menu for UNDELETE Help Screens

The Help for Help and Contents options are the same as the those described above. The Backtrack option takes you to the last Help screen you looked at, and the Next and Previous options take you to the next and previous screens in the order they exist in the program. The

Glossary option takes you into an on-line glossary of terms relevant to file recovery.

UNDELETE is an external command.

The RECOVER command extracts information from damaged disks. When a disk becomes damaged, either by physical stress or exposure to a magnetic field, parts of the files stored on it can be lost. Even though some disks are manufactured as having lifetime guarantees, all disks will fail, sooner or later. When this happens, one or more of the files on the disk becomes unreadable. DR DOS 6.0 therefore provides the RECOVER command to extract as much information as possible from these damaged disks. RECOVER cannot completely restore the parts of files that are written on damaged parts of the disk, but it can often restore the other parts of the file, both before and after the damaged area.

The root directory of a disk occupies a specific area of the disk. This area is set up when the disk is formatted and cannot be changed, so the root directory has a finite number of entries it can contain. The actual number of entries is dependent on the size and type of disk. (Root directory capacities are discussed in Chapter 7.)

This limitation on the number of entries in the root directory is significant for using the RECOVER command, because RECOVER always restores files to the root directory. Thus, if you attempt to recover more files than will fit in the root directory, you may permanently lose any files that RECOVER attempts to put into the root directory after it is full. Therefore, RECOVER must be used carefully. It is generally best to recover just one file at a time. That file can then be moved out of the root directory before recovering the next.

RECOVER should only be used when absolutely necessary, and it should never be used to undelete a file. If a program such as a word processor, spreadsheet, or database, cannot access a file it created, then the DOS COPY command should be tried. DOS can frequently copy a file that a program cannot read, and make the copy readable by the program. If this fails, then RECOVER may be your only hope. A more disastrous occurrence is the destruction of the root directory or FAT on a disk. When this happens, none of the files on the disk can be accessed, and they must all be recovered with the RECOVER command. However, if the files were lost due to an accidental FORMAT of the disk, it may be possible to recover them using the UNFORMAT command, discussed in Chapter 7. If UNFORMAT will work, it is preferable to RECOVER.

Some files are unusable after they have been recovered, because they will work only if the entire file is intact. This is generally true of binary files—those that end with BIN, COM, EXE, LIB, OBJ, or SYS extensions. In addition, many programs, such as most databases and spreadsheets, build internal linkages in their data files. These linkages maintain the relationships between various parts of the file, and are required for the program to use the file. Consequently, these programs often cannot work with a partially recovered file, since the missing part of the file will have contained linkages to other parts of the file. In this case, the program may be able to work with the first part of the file—up to the first broken link—or it may not be able to use the file at all. In this case, you are left with the choice of either attempting to view the file with a word processor, to extract what information you can manually, and re-enter it into a new data file, or throwing the file away and starting over again. The best candidates for partial recovery are plain ASCII text files, and word processing files.

There are commercial file recovery programs available from software dealers that provide more effective and complete tools for recovering files from damaged disks than the RECOVER command. These programs also include more powerful undelete tools than the UNDELETE command does. If you have an important file that must be recovered from a damaged disk, it may be worth investing in one of these packages.

There are two forms of the RECOVER command. The first is:

```
RECOVER filespec
```

Filespec identifies the file or files to be recovered. A drive identifier and directory may be included, but wild cards are not permitted. When a file is recovered, the sections of the file that are readable are pieced together and stored in a new file named FILE0001.REC, in the root directory. You can then copy this file to its original name, in its original directory, and attempt to use it with the program that created it.

The second form of the RECOVER command is:

```
RECOVER drive:
```

Drive refers to a drive letter. The colon is required. This form of the command is used when the FAT and/or root directory have been damaged, and you must recover all files on the disk. This is very risky, particularly with hard disks, since the root directory can hold only a limited number of files, and there may be more than that number on the disk. It is best to use the first syntax of the command to recover individual files, unless you are absolutely certain that the number of files on the disk does not exceed the maximum number that the root directory can hold. Capacities of root directories for different disk types are discussed in Chapter 7.

What happens to bad clusters after a file has been recovered? When RECOVER restores a file, it reads the file one cluster at a time. If the cluster is good, it copies the information in the cluster to the FILExxxx.REC file that it is building. If the cluster is damaged, RECOVER marks it as unusable in the FAT. When a cluster is marked as unusable in the FAT, DOS will not attempt to use that cluster. You can see how many bad clusters there are on a disk with the CHKDSK command. A few bad clusters are not cause for alarm; some hard drives actually come with a few clusters marked bad. But if a large percentage of your disk is ending up in bad clusters, you should have your computer (or the disk) checked for a malfunction.

RECOVER does not work on drives that have been affected by the ASSIGN, JOIN, and SUBST commands, or on network drives.

RECOVER is an external command.

The REPLACE command replaces files on one disk or directory with files of the same name on another disk or directory. Several switches let you control how files are replaced. The most common use of REPLACE is to replace files on one disk or directory with more recent versions of the same files on another disk or directory. If there are multiple copies of a file in different directories of a disk, REPLACE can replace each of them with an updated copy in one step. REPLACE can also add files that appear on one disk or directory to another disk or directory on which they do not appear. REPLACE is a safer way to maintain a disk with backup copies of files than the COPY command, since REPLACE can be set to only overwrite older copies of a file.

The simplest form of the REPLACE command is:

```
REPLACE source target
```

Source is the source file that will replace the target file. Drive letters, directory paths, and wild cards may all be used in the source and target specifiers. For example, the following command replaces a file named ROBERT1.LET in the current directory of drive A: with a file of the same name in the \ WP \ LETTERS \ PERSONAL directory of the C: drive:

```
REPLACE C:\WP\LETTERS\PERSONAL\ROBERT1.LET A:
```

This command replaces the file on drive A: with the file on drive C: regardless of the date and time stamps on the two files. When it is finished, REPLACE displays the message "1 file(s) replaced."

If the source file does not exist on the target drive, the source file is not copied. REPLACE displays the message "No files replaced" instead. The REPLACE command can be used to add files to a drive or directory on which they do not already exist by using the /A switch. Appending /A to the above command would cause the file on drive C: to be copied to the A: drive, but only if there was no file with the same name already on the A: drive. In this case, REPLACE displays the message "1 File(s) added."

The /U switch enables you to replace the target file only if it is older than the source file. Appending /U (for Update) to the above command would cause the file on drive A: to be replaced with the file on drive C: if, and only if, the file on drive C: were more recent than the file on drive A:. REPLACE determines which file is more recent by comparing the date and time stamps of the two files. /A and /U cannot both be used on the same command line.

When replacing a large number of files with one command, it is sometimes desirable to have REPLACE prompt you for confirmation before replacing each file. This is accomplished with the /P switch. The following command replaces all files with an extension of LET on drive A: with more recent versions of the correspondingly named files on the C: drive, and prompts you for confirmation before each replacement:

```
REPLACE C:*.LET A: /U /P
```

For each file that matches the source specification, REPLACE displays the file name, followed by a (Y/N)? prompt. Pressing N causes REPLACE to skip the file, while pressing Y causes it to replace the file. When REPLACE is done, it displays a count of the actual number of files replaced.

If you attempt to replace a file whose Read-only attribute is set on the target drive, REPLACE displays the message "filespec...access denied" where filespec is the target file specifier. REPLACE then terminates and does not process any more files identified by the source specifier. If you want REPLACE to replace Read-only files, the /R switch can be used. This switch should be used with caution, since files are typically marked read-only specifically to prevent them from being overwritten or deleted.

Sometimes there are multiple copies of a file in various subdirectories on a disk, and you want to update all of those copies with a single copy on another disk and/or directory. This can be done with the /S switch. The following two commands demonstrate this. The first updates all files named SALES.RPT in all directories of the C: drive with a file of the same name in the A: drive. The second updates all files named ROBERT1.LET in the C: \ WP \ LETTERS directory, and all of its subdirectories, with a file of the same name in the A: drive.

```
REPLACE A:ROBERT.LET C:\ /S
REPLACE A:ROBERT.LET C:\WP\LETTERS /S
```

The /S switch cannot be used with the /A switch, and it does not search subdirectories on the source drive.

If you are using a floppy drive for either the source or target, or both, the /W switch can be used to cause REPLACE to wait until you press a key. The /W switch is most often used when REPLACE is used in a batch file. The following command replaces all files on the A: drive that have a BAT extension, with the corresponding files on the C: drive, and instructs REPLACE to pause until a key is pressed before starting to copy files:

```
REPLACE C:*.BAT A: /W
```

When this command is entered, REPLACE displays the message "Press [Enter] to begin copying file(s)...." When a key is pressed, REPLACE begins searching the source for the specified files.

REPLACE does not normally copy files whose Hidden and/or System attributes are turned on. If you want to copy Hidden or System files, the /H switch should be used.

The /M switch is used to copy files that have changed since their last backup, providing the copies on the target have not changed since the last backup. For example, suppose that the C:\WP\LETTERS directory contained the files MARY.LET, ROGER.LET, and BILL.LET, and that BILL.LET already exists on the disk in drive A:. If the Archive attribute is turned on for MARY.LET and off for ROGER.LET, indicating that MARY.LET has changed since the last backup but ROGER.LET has not, then the following command will copy MARY.LET to drive A:

```
REPLACE C:\WP\LETTERS\*.LET A: /M
```

This command copies MARY.LET to the A: drive because it does not already exist there, and its Archive attribute is turned on. ROGER.LET is not copied because its Archive attribute is turned off, indicating it has not changed since the last backup. BILL.LET will be copied regardless if the following two conditions are met: its Archive attribute is turned on, and the Archive attribute for the BILL.LET file on the A: drive is turned off. The requirement that both of these conditions are met assures that files that have been changed will be copied, but only if they do not overwrite files that may have been changed themselves on the target.

The /N switch is used to display what the effects of the REPLACE command will be, without actually executing it.

The switches for the REPLACE command are summarized in Table 6.16.

Table 6.16 Switches Used with the REPLACE Command

Switch	***Effect***
/A	Copies only files that do not already exist on the target.
/II	Includcs filcs with Hidden and/or System attributes set.
/M	Merges changed files on the source with unchanged files on the target.
/N	Shows what the effects of the command will be, without actually executing it.
/P	Prompts you before copying each file.
/R	Overwrites Read-only files on the target.
/S	Replaces files in subdirectories of the specified target directory.

Table 6.16 continued ...

Switch	Effect
/U	Replaces only files on the target that are older than those on the source.
/W	Causes REPLACE to wait for a key to be pressed before continuing—usually used to provide an opportunity to insert a new disk.

REPLACE is an external command.

The VERIFY command adds an extra measure of protection to the process of storing information on a disk. The VERIFY command is actually a switch: it turns disk write verification on and off. Verification is off when you start your computer, until a VERIFY ON command is entered. There are three forms of the VERIFY command:

```
VERIFY
VERIFY ON
VERIFY OFF
```

The first form of the command responds with a message that indicates the status of verification: "VERIFY is on" or "VERIFY is off." The second form turns it on, and the third form turns it off.

When verification is on, every time anything is written to the disk, DOS double checks to make sure it can be read. If a sector has become damaged on the disk, but has not yet been marked as bad, DOS will normally go ahead and use the sector. You may not find out it was bad until you try to retrieve information from it. With VERIFY on, DOS will recognize a bad sector and will not write to it.

Having VERIFY on significantly slows the disk performance of a computer, so in general it is best to leave it off. However, for critical processes, it can be worth turning it on. A prime example is the use of the BACKUP command. Since backup files are your only source of recovery from disasters, it is essential that they be readable. Consequently, it is a good idea to turn VERIFY on before using BACKUP.

VERIFY is an internal command.

File Security—The PASSWORD Command

The PASSWORD command is used to assign passwords to files and directories. A password can be up to eight characters long. When entered by itself, the password command lists the passwords assigned to files in the current directory. There are three levels of password protection that can be assigned to a file. The first is Delete protection, which means the password must be used in order to delete the file, to rename it, or to change its attributes. However, files protected with a Delete password can be read and modified without the password.

The second level of password protection is Write protection. Files protected with a Write password can be read without the password, but it is required to modify the file, to rename it, to change its attributes, or to delete it.

The highest level of password protection is Read protection. Files protected with a Read password cannot be read, modified, or deleted, without the password.

To assign a password to a file, the following syntax is used:

```
PASSWORD filespec switches
```

You may assign the same password to groups of files using wild cards in the filespec, or by using a filelist for the filespec.

Switches are used for a variety of purposes, including setting the level of protection. The /R: switch specifies a Read password, /W specifies a Write password, and /D specifies a Delete password. For example, the following command assigns the Read password SECRET to a file named MARY.LET:

```
PASSWORD MARY.LET /R:SECRET
```

DR DOS responds with the following message:

```
rwd  c:mary.let
```

The "rwd" means that read, write, and delete protection has been assigned. If /W had been used, the message would appear as follows:

```
-wd  c:mary.let
```

When you enter the PASSWORD command, the password you assign appears on the screen, so it is a good idea to use the CLS command to clear the screen immediately after entering the password. Alternatively, the following batch file can be used to assign passwords:

```
ECHO OFF
CLS
PASSWORD %1 %2
```

If this file were named SETP.BAT, then the following command would assign the Read password SECRET to the file MARY.LET:

```
SETP MARY.LET /R:SECRET
```

The advantage of using SETP.BAT is that it clears the screen before executing the PASSWORD command, so the password you type is only on the screen briefly. The disadvantage, however, is that you won't see any typing errors. For example, if the command were entered as SETP MARY.LET /R:SECTET, you may not notice the error because it would be cleared from the screen as soon as you pressed the Enter key. You would then be unable to access the file.

Once a file is password-protected, you will not be able to access the protected rights (read, write, delete) unless you enter the password for the file. How you enter the password depends on how you want to access the file. Some DOS commands, such as the ATTRIB command, will prompt for a password. For example, entering the command ATTRIB +R MARY.LET will result in the following prompt:

```
c:\mary.let ...file password?
```

When you enter the password, DOS echoes your keystrokes with asterisks (*) rather than the characters you are typing. This allows you to see how many characters you have typed, but does not reveal the password itself.

If you are using a DOS command that does not prompt for a password—which is most DOS commands—you can append the password to the filename, separated by a semi-colon. For example, if the file MARY.LET had the Read password SECRET assigned to it, then the following command would display the contents of MARY.LET on the screen:

```
TYPE MARY.LET;SECRET
```

If you do not include the password, or use the wrong password, DOS responds with the message "Invalid password" and does not execute the TYPE command.

Again, it is a good idea to enter a CLS command to clear the screen after the command is executed, in order to prevent unauthorized users from seeing the password. Alternatively, the following simple batch file can be used to enter DOS commands for files with passwords. The batch file takes the DOS command, the filename, and the password as parameters, and clears the screen before executing the command:

```
ECHO OFF
CLS
%1 %2;%3
```

If this file were named GO.BAT, then the following command would execute the TYPE command for the file MARY.LET, with the password SECRET:

```
GO TYPE MARY.LET SECRET
```

When this command executes, the screen is cleared, then the contents of MARY.LET are displayed on the screen. The GO.BAT file will work with any DOS command that accepts a single file specifier as its parameter. A similar batch file could be constructed for commands that accept two file names:

```
ECHO OFF
CLS
%1 %2;%3 %4
```

This batch file takes the DOS command as the first parameter, the first filename as the second parameter, the password for the first filename as the third parameter, and the second filename as the fourth parameter. For example, if this file were named GO2.BAT, then the following command would copy a password-protected file named MARY.LET, with the password SECRET, into a nonpassword-protected file named MARY1.LET:

```
GO2 COPY MARY.LET SECRET MARY1.LET
```

It can become a nuisance to have to enter a password for every file you want to access, so DR DOS provides the ability to set a *global password.* A global password is a password that DOS remembers as long as the computer remains running, unless you specifically turn it off. Every time a password protected file is accessed, whether by a DOS command or a software program, DR DOS automatically checks the file's password against the global password. If it matches, you are granted access to the file without having to enter the password. The /G switch is used to enter a global password. The following command sets the global password to SECRET:

```
PASSWORD /G:SECRET
```

After this command is entered, any file with the password SECRET can be accessed without entering the password. Files with other passwords will still require that their passwords be entered before they can be accessed.

The global password also makes it possible to access a password-protected file from a software program. Software programs themselves are oblivious to passwords, so passwords are handled entirely by DOS. You cannot append a password to a filename that is passed as a parameter to a software program, because the program won't know what to do with it. For example, if your word processor is started with the command WP, the following command would not work to load the file MARY.LET into your word processor:

```
WP MARY.LET;SECRET
```

However, if the global password is set to match the file's password, then DR DOS will automatically handle the password checking without the program ever being aware of it. In this case, the following command would start your word processor and load the MARY.LET file:

```
WP MARY.LET
```

You must be cautious when using passwords on files that may be accessed by software programs. When a password is assigned to a file, the Hidden attribute is turned on, so most software programs won't even know the file exists unless the global password matches the file's password. When DOS encounters a password-protected file, it ignores the Hidden attribute, so that the file still shows up in DIR listings, but software programs will not ignore it. However, the hidden attribute is rarely used on data files for software programs, so some programs will actually create a new file with the same name as a hidden file, overwriting the hidden file. If this happens the contents of the hidden file are lost. The new file will not have a password assigned to it. To guard against this happening, you should test your software programs to see how they handle password-protected files before using passwords on their data files. It is wise to test their behavior with and without the global password set.

You may set a password for directories as well as for files. When a directory has a password assigned to it, you cannot change to the directory or access any of its files without the password. To set a password for a directory, the /P switch is used. Directory passwords always assign full Read protection to the directory. The following command assigns the password SECRET to the \WP\LETTERS directory:

```
PASSWORD \WP\LETTERS /P:SECRET
```

To change to a directory that has a password assigned to it, append the password to the directory name:

```
CD \WP\LETTERS;SECRET
```

Alternatively, to protect the password from being seen by unauthorized users, the GO.BAT file described above may be used:

```
GO CD \WP\LETTERS SECRET
```

This will clear the screen before changing directories.

The /S switch may be used to set the same password to all files in the current directory, as well as to all files in any subdirectories of the current directory. For example, suppose that the \WP directory has a subdirectory named LETTERS, and that LETTERS has a subdirectory named PERSONAL. Assuming that WP is the current directory, the following command assigns the Read password SECRET to all files that have a LET extension in the \WP, \WP\LETTERS, and \WP\LETTERS\PERSONAL directories:

```
PASSWORD /R:SECRET /S
```

Just as there are switches for assigning passwords, there are several switches for removing passwords. You will always be prompted for the current password before it is removed. The /N switch is used to remove all passwords from files in the current directory. This switch can be used with /S to remove passwords from all files on a disk:

```
PASSWORD /N /S
```

If the current directory is the root when this command is entered, the PASSWORD program scans every file on the disk. Whenever it encounters one with a password, it prompts you for the password for that file.

The /NP switch removes the password from a directory, and the /NG switch removes the global password. For example, suppose the global password is set to SECRET. Entering the command PASSWORD/NG will remove the global password. This is the only /N switch that does not prompt you for the password. It does not need to, because the global password is simply stored temporarily in memory for comparing to file passwords.

PASSWORD is an external command.

Commands to Create, Delete, and Navigate in, Directories

Since directories are central to the management of files on a PC, DR DOS 6.0 provides a variety of commands for managing directories, and for moving quickly from one directory to another.

The CHDIR, or CD, command is a navigation command that changes the current directory. The current directory for a drive is the one to which DOS refers whenever a command or program references the drive. Thus, by default, all read and write operations to a drive go the current directory in that drive, unless another directory is explicitly specified. CHDIR can be abbreviated to just CD, which is how it is usually used. There are three forms of the CD command:

```
CD
CD NEWDIR
CD DRIVE:NEWDIR
```

The first form of the command displays the current drive and directory. For example, if C: is the current drive, and the current directory is the root, the CD command will display the following:

```
C:\
```

Since most people set up their computer to display the current drive and directory as part of the prompt, this form of the command is usually used to quickly see what the current directory is for another drive. To see the current directory for the A: drive, the following command would be used:

```
CD A:
```

The second form of the command changes the current directory for the current drive. The following commands both assume that C: is the current drive, and that the current directory is C: \ GV. The first command changes the current directory to WP \ LETTERS, while the second changes the current directory to \ GV \ DATA:

```
CD \WP\LETTERS
CD DATA
```

It is worth analyzing how the CD command interprets the new path. CD always assumes that the current directory is the starting point, so that in the second command above, it knows that DATA is a subdirectory of the current (GV) directory. In the first command, however, the new directory path starts with a backslash, which indicates the root directory. So even though CD assumes that it should start with the current directory, the initial backslash says "Jump from the current directory to the root, then continue reading the new directory path from there." So an initial backslash can be used as a quick way to start from the root, if the new path is not in the same chain of directories as the current one. In fact, a quick way to change to the root directory is:

```
CD \
```

There is one other shorthand technique, which is used for changing to a directory that is above the current directory, but is in the same branch as the current one. This is the use of two periods to specify the immediate parent of a directory. The following commands demonstrate, assuming C: is the current drive and the current directory is \ WP \ LETTERS, and using the directory tree shown in Figure 6.2:

```
CD ..
CD ..\..
CD ..\BILLS
```

The first command changes the current directory to the C: \ WP directory. The second command changes the current directory to the root directory—the parent of the parent of the current directory. The third command changes the current directory to the C: \ WP \ BILLS directory—it first moves back to the parent of the current directory, then moves down to the BILLS directory.

DOS keeps track of a current directory for every drive on the computer. Thus, if you have a computer with a C: drive and an A: drive, DOS remembers the current directory for each of these drives independently. It is therefore possible to change the directory for a drive other than the current drive, without changing the current directory on the current drive. For example, suppose that the current directory on drive A: is the root, and the current directory on drive C: is C: \ WP \ LETTERS. You may want to access some files in the \ DATA directory on the A: drive. For referencing one or two files, it may be easy enough to simply add the path name to the command that references the file, but if you want to repeatedly access that directory, it is easier to change the current directory on A: to \ DATA. The following command accomplishes this:

```
CD A:\DATA
```

This command leaves the current directory on C: unchanged, but changes the current directory on the A: drive. Now, when a command or program references the A: drive, it will automatically look in the \ DATA directory, unless another directory is explicitly specified.

CD is an internal command.

The MKDIR, or MD, command creates a new directory. This command enables you to build the subdirectory structures used for organizing and managing files. MKDIR can be abbreviated as MD, which is how it is usually used.

The following command creates a new directory named NEW beneath the current directory:

```
MD NEW
```

As with the CD command, you may use a drive specifier and a directory path specifier to create subdirectories on disks and directories other than the current one. The same shorthand symbols as used with CD can be used with MD: backslash (\ ) for the root directory, and two periods (..) for a parent directory.

Directory names follow exactly the same rules as file names. While it is legal to include an extension on a directory name, it has become a convention never to do so. File names are discussed earlier in this chapter, in the section titled, *File Names*.

MD is an internal command.

The RMDIR, or RD, command is used to remove or delete an existing directory. The RMDIR directory can be abbreviate to RD, which is how it is usually used. The following command removes a directory named OLD from the current directory:

```
RD OLD
```

You may specify a drive and/or path to directories in locations other than the current directory of the current drive.

A directory must be empty before it can be removed. It may not contain any files or subdirectories. If you attempt to remove a non-empty directory, RD will respond with the message "Invalid path, not directory, or directory not empty." If this message appears, and the name you specified is indeed a directory, then you should make sure you have deleted all files from the directory. If there are files you want to keep, they can be copied to another directory before deleting them. If there are subdirectories, they must be emptied of all files and subdirectories and removed as well. If you believe you have completely emptied a directory, yet continue to get this message, there may be files in the directory whose Hidden and/or System attribute is on. Hidden and System files do not show up with a normal DIR command, so if these are the only files in the directory, it will appear to be empty. Furthermore, the DEL command cannot delete them. Using the DIR /A command will display these files, and the ATTRIB command can be used to turn off these attributes, so they can be deleted.

RMDIR is an internal command.

The RENDIR command is used for renaming directories. It is discussed above, in the section *Renaming Files and Directories*.

The PATH command sets the internal PATH that DOS will use to search for files. The *internal path* is a list of directories that DOS searches when you attempt to run a program or enter an external DOS command. DOS can only search the path for files that have BAT, COM, or EXE extensions, and then only when it is trying to execute them—when the file names have been entered as commands, not as parameters to another command. The PATH command is discussed in detail in Chapter 4.

DOS only keeps track of a single path, regardless of how many drives your computer has, so a single path may contain references to more than one drive. Be cautious when including a floppy drive in the path, since the specified directory may only exist on a single disk that may not be in the drive. All directories on the path should be available at all times.

The current path can be viewed by entering the PATH command by itself:

```
PATH
```

To change the path, enter the command PATH, followed by the list of directories that should constitute the new path. For example, the following command creates a path that contains the C:\WP\LETTERS, C:\GV, C:\, and C:\DRDOS directories:

```
PATH C:\WP\LETTERS;C:\GV;C:\;C:\DRDOS
```

Note that the directories are separated by a semicolon, and that there are no spaces between the directories. The semicolon is the only separator needed. The total number of characters in the PATH cannot exceed 127, so it is important to keep the PATH as concise as possible. If you find you cannot fit all of the necessary directories in 127 characters, you may use the SUBST command to assign a directory to a drive letter. The substituted drive letter may then be used in place of the complete directory name, thus shortening the path. However, beware that drives created by SUBST cannot be used with certain DOS commands, a few examples of which are BACKUP, RESTORE, and RECOVER. The APPEND command can also be used to effectively increase the length of the path, by using the /X:ON switch with APPEND. The SUBST and APPEND commands are discussed in detail in Chapter 7.

The existing path can be cleared completely, so that only the current directory is searched for executable files, by entering the following command:

```
PATH;
```

Regardless of what directories the path contains, DOS always searches the current directory before it searches any of the path directories. If there are two executable files in the same directory with the same name but different extensions, DOS will determine which to execute according to the following precedence: COM files are executed before EXE files, which are executed before BAT files. This precedence can be overridden by including the extension in the command. For example, if the current directory contained three executable files, named TEST.COM, TEST.EXE, and TEST.BAT, to execute the TEST.BAT file, you would enter the command TEST.BAT on the command line.

Since creating a new path destroys the old one, you must make sure any directories in the old path that you still want DOS to search are included in the new one. If you have a long path, and just need to add a single directory to it, it is a nuisance to have to retype the entire path. It is not possible to directly append a new directory to the existing path, but the following batch file allows you to do this:

```
SET PATH1=%PATH%
PATH=%PATH%;%1
```

This batch file uses the DOS environment variable named PATH, which contains the current path, and the batch file parameter %1, which contains the first parameter passed on the command line when the batch file is run, to reset the PATH with the command line parameter appended to it. If this file were named NEWPATH.BAT, then the following command would add a directory named \ DB to the path:

```
NEWPATH \DB
```

In this batch file, the old path is saved in an environment variable named PATH1, in case you need to restore it. Batch files are discussed in detail in Chapter 9.

Another consideration in creating a path is that the longer the path is, the longer it will take DOS to find files that are not in the current directory. DOS searches the path directories in the order they appear, so you can speed up the performance of your computer by placing the directories with frequently used programs early in the path.

PATH is an internal command.

Interrupting DOS Commands

DOS commands may be interrupted by holding down Ctrl and pressing either C or Break. Occasionally, Ctrl-Break will work where Ctrl-C won't, but the reverse is never true, so Ctrl-Break is the best. This technique should not be used too freely, since interrupting a command can leave behind partial files, which you might later think are usable. For example, interrupting the BACKUP and COPY command can result in incomplete file copying, so that only part of the file is backed up or copied. However, it is extremely useful to be able to interrupt a DEL *.* command that was entered by accident.

Advanced Topics

The information covered so far in this chapter is sufficient for the file and directory management requirements of most PC users. However, understanding in more detail how directories are actually configured, and what information they keep about each file, can enhance your use of the commands discussed earlier. The ATTRIB command is also presented in detail in this section.

How Files are Stored in Directories

For each file in a directory, the directory reserves 30 bytes of space, in which it stores the following eight items, in the order shown:

1. The file name, which occupies the first eight bytes. Thus, the file name can be up to eight characters long. When a file name has fewer than eight characters, its name is left-justified, with the rest of the eight bytes being filled with blanks.
2. The file extension, which occupies the next three bytes. Thus, the extension can be up to three characters long. When a file extension has fewer than three characters, it is left-justified, with the rest of the three bytes being filled with blanks. The period that separates the file name from the file extension is not stored. DOS uses the period when file names are entered to tell where the name ends and the extension begins.
3. The file attributes occupy the next byte. The attributes will be discussed later.
4. The next 10 bytes are reserved. They are not currently in use, but the developers of DOS recognize that additional space will be needed in the future, so they've reserved it now. That way, when more information is added to the directories in the future, directories created under today's version of DOS won't have to be reconstructed.
5. The next two bytes are reserved for the time stamp of the file. The time is recorded using a code that DOS interprets when it displays a directory listing.
6. The next two bytes are reserved for the date stamp of the file. The date is recorded using a code that DOS interprets when it displays a directory listing.
7. The next two bytes are reserved for the beginning FAT entry. This number indicates the cluster that is assigned to the first part of the file. Given the first cluster, the FAT can be used to build the chain of clusters that constitute the rest of the file.

8. The last four bytes are reserved for the file size. This allows files to grow to 4,294,967,295 bytes, which is one less than four gigabytes.

File attributes are special markers that DOS uses to determine how a file should be interpreted, and what access should be granted to it. An attribute can either be on or off. An attribute that is on is said to be *set*. If the attribute is on, the file is considered to have that attribute; otherwise it does not. Every file can have any of the following six attributes:

1. Read-only: When this attribute is set, the file cannot be deleted or modified. If an attempt is made to modify it, the message "access denied" is displayed. Files that are marked Read-only are generally files that are crucial for the performance of a program, and that should never be modified.
2. Hidden: When the Hidden attribute is set, the file is not displayed in normal DIR command listings, or when software programs display a directory listing. (Some software programs are designed to let you display directory listings that include hidden files, but most do not.) Hidden files are generally files that are so vital to a program's operation that it is considered best to not even let people know they are there. Hidden files are also sometimes used in copy-protection schemes—techniques that make it difficult to duplicate a file, thus preventing software piracy.

   When a file is hidden, it is treated as a Read-only file—if you know it's there, you can read it. Most programs will actually load and display a file that is marked as hidden, but if you attempt to save the file to the disk, an "Access denied" message will appear. It is interesting to set a file's Hidden attribute to on, then attempt to see it with a DIR command—it doesn't show up. But when you enter a TYPE command, its contents are displayed on the screen.
3. System: The System attribute indicates that a file is used as part of the operating system. Thus, when you install DR DOS 6.0 on a disk, there are two files placed on the disk with the

System attribute set: IBMBIO.COM and IBMDOS.COM. If you use the SYS command to create a boot disk, these files are transferred to that disk. A file with the System attribute set is treated as though the Hidden attribute is set. It does not show up in directory listings, and it cannot be modified. However, like a Hidden file, its contents can still be viewed, if you know it's there. Some software programs create files and turn on their System attributes, even though they are not a part of DOS. These programs are generally utilities that provide deletion and formatting protection that goes beyond the protection provided by DOS.

4. Volume Label: The Volume Label attribute is used to indicate that a file should not be treated as a normal file, but instead contains the volume label for the disk. When you enter a DIR command for a disk, say the C: drive, you will either see the message "Volume in drive C has no label," or "Volume in drive C is xxx," where xxx represents a volume label. A volume label may be up to 11 characters long. The 11 characters may seem like a strange number because numeric limits in computers are usually in powers of two, like 8, 16, 32, or 64. However, note that 11 is the total number of characters in a file name—eight for the name, and three for the extension. When a file has the VolumeLabel attribute set, DOS combines the name and extension to generate the volume label. There should only be one such file entry per disk, and it should appear only in the root directory. In this special case, the directory entry does not apply to a true file: there is no pointer to the first cluster in the FAT, and no space is reserved on the disk for the contents of this file. Unlike Read-only, Hidden, and System files, the Volume Label file cannot be viewed in any way: the file-handling commands will treat it as though it were not there. The only way to see any part of this file is to use the DIR and LABEL commands to display and change the label itself.

5. Subdirectory: The Subdirectory attribute tells DOS that the file is actually a subdirectory. Subdirectories are really just

files, which is why there is no limit to how many entries they can hold. But unlike most files, DOS requires their contents to have a very precise format, described earlier in this chapter in the section titled *Directories*.

6. Archive: The final attribute is the Archive attribute. This attribute keeps track of which files have been modified since their last backup. When a file is backed up, either using the BACKUP command, the XCOPY command with the /M switch, or a commercial backup utility, the Archive attribute is turned off, indicating that the file has been backed up. As soon as the file is modified in any way, DOS turns the Archive attribute back on, indicating that the file has changed.

You may be wondering how DOS manages to store six attributes, given that only a single byte is reserved for attribute settings. In general, a byte is considered the smallest unit of information that can be stored in a computer. But remember that a byte is actually eight bits, and that each bit can be either on or off. Each attribute setting is a single binary value, so it is possible to store up to eight attributes in this one byte. This leaves two unused attributes, and in fact there are two attributes reserved for future use.

While it is true that the computer must access an entire byte at a time, by using special binary operators built into the processor, it is possible to figure out how each bit in a byte is set. Thus, DOS can test each attribute bit individually, to determine the attribute settings for each entry in a directory.

Although each attribute has a particular meaning, DOS exercises no control over who can turn the Archive, Hidden, Read-only, and System attributes on and off, or which files can have which attributes set. Thus, you could create a file with your word processor, then mark it as a system file. The only attributes DOS maintains control over are the Label and Subdirectory attributes. This is wise, because if either of these attributes is set incorrectly you could damage the disk, resulting in the loss of important files.

The ATTRIB command can be used to view those attributes that you are allowed to adjust. The syntax is:

```
ATTRIB filename
```

For example, from the root directory of a bootable disk, you could enter the command ATTRIB IBMBIO.COM. The following response will appear:

```
SH   C:\IBMBIOS.COM
```

This indicates that the file is a System file, and that it is Hidden. The attributes that may appear to the left of a file name are: R for Read-only, H for Hidden, S for System, and A for Archive. The Volume Label and Subdirectory attributes do not appear, because you are not allowed to manipulate them.

The syntax for changing a file's attributes is as follows:

```
ATTRIB +/-x filename
```

Where the x stands for A, H, R, or S (for Archive, Hidden, Read-only, or System). The plus sign turns on the attribute, and the minus sign turns it off. Drive letters, directory paths, and wild cards may be used as part of the file name. You may also include all of the files in subdirectories of the specified directory that match the file specifier by using the /S switch. The following command turns off the Archive attribute in all files that have an extension of BAK in the C: \ WP \ LETTERS directory, and in all of its subdirectories:

```
ATTRIB -A C:\WP\LETTERS\*.BAK /S
```

The first byte of a file name has special meaning to DOS. When a file is deleted, this byte is changed from the first letter of the file name to an ASCII code 229 (E5h), which happens to be the Greek Sigma character. So if the first byte contains a legal file name character, DOS knows there's a file represented by this item. If it contains an ASCII 229, DOS knows the file has been deleted. There are three other possible values that DOS may store in the first character of a file name: an ASCII 5, which marks it as a pending delete; a period, which indicates that DOS is using that entry for some internal data it needs to maintain and manage the directory structure; or a zero, which indicates that the entry has never been used.

When a directory is created, it is allocated one cluster of disk space, just like any other file. However, unlike other files, this cluster is then initialized with blank directory entries. All of the entries in the directory are initialized to have a zero in the first byte of the file name. When files are added to a directory, DOS places them in the directory sequentially. Consequently, DOS can always tell when it has read the entire contents of a directory. It reads until it comes to the first entry for which the first byte of the file name is zero. This is the first entry that has not been used, and is therefore at the end of the directory. As the directory grows, additional clusters are allocated and initialized as needed to store more entries.

The MOVE command transfers a file from one directory to another, but it never actually moves the physical file, as long as the file remains on the same disk. Now that it is clear how directories store file information, it is easy to understand how this can be accomplished. All that MOVE does is copy the directory entry from the source directory to the target, then delete it from the source. Some software packages also include MOVE utilities that work the same way.

Understanding the Root Directory

For most purposes, the root directory can be considered the same as any another directory. But it is unlike other directories in three important ways: it is created during the formatting process, it is placed in a special region of the disk immediately following the File Allocation Table, and it has a fixed size—it cannot grow as it fills up—it can only hold a fixed number of entries. Most hard disks have a root directory large enough to hold 512 files, including subdirectories. 360K floppies have root directories that will hold 112 entries, including subdirectories. The rest of the directory structure grows out of the root directory.

Chapter 7

Understanding and Managing Disks

Disk drives store the information and programs that personal computers use. There is a growing variety of disk drives found on PCs, but all of them perform essentially the same task, and almost all of them do it in essentially the same way. This chapter discusses the different types of disk drives available, their physical and logical organization, and the DOS commands that can be used to configure and use them. This is a fairly technical subject, and for most users it isn't necessary to master it—many people who use computers have little or no understanding of this subject. On the other hand, the more completely you understand how your computer works, the better you will be able to use it to its full potential.

Even if you don't want to read the entire chapter, you should review the sections on the DISKOPT, FILELINK, and SUPERSTOR programs. These are very useful utilities that DR DOS 6.0 provides to improve the performance of your system.

What Disks Are and What They Do

Disks are the primary storage media for information on personal computers. They have two characteristics that make them ideal for this purpose: they are non-volatile, which means that the information on them does not go away when the computer is turned off, and they can be manufactured in portable forms, making it easy to transfer information from one computer to another.

The Physical Structure of Disks

Most disks today are magnetic, which means they use magnetic particles to store information. However, there are alternative technologies emerging. One of these is the optical disk. This is a disk that uses the recording principles developed for musical compact disks, also referred to as *compact discs*, or CDs. Optical disks are read and written using a laser beam, and information is stored on them as tiny distortions in a plastic medium. There are two advantages to optical disks: they can store an enormous amount of information on a small, portable disk, and they are not sensitive to magnetic fields, which can destroy the information on a magnetic disk. However, there are also two drawbacks to optical disks: they are expensive to manufacture in a way that allows them to be written to more than once, and they are still significantly slower than magnetic disks. As these limitations are overcome, optical disks may become the standard technology for information storage in personal computers.

For the rest of this chapter, the term *disks* is used to mean magnetic disks. Other technologies that are used to produce disks use the same logical organization as magnetic disks, since all of the disk-access logic in the computer depends on this organization. Therefore, much of the material in this chapter holds true for all types of disks, regardless of the type of media.

A computer disk is a flat, spinning plate coated with tiny magnetic particles. Reading and writing information on a disk uses the same principle that audio and video tape recording uses. The magnetic particles can be arranged in a particular order that reflects some information about the world. This is the recording process, or the *write* process in computer jargon—information is written to the disk by arranging the magnetic particles. Once this has been done, the order of the magnetic particles can be analyzed to reproduce the information. With video tapes, this is the playback process. With computer disks, it is the *read* operation—the information that was stored on the disk is read by the computer.

All of the information a computer works with is stored as a series of ones and zeros, or bits. This has been said elsewhere in this book, but bears repeating because it is the single most important fact to keep in mind when understanding how computers work. To a computer, everything is handled in terms of bits.

Disks store files. A file is simply a discrete chunk of information, much like a book. It has a beginning, a middle, and an end. There are various ways to organize information within a file, depending on what software program created the file. But how the file is organized internally is not important to the disk. What is important is where the file begins, where the middle parts are, and where it ends. In addition, the disk must be concerned with making sure the contents of the file are stored accurately. If the information that created the file began with the letter A, then the first byte of the file should contain an A. Almost everything on a disk is a file of one sort or another. The only things that are not files are some of the structures that the computer uses to manage the disk. These are discussed throughout the rest of this chapter.

Types of Disks

There are basically two kinds of magnetic disks: floppy disks and hard disks. The term *floppy disk* refers to any of the small, removable, relatively low-capacity disks. The common physical sizes for floppy disks are 5.25-inch and 3.5-inch. The term *floppy* stems from the 5.25-inch disks, which are somewhat flexible because they are enclosed in flexible plastic cases. The more recent 3.5-inch disks are enclosed in hard plastic cases. These disks have the advantages of being small enough to fit in a shirt pocket, being more rugged because of their stronger case, and having a higher storage capacity than the 5.25-inch disks.

For each size of floppy disk, there are two densities, *low-density* and *high-density*. For 5.25-inch disks there are five different capacities supported by DR DOS 6.0, depending on the number of sides of the disk that can be used and the density of the magnetic particles. For 3.5-inch disks there are three different capacities supported. Both sides of 3.5-

inch disks are always usable. The different sizes and capacities are shown in Table 7.1.

Table 7.1 Floppy Disk Capacities

Disk Size	***No. of Sides***	***Capacity***
5.25"	1	160K
5.25"	1	180K
5.25"	2	320K
5.25"	2	360K
5.25"	2	1.2M
3.5"	2	720K
3.5"	2	1.44M
3.5"	2	2.88M

The 160K, 180K, 320K, and 360K 5.25-inch disks, and the 720K 3.5-inch disk, all have a low density of magnetic particles, and are therefore used with low density drives. The 1.2M 5.25-inch and 1.44M 3.5-inch disks both have a high density of magnetic particles and require high density drives. The 2.88M 3.5-inch disk requires yet another type of drive, specially made to handle its very high capacity. High density disk drives can read and write both low and high density disks, but low density drives can only read and write low density disks. As costs on high density disks come down, low density disks are being used less frequently, and as 3.5-inch disk drives become more common, 5.25-inch disks are being used less frequently.

Unlike floppy disks, which can be easily removed, hard disks are permanently installed in the computer. They have two main advantages over floppy disks: they can store much more information, and they can move information to and from electronic memory much faster. Remember that the computer can only operate on information that has been copied from a disk into memory. Since the computer operates at electronic speeds, the mechanical process of reading from and writing to a disk is the slowest operation the computer performs. Because hard disks are extremely fast at reading and writing, compared to floppy disks, this speed increase alone is enough to justify their existence. Their large capacity is also essential for many of today's programs.

Hard disks come in many sizes. The smallest is 10 megabytes, but hard disks that small are rarely encountered anymore. Sizes today typically range from 20 to 650 megabytes and more.

DOS refers to disk drives by letters of the alphabet. If a computer contains two floppy drives, they are usually referred to as drive A and drive B. If a computer contains a hard drive, that drive is almost always referred to as drive C. If a computer contains only one floppy drive and a hard drive, the floppy drive is generally designated to be both A and B, while the hard drive is still drive C. Additional drives are referred to as D, E, F, etc. When specifying a drive, the letter is followed by a colon. Thus, you type A: to reference drive A.

The Logical Structure of Disks

Disks are physically simple—just platters with a magnetic coating. However, to store information accurately, in a way that the computer can understand and access, requires that a more complex logical structure be imposed on the physical structure.

Tracks, Cylinders, and Sectors

To provide a consistent pattern to where information is stored on a disk, the surface of a disk is divided into concentric circles, called tracks. The number of tracks on a disk depends on what type of disk it is. On a 1.44 meg floppy disk, the surface is divided into 80 tracks. The outermost track is referred to as track 0, and the innermost track is track 79. Thus, on a 1.44 meg floppy, there are 80 concentric circles, starting near the outer edge and ending near the center. The tracks are where information is actually stored on the disk.

To read and write information on a disk, some mechanism must be provided that can locate the tracks and sense the magnetic charge of the particles on them. This mechanism is called a read-write head, or just head for short. The head is attached to an arm that moves back and forth across the disk, positioning the head precisely over each track.

Since there are two sides to a disk, it makes sense to use both sides for storing information. The top side of the disk is side 0, and the bottom side is side 1. Therefore, there are 160 tracks on a 1.44 meg floppy disk—tracks 0 through 79 on side 0, and tracks 0 through 79 on side 1. The read-write head actually consists of two heads, one on each side of the disk. As the disk is used, information is written first to side 0, track 0, then to side 1, track 0, then to side 0, track 1, and so on. It makes sense to use the same track on both sides of the disk before moving on to the next track, because the slowest operation the disk performs is moving the head from one track to another. By going from side 0 to side 1, the head does not have to be repositioned.

When your disk malfunctions and someone says it needs alignment, what they mean is that the heads are no longer accurately positioning themselves over the tracks. They need to be re-aligned with the tracks, so that they can again read and write accurately.

If you imagine several rings stacked up on top of each other, they make a cylinder. Many hard disks use several disks. This is a relatively inexpensive and compact way to increase the amount of storage provided by a drive, since the only additional parts are the extra platters and heads. DOS treats the entire set of platters as one disk. For each disk, there is a pair of read-write heads attached to a moveable arm. The correspondingly numbered tracks on the two sides of the different disks are referred to together as a *cylinder*. Thus, on a 1.44 meg floppy disk, cylinder 0 consists of two tracks: track 0 on side 0, and track 0 on side 1. The number of platters on hard drives varies with the manufacturer and model of drive. Some have just one, while others have several.

On floppy disks, the head actually sits on the magnetic media. This restricts the speed at which the disk can rotate, and therefore the speed with which information can be transferred to and from the disk. On hard disks, the head floats on a thin layer of turbulent air created by the rotating disk. Since this layer is very thin, dust and other small particles could create problems, so they must be kept out. Hard disks are therefore manufactured in *clean rooms* and their assemblies sealed so that no particles can creep in after they leave the clean room. You should never attempt to disassemble a hard disk unit, though you may decide to install or remove the entire unit yourself.

When a disk drive performs a disk access operation (either a read or write), it must access a specific amount of information—it cannot arbitrarily read 10 bytes one time, and 50 the next. The ideal amount of information to be accessed at once would be enough so that most access operations would be accomplished in one step, but not so much that a lot of extra information was accessed. A full track generally contains too much information. To read and write entire tracks would make the disk drive very slow, and would usually require reading or writing much more information than is required by the computer. Tracks are therefore divided into units called *sectors* to provide a sensible size for reading and writing.

Most disks are manufactured to support a variety of sector sizes, so that they can be used with many different types of computers. The actual sector size used is set by the computer's operating system, during a process known as *low-level formatting*. All versions of the DOS operating system for IBM-compatible PCs use 512 byte sectors for both hard disks and floppy disks. Sector numbering starts with 1, so a disk that has 18 sectors per track will have sectors numbered from 1 to 18. Sector numbering starts over again for each track. 1.44 meg floppy disks have 18 sectors per track. On a hard disk, the number of sectors per track varies with size and type of disk; 17 sectors per track is common.

It is now apparent how the capacities of disks are determined: the number of bytes per sector, times the number of sectors per track, times the number of tracks, times the number of disk sides, gives the total number of bytes available on a disk. For example, consider the high density 3.5-inch floppy disk. It has 512 bytes per sector, 18 sectors per track, 80 tracks per side, and two sides. This gives the following calculation:

$$512 \times 18 \times 80 \times 2 = 1{,}474{,}560 \text{ bytes}$$

1,474,560 divided by 1,024 (the number of bytes in a kilobyte) gives 1,440 kilobytes. Since 1,000 kilobytes are referred to as a *megabyte* (or meg), these disks are referred to as 1.44 meg disks. Since the number of bytes per sector is fixed at 512, the three variables that allow manufacturers to create disks of different capacities are the number of sectors per track, the number of tracks per disk side (which is the same as the number of cylinders), and the number of physical platters per disk drive (which corresponds to the number of disk sides).

Interleave

So far, sectors have been discussed as though they are numbered sequentially around the disk, starting with one and, for a typical 40-megabyte hard drive, ending with 17. When DOS accesses the disk, say, to write a new file, it writes to sequentially numbered sectors. Thus, if sectors 9, 10, and 11 are all available, a 1,500-byte file will be written on those sectors. But think for a minute how the disk is operating: it is spinning at high speeds, with the head floating over the track. Now consider that DOS can only transfer data in 512-byte chunks—one sector at a time. So it transfers the first 512 bytes to sector 9, then goes back to the electronic memory to fetch the next 512 bytes. But if the computer's transfer time is not fast enough, by the time DOS has retrieved the next 512 bytes from memory and is ready to write to sector 10, that sector has flown by. So now DOS must wait until sector 10 comes around again. This slows down the computer considerably. To write all 17 sectors of a track would require 17 revolutions of the disk.

To get around this problem, sectors are not always numbered sequentially. Instead, the sequence of numbers may proceed to every other sector, so that the physical third sector is sector number two, the physical fifth sector is sector number 3, and so on. Only when the numbering gets back to sector one does the second physical sector get assigned a number. This scheme is called *interleaving*; when every other sector is numbered sequentially, it is referred to as a *2:1 interleave*. If every third sector is numbered sequentially, it is a *3:1 interleave*. Matching the interleave of a drive to the speed at which its computer can transfer data to it is a critical part of designing computers—and one that is not always done correctly.

Disk Performance

When discussing disk drives, particularly hard disks, you will often hear reference made to the *speed* of the disk. This term refers to the average access time, and is measured in milliseconds. It is one of the critical measurements of a disk drive's performance, and is often considered to be as important as the capacity of the disk.

Average access time refers to the amount of time it takes the drive, on the average, to move the head from its current position, to the track you want to access. If the head always started at one edge of the disk, then the average access time would be the time it takes to travel across half of the tracks, since half of the tracks would be less than half way away, and half would be more. If it always started at the middle of the disk, then the average access time would be the time required to move across one quarter of the tracks. However, neither of these numbers is accurate because there is no telling where the head is going to be, before a particular access request. The average access time is actually taken to be the time it takes to move across one-third of the tracks. This number bears out in testing as an accurate measure of average access time.

The average access time of hard disks varies tremendously, from less than 10 milliseconds, to over 100. Generally, a time in the 25-millisecond range is considered good.

Disk access is the greatest bottleneck in terms of how fast a computer operates, and moving the head from one track to another is the slowest part of disk access. Anything that can be done to increase disk performance can have significant payoffs for the overall performance of the computer. There are many ways in which both you and the operating system can increase the efficiency with which disk accesses are handled, regardless of the average access time. For example, if files are arranged so that each one is in contiguous sectors on the disk, then less time will be spent moving the head around the disk to locate all the sectors for a particular file. These techniques are discussed in the *Managing Disks* section of this chapter.

Formatting Disks

So far the discussion has centered on relatively low-level characteristics of disks—the size and number of sectors per track, the number of platters per drive, and so on. These characteristics are generally set once and not changed. Setting the number of bytes per sector, and the interleave, are part of a process called *hard formatting*, or *low-level formatting*. All of this provides the background for the disk to do what it is supposed to do—store and retrieve information. But in order to efficiently store and retrieve information, there must be a way to keep track of what information is where on the disk—to build the directory structure discussed in Chapter 6. In addition, part of a disk may become damaged, disabling a particular sector. Rather than throw away an entire disk drive because a very tiny percentage of the capacity is disabled, it should be possible to detect and mark those damaged areas so that they are ignored. Setting the disk up for actually handling files and directories, and marking bad sectors, is called a *high-level format*. A high level format is what is usually referred to when people speak of formatting a disk.

To provide the necessary logical organization to manage all of the information on a disk, when a disk is formatted DOS divides it into four main areas: the *Boot Record*, the *File Allocation Table* (*FAT*), the *Root Directory*, and the *Data Area*. It makes no difference what kind of disk it is, or how large it is. All disks that can be used on a DOS-based computer have these four areas.

The term *Boot Record* comes from the fact that the information stored here is used by the computer during the start-up, or *boot,* operation. The Boot Record contains a small program that the computer reads when it is started. This program provides the computer with the essential information it needs to continue the boot operation, as well as with information about the disk it is on—the number of sectors per track, the number of sides, and so on. An example of a boot record is shown in Figure 7.1.

Description		***Boot Record Data***
OEM ID	:	DRDOS6.0
Bytes per sector	:	512
Sectors per cluster	:	4
Reserved sectors at beginning	:	1
FAT Copies	:	2
Root directory entries	:	512
Total sectors on disk	:	(Unused)
Media descriptor byte	:	F8 Hex
Sectors per FAT	:	80
Sectors per track	:	17
Last side number	:	5
Special hidden sectors	:	17
Big total number of sectors	:	81923
Physical drive number	:	128
Extended Boot Record Signature	:	29 Hex
Volume Serial Number	:	376387808
Volume Label	:	
File System ID	:	FAT16

Figure 7.1 A Typical Boot Record

This Boot Record indicates, among other things, that the disk it is stored on can contain up to 512 root directory entries, that there are 17 sectors per track, and that the last side number is 5 (which means there are 3 platters, with sides numbered 0 through 5). It also indicates that there are four sectors per cluster on this disk. Recall from Chapter 6 that DOS actually works with clusters as the smallest allocation units on a disk. The number of sectors per cluster varies with different types of disks; floppy disks usually have one or two sectors per cluster, while hard disks typically have four or more. You may have noticed that the free disk space on a disk usually goes down by more than the size of a file that has been added. The reason is that a file may only be one byte in size, but on a disk that has four sectors per cluster, a full cluster, or 2048 bytes, is allocated at once. If you go back to this file and add, say, 1000 bytes, the free disk space will not change because you are only filling up space that has already been assigned to the file.

Since the number of tracks on a disk, and the number of sectors per track, is set during a high-level format, it is possible to adjust these numbers with the FORMAT command, discussed below. However, it is not recommended that you do so.

The Boot Record is always written at the very beginning of a disk on side 0, track 0, sector 1. It is written to every disk that DOS uses, whether it is a bootable disk or not. Bootable disks have, in addition to the four areas of the disk discussed here, three special system files copied to them.

To read and write information to disks, DOS must know the status of all the clusters on the disk. It must know whether a cluster is available for use, or whether it has already been assigned to a file. In addition, DOS should be able to keep track of sectors that have been damaged and therefore should not be used. All of this information is stored permanently in the second logical area of the disk—the File Allocation Table, or FAT. The FAT is stored immediately following the Boot Record on a disk.

When you boot your computer the FAT is read into memory. This speeds up the disk performance, since the drive does not have to locate and read the FAT each time you access the disk. However, on a large disk a FAT that kept track of all the sectors on the disk would be quite large. This is why DOS groups sectors into clusters.

The FAT stores a code for every cluster on a disk. On large disks, DOS stores a two-byte code for each cluster, while on floppy disks a

1.5-byte, or 12-bit, code is used. From the value of this code, DOS can determine everything it needs to know about a cluster. If the code is zero, then the cluster is available for use. Assuming a two-byte code, if the code is a number between 2 and 65,519, then the cluster is already in use by a file. In this case, the number points to the next cluster assigned to the file. If the number is between 65,528 and 65,535, then the cluster is assigned to a file, and is also the last cluster for the file.

You may notice that there are a few missing numbers in this sequence. If the FAT entry for a cluster is 65,527, then the cluster is bad and should not be used. The numbers between 65,520 and 65,526 are reserved for use in future versions of DOS. The number 1 cannot be used, because the first cluster of the disk is used by the system information: the Boot Record, the FAT, and the Root directory.

Obviously, the FAT is essential to maintaining the integrity of a disk. If a cluster is damaged, you may lose all or part of a file. But if the FAT is damaged, you lose the whole disk. Consequently, DOS actually creates and maintains two identical FATs on each disk. If one is damaged, there is a reasonable chance that the second will be usable.

The Root directory holds the same information as other directories, which were discussed in detail in Chapter 6. However, the Root directory is unique in that it is assigned a specific, fixed location in the system area of the disk. It immediately follows the FAT, and can never grow or shrink. Consequently, the Root directory can only hold a specified number of entries. This number is stored in the Boot Record, and is determined during low-level formatting, and cannot be changed. For the disk in Figure 7.1, there is room for 512 entries in the Root directory. This is a typical value for hard disks.

Among the items of information stored for each file in a directory is the number of the starting cluster for the file. This is why DOS can manage to find files accurately, even if they are highly fragmented and stored in non-contiguous clusters. DOS reads the first cluster number from the directory, then looks in the FAT to find the subsequent clusters. Each cluster points to the next one, until the end of the file is reached.

Following the Root directory is the data area, which occupies the rest of the disk.

Disk Partitions

The last aspect of disk organization that should be reviewed is partitions. Partitioning is a way of taking one physical disk, and making it behave as though it were two or more disks. There are two reasons for doing this. The first is that some people want to use more than one operating system with the computer. Since the formatting of a disk is entirely dependent on the operating system, and every operating system requires disks that were formatted with its own particular needs in mind, the only way to use one hard disk with two operating systems is to partition it.

The second reason for partitioning a hard disk is that many earlier versions of DOS could only handle disks that were 32 megabytes or smaller. The reason is that these versions of DOS used two bytes to refer to sector numbers on a disk. The largest number two bytes can store is 65,536. Since each sector has to be 512 bytes, this gives 65,536 X 512, or 33,554,432 bytes as the largest possible size for a disk. This is precisely 32 megabytes. DR DOS 6.0 uses a larger number of bytes to store a sector number, and therefore permits partitions of up to 512 megabytes, or 536,870,912 bytes. If you have a hard disk that is larger than 512 megabytes you will need to partition it. Some people still prefer to partition hard drives that are less than 512 megabytes into multiple smaller drives, though it is no longer necessary.

To partition a drive, a partition table is added to the system area of a disk. It was stated earlier that the Boot Record always occupies the very first sector of the first track of side 0 on a disk. This is actually only the case with non-partitionable disks. Partitionable disks, which includes all hard disks but not floppies, place the partition table in the first sector. The partition table is independent of the operating system, so it is set up in the low-level formatting of the disk. The rest of the system area is then bumped forward. Since the computer requires a boot program to be in the first sector of a boot disk, the partition table includes a boot program. All hard disks have partition tables, and technically all hard disks are partitioned, even though some have only one partition that comprises the entire disk.

Managing Disks

Managing disks involves keeping the files that are on them organized so that the disk does not become fragmented, and so that most files occupy clusters that are either contiguous or at least close together on the disk. It also involves configuring your PC to use your hard drive as efficiently as possible.

It is obvious, but bears stating nonetheless, that the most useful thing you can do to keep a disk from running out of space is to delete files that are no longer needed. If there are files you do not want to delete, in case they are needed again in the future, but that are not being actively used, they should be copied to floppies and deleted from the hard disk. Other files to watch out for are temporary files that programs create, and normally delete when the program terminates. These files can be left on the disk if the computer is unexpectedly turned off while the program is running. For example, many word processors create temporary backup files as you work. These are deleted when the word processor is exited, but if the power is shut off while the word processor is still running, these temporary files are left behind. It is worth checking for these files whenever the power fails unexpectedly. Finally, there are several files that come with DR DOS 6.0 that you may never use. If you will not need one or more of these files, it is worth deleting them to free up disk space. These files are:

EMM386.SYS is an expanded memory manager that can only be used with computers that have a 386 or later CPU. If your computer has a 286 or earlier chip, or if it is a 386 or later but you do not want to use expanded memory, this file can be deleted. This file occupies about 10K of disk space.

EXE2BIN.EXE is a programming tool used to convert files with an EXE extension to a binary file. This is a tool used exclusively by programmers, and even most programmers don't use it. This file occupies about 8K of disk space.

PCKWIK.SYS and *PCKWIN.SYS* are device drivers used to provide a disk cache for hard disks, on computers that have extended or expanded memory. A disk cache is used to speed up the performance of hard disks, but chews up memory resources in the process. PCKWIN.SYS is for use with WINDOWS 3.0. If you do not have extended or expanded memory, or do not want to create a disk cache, you can delete these files. They occupy about 2K of disk space each. These drivers are discussed later in this chapter.

TASKMAX.EXE is the program file for TaskMAX, and TASKMAX.INI is the initialization file for TaskMAX. If you do not intend to use TaskMAX, these files may be deleted. They occupy about 17K and 3K, respectively. TaskMAX is the subject of Chapter 3.

VDISK.SYS is a device driver used to set up a RAM disk, which is a pseudo-disk in memory. RAM disks can be used to greatly increase the speed at which some programs run, but they can also take up considerable memory resources. If you do not want to set up RAM drives, you can delete this file. This file occupies about 5.5K of disk space. The VDISK.SYS driver is discussed later in this chapter.

There are several files that have VIEWMAX for the name, with different extensions. If you do not intend to use ViewMAX, you may delete these files from the disk. They occupy a total of about 173K of disk space. ViewMAX is the subject of Chapter 2. In addition, the following files are used to provide international standards support. This allows you to change the keyboard to reflect French usage, or to change the internal character set to that used by a foreign language. If you do not need international support, these files can be removed:

File Name	*Approximate Size*
COUNTRY.SYS	10K
DISPLAY.SYS	4K
GRAFTABL.COM	2K
KEBY.COM	34K
NLSFUNC.EXE	2K
PRINTER.SYS	5K
Any DOS file with an extension of CPI	0.4K - 24K

FORMAT

When a disk is new it must be given both a low-level format and a high-level format. The low-level format sets up the number of bytes per sector, the system area, and other details that define how the disk will interact with the operating system. When the term *format* is used with a hard drive, it usually refers just to the high-level format, because the FORMAT command only performs a high-level format on hard disks. When the term is used with floppy disks, however, it means a combined low-level and high-level format because FORMAT performs both of these operations on floppy disks. Hard disks are normally formatted before being sold, while floppy disks need to be formatted after they are purchased.

When a disk is formatted, four things happen: images of the FAT and Root directory are saved (if the disk had been previously formatted), a new FAT is created, a new Root directory is created, and the disk is checked for bad clusters, which are marked as bad in the FAT. This is sometimes referred to as a *safe format* because it saves an image of the current FAT and Root directory before overwriting them, and it does not affect existing information in the Data Area of the disk. Consequently, a disk that has been reformatted can be unformatted, recovering the information that was there before it was reformatted. The /U switch, discussed below, can be used to perform an Unconditional format, which does not save an image of the FAT or Root directory. The FORMAT command is used to format a new disk, and to reformat disks that have already been formatted. Reformatting can sometimes correct errors that have crept into a disk.

Reformatting a disk to a format other than its current one makes it impossible for DOS to save the FAT and Root directory. It is therefore impossible to unformat a disk whose format has been changed.

If a disk has given you read and write error messages, reformatting it may solve the problem. In this case, you should use the /U switch. The /U switch tells FORMAT to destroy all information on the disk. This makes it impossible to recover the previous state of the disk with the UNFORMAT command, since no existing information is saved, but it may also eliminate whatever was causing the problems with the disk.

FORMAT automatically senses the maximum number of tracks and sectors per track that a floppy drive can handle. It uses those numbers for any disk formatted in that drive, so it is not usually necessary to specify those values. However, it is sometimes desirable to format a disk that has a lower capacity than the maximum the drive can provide, and in some special circumstances, you may want to format a disk that has an unusual number of tracks and/or sectors per track. You can specify a different capacity in one of two ways: with the /F switch (to specify a different DOS capacity), or with the /T and /N switches (to specify the number of tracks and sectors). Using the /F switch is the recommended method. You cannot use the /F switch with either the /T or the /N switch.

The /F switch takes the form /F:capacity, where capacity specifies one of the capacities shown in Table 7.2.

Table 7.2 Values for the FORMAT /F:capacity Switch.

Physical Size	***Number of Sides***	***Storage Size***	***Capacity***
5.25"	1	160K	160
5.25"	1	180K	180

Table 7.2 continued ...

Physical Size	***Number of Sides***	***Storage Size***	***Capacity***
5.25"	2	320K	320
5.25"	2	360K	360
3.5"	2	720K	720
5.25"	2	1.2M	1.20
3.5"	2	1.44M	1.44
3.5"	2	2.88M	2.88

The following command formats a 3.5" diskette in the A: drive to 720K:

```
FORMAT A: /F:720KB
```

The /F switch sets the capacity of a disk by adjusting the number of tracks, and the number of sectors per track, that the disk uses. Thus, it is an indirect way of adjusting these values. It is the preferred method because it can only use standard DOS values. Furthermore, with /F you don't need to know the number of tracks and sectors, just the capacity you want the formatted disk to have.

The /T and /N switches must be used together. The /T switch specifies the number of tracks, and /N specifies the number of sectors per track. The following command can be used on a high density 3.5" drive (1.44 meg) to format a disk to 720K:

```
FORMAT A: /N:9 /T:80
```

This command creates a disk with nine tracks, and 80 sectors per track, which is the format of a 720K disk. The /F:720 switch would have the same effect.

> ***Caution:*** When using the /T and /N switches, there is the possibility of formatting a disk to a non-standard number of tracks and sectors per track. This could make the disk unreadable.

> ***Note:*** When formatting a disk that has been previously formatted, using any switch that changes the capacity of the disk performs an unconditional format, just as though the /U switch had been used. Previously recorded data then becomes unretrievable.

Formatted disks are not automatically *bootable* disks. A bootable disk is one that can be used to boot the computer. For a disk to be bootable, it must have three special system files on it: IBMBIO.COM, IBMDOS.COM, and COMMAND.COM. The first two files have the Hidden and System attributes turned on, so they do not show up in a directory listing produced with the DIR command. They can be seen, however, by using the XDIR command.

All three of these files are stored in the root directory of a bootable disk, and contain instructions that the computer needs in order to function properly. To create a bootable disk during the FORMAT operation, the /S switch is used, which copies these files to the disk after formatting is complete. The following command formats a disk in drive A:, and transfers all three system files to it:

```
FORMAT A: /S
```

In many previous versions of DOS, the two hidden system files, IBMBIO.COM and IBMDOS.COM, were required to be located in a particular area of the disk, just as the Boot Record and FAT are. This is not true in DR DOS 6.0; these files may be located anywhere on the disk. The SYS command, discussed below, is used to transfer these files to a disk that is already formatted. The only requirement is that there be enough free space on the disk to hold them.

You may specify a volume label for a disk during the FORMAT process by using the /V switch. A volume label may be up to 11 characters, and appears when a DIR command is issued for the disk. The following command formats the disk in drive A:, and gives it a volume label of WP-FILES:

```
FORMAT A: /V:WP-FILES
```

If the /V switch is not used, or if it is used but no label is specified, FORMAT will prompt you for a label. You will still have the choice of leaving it blank. The volume label can always be added or changed later, using the LABEL command.

Three switches are used to deal with older disk technologies that are becoming less and less common. The first is the /1 switch, which is used to format a single-sided floppy disk. The /4 switch is used to format a 5.25" 360K floppy disk in a high density (1.2 meg) drive. Disks that are formatted to low density in a high-density drive are not always readable by low-density drives, so this switch should be used with caution. The /8 switch formats a 5.25" double-density disk to have eight sectors per track (320K). This is the format used by very early versions of DOS.

The /X switch tells DOS that you are formatting a hard disk; it should never be used with a floppy disk. When /X is used, FORMAT prompts you with the following message:

```
WARNING ALL existing data on non-removable disk will
be destroyed! – Continue (Y/N)?
```

The /A switch causes the computer to beep when the format operation is complete.

UNFORMAT

If a formatted disk is reformatted, it may be possible to restore it to its condition before the FORMAT command was issued, by using the UNFORMAT command. UNFORMAT will not work on network drives. It can only be used on local hard drives and floppy drives.

When the FORMAT command is used to reformat a disk that was previously formatted, it performs a *safe format*, unless the /U switch was used or the format of the disk is changed. When a safe format is performed, the information in the FAT and Root directory is saved in the last two clusters of the disk, and information in files remains on the disk. A safe format replaces the FAT and Root directory after copying them, but does not overwrite any of the data area. For most purposes, the files are gone, since the pointers to them in the directory and the FAT are gone, and DOS will overwrite them, because the FAT has all of the clusters in the data area marked as available. But if you know where to look, the data is still there, and the UNFORMAT command knows where to look. This is because the safe format always writes the copy of the FAT and Root directory to the last two clusters on the disk.

The reason that the copies of the FAT and Root directory are placed in the last two clusters on the disk is that these are the last clusters used, and on a disk that is periodically optimized anything that may have been written to them will be moved to earlier clusters. Consequently, the last two clusters are more likely to be available than any other area of the disk. If the last two clusters are occupied by a file, then FORMAT moves backward through the clusters, searching for whichever free clusters are closest to the end of the disk.

If the disk is full, then there is not room for copies of the FAT and Root directory to be saved without overwriting some information. If this happens, FORMAT displays the following message:

```
Insufficient space to save UNFORMAT
information without destroying some data –
Continue (Y/N)?
```

If you answer N, the FORMAT operation is aborted. If you answer Y, FORMAT continues with a safe format and overwrites whatever is in the last two clusters with copies of the FAT and Root directory. If you UNFORMAT such a disk, it may appear that all of the files have been restored—they may all show up in the directory listing, and they may all have the correct size. However, if you do a COMP command to compare the files with copies of them that were made before the FORMAT, you will find that one or more of them have been corrupted. Consequently, the best thing to do if the above message appears is to abort the format operation and delete some files from the disk, then try again.

Since UNFORMAT knows where to find the information for the former FAT and Root directory, it can completely reconstruct them. From there, it can go on and reconstruct the rest of the directory and file structure.

Obviously, if files have been created on a disk after it has been reformatted, they may have overwritten some of the data area that stored files from before the reformat. These files will not be recoverable. If a directory has been overwritten, then the files that were contained in it will not be recoverable. Worse yet, they may overwrite the copies of the original FAT and Root directory. Consequently, it is essential that UNFORMAT be used as soon after an accidental reformatting as possible. If the copies of the FAT and Root directory have been overwritten, when you attempt to unformat the disk the following message will appear:

```
UNFORMAT information has been overwritten
```

UNFORMAT will be completely useless with a floppy disk that has been unconditionally formatted, and with any disk that has been completely filled up with new files after any type of format.

To unformat a disk, enter the following command:

```
UNFORMAT X:
```

where *X* is the drive letter for the disk to be unformatted.

FDISK—Partitioning a Hard Drive

Partitioning a disk is the process of dividing the disk into distinct units that are each treated as though they were separate drives. Only hard disks may be partitioned. The reasons for partitioning a hard disk were discussed earlier in this chapter.

The FDISK command is used to partition a drive. This command should only be used if you are quite confident of what you are doing. When it is used to change a partition on a disk, all of the information in the modified partition is lost. You should always back up your disk before using the FDISK command for anything other than viewing the current partition table.

There are three types of partitions that a disk can have: a primary DOS partition, an extended DOS partition, and non-DOS partitions. Non-DOS partitions are for use by operating systems other than DOS, such as Unix or Xenix. With DR DOS 6.0, you may have two DOS partitions on a single hard drive: one primary partition, and one extended partition. The primary DOS partition is a partition that contains the system files required for booting the computer—IBMBIO.COM, IBMDOS.COM, and COMMAND.COM.

The extended DOS partition may be subdivided into multiple logical drives, or may be used as a single drive. Consider a 120-megabyte hard drive. Using FDISK, you could create a primary DOS partition that is 40 megabytes in size, and is referenced as the C: disk. This would be the logical disk that the computer would boot from. The other 80 megabytes would then be used to create an extended partition. In order to use the extended partition, one or more logical drives must be created on it. If you create more than one logical drive, the sum of the drive sizes should total the size of the extended partition.

When the FDISK command is entered, the screen shown in Figure 7.2 is displayed.

```
FDISK R1.60     Fixed Disk Maintenance Utility
Copyright (c) 1986,1988,1990 Digital Research Inc. All rights reserved.
 Partitions on 1st hard disk (40.5 Mb, 976 cylinders):
 No  Drive  Start    End    MB      Status   Type
  1    C:     0      963    40.0       A     DOS 3.31



 Select options:
 1) Create DOS partition
 2) Delete DOS partition
 3) Select bootable partition
 Enter desired option: (ESC = exit) [?]
```

Figure 7.2 The FDISK Menu

This screen provides several pieces of information about the hard drive—the number of partitions, the drive letter that corresponds to each of them, the starting and ending cluster for each drive, the total capacity of each drive, its status (A indicates Active; N indicates Non-active), and the type of partition. The type of partition will indicate whether it is a non-DOS partition or, if it is a DOS partition, what version of DOS the partition was created with. The disk in Figure 7.2 was partitioned using DOS 3.1.

If you choose one of the three options shown in Figure 7.2, remember that modifying any existing partition will destroy the information in it. It is not possible to simply change a partition by enlarging or shrinking it. Rather, you must delete it and create a new partition with the characteristics you desire.

Option 3 refers to the *bootable* partition. When a disk has partitions for more than one operating system, each operating system must have one partition that contains its system files. To use the partition(s) that are compatible with that operating system, the partition that has the system files must be active. For example, suppose you had both DOS and Unix operating systems on your computer. Each of these would have a partition that contained their operating system files. For DOS, this would be the Primary DOS partition. If this was assigned to be the bootable partition, then when the computer was started it would boot with the DOS operating system. If you wanted to boot with the Unix operating system, you would have to change the bootable partition.

A partition does not have to be bootable in order to use it. For example, if the bootable partition is the primary DOS partition, then an extended DOS partition can also be used. The bootable partition is the partition that contains the operating system files, and therefore determines the operating system that will boot the computer.

The default FDISK menu, shown in Figure 7.2, does not include an option to delete a non-DOS partition. This can be done by starting FDISK with the /D switch:

```
FDISK /D
```

The FDISK menu will be the same, but you will now be able to delete both DOS and non-DOS partitions by choosing option 2.

You should not use FDISK unless you are quite experienced in working with hard disks, and have a good reason for wanting to modify the partitions on your hard drive.

FDISK is an external command.

SYS—Creating a System Disk

A system disk is a disk that can be used to boot your computer. This requires that three files be present on the disk: IBMBIO.COM, IBMDOS.COM, and COMMAND.COM. IBMBIO.COM and IBMDOS.COM are both hidden and system files, which means that they normally do not show up in directory listings. When a disk is formatted, it can be made a system disk by including the /S switch. If a disk was formatted without /S, and you now want to make it a system disk, use the SYS command.

The system files are always placed in the root directory. To create a system disk, the following command copies the files from the root directory of the current disk to the disk in the A: drive:

```
SYS A:
```

SYS copies the files in the following order: IBMBIO.COM, IBMDOS.COM, and COMMAND.COM. In many earlier versions of DOS, the IBMBIO.COM and IBMDOS.COM files had to be located in specific positions near the beginning of the data area on the disk. Consequently, if a disk had files already on it, those files could occupy the locations needed by the system files, and the system files could not be transferred. However, this is not the case with DR DOS 6.0, so any disk that has enough space to hold the three files can be made a system disk. The IBMBIO.COM file is about 24K, IBMDOS.COM is about 39K, and the COMMAND.COM is about 50K, so a disk must have about 113K free to store these files.

The SYS command cannot be used on drives that have been affected by the ASSIGN, JOIN, or SUBST command, or on network drives.

SYS is an external command.

LABEL—Modifying the Volume Label

Every disk may be assigned a volume label. This is a name that can be stored on the disk, and that shows up when a DIR command is used to list the contents of the disk. The LABEL command can be used to display, add, or replace a disk's volume label.

If no drive is specified on the command line, the LABEL command applies to the current drive. The following two commands demonstrate this: the first changes the label of the disk in the current drive to TEST-DISK, while the second changes the label of the disk in the A: drive to TEST-DISK:

```
LABEL TEST-DISK
LABEL A: TEST-DISK
```

If no label is specified with the LABEL command, it displays the current label, and the volume serial number if there is one, and prompts you for a new label with the following messages:

```
Volume in drive C: is DOS500
Enter Volume label (0 to 11 characters):
```

Entering a new label and pressing Enter replaces the label. If you press Enter without entering a new label, the following message appears:

```
Delete current volume label (Y/N)?
```

Responding with a Y removes the current label, leaving the disk with no volume label. Respond with N leaves the current label intact.

LABEL is an external command.

VOL—Displaying the Volume Label

The VOL command is used to display the volume label. If no drive is specified, the current drive is assumed. The following command displays the volume label of the disk in drive A:

```
VOL A:
```

VOL is an internal command.

CHKDSK—Checking Disk Integrity

The CHKDSK command is used to display information about the capacity and available space on a disk and about the status of memory usage, and to check the integrity of the FAT and directory structure of a disk. The number of pending delete files, and the number of bytes in them, are also displayed.

Recall that the FAT keeps track of the status of every cluster on the disk. Each cluster can be labeled as available for use, in use by a file, or defective. It sometimes happens that an error creeps into the FAT, leaving a cluster marked as in use, when in fact it is no longer part of a file. This can be determined by studying the starting clusters for files, as listed in the directories, and following the chains that start with those clusters to the end of the file. A cluster that does not fall into one of these chains is lost; it cannot be assigned to a new file, and it does not belong to an existing file.

To run CHKDSK for the current drive, just type CHKDSK and press Enter. To run it for another drive, append the drive letter to the command. Running CHKDSK for the C: drive produces a report similar to that shown in Figure 7.3.

```
Volume DRDOS6 created Dec-17-1991 18:14

41,844,736 bytes total disk space.
   329,728 bytes in 3 hidden files.
   131,072 bytes in 56 directories.
37,462,016 bytes in 1419 user files.
   900,020 bytes in 13 pending delete user files.
    11,400 bytes in bad sectors.
 3,011,500 bytes available on disk.

   588,800 total bytes of memory.
   498,272 total bytes of free memory.

   497,792 bytes in largest free memory block.
```

Figure 7.3 Output from CHKDSK Command

If there had been lost clusters on the disk, CHDKSK would have displayed the following messages:

```
XX lost clusters found in YY chains.
Convert lost chains to filennnn.chk files (Y/N)?
```

Where *XX* is a number that indicates how many lost clusters were located, and YY indicates that some of those clusters are chained together, which means they once belonged to the same file. For example, suppose a file occupies clusters 10, 15, and 20, in that order. The directory entry for the file will indicate that the first cluster in the file is cluster 10. The FAT entry for cluster 10 will point to cluster 15, and the FAT entry for cluster 15 will point to cluster 20. The FAT entry for cluster 20 will be marked as the end of the chain. Now suppose you delete the file, so the directory entry is marked as deleted, but something goes wrong so that only cluster 10 is marked as deleted in the FAT. Clusters 15 and 20 continue to be marked as occupied, but they no longer belong to a file. Since cluster 15 points to cluster 20, and cluster 20 is marked as the end of the file, CHKDSK would report 2 lost clusters in one chain.

Lost clusters can result from a bug in a program, or a power failure while a file is being written, or some other problem. A lost cluster may contain important data. CHKDSK can be used to recover these clusters and chains, so that you may examine them and decide whether or not to keep them. In the messages shown above, CHKDSK prompts you as to whether or not it should convert lost chains to files.

This can be a misleading question, because answering Y only works if the /F switch was used with CHKDSK. If /F was not used, then CHKDSK takes no action, even if you press Y. However, if /F was used, pressing Y will cause CHKDSK to convert each chain of lost clusters to a file in the root directory. The names of the files will be FILExxxx.CHK, where xxxx is a number. The first file converted is FILE0001.CHK, the second is FILE0002.CHK, and so on.

When a program needs to access a file, the file must first be *opened.* When a file is opened, DOS assigns it a number, known as a file handle, and tells the program what the file handle number is. The program then refers to the file by its handle. When DOS closes a file, it releases the handle so it can be used by the next file.

Normally, there will be no open files when you run CHKDSK, because it is run at the command prompt. However, if you are running a multi-tasking environment like DESQview or Windows, then there may be open files. CHKDSK should not be used in these cases, because the presence of open files may result in erroneous reporting of lost clusters.

If CHKDSK frequently reports lost clusters, you may want to consider having your disk checked for servicing. Lost clusters should be a relatively rare occurrence.

If CHKDSK reports bad sectors on the disk, this is because it detected clusters that were marked as bad in the FAT. This is not something you need to worry about, since they have been marked in the FAT and they will not be used. This information is provided simply as one of the statistics about the disk.

You can save the output from the CHKDSK command to a file by using the output redirection symbol (>), but you should not do so when using the /F switch. The following command performs a CHKDSK on the current drive, and stores the output in a file named CHECK.DAT:

```
CHKDSK > CHECK.DAT
```

The /V switch can be used to tell CHKDSK to display each file name on the disk as it checks the files.

Note that CHKDSK only checks for logical errors in the FAT. It does not check the physical integrity of the disk, nor does it recover files from a physically damaged disk. The RECOVER command must be used if the disk is physically damaged.

CHKDSK cannot be used on drives affected by the ASSIGN, JOIN, or SUBST commands, or on nctwork drivcs.

CHKDSK is an external command.

DISKCOMP—Comparing Two Floppies

DISKCOMP compares the exact contents of two floppy disks. The two disks must be the same size and format. DISKCOMP performs a track-by-track comparison, so it is not sufficient for two disks to contain the same set of files. The files must occupy the same clusters on each disk. It is useful to perform a DISKCOMP after performing a DISKCOPY command, to ensure that the DISKCOPY accurately reproduced the source disk. DISKCOPY can produce an exact image of a disk in a file, called an image file, and DISKCOMP can also be used to compare the contents of a disk with an image file. This is useful if you want to compare one disk to several others, because it is faster to compare from a file on the hard disk than from a floppy. You may not, however, compare two image files.

The following command compares the disk in drive A: with the disk in drive B:

```
DISKCOMP A: B:
```

Since the entire contents of a disk usually won't fit in conventional memory, DISKCOMP will automatically use any system resources available to store the entire contents of the source disk the first time it is read. This minimizes the number of times you have insert and remove the disks, if you are using the same drive for the source and target. The system resources DISKCOMP will use, if available, to store the contents of the source disk are: expanded memory, extended memory, and temporary files on the hard disk, in that order. An appropriate device driver, such as EMM386.SYS or HIDOS.SYS, must be loaded before DISKCOMP can make use of expanded or extended memory.

There are five switches that may be used with DISKCOMP: /1, /8, /A, /M, and /V. The /1 switch instructs DISKCOMP to compare only the first side of the disks, even if they are two-sided disks. The /8 switch tells DISKCOMP to compare only the first 8 sectors per track, regardless of how many sectors the disks have.

/A causes the computer to beep when the comparison is completed.

/M is used to compare multiple disks against an image file. After the first disk has been compared, you are asked if you want to compare another disk to the image file. If you enter Y, for Yes, you are prompted to insert the next disk. This continues until you enter an N, for No.

The /V switch is used to verify that the entire source disk or image file can be read accurately. This slows down the process, and is usually not necessary, but in critical situations it may be worth the extra time it takes.

If the two disks are identical, DISKCOMP displays the message "Compare OK." If they are not, it displays a message indicating the side and track on which the mismatch occurred.

You may perform a DISKCOMP using only one drive by specifying the same drive letter for both the first and second drives. DISKCOMP will then prompt you to put the first and second disks in the drive as it needs them.

DISKCOMP is an external command.

APPEND

The APPEND command is similar to the PATH command, only it operates on data files instead of executable files. Recall that the PATH sets up a list of directories in which DOS will search for executable files, when a command is entered that is neither an internal DOS command, nor a program in the current directory. The APPEND command sets up a list of directories that DOS will search for data files that programs attempt to open, if those files are not found in the current directory. The command is called APPEND because for the purpose of looking for data files, the files in these directories are treated as if they were appended to the current directory. The DIR command does not show files in appended directories.

You may use different drives as well as different directories with the APPEND command. When you are appending two or more directories, they should be separated by a semicolon. For example, the following command appends the root directory in drive A: and the \LETTERS directory in drive B: to the current directory:

```
APPEND A:\;B:\LETTERS
```

If APPEND is entered by itself, it will display the list of currently appended directories. To cancel the effect of the APPEND command, enter the command with a semicolon:

```
APPEND ;
```

When you specify a data file in a program, you may usually include a path if the file is not in the current directory. This normally does not disable the effect of APPEND—if the file is not found in the specified directory, DOS will go ahead and search the appended directories for it. However, you may want DOS to ignore appended directories when a path is included with the file specification. This can be accomplished with the /PATH switch. When /PATH:ON is specified, DOS searches the appended directories, regardless of whether a path is specified with the file name. When /PATH:OFF is specified, DOS only searches appended directories when there is no path specified with the file name. The default is ON.

Normally, DOS searches the path for program files and appended directories for data files. However, you can instruct DOS to use the appended directories as though they are a part of the path—to search them for programs as well as for data files—by using the /X switch. If you want to do this, you must use /X:ON the first time APPEND is used after booting your computer. You can then specify /X:OFF to turn APPEND off, and /X:ON to turn it back on. If /X:ON is not specified the first time APPEND is used, X:ON and X:OFF will have no effect.

You may store the list of appended directories in a DOS environment variable named APPEND by using the /E:ON switch. Programs that are designed to do so can then access this variable, to see what directories are appended. The following command creates the environment variable, and appends the A:\ and B:\LETTERS directories to the current directory:

```
APPEND /E:ON A:\;B:\LETTERS
```

/E:OFF can be used to turn off this feature. OFF is the default.

> ***Note:*** APPEND shoul be used only with data files that will not be copied by a program. For example, suppose your word processor saves a file by copying a new file with the same name. If the file that you are working on is in an appended directory, then when it is saved, a new file of the same name will be created in the current directory, since APPEND does not affect the location of files being created. This leaves two files of the same name on the drive, but you will be unaware that this has happened. This can result in confusion, and in the wrong file being used at a later time. If the program you are using modifies a file without replacing it, then it is okay to use it with appended directories. Database programs and spreadsheets generally modify files without making new copies, while word processors often create new copies of files when they are saved.

You should clear any appended directories with the APPEND; command before using the BACKUP command.

APPEND is an external command.

ASSIGN—Reassigning Drive Letters

Some software programs, particularly older ones, insist on disks being in a certain drive, usually A: or B:. However, you may want the disk in some other drive. One of the most common occurrences is when software comes on a 5.25-inch disk, and insists that the disk be in the A: drive. Many PCs today have a 3.5-inch drive as the A: drive, and a 5.25-inch drive as the B: drive. The ASSIGN command gets around this problem by tricking DOS into thinking that a reference to one drive letter is really a reference to another drive letter. The following command assigns drive B: to drive A:

```
ASSIGN A=B
```

The effect of this command is that whenever a program references either the A: drive or the B: drive, DOS will interpret it as a reference to the B: drive. This can be demonstrated by performing a DIR command on drive A:—DOS will display the directory of the disk in the B drive.

You may enter colons after the drive letters if you wish, but they are optional.

To clear all assignments and restore the original meaning of drive letters, enter the ASSIGN command by itself, with no drive letters. To see the current assignments, enter the following command:

```
ASSIGN /A
```

Any given drive letter can only have one other drive letter assigned to it at a time. For example, if you enter the command ASSIGN A=C, then enter the command ASSIGN B=C, after the second command, drive A will no longer be assigned to drive C. You may, however, use the SUBST command to substitute the C drive for the A drive, and still use the ASSIGN command to reassign B to C.

You should not attempt to assign a hard disk to another drive, though you can assign a floppy drive to a hard drive. Also, you may not use a drive letter that does not exist, as you can with the SUBST command. Furthermore, although it may work, you should never use ASSIGN with the BACKUP, DISKCOMP, DISKCOPY, FORMAT, JOIN, LABEL, PRINT, RESTORE, or SUBST commands. ASSIGN may be used with network drives.

The SUBST command is preferred over ASSIGN, and should be

used instead whenever possible, since the ASSIGN command may be dropped from future versions of DOS.

ASSIGN is an external command.

JOIN—Joining Two Drives

The JOIN command makes a drive behave as if it were a subdirectory of the root directory on another drive. For example, the following command makes the A: drive behave as if it were the C:\ADRIVE directory:

```
JOIN A: C:\ADRIVE
```

Now, when the C:\ADRIVE directory is referenced, the A: drive will be accessed. When this JOIN command is entered, the \ADRIVE directory must either not exist, or be an empty directory, on the C: drive. If the \ADRIVE directory does not exist, the JOIN command creates it. Any legal directory name could be used in place of \ADRIVE, as long it is either empty or non-existent. The requirement that the directory be empty makes sense; if there were files in the directory, DOS would have no way of knowing whether you wanted to reference the files in the real directory, or on the joined drive. If you create a JOIN with a non-empty directory, JOIN assigns the drive to the directory, and ignores the actual directory. For example, if the C:\ADRIVE directory existed when the above JOIN command was executed, then executing the command DIR C:\ADRIVE would display the contents of the disk in the A: drive, not the contents of the actual C:\ADRIVE directory.

The drive that is joined to a directory on another drive becomes invalid. In the example above, if an attempt was made to reference the A: drive, the message "Invalid drive specified" would be shown.

If you want to see a list of the currently joined drives and directories, enter the command JOIN by itself. For each joined drive, a message similar to the following will be displayed:

```
A: => C:\ADRIVE
```

A JOIN may be deleted with the /D switch. When /D is used, only the drive letter is specified, not the joined directory. The following command removes the JOIN defined above:

```
JOIN A: /D
```

There are several DOS commands that should never be used when the JOIN command is in effect: ASSIGN, BACKUP, CHKDSK, DISKCOMP, DISKCOPY, FDISK, FORMAT, LABEL, RECOVER, RESTORE, SUBST, and SYS.

JOIN cannot be used with networked drives.

JOIN is an external command.

SUBST—Substituting Drive Letters

The SUBST command is similar to the ASSIGN command, but is more flexible. SUBST allows you to assign a subdirectory path from any real drive to another real drive, or to a *virtual drive*—a legal drive letter for which there is no physical drive on the computer. SUBST should be used in place of ASSIGN whenever possible, as the ASSIGN command may be dropped from future versions of DOS.

To substitute the root directory of the C: drive for the A: drive, enter the following command:

```
SUBST A: C:\
```

This is equivalent to the command:

```
ASSIGN A=C
```

However, SUBST will also work with this command:

```
SUBST A: C:\WP\LETTERS
```

Now, references to drive A: will be translated into references to the \WP\LETTERS directory of the C: drive. Furthermore, you may substitute a drive that does not exist for a subdirectory on one that does exist. For example, the following command substitutes the drive letter E: for the C:\WP directory:

```
SUBST E: C:\WP
```

Now, references to drive E: will be interpreted as references to the C:\\WP directory. With this substitution in place, the following command would display the files in the C:\WP\LETTERS directory:

```
DIR E:\LETTERS
```

The drive E: in this example is referred to as a *virtual drive*, since there is no physical drive labeled E:. Virtual drives may use any letter of the alphabet that is not already assigned to a physical drive. However, they must be in the range specified by the LASTDRIVE command in your CONFIG.SYS file. The LASTDRIVE command is discussed in Chapter 10.

A drive substitution may be deleted with the /D switch. The following command deletes the above substitution:

```
SUBST E: /D
```

If you want to list the current substitutions, enter the SUBST command by itself.

The following commands should not be used with drives affected by SUBST: BACKUP, CHKDSK, DISKCOMP, DISKCOPY, FDISK, FORMAT, LABEL, RECOVER, RESTORE, SYS.

SUBST is an external command.

BUFFERS

When DOS reads information from a disk, it reads at least one sector of information at a time. For example, if you request that a database retrieve the name of a person—say, John Smith—DOS will not only read the name John Smith from the disk, but will also read the rest of the information that is in the sector that stores the name on the disk. This is done intentionally because disk reads, even with a hard disk, are the slowest operation your computer has to carry out. By reading in extra information, DOS minimizes the number of disk accesses it must carry out. The information that DOS reads from the disk is stored in areas of memory that are set up when you boot the computer. These areas are known as buffers.

The next time DOS receives a request to read information from the disk, it will first look in the buffers to see if the information is there. If it is, DOS reads it from the buffers and saves the time required to physically access the disk. There is a reasonably good chance the information will be in a buffer, since it is common for two disk reads to be retrieving related information, and related pieces of information are often stored near each other on the disk. If you pay attention to your disk drive indicator light you will notice that it does not always go on when you request information from the disk. When it does not, DOS is finding the requested information from the buffer. You will also notice that information retrieved from a buffer appears on the screen more quickly than information that requires a disk access. DOS will also use the buffers when writing to a disk, which further minimizes disk accesses.

DOS can have more than one memory buffer for storing information from the disk. Each buffer can hold one 512-byte disk sector. The more buffers DOS has, the more likely it is that the needed information will be in memory, thus avoiding additional disk accesses. However, as the number of buffers goes up so does the amount of memory required for them. This memory is permanently set aside for these buffers, so it is taken away from the memory available to programs.

The number of buffers that DOS will set up is determined by the BUFFERS command in the CONFIG.SYS file. This number cannot be changed after the computer is booted, except by modifying the CONFIG.SYS file and rebooting the computer. The following line in the CONFIG.SYS file instructs DOS to set up 15 buffers:

```
BUFFERS=15
```

You may specify anywhere from three to 99 buffers. If you do not include a BUFFERS command in your CONFIG.SYS file, DOS will use a default value based on the configuration of your computer. For a computer that has 640K of memory, the default is 15.

Each buffer consumes about 532 bytes of memory. Thus, 10 buffers consumes a little over 5K. The trick in setting the number of buffers is to find a number that provides the maximum performance increase, but is not so large that some of the buffer space is never used effectively. The default values for buffers are based on the amount of memory in your computer, but in fact a more important consideration is probably the size of your hard disk—the larger the disk, the more buffers you are likely to need. Table 7.3 provides guidelines for setting the BUFFERS command based on the capacity of your hard disk.

Table 7.3 Recommended BUFFERS Settings for Various Hard Disk Capacities

Hard Disk Capacity	***Recommended BUFFERS Setting***
Under 40 megabytes	20-25
40 to 80 megabytes	30-35
80 to 120 megabytes	40-45
More than 120 megabytes	50-60

Another factor in considering how to set your BUFFERS command is the type of software you will use. If you use a database system or another application that reads and writes large amounts of information to and from the disk it may help to increase the number of buffers. This is because these systems frequently access different sectors of the disk on each read or write, so having more buffers available increases the likelihood that a requested sector will be in memory. For most database applications setting 20 buffers is a good place to start.

Some programs require that a certain number of buffers be specified in order to run properly. The number specified is always the minimum number required, so if one program you use requires 15 buffers, and another program requires 20, then 20 will work for both programs.

If you have a performance problem that you believe may be alleviated by adjusting the BUFFERS command, the best thing to do is to try different values and see how they affect the problem. For example, if your database seems to be performing poorly it could be because you do not have enough buffers available, resulting in more disk accesses than necessary. It could also be because you have too many buffers specified, not leaving enough memory for the database application to efficiently perform its processing, in which case it will have to use the disk for tasks it would otherwise use memory for. The only way to determine whether adjusting the BUFFERS command will help is to try different numbers of buffers and see what effect this has.

If your computer takes a very long time to carry out some task, changing the BUFFERS command can help only if the disk is being accessed during the task. If the disk is never read or written to, the problem is not one of disk access but rather of processor speed. Adjusting the BUFFERS command will not help with this problem.

You may use the HIBUFFERS command instead of BUFFERS. HIBUFFERS tells DOS to load the buffers into high memory. This means that the buffers will not use memory that could be used by applications, and thus leaves more memory available for running your programs. The HIBUFFERS command is discussed in Chapter 6.

BUFFERS is a CONFIG.SYS command.

FASTOPEN

The FASTOPEN command increases the performance of your hard disk by keeping track of the names and locations of files and directories that you access. Without FASTOPEN, each time you access a file on a hard disk, DOS must search the directory structure to locate the starting position of the file, then retrieve the file's chain of disk cluster addresses from the FAT, before it can actually access the file. FASTOPEN keeps this information in memory for recently opened files. When you then go back to those files, DOS does not have to search around various areas of the disk for this information. This can result in a significant improvement in the speed with which your computer retrieves information from the disk. FASTOPEN only stores information for files on hard disks; it has no effect on floppy drives.

The FASTOPEN command goes in the CONFIG.SYS file; the following command directs FASTOPEN to track 256 files:

```
FASTOPEN = 256
```

You may specify anywhere from 128 to 32,768 files; the default is 512. Since FASTOPEN goes in the CONFIG.SYS file, you must restart your computer to change the settings.

Some versions of DOS supply FASTOPEN as an executable program that can be run from the command line. However, even in these versions of DOS it can be run only once. Because FASTOPEN is sometimes included as an executable program, some software programs expect a file named FASTOPEN.EXE to exist in a directory that is included in the current path. Consequently, DR DOS 6.0 includes a program named FASTOPEN.EXE, which is stored in the DRDOS directory. This program does not perform any function other than satisfying the requirement that such a program file exist.

FASTOPEN is most effective with programs that open and close a lot of files, such as database management systems and computer language compilers. Other types of software may benefit more from the BUFFERS command or the VDISK device driver. The best way to determine whether FASTOPEN is useful is to experiment with it. Try loading it, then run the programs you commonly work with. If you notice a speed increase, FASTOPEN is helping out. If you do not, your programs probably do not make use of the disk in ways that FASTOPEN can help with, so it should be removed to save the memory it occupies. Each file specified in FASTOPEN takes up two bytes of memory.

FASTOPEN is a CONFIG.SYS command.

VDISK—Speeds Up Your System

VDISK is a program that allows you to create a *RAM disk.* A RAM disk is an area of memory that is set up to simulate a disk drive. Once a RAM disk is set up, you can reference it just as you would any other drive. However, because it consists of electronic memory instead of a mechanical drive, a RAM disk operates at many times the speed of even a very fast hard disk.

VDISK is not generally as useful as Super PC-Kwik, because a RAM disk has to have specific files copied to it, and it is then only useful for speeding up access to those files. Super PC-Kwik, on the other hand, speeds up access to all disks, regardless of which files are being accessed.

However, if you have a program that frequently accesses one or more fairly small files, you may achieve a greater performance increase by using VDISK than Super PC-Kwik.

Since VDISK creates a drive in memory, the drive is volatile—if the computer is turned off, the contents of the drive are lost. Consequently, RAM disks should never be used to store data files. They should be used for files that are referenced, such as spell-checking dictionaries in word processors. If you want to use a RAM disk to speed up access to a data file for an operation like spell-checking, the file should be copied to the RAM disk before the operation, then, if it was changed during the operation, back to the physical disk as soon as the spell-checking is completed.

One of the most useful ways to use a RAM disk is with programs that create temporary files in a directory specified by an environment variable. An environment variable is a name that resides in the DOS environment, and that contains some value. Programs can reference environment variables. Many programs will look for an environment variable named TEMP that will identify the directory in which they should store their temporary files. You can define this variable to contain the C:\TEMP directory by entering the following command:

```
SET TEMP=C:\TEMP
```

If you are using a RAM drive, then you can store the name of a directory on the RAM drive in the TEMP environment variable. Now these programs will store their temporary files on the RAM drive, which can greatly increase the speed of the programs.

VDISK is actually a device driver, so it is loaded from the CONFIG.SYS file when the computer is booted. The following command in CONFIG.SYS loads VDISK and specifies a 200K RAM disk in conventional memory:

```
DEVICE=C:\DOS\VDISK.SYS 200
```

The size parameter, 200 in the above command, indicates the capacity of the RAM disk in kilobytes. You may specify any number from 1 through 256, unless you are using expanded memory for the disk, in which case it may be up to 32,768. The use of expanded memory with VDISK is discussed below. The default value is 64.

When VDISK creates a RAM disk, it determines the last drive letter in use by your computer, and assigns the next drive letter to the RAM disk. Thus, if the last drive letter in use by your computer is C:, then VDISK will assign the letter D: to the RAM disk.

RAM disks are set up to have 128 byte sectors, just like all physical disks that are found on PCs. You may optionally specify an alternative sector size for the RAM disk, though there is rarely any reason to do this and it is strongly recommended that you do not. This is done by specifying the sector size immediately after the disk capacity. Valid sector sizes are 128, 256, and 512 bytes. The following command specifies a 200K RAM disk with 256 byte sectors:

```
DEVICE=C:\DOS\VDISK.SYS 200 256
```

Just as physical disks have a specified number of entries that can be stored in the root directory, so do RAM disks. The default number of root directory entries for a RAM disk is 64. You may change this value by appending the maximum number of root directory entries to the end of the command. The following command sets up a 200K RAM drive that has 512 byte sectors and a root directory that can store up to 100 entries:

```
DEVICE=C:\DOS\VDISK.SYS 200 512 100
```

You may specify anywhere from 2 to 512 root directory entries. Increasing the size of the root directory increases the total amount of memory used for the RAM drive. Consequently, you should set up your RAM drive to contain as many root directory entries as you think it will need, but no more.

By default, VDISK creates the RAM disk in conventional memory. This is the worst place to put it, since conventional memory is needed to run programs. However, it is also the only type of memory that every computer is guaranteed to have, so it makes sense to default to this and then let you change it. To specify that the RAM disk should go into expanded memory, the /X switch is used. When /X is used, the size of the disk may go up to 32 megabytes.

There is no way for programs to access a RAM disk that is entirely stored in extended memory, so if you use extended memory for the RAM disk, the contents of the disk are swapped back and forth between a window in conventional memory and the entire disk contents in extended memory. If you want to put the RAM disk into extended memory, the /E:nn switch is used, where nn is the number of sectors that should be transferred between conventional memory and extended memory. You may specify anywhere from 1 to 8 sectors (8 is the default).

You may create as many RAM disks as you like, by specifying multiple DEVICE=VDISK.SYS lines in the CONFIG.SYS file.

In most cases, setting up a RAM disk in conventional memory is not recommended. The performance gains are generally not worth the lost memory. However, if your computer has expanded or extended memory, a RAM disk may be worth using.

VDISK may be loaded into the upper memory area using the HIDEVICE command:

```
HIDEVICE=C:\DRDOS\VDISK specs
```

Using DISKOPT to Eliminate Disk Fragmentation

Disk fragmentation is the most common cause of deteriorating disk performance, and is also one of the simplest problems to overcome. Disk fragmentation occurs as files are added, deleted, and expanded on a disk. For example, consider a hard disk that has four sectors per cluster. Disk space is allocated in 2,048-byte chunks. Say you create a 2000-byte file that is stored in cluster 5, then you create another 2000-byte file that is stored in cluster 6. So far so good, but what happens when you want to add more information to the first file? Since cluster 6 is in use, cluster 7 gets allocated to the first file. As some files grow, others shrink, and yet others are deleted, the pattern of available clusters on the disk becomes more and more fragmented.

On a floppy disk, this problem is easy to fix: simply use the COPY or XCOPY command to copy all of the files to another disk. These commands copy the files into contiguous sectors on the new disk, thereby eliminating fragmentation. If you have two hard disks available, and there is enough free space on one to duplicate the other, this technique can be used there as well. But this is rarely the case, and even when a second hard disk is available, this is a clumsy approach. For this reason, the DISKOPT program is provided with DR DOS 6.0. DISKOPT can unfragment a disk without copying everything to a second disk.

Before running DISKOPT, you should delete unnecessary files. Deleting them after the compression is done will simply fragment the disk again. It is also a good idea to run the CHKDSK command, discussed above, to recover any lost clusters. You should keep in mind that DISKOPT can take a long time to run, since it may have to move a tremendous amount of information to get a large hard disk organized. Its operation can safely be stopped by pressing the Esc key, but it is better to use it when you know there will be plenty of time. Some people choose to run it overnight.

DISKOPT should never be run when any other program is active. For example, you should not use DISKOPT when TaskMAX is running. You should also be sure to back up your disk before running DISKOPT. It is a very reliable program with good safety checks built in, but any time you are rearranging the organization of your hard disk a backup should be made first.

There is one type of file that will not be moved by DISKOPT: system files. If you want DISKOPT to move system files along with the rest of your files you must first turn off the System attribute for those files.

DISKOPT is a menu-driven utility. To start it, enter the command:

```
DISKOPT drive
```

at the command prompt, where *drive* is the letter of the drive you want to optimize. If you do not specify a drive, a menu of available drives will be displayed. The screen in Figure 7.4 will then appear.

The DISKOPT startup screen shows a map of the current physical layout of the disk to be optimized. The map is divided into blocks, each of which represents one cluster. There are three symbols that may appear in a cluster. An X represents a cluster that cannot be moved, because it contains a system file. A small dot represents a cluster that is in use by a file. A shaded block represents an unused cluster. In Figure 7.4 there are 12 clusters occupied by unmoveable files, and 88 unused clusters. The rest of the disk is filled with moveable files.

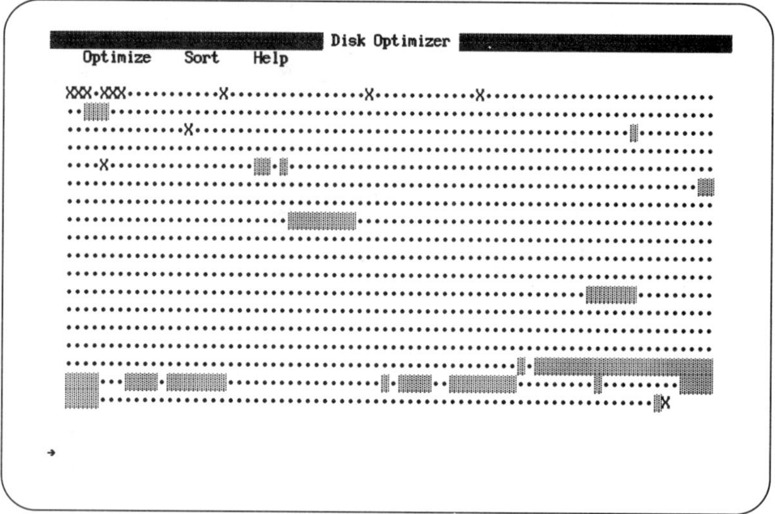

Figure 7.4 Typical DISKOPT Startup Screen

When the DISKOPT startup screen appears, you may choose an option from one of the drop-down menus on the menu bar at the top of the screen. To drop down the Optimize menu, hold down the Alt key and press the O. To drop down the Sort menu, hold down the Alt key and press the S. To drop down the Help menu, hold down the Alt key and press the H.

The Help menu serves as an entry point to a complete on-line system of documentation for the DISKOPT program. This Help system works in exactly the same way as that for the UNDELETE program described in Chapter 6.

The Sort menu provides options for sorting the files in directories. Since a directory is simply a file whose contents are the names and descriptions of other files, they can be sorted in any order you want. The order in which the files appear in the directories has nothing to do with their order on the disk, so sorting them is done simply to make it easier to find them. The Sort menu provides options for sorting by name, extension, date, size, or starting cluster, or for leaving them unsorted.

The Optimize menu provides three options: you may change to a different drive, start the optimization process, or exit from DISKOPT. When you start the optimization process, you will see a message that DISKOPT is analyzing the disk. You will then see the blocks on the screen rearrange themselves as DISKOPT reorganizes the file organization on the disk. You may interrupt this process at any time by pressing the Esc key, but you should never reboot the computer while optimization is in process.

Adjusting the Interleave

DR DOS 6.0 does not provide any programs or commands for changing the interleave of a disk. However, adjusting the interleave to be appropriate for your PC can make a significant difference in the performance of your hard disk. There are programs available from software dealers that can be used to adjust the interleave. These programs are usually capable of analyzing the current interleave as well, and determining what interleave will work best on your computer.

Using the SuperStor Program to Increase Your Hard Disk Capacity

One of the most common problems encountered with PCs that have been in use for awhile is that they don't have enough hard disk space to contain all of the programs and data that the computer is being used for. DR DOS 6.0 addresses this problem by including the SuperStor program, which can effectively increase your available hard disk space by anywhere from two to eight times.

How SuperStor Works

SuperStor is able to increase hard disk capacity by removing inefficiencies in the way in which files are stored. Virtually no files are stored in the most efficient way possible, and many are stored in extremely inefficient formats. To take a simple example, suppose a database has room to store up to 50 characters for the name of a business. There will always be space for 50 characters reserved on the disk, regardless of how many are actually used. If the name of a company in the database is Acme Inc., then there are 41 blank spaces that are never used. Clearly it would more efficient to store the name, followed by the number 41 and a symbol for blank spaces.

SuperStor examines the files on a disk and compresses out the unnecessary spaces. The amount of compression that can be achieve varies with the type of file. Executable program files may be compressed by a factor of from 1.4:1 to 2:1, while most other files can be compressed by factors of between 2:1 and 8:1. Overall, you will usually see the disk capacity of a hard drive approximately doubled when you use SuperStor. SuperStor cannot be used on floppy disks.

There is another way in which SuperStor saves you disk space. You may have noticed that when you create a tiny file, say just a few bytes in size, the free disk space still goes down by 2048 bytes or more. On a hard disk, space is typically allocated in clusters of sectors. Clusters are typically between 2048 and 4096 bytes. Consequently, regardless of how much information is being stored, 2048 bytes are more is the minimum being consumed. When SuperStor controls a disk, it allocates space in sectors, rather than clusters. Sectors are usually 512 bytes each. Consequently, if you are saving a file that is 512 bytes or smaller, you will automatically save at least 75% of the space reserved for the file.

When SuperStor is used on a disk, the entire disk must be converted. This means that all of the files on it are converted to a compressed format. SuperStor then loads a small TSR (Terminate and Stay Resident) program into memory that automatically decompresses information as it comes off the disk, and compresses information as it goes on. This TSR must always be loaded in order to access the disk.

You may leave some of the disk space uncompressed, but when this is done the disk is actually partitioned into two drives, one of which is compressed and the other which is not.

Precautions Before Using SuperStor

The SuperStor program has been designed to be as safe as possible. However, it is making radical changes to the way information is stored on your hard disk, so you should take the following precautions before converting a drive to a SuperStor drive:

1. Make two complete backups of the hard disk before converting it to a SuperStor drive. You want to have two in case something goes wrong with one of them.

2. Remove any copy-protected software from your hard disk before converting the disk, then reinstall the software after the conversion. Copy-protected software has files that must remain intact, and they will almost certainly be corrupted by the SuperStor conversion process. This will render the software unuseable. After SuperStor has been run, copy-protected software can safely be reinstalled on the drive.
3. If you run any programs that create permanent swap files, such as Microsoft Windows, you should remove the swap files before converting the disk. They can be recreated after the conversion.
4. After the above steps have been taken, you should run CHKDSK to make sure your disk is functioning properly. If CHKDSK reports errors, they should be corrected before converting the disk.
5. Make sure that there are no multi-tasking programs, such as TaskMAX, Windows, or DESQview, or TSR programs, loaded when the conversion is done.
6. There must be at least 1.5 megabytes of free disk space, to hold temporary files that SuperStor creates during the conversion. If there is not enough free disk space SuperStor will abort the conversion.

Setting Up a SuperStor Drive

To start SuperStor, enter the command SSTOR at the command prompt. Normally the SuperStor screens will be in color; if you want to force them into black and white mode, enter the command with the /B switch: SSTOR /B. The screen in Figure 7.5 will appear.

Before a drive can be used as a compressed drive, it must be prepared. Preparation involves converting all of the files on the drive to compressed format. To prepare a drive, choose the Prepare option on the SuperStor menu. If there is more than one hard disk partition on your computer you will be provided a menu from which to choose the partition you want to convert.

After you have selected the drive to convert, you are prompted for the amount of space to be saved in uncompressed format. If you specify that some space should be left uncompressed, that space will be set up as a separate drive letter. For all intents and purposes, you will now have two drives where previously you had one. SuperStor will now go ahead and convert your disk. If the disk is empty, conversion will take only a few seconds, but if there are files to be converted then it may take several minutes.

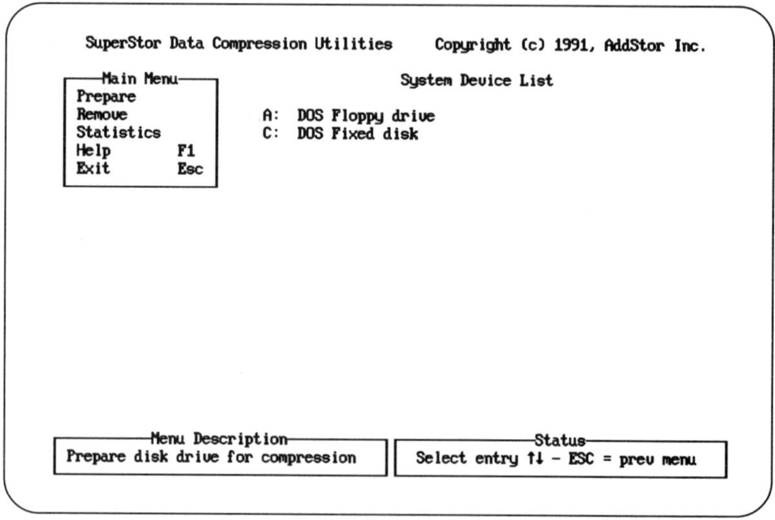

Figure 7.5 SuperStor Startup Screen

Removing a SuperStor Drive

You may remove a SuperStor drive by choosing the Remove option on the menu (Figure 7.5). When you remove a SuperStor drive, all the information on it is lost, so you must back it up before removing it, then restore the contents to the uncompressed drive after it has been removed. You may not remove the current drive, so you must start SuperStor from a drive other than the one you want to remove.

Analyzing the Effect of SuperStor

You may choose the Statistics option on the menu in Figure 7.5 to see the effects of using SuperStor. The following statistics are displayed:

1. *SSTOR Bytes Used.* This is the total number of bytes being used to store data in compressed format.

2. *SSTOR Free (est.).* This is an estimate of how many more bytes can be stored on the disk, assuming that anything new that gets stored on the disk will have the same degree of compression as the existing data.
3. *SSTOR Total (est.).* This is the total number of bytes that SuperStor estimates can be stored on the compressed drive.
4. *Actual Total.* This is the physical size of the disk.
5. *Actual Bytes Used.* This is the number of bytes used, in units of physical sectors, that are being used to store files on the disk.
6. *Actual Free.* This is the number of physical bytes available for storing information on the disk.
7. *Compression Ratio.* This is the efficiency with which data is being compressed. It is obtained by dividing SSTOR Bytes Used by Actual Bytes Used.
8. *Space Savings.* This number is obtained by dividing the Actual Bytes Used by the SSTOR Bytes Used, then subtracting from 100 percent.

Warnings

SuperStor can provide great benefits in terms of your available hard disk space, but the following points should be kept in mind when it is used:

1. SuperStor radically changes the contents of your disk, and you cannot undo these changes without backing up the contents of the SuperStor disk before converting it to SuperStor format, deleting the disk, which destroys its contents, then restoring the contents from the backup disk. Furthermore, if anything causes your computer to shut down while the conversion process is taking place, SuperStor will corrupt at least some of the files on the disk. Consequently, you should make two backups of your disk before converting it, then experiment extensively with the converted disk to make sure it will work properly for you.
2. The CONFIG.SYS file cannot be compressed, because DOS must be able to read it before the SuperStor device driver is loaded. Consequently, SuperStor creates a special area of the

disk that contains the uncompressed CONFIG.SYS file. SuperStor also creates a file named DCONFIG.SYS in this area, which contains the configuration statements. If you want to edit your CONFIG.SYS file, you must use a different drive letter to access it, and you must edit the DCONFIG.SYS file. SuperStor will then copy this into the actual CONFIG.SYS file on the original uncompressed disk.

3. SuperStor will not work with applications that create Fixed Length Files.
4. If you installed DR DOS 6.0 on a computer that had a different version of DOS, you may have reserved the ability to uninstall DR DOS 6.0 and restore the previous operating system. If this case, converting your bootable hard disk (usually drive C:) to a SuperStor disk will make it impossible to do this.

Using Super PC-Kwik to Speed Up Your Disk

Super PC-Kwik is what is known as a *disk-caching* program. Disk caching programs are used to speed up the performance of hard drives, and they often show dramatic improvement in the speed at which certain programs operate. These programs are termed disk-intensive because they perform a lot of disk accesses. Since disk accesses are by far the slowest operation the computer performs, speeding them up can be very beneficial.

Super PC-Kwik is a program that was actually developed and marketed by Multisoft Corporation. It has been around for several years and is generally recognized as one of the best disk caching utilities available. Digital Research has licensed it from Multisoft for inclusion in DR DOS 6.0.

Understanding Super PC-Kwik

A disk cache is like a huge disk buffer, as defined earlier for the BUFFERS command. When a disk cache is set up, the first time a sector is read from the disk, it is stored in the cache. Since the cache is much larger than buffers defined by the BUFFERS command, much more information is stored, thus increasing the likelihood that information needed from the disk will be found in memory. When using Super PC-Kwik, keep in mind that you are storing a lot of information in memory that would normally be written to disk. When the cache fills up, Super PC-Kwik automatically writes some of the information to disk in order to free up some of the cache. However, if your system fails while Super PC-Kwik is running, you may lose substantial amounts of data.

Super PC-Kwik can be installed in conventional, extended, or expanded memory. If you have both extended and expanded memory available, expanded memory is faster because Super PC-Kwik is optimized for it. However, if you have significantly more extended memory than expanded, then you may want to use extended for Super PC-Kwik, in order to conserve the expanded memory for other purposes. The SUPERPCK command is used to install a disk cache, to modify it, and to remove it from memory.

During installation of DR DOS 6.0 you may have specified that Super PC- Kwik be loaded automatically when your computer starts. If you did so, then Super PC-Kwik automatically determined the optimum configuration for your system. If you did not, you may do so at any time using the SETUP program to achieve the same result. Normally, the settings that Super PC-Kwik determines for itself during installation or setup are the best settings, so you don't need to do anything else. However, there are many options available for adjusting the performance and behavior of Super PC-Kwik that you may choose to adjust on your own, using the SUPERPCK command at the command line, with the switches discussed below.

Super PC-Kwik is not a simple program. It provides a remarkable degree of flexibility over how your system resources are used. The following discussion is fairly technical, and assumes some familiarity with the organization of disks, and with the types of memory found on Personal Computers. You may want to review Chapter 4, and the first part of this Chapter, if you are not familiar with these topics.

How Super PC-Kwik Uses Memory

Super PC-Kwik uses memory for three different purposes: to store its own program code, to store a *track buffer*, which contains portions of the disk track before and after the disk sector that it has retrieved for an application, and to store a *cache buffer*, which contains the actual sectors requested. If your system has expanded memory, Super PC-

Kwik will automatically store most of its program code, the track buffers, and the cache buffers in expanded memory. Only a small amount of the Super PC- Kwik program will be stored in conventional memory. If your system has extended memory, but not expanded, then Super PC-Kwik will store the cache buffers in extended memory, but the program code and track buffers will be stored in conventional memory. If your system has neither expanded nor extended memory, then the program code, track buffers, and cache buffers will all be stored in conventional memory.

If Super PC-Kwik is using either expanded or extended memory, it will *lend* some of the memory allocated to the cache buffers to other programs as they need it. Super PC-Kwik is smart enough to observe when a program wants expanded or extended memory and automatically provide it, then retrieve it when the program no longer needs it. By default, half the total cache memory will be available for lending. This amount can be adjusted using the /L switch, discussed below.

If upper memory blocks are available, Super PC-Kwik will automatically use them to reduce the amount of conventional memory it needs.

In the following discussions of the various options, switches can be turned on by following them with a plus sign (+) and turned off by following them with a minus sign (-). The default, if neither is specified, is +, unless otherwise indicated.

The options fall into two broad categories: those that are used only when Super PC-Kwik is loaded, and those that are used while it is running. The options used for loading Super PC-Kwik are discussed first, followed by those that are used while it is running.

The syntax for Super PC-Kwik is:

```
SUPERPCK switches
```

where *Switches* can be any of the switches discussed in the following sections.

Specifying the Drive(s) to Cache

Normally, Super PC-Kwik caches all floppy and hard drives on your computer. RAM drives and network drives are not cached. However, you may wish to prevent it from caching one or more of the drives on your computer. This can be done with the /-d switch, where d is a drive letter.

/-d may only be specified at load time.

Controlling the Use of Upper Memory Blocks

Normally, Super PC-Kwik uses Upper Memory Blocks (UMBs) wherever possible to increase the amount of conventional memory that is available for applications. For example, if you are loading Super PC-Kwik into expanded memory, the small part of the Super PC-Kwik program code that would go into conventional memory is stored in a UMB, if one is available. If you are loading Super PC-Kwik into extended memory, then the track buffers and all of the program code will be loaded into UMBs, if enough are available. You may want to disable this, and preserve your UMBs for other purposes. This can be done using the /&U- switch. The default is /&U+. /&U may only be specified at load time.

Specifying the Use of Expanded memory

The /A+ switch is used to specify that expanded memory should be used. This is the default when no other type of memory is specified. To disable the use of expanded memory, use the /A- switch. /A may only be specified at load time.

Specifying the Use of Extended memory

The /EM+ switch is used to specify that extended memory should be used. Normally, extended memory is automatically used only if expanded memory is not present on your computer. To disable the use of extended memory, the /EM- switch is used. /EM- is required only if your computer has extended memory and no expanded memory. /EM may only be specified at load time.

Controlling Memory Lending

Normally, when either expanded or extended memory is used for disk caching, Super PC-Kwik will lend up to 50% of the memory reserved for the cache buffers to programs that require the type of memory used. This feature may be turned off, or the amount of memory to be lent can be modified, using the /L switch. To specify a certain number of kilobytes of memory that can be lent to programs, use the /L:nnnnn syntax. For example, the following switch setting specifies that up to 512K of expanded or extended memory be lent to applications:

```
/L:512
```

The maximum amount of memory that may be specified with the /L switch is determined dynamically by Super PC-Kwik, depending on your computer's configuration. If you specify more memory than Super PC-Kwik determines for the maximum, it will lend the maximum amount. For example, if the above switch were used and Super PC-Kwik determined that the maximum amount that could be lent was 256K, then it would lend up to 256K.

To disable memory lending altogether, the /L- syntax is used. /L may only be specified at load time.

There may be times when memory lending does not work with a specific program. Even though memory lending is turned on, the program will not be able to borrow memory from the cache. When this happens, you may use the /R switch to specify a particular amount of memory to be reserved for applications. The type of memory reserved will automatically be whatever type is used for the cache. The rest of that type of memory will then be used for the cache. The following switch specifies that 256K is to be reserved for use by applications:

```
/R:256
```

Note that /L is a better choice when it works, because it allows the cache to use the memory when an application is not using it. /R reserves the memory exclusively for applications, so the cache is never able to use it.

The default values, if /R is not specified, are 480K for conventional memory and 0K for expanded and extended memory. /R may only be specified at load time.

There is another technique for insuring that extended memory will be available for your applications. When Super PC-Kwik allocates extended memory for use in the cache, it allocates it from the top down. For example, suppose you had one megabyte of extended memory. The addresses for that memory would go from 1024K to 2048K. If Super PC-Kwik allocated 512K of extended memory, it would use the addresses from 1536K to 2048K. If Super PC-Kwik does not recognize that an application you are running needs extended memory, you may tell Super PC-Kwik what the lowest address is that it should use for the cache. All extended memory below that address will then be available for applications. This is done with the /EM:nnnnn and /EP:nnnnn switches. The nnnnn specifies the lowest extended memory address to be used for the cache.

Since these switches limit the amount of extended memory that will be used for the cache, Super PC-Kwik may have to do one of two things to compensate: either it will reduce the cache size, and thereby lower the performance benefits gained by the cache; or it will keep the same cache size by using conventional memory, thereby lowering the amount of conventional memory available to applications. The letters M and P stand for Memory and Performance—the /EM:nnnnn switch tells Super PC-Kwik to conserve memory by reducing the cache size, while the /EP:nnnnn switch tells it to conserve performance by reducing available conventional memory.

This switch should not be used unless you are absolutely certain it is the only way to allocate memory the way you want to. The /R and /S options are preferred (/S is discussed below). The default value is /E:1024, which means that all extended memory is used by Super PC-Kwik. Since this specifies all extended memory, the M and P specifiers are not needed.

/E may only be specified at load time.

The /S switch is the opposite of /R. Where /R specifies the amount of memory to be reserved for applications, and leaves the rest to Super PC-Kwik, /S specifies the amount of memory to be used by Super PC-Kwik and leaves the rest for applications. The syntax for /S is /S:nnnnn, where nnnnn is the number of kilobytes to allocate. To specify 512K of memory for Super PC-Kwik, the following switch would be used:

```
/S:512
```

Normally, it is best to let Super PC-Kwik take over all of the memory and lend it out to programs as they need it. This is the default setting, if none of the memory control switches are set. However, under some circumstances you may have reason to want a cache of a specific size, in which case /S is the appropriate switch. There is no default setting for /S; if it is not specified then the default /R switch is used. If you are using /S and Super PC-Kwik is loading into conventional memory, then nnnnn should be between 64 and 512. If you are using it with expanded or extended memory, nnnnn should be between 64 and 16,384. /S may only be specified at load time.

Displaying a Drive Table During Loading

The /I+ switch may be used to display the drive table shown in Figure 7.6 when Super PC-Kwik loads. /I may only be specified at load time.

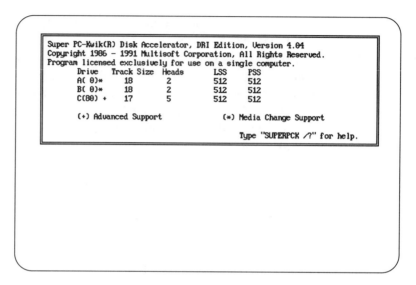

```
Super PC-Kwik(R) Disk Accelerator, DRI Edition, Version 4.04
Copyright 1986 - 1991 Multisoft Corporation, All Rights Reserved.
Program licensed exclusively for use on a single computer.
         Drive     Track Size  Heads         LSS     PSS
         A( 0)*       18         2           512     512
         B( 0)*       18         2           512     512
         C(80) +      17         5           512     512

         (+) Advanced Support              (*) Media Change Support

                                      Type "SUPERPCK /?" for help.
```

Figure 7.6 Drive Table Displayed by /I+ Switch with Super PC-Kwik

Controlling the Data Transfer Method

There are two ways in which Super PC-Kwik can transfer information between the disk and the cache: either one sector at a time, or in batches of sectors. It is much faster to transfer batches of sectors, so that is how Super PC-Kwik does it by default. However, when copying is taking place, the rest of the machine's operation is suspended. This is not normally a problem, but if you are transferring data over a high-speed communication line, such as a 2400 baud modem, suspending the data transfer long enough to perform a batch read or write may create problems with the communication. If this happens, you may force Super PC-Kwik to perform single-sector transfers between the cache and the disk with the /B- switch. The default, if /B is not specified, is /B+, which turns on batch transfers. /B may only be specified at load time.

Controlling Advanced Support for Floppy Disk Drives

If the diskette drives in your computer are 100% IBM compatible, then it is possible for Super PC-Kwik to use special techniques for speeding up the data transfer rate between the cache and floppy disks. The /D+ switch turns on this advanced support, and /D- turns it off. Super PC-

Kwik will automatically determine whether your floppy disk drives can take advantage of these techniques, and set the default accordingly. Consequently, it is not normally necessary to use this switch. /D may only be specified at load time.

Controlling Advanced Support for Hard Disk Drives

Just as floppy drives that are 100% IBM compatible may use advanced techniques for speeding up the transfer of information between the cache and the disk, so can hard drives that are 100% IBM compatible. AT-style computers can take advantage of this even if their hard drives are not 100% IBM compatible. The /H+ switch turns on this advanced support, and /H- turns it off. Super PC-Kwik will automatically determine whether your hard disk can take advantage of these techniques, and set the default accordingly. Consequently, it is not normally necessary to use this switch. /H may only be specified at load time.

Giving Disk Reads Priority Over Disk Writes

When either /D+ or /H+ is used, the /O+ switch can be set to make use of an optional algorithm that gives disk read operations priority over disk write operations. Depending on the speed of your disk drives, and the type of applications you are running, this may increase the performance even further than /D+ or /H+ alone. It will also usually improve the effect of the /Q+ switch, which is used to speed up the return to the DOS prompt. /Q+ is discussed below. The default value of /O is /O-, which does not use the optional algorithm to give read operations priority over write operations. /O may only be specified at load time.

Using /Q+ to Quickly Return to the DOS Prompt

Like /O+, this option can only be used when either /D+ or /H+ is also being used. When the last step in a command or application execution is a disk read or write, /Q+ can cause the computer to return to the DOS prompt more quickly than it would otherwise. This allows you to start another application or execute another command while the previous disk transfer is still completing.

When you use this option, it is possible that you will start another operation that uses a diskette drive that is still transferring data to or from the cache. You must be sure to wait for the drive light to go off before removing the diskette that is in the drive.

If you use /Q+, you may find that /O+ increases its effectiveness. The default value of the /Q switch is /Q-. /Q may only be specified at load time.

Controlling Track Buffering

When a command or program requests information from the disk, Super PC-Kwik automatically reads the entire track into the cache. It is common that a disk request will be for information that is physically near the previous and next requests, so by reading the entire track into the cache at once, Super PC-Kwik is able to speed up overall disk access. However, reading the entire track increases the memory overhead of Super PC-Kwik by about 8K. Under most circumstances, this is worth the extra memory.

However, if your disk accesses are for many small files that are scattered around the disk, or if you need the extra memory, you can adjust the amount of track buffering with the /T switch. You can disable track buffering altogether by specifying /T-. Alternatively, you may specify a maximum number of sectors per track to use by using the /T:nn syntax, where nn is the number of sectors per track.

The default setting is /T+, which tells Super PC-Kwik to automatically choose a buffer size. When this is done, Super PC- Kwik usually chooses the best balance of buffer size and memory use, with a maximum of 72 sectors. If you have a lot of extra memory and a disk with a larger track size, the /T:nn switch can be used.

The third way of using the /T switch is to specify /TL, which tells Super PC-Kwik to examine the entire disk to determine the largest track it contains, and use the number of sectors on that track as the maximum. /T may only be specified at load time.

Detecting Changed Disks in Floppy Drives

High-capacity 5.25-inch drives, and 3.5-inch drives, often have special hardware built in that generates a signal when the drive door is opened. When this is the case, Super PC-Kwik can use this signal to update itself automatically to work with the contents of the new disk. The /V+

switch is used to turn on volume-change detection. This option will never affect 360K drives, because they never have volume change detection hardware. /V is on by default—to turn it off, specify /V-. You normally do not need to use /V because Super PC-Kwik automatically detects whether or not the appropriate hardware is present, and set /V accordingly. /V may only be specified at load time.

Suppressing Unnecessary Write Operations

When Super PC-Kwik performs a write operation, it first checks to see if the information on the disk is identical to what will be written. If it is, the write operation is cancelled. This speeds up the performance of Super PC-Kwik. You can turn this feature off, which forces Super PC-Kwik to always write data even if the disk contains identical data, with the /W- switch. The default is /W+, which suppresses the writing of identical data. /W may only be specified at load time.

Managing Conflicts Between BIOS and Boot Sector Information

Super PC-Kwik has to know some things about each drive that it works with, such as the size and format. When Super PC-Kwik starts, it reads the boot sector on the disk, where this information is stored. The information can also be obtained from the computer's BIOS (Basic Input Output Services). Occasionally, a computer will have conflicting information in these two places—the boot sector will describe the number of heads, or the number of sectors per track, differently than the BIOS does. When Super PC-Kwik encounters this situation, it displays a warning message and uses the information in the boot sector. The /G- switch tells Super PC-Kwik to use the BIOS information instead of the boot sector information. The default value is /G+, which tells Super PC-Kwik to use the information in the boot sector. /G may only be specified at load time.

Controlling the Display of Warning Messages

Whenever Super PC-Kwik displays a warning message during loading, it pauses and waits for you to press a key. This is helpful when you need to do something about the warning, but sometimes you will know that the configuration you are using will generate one or more warning messages, and you want to use it anyway. In this case, it is a nuisance to have to press a key to get Super PC-Kwik started again. The /K- switch can be used to turn off this pause feature. The default value is /K+, which causes Super PC-Kwik to pause. /K may only be specified at load time.

Displaying Switch Settings

The /P+ switch is used to display all of the switch settings used by Super PC-Kwik when it loads. Since Super PC-Kwik sets many switches with default values, unless you explicitly set them on the command line, it can be useful to see what Super PC-Kwik is using for default values. Figure 7.7 shows a typical display produced by the /P+ switch. /P may only be specified at load time.

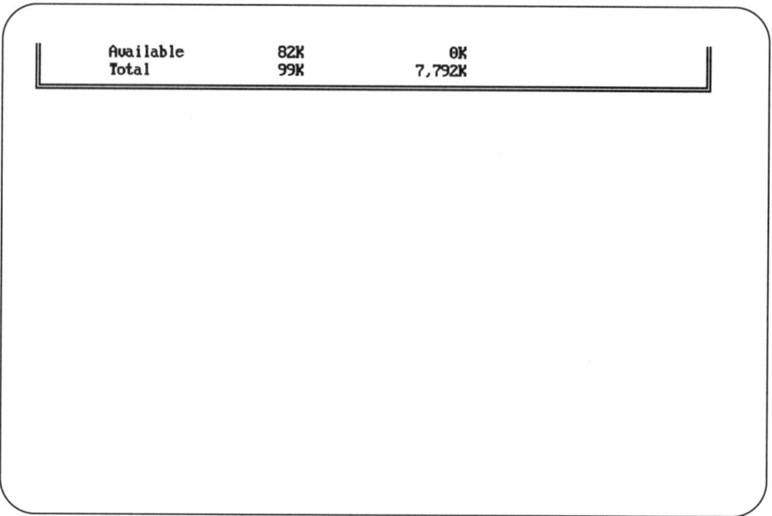

Figure 7.7 Switch Settings Displayed by /P+ Switch with Super PC-Kwik

Temporarily Disabling and Enabling the Super PC-Kwik Cache

Under some circumstances you may find that Super PC-Kwik interferes with the proper functioning of an application. When this happens, you may use the /D switch to disable the cache, and all other Super PC-Kwik functions. When you want to use it again, the /E switch can be used to make it active. /D and /E may only be specified after Super PC-Kwik is running.

Flushing the Cache

Normally Super PC-Kwik will automatically keep your disks up to date, writing information to them as necessary. However, you may use the /F switch to force Super PC-Kwik to write the contents of the cache to disk. This does not remove any data from the cache, but does make the disks current with the cache. /F may only be specified after Super PC-Kwik is running.

Displaying Disk Cache Measurements

The /M switch may be used to display the following cache measurements: the number of disk transfer requests, the number of physical disk transfers, the number of disk transfers saved, and the percentage of disk transfers saved. A typical screen resulting from this switch is shown in Figure 7.8. /M may only be specified after Super PC-Kwik is running.

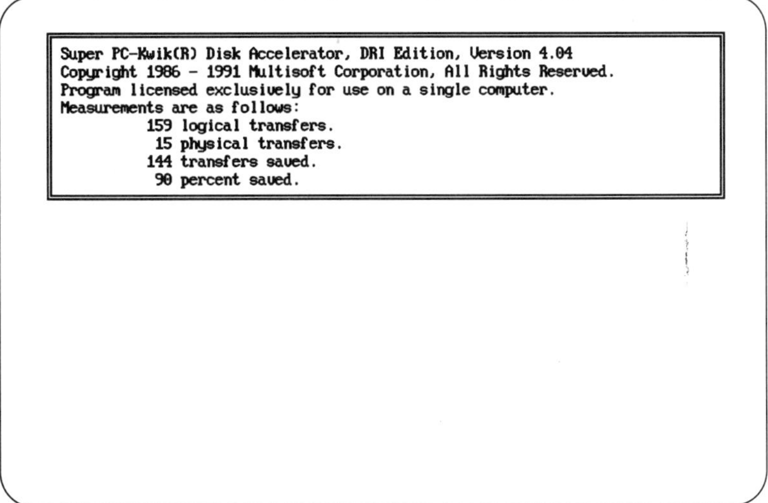

```
Super PC-Kwik(R) Disk Accelerator, DRI Edition, Version 4.04
Copyright 1986 - 1991 Multisoft Corporation, All Rights Reserved.
Program licensed exclusively for use on a single computer.
Measurements are as follows:
          159 logical transfers.
           15 physical transfers.
          144 transfers saved.
           90 percent saved.
```

Figure 7.8 Output of /M Switch with Super PC-Kwik

Unloading Super PC-Kwik from Memory

The /U switch is used to remove Super PC-Kwik from memory. After using /U, the computer is left configured as though Super PC-Kwik had never been loaded. /U may only be specified after Super PC- Kwik is running.

Tips for Using Super PC-Kwik

If you find that Super PC-Kwik is taking up more conventional memory than you want, you can save some by using the /T:nn option to specify 4 or 8 track buffers. This will slow down Super PC-Kwik a little, but gives you more conventional memory.

If you are using extended memory with Super PC-Kwik, and it appears that applications that need extended memory are not able to borrow it from Super PC-Kwik, try using the /R switch to reserve extended memory for applications. Note that this will make the specified amount of extended memory unavailable to Super PC-Kwik.

Since Super PC-Kwik is caching the hard disk for you, you probably don't need to have as many disk buffers as you would without it. This can only be determined by experimentation. A good place to start is to set BUFFERS equal to 3, and see if your disk performance decreases. If it does, gradually increase the BUFFERS until disk performance no longer improves. If you are running Microsoft Windows, you may want to start with 10. Eliminating disk buffers saves memory.

If you are running TaskMAX with Super PC-Kwik, be sure to load Super PC-Kwik before TaskMAX. Otherwise, you will be switching the cache in and out of action whenever you switch in and out of the task it was loaded in. This can result in the cache and the disk getting out of sync.

IOMEGA Bernoulli drives can also be cached using Super PC-Kwik, but they require that a special device driver be installed in the CONFIG.SYS file. If you have a Bernoulli drive, follow these steps:

1. Look in your CONFIG.SYS file for the line that specifies the device driver for the Bernoulli drive; this driver may be named IDRIVE.SYS or RCD.SYS. Place the following line immediately after it:

   ```
   DEVICE=C:\DRDOS\PCKWIK.SYS
   ```

   If the PCKWIK.SYS file is in a directory other than DRDOS, then specify that directory.

   You may not load the PCKWIK.SYS driver into high memory with the HIDEVICE command, even if the Bernoulli driver is loaded high. PCKWIK.SYS must be loaded into conventional memory.

2. Reboot your computer. A sign-on message from the PCKWIK.SYS driver should appear during the boot process.
3. Start Super PC-Kwik the same you normally would. The Bernoulli drive will now be cached.

Note that some Bernoulli drives come with a disk cache utility named IOMCACHE. You cannot run two disk cache utilities at the same time. Super PC-Kwik provides all of the functions that IOMCACHE provides, and much more, so if you are using IOMCACHE it should be replaced with Super PC-Kwik.

Since Super PC-Kwik will run in any type of memory, you may use it regardless of what type of memory you have in your PC. In general, however, it is advisable to use Super PC-Kwik only if you have expanded or extended memory. You must be sure to leave sufficient extended or expanded memory for whatever other purposes you want to use them for, then provide the largest possible cache. To determine how large a cache your system can handle, install the largest possible cache and test your programs. If they don't run, reduce the size of the cache a little and try again. When all of your programs run successfully, you have found the largest cache you can have for that set of programs.

It is a good idea to use the DISKOPT disk compaction program to keep your disk well organized, whether or not you are using Super PC-Kwik. If you are using Super PC-Kwik, DISKOPT will keep Super PC-Kwik performing as efficiently as possible, because it keeps related information in the same area of the disk.

Transferring Files Between Computers Using FILELINK

With the increasing variety of disk drives found in computers today, and with laptops becoming ever more common, a frequent problem is how to quickly transfer files between two different computers that may have different size disk drives. DR DOS 6.0 addresses this problem by providing the FILELINK program, which allows you to connect two computers together with a serial cable and copy files back and forth. You may also use FILELINK to use one computer to examine the files on another.

In order for FILELINK to work, it must be running on both computers. One of its useful features is that it can be installed on one computer through a serial communications port that is connected to a computer on which it is already installed.

To use FILELINK you must understand the notion of a master computer and a slave computer. When two computers are connected together with FILELINK, you may only enter commands on one of them. This one is called the master computer. The other computer, called the slave, is connected to the master. You may use the master to examine and copy files on either computer; the slave cannot be used while FILELINK is running.

FILELINK Command Syntax

The FILELINK syntax is:

```
FILELINK command filespec1 filespec2 comparm /switches
```

The command may be any one of the following: DIRECTORY, DUPLICATE, QUIT, RECEIVE, SETUP, SLAVE, and TRANSMIT. Filespec1 is the source file specifier of the file(s) to be copied; it may include wildcards or a filelist. Filespec2 is the destination drive, path, and name. If filespec2 contains a name other than that on the source specifier, the files are renamed during the copy operation.

Setting the Communications Port and Baud Rate

The comparm is a combination of specifiers that indicate what communications port the serial cable is plugged into, and the baud rate. The COM port number is typically either 1 or 2; the baud rate may be any of those shown in Table 4. Either the full baud rate or the abbreviation may be used.

Table 7.4 Standard Baud Rates and Abbreviations for FILELINK Command

Baud Rate	**Abbreviation**
115,200	115
57,600	57

Table 7.4 continued ...

Baud Rate	***Abbreviation***
38,400	38
19,200	19
9,600	96
4,800	48
2,500	24
1,200	12
600	60
300	30
150	15
110	11

The higher the baud rate, the faster the data transfer rate will be. Most computers work fine with a 9600 baud rate, so that is a good place to start. Once you have that working, you can try increasing the rate to find the fastest possible speed for your computer. It is ESSENTIAL that both computers run at the same baud rate—FILELINK will not work otherwise.

You may set up a default communications port and baud that FILELINK will always use, so you don't have to specify them every time you use FILELINK, with the following SETUP command:

```
FILELINK SETUP comparm
```

For example, the command FILELINK SETUP com1:9600 would set up FILELINK on your computer to always use com port 1, and a baud rate of 9600.

Entering FILELINK SETUP by itself displays the current setup for FILELINK.

Installing FILELINK on a Slave Computer

If you have FILELINK installed on one computer, you may install it on a second computer by connecting them with a serial port and entering the following command:

```
FILELINK DUPLICATE comparm
```

where *Comparm* is the communications port on the MASTER computer. You will then be prompted through a number of steps to install FILELINK on the slave.

Transferring Files with FILELINK

In order to transfer files between the master and slave computers, you must first execute the following command on the slave computer:

```
FILELINK SLAVE comparm
```

The /X switch may be appended to this command to prevent files from being overwritten on the slave.

Once this command has been entered on the slave, the FILELINK TRANSMIT command may be used on the master computer. The TRANSMIT command accepts the switches shown in Figure 7.9.

Switch	*Effect*
/A	Copies only files that have the Archive attribute set.
/D:date	Copies only files that have been modified since the specified date.
/H	Includes files with the Hidden and/or System attributes set.
/M	Copies only files that have the Archive attribute set on the source, and either do not exist or do not have their Archive attribute set on the target. This is the same as the /M switch for the REPLACE command.
/P	Causes FILELINK to prompt you before each file is copied.
/R	Causes FILELINK to overwrite files on the slave that have the Read-only attribute set. By default, FILELINK will not overwrite these.
/S	Causes FILELINK to include files in subdirectories that stem from the source directory.
/U	Causes FILELINK to copy only those files that either do not exist on the slave, or that exist but have an earlier date stamp.

Figure 7.9 Switches for FILELINK TRANSMIT Command

Displaying the Directories and Files on the Slave

The FILELINK DIRECTORY command is used on the master computer to display the files on the slave. This command uses the following syntax:

```
FILELINK DIRECTORY filespec comparm switches
```

The switches for this command are summarized in Figure 7.10.

Switch	*Effect*
/A	Shows only files that have the Archive attribute set.
/D:date	Shows only files that have been modified since the specified date.
/H	Includes files with the Hidden and/or System attributes set.
/P	Causes FILELINK to pause after each screenful.
/S	Causes FILELINK to display files in subdirectories that stem from the source directory.

Figure 7.10 Switches for FILELINK DIRECTORY Command

Chapter 8

The DR DOS 6.0 Editor

DR DOS 6.0 comes with a full-screen text editor named, appropriately, *EDITOR*. EDITOR produces plain ASCII text files, which means they have only the standard and extended ASCII characters in them. A complete table of the ASCII characters and their codes appears in the appendix. Batch files, the CONFIG.SYS file, the DR DOS 6.0, TaskMAX, and ViewMAX initialization files, and other files used by DOS, all must contain standard ASCII codes only. Most word processors do not produce plain ASCII files unless you specifically tell them to.

EDITOR is a command line editor, which means that commands are entered as keystrokes, rather than from menu choices. In fact, EDITOR is very similar to the original WordStar editor. If you are familiar with the basic WordStar commands you already know how to use Editor.

If you have a VGA or EGA monitor, EDITOR will write information directly to the screen memory rather than use BIOS function calls to display your file's contents. If you have some other type of monitor, EDITOR will use the BIOS calls. You may force EDITOR to use the BIOS calls with EGA and VGA monitors by specifying the /D switch for the EDITOR command.

Starting and Leaving EDITOR

You start EDITOR with the EDITOR command. You may include a file name as a parameter on the command line, in which case the specified file is loaded when EDITOR starts. If no file name is specified, the EDITOR Startup Screen shown in Figure 8.1 will be displayed.

```
EDITOR R2.00    Full Screen Text Editor    Copyright (c)
1988,1989,1990 Digital Research Inc. All rights reserved.



Please enter the name of the text file you wish to edit. If the
file does not already exist it will be created. Press the Esc key
to leave this program.
File name?
```

Figure 8.1 EDITOR Startup Screen

You may press the Esc key from the screen in Figure 8.1 to abort the EDITOR program and return to the command prompt. Alternatively, if this screen is displayed after you have been editing a file, holding down the Ctrl key and pressing R will play back the previous file name. If you enter the name of a file that does not exist, the screen clears and the following message appears:

```
filespec ...file not found
Create new file (Y/N)?
```

Responding with an N returns you to the screen in Figure 8.1; responding with a Y causes EDITOR to create the file and take you to a blank editing screen, where you can start entering text. If you specify a file that already exists, then the editing screen will contain that file.

There are several keystrokes that can be used to end an editing session. When an editing session is ended, you are usually returned to the EDITOR Startup Screen (Figure 8.1), from which you may press Esc to return to the command prompt. All of the keystrokes for ending editing sessions involve a Ctrl + K keystroke, followed by one more keystroke. The Ctrl + KQ command will terminate the current editing session without saving any changes you have made to the file and return you to the Startup Screen. The Ctrl + KX command saves any changes you have made and exits EDITOR, returning you to the command prompt rather than the Startup Screen. The Ctrl + KD command saves any changes you have made and returns you to the Startup Screen. The Ctrl + KS command saves any changes and continues editing the same file. This is useful when you are working for a long time in a single file, and want to make sure changes are saved periodically in case of a system failure.

The EDITOR Screen

The EDITOR screen is primarily reserved for displaying files that are being edited. However, the top line of the screen contains several items of information. A typical example is shown in Figure 8.2.

```
c:\wp\letters\mary.let  chr=1 col=1     ins. ^J=help
```

Figure 8.2 Top Line of EDITOR Screen

At the left end of this line is the complete path and filename for the file being edited. Following that are two numbers, one labeled *chr* and the other, *col*. The chr number is the number of characters from the start of the file to the current cursor position, including that position. Tab stops and carriage-return line feeds, which are inserted when you press the Enter key, count as single characters. The col number represents the horizontal position of the cursor. When EDITOR is first started, as in Figure 8.2, the cursor is in the first position of the file.

Following the col number is the term *ins.* This indicates that the computer is in Insert mode. If you press the Insert key, this term disappears, indicating that the computer has changed to Overwrite mode. Pressing Insert again turns it back on. Insert and Overwrite modes are discussed below.

At the far right of the screen is the phrase *^J=help*. The caret in front of the J means that you should hold down the Ctrl key and press the J. This phrase tells you that holding down the Control key and pressing J will bring up a Help screen.

On-line Help for EDITOR

Pressing Ctrl + J or F1 brings up the help screen in Figure 8.3.

```
Entering text
Type text as at a typewriter. Press the Enter key to begin a new line.
In insert mode existing text is moved aside to accommodate text you
              type.
In overwrite mode the text you type replaces existing text.
Ctrl-V        Switch between insert and overwrite modes
Ctrl-N        Insert new line at cursor
Ctrl-P        The next character you type is entered as a control
              code
Ctrl-Qn       Enter character code directly (0..255 or 0x00..0xFF)
Deleting text
Ctrl-H        Delete the character immediately before the cursor
Ctrl-G        Delete the character at the cursor
Ctrl-T        Delete the "word" at the cursor
Ctrl-Y        Delete the line containing the cursor



Press Enter for next page, or Esc to resume editing...
```

Figure 8.3   First Help Screen for EDITOR

There is a total of three such Help screens, which are displayed consecutively if your press the Enter key. They provide information on entering text, deleting text, moving the cursor, finishing an edit session, working with blocks of text, and miscellaneous commands. When the third Help screen is displayed, pressing the Enter key again displays the following prompt:

```
Do you wish to have the quick reference display (Y/N)?
```

If you answer N, you are returned to the screen just as it was before you pressed Ctrl + J. However, if you answer Y, you will be returned to the editing screen with the top six lines occupied with a quick reference to the most commonly used keystrokes. This quick reference section is shown in Figure 8.4.

To Move the Cursor		To Delete Text	To Finish Editing
^Qr Top of file	^Qc Bottom of file	^H char left	^Ks save text & resume
^R Previous page	^C Next page	^G char	^Kd save text & edit new
^E Previous line	^X Next line	^T word	^Kx save text & exit
^A Previous word	^F Next word	^Y line	^Kq don't save, edit new
^S Previous char	^D Next character		

Figure 8.4 Quick Reference Display in EDITOR Screen

There are many commands that begin with either Ctrl + K or Ctrl + Q. Consequently, when the Quick Reference Display is turned on, pressing Ctrl + K shifts it to display all of the commands that begin with Ctrl + K, and pressing Ctrl + Q shifts it to display all of the commands that begin with Ctrl + Q.

When you are first learning to use EDITOR it is a good idea to keep this Quick Reference Display turned on. However, once you have become familiar with these commands it should be turned off to provide a larger screen for editing your files.

Entering Text

When the EDITOR screen appears you can begin entering text. Assuming you arc starting a new file, the screen will be blank and whatever you type will appear starting in the upper left corner of the screen. If you are used to using a word processor, there is one important difference with EDITOR that you should be aware of: EDITOR does not have a word wrap feature, which means that when it comes to the right edge of the screen, it simply keeps going. The display scrolls 25 characters to the left, so that the characters you type continue to appear on the right side of the screen. The column number at the top of the screen (col) will let you know how far over you have typed. To avoid this, press the Enter key when you get near the right edge of the screen to start a new line.

Switching Between Insert and Overstrike Mode

When EDITOR starts it is in insert mode, which means that if you move the cursor to the middle of a line and start typing, whatever you type is inserted into the line, pushing everything beyond it to the right. You can switch to Overstrike mode by pressing the Insert key. You will notice that the term *ins.* in the upper right corner of the screen disappears. In Overstrike mode, anything you type overwrites whatever is already there. Pressing Insert again switches Insert mode back on.

Use of the Tab Key

The Tab key generates a tab character, which is ASCII code 9. When a tab character is encountered in EDITOR, the cursor jumps eight spaces to the right. In most word processors you can set the tab spacing to move any number of characters you want, though eight is the usual default. You cannot modify the tab setting in EDITOR. Note that although the tab character appears to place eight blanks in your file, it doesn't—it simply places a single tab character. You will notice that the *chr* number at the top of the screen changes by one, not eight, when a tab is entered.

Entering Control Characters

Control characters are part of the ASCII table of standard characters, but they are not alphanumeric characters. Instead, they are special codes that are used for a variety of purposes—sending a form feed to the printer and causing the computer to beep are two examples. In fact, the tab character is also a control character—it tells the current display device to move the cursor the number of characters defined as the current tab setting.

Control characters are often entered by holding down the Control key and pressing one of the letters. The control characters and their meaning can be seen in the ASCII table in the appendix, where the letter that corresponds to them is also shown. For example, ASCII 7 is the *BEL* character, which causes the computer to beep. It is referred to as Control-G, because it is generated by holding down the Ctrl key and pressing the G.

You can include Ctrl characters in your EDITOR files, but because the Ctrl key is used in conjunction with commands, you must use a special technique to do it. To enter a control character, hold down the Ctrl key and press the P. The ^P symbol will appear in the upper left corner, with the cursor flashing after it, indicating that it is waiting for the rest of the control character. Now press the letter G. The ^G symbol will appear in the last cursor position in your file. Note that this is a single character—backspacing over it deletes both the caret and the G, and it only counts for one character in the *chr* number at the top of the screen.

Control codes can also be entered in EDITOR using the Ctrl + QN keys, as described below in the section *Entering Extended ASCII Codes.* However, the Alt + number technique described in the same section does not work for all control codes.

Entering Extended ASCII Codes

The standard ASCII table consists of 128 codes, numbered 0 through 127. The number 128 derives from the fact that seven bits are used to store them, and the largest number that can be stored in seven bits is 128 (2 to the 7th is 128). However, IBM-compatible personal computers work with eight-bit bytes. 2 to the 8th is 256, so sticking with the standard ASCII codes leaves 128 codes unused. Consequently, when the first PC was developed, IBM defined an *extended ASCII table* which uses the codes from 128 through 255 to store special symbols, such as line drawing symbols, letters of the Greek alphabet, and others. These can be seen in the Appendix.

The extended ASCII codes can also be entered in your EDITOR files, using the Alt key and the numeric keypad. In fact, almost any symbol in the ASCII table can be entered this way, in EDITOR as well as at the command prompt and in most application programs. The technique is simple: hold down the Alt key and enter the numeric ASCII code for the character, on the numeric keypad, then release the Alt key. You cannot use the number keys at the top of the keyboard for this purpose. For example, to enter the letter A you can hold down the Alt key and enter the number 65. You do not have to press the Enter key—releasing the Alt key sends the code to the computer. Using this technique with ASCII codes 179 through 223, you can draw boxes and figures in your files.

EDITOR does not allow you to enter all of the control codes using this technique, though most programs will. To enter control codes, use the technique described in the preceding section, or the following technique.

Some computers, particularly notebooks and laptops, do not have a numeric keypad. If your keyboard does not have a numeric keypad, or if you want to enter control codes using their ASCII codes instead of the Ctrl + P technique described above, you can enter the command Ctrl + QN. When this command is entered, EDITOR displays the following prompt:

```
Character code number (0..255 or 0x00..0xFF)?
```

At this prompt, you may type the decimal ASCII code, or the hexadecimal ASCII code preceded with a 0x. For example, the ASCII code for a double line in the lower left corner of a box is 200 decimal, and C8 hex. Either of the following two responses to the above prompt would produce this character:

```
200        0xC8
```

After entering the ASCII code, press the Enter key to insert the character at the cursor position.

Moving the Cursor

There are a variety of keys available for moving the cursor around on the screen and through your file. Which to use is sometimes a matter of personal preference, while other times it is dictated by how far you want to move the cursor.

Moving the Cursor to the Right

There are three ways to move the cursor to the right. The Ctrl + D and right arrow keys move the cursor *one character* to the right, the Ctrl + F and Ctrl + right arrow keys move the cursor *one word* to the right, and the Ctrl + QD and Ctrl + Q + right arrow move the cursor to the *end of the line*.

Moving the Cursor to the Left

There are three ways to move the cursor to the left. The Ctrl + S and left arrow keys move the cursor *one character* to the left, the Ctrl + A and Ctrl + left arrow keys move the cursor *one word* to the left, and the Ctrl + QS and Ctrl + Q + left arrow keys move the cursor to the *beginning of the line*.

Moving the Cursor Up

There are three ways to move the cursor up. The Ctrl + E and up arrow keys move the cursor up *one line*. The Ctrl + R and PgUp keys move the cursor up *one screen*. The Ctrl + QR and Home keys move the cursor to the *beginning of the file*.

Moving the Cursor Down

There are three ways to move the cursor down. The Ctrl + X and Down arrow keys move the cursor down *one line*. The Ctrl + C and PgDn keys move the cursor down *one screen*. The Ctrl + QC and End keys move the cursor to the *end of the file*.

How to Remember the Cursor Movement Keys

The arrow, PgUp, PgDn, Home, and End keys are fairly easy to remember, as there is some logic to their use. There is logic to the other keys as well, but it isn't quite as obvious. If you examine the positions of the E, S, X, and D keys you will see that they form a diamond on the keyboard. The E key is at the top, the X key is at the bottom, the S key is at the left, and the D key is at the right. Consequently, holding down the Ctrl key and pressing one of the keys in this diamond moves the cursor in that direction.

The A key is further to the left than the S key, so it moves the cursor further to the left—a whole word, rather than a single character—when the Ctrl key is held down. Likewise, the F key is further to the right than the D key, so it moves the cursor further to the right—a whole word, rather than a single character—when the Ctrl key is held down.

The R and C keys are not quite as intuitive, since they are not further up or down than the E and X keys.

The letter Q is short for *Quick*, and it has the effect of extending a keystroke, as though you repeated it very quickly a number of times. For example, Ctrl + QR moves you quickly to the top of the file and Ctrl + QC moves you quickly to the bottom of the file.

Moving the Cursor to the Beginning and End of Blocks

Marking and working with blocks is discussed below, in the section *Editing a File*. When a block is marked, you may move to the beginning of the block by pressing Ctrl + QB, and you may move to the end of the block by pressing Ctrl + QK.

Moving The Cursor To Tagged Positions

You may define up to ten *tags* in a file. A tag is place marker—a position you can jump to quickly. To place a tag, hold down the Ctrl + K key and press a number between 0 and 9. The tag is now set. To jump to it from any place in the file, press the Ctrl + Q key and press the corresponding number. The cursor will jump to the tagged position.

Scrolling the Screen

The screen may be scrolled up one line at a time by pressing the Ctrl + Z keys, and down by pressing the Ctrl + W keys. These keys can be held down for continuous scrolling. The cursor will stay in the same position in the text until it reaches the top or bottom of the screen.

Editing a File

Editing a file involves entering text, deleting text, moving part of the text from one place to another, and duplicating text in different parts of the file. Commands for carrying out these operations are discussed in the following sections.

Deleting Text

There are five ways to delete text, depending on how much you want to delete. The Backspace key deletes the character to the left of the cursor, and moves the cursor back one space. The Ctrl + H keys have the same effect as Backspace. The Ctrl + G and Del keys delete the character at the cursor position.

The Ctrl + T keys delete everything from the current cursor position to the beginning of the next word. For example, consider the following line:

```
This is a test line for EDITOR.
```

If the cursor is under the l at the beginning of the word *line*, pressing Ctrl + T will remove the word *line* and move the word *for* forward, so that the f will be where the l is now. If the cursor is under the letter i in *line*, then pressing Ctrl + T will move the word *for* up to where the i is, so that the term *lfor* will appear where the word line is.

You can delete an entire line by pressing the Ctrl + Y keys. It does not matter where in the line the cursor is.

You can delete an entire block of text by marking the block using the techniques in the following section, and pressing the Ctrl + KY keys.

Defining Blocks of Text

In order to edit text efficiently it is often helpful to define an area of the file that you will work with as a block, so that subsequent commands will affect the entire block. For example, you may want to delete an entire section of a file, or you may want to move it or copy it to another location.

Marking and working with blocks always involves holding down the Ctrl key and pressing the letter K. The next letter you press defines the specific block command. If you have the Quick Reference Display turned on (Figure 8.4), when Ctrl + K is pressed you will see it change to display all of the block commands.

There are two commands used to define blocks, one to mark the beginning of the block and the other to mark the end of it. To mark the beginning of a block, put the cursor under the first character in the block and press Ctrl + KB. A <B> symbol will appear in the text to show you where you have placed the beginning of the block. Now move the cursor to the last character in the block, and press Ctrl + KK. The <B> symbol will disappear, and the entire block will be reverse highlighted. You may now go ahead and work as you normally do, or you may enter one of the block commands discussed below. The block commands work any time that a block is marked and displayed in reverse highlight. You may turn off the block display, so that it is no longer reverse highlighted, by pressing the Ctrl + KH keys. The H stands for *Hide*. The block commands do not affect a block when the block display is hidden. Pressing the Ctrl + H again turns the block display back on.

To copy a block of text, mark the block and move the cursor to the position you want it copied to. Now press the Ctrl + KC keys. The block will be duplicated at the cursor position. The new block will now be the marked block. Pressing Ctrl + KH will hide the marking. When a block is copied, the original block is left unchanged.

To move a block of text, mark the block and move the cursor to the position you want it moved to. Now press the Ctrl + KV keys. The block will be removed from its original position and inserted at the new position. It will still be reverse highlighted.

You may copy a block of text to a new file by marking the block and pressing Ctrl + KW (for Write). The following prompt will appear:

```
Name of file to write to?
```

You should type in the name of the file, including a path if you don't want it in the current directory, and press the Enter key. If the file already exists, this prompt will appear:

```
File already exists, overwrite (Y/N)?
```

Pressing Y will cause the contents of the file to be replaced with the marked block. The marked block is not removed from the file being edited—this is a copy, not a move. Pressing N will abort the copy operation, but leaves the block marked.

Just as you can write a block of text to a file, you can read the contents of a file and insert it at the current cursor position. This is done with the Ctrl + KR (for Read) command. First, position the cursor at the point where you want the file's contents inserted, then press Ctrl + KR. The following prompt will appear:

```
Name of file to read in?
```

You should type the name of the file, with a path if it is not in the current directory, and press the Enter key. The contents of the file will be inserted. If the file does not exist, the following message will appear:

```
Disk error - file not found
File - filespec
Press Esc to continue
```

Filespec will be the filename you typed in. Pressing Esc will return you to the editing screen.

You may delete a block of text by marking it, then pressing the Ctrl + KY keys.

Moving the End of a Line Down

The Ctrl + N keys are used to move everything beyond the cursor down to the next line. The effect of this is the same as pressing the

Enter key, then the up arrow, then the Ctrl + QD keys. The part of the line that is moved down appears on its own line, and everything beneath the current line is moved down one.

How EDITOR Creates Automatic Backups

Whenever you save a file, EDITOR first renames the original copy of the file to the same name with a BAK extension, then saves your changed file under the original name. This provides a measure of protection against accidentally overwriting a file with changes that you did not want to keep. For example, suppose you were editing a letter named MARY.LET, and decided you didn't like the changes you made. Pressing Ctrl + KQ will exit the editing screen without saving your changes. But if you press Ctrl + KX instead, the changes will be saved.

Since EDITOR saved the original in a backup file before saving your changes, you can recover from this situation by exiting EDITOR, deleting the file that has the changes in it, and renaming the backup file to the original name.

EDITOR will not allow you to edit a file that has a BAK extension.

Command Summary

Table 8.1 summarizes the EDITOR commands.

Table 8.1 Keys Used in EDITOR

Keystroke(s)	***Effect***
For On-line Help	
F1 or Ctrl + J	Displays on-line help.
For moving the cursor	
Home/Ctrl + QR	Moves cursor to start of file.
End/Ctrl + QC	Moves cursor to end of file.
Ctrl + QS	Moves cursor to start of line.
Ctrl + QD	Moves cursor to end of line.
Left arrow/Ctrl + S	Moves cursor one character to left.
Ctrl + A	Moves cursor one word to left.
Right arrow/Ctrl + D	Moves cursor one character to right.

Table 8.1 continued ...

Keystroke(s)	***Effect***
Ctrl + F	Moves cursor one word to right.
Up arrow/Ctrl + E	Moves cursor up one line.
Down arrow/Ctrl + X	Moves cursor down one line.
Ctrl + W	Scrolls text down one line.
Ctrl + Z	Scrolls text up one line.
PgUp/Ctrl + R	Moves cursor up one page.
PgDn/Ctrl + C	Moves cursor down one page.
For Deleting Text	
Del/Ctrl + G	Deletes the character at the cursor.
Ctrl + Y	Deletes the line the cursor is on
Backspace/Ctrl + H	Deletes the character to the left of the cursor.
Ctrl + T	Deletes from cursor to beginning of the next word.
For Working With Blocks	
Ctrl + KB	Marks the beginning of a block.
Ctrl + KK	Marks the end of a block.
Ctrl + KC	Copies the marked block to the current cursor location.
Ctrl + KV	Moves the marked block to the current cursor location.
Ctrl + KY	Deletes the marked block.
Ctrl + KW	Writes the marked block to a file.
For Inserting Another File	
Ctrl + KR	Reads contents of a file into the current cursor location.
For Saving Files	
Ctrl + KX	Saves file and returns to command prompt.
Ctrl + KD	Saves file and returns to Startup Screen.
Ctrl + KS	Saves changes and returns to editing the file.
Ctrl + KQ	Returns to Startup Screen without saving file.

Table 8.1 continued ...

Keystroke(s)	***Effect***
Miscellaneous	
Ctrl + N	Inserts a new line after cursor, without moving cursor.
Ctrl + P	Inserts a control character at the cursor position.
Ctrl + QN	Enters characters using ASCII codes.
Alt+number	Enters characters using ASCII codes.

Chapter 9

Batch Files

s you use your computer, you'll find that you execute certain sequences of commands over and over, particularly if you work frequently at the command prompt. For example, if your word processor document files are in a directory named C:\WP\DOCS, then to work on a document in your word processor you will need to enter a CD \WP\DOCS command to change to that directory, then the command that executes the word processor. When you are finished working in your word processor you may want to return to the root directory, which will require a CD \ command.

So there are two or three commands that you must remember and enter every time you edit a file in your word processor. Batch files are files that contain *batches* of DOS commands that can be used to automate these repetitive tasks. Batch files may contain any set of commands that you enter at the command prompt. These commands are then executed sequentially by simply entering the name of the batch file as though it were a command.

In addition to the usual DOS commands, there are some special commands for use only in batch files. These provide a limited form of programming power in batch files. All of these commands are internal commands.

This chapter will explore the creation and use of batch files. Familiarity with the DOS commands discussed in Chapters 4 and 6 is assumed.

A batch file is identified by the extension BAT. Batch files are executable files—DOS interprets their contents as instructions, and carries them out. When you type a command at the DOS prompt, DOS searches in the current directory and in any directories identified by the current path for a file that has the name you typed in, followed by an extension of COM, EXE, or BAT. DOS will only attempt to execute files with these extensions, and it does so in a different way for each extension. You could not name a batch file with a COM extension and have it execute. Batch files must only have BAT extensions, and you should avoid naming batch files with the same name as programs that have COM or EXE extensions.

Most DOS commands can be included in batch files, and so can commands that run software programs. For example, if a word processor is started by typing WP at the DOS prompt, then the command WP may be included in a batch file. When DOS executes a batch file, it stores the entire file in memory until all of the commands have been executed. This means you can include commands that will execute both before and after a program that is run from within a batch file.

Creating Simple Batch Files

The simplest batch files have only a few commands in them. A common application for a simple batch file is to change the current directory to one that contains a program you want to use, start the program, then when it is finished return to the root directory. For example, if the command that starts your word processor is WP, and you want to start it from the C:\WP\LETTERS directory, then the following batch file will take you to that directory, run the word processor, and return you to the root directory when you exit the word processor.

```
CD C:\WP\LETTERS
WP
CD \
```

Each command in a batch file appears on its own line. As each line executes it appears on the screen. This is called *echoing*—the commands are echoed on the screen as they are processed.

Using Echo and Pause Commands in Batch Files

The ECHO command is used in batch files to cause a message to display on the screen. The PAUSE command is used to suspend the batch file from executing until a key is pressed. ECHO has an additional use in batch files: it acts as a switch that either prevents or causes the commands within a batch file to appear on the screen as they execute. The following batch file demonstrates this:

```
ECHO OFF
CLS
ECHO Make sure the word processor disk is in drive A:
PAUSE
A:WP
```

If this batch file was named WP.BAT, entering the command WP would cause the screen to clear and the following two messages to appear:

```
Make sure the word processor disk is in drive A:
Strike a key when ready . . .
```

After a key is pressed the WP program in drive A: will execute.

In this batch file, the ECHO OFF command turns off echoing. This means that as the subsequent batch file commands execute, they are not displayed on the screen. However, any output they may produce does appear on the screen. The next command, CLS, causes the screen to clear. It is a good idea to start batch files with CLS in order to remove any distracting information that may still be there from the last command.

The next ECHO command is used to display a message on the screen—in this case, a prompt to put a disk in drive A. The PAUSE command causes DOS to stop executing the commands in the DOS file and display the message "Strike a key when ready . . . ." When you press a key, DOS resumes executing the batch file. The last command, (A:WP), executes a program named WP on the A: drive.

When a batch file finishes executing, DOS restores the ECHO state to whatever it was when the batch file was called. Thus, if ECHO is on when a batch file is called, ECHO will be turned on when the batch file finishes. If ECHO is off when the batch file is called it will be switched off when the batch file finishes.

In the above example, the PAUSE command is used to wait for you to put a disk in drive A:. Another use of the PAUSE command is to display more than one screen of information, but to permit the user to finish reading the first screen before the next one displays. For example, there may be two screens of help information that you want to make available to users. The information could be in two files, called HELP1.FIL and HELP2.FIL. The following batch file, named HELP.BAT, will display the help information one screen at a time, when the command HELP is entered:

```
CLS
TYPE HELP1.FIL | MORE
PAUSE
TYPE HELP2.FIL | MORE
```

The first TYPE command types the information in the file HELP1.FIL on the screen, and the MORE filter causes it to pause whenever the screen fills up. However, the last part of the HELP1.FIL file could be scrolled off the screen without a pause by the start of the second TYPE command. So the PAUSE command is used to halt the execution of the batch file after the first file is displayed, until you press a key. DOS then goes on to display the second screen of information.

Parameters and Environment Variables in Batch Files

The term *parameters* refers to variables in your batch files—items that are referenced within the file, but whose specific value can change each time the file is run. A batch file that clears the screen and then lists the WP directory on drive C could contain the following two commands:

```
CLS
DIR C:\WP /P
```

If this file was named D.BAT, you could simply type the letter D to list the files in the C:\WP directory. However, if you wanted to list the files in different directories, you would need a separate batch file for each directory, and you would have to remember the name of each file. It would probably be easier to just type the DIR command each time, specifying the directory you want to see.

A better solution is to use a batch file that accepts a parameter to tell it which directory to list. The following batch file demonstrates this:

```
CLS
DIR %1 /p
```

Batch file parameters are represented within the batch file by the % sign followed by a number from 1 to 9. When the file is executed, each parameter is replaced by the corresponding item from the DOS command that called the file. For example, if the above two commands were in a file named D.BAT, then entering the command D C:\WP would cause the %1 to be replaced by the letters C:\WP. This results in the command DIR C:\WP /P being executed. The next time the file is run, it can be entered as D A:, which displays the directory of drive A. More than nine parameters may be referenced in a batch file, with some limitations, using the SHIFT command. SHIFT is discussed in Chapter 11.

An example of a batch file using two parameters follows. It creates a new directory, then copies files from an existing directory to the new one.

```
MD %1
COPY %2 %1
```

If this batch file is named MC.BAT, the following command will create a new directory named NEWDIR and copy all of the batch files from the C:\ directory into the NEWDIR directory:

```
MC NEWDIR C:\*.BAT
```

Environment variables may be referenced from batch files, by enclosing them in percent signs (%). In Chapter 6, the following batch file was presented as a means of appending a new directory onto an existing path:

```
SET PATH1=%PATH%
PATH=%PATH%;%1
```

This batch file refers to the PATH environment variable, by enclosing it with % percent signs. The first line sets a new environment variable, named PATH1, to contain the existing path, and the second line appends the first parameter passed to the batch file onto the end of the existing path. For example, if this batch file is named SP.BAT, the following command will append the C:\GV directory to the end of the current path:

```
SP C:\GV
```

Creating Batch Files that Call Themselves

The names by which batch files refer to parameters start with %1 and end with %9. However, you may also use %0 in your batch files. %0 is a special parameter symbol that refers to the name of the batch file in which it occurs. This allows you to call a batch file from within itself. It might not seem useful at first to do this, but there are circumstances in which it can be a very efficient way to accomplish a task which must be repeated many times. The following batch file demonstrates this:

```
ECHO OFF
ECHO Place source disk in drive A and target disk in drive B
PAUSE
COPY A: B:
%0
```

If this file is called CCOPY.BAT, for Continuous COPY (note that you should not give batch files the same names as DOS commands, in this case COPY), then entering the command CCOPY will result in the message, "Place source disk in drive A and target disk in drive B" being displayed on the screen. Below that will be the message, "Strike a key when ready . . ." After you have placed the disks in drives A and B and pressed a key, all of the files will be copied from drive A to drive B.

The %0 command will cause this sequence to repeat and the message "Place source disk in drive A and target disk in drive B" will again be shown, followed by the "Strike a key when ready . . ." message. The batch file will continue executing like this until you press Ctrl-Break. This will always cause a batch file to stop execution. Pressing Ctrl-Break causes the following prompt to be displayed:

```
Halt Batch Process (Y/N) ?
```

Pressing Y will return you to the DOS prompt and the screen should look similar to that shown in Figure 9.1.

```
Place source disk in drive A and target disk in drive B
Strike a key when ready . . .
A:JOHN.LET
A:MARY.LET
A:BILL.LET
A:GEORGE.LET
     5 File(s) copied
Place source disk in drive A and target disk in drive B
Strike a key when ready . . .
A:ACCNTS1.RBF
A:ACCNTS2.RBF
A:ACCNTS3.RBF
     3 File(s) copied
Place source disk in drive A and target disk in drive B
Strike a key when ready . . .
A:JULY.WK2
A:AUGUST.WK2
A:SEPT.WK2
     2 File(s) copied
Place source disk in drive A and target disk in drive B
Strike a key when ready . . . ^C
Terminate batch job (Y/N)? y
C:\_
```

Figure 9.1 Result of Running CCopy Batch File

Halting the Execution of a Batch File

You may encounter situations in which you want to stop a batch file before it is finished executing. This could be because you realize after starting that it is going to take too long to complete, or that it is going to do something you do not want it to do. You may even have created a batch file that never terminates on its own, such as the previous example for copying large numbers of disks from drive A to drive B. Batch file execution may always be stopped by holding down Ctrl and pressing Break. This is known as a *control-break*, a special signal that DOS recognizes as a command to stop whatever it is doing and return to the DOS prompt.

Use of the IF Command in Batch Files

One of the powerful features of DOS batch files is the ability to execute a command only if some condition is true, or alternately if some condition is not true. Conditions that can be tested are:

1. The existence or nonexistence of a file or directory that is named in the batch file.
2. The existence or nonexistence of a file or directory passed as a parameter.
3. Whether a parameter matches a value that is specified in the batch file.
4. Whether or not a previous command terminated normally.

1. The first condition can be demonstrated with a batch file that displays the directory information for a file named TEST.FIL only if the file exists in the current directory. This file contains the following commands:

```
ECHO OFF
CLS
IF EXIST TEST.FIL DIR TEST.FIL
IF NOT EXIST TEST.FIL ECHO Test.fil does not exist
```

You may include a drive and/or path for the filename, if the file is not in the current directory of the current drive.

Note that in the above example, echo is turned off with the ECHO OFF command, and the screen is cleared with the CLS command, at the start of the file. It can be desirable to have commands display on the screen when a batch file executes, but in general it is good style to not display them. They tend to be confusing, especially since they often flash by too quickly to read. Clearing the screen is a good idea because it removes clutter that makes it difficult to locate important messages or other information.

You may change this file to check for the existence of a directory rather than a file by using the DIREXIST phrase instead of EXIST. You may check for a directory anywhere on any drive in the machine. For example, the following batch file checks for the existence of a subdirectory named TEST, in the root directory of the A: drive:

```
ECHO OFF
CLS
IF DIREXIST A:\TEST DIR TEST
IF NOT DIREXIST A:\TEST ECHO Test does not exist on A:
```

These files demonstrate the use of the NOT operator. You may place NOT in front of any of the IF condition tests in batch files. The effect is to test for the failure of the condition, rather than its success. When the first file above is executed, if TEST.FIL exists in the current directory the DIR listing for it will be displayed. If it does not exist, the message "Test.fil Does Not Exist" will be shown instead.

2. Checking for the existence of a file name entered as a parameter can be demonstrated with a batch file that starts a word processor named WP with the specified file loaded, if the file exists. If the file does not exist the batch file displays an error message. The following batch file demonstrates:

```
ECHO OFF
CLS
CD C:\WP\LETTERS
IF EXIST %1 WP %1
IF NOT EXIST %1 ECHO %1 Does Not Exist - Check The Name
CD C:\
```

This batch file changes directories to the word processing directory C:\WP\LETTERS before checking for the existence of the file that is passed as a parameter. It is important to include a CD (Change Directory) command in batch files that serve the type of function demonstrated here, since the batch files are usually in the root directory and the program and data files are generally in subdirectories. It is also a good idea to return to the root directory at the end of the batch file, as is done here with the CD C:\ command, since that is where other batch files you might want to execute will most likely be found.

If this batch file is named WP.BAT, and a file named MYFILE.LET exists in the C:\WP\LETTERS directory, then the following command will result in the word processor WP starting up with the file MYFILE.LET loaded:

```
WP MYFILE.LET
```

If MYFILE.LET does not exist in the C:\WP\LETTERS directory, the message "MYFILE.LET Does Not Exist - Check The Name" will be displayed.

This file can be changed to check for a directory rather than a filename in the following way:

```
ECHO OFF
CLS
CD C:\WP\LETTERS
IF DIREXIST %1 WP %1\%2
IF NOT DIREXIST %1 ECHO %1 Does Not Exist - Check The Name
CD C:\
```

In this example, two parameters are passed: the directory to check for, and the filename in that directory, which should be opened in the word processor.

3. Testing whether a parameter matches a value that is included in the batch file can be demonstrated with a batch file that carries out one command if the name Mary is entered as a parameter, and another command if the name Bill is entered. The commands for this batch file are:

```
IF %1 == "Mary" WP
IF %1 == "Bill" DB
ECHO A valid name was not entered. Try again.
```

If this batch file is named NAME.BAT, then the following command will cause a program named WP to be run:

```
NAME MARY
```

If the name entered is neither Mary nor Bill, the ECHO command will execute, displaying the message "A valid name was not entered. Try again." Notice that there are two equal signs in these condition tests. If you use only one equal sign, DOS will terminate execution of the batch file and display the message "Syntax error." It is a good idea to use the double quotes around the text string being compared, in order to insure that DOS will correctly interpret the string as simply a string, and not a command.

The WP and DB programs could be batch files, or they could be EXE or COM files. If WP and DB were COM or EXE files, then the

ECHO command would always execute. This is because when the WP or DB programs ended, control would return to the NAME.BAT file, and the ECHO command would execute before the batch file terminated. However, when one batch file executes a second batch file in the manner demonstrated here, control will not return to the first batch file. If you want control to return to a batch file after it runs another batch file you must use the CALL command, discussed later in this chapter.

The names Mary and Bill must be spelled exactly the same on the parameter line and in the batch file. This includes case sensitivity. If you entered the command NAME MARY or NAME mary, the IF condition would fail and the ECHO command would execute.

4. Testing for normal termination of the previous command only works with certain DOS commands and certain programs. When these commands terminate, they leave a code known as the EXIT CODE in the DOS environment ERRORLEVEL variable. Batch files may access this code to determine the status of the last command's termination—whether it terminated normally or abnormally.

Usually an exit code of 0 means the command terminated normally—it carried out its intended purpose with no interruption or error. A nonzero exit code will indicate an abnormal termination. This can be caused by the user interrupting the operation or by an error occurring during the operation. The exit code will indicate what caused the interruption. Generally, the higher the exit code the more serious the problem. DOS exit codes are shown in Chapter 11, for those DOS commands that generate exit codes.

One of the DOS commands that sets an EXIT code is the BACKUP command (see Chapter 7). This command is used to back up a disk, usually a hard disk, onto onc or more floppy disks. The following batch file tests for an exit code from the BACKUP command and takes an action based on that code.

```
BACKUP %1
IF ERRORLEVEL 0 ECHO Backup finished normally.
IF ERRORLEVEL 1 ECHO No files were found for backing up.
IF ERRORLEVEL 1 ECHO Check the file specification and try again.
IF ERRORLEVEL 2 TYPE BUERR.2
```

(continued ...)

```
IF ERRORLEVEL 3 ECHO You have terminated the backup.
IF ERRORLEVEL 4 TYPE BUERR.4
```

This file relies on two text files, BUERR.2 and BUERR.4, that could contain lengthy error messages and instructions if the **BACKUP** command returns an exit code of either 2 or 4.

Placing Comments in Batch Files

As batch files become larger and more complex, they also become harder to understand. The REM command helps make batch files easier to understand. REM stands for *remark*. When a batch file line begins with the letters REM, everything on that line is ignored when the batch file executes. The line is used for a comment that explains something about the batch file. REM lines can also be used to separate commands from one another, making the batch file easier to read.

Remarks will be echoed to the screen if ECHO is set on, so it is a good idea to always start your batch files with the ECHO OFF command. If there are particular lines in your file you want echoed, you can turn ECHO back on for those lines. Many of the examples in the rest of this chapter will make use of REM lines to help explain how the files work.

Developing Complex Batch Files

To demonstrate more sophisticated batch file techniques, an on-line help system for three programs—a word processor, a spreadsheet, and a database program—will be developed entirely with batch files. This system will use three files to contain help information for the respective programs. The file that contains the help for word processing should be named WP1.FIL; the file that contains the help for the database system should be called DB1.FIL; and the file that contains the help for the spreadsheet system should be called SS1.FIL. Each of these files should contain less than one screen of text. If you want to provide more than one screen of information for a subject, enter the second screen into an xx2.FIL file—a second screen of information for the spreadsheet goes in the SS2.FIL. A third screen would go in the SS3.FIL, and so on.

The name of the on-line help batch file is HELP.BAT. Figure 9.2 contains the contents of HELP.BAT.

```
@ECHO OFF
REM filename: HELP.BAT
REM This file is used to display help screens that are stored
REM in files named XX1.FIL, XX2.FIL, and so on. The XX's stand
REM for the application for which the help is provided. For
REM example, the word processor help screens are stored in files
REM named WP1.FIL, and WP2.FIL. This file is executed by entering
REM the command HELP XX - e.g. HELP WP
CLS
IF NOT EXIST %11.FIL ECHO No help files for that command.
IF EXIST %11.FIL TYPE %11.FIL
IF EXIST %12.FIL PAUSE
IF EXIST %12.FIL TYPE %12.FIL
IF EXIST %13.FIL PAUSE
IF EXIST %13.FIL TYPE %13.FIL
```

Figure 9.2 Batch File for an On-line Help System

To use this help system for assistance with starting the word processing system, a user would enter the command HELP WP. The HELP.BAT file then checks for the existence of a file named WP1.FIL. If the file does not exist, it will display the message "No help files for that command." If the file does exist, HELP.BAT will display the contents of the file on the screen, then check for the existence of a file named WP2.FIL. If WP2.FIL exists, the PAUSE command will execute, displaying the message "Press any key to continue . . ." on the screen. When a key is pressed the contents of WP2.FIL will be displayed. The process will then repeat for the file named WP3.FIL.

This system may be expanded to provide as many HELP screens as you like, for as many applications as you like. You must make sure that you allow for the maximum number of help files you have written for any one of the commands. If you have five help files for the database system (DB1.FIL, DB2.FIL, DB3.FIL, DB4.FIL, and DB5.FIL), and three for each of the others, then you must have IF EXIST commands for five files.

If you have been typing in and executing the examples up to now, you may have noticed that whenever there is an ECHO OFF command, it echoes on the screen. This makes sense, since ECHO is ON when the command is executed. But it can also be annoying because one of the goals is to make the batch file commands transparent to the end user. You can't do that if they echo on the screen. The ECHO OFF command in the example for the on-line help system did not appear on the screen. The reason is that it begins with an @ sign. The @ sign tells DOS not to echo the command on the screen, regardless of the ECHO status. You can use this in front of any batch command to selectively suppress it from echoing.

This Help system demonstrates the ability to insert a parameter into a text string. When DOS executes a batch file that contains parameters it literally inserts the parameter values directly into the command.

Branching of Program Control with the GOTO Command

The GOTO command can be used in conjunction with the IF command to add great flexibility and power to batch files. GOTO causes control to jump from one line in the file to another. It is used in conjunction with a label that indicates the point in the file to jump to. For example, the batch file in Figure 9.3 uses a GOTO to display one message if the file passed as a parameter exists, and another message if the file does not exist.

```
1      @ECHO OFF
2      REM This file is named JUMP.BAT. It tells the user whether
3      REM or not the file passed as a parameter exists.
4      REM
5      IF NOT EXIST %1 GOTO NOFILE
6      ECHO The file %1 exists.
7      GOTO :END
8      :NOFILE
9      ECHO The file %1 does not exist.
10     :END
(Line numbers are for reference only; they should not be included in
the batch file.)
```

Figure 9.3 Batch File with GOTO Command

This batch file first checks to see if the file passed as a parameter exists. If it does, the GOTO on line 5 does not execute and control continues with line 6. This displays the message, "The file [filename] exists." Then the GOTO on line 7 executes, causing control to jump past lines 8 and 9 to line 10, which is the end of the file.

On the other hand, if the file that is passed as a parameter does not exist, then the GOTO on line 5 executes, causing control to jump past lines 6 and 7 and continue on line 9 (line 8 is a label line, which does not execute—it simply marks the point to jump to). This displays the error message, "The file (filename) does not exist."

The line on which the label appears must begin with a colon (:), and the label must be the only thing that appears on the line after the colon. Lines containing a label in a batch file are not echoed on the screen, even if ECHO is on. This provides an alternative to the REM command for including remarks in a batch file: start the line with a colon, which identifies it as a label to DOS, then place your remark after the colon. The line will not be echoed on the screen, as REM lines are if ECHO is on. The only thing you must guard against if you use colons instead of REM is having a comment that matches a label. This may cause control to jump to the comment, rather than the true label.

The batch file in Figure 9.4 sets up the same on-line help system described in Figure 9.2, only Figure 9.4 uses the GOTO command to reduce the number of IF commands.

```
@ECHO OFF
REM filename: HELP.BAT
REM This file is used to display help screens that are stored
REM in files named XX1.FIL, XX2.FIL, and so on. The XX's stand
REM for the application for which the help is provided. For
REM example, the word processor help screens are stored in files
REM named WP1.FIL and WP2.FIL. This file is executed by entering
REM the command HELP XX - e.g. HELP WP
CLS
IF NOT EXIST %11.FIL GOTO NOFILE
TYPE %11.FIL
IF NOT EXIST %12.FIL GOTO END
PAUSE
TYPE %12.FIL
IF NOT EXIST %13.FIL GOTO END
PAUSE
TYPE %13.FIL
:NOFILE
ECHO No help files for that command.
:END
```

Figure 9.4 Use of GOTO to Improve the On-line Help System

Branching with Subroutines Using GOSUB and RETURN

The GOTO command gives a limited amount of flexibility in changing the point of control in a batch file. The GOSUB and RETURN commands provide much more flexibility, and permit you to modularize your batch files. The term GOSUB means *go to subroutine* where *subroutine* is a block of code that begins with a label and ends with a RETURN command.

When DOS encounters a GOSUB command, it looks for the matching label and shifts control to the command that follows the label, just as GOTO does. However, when a RETURN command is subsequently encountered, control returns to the line following the GOSUB. The logic of programs using GOSUB and RETURN commands is usually clearer and easier to grasp than when GOTO is used. The batch file in Figure 9.4 can be improved using GOSUB and RETURN, as shown in Figure 9.5.

```
@ECHO OFF
CLS
IF EXIST %11.FIL GOSUB HELPFILE
IF NOT EXIST %11.FIL GOSUB NOFILE
EXIT
:
:HELPFILE
TYPE %11.FIL
PAUSE
IF EXIST %12.FIL TYPE %12.FIL
PAUSE
IF EXIST %13.FIL TYPE %13.FIL
PAUSE
RETURN
:
:NOFILE
ECHO No help files for the %1 command.
PAUSE
RETURN
```

Figure 9.5 Use of GOTO to Improve the On-line Help System

In this figure, the basic control logic is clear—simply to test whether or not there is a helpfile for the command passed as a parameter. If there is, the program executes the HELPFILE subroutine; if there isn't, it executes the NOFILE subroutine. The logic for each of these possibilities is also segregated from the rest of the code, so you can quickly read this batch file and see what it does and how it works.

You may also nest GOSUB and RETURN commands, to achieve an even greater degree of modularity. Nesting means that within one subroutine, there is another GOSUB, which shifts control to another subroutine. When the second subroutine ends, control is returned to the first subroutine, and when that one ends, control is returned to the part of the file that called it. Nesting may go several levels deep. Figure 9.6 shows sample code that illustrates nesting.

```
@ECHO OFF
ECHO START HERE
GOSUB ONE
ECHO RETURNED FROM ONE
EXIT
:ONE
ECHO IN ONE NOW
GOSUB TWO
ECHO RETURNED FROM TWO
PAUSE
RETURN
:TWO
ECHO IN TWO NOW
GOSUB THREE
ECHO RETURNED FROM THREE
PAUSE
RETURN
:THREE
ECHO IN THREE NOW
PAUSE
RETURN
```

Figure 9.6 Sample Code that Demonstrates Nested Subroutines

You should be sure to have one RETURN command for each GOTO command, and vice versa.

Dynamically Switching Between Labels with the Switch Command

The SWITCH command can be used to accept input from the keyboard, and switch to a label based on what was typed. This can be very useful for creating menu systems from batch files. The batch file named MENU.BAT in Figure 9.7 demonstrates how this works. The text file in Figure 9.8 is referred to on the third line of MENU.BAT.

```
@ECHO OFF
CLS
TYPE SAMPLE.MNU
ECHO Enter the number of your choice:
SWITCH ONE TWO THREE
EXIT
:ONE
ECHO This is where the WP command goes.
RETURN
:TWO
ECHO This is where the SS command goes.
RETURN
:THREE
ECHO This is where the DB command goes.
RETURN
```

Figure 9.7 Batch File for Menu System Using SWITCH Command

```
1.   Word Processing
2.   Spreadsheet
3.   Database
```

Figure 9.8 Text File for Menu Options

Using FOR to Repeat Commands for Processing Several Files

The FOR command is used in batch files to cause a command to repeat once for each file in a specified set of files. It does this by specifying a variable that takes on each of the values in a set of filenames that is specified in the command. The variable is named with two percent signs followed by any one character, for example %%A. The set of filenames that the variable will take on is specified by placing them within parentheses in the FOR command. Figure 9.9 contains a simple batch file, named SHOW.BAT, that uses the FOR command.

```
@ECHO OFF
REM This file is named SHOW.BAT. It is used to display the
REM directory listing of the three files entered in the
REM parentheses.
REM
FOR %%F IN (FILE1 FILE2 FILE3) DO DIR %%F
```

Figure 9.9 Use of the FOR Command

When the SHOW.BAT file is called, the FOR command gets translated by DOS into three separate commands that look like this:

```
DIR FILE1
DIR FILE2
DIR FILE3
```

The variable %%F takes on each value in the set (FILE1 FILE2 FILE3), and is passed to the DIR command for each of these values. This may not seem useful at first, but the values in parentheses (called the SET of the FOR command) can be replaced by parameters passed to the batch file on the command line. Figure 9.9 could be rewritten as shown in Figure 9.10.

```
@ECHO OFF
REM This file is named SHOW.BAT. It is used to display the
REM directory listing of the three files entered in the
REM parentheses.
REM
FOR %%F IN (%1 %2 %3) DO DIR %%F
```

Figure 9.10 Use of Parameters with the FOR Command

With the SHOW.BAT file shown in Figure 9.10, you could enter the command SHOW FILE1 FILE2 FILE3, and DOS would display the directory listing for each of the three files specified on the command line. You could also use directories rather than filenames, to display several complete directories. In this case, you would probably want to use the /P parameter on the DIR command.

You could take this a step further and, as shown in Figure 9.11, display messages about files that do not exist, and display the directory listing for files that do exist, all with only two commands.

```
@ECHO OFF
REM This file is named CHECK.BAT. It is used to display the
REM directory listing for files that are entered on the command
REM line. If a file does not exist, a message is displayed that
REM lets the user know a non-existent file name was entered.
REM
FOR %%F IN (%1 %2 %3 %4) DO IF EXIST %%F DIR %%F
FOR %%F IN (%1 %2 %3 %4) DO IF EXIST %%F ECHO %%F does not exist
```

Figure 9.11 Combining FOR and IF Commands

If the CHECK.BAT file shown in Figure 9.11 were executed with the command CHECK FILE1 FILE2 FILE3, and only FILE2 existed, the result would appear similar to the following:

```
C:\DRDOS>TEST FILE1 FILE2 FILE3
   Volume in drive C is DRDOS 6.0
   Directory of C:\DOS
FILE2     7 11-21-91     5:23p
     1 File(s) 9166848 bytes free
FILE1 does not exist
FILE3 does not exist
```

Notice that only three file names were entered, even though the batch file allows for four parameters. The fourth parameter is ignored if nothing is entered for it, so you should make sure you allow for the maximum number of parameters in the FOR command set.

The on-line help system shown in Figures 9.2, 9.4, and 9.5 can be greatly simplified using a single FOR command and two batch files. The batch files are shown in Figures 9.12 and 9.13.

```
@ECHO OFF
REM This file is named HELP.BAT. It is used to display help
REM files that have been prepared for one of the applications
REM available to users of this computer. There can be up to
REM four help files per application. This number can be
REM increased simply by adding additional parameters to the
REM FOR command set.
REM
CLS
FOR %%F IN (%11.FIL %12.FIL %13.FIL %14.FIL) DO CALL SHOW %%F
```

Figure 9.12 Use of FOR Command to Improve On-line Help System

```
REM This file is named SHOW.BAT. It is called from the file
REM HELP.BAT. It displayes the help screen file that is passed
REM to it as a parameter, then pauses so the user will have time
REM to read the screen. It checks for the existence of the file
REM because HELP.BAT is going to pass four file names, even if
REM they don't all exist. Checking for their existence prevents
REM the appearance of extraneous messages appearing on the
REM screen.
REM
IF EXIST %1 TYPE %1
IF EXIST %1 PAUSE
```

Figure 9.13 SHOW.BAT File Called from HELP.BAT

After you take out the remarks, there are only five commands in these two files taken together, as opposed to eight and thirteen commands in Figures 9.2 and 9.4, respectively. The CALL command in this version of HELP.BAT is discussed in the next section.

The most important improvement in the system shown in Figures 9.12 and 9.13 is that it is much easier to understand and modify. If you want to add additional help files you simply increase the number of parameters in the SET of the FOR command.

As you can see, the FOR command can be very useful for concisely repeating the processing of a file.

Batch Files that Call Other Batch Files

As seen in some of the examples above, a batch file can cause another batch file to execute simply by having the name of the second batch file occur as a command in the first. When this happens, the first batch file gives up control to the second one. Commands will not execute appear in the first batch file after the command that calls the second batch, unless there is a GOTO that can cause control to branch around the reference to the second batch file. The batch files in Figures 9.14 and 9.15 demonstrate this.

When the command GREETING is entered, the following two messages will appear on the screen:

```
Hello.
You'll never say goodbye.
```

```
@ECHO OFF
REM This file is named GREETING.BAT
REM
ECHO Hello.
FILE2
ECHO Goodbye.
```

Figure 9.14 GREETING.BAT File with Nonreturnable Call to RESPONSE.BAT

```
REM This file is named RESPONSE.BAT
REM
ECHO You'll never say goodbye.
```

Figure 9.15 RESPONSE.BAT File

This happens because when GREETING passes control to RESPONSE, it gives up control altogether. There is no way for the ECHO Goodbye command to execute. If you want control to return to the calling file you must execute the second batch file with a CALL command. When the second batch file finishes executing, control then returns to the first batch file, at the line immediately following the CALL command. The batch file in Figure 9.16 illustrates this.

```
@ECHO OFF
REM This file is named GREETING.BAT
REM
ECHO Hello.
CALL RESPONSE
ECHO Want to bet?
ECHO Goodbye!
```

Figure 9.16 GREETING.BAT File with Returnable Call to RESPONSE.BAT

Now when the command GREETING is entered, the following messages appear on the screen:

```
Hello.
You'll never say goodbye.
Want to bet?
Goodbye!
```

As you can see, the CALL command causes control to return to the calling file. You also may have noticed that there is no ECHO OFF command at the beginning of RESPONSE.BAT. The ECHO state is passed from one batch file to another, and restored when control returns. This means that when GREETING.BAT sets ECHO OFF, it remains off in RESPONSE.BAT unless an ECHO ON command is encountered. If RESPONSE.BAT sets ECHO ON, it will be restored to its off status when control returns to GREETING.BAT.

You may pass parameters from one batch file to another. For example, the batch files in Figures 9.17 and 9.18 both accept parameters. The file in Figure 9.17 calls the file in Figure 9.18, passing its second parameter to the called batch file's first parameter:

```
@ECHO OFF
REM This file is named BATCH1.BAT
COPY %1 %2
BATCH2 %2
```

Figure 9.17 Passing Parameters from One Batch File to Another

```
REM This file is named BATCH2.BAT
DIR %1
```

Figure 9.18 Batch File that Receives Parameters from Another Batch File

The first file, BATCH1, can be called with the following command:

```
BATCH1 TEST.FIL C:\DRDOS
```

This will copy the file named TEST.FIL to the DRDOS directory. TEST.FIL will become parameter %1 in this file and C:\DRDOS will become parameter %2. The second batch file will then be called with the command BATCH2 C:\DRDOS, which will result in the C:\DRDOS directory being displayed.

Batch files that call each other may be nested as deep as you like—there is no limit to how many you may have. You may even have a batch file that calls itself, as demonstrated earlier, or two batch files that call each other. However, there are a few important considerations to keep in mind.

Each time a batch file calls another batch file, the first file must be stored in memory until control returns to it, so that DOS will know what command to execute at that time. If the second batch file calls a third batch file, the second batch file must be stored in memory as well. Eventually all of the available memory could be used and the computer will lock up and stop responding to the keyboard. You will have to reboot in order to get started again. Consequently, if you are going to use the CALL command you must think through its logic very carefully, to make sure that control will eventually be passed back to the first execution of the first file in the calling sequence, so the whole process can terminate.

If you suspect that a batch file sequence has gone into an endless loop, or is in danger of running out of memory, you can always stop it with Ctrl-Break.

There is an important difference between using CALL to call another batch file, and using %0 in a batch file to recursively reference itself. Since no CALL command is involved with %0, DOS does not save the calling file in memory in order to return control to it. The calling file is discarded when the %0 command is encountered, so there is no danger of running out of memory.

Chapter 10

Configuring and Customizing DR DOS

DOS commands can be thought of as falling into two broad categories: commands that do some kind of work for you, and configuration commands. Most of the commands discussed up to this point fall into the former category. Some were configuration commands, but they related to very specific aspects of DOS, which warranted their own chapters (such as memory configuration commands). The rest of the configuration commands do not fit neatly into one subject area, but instead comprise a sort of grab bag of functions that influence various aspects of DOS.

The first thing DOS does when you start your computer is read the contents of the CONFIG.SYS file and execute the commands it finds there. The second thing it does is read the AUTOEXEC.BAT file and execute the commands it finds there. The CONFIG.SYS file contains commands that can generally be executed only at boot time, while the commands in AUTOEXEC.BAT are standard DOS commands that could be entered at the command prompt. Configuring DOS consists primarily of altering the contents of these two files.

There are two ways to modify these files: directly, using a text editor; and via SETUP, which provides menus of choices and then automatically updates these files based on your choices. Setup is easier to use and has on-line help, but does not provide as fine a level of control as manually adjusting the files does. To configure your computer using setup, type SETUP at the command prompt and press the Enter key. SETUP is an external command, so the DRDOS directory must be current or in the path for it to work.

This chapter discusses techniques for manually adjusting these files to configure DOS. If you understand how to do this manually, you will also have a better understanding of the SETUP options.

The DOS Environment

When the computer is booted, DOS sets up an area of memory known as the *environment*. This is an area that contains common values that DOS and some software programs will need to find. The format of the DOS prompt is stored in the environment, as is the current path. In addition, the environment contains variables, called *environment variables*. They are called environment variables because they are stored in the environment space, and they can be created, modified, and dropped at will. An environment variable that is used with DR DOS 6.0 is COMSPEC, which tells DOS where to locate the COMMAND.COM file.

A common use of an environment variable by a program is to store the name of a directory that a program needs to reference. Rather than force you to use a particular name for a directory, the program will simply require that you put the name of whatever directory you want to use in an environment variable. The program then refers to that environment variable when it needs to find the directory. For example, the Microsoft C language compiler needs to know where a set of files known as *library files* are stored. The instructions for the compiler tell you that you may use whatever directory you want, but you should enter the following command before starting the compiler:

```
SET LIB=dirname
```

where DIRNAME is the complete path specification for the directory in which the library files will be stored. If you wanted to store them in the C:\C600\LIB directory, then you would enter this command:

```
SET LIB=C:\C600\LIB
```

This allows you to name your directories whatever you want, and still let the compiler know where the library files are stored.

Environment variables may be referenced within batch files, by surrounding them with percent signs. An example of this can be seen in Chapter 9.

Creating Environment Variables with the SET Command

As seen above, the SET command is used to define environment variables, and to change or remove them. When SET is entered by itself, it displays the current environment. A typical environment displayed by the SET command is shown in Figure 10.1.

```
OS=DRDOS
VER=6.0
PROMPT=$p$g
PATH=C:\DRDOS;C:\UTILITY;C:\WP;C:\RBFILES
COMSPEC=C:\DRDOS\COMMAND.COM
```

Figure 10.1 A typical DOS Environment Displayed by SET Command

The first environment variable shown in Figure 10.1 is OS, and the second is VER. These two together tell which operating system is being used, and which version of it is being used.

The next line shows the current definition of the prompt, followed by the current path. The path and prompt appear to be the same as environment variables, and indeed they are—when DOS needs to know how one of these is defined, it looks up the appropriate environment variable.

The last environment variable is COMSPEC, which contains the path to the file COMMAND.COM. Under some circumstances, it is necessary for DOS to reload part of the COMMAND.COM file because it was overwritten in memory. The COMSPEC environment variable tells DOS where to find the COMMAND.COM file.

The SET command is used to create new environment variables by following the word SET with an equal sign, then a text string that should be contained in the variable. There can be no spaces on either side of the equal sign.

To remove an environment variable, enter the SET command with nothing following the equal sign. For example, to remove the VER environment variable, enter the following command:

```
SET VER=
```

Environment variables remain in the environment until they are either removed in this way, or the computer is turned off. These variables take up memory, and there is only a specific amount of memory available for the environment. If you attempt to create an environment variable, or do something else that requires environment space, like defining a larger path or prompt, and receive the message "Out of environment space," it means that all of the memory reserved for the environment is being used. Removing some environment variables may fix the problem.

It is important to understand that all of the space for the environment is allocated when the computer is booted. Thus, adding environment variables does not reduce the amount of space available to programs, but instead reduces the amount of environment space available for other environment variables. Increasing the amount of environment space, on the other hand, does reduce the amount of memory available to programs. If you need more environment space than you have, you may specify more with the SHELL command.

Changing the Environment Size with SHELL

The SHELL command defines the command interpreter that DOS uses to interpret the commands entered on the command line. The parameters and switches used with SHELL follow the name of the command interpreter, and some of them are actually accepted by the command interpreter rather than SHELL. The standard DOS command interpreter is COMMAND.COM, and if no SHELL command is found in the CONFIG.SYS file, DOS automatically looks for COMMAND.COM in the root directory of the boot disk.

SHELL can also be used to change the amount of memory available for the DOS environment. Note that SHELL is a CONFIG.SYS command, and only executes at boot time. Its effects cannot be changed or undone except by modifying the CONFIG.SYS file and rebooting the computer. The DOS environment is normally set to 512 bytes. To change the size of the environment, use a SHELL command similar to the following:

```
SHELL=C:\DRDOS\COMMAND.COM /E:xxxx /P
```

Whenever DOS sees a SHELL command in the CONFIG.SYS file, it expects to be told what command interpreter to use. The command interpreter must, therefore, be fully defined (path and file name). In this case, the command interpreter is COMMAND.COM, located on the C drive in the DRDOS directory. The /E switch specifies the environment size, and xxxx specifies the size in bytes. The range for this value is between 512 and 32,751. The size of the environment should be large enough to store all of the environment variables that you need, but no more. Memory allocated to the environment is taken away from the memory available for running programs.

Setting an Alternate Command Interpreter and AUTOEXEC File

The /P switch must always be used with the SHELL command. Without it, it would be possible to exit the permanent command processor with an EXIT command, and DOS would have nowhere to go from there. /P causes the copy of COMMAND.COM to remain in memory, and causes the AUTOEXEC.BAT file to execute. You may also specify a file other than AUTOEXEC.BAT to execute by specifying a filename after the /P command, as in the following example:

```
SHELL=C:\DRDOS\COMMAND.COM /P:ALTAUTO.BAT
```

This command will execute a file named ALTAUTO.BAT at boot time, instead of the AUTOEXEC.BAT file.

SHELL can be used to define a different command interpreter, if you do not want to use COMMAND.COM. This is a rare occurrence, but if you want to do it, all you have to do is include the following line in your CONFIG.SYS file:

```
SHELL=path\filename
```

where PATH\FILENAME represents the complete path and file name of the command interpreter you want to use.

Controlling the Memory Location of COMMAND.COM

Chapter 5 discussed a variety of techniques for loading most of DOS into the upper and high memory areas. These techniques are generally sufficient to get the best possible memory configuration, but you may also use the SHELL command to force COMMAND.COM to load into a specific area of memory. This is done with the /ML, /MH, and /MU switches for the SHELL command. These force COMMAND.COM to load into low, high, and upper memory, respectively. The following command directs SHELL to load COMMAND.COM into upper memory:

```
SHELL=C:\DRDOS\COMMAND.COM /P /MU
```

Note that in order for COMMAND.COM to load into upper or high memory, there must be a device driver loaded that supports upper or high memory. EMM386.SYS, EMMXMA.SYS, and HIDOS.SYS are device drivers that are come with DR DOS 6.0 and that provide these functions.

Rather than specify either high or upper memory, you may use the /R switch to specify either. The following command tells SHELL to load COMMAND.COM into either high or upper memory, if enough of one of them is available:

```
SHELL=C:\DRDOS\COMMAND.COM /P /R
```

If there is not sufficient high or upper memory available, then DOS will ignore any memory switches on the SHELL command and load COMMAND.COM into conventional (low) memory.

Understanding and Controlling the CONFIG.SYS File

Some of the commands discussed in other parts of this book are used in the CONFIG.SYS file for specific purposes. However, there are many commands available for choosing the commands that CONFIG.SYS will execute, and for controlling the way in which those commands are executed.

Including Comments in CONFIG.SYS Files

CONFIG.SYS files can become quite complex, particularly with the ability to control the flow of execution using the commands discussed below. You may include comments in your CONFIG.SYS file, just as you can in batch files, using the REM command. Any lines that begin with the letters REM followed by a space are interpreted as comments, and are therefore ignored by DOS. Comments can make it easier to understand the logical structure of the commands in a CONFIG.SYS file, and to see quickly what a particular command is doing. The REM command can be seen in the examples below.

Controlling the Execution of CONFIG.SYS Commands

DR DOS 6.0 provides a variety of commands that allow you to actually program the CONFIG.SYS file, just as you can program a batch file. In fact, many of these commands are identical to batch file commands. Many of these commands use labels, like those in batch files, to identify the subroutine to jump to. A label begins with a colon, followed by an identifier of up to eight characters. (You may actually use labels longer than eight characters, but DOS looks at only the first eight to identify the label, so the first eight characters must be unique.)

CONFIG.SYS commands do not appear on the screen as they are executed. It is sometimes useful to display messages during the processing of CONFIG.SYS commands. This can be helpful in debugging a CONFIG.SYS file, and in providing prompts for use with the SWITCH command (discussed below). The ECHO command is used for this purpose; the following command will cause the message "Switch to alternate configuration?" to appear:

```
ECHO=Switch to alternate configuration?
```

Everything following the equal sign will be included as part of the message. If you include a blank space between the equal sign and the message, then the message will be indented by one blank space.

The ? command is used to display a prompt, and allow you to decide whether or not a particular CONFIG.SYS command should be executed. For example, under some circumstances you may want the ANSI.SYS device driver loaded, and under other circumstances you may not want it loaded. The following command will allow you to choose each time the computer is booted:

```
?"Load ANSI.SYS?"DEVICE=C:\DRDOS\ANSI.SYS
```

When this command is encountered, the prompt “Load ANSI.SYS?” is displayed (without the quotes), and the computer pauses until you press a Y or an N.

You may omit the message, and simply precede the command with a question mark:

```
?DEVICE=C:\DRDOS\ANSI.SYS
```

In this case, when the ? is encountered the following prompt appears:

```
DEVICE=C:\DRDOS\ANSI.SYS (Y/N) ?
```

You may include up to 128 characters on a CONFIG.SYS command line. This includes the question mark and message. If a command line is longer than 128 characters it is ignored.

The SWITCH command provides a greater degree of programming power than the ? does. SWITCH functions the same way in CONFIG.SYS files as it does in batch files—it allows you to prompt for an input, then switches to a subroutine based on what is entered. When the subroutine is finished executing, control returns to the command immediately following the SWITCH command. Unlike the ? command, SWITCH does not include a message, so you must use the ECHO command in conjunction with it.

Figure 10.2 contains a sample CONFIG.SYS file that uses the SWITCH command to determine which of three possible memory configurations should be used (this example assumes a 386 PC with extended memory).

The first line in Figure 10.2 uses the CLS command to clear the screen. Several ECHO commands then set up a small menu and prompt you to enter the menu item of your choice. Based on the choice you make, SWITCH then jumps to the appropriate subroutine. When the selected subroutine is finished executing, control is returned to the command following SWITCH—the ECHO command that informs you that the requested configuration has been implemented. The EXIT command then terminates the CONFIG.SYS file. EXIT is necessary, because without it DOS would continue into the commands in the subroutines.

You may use up to nine labels with a SWITCH command.

```
REM First set up a menu of possible memory configurations, then
REM get the user's choice of which one they want. Finally,
REM switch to the code for that choice, then return and exit.
CLS
ECHO
ECHO
ECHO
ECHO
ECHO 1. Configure Extended Memory Only
ECHO 2. Configure Expanded And Extended Memory
ECHO 3. Configure Only Conventional Memory
ECHO
ECHO
ECHO
ECHO
ECHO Enter the number of your choice:
SWITCH EXTENDED EXPANDED CONVNTL
ECHO Your requested memory configuration has been implemented.
EXIT
:EXTENDED
REM Install emm386.sys for extended memory only
DEVICE=C:\DRDOS\EMM386.SYS /F=NONE /B=FFFF
RETURN
:EXPANDED
REM Install emm386.sys for expanded memory emulation
DEVICE=C:\DRDOS\EMM386.SYS /F=AUTO /K=1280 /B=FFFF
RETURN
:CONVNTL
REM Don't install emm386.sys
ECHO Neither extended nor expanded memory will be available
RETURN
```

Figure 10.2 SWITCH Command in CONFIG.SYS File

The EXIT command can be used anywhere in a CONFIG.SYS file to terminate it. It is generally used with either a SWITCH or ? command. EXIT can be placed in a subroutine or in the main body of the CONFIG.SYS file.

There is one aspect of the ? and SWITCH commands that can be annoying: you are required to interact with the computer in order for it to complete the boot process. It is often convenient to start the computer, then go about some other task while it boots. The TIMEOUT command is used to get around this inconvenience.

TIMEOUT is used to specify a number of seconds that the computer will wait for a response to a ? or SWITCH command. If the specified number of seconds elapses without a response, TIMEOUT ignores ? commands and executes the first option on SWITCH commands. The following command tells TIMEOUT to wait 10 seconds for a reply:

```
TIMEOUT 10
```

You may use an optional equal sign for readability if you like. The following command is equivalent to the one above:

```
TIMEOUT = 10
```

TIMEOUT applies to all ? and SWITCH commands that follow it. Any that come before it will not be affected.

The GOSUB command is similar to SWITCH in that it jumps to a subroutine, and when the subroutine is done control returns to the command following GOSUB, but it does not prompt for a response to determine the point to jump to. Instead, the point to jump to is identified in the CONFIG.SYS file. The following code demonstrates the use of GOSUB:

```
REM First configure memory
GOSUB mem
REM Now load the network drivers
GOSUB nw
REM Now load all other drivers
GOSUB miscdrvr
EXIT
:mem
ECHO Memory configuration commands go here
RETURN
:nw
ECHO network configuration commands go here
RETURN
:miscdrvr
ECHO Miscellaneous drivers go here
RETURN
```

Figure 10.3 Sample CONFIG.SYS File Using GOSUB Commands

GOSUB is useful for organizing your CONFIG.SYS file, so that the logic for it is clear. If your CONFIG.SYS file does a lot of jumping around using GOTOs, its readability can probably be improved by using GOSUBs to place the main logic at the top of the file, and organize the secondary logic in subroutines. Figure 10.3 shows a sample CONFIG.SYS file organized with GOSUB commands.

The GOTO command is used to jump from one location in a CONFIG.SYS file to another. Unlike TIMEOUT and GOSUB, control does not return to the command following the GOTO. The location to jump to is identified by a label. The following code demonstrates the use of GOTO:

```
?"Do you want to load the network driver (Y/N)?" GOTO nw
.
.
.
EXIT
.
.
.
:nw
DEVICE=netdriver
```

The EXIT command is included because the network drivers will be loaded even if you answer N to the prompt, unless you force an exit from CONFIG.SYS.

The CHAIN command is used to transfer control from one CONFIG.SYS file to another. CHAIN is most commonly used with computers that boot from read-only or ROM disks, which are disks whose contents cannot be changed. By including the CHAIN command in a CONFIG.SYS file on such a disk, the user has the option of providing an alternative CONFIG.SYS file on a normal disk. If the CONFIG.SYS file specified on the CHAIN command does not exist, DOS goes ahead and executes the rest of the original CONFIG.SYS file.

After the second CONFIG.SYS file is done executing, control does not return to the original. Commands prior to the CHAIN command execute normally. The following command tells DOS to switch control to a CONFIG.SYS file in the root directory of the A: drive:

```
CHAIN = A:\CONFIG.SYS
```

Note that when CHAIN is used to switch to a CONFIG.SYS file on another drive, the full path, including the drive, must be used on all DEVICE and HIDEVICE commands.

Controlling the Display from CONFIG.SYS

There are two commands that let you control the appearance of the screen from the CONFIG.SYS file: the CLS and CPOS commands. CLS is the same as the command-line CLS command—it clears the screen.

CPOS is used to position the cursor on the screen. You must specify both a row and a column. The following command places the cursor at row 10, column 40:

```
CPOS 10, 40
```

You may specify any row number from 1 to 25, and any column number from 1 to 80. Once the cursor has been positioned using CPOS, a subsequent ECHO command will display its message at the cursor position. The menu-definition commands in the CONFIG.SYS file in Figure 10.2 could be modified to center the menu as follows:

```
CPOS 10,15
ECHO 1. Configure Extended Memory Only
CPOS 11,15
ECHO 2. Configure Expanded And Extended Memory
CPOS 12,15
ECHO 3. Configure Only Conventional Memory
```

Configuring File and Drive Characteristics

A number of CONFIG.SYS commands are provided to set characteristics related to files and disk drives. The BUFFERS, HIBUFFERS, FASTOPEN, and FILES commands all affect file characteristics; these commands were discussed in Chapters 5 and 7.

VDISK.SYS is a device driver that can be used in CONFIG.SYS to set up a RAM disk. VDISK.SYS is discussed in detail in Chapter 7.

The term *logical drive* refers to any device or structure that appears to DOS as a disk drive. Thus, setting up a RAM drive creates a logical drive, and partitioning a single hard disk into several smaller drives creates multiple logical drives. A logical drive is anything referenced by its own drive letter.

You may have to up 26 logical drives on your computer—one for each letter of the alphabet. But for each drive letter that is supported, a small amount of memory is required. When the computer is booted, DOS assigns a drive letter to every logical drive it locates, including RAM drives. (If DOS only finds one floppy drive, it assigns both A: and B: to it.) It then sets the last drive letter used as the last drive on the machine. By limiting the number of drives that can be supported, memory is conserved.

The LASTDRIVE command is used to set a different last drive letter. This allows you to reserve drive letters that will be used after boot time. The only reason for providing extra drive letters is if you expect to create a new logical drive with the SUBST command, or if you will be creating a RAM drive after the CONFIG.SYS file has been processed. SUBST is discussed in detail in Chapter 7. SUBST is used to assign a logical drive letter to replace a directory path. These substituted drive letters are sometimes called *virtual drives*. If you want to do this, you will need to adjust the LASTDRIVE value to leave enough free drive letters for as many virtual drives as you want to create. The following command sets the last legal drive letter to G:

```
LASTDRIVE = F
```

If your computer has one or two floppy drives and a hard drive, then the letters A, B, and C will be assigned by DOS. The above command will permit the letters D, E, and F to be used for additional logical drives.

Device Drivers

Any piece of hardware that is attached to the computer, and provides some form of input or receives some form of output, is referred to as a *device*. Each device is unique, and requires its own software, called a *device driver,* to manage its communications with the computer. Some device drivers are built-in, and others can be installed by including them in the CONFIG.SYS file, using the DEVICE= command. The DEVICE= command was explained in Chapter 5, where it was used to install the EMM386.SYS device driver. There are several other standard device drivers provided with DR DOS 6.0, including ANSI.SYS, DISPLAY.SYS, DRIVER.SYS, EGA.SYS, and PRINTER.SYS.

There is one file provided with DR DOS 6.0 that would appear from its name to be a device driver: COUNTRY.SYS. This is not a device driver, and attempting to load it with the DEVICE= command will lock up your computer. Since the command is in the CONFIG.SYS file, you will have to boot the computer with a different disk and edit CONFIG.SYS before that disk can be used again to boot the computer. The COUNTRY= command is used to load this file, rather than the DEVICE=command.

The DEVICE= and HIDEVICE= commands are discussed in detail in Chapter 5.

Using ANSI.SYS to Customize the Screen and Keyboard

One of the standard device drivers provided with DR DOS 6.0 is the ANSI.SYS driver. This driver allows you to modify the way the CPU responds to the keyboard and the way it displays characters on the screen. One of the ways of sending commands to this driver is through the PROMPT command, using the $E parameter. $E inserts into the command line a character known as the Escape character. The Escape character tells DOS that what follows is one or more commands that should be sent to the ANSI.SYS device driver. The combination of the Escape character and ANSI.SYS commands is known as an *escape sequence*.

It is worthwhile to keep in mind how these escape sequences work. They are not really PROMPT commands. Rather, they use the PROMPT command to send a command sequence to the ANSI.SYS driver. For this reason, entering another PROMPT command does not automatically cancel them, the way it would cancel previous PROMPT commands. The only time a PROMPT command communicates with the ANSI.SYS device driver is when an escape sequence is included in the command, and the only time a previous command to ANSI.SYS is canceled is when a specific cancellation command is sent to ANSI.SYS.

The ANSI.SYS device driver can also receive commands from programs written in programming languages like BASIC, PASCAL, and C, but a discussion of these uses is beyond the scope of this book.

PROMPT Parameters Used for Positioning the Cursor

The escape sequence $E[row;columnH places the cursor at the point on the screen specified by the row and column values. The H tells ANSI.SYS to interpret the preceding numbers as cursor positions. You must be certain to use a capital H; using a small h will change your screen display. (If this happens, refer to the next section, titled *PROMPT Parameters Used for Modifying the Screen Display*, to restore your display.)

The following command demonstrates the use of PROMPT to position the cursor:

```
PROMPT $E[10;31HThis Is The DOS Screen$E[12;1H$P$G
```

This command displays the message "This Is The DOS Screen" on row 10, starting at column 31 (which centers the message horizontally, slightly above the middle of the screen). It then moves the cursor to the beginning of line 12 and displays a common DOS prompt—the current directory followed by a greater than sign.

This prompt appears at the specified location, regardless of whatever else is on the screen. It does not clear the screen first, so the prompt may appear in the middle of other information already being displayed. Whether this is a problem depends on your anticipated use of the DOS command line. You may clear the screen before the message is displayed, or only clear the lines on which the prompt will appear, using the escape sequences discussed in the next section. If you enter the CLS command, which clears the screen, after entering this PROMPT command, the screen will appear as in Figure 10.4.

```
This Is The DOS Screen



C:\DRDOS
```

Figure 10.4 DOS Prompt Using ANSI.SYS for Cursor Positioning

If the screen is not cleared first, the message could appear in the middle of information displayed by the last command, as shown in Figure 10.5.

```
NC                  <DIR>        01-04-91     11:29a
NORTON              <DIR>        01-04-91     10:50a
PROCOMM             <DIR>        01-05-91      3:37p
QC25                <DIR>        01-03-91     10:38P
QEMM                <DIR>        01-04-91     11:55a
RBFILES             <DIR>        01-03-91      9:51p
SPRINT              <DIR>        01-03-91     10:20p
APPDIR     BAT            3404-29-This Is The DOS Screen
AUTOEXEC   CLR           160     04-20-91      7:25a
AUTOEXEC   50            427     04-15-91      8:33a
AUTOEXEC   BAT           385     05-04-91      8:00p
AUTOEXEC   ORG           326     01-04-91     11:56a
AUTOEXEC   DV            385     05-04-91      8:00p
CONFIG     DV            210     03-02-91      1:14p
CONFIG     ORG           192     01-04-91     11:56a
CONFIG     50            236     04-17-91      7:22a
CONFIG     SYS           253     05-05-91     10:38p
CONFIG     CLR           221     04-20-91      7:44a
DV         BAT            55     01-04-91     11:58a
MIRROR     BAK         58880     05-05-91     10:33p
MACS       BAT            96     03-30-91     11:42a
MIRROR     FIL         58880     05-05-91     10:38p
OPT3       BAT           642     01-04-91     12:28p
HELP       BAT           603     05-05-91      6:03p
SETCL      BAT            62     04-20-91      7:00a
```

Figure 10.5 ANSI-defined DOS Prompt without First Clearing Screen

The following four escape sequences may be used with the PROMPT command to move the cursor up, down, left, and right:

$E[numA] Moves the cursor up num rows without changing the column it is in.

$E[numB] Moves the cursor down num rows without changing the column it is in.

$E[numC] Moves the cursor to the right num spaces without changing the row it is in.

$E[numD] Moves the cursor to the left num spaces without changing the row it is in.

One use of the C and D sequences is to make detailed changes to the appearance of the date and time in the DOS prompt, as demonstrated in the following command:

```
PROMPT $D$E[10D$H$H$H$HDate$E[9C$G
```

This command replaces the day of the week with the word "Date". The result is the following prompt:

```
Date11-01-1991>_
```

The first parameter, $D, inserts the date into the prompt. The prompt is now "Sat 11-01-1991." The first escape sequence, $E[10D, moves the cursor to the left 10 spaces, which puts it under the first 0 at the beginning of the date. The following four parameters are all $H, which erases four characters (the day of the week and the space that separates it from the date) and leaves the cursor at the beginning of the line. Then the word "Date" is inserted, followed by the escape sequence $E[9C, which moves the cursor to the right nine spaces, placing it at the end of the date. Finally there is a $G parameter, which causes the prompt to terminate with a greater than sign.

PROMPT Parameters Used for Modifying the Screen Display

You may use escape sequences to modify the screen display itself, as well as to position the cursor. The extent to which you can modify the display is dependent on the type of monitor you have. If you have a color monitor, you may set the foreground and background colors of characters that appear in the prompt, as well as the colors of anything that is displayed as the result of a command. This includes information such as directory displays. The escape sequence settings do not, however, affect the display of the shell or other programs you run—they only affect displays generated by DOS commands. On monochrome displays you can define the underline characters.

The escape sequence $E[2J is used to erase the entire screen and position the cursor in the upper-left corner. You may then use the cursor positioning sequences to place it elsewhere if you desire. This would be a useful sequence to add to the example above that displays a message in the middle of the screen using the $E[row,columnH sequence.

The escape sequence $E[K erases the screen from the current cursor position to the end of the line. This erases whatever is at the cursor position as well, so before using this sequence, you may want to move the cursor to the right one space to avoid erasing the last character of the prompt.

The format of the escape sequences for setting colors and other display attributes is:

```
$E[setting1;setting2;...m
```

There may be any number of settings; the last setting is terminated with a small m rather than a semi-colon. This indicates the end of the escape sequence. Each setting is a number between 0 and 47, though not all numbers are available. The available settings are as follows:

Setting	*Description*
0	Turns all other settings off. This sets all new displays off the screen to the default of white letters on a black background. Information on the screen is unaffected.
1	Turns on bold. Everything displayed after this setting will appear in bold (high intensity). This will affect everything displayed until an "all settings off" (setting 0) turns bold off. Anything displayed in bold will remain in bold on the screen; new characters will not be in bold.
4	Turns on underscore. This is effective for monochrome displays only—color displays cannot show a character as underlined. This will remain in effect until an "all settings off" (setting 0) turns off underlining.
5	Turns on blinking. Everything displayed/entered after this setting will blink. This will affect everything displayed/entered until an "all settings off" (setting 0) turns blinking off. Anything displayed before the $E0m will continue to blink, but new displays will not blink.
7	Turns on reverse video. Everything displaye/ entered after this setting will appear in black letters on a white background. This setting will remain in effect until an

	"all settings off" (setting 0) turns off reverse video. Anything displayed in reverse video will remain in reverse video after it is turned off.
8	Turns off the display screen. Anything typed at the keyboard and anything that would normally appear on the screen will not appear. This is useful for entering passwords that you do not want to have appear on the screen when you enter them. This remains in effect until an "all settings off" (setting 0) resets the display mode.
30	Sets the foreground color to Black.
31	Sets the foreground color to Red.
32	Sets the foreground color to Green.
33	Sets the foreground color to Yellow.
34	Sets the foreground color to Blue.
35	Sets the foreground color to Magenta.
36	Sets the foreground color to Cyan.
37	Sets the foreground color to White.
40	Sets the background color to Black.
41	Sets the background color to Red.
42	Sets the background color to Green.
43	Sets the background color to Yellow.
44	Sets the background color to Blue.
45	Sets the background color to Magenta.
46	Sets the background color to Cyan.
47	Sets the background color to White.

You can also use escape sequences to set the screen *mode*; mode refers to how the screen as a whole displays information. There are two classes of modes: text and graphics. Text modes display only text and limited figures, but the resolution is very high. Graphics modes can display very complex graphic images, but when displaying text characters the resolution is sometimes not as high.

Text modes divide the screen into either 40 characters per line and 25 lines per screen, or 80 characters per line and 25 lines per screen.

Graphics modes divide the screen into much smaller units called *pixels*. The number of vertical and horizontal pixels varies with the type of monitor and video card in your computer. The various types of cards are reviewed in Chapter 1. Pixels can either be in color or black and white.

In addition to setting either graphics or text mode, there is one additional use of the Set Mode escape sequence: to turn on or off the line wrapping feature. By default, if you type past the end of the DOS command line, the cursor moves to the beginning of the next line and you can continue typing there. You may enter up to 128 characters on the DOS command line, so depending on the length of the prompt the line may wrap once or twice. If you do not want to allow line wrapping you may use the Set Mode escape sequence to cause the cursor to stop at the end of the line. Whatever you type at that point overwrites the last character on the line.

Which modes are available on your computer depends upon your hardware configuration: some monitors can only display in one or two modes, while others can display in all of them. All monitors will display in 40 x 25 and 80 x 25 text modes, and all monitors will allow the line-wrapping feature to be switched on and off. If you aren't sure which modes are available on your computer, the simplest way to find out is to try out the commands and see which ones affect your display.

The mode is set with the escape sequence $E[=numh, where num is a number that specifies the mode and the h marks the end of the command. The h must be lowercase. The allowable numbers and their effects are specified in Table 10.1.

Table 10.1 Screen Mode Settings Using the ANSI.SYS Driver

Setting	*Description*
0	40 x 25 characters text mode—black and white
1	40 x 25 characters text mode—color
2	80 x 25 characters text mode—black and white
3	80 x 25 characters text mode—color
4	320 x 200 pixels graphics mode—black and white
5	320 x 200 pixels graphics mode—4 colors
6	640 x 200 pixels graphics mode—black and white
7	turns on line wrapping (the default)

PROMPT Parameters Used for Modifying the Keyboard

The $E escape sequences may be used for modifying the way the CPU responds to the keyboard. Specifically, you can assign any key (including shift-key combinations and function keys) to print a different letter than was originally assigned to it, or even to print a string of letters, numbers, and symbols. For example, you could assign F1 to automatically perform a DOS command, such as DIR, which lists the files in the current directory. You may also use this feature to cause a message to display whenever a particular keystroke is entered.

These keyboard commands work only for keystrokes entered at the DOS prompt. They will not affect the keystrokes entered within the ViewMAX or within your software programs, such as your word processor. They can therefore be used to customize the DOS interface without worrying about interference with other programs.

To understand how this works you must know a little about how the computer responds to the keyboard. Each key, and each Shift, Alt, and Ctrl key combination, produces a numeric code that gets sent to the CPU. These codes are translated by the computer into ASCII codes. ASCII codes are codes that correspond to the common characters and symbols that we use for communicating—the upper- and lowercase alphabetic characters, numbers, punctuation symbols, and so on. When the CPU sees one of these ASCII codes it displays the appropriate character on the screen. For example, the ASCII code for capital A is 65, so when the CPU sees an ASCII code of 65 it displays a capital A on the screen.

There are 256 ASCII codes altogether. The first 128 of them (codes 0 through 127) are known as standard ASCII. They share a common meaning among computer systems that use ASCII codes, and they represent such common symbols as the letters of the alphabet or numbers.

The use of the last 128 codes (codes 128 through 255) is not shared among computer systems. IBM-compatible PCs use these codes for special symbols that can be displayed on the screen. They include letters of foreign alphabets, arrow symbols, and symbols that can be used for drawing lines and boxes on the screen. The entire 256-code ASCII table for IBM-compatible PCs appears in the appendix. Some of the ASCII codes produce two symbols—a caret (^) followed by a capital letter.

Some of them do not produce printable characters at all—they are used for sending special messages to the display device (either a printer or the screen). An example of such a message is CR, for Carriage Return. This tells the printer or screen to move to the beginning of the next line.

Escape sequences can be used to change the ASCII code that is assigned to a key. The escape sequence used for this purpose is:

```
$E[num;replacementp
```

In this escape sequence, *num* stands for the ASCII code for the key, *replacement* stands for the new code or codes to be assigned to that key, and *p* indicates the end of the sequence. The re-assignment codes may be either in the form of another numeric code or actual letters enclosed in double quotes. For example, the letter *A* (uppercase A) has an ASCII code of 65 and the letter *B* has an ASCII code of 66. Both of the following PROMPT commands will cause the letter *B* to appear when the letter *A* is entered:

```
PROMPT $E[65;66p
PROMPT $E[65;"B"p
```

Since these are PROMPT commands, as well as commands sent to ANSI.SYS, they will change the DOS prompt—in fact, they will eliminate it, since there are no PROMPT parameters other than $E in the command. To send this keyboard command to ANSI.SYS and also leave a DOS prompt that shows the current directory followed by a greater than sign, you must enter one of the following commands:

```
PROMPT $E[65;66p$P$G
PROMPT $E[65;"B"p$P$G
```

After either of these PROMPT commands has been entered, typing a capital *A* at the DOS prompt will result in a capital *B* appearing on the screen. You may assign more than one ASCII code to a key. This allows you to have entire messages or commands appear at the touch of a key. These messages may be entered as either ASCII numeric codes or as character strings enclosed in quotes. Both of the following commands assign the word HELP to the *A* key:

```
PROMPT $E[65;72;69;76;80p$P$G
PROMPT $E[65;"HELP"p$P$G
```

Again, the PROMPT is terminated with PG to leave a reasonable prompt appearing on the screen.

You may assign codes to the function keys rather than the regular keys by starting the numbers in the escape sequence with a 0. This tells ANSI.SYS that the next number refers to what is known as an *extended code*. The function keys are numbered with extended codes 59 through 68. The following PROMPT reassigns F1 to type the message "HELP":

```
PROMPT $P$G$E[0;59;"HELP"p
```

If you examine the ASCII table, you will see that ASCII code 13 has the letters CR corresponding to it. CR stands for Carriage Return, and whenever the CPU sees the ASCII code 13 it sends a carriage return signal to the output device. This is the same as having pressed Enter. An ASCII code 13 can be included in the keyboard reassignment escape sequence to cause a keystroke to carry out a DOS command. For example, the following PROMPT command results in the letters DIR, followed by a carriage return, to be typed out whenever F1 is pressed:

```
PROMPT $P$G$E[0;59;"DIR;"13p
```

This will cause the DOS DIR (directory) command to be entered when F1 is pressed, resulting in a directory listing of the current directory. You can extend this to have function keys execute batch files.

A particularly useful application of this technique is to use it with an appropriate DOS prompt to make sure you or other users of your computer always know how to get back to the Shell. The following PROMPT command will set this up:

PROMPT Press F1 to return to the Shell$G$E[0;59;"EXIT;"13p

This will result in the following DOS prompt:

```
Press F1 to return to the Shell>
```

It will also assign the word EXIT, followed by a carriage return, to F1, which is what is required for returning to the Shell when you have temporarily exited from it. For this prompt to remain in effect when you exit and re-enter the Shell, you must enter the PROMPT command at the DOS prompt (while the Shell is not running in the background).

Fine-tuning the Keyboard Response Rate with the MODE Command

The MODE command can be used to adjust the rate at which the computer repeats a key that is held down, and the amount of time it waits after the key is pressed before beginning to repeat. The first of these two characteristics is called the *typematic rate*, and the second is called the *keyboard delay*. However, some keyboards, particularly older ones, will not recognize this command.

To adjust the rate, enter the following command:

```
MODE CON RATE=xx DELAY=yy
```

The value of xx may be anywhere from 1 to 32, representing about 2 to 30 repetitions per second. The default value is 20 or 21, depending on the keyboard.

The value of yy may be 1, 2, 3, or 4. These correspond to 0.25, 0.50, 0.75, and 1.00 seconds, respectively. The default value is 2 (0.50 seconds).

You must either set both values, or neither. You cannot set just one of them.

Managing the Print Queue

When you use the PRINT utility, all files that are sent to the printer are put into the print queue. The print queue is an area of memory, that stores the names of files to be printed. When one file finishes printing the next one in the queue is sent to the printer.

The PRINT utility is enabled by including a PRINT command in the AUTOEXEC.BAT file. You may modify the PRINT command in the AUTOEXEC.BAT file using the switches discussed below. Many of the switches can only be executed the first time the PRINT command is invoked. These should be set in the AUTOEXEC.BAT file, since that is where the PRINT command is first called. These may only be set once because the first time PRINT is executed a portion of the program is loaded into memory, and these switches are set in that portion of the program. They cannot be manipulated after being loaded.

The other switches are used for manipulating the queue after it has been called. They allow you to remove files from the queue and add files to the queue, and they can be invoked as often as you wish. These are available by going to the command prompt and executing the PRINT command.

You may use as many or as few of the switches as you like. If you do include switches the first time you invoke PRINT, DOS will prompt you for the device to print to (discussed in the next section, *Specifying the Printing Device*). If you invoke PRINT without any switches after the first time it has been invoked, it will simply list the files currently in the print queue.

If you want control over the PRINT utility startup switches, you should remove the PRINT command from your AUTOEXEC.BAT file. You can then load the resident part of PRINT the first time you execute the PRINT command. You may specify the load switches at this time.

After a file has been added to the print queue, you must not make any changes to it until after it has finished printing. If the file is on a floppy disk you must leave the disk in the drive until the file has been printed. If a disk error occurs when DOS attempts to read a file for printing, the following sequence of events occurs:

1. The file being printed is canceled from the queue.
2. The disk error message is printed on the printer.
3. The printer paper is advanced to the next page.
4. The printer alarm is sounded.
5. The remaining files in the print queue are printed.

You must not attempt to use the printer for any other purpose while the Print command is operating. For example, you must not press the Shift-Print Screen combination to print a screen image. Doing so will cause the message "out-of-paper" to appear until all files have been printed or printing is terminated with a /C or /T switch (discussed below).

Specifying the Printing Device

Devices such as printers are attached to the computer through connections called *ports*. The print program must know which port should receive information that is to be printed. For instance, you may have two printers attached to your computer at ports named LPT1 and LPT2 (for Line Printer 1 and Line Printer 2). When you run PRINT the first time, you may specify where the information should be sent. This is done with a /D switch. The /D switch can only be entered the first time you run the PRINT command. If you use /D, it must be the first switch specified. The following command installs the resident part of the print program and tells it to send all files in the print queue to the LPT1 port:

```
PRINT /D:LPT1
```

If you do not include a /D switch, the first time you invoke PRINT the computer will respond with the message:

```
Name of list device [PRN]:
```

Pressing Enter will accept the default value of PRN, which in most cases is the correct choice. If you have one printer attached to your computer on the LPT1 port, this default value will work. Otherwise, you may specify any other port to which you would like to send the print queue output. Common choices are shown in Table 10.2.

Table 10.2 Common Ports for Printer Connections

LPT1	Line printer 1
LPT2	Line printer 2
LPT3	Line printer 3
PRN	Same as line printer 1
COM1	Communications port 1
COM2	Communications port 2
AUX	Auxiliary port

You must make sure that the port identified by the /D switch exists on your computer, and that there is some device attached to it that can receive the output. If there is no such port, or if there is nothing attached to it, using the PRINT command may cause your computer to hang up or to work erratically. For example, if you specify LPT2 your computer must have a port named LPT2 and there must be a printer attached to it.

Specifying the Size of the Print Buffer

When you run Print the first time after booting your computer, it sets up an area of memory known as a print buffer. Many printers can only receive a small number of characters at a time, and after they have printed these characters they request more from the computer. The computer must then suspend whatever it is doing, read the next characters to be printed from the disk, and send them to the printer. This ends up causing large portions of the computer's time to be spent communicating with the printer.

The print buffer is used to alleviate this problem. It stores a large number of characters that are ready to go to the printer, so when the printer is ready for more characters the computer does not need to suspend other operations in order to read them from disk. The only time the computer needs to suspend other operations for the printer is when the print buffer is empty.

The /B switch is used to specify the number of bytes set aside for the print buffer. It can only be entered the first time you invoke the PRINT command. If you do not include the /B switch, a 512-byte buffer is used. You may specify anywhere from 512 bytes to 16K bytes. A larger value may noticeably increase the performance of the PRINT command, especially if you have a high-speed printer.

The following command demonstrates the /B switch:

```
PRINT /B:1024
```

This specifies a print buffer of 1024 bytes—twice the default value of 512. Since /B can only be used the first time you invoke PRINT you will probably include a /D switch, as follows:

```
PRINT /D:LPT1 /B:1024
```

Remember that the /D switch must be the first switch if it is to be included. The order in which the other switches appear is not important.

Specifying the Maximum Number of Files in the Queue

The /Q switch is used to specify the maximum number of files you may have in the queue at any one time. If you reach this maximum, DOS will not allow you to add any more until the first one finishes printing. Then you may add one more, until the next one finishes, and so on.

The /Q switch can only be added the first time PRINT is invoked. You may specify anywhere from 4 to 32 files. If /Q is not included, the default value is 10. The following command demonstrates the use of /Q:

```
PRINT /D:LPT1 /B:1024 /Q:15
```

This command specifies LPT1 as the printer port, 1024 bytes for the print buffer, and a maximum of 15 files in the queue at any one time.

Managing PRINT Time

When the print queue is in use, it slows down the operation of your computer. There is no way around this. The computer can only do one thing at a time, so when it tends to the print queue it cannot tend to your other tasks. It is important, therefore, to have some control over how much of the computer's time is devoted to managing the print queue and how much of it is available for your other tasks.

There are three factors that determine how much of the computer's time is spent managing the print queue. But to understand these you must understand a little bit about how the computer's clock controls what the computer does.

Like any clock, the computer's clock operates by "ticking" time away. It ticks very fast—millions of clock ticks per second. Since a tick is such a tiny amount of time, the computer allocates much of its time in terms of *time slices* rather than clock ticks. A time slice consists of 255 clock ticks, just as a minute consists of 60 seconds.

The computer operates in *time cycles*. People also operate in time cycles, called days. A person may get up at 6:30, have breakfast at 7:00, arrive at work at 7:45, leave work at 4:45, and so on. Each day repeats the cycle. Certain time slices of the day are allocated to particular tasks, such as having breakfast. In the same way, the computer breaks its cycle into different tasks.

If you are working in your office on three projects, you may allocate the time from 1:00 to 3:00 for a particular project. Each day you work on that project from 1:00 to 3:00, and each day a little more of it gets done. In the computer's cycle, each time it gets around to the point where a particular task gets some time, a little more of that task gets done.

It is important to keep in mind that in the computer all of this is happening very fast—thousands of times per second—so you rarely notice the computer pausing in one task to give time to another.

In your computer's cycle there are 255 slices available for all tasks. This means that the smallest amount of time the computer can allocate to any one task is 1/255th of its cycle. You can specify how many time slices per cycle get allocated to managing the print queue with the /S switch. This switch can only be entered the first time you run the PRINT command. You may specify anywhere from 1 to 255 time slices. If you do not specify the /S switch the default value of 8 is used. The following command demonstrates the use of the /S switch:

```
PRINT /D:LPT1 /S:16
```

This command specifies the LPT1 port, and 16 time slices per cycle—(double the default value). The effect of this is that more of the computer's time will go to making sure your files print as fast as possible, but less time will be available to whatever other task you are performing while the files are printing.

When you specify a number of time slices (16 in this example), the computer does not bunch all of them together (give the printer 16/255ths of its time all at once, then wait for a complete cycle to come around before the PRINT program gets any time again). Rather, it distributes the slices evenly throughout the cycle. This helps make the print operations more transparent to you, since only very small amounts of time are being taken away from your other tasks. But those small amounts are taken away more frequently.

When a time slice for the print queue comes around, DOS checks to see if the printer is still printing the last characters sent to it or if it is waiting for some more characters. If it is waiting for more, DOS starts sending them.

However, DOS can send characters to the printer much faster than the printer can print them, so much of the time slice allocated to printing may be wasted. DOS may be able to send all of the characters the printer can print between now and the next printer time slice in the first few clock ticks of this slice, so the rest of the clock ticks for this slice are wasted. The /M switch is used to recover those ticks for the next task in the computer's cycle.

The /M switch specifies the number of clock ticks that DOS will use to send characters to the printer. If the printer is waiting for characters when a printer time slice starts, only the number of ticks specified with /M will be used to send characters to the printer. The rest of the time slice is released for the next task in the computer cycle.

You only specify /M the first time the PRINT command is invoked. You may specify anywhere from 1 through 255 ticks. The default value used if /M is not included is 2. The following command demonstrates the use of /M:

```
PRINT /D:LPT1 /M:10
```

This command specifies the LPT1 port, and allocates 10 clock ticks per printer time slice for sending characters to the printer. Since no /S switch is included in the command, the default of 8 time slices per cycle is used.

If the printer is still printing when a printer time slice comes around, DOS will continue checking the printer during the time slice. This can end up wasting the entire time slice if the printer does not complete its printing task during that time. The /U switch prevents this. It specifies how many clock ticks DOS will wait for the printer to complete its printing so it can receive new characters. If the printer does not finish in the number of ticks specified the rest of the time slice is released for the next task in the computer's cycle.

The /U switch can only be specified the first time PRINT is invoked. You may specify anywhere from 1 to 255; the default value if /U is not specified is 1. The following command demonstrates the use of the /U switch:

```
PRINT /D:LPT1 /U:10
```

This command specifies the LPT1 port, and 10 clock ticks to wait for the printer to be freed up. Since no /S or /M switches were specified, the default values of 8 and 2 will be used for these values.

The best use of the /S, /M, and /U switches is totally dependent on both your hardware configuration and the use you will make of the Print utility. In most cases, the default values are satisfactory. However, if you find that the computer is taking too long to print your files, or that it is taking too much time away from your other tasks, you may want to try adjusting them.

The switch that is most likely to have an impact on how much the Print utility is slowing down your other tasks is the /S switch, since that determines how much total time out of each cycle is devoted to PRINT. The /M and /U are for fine-tuning—they determine how much of the time slices allocated to the printer can be wasted before releasing the rest of the slice for other tasks.

If your printer is pausing frequently and for long periods of time, try increasing /M first. This will provide a larger portion of the available time slice for sending characters to the printer without taking up more time slices for printing. If that does not work increase /S. You may need to try several combinations of /M and /S before finding the one that provides the best printing speed with the least degradation of other computer performance.

The /U switch should only be used if maximizing printer throughput is very important, since it almost guarantees that time will be wasted waiting for the printer to become ready for more characters.

Managing Files in the Queue

There are three switches used to manipulate the files in the queue. These switches may be used at any time—they do not have to be included in the PRINT command the first time it is invoked.

The /T switch terminates printing from the queue. When you enter the PRINT command with the /T switch, all files in the queue are removed from the queue. The following command demonstrates the use of the /T switch:

```
PRINT /T
```

If a file is printing when the /T command is entered, the following sequence of events occurs:

1. The file being printed is canceled from the queue.
2. A file cancellation message is printed on the printer.
3. The printer alarm sounds.
4. The printer paper is advanced to the next page.
5. Any files specified on the command line after the /T switch are printed.

If no files are in the queue when this command is entered the message "PRINT queue is empty" will appear on the screen.

You may also specify one or more files to print after emptying the queue. These are included on the command line after the /T switch. Often you will wish to cancel the print queue because you want to print a file immediately, without waiting for all the other files in the queue to complete. The following command demonstrates this:

```
PRINT /T letter1.fil letter2.fil
```

This command will cancel all files in the queue and put the files letter1.fil and letter2.fil into the queue. Letter1.fil will then print, followed by letter2.fil.

The /C switch is used to cancel specified files from the queue. You may include one file name before the /C and as many as you like following it. Both of the following commands will remove the files letter4.fil and letter6.fil from the print queue:

```
PRINT letter4.fil /C letter6.fil
PRINT /C letter4.fil letter6.fil
```

You do not have to specify the file names in the order that they occur in the queue. If /C is used to cancel a file that is currently being printed, the following sequence of events occurs:

1. The file being printed is canceled from the queue.
2. A file cancellation message is printed on the printer.
3. The printer alarm sounds.
4. The printer paper is advanced to the next page.
5. The remaining files in the print queue are printed.

The /P switch adds files to the print queue. The file name preceding the /P and all file names following it will be added to the print queue. Files are added in the order in which they occur on the command line. Both of the following commands will add the files letter4.fil and letter6.fil to the queue:

```
PRINT letter4.fil /P letter6.fil
PRINT /P letter4.fil letter6.fil
```

The /P switch is the default: if no switches are specified, but file names are included on the command line, then the files are added to the print queue. The following two command lines are functionally identical:

```
PRINT letter4.fil /P letter6.fil
PRINT letter4.fil letter6.fil
```

The /C and /P switches may be combined on one command line. The switch specified first will be in effect up to the file name that precedes the switch specified second. Either of the following command lines will remove the file letter4.fil from the queue, and add the files letter5.fil and letter6.fil:

```
PRINT letter4.fil /C letter5.fil /P letter6.fil
PRINT letter4.fil /C /P letter5.fil letter6.fil
```

To experiment with the commands, you can turn off your printer and enter the PRINT command with various switches. If you turn off your printer the print queue will not empty out. Whenever any Print command executes, the entire queue is listed, so you can see what effect the command had.

Use of Wild Cards in Print Command File Names

You may use the wild cards * and ? in the file names entered in the PRINT command. The * is used to replace groups of characters, the ? is used to replace individual characters. For example, the file name *.fil refers to all files that have an extension of FIL. The file name letter?.* refers to all files that begin with letter plus one more character, and any extension. This would include letter1.fil, letter2.dat, etc. You may also embed the asterisk within a file name: let*.fil will include letter.fil, let.fil, lettuce.fil, etc. However, if you begin the file name with *, all file names will be included. The designation *etter.fil will include all files with the extension fil.

If you wanted to print all files with an extension of fil you could enter the following command:

```
PRINT *.fil
```

To print all files that begin with letter followed by a number and the extension FIL you could enter the following command:

```
PRINT letter?.fil
```

You could also print all files that begin with LET followed by any group of characters and the extension fil with the following command:

```
PRINT let*.fil
```

The wild card symbols may be included with any of the PRINT switches. The following command will remove all files that are named letter followed by an extension:

```
PRINT letter.*/C
```

Controlling the Effects of Control-Break

Pressing Ctrl-C, or Ctrl-Break, interrupts the activity of the CPU and terminates whatever process is taking place. For example, if a very long directory listing is in progress, you can interrupt it by pressing Ctrl-C. This is because DOS scans the keyboard for these keystrokes. However, normally DOS only watches for Ctrl-C when it is reading keyboard input or writing something to the screen or printer. During other operations, like disk reads and writes, it does not check for Ctrl-Break. This makes sense, since these are operations that should not normally be interrupted. However, you can tell DOS to scan for Ctrl-Break during all DOS operations by entering the following command at the command prompt:

```
BREAK ON
```

You may turn this extended checking off again by entering this command:

```
BREAK OFF
```

By default, BREAK is off. Turning it on slows down the performance of your computer slightly, because DOS is scanning for Ctrl-Break more frequently.

The effect on your software programs of turning on Ctrl-Break is not predictable. On some, it may permit you to interrupt some processes that would otherwise not be interruptible, while for other programs there will be no effect.

System Security

In addition to the LOCK command discussed in Chapter 4, and the PASSWORD command discussed in Chapter 6, there is one additional security feature available in DR DOS 6.0, called System Security. System Security is used to provide a password that must be entered before the computer can be booted. This prevents all unauthorized users from gaining access to the computer.

When System Security is enabled, attempting to boot from a floppy disk will work, but you will not be able to access the hard disk until you run the LOGIN program from a floppy disk.

As with any password system, there is the danger that you will forget your password. Recovering from a lost password is impossible; if you lose your password you will have to have a low-level format of your hard disk performed, which will destroy all of the information on it. Consequently, you must be sure to use a password that you will remember. Furthermore, it is best to only use the security features if you really need them. They slow down access to your PC, since you must enter passwords, and they create the risk that you will forget your password.

To install System Security, select the System Security option on the Installation or SETUP program menu. You will be prompted for a Master Key and a User Key. The User Key is the password that will be used to gain access to the computer. The Master Key is the password that is required to enable and disable System Security.

Either password can be changed by running SETUP. The passwords should be changed frequently if there is any possibility that someone could learn what they are.

System Security can be disabled by running SETUP and choosing the System Security option. When you choose the Disable Security option, you will be prompted for the Master Key.

Chapter 11

The DR DOS Command Dictionary

This chapter provides a command dictionary of all commonly used DR DOS commands. A statement of each command's purpose and its syntax are given. Most of these commands are discussed in greater detail in other chapters of this book. You may locate these discussions by checking the index.

A type is also specified for each command, and it will be one of the following:

- Internal
- External
- External/Internal
- CONFIG.SYS
- Batch

Internal commands are loaded into memory when you boot your computer. It is not necessary to have a DOS disk or directory available when you invoke these commands, since they are located in memory.

External commands are not loaded into memory when the computer is booted. Consequently, you must have a DOS disk available on a floppy disk system, or have the DOS directory available (via a PATH or APPEND if it is not the current directory) in order to use the command.

External/Internal commands are external the first time they are invoked. The DOS disk or directory must therefore be available when they are used for the first time. After their first use they become internal commands—they are then retained in memory and can be used without access to a disk. When you reboot your computer they become external until they are invoked again.

CONFIG.SYS commands must be specified in the CONFIG.SYS file. In general, these commands cannot be entered at the command prompt, though there are some exceptions to this. If they can be entered at the command prompt as well, they will have two labels—Internal and CONFIG.SYS.

Batch commands are used either exclusively or primarily in batch files.

On-line help can be obtained for any DOS command by typing HELP cmd on the command line, where cmd is the command you want help with.

@

Type: *Internal*

Purpose: Used in batch files to suppress the echoing of a command, even if ECHO is set to on; has no effect if ECHO is set to off. Also used as a prefix to filenames, to identify them as containing filelists.

Syntax: @ command

Parameters: *command* is any legal batch file command.

Comments: Useful if you do not want to set ECHO OFF, but do want to suppress the display of a batch file command.

APPEND

Type: *External/Internal*

Purpose: Sets a path of directories that DOS will search when it cannot locate a file in the current directory. The /X parameter can be specified to tell DOS whether or not to use the appended directories when searching for executable files (files with a COM, EXE, or BAT extension). The appended directories will always be used when searching for non-executable files. The /PATH parameter may be used to tell DOS whether to search appended directories for files that included a drive or path specification.

Syntax: APPEND path1; path2 ... /X:OFF /PATH:OFF

ON ON

APPEND /E /X:OFF /PATH:OFF ON ON

APPEND ;

APPEND

Switches: */X* same as /X:ON.

/X:ON turns on the use of appended directories when searching for executable files. /X:OFF turns off the use of appended directories when searching for executable files. The default is /X:OFF.

/PATH:ON tells DOS to search appended directories even if a drive and/or path is specified with the file name. The default is /PATH:ON. /PATH:OFF tells DOS not to search appended directories when a drive and/or path is specified with the file name.

/E tells DOS to keep the append paths in the DOS environment. This permits the append paths to be viewed with the SET command as well as with the append command. /E can only be used the first time append is invoked. If /E is used then you may not specify any paths to be appended the first time it is invoked; you may specify paths to be appended only on subsequent calls to append.

; The semicolon is used to separate paths that are being appended. If the append command is entered with just the semicolon, the previous append command is canceled.

Comments: Each time you enter a new APPEND command, the preceding one is canceled. Consequently, only the most recent APPEND command is in effect at any time. If APPEND is entered with no parameters the first time, it is loaded into memory and becomes an internal command. If APPEND is entered with no parameters after the first time, a list of appended paths is displayed.

If a file is found in an appended path by a program and is then saved, it will be saved in the current directory. This can lead to multiple versions of the same file existing in different directories.

If the ASSIGN command is to be used, as well as the APPEND command, the first APPEND command must be entered before the ASSIGN command

If a path that does not exist is included in a list of APPEND paths, DOS will ignore that path and go on to the next. However, if a path cannot be found because the drive on which the path exists is not ready, then DOS terminates the APPEND search.

ASSIGN

Type: *External*

Purpose: Causes a reference to a drive to access a different drive.

Syntax: ASSIGN drive1=drive2 drive3=drive4 .../A

Parameters: *drive1* and *drive3* refer to drives being reassigned;

drive2 and *drive4* refer to drives that *drive1* and *drive3* are being reassigned to.

Switches: /A displays the current status of any ASSIGN.

Comments: You should not use the JOIN or SUBST commands if ASSIGN is in effect. Some programs will ignore the effect of ASSIGN and use the drive specified even if it has been reassigned.

ASSIGN commands are cumulative. If you assign drive A to drive B, then later assign drive C to drive B, drive A will continue to be assigned to drive B. You can reset all drive assignments to their normal meanings, by entering the command ASSIGN with no parameters.

The SUBST command provides the same functionality as ASSIGN, with more flexibility. ASSIGN may disappear in future versions of DOS. It is therefore recommended that you use SUBST instead.

ATTRIB

Type: *External*

Purpose: Used to switch the Read-only, Archive, System, and Hidden attributes on and off; can be used on one file or on multiple files using * and ? wild cards; can also be used to display a file's attribute settings.

Syntax: ATTRIB +/-R +/-A +/-H +/-S /P filespec /S

ATTRIB filespec

Switches: *+R* turns on the Read-only attribute.

-R turns off the Read-only attribute.

+A turns on the Archive attribute.

-A turns off the Archive attribute.

+S turns on the System attribute.

-S turns off the System attribute.

+H turns on the Hidden attribute.

-H turns off the hidden attribute.

/P pauses the display after each screenful.

filespec specifies the file or files whose attributes should be set. Wild card symbols * and ? can be used to change attributes in sets of files. Filelists may also be used to changes attributes in sets of files. Drive and path specifiers may be included.

/S causes all files in a specified directory and its subdirectories to be affected by the settings. For example, ATTRIB +A C:\WP*.* /S will turn on the Archive attribute for all files in the directory WP and all of its subdirectories.

Comments: When the only parameter is a file name, DOS displays the attribute settings for that file. For example, entering ATTRIB MYFILE.LET will result in a message similar to: R C:\MYFILE.LET This indicates that MYFILE.LET has the Read-only attribute set on and the other attributes set off.

If you attempt to delete a file that has the R, H, or S attribute set, DOS will display the message "Access denied." You may use the ATTRIB command to turn off these attributes.

The /S parameter may be used to locate all occurrences of a file on a disk. For example, the command ATTRIB C:\MYFILE.LET /S will cause DOS to display all occurrences of the file MYFILE.LET on drive C.

BACKUP

Type: *External*

Purpose: Used to back up files from one disk to another disk. The files may be restored with the RESTORE command.

Syntax: BACKUP source-filespec target-drive /S /M /A /F:size/D:mm-dd-yy /T:hh:mm:ss /L:filename

Parameters: *source-filespec* specifies the file(s) to be backed up; a drive and path may be included. If only a drive is specified, all files in the current directory of that drive will be backed up. If a drive and path are specified, all files in the specified directory will be backed up. If a file name is specified, only the file(s) specified by the file name will be backed up. The handling of subdirectories is determined by the /S parameter.

/S backs up all files that match the file name specification in the current directory and its subdirectories.

/M backs up those files that have been modified since the last backup. This is determined by checking the Archive attribute of the file(s).

/A adds the files being backed up to files that already exist on the target disk. If /A is not specified all existing files on the target disk will be erased by the BACKUP command.

/F:size formats the disk to the specified size. Possible values of size are: 160, 180, 320, 360, 720, 1.2, 1.44, 2.88.

/D:mm-dd-yy backs up files that were modified on or after the date specified. The format of the date depends on the Country setting. This setting is determined during the installation of DR DOS 6.0. It may be modified with the COUNTRY command.

/T:hh:mm:ss backs up files that were changed at or after the time specified on the date indicated with the /D parameter. If /D is not used with /T then all files changed at or after the time specified on any date are backed up. Whether the time is interpreted as a 12-hour format or 24-hour format is dependent on the Country setting. This setting is determined during the installation of DR DOS 6.0. It may be modified with the COUNTRY command.

/L:filename creates a log file. If the /L parameter is used without a file name, the name BACKUP.LOG is used. If the specified log file already exists the new information is appended to it. The first line in the log file indicates the date and time of the backup. Subsequent lines contain the backup disk number, path, and file name of each backup file.

Comments: BACKUP will automatically format a floppy disk if it is not already formatted. For it to do this, the FORMAT program must be in the current directory or in a directory specified by the path. If the FORMAT program cannot be located the BACKUP command will display an error message and terminate the backup process.

Files can be backed up from:

1. A fixed disk to a floppy disk;
2. One floppy disk to another floppy disk;
3. A floppy disk to a fixed disk;
4. One fixed disk to another fixed disk.

When one floppy disk is filled up, BACKUP automatically prompts you to put in the next disk. The disks are numbered by BACKUP to indicate the order in which they occur.

Files created with the BACKUP command are not ordinary files. They cannot be accessed directly by DOS or by your programs. You must use the RESTORE command to make them accessible.

The BACKUP command sets an Exit code that can be accessed by the BATCH command IF ERRORLEVEL .... The Exit code is set according to the following table:

Exit code	*Meaning*
0	The BACKUP completed normally.
1	There were no files found to back up.
2	Some of the specified files were not backed up due to file-sharing conflicts on a network.
3	The BACKUP operation was terminated by the user pressing Ctrl-Break.
4	The BACKUP operation terminated due to an error.

BREAK

Type: *Internal*

Purpose: Tells DOS whether to check for a Ctrl-Break key stroke whenever a program requests any DOS function.

Syntax: *At the command line:*

BREAK ON

BREAK OFF

In the CONFIG.SYS file:

BREAK=ON

BREAK=OFF

Parameters: ON tells DOS that whenever a DOS function is requested from an application program, DOS should check to see if the user has pressed Ctrl-Break. If the user has pressed Ctrl-Break, DOS will terminate the program and return the user to the DOS prompt.

OFF tells DOS to check for a Ctrl-Break combination only when one of the following operations is occurring:

1. Standard input operations;
2. Standard output operations;
3. Standard print device operations;
4. Standard auxiliary device operations.

OFF is the default condition.

Comments: Setting BREAK on allows you to terminate some programs that use few or no standard device operations.

You may type BREAK at the command prompt to see the current BREAK setting.

BUFFERS

Type: *CONFIG.SYS*

Purpose: Specifies the number of internal disk buffers that DOS should allocate.

Syntax: BUFFERS=num

Parameters: *num* specifies the number of disk buffers to be used; the minimum is 3 and the maximum is 99.

Comments: The default number of buffers is set to 15 on a 640K computer.

Each regular buffer increases the amount of memory required for DOS by 532 bytes. Each look-ahead buffer increases the amount of memory by 512 bytes.

CALL

Type: *Internal* (used only in Batch files)

Purpose: Used in a batch file to execute another batch file and have control return to the first batch file when the second is finished executing.

Syntax: CALL filespec

Parameters: Drive and path specifiers may be included in the filespec. They are not necessary if the batch file being called is in the current directory or a directory specified in the current path.

Comments: When one batch file calls another, the first may pass parameters to the second. For example, if the line CALL BATCH2 %2 %4 appeared in a batch file, the %2 parameter of the first file would become the %1 parameter in the second file, and the %4 parameter in the first file would become the %2 parameter in the second.

The ECHO mode is passed to the called batch file. If that batch file changes the ECHO mode, it is restored when control returns to the first. Thus, if the first file sets ECHO to off and the second file sets ECHO to on, when the second file is called ECHO is initially off, and when control returns to the first file ECHO is reset to off even though the second file set ECHO to on.

Two or more batch files may repetitively CALL each other, or one batch file may CALL itself. However, it is essential that the cycle eventually ends, and that control is returned to the first batch file so it may finish executing.

If a batch file has the same name as an internal command (such as COPY), then attempting to CALL the COPY batch file will result instead in the internal COPY command executing. It is recommended that batch files be given unique names.

CD or **CHDIR**

Type: *Internal*

Purpose: Changes or displays the current directory of the specified drive.

Syntax: CHDIR drive:path

CD drive:path

CHDIR drive:

CD drive:

Parameters: *drive* specifies the drive for which the current directory should be changed. If no drive is specified, the current drive is used. When only a drive is specified, the current directory for that drive is displayed without being changed.

path is the path to which the current directory for the specified drive should be changed. Path may not be more than 63 characters long, starting from the root directory.

Comments: Each drive has its own current directory. Thus, the commands CD C:\DOS and CD A:\WP will cause the current directory of drive C to be C:\DOS and the current directory of drive A to be A:\WP. When you change drives, the current directory is the one you are in.

If your prompt does not show the current directory, the CD command can be useful for determining the current directory.

A leading backslash tells DOS to start at the root directory.

CHAIN

Type: *CONFIG.SYS*

Purpose: Switches control to the specified CONFIG.SYS file.

Syntax: CHAIN = filespec

Parameters: *filespec* indicates the complete drive and path name for the alternate CONFIG.SYS file.

CHKDSK

Type: *External*

Purpose: Displays the current status of the specified directory, the total amount of memory on the computer, and the amount of memory that is available for programs.

Syntax: CHKDSK drive:path\filename /F /V

Parameters: *drive* indicates the drive to be checked

path\filename tells DOS to give additional report about the specified files (wild cards may be used to specify more than one file). For example, if a file named MYFILE.LET existed in the WP directory of drive C, the command CHKDSK C:\WP\MYFILE.LET would result in a report similar to the following:

Volume DRDOS6 created Oct-30-1991 13:00 Errors detected, /F option required to update disk.

9 lost clusters in 1 chain.
324,444,160 bytes total disk space.
25,329,664 bytes in 8 hidden files.
1,179,648 bytes in 144 directories.
132,202,496 bytes in 3115 user files.
165,658,624 bytes available on disk.
645,120 total bytes of memory.
450,000 total bytes of free memory.
449,520 bytes in largest free memory block.
C:\SPRINT\DRD\DRD.GV contains 3 non-contiguous blocks.

Switches: /F tells DOS to correct any errors it finds in the directory and file allocation table and to write the corrections on the disk. If you do not specify /F, DOS will go through the motions of correcting the errors, which gives you an indication of what effects the correction might have without actually writing the correction to the disk. If CHKDSK reports that there are *lost clusters* on the disk, the /F parameter will cause CHKDSK to ask you if you want to recover them. Lost clusters are sections of files that have become *orphaned* on a disk—DOS can no longer identify what file they belong to. Consequently the space they occupy is no longer available for other purposes. There are several possible causes of lost allocation units, but a power failure during operation is a common one. If you respond with a Y (Yes) to indicate that you want DOS to recover them, it will convert them to ASCII text files with names FILEnnn.CHK, where nnn represents a number. You can then examine them to determine whether the data in them is valuable.

/V tells DOS to display the names of all files on the specified drive. The path name for each file is displayed; as well as the file name. DOS does not pause when the screen fills up, but pressing Ctrl-S will stop the screen from scrolling until you press another key.

Comments: The disk status information includes the total disk space, the number of hidden files on the disk and the number of bytes they occupy, the number of directories on the disk and the number of bytes they occupy; the number of user files on the disk and the number of bytes they occupy, the number of bad sectors on the disk, the number of bytes of available space on the disk, the size of the allocation units on the disk, the total number of allocation units on the disk, and the number of available allocation units on the disk.

When you use CHKDSK to check a floppy drive, DOS assumes the drive is ready, so you must be sure to have a disk in the drive before executing this command.

It is a good idea to run CHKDSK periodically against any disks that are in regular use. This will alert you to problems that may be developing in your files before you lose a lot of valuable information.

If a file is badly fragmented (if it contains a large number of non-contiguous blocks), it can cause the computer to take longer than necessary to access the file.

CLS

Type: *Internal* and *CONFIG.SYS*

Purpose: Clears the screen.

Syntax: CLS

Parameters: None.

Comments: This command is used to clear the screen. After the command executes, the cursor and prompt appear at the top left corner of the screen. It is useful in batch files to avoid having clutter obscure messages generated by the batch file. CLS can also be used as a CONFIG.SYS command.

COMP

Type: *External*

Purpose: Compares the contents of one set of files to the contents of a second set of files.

Syntax: COMP filespec1 filespec2 /A /M:num

Parameters: *filespec1* specifies the first set of files to compare. It may include wild cards and a drive and path specification. If you specify a drive and path with no file name, DOS assumes a file name of *.*; filespec2 specifies the second set of files against which the first is compared. It may include wild cards and a drive and path specification. If you specify a drive and path with no file name DOS assumes a file name of *.*.

Switches: */A* displays differences as characters.

/M:num sets the maximum number of mismatches that can occur before COMP aborts. The default value is 10. Setting num to 0 specifies an unlimited number of mismatches.

Comments: This command compares the contents of files to determine whether or not they are identical. If filespec1 and filespec2 are individual file names—containing no wild cards—then the contents of the two files are compared. If filespec1 contains wild card symbols and filespec2 does not, then each file specified in filespec1 is compared with the file named in filespec2 that meets the criteria specified below. If both filespec1 and filespec2 contain wild cards, then only files with the same name are compared.

COMP expects files it is comparing to be the same size. If they are not, it displays the following message:

```
Comparing filespec1 with filespec2
Files are not the same size. Compare them anyway (Y/N)?
```

If a parameter is missing or does not adequately specify a set of files, DOS will prompt you for the missing information.

If you specify a floppy disk drive in one of the filespecs, DOS assumes the drive is ready. You should therefore be sure the drive has the necessary disk in it before entering this command.

If two files that are being compared do not match, DOS displays an error message in the following format:

```
Comparing filespec1 with filespec2 - Compare failure.
Offset xx Source = yyh Destination = zzh
```

Where xx indicates the number of bytes (in hexadecimal) into the files at which a mismatch occurred, yy indicates the hexadecimal value of the first mismatched byte in file1, and zz indicates the hexadecimal value of the first mismatched byte in file2.

If the message "EOF mark not found" appears it means that the files may be identical even if they produced "Compare error" messages. This occurs because some types of files have directory entries that indicate they are a multiple of 128 bytes in length, when in fact they terminate before the end of the last 128 byte block. COMP still attempts to compare these files out to the end of the last 128 byte block, and it may be that the Compare error occurred beyond the true end of the file. In that case, the files would be identical but still produce an error message.

Note that this command is distinctly different from the DISKCOMP command. DISKCOMP compares two complete disks to see if they are identical in all respects, while COMP compares the contents of two files.

COPY

Type: *Internal*

Purpose: Used to copy one or more files from one location to another. Also used to combine two or more files into one file.

Syntax: COPY filespec1 /B filespec2 /B /V /S /C /Z /A /A

COPY f1 + f2 + ... + fn /A target /A /V /S /C /Z /B /B

Parameters: *filespec1* specifies the file or files to be copied. Wild card symbols may be used; filespec2 specifies the destination of the new copies. Wild card symbols may be used; f1, f2, and fn represent files that will be combined to create one new file, specified by target.

Switches: */A* and */B* are optional parameters. They are used to tell DOS where in the source file to stop copying, and how to specify the end of the destination file. When /A is specified for the source file, DOS expects the source file to be an ASCII text file and copies everything up to the first control-Z character it encounters (Ctrl-Z is the ASCII end-of-file character). The Ctrl-Z character itself is not copied. If neither /A nor /B is specified, /A is taken as the default if two or more files are being combined.

When /B is specified for the source file, DOS determines the size of the file by the number of bytes specified for it in the directory. If neither /A nor /B is specified, /B is taken as the default unless two or more files are being combined (see the *Comments* section below).

When /A is specified for the target file, DOS adds a Ctrl-Z character to the end of the file.

When /B is specified for the target file, DOS does not add a Ctrl-Z character to the end of the file.

/V makes absolutely certain that the new file is written to the disk without any errors. The V stands for Verify. This slows down the copy process considerably, since DOS must read and check each sector after it is written. In most cases, it is

unnecessary since errors rarely occur during a copy process, but if the occurrence of an error will result in a serious loss then it is worth the extra time.

/S tells COPY to include System and Hidden files in the copy operation; normally these are ignored.

/C tells COPY to prompt for confirmation before each file it copies. If you are using COPY to combine groups of files, /C causes COPY to confirm each group by the name of the first source file in the group.

/Z Changes the eighth bit of every character to 0. This is done because the standard ASCII set only uses the first seven bits, and some older word processors used the eightth bit to mark the beginning and ending of words. This is not compatible with with current word processors, which use the eighth bit to define line drawing and other characters in the Extended ASCII Set (see Appendix). By specifying /Z, you can reduce files produced on the older word processors to simple ASCII files that use only the first 128 characters in the standard ASCII table.

Comments: All file specifications (indicated in the syntax by filespec1, filespec2, f1, f2, fn, and target) may include a drive and path specification. COPY copies only files in the specified directory, or in the current directory if no directory is specified. Files in subdirectories are not copied. If you want to copy files in subdirectories you should use the BACKUP or XCOPY command.

If the target directory (filespec2 and target in the syntax) is not the same as the source directory the files will be copied with their same names, unless a new name is specified. If the target directory is the same as the source directory then new names must be specified, since a file cannot be copied to itself.

If the target file name already exists, the old file is replaced by the new one. DOS does not issue a warning before replacing the old one, so you must be careful not to overwrite a file you want to keep.

The target file will never be created with the Read-only attribute set on, even if the source file has Read-only set on.

You may use COPY to transfer information between devices. For example, the command:

```
COPY CON: filename
```

will copy whatever you type at the keyboard into the file named file name. Copying will end when you press Ctrl-Z, then E. This will create a file named filename that contains whatever you typed at the keyboard, up to the Ctrl-Z. The command:

```
COPY filename PRN:
```

will copy the file filename to the printer, causing it to be printed.

When combining files, if you do not specify a target file, then all files following the first one named are appended to the first one named. For example, the command:

COPY file1 + file2 + file3

will result in the files file2 and file3 being appended to file1.

COUNTRY

Type: *CONFIG.SYS*

Purpose: Specifies the country that country-specific formats are used for. Formats include date and time formats, collating sequence, capitalization, folding format, currency symbol, and decimal separator.

Syntax: COUNTRY=code, codepage, filespec

Parameters: *code* refers to a three-digit number that specifies a particular country, as specified in Table 11.1.

codepage refers to the three-digit code page to use with the specific country. Code pages determine how the ASCII codes will be translated into characters. The code pages for each country are specified in Table 11.1. The code page is optional in the

COUNTRY command. If it is not used DOS will use the primary code page for the country specified by code. The primary code page for each country is the first one listed in Table 11.1 (the primary code page for the U.S. is 437).

filespec indicates the file that contains the country-specific information. In DR DOS 6.0, this file is named COUNTRY.SYS. If the filespec parameter is omitted, DOS assumes that COUNTRY.SYS is located in the root directory of the boot disk. COUNTRY.SYS is normally stored in the DRDOS directory; if this is the case on your computer, you must specify the filespec. If DOS cannot locate the file, it produces an error message when it encounters the COUNTRY command.

Comments: If you specify the filespec parameter you must use the code page parameter, or replace it with a comma so that DOS will know not to interpret the filespec as a code page. For example:

```
COUNTRY=001,,C:\DOS\COUNTRY.SYS
```

Notice that two commas are used—one replaces the code page, and the other is the command that follows the code page parameter.

It is important to understand that the COUNTRY command does not translate DOS messages or other information into another language, it simply defines the format for such information as date and time.

The Country setting affects the BACKUP, DATE, RESTORE, and TIME commands.

Table 11.1 *Country Codes and Code Pages.*

Country Code	***Code***	***Pages***
Australia	061	437, 850
Belgium	032	437, 850
Canada (French-speaking)	002	863, 850

Table 11.1 continuted ...

Country Code	***Code***	***Pages***
Denmark	045	865, 850
Finland	358	437, 850
France	033	437, 850
Germany	049	437, 850
Hungary	036	852, 850
Israel	972	862, 850
Italy	039	437, 850
Japan	081	932, 437
Korea	082	934, 437
Latin America	003	437, 850
Middle East	785	864, 850
Netherlands	031	437, 850
Norway	047	865, 850
Portugal	351	860, 850
Russia	007	866, 850
Spain	034	437, 850
Sweden	046	437, 850
Switzerland (French)	041	437, 850
Switzerland (German)	041	437, 850
Turkey	090	857, 850
United Kingdom	044	437, 850
United States	001	437, 850

DATE

Type: *Internal*

Purpose: Sets the date that is stored in the internal clock.

Syntax: DATE mm-dd-yy

DATE dd-mm-yy

DATE yy-mm-dd

DATE

Parameters: *mm* stands for the month (01 - 12).

dd stands for the day of the month (01 - 31).

yy stands for the year. yy may be entered as a two-digit or four-digit year. If entered as a four-digit year, the century must be 19 or 20.

Comments: If you type an incorrect date, DOS will display the message.

```
Invalid date
Enter new date (mm-dd-yy)
```

If you press Enter at this point, the date will be left unchanged.

You may use the forward slash (/) in place of the hyphens to separate the month, day, and year.

Entering DATE with no parameters causes DOS to display the current date, then prompt for a new date. A three-letter abbreviation of the day of the week will also be displayed:

```
Date: Mon 10-28-1991
Enter date (mm-dd-yy):
```

Pressing Enter will leave the date unchanged.

DEL

Type: *Internal*

Purpose: Deletes one or more files from a disk.

Syntax: DEL filespec /C /S

Parameters: *filespec* is the name of the file(s) that you want to delete. Wild cards may be used. A drive and path specifier may be included.

Switches: */C* causes DOS to display each file name then pause with a prompt that asks you to confirm the deletion before it is carried out.

/S causes DEL to include system files in the delete operation. Normally system files are not included in deletions.

Comments: The DEL command is functionally identical to the ERASE command.

DEL will not remove files whose Hidden attribute is set to ON.

If the DEL command is entered with a drive and path specifier, but no file name, it assumes *.* for the file name.

If you enter a DEL command to delete all files in a directory or all files on a disk, DOS will pause and display the message:

```
Are you sure (Y/N)?
```

This is to prevent you from accidentally deleting a large number of files by accident. Press either Y for Yes or N for No and press Enter.

The DEL command cannot be used to delete a subdirectory; you must use the XDEL (Extended Delete) command for that purpose.

DELPURGE

Type: *External*

Purpose: DELPURGE is used to actually delete those files that have been marked as pending deletes when files DELWATCH was running.

Syntax: DELPURGE filespec /A /L /S /P /D:date /D:-nn /T:time

Parameters: *filespec* is the file specifier for the pending delete files to be purged.

Switches: */A* is used to turn off prompting. Normally DELPURGE prompts you before deleting each file; with /A no prompting occurs.

/L lists the pending delete files that match the filespec, but does not actually purge them.

/S purges files in subdirectories as well as in the specified directory.

/P causes DELPURGE to pause until a key is pressed after each screenful of information is displayed.

/D:date purges files that were deleted before the specified date.

/D:-nn purges files that were deleted more than nn days ago.

/T:time purges files that were deleted before the specified time.

Comments: When loaded, the DELWATCH utility intercepts all attempts to delete files, and instead marks them as pending deletes. This makes them functionally identical to deleted files, except that they may be fully recovered with the UNDELETE command unless DELPURGE is used to actually delete them. Once a pending delete file has been removed with DELPURGE, it cannot be recovered using UNDELETE, though some third-party utilities will still be able to recover these files. DELPURGE is discussed in detail in Chapter 6.

DELQ

Type: *Internal*

Purpose: Used to delete files, but causes DOS to query you before each deletion.

Syntax: DELQ filespec /S

Parameters: filespec is the file identifier of the file(s) to be deleted. It may contain a drive, path, and wild cards. Files in subdirectories are not affected by DELQ.

Switches: */S* tells DELQ to include system files in the delete operation.

Comments: DELQ is identical to ERAQ. These commands are useful when you want to delete a subset of a set of files that have similar names. For example, if you had ten files that had the extension BAK, and wanted to delete eight of them, DELQ could be used to select those BAK files you wanted to delete.

DELWATCH

Type: *External*

Purpose: DELWATCH is used to protect files from accidental deletion, and to make it possible to fully recover any files that are deleted.

Syntax: DELWATCH drive1 drive2 ... /S /D /B:nnn

/O:ext1+ext2+... /E:ext1+ext2+... /F:nnn /MU /ML

Parameters: drive1, etc. are the drives that DELWATCH should protect.

Switches: Summarized in Table 11.2.

Table 11.2 Switches Used with DELWATCH Command

Switch	***Effect***
/B:nnn	Sets the number of files with the same name in the same directory to save as pending delete files. The default value is 1.
/D	Disables DELWATCH for the specified drive(s). No other switches can be used with /D.
/E:ext[+ext...]	Tells DELWATCH to save all deleted files as pending deletes, except for those specified by the extensions. Up to 10 extensions may be specified.
F:nnn|ALL	Determines the maximum number of files that DELWATCH will save as pending delete files. nnn may be anywhere from 1 to 65,534. 65,535 specifies that the disk capacity is the limit at which to start removing pending deletes to make room for new ones. ALL specifies no limit, and pending deletes are never removed, even if the disk becomes full.
/ML	Forces DELWATCH to load into low memory, even if high memory is available.
/MU	Forces DELWATCH to load into high memory. If insufficient high memory is available, DELWATCH does not load.

Table 11.2 continued ...

Switch	***Effect***
/O:ext[+ext...]	Tells DELWATCH to save only deleted files that have the specified extensions. All other files are deleted as though DELWATCH were not loaded. Up to ten extensions may be specified.
/S	Displays the current status of DELWATCH.

Comments: DELWATCH is a TSR that, when loaded, constantly monitors the deletion of all files on the specified disk(s). Whenever a file is deleted, DELWATCH marks it as a "pending delete," which makes the file behave like a deleted file. DELWATCH is discussed in detail in Chapter 6.

DEVICE

Type: *CONFIG.SYS*

Purpose: DEVICE is used to install a device driver when you boot your computer.

Syntax: DEVICE=filespec parameters

Parameters: *filespec* is the file name of the device to be installed. It may include a drive and path specification; parameters represents any parameters required by the device driver.

Comments: A separate DEVICE= command is required for each device driver you want to install. The HIDEVICE command may be used to install devices into high or upper memory.

DIR

Type: *Internal*

Purpose: Displays a directory listing for a specified directory.

Syntax: DIR filespec /W /L /2 /D /S /A /N /P /R /C

Parameters: filespec specifies the directory to be displayed. A drive and path may be included. A file name and wild cards may be used to display only selected files. If no filespec is provided the current drive is assumed, and the file name *.* is assumed.

Switches are suummarized in Table 11.3.

Table 11.3 Switches for the DIR Command

Switch	***Effect***
/A	Displays all files and subdirectories in the current directory, except those with the Hidden attribute set.
/C	Sets default switches for use with subsequent DIR commands.
/D	Displays those files for which the system attribute is off. This switch is on by default.
/L	Displays the file size, and the date and time of last modification. This switch is on by default.
/2	Produces the same display as /L, except it produces two columns side by side, instead of one.
/N	If you have changed the default DIR switch using /C or /R, /N returns you to the default switches for the current DIR command.
/P	Causes the display to pause after each screenful of information.
/R	Should be specified as the last switch in a series; executes the DIR command with the preceding switches, and remembers them for future DIR commands.
/S	Displays files that have the System attribute set.
/W	Displays just the names of files and directories in five columns across the screen. Subdirectories are indicated by a backslash (\) in front of the name.

Comments: Subdirectory names are shown, but not their contents. Subdirectories are labeled with <DIR> in the file size area.

In addition to the files contained in the specified directory, the DIR command displays the volume label. The number of bytes free on the specified drive is shown at the end of the file listing.

This command is discussed in detail in Chapter 6.

DISKCOMP

Type: *External*

Purpose: Compares two floppy disks to determine whether they are identical in all respects.

Syntax: DISKCOMP source target /1 /8 /A /M /V

Parameters: *source* is the source drive to compare to target.

target is the target drive against which source is compared.

/1 tells DOS to compare only the first side of the disks even if they are double-sided.

/8 tells DOS to compare only 8 sectors per track, even if the source disk has 9 or 15 sectors per track.

/A causes the computers to beep when the comparison is finished, or when you need to switch disks.

/M causes DISKCOMP to automatically repeat the comparison operation for multiple disks. This is particularly useful when comparing multiple disks against an image file.

/V causes DISKCOMP to verify that the entire source disk or image file can be read.

Comments: DISKCOMP compares two floppy disks sector by sector. If two disks do not compare exactly, DOS will display a message indicating the track and side at which they first differed.

If two disks contain identical sets of files (as determined by the COMP command), but the files do not occupy identical sectors on each disk, the disks will not compare as identical with the DISKCOMP program. For example, on the source disk FILE1 may occupy sectors 1, 2, and 3 of track 1, while on the target disk FILE1 may occupy sectors 4, 5, and 6 of track 2.

If you have only one floppy drive, the DISKCOMP command can be used by omitting the target drive specification. DISKCOMP will then compare two disks on the same drive, prompting you to change disks at the appropriate times.

Unless you use the /1 or /8 parameters, DISKCOMP will automatically determine the maximum number of sides and sectors per track supported by the source drive and uses those values.

You can use the DISKCOPY command to create an *image file*, which contains an exact duplicate of a diskette. The image file can then be used with DISKCOMP in place of the source diskette. This can speed up the comparison operation, particularly if you want to compare multiple disks to the same source disk.

DISKCOMP automatically uses expanded and extended memory, and temporary disk files, to store the contents of the source disk. This speeds up the comparison and eliminates the need to be switching disks when comparing two disks on the same drive.

DISKCOPY

Type: *External*

Purpose: Used to create an exact duplicate of a floppy disk, either on another disk of the same size and format, or in an image file.

Syntax: DISKCOPY source target /1 /A /M

Parameters: *source* is the drive to be copied from.

target is the drive to be copied to.

/1 copies only side 1 of the source disk, even if it is a two-sided disk.

/A causes the computer to beep when the copy is done, or when you need to change disks.

/M causes DISKCOPY to make multiple copies. After each copy, you are prompted if you want to make another.

Comments: DISKCOPY creates a copy of a disk that is identical in all respects. A disk that has been created with DISKCOPY will DISKCOMP successfully with the original disk.

If the target disk is not formatted, DISKCOPY will format it during the copy process.

Any existing files on the target disk will be erased during a DISKCOPY.

If you have only one floppy drive, omit the target drive. DOS will then perform the copy using a single drive. You will be prompted when to change disks.

If an error occurs during the copy, DOS displays a warning message indicating the drive, side and track on which the error occurred, then proceeds to complete the copy.

DISKCOPY will ignore any ASSIGN commands that are in effect.

In general, it is better to use the COPY command, since this will unfragment files, and will not erase any additional files on the target disk. DISKCOPY does not unfragment files.

DISKMAP

Type: *External*

Purpose: Used to create a copy of the FAT in a file named DISKMAP.DAT, which can be used to recover deleted files using the UNDELETE command.

Syntax: DISKMAP /D

Parameters: None.

Switches: */D* causes DISKMAP to delete the existing DISKMAP file and create a new one. Without /D, if a

	DISKMAP file already exists it is updated rather than replaced. Using /D will remove information about any files that were deleted after the last DISKMAP was performed.
Comments:	DISKMAP is discussed in detail in Chapter 6.

DISKOPT

Type:	*External*
Purpose:	Arranges the information in a disk so that all of the information for each file lies in contiguous clusters on the disk.
Syntax:	DISKOPT drive
Parameters:	*drive* specifies the drive that contains the disk to be optimized. If omitted, the current drive is assumed.
Comments:	Running DISKOPT regularly speeds up the performance of the disk and reduces wear and tear. DISKOPT should never be run when multi-tasking utilities are in operation, or when TSRs are loaded. DISKOPT is a menu-driven program, and is discussed in detail in Chapter 7.

DOSBOOK

Type:	*External*
Purpose:	Provides complete online help for all aspects of DR DOS 6.0.
Syntax:	DOSBOOK command /B
Parameters:	*command* is the name of a command that you want help with. DOSBOOK is a menu-driven program; entering DOSBOOK without a command name takes you to an opening menu.
Switches:	*/B* forces DOSBOOK to display its menus and screens in black and white mode. The default is color.
Comments:	DOSBOOK is discussed in detail in Chapter 4.

DRIVPARM

Type:	*CONFIG.SYS*

Purpose: Allows you to assign the physical characteristics of a logical drive. For example, some computers are not designed to recognize 3.5 inch drives. If you install a 3.5 inch drive on such a computer, DRIVPARM can be used to define the drive parameters that will allow DR DOS to bypass this limitation.

Syntax: DRIVPARM = /D:d /C /F:f /H:h /N /S:ss /T:tt

Parameters: None.

Switches: */D:d* d is a single digit that identifies the drive being defined. Normally, drive A is 0, drive B is 1, and so on.

/C indicates that the drive has the intelligence built in to detect when a disk is being changed.

/F:f specifies the drive type, where f is 0 for a 360K drive, 1 for a 1.2M drive, 2 for a 720K drive, and 7 for a 1.44M drive. The default value is 2.

/H:h specifes the number of drive heads, where h is either 1 or 2.

/N indicates that the drive uses permanent media.

/S:ss specifies the number of sectors the drive can support. ss can be any number from 1 to 63.

/T:tt specifies the number of tracks that the drive supports. tt may be either 40 or 80.

Comments: The drive specified in the DRIVPARM command must already exist.

ECHO

Type: *Batch, CONFIG.SYS*

Purpose: Turns the screen display of batch file commands on and off. Also used to force the display of a message in a batch file or in a CONFIG.SYS file.

Syntax: ECHO ON

ECHO OFF

ECHO message

ECHO

ECHO=message

Parameters: *ON* turns on ECHO mode. ON is the default mode; *OFF* turns off ECHO mode.

message is a message that you want displayed, even if ECHO is set off.

Comments: When the ECHO command is entered with no parameters, the current ECHO state is displayed.

ECHO ON and ECHO OFF are useful in batch files for causing or suppressing the display of batch file commands.

ECHO message displays the specified message. This command is useful in batch files.

The only form of the command that may be used in CONFIG.SYS is ECHO=message, and the CONFIG.SYS file is the only place this syntax may be used. This causes the message to be displayed on the screen during the processing of the CONFIG.SYS file. It can be used to prompt the user, or to let you know when a particular part of the CONFIG.SYS file is reached.

ERAQ

Type: *Internal*

Purpose: Used to delete files, but to prompt you before each file is deleted. Functionally identical to DELQ.

ERASE

Type: *Internal*

Purpose: Used to delete files without confirmation. Functionally identical to DEL.

EXIT

Type: *Internal, CONFIG.SYS*

Purpose: At the command line, EXIT terminates the processing of a secondary command processor and returns you to the calling program. In CONFIG.SYS, it is used to stop the processing of CONFIG.SYS commands and continue with the boot process.

Parameters: None.

Comments: At the command line, EXIT is typically used to return to a program after shelling out to DOS.

FASTOPEN

Type: *CONFIG.SYS*

Purpose: Increases the speed with which you can access disk files, when the same files are used repeatedly.

Syntax: FASTOPEN=nnn

Parameters: *nnn* is the number of files to keep track of. The default value is 512.

Comments: FASTOPEN works by setting up buffers in memory that contain the directory information for recently opened files. This information includes the location of the directory information and continuous space information. Retaining this information in a memory buffer allows it to be retrieved much faster than if it is read from the disk.

There is one drawback to using FASTOPEN: it reduces the amount of memory available to applications.

FC

Type: *External*

Purpose: Finds and displays the differences between two files.

Syntax: FC source target /A /B /C /Gn /L /Mn /W

Parameters: *source* is the file that is compared to target.

target is the file that source is compared to.

Comments: FC is used to identify the differences between two files, where COMP is used to verify that two files are identical. The FC command is discussed in detail in Chapter 6.

You may use filelists for the source file.

FILES

Type: *CONFIG.SYS*

Purpose:	Sets the maximum number of files that can be open at any one time.
Syntax:	FILES=num
Parameters:	*num* specifies the maximum number of files that can be open at any one time. The minimum is 20 and the maximum is 255.
Comments:	If no FILES= command is included in your CONFIG.SYS file the default value of 20 is used.
	Each time a program is run the file that contains the program is opened. Each data file that must be accessed by a program must be opened. If a program uses overlay files, they will also have to be opened. 20 files is usually sufficient, but it is becoming more and more common for a larger number to be needed. FILES is used when more than 20 files must be open at one time.

FILELINK

Type:	*External*
Purpose:	Used to transfer files between computers, using their serial ports.
Syntax:	FILELINK command filespec1 filespec2 comparm switches
Comments:	The switches that may be specified depend on the command entered. You may use a filelist for filespec1. The FILELINK command is discussed in detail in Chapter 7.

FIND

Type:	*External*
Purpose:	Locates text strings in files.
Syntax:	FIND /B /C /F /N /S /U /Vstring filespec1 filespec2 ...
Parameters:	*filespec1*, *filespec2*, etc. specify the files to be searched for the string. They may contain wild cards, or they may be filelists.
Switches:	*/B* displays headings for each file.
	/C displays a count of the lines that were found to contain the string.

/F shows only the names of the files that contain the search string.

/N displays the line number and the line that was found to contain the string.

/S searches files in subdirectories.

/U makes the search case-sensitive.

/V displays all lines that do not contain the string.

Comments: Files are assumed to be ASCII text files, so they are searched up to the first control-Z character encountered.

The search is not case-sensitive, unless the /U switch is specified.

The string to be searched for must be enclosed in double quotes.

FOR

Purpose: Used in batch files and at the command line for repetitively executing a command.

Syntax: FOR %%variable IN (set) DO command

FOR %variable IN (set) DO command

Parameters: *%%variable* is the %% sign followed by any single character, including 0 through 9. %%variable is used in batch files to indicate a variable name that will take on each value in (set), one at a time, and execute command for each value.

%variable is the same as %%variable, except it is used at the command line instead of in a batch file.

(set) contains one or more values that the variable takes on, each for one execution of the command.

command represents the DOS command that will be executed once for each value in (set).

Comments: FOR is useful when a single command must be executed several times, with one value in the command changing. The following command entered at the command prompt will display the directory listing of DIR1, DIR2, and DIR3:

```
FOR %D IN (DIR1, DIR2, DIR3) DO DIR %D
```

The same command could be executed in a batch file as follows:

```
FOR %%D IN (DIR1, DIR2, DIR3) DO DIR %%D
```

FORMAT

Type: *External*

Purpose: Prepares a new floppy or fixed disk for use.

Syntax: FORMAT drive: /A /U /S /V:label /8 /4 /1 /N:xx /T:yy /F:size /X

Parameters: *drive* is the drive on which the disk will be formatted.

Switches: */A* causes the computer to beep when the format operation is complete.

/U specifies an unconditional format. This does not create a mirror image of the FAT and root directory before formatting. Therefore, it makes the disk impossible to unformat.

/S copies the operating system files to the disk so that the computer may be booted from the disk.

/V:label specifies a volume label for the disk. If /V is not specified, you will be prompted to enter a label after the format is complete. If you press Enter, no label will be created.

/8 is used to format a 5.25-inch floppy disk with eight sectors per track (as opposed to the default of 9).

/4 is used to format a 360KB or 180KB 5.25-inch floppy disk in a high capacity (1.2 megabyte) drive. This does not produce a disk that can be reliably read or written in a 360KB drive.

/1 formats side one only on a 5.25-inch floppy disk.

/N:xx /T:yy specifies the number of sectors per track and the number of tracks per disk. If either parameter is used, then both parameters must be specified or DOS will terminate the command with an error message.

/F:size allows you to specify an alternate media size for a floppy disk. Valid values for size are: 160K,

180K, 320K, 360K, 720K, 1200K, 1440K, and 2880K.

/X specifies that a hard disk should be formatted. FORMAT will not format a hard disk without this switch.

Comments: In DR DOS 6.0, the normal format is a safe format, which means that a copy of the FAT is copied to the disk before the format is carried out. This allows the UNFORMAT command to recover a disk that has been accidentally formatted.

GOSUB

Type: *Batch* and *CONFIG.SYS*

Purpose: Used to jump to a subroutine in a batch or CONFIG.SYS file, then have control return when the subroutine is done.

Syntax: GOSUB label

Parameters: *label* refers to a line in the file that contains a colon followed by the label. When the GOTO command executes, control jumps to the line following the label.

Comments: Only the first eight characters of a label are examined, so if more than one label is used in a batch file, they must not contain the same first eight characters.

Labels are never displayed, even if ECHO is set to on, so you may use the colon to add comments to a batch file instead of the REM command, which is echoed unless ECHO is set to off. If you use the colon in this way make sure the first eight characters of the comments do not match the first eight characters of a legitimate label.

When control branches to a subroutine, commands are executed in sequence within the subroutine until a RETURN command is encountered, at which point control returns to the command following GOSUB.

GOTO

Type: *Batch* and *CONFIG.SYS*

Purpose: Used in batch files to create a branching flow of control.

Syntax: GOTO label

Parameters: *label* refers to a line in the file that contains a colon followed by the label. When the GOTO command executes, control jumps to the line following the label.

Comments: Only the first eight characters of a label are examined, so if more than one label is used in a batch file, they must not contain the same first eight characters.

Labels are never displayed, even if ECHO is set to on, so you may use the colon to add comments to a batch file instead of the REM command, which is echoed unless ECHO is set to off. If you use the colon in this way make sure the first eight characters of the comments do not match the first eight characters of a legitimate label.

GRAPHICS

Type: *External*

Purpose: Allows you to use the PrintScreen key to print a graphics display on IBM-compatible printers.

Syntax: GRAPHICS color /R

Parameters: *color* enables GRAPHICS to print color output on IBM-compatible color graphics printers, with up to eight colors.

/R specifies that black and white should not be reversed. Normally everything that appears black on the screen is not printed, and everything that appears white is printed in black. /R is used to turn off this reversal.

Comments: Your printer must have the ability to print graphics for this command to work. GRAPHICS is a TSR, so it only needs to be loaded once. Once loaded, it reduces the amount of memory available to applications by a small amount.

HELP

Type: *External*

Purpose: Starts the DOSBOOK on-line help system.

Syntax: HELP HELP command

Parameters: *command* is any DOS command.

Comments: See the DOSBOOK command, and Chapter 4.

HIBUFFERS

Type: *CONFIG.SYS*

Purpose: Loads buffers into high or upper memory.

Syntax: HIBUFFERS=xx

Parameters: None.

Comments: This command is the same as the BUFFERS command, except that it loads the buffers into high or upper memory, thereby conserving conventional memory for applications.

HIDEVICE

Type: *CONFIG.SYS*

Purpose: HIDEVICE is used to install a device driver into a UMB (*Upper Memory Block*) when you boot your computer.

Syntax: HIDEVICE size=hexsize=filespec parameters

Parameters: *size=hexsize* is an optional specification of the minimum amount of memory that must be available in a UMB before HIDEVICE will attempt to load the driver into high memory.

filespec is the file name of the device to be installed. It may include a drive and path specification.

parameters represents any parameters required by the device driver.

Comments: For HIDEVICE to work, you must have an upper memory manager installed. If you have a 386 or later CPU, then the EMM386.SYS memory manager that is provided with DR DOS 6.0 can be used to manage the upper memory area. If you have a 286 PC, then the HIDOS.SYS device driver can be used.

HIDEVICE can save conventional memory resources by loading device drivers into high memory. However, some device drivers will not work in high memory.

This command is discussed in detail in Chapter 5.

HIDOS

Type: *CONFIG.SYS*

Purpose: Loads as much of the DOS operating system data structures as possible into upper memory.

Syntax: HIDOS=ON HIDOS=OFF

Parameters: None.

Comments: HIDOS is discussed in Chapter 5.

HIINSTALL

Type: *CONFIG.SYS*

Purpose: Loads TSRs into upper memory. This fills the same function as HILOAD, except that it is processed as part of the CONFIG.SYS file instead of at the command line.

Syntax: HIINSTALL=filespec parameters

Parameters: *filespec* is the name of the TSR to load into high memory.

parameters are any parameters or switches that filespec uses.

HILOAD

Type: *CONFIG.SYS*

Purpose: Loads TSR programs into high or upper memory, thereby saving space in conventional memory for applications.

Syntax: HILOAD filespec parameters

Parameters: *filespec* the name of the TSR program to load into high memory.

parameters are any parameters that the TSR program accepts.

Comments: HILOAD is discussed in detail in Chapter 5.

HISTORY

Type: *CONFIG.SYS*

Purpose: Used to keep a command stack of previously entered DOS commands; also provides extended editing facility for DOS commands.

Syntax: HISTORY = ON, nnn, ON OFF OFF

Parameters: None.

Switches: *ON* or *OFF* immediately after the equal sign turns HISTORY on or off.

nnn specifies the size in bytes of the memory buffer for storing commands. nnn may be 128 to 4096; the default is 512.

ON or *OFF* at the end of the command sets the insert mode ON or OFF. The default is OFF.

Comments: When insert mode is off, typing new characters in the middle of the command line overwrites whatever was there before. When insert mode is on, new characters are inserted. After HISTORY is loaded, you may toggle insert mode on and off by pressing the insert key.

HISTORY is discussed in detail in Chapter 4.

IF

Type: *Batch*

Purpose: Provides logical IF - THEN programming logic in batch files.

Syntax: IF (NOT) condition command

Parameters: *NOT* is used to cause the command to execute only if the condition is not met.

condition may be one of the following:

1. The existence of a file that is named in the batch file;
2. The existence of a file passed as a parameter;
3. A parameter matches a value is specified in the batch file;
4. Whether the previous command in the batch file terminated normally.

command is any DOS command.

Comments: The IF command is discussed in detail in Chapter 9.

INSTALL

Type: *CONFIG.SYS*

Purpose: Can be used in the CONFIG.SYS file to load TSR programs.

Syntax: INSTALL=command

Parameters: *command* is a DOS or other program command for a TSR program.

JOIN

Type: *External*

Purpose: Makes one drive appear to be a subdirectory of another drive.

Syntax: JOIN drive1 drive2:path JOIN drive/D

Parameters: *drive1* is the drive that will appear as a directory on *drive2*.

drive2:path is the drive and optional path that will refer to drive1.

drive/d deletes the join for the specified drive. The drive referenced here should have been drive1 in an earlier JOIN command.

Comments: When used with no parameters, JOIN displays a list of joins in effect.

The directory specified for drive2 must either not exist or be empty. If it does not exist, an empty directory of the specified name is created, and left on drive2 after the JOIN is ended. If the directory does exist, and is not empty, JOIN will will ignore the actual directory and refer to the joined drive when the directory is referenced.

When a join is in effect, references to drive1 will not be recognized, and will generate the message "Invalid drive specified."

The following commands do not work with a drive formed by JOIN: ASSIGN, BACKUP, DISKCOMP, DISKCOPY, FORMAT, and SUBST.

KEYB

Type: *External*

Purpose: Defines a keyboard layout that corresponds to that used in a country other than the United States.

Syntax: KEYB code+ , codepage /ML - /MH /ML

Parameters: *code* a two-letter code from Table 11.4 that defines the country for which the keyboard should be defined.

+ is an optional specifier to force the KEYB program to assume an extended (101/102/104 key) keyboard.

- is an optional specifier to force the KEYB program to assume a standarad (83/84 key) keyboard.

codepage specifies the code page to use. Two code pages are available for each country. If codepage is not specified the first code page listed in Table 11.4 is used.

Table 11.4 Keyboard Codes and Code Pages

Country	***Abbreviation***	***Code Pages***
Belgium	BE	437, 850
Canada (French-speaking)	CF	863, 850
Denmark	DK	865, 850

Table 11.4 continued ...

Country	*Abbreviation*	*Code Pages*
Finland	SU	437, 850
France	FR	437, 850
Germany	GR	437, 850
Hungary	HU	852, 850
Italy	IT	437, 850
Latin America	LA	437, 850
Netherlands	NL	437, 850
Norway	NO	865, 850
Portugal	PO	860, 850
Russia	RU	866, 850
Spain	SP	437, 850
Sweden	SV	437, 850
Switzerland (French)	SF	437, 850
Switzerland (German)	SG	437, 850
Turkey	TF/TQ	857, 850
United Kingdom	UK	437, 850
United States	US	437, 850

/ML forces KEYB to load into low (conventional) memory.

/MH forces KEYB to load into high memory.

/MU forces KEYB to load into upper memory.

Comments: If there is not enough high or upper memory available when /MH or /MU is specified, then KEYB loads into conventional memory.

You must have a device driver loaded that supports high and upper memory before the /MU and /MH switches can be used.

The default keyboard, if none is specified, is the U.S.

When KEYB is entered without any parameters the current alternate keyboard is displayed.

You may change the alternate keyboard by entering the KEYB command. When the alternate keyboard is in effect, pressing Ctrl+Alt+F1 will switch to the U.S. keyboard. Pressing Ctrl+Alt+F2 will switch back to the alternate keyboard.

If you are using the Russian character set, the right-hand Ctrl key toggles you between the Russian and U.S. keyboard layouts.

Example: KEYB FR+,437 specifies the French keyboard layout, insures that the keyboard will be recognized as an extended keyboard, and uses code page 437.

LABEL

Type: *External*

Purpose: Defines a disk volume label. If a disk does not have a label, the LABEL command adds one. If the disk does have a label, the LABEL command is used to changes or deletes the label.

Syntax: LABEL drive label

Parameters: *drive* is the drive containing the disk whose label will be defined. If the drive is not specified, the current drive is assumed.

label is the label that will be placed on the disk. The label can be from 1 to 11 characters. The same characters as used for file names can be used, but no period should be used to separate an extension. Spaces may also be used.

Comments: If no label is specified a message similar to one of the following messages will appear:

```
Volume in drive A: does not have a label
Enter Volume label (0 to 11 characters):
```

```
Volume in drive C: is DRDOS6
Enter Volume label (0 to 11 characters):
```

LASTDRIVE

Type: *CONFIG.SYS*

Purpose: Defines the maximum number of drives that may be accessed.

Syntax: LASTDRIVE=driveletter

Parameters: *driveletter* is any alphabetical character from A to Z. Uppercase and lowercase are treated identically. This is the last drive letter that DOS will allow you to reference.

Comments: If no LASTDRIVE command is included in your CONFIG.SYS file the default letter E is used.

LASTDRIVE is often used in conjunction with the SUBST command. It determines the last drive letter you may use when SUBST is in effect.

LOCK

Type: *External*

Purpose: Temporarily locks the operating system on the computer, without shutting off the computer. This prevents anyone from using the computer until the correct password is entered.

Syntax: LOCK password

LOCK

Parameters: *password* specifies the password that must be used to unlock the computer.

Comments: If LOCK is entered without a password, the existing system password will be used.

LOCK is particularly useful when running TaskMAX, because you can leave all of your work active, but suspended, by switching to the LOCK task.

LOCK is discussed in detail in Chapter 4.

MEM

Type: *External*

Purpose: Displays a report of the amount of memory used by the system, the contents of memory in use, and the amount of memory available for programs.

Syntax: MEM /H /B /D /S /P /M /A

Parameters: None.

Switches: */B* displays the areas of memory used by the operating system, including device drivers, BIOS, and the DOS Memory Control Block (MCB) chain. The MCB chain shows how memory is allocated to different programs, so you can see what programs are loaded, and where they are located in memory.

/D shows the names of all device drivers, including those that are built-in.

/S shows the DOS disk buffer chain, with adjacent buffers grouped together.

/P causes MEM to pause after each screenful, until a key is pressed.

/M shows a graphical display of the location of RAM, ROM, and EMS memory.

/A shows all of the information provided by the above switches.

Comments: The /M switch is useful when fine-tuning the use of the EMM386.SYS driver.

MEMMAX

Type: *External*

Purpose: The MEMMAX program is used to enable and disable various aspects of the memory management utilities that are provided with DR DOS 6.0, and to display the status of the different memory areas.

Syntax: MEMMAX +L +U +V /U /L /V - - -

Parameters: None.

Switches: *+L* enables access to lower memory.

-L disables access to lower memory.

+U enables access to upper memory.

-U disables access to upper memory.

+V enables access to memory reserved by the / VIDEO option that can be specified with the EMM386.SYS and HIDOS.SYS device drivers.

-V disables access to memory reserved by the /VIDEO option that can be specified with the EMM386.SYS and HIDOS.SYS device drivers.

/L displays the status of lower memory.

/U displays the status of upper memory.

/V displays the status of video memory.

Comments: MEMMAX is discussed in detail in Chapter 5.

MKDIR or **MD**

Type: *Internal*

Purpose: Creates a new subdirectory on the specified drive, under the specified directory.

Syntax: MKDIR drive:path

MD drive:path

Parameters: *drive* indicates the drive on which the new subdirectory should be created. If omitted, the current drive is used.

path is the complete path specification for the new subdirectory, including the new subdirectory name. If only the new subdirectory name is specified the current directory is used.

Comments: The commands MKDIR and MD are functionally identical.

Naming subdirectories follows the same rules as naming files. It is conventional, however, to omit extensions from subdirectory names.

The number of subdirectories that may exist on a disk is limited only by disk space. Each subdirectory created on a hard disk requires 2,048 bytes.

The complete path specification from the root directory to the subdirectory, including the backslash characters required to separate subdirectories, must not exceed 63 characters.

MORE

Type: *External*

Purpose: Causes the screen display to pause whenever it fills up, and waits for a key to be pressed before scrolling up the next screen of information.

Syntax: MORE < filename

command | MORE

Parameters: < *filename* causes the contents of the file filename to be displayed on the screen in the same way as the TYPE command, except that when the screen fills up, it pauses with the message — *More*— at the bottom of the screen. Pressing any key will cause the next screen to be displayed.

command | MORE causes the output of the command to be processed by MORE, resulting in the display pausing when the screen fills up and the message — *More*— appearing at the bottom of the screen. Pressing any key will cause the next screen to be displayed.

Comments: An example of the first syntax is:

MORE MYFILE.LET

This will cause the contents of MYFILE.LET to appear on the screen. MYFILE.LET should be an ASCII text file.

An example of the second syntax is:

DIR | MORE

This will cause the screen to pause, scrolling each time it fills up with directory information. The effect is similar to the /P parameter on the DIR command.

MOVE

Type: *External*

Purpose: Moves one or more files or subdirectories to another location on the same disk, or to another disk.

Syntax: MOVE filespec dir /A /D:date /H /M /P /R /S /T /V /W

Parameters: *filespec* is the file specifier of the file(s) to be moved. It may include wild cards, or it may consist of a file list.

dir is the source directory for the file(s) being moved.

Switches: Summarized in Table 11.5.

Table 11.5 Switches for Use with the MOVE Command

Switch	***Effect***
/A	Only moves files that have the Archive attribute set, and leaves the Archive attribute set after moving the file.
/D:date	Only moves files whose date is on or after the one specified. The format of the date is determined by the current country code.
/H	Includes hidden and system files in the move operation.
/M	Turns off the Archive attribute after moving the file.
/P or /C	Pauses for confirmation before moving each file.
/R	Causes MOVE to overwrite files with the same name as the source, even if they have the Read-only attribute set.
/S	Duplicates source subdirectories on the target, but does not delete the source subdirectories after moving their files.
/T	Duplicates source subdirectories on the target, and deletes the source subdirectories after moving their files.
/V	Performs a verification of the moved file. This slows down the process but increases reliability.
/W	Pauses after the MOVE command is entered and waits for a disk to be inserted. You may interrupt the command at this point by pressing Ctrl+C or Ctrl+Break.

Comments: When MOVE is used to move files from one directory to another on the same disk, only the directory entries need to be moved. The files themselves are not touched. This makes moving a file much faster than copying and deleting it.

When MOVE is used to move files from one disk to another, they must be copied and deleted.

PASSWORD

Type: *External*

Purpose: Used to assign passwords to files and directories. Access to those files and/or directories is then restricted to users who know the password.

Syntax: PASSWORD filespec /R /W /D /P /G :password /N /NP /NG /S

Parameters: *filespec* is the file specifier that the specified password should be assigned to. It may include wild cards, or it may be a file list.

password is the password assigned to filespec.

Switches: */R:password* sets a Read password for filespec.

/W:password sets a Write password for filespec.

/D:password sets a Delete password for filespec.

/P:password sets a password for the specified directory. Directory passwords are always Read passwords.

/G:password sets a global default password. This password will be automatically checked against any password-protected file or directory. Thus, files and directories that have this password can be accessed without entering a password. For example, if /G:SECRET were entered, then any file or directory that had a password of SECRET could be accessed without having to first enter the password.

/N removes password protection from files. You will be prompted for the password before it is removed.

/NP removes password protection from directories. You will be prompted for the password before it is removed.

/NG removes the global default password. You will not be prompted for the password.

/S sets the same password to all files in the current directory, as well as to all files in any subdirectories of the current directory. For example, assume that the \WP directory has a subdirectory named LETTERS, and that LETTERS has a subdirectory named PERSONAL. Assuming that WP is the current directory, the following command assigns the Read password SECRET to all files that have a LET extension in the \WP, \WP\LETTERS, and \WP\LETTERS\PERSONAL directories:

PASSWORD /R:SECRET /S

Comments: Passwords should only be set when they are really needed. They slow down access to files because they must be entered before the file can be accessed, and they create the danger that they will be forgotten. If you forget your password you will not be able to access or delete the protected file.

PASSWORD is discussed in detail in Chapter 6.

PATH

Type: *Internal*

Purpose: Defines a set of directories that DOS will search for executable files if they are not found in the current directory. Executable files are those that have extensions of COM, EXE, and BAT. Also used to display the current path setting.

Syntax: PATH path1; path2; ... PATH ;

Parameters: *path1*, *path2*, etc. are the directories to be searched. They should include the complete path starting from the root directory.

; removes all subdirectories from the path. DOS will only search the current directory for executable files.

Comments: PATH entered with no parameters will display the current path without changing it.

Each time a new path is specified the previous path is removed, so to define multiple subdirectories as part of the path you must include all of them in one PATH command.

If there is an error in a subdirectory specification, DOS will not detect the error until it attempts to access the directory.

If a subdirectory specified in the PATH command does not exist, DOS will ignore that directory and go on to the next.

PAUSE

Type: *Internal*

Purpose: The PAUSE command is used in batch files to suspend execution of the batch file until a key is pressed.

Syntax: PAUSE message

Parameters: *message* is an optional message that will display when the program pauses. This will only display if ECHO is on, and the PAUSE command itself is also displayed.

Comments: PAUSE is useful in batch files, especially when the ECHO command is used to display a message instructing the user to perform some action. PAUSE allows the user to read the message before the program continues executing.

When the PAUSE command executes it suspends the execution of the batch file and displays the message, "Press any key to continue... ."

PRINT

Type: *External*

Purpose: Used to establish and manipulate a print queue for printing one or more files while you continue to use the computer for other purposes.

Syntax: PRINT filespec /D:device /Q:num /B:size /S:timeslice /U:busy M:max /C /T /P

Parameters: *filespec* specifies the file(s) to print.

Switches: The switches are described in detail in Chapter 10.

Comments: The PRINT command is discussed in detail in Chapter 10.

PROMPT

Type: *Internal*

Purpose: Defines the format of the DOS prompt.

Syntax: PROMPT text PROMPT

Parameters: *text* can be constructed of regular text and parameters. The text and parameters may be intermixed as much as desired, though the entire command cannot exceed the DOS limit of 128 characters. The parameters that may be interspersed with text are:

$$ includes a dollar sign in the prompt.

$t includes the current time in the prompt.

$d includes the current date in the prompt.

$p includes the current directory of the current drive in the prompt.

$v includes the DOS version number in the prompt.

$n includes the default drive letter in the prompt.

$g includes a greater than sign (>) in the prompt.

$l Includes the less than sign (<) in the prompt.

$b includes the bar (|) symbol in the prompt.

$q includes the equal sign (=) in the prompt.

$h inserts a backspace into the prompt, deleting the character immediately preceding the backspace.

$e includes the Escape character in the prompt. This can be used to send commands to the ANSI.SYS device driver.

$_ includes a Carriage Return/Line Feed sequence in the prompt, allowing you to develop multi-line prompts.

$x tells DOS to run the command identified by the PEXEC environment variable every time you return to the command prompt. For example, the following

two commands would cause DOS to execute the DIR command every time you returned to the command prompt:

```
SET PEXEC=DIR PROMPT $P$G$X
```

Comments: When PROMPT is entered with no parameters, the DOS prompt is reset to its default, which shows the current drive followed by a greater-than sign.

The PROMPT command is discussed in detail in Chapters 4 and 10.

RECOVER

Type: *External*

Purpose: Helps in recovering files that occupy a bad disk sector. Also useful in recovering all the files on a disk that has a damaged directory.

Syntax: RECOVER filespec

RECOVER drive

Parameters: *filespec* is a file identifier that indicates which file to attempt to recover. It may include a drive and path specification. If no drive or path is specified, the default drive and path are assumed.

drive is a drive that contains a disk with a damaged directory.

Comments: If a file contains a bad disk sector, using RECOVER on the file will recover all of the data in the file except that which occurs in the bad sector. For this reason non-text files (program files) are not good candidates for using RECOVER, since you have no reasonable way to restore the missing part of the file.

The same is true of spreadsheet files and database files, since the missing data will probably make at least the last part of the file unreadable by the database or spreadsheet program. However, you may be able to see what the data is and re-enter it.

When a file is recovered, DOS often includes some extra information at the end of the file. This is because DOS recovers complete allocation units, even if the end of the file does not occupy a complete allocation unit.

You are not allowed to recover more files than will fit in the root directory of the disk in one operation. On double-sided floppy disks, this is 112 files. If the total number of files being recovered exceeds this, you must enter multiple RECOVER commands. After the first RECOVER operation, copy the files you want to keep to a new disk and delete them from the damaged disk. Then issue the next RECOVER command, and so on, until all damaged files have been recovered.

The form RECOVER drive should only be used if the disk directory has become unusable. DOS will then ignore all information in the directory and attempt to recover everything on the disk. This is done by determining what allocation units belong together to make a file, and copying those allocation units into files named FILExxxxx.REC, where xxxxx is a sequential number starting with 00001. Each REC file represents one recovered file.

RECOVER is not a miracle program, and it will not necessarily produce useful files. It should be used only in extreme situations, where there is no other chance of recovering files.

REM

Type: *Batch files* and *CONFIG.SYS*

Purpose: Used to include lines in batch files and the CONFIG.SYS file that DOS does not attempt to execute, but that contain information helpful to someone reading the file.

Syntax: REM comment

REM

Parameters: *comment* is any text message up to 123 characters long that explains some aspect of the commands in the file.

Comments: Using REM by itself helps to space out the lines in a batch file or CONFIG.SYS file, making it easier to read.

If ECHO is on the entire REM line, including the letters REM, will be displayed when DOS encounters the line in a batch file. If ECHO is off, the REM lines will not display on the screen.

RENAME or **REN**

Type: *Internal*

Purpose: Changes the name(s) of one or more files.

Syntax: RENAME oldname newname

REN oldname newname

Parameters: *oldname* is the name of the file being renamed.

newname is the new name of the file being renamed.

Comments: If a file named newname already exists, DOS will display a message and terminate the command without changing the file name.

There are two ways in which wild card symbols may be used. The first is to change only the name or only the extension of a file. For example, the command REN TEST.BAT *.TMP will rename the file TEST.BAT to TEST.TMP .

The second way in which wild cards may be used is to rename a set of files by replacing only certain letters of their name. For example, the files TEST1.BAT, TEST2.BAT, and TEMPEST.BAT could be renamed with the command REN T*.BAT XY*.BAT The result of this command is that the three files are given the new names XYST1.BAT, XYST2.BAT, and XYMPEST.BAT . In other words, the number of letters replaced is defined by the number of letters in the new file name.

RENDIR

Type: *External*

Purpose: Renames directories.

Syntax: RENDIR oldname newname

Parameters: *oldname* is the name of the directory to be renamed.

newname is the name the directory should be renamed to.

REPLACE

Type: *External*

Purpose: Used to copy files from one disk to another, choosing files based on one or more of several selection criteria as discussed below.

Syntax: REPLACE source target /P /R /W /S /U /A /H /M /N

Parameters: *source* is the file specifier of the files to be copied. It may include wild cards, or it may be a filelist. A drive and path specifier may also be included.

target is the target drive to copy to. Target file names are not allowed, since the files will be given the same name as they have on the source.

/P causes DOS to prompt you before copying any files that match the specified criteria. This allows you to perform a file-by-file replacement of old files or addition of new files.

/R causes DOS to replace files on the target that have the Read-only attribute set ON. If /R is not specified read-only files will not be replaced.

/W causes DOS to wait for you to insert a floppy disk into the source drive before it starts to search for the files.

/S causes DOS to search subdirectories of the target disk, as well as the current directory, to locate files that match the source file name.

/U causes DOS to replace files on the target if the date and time on the source are more current.

/A causes DOS to copy all specified files on the source that do not exist on the target. This is used to add files to the target without overwriting existing files. /A may not be used if /S or /U is used.

/H includes hidden and system files in the replacement.

/M is used to copy files that have changed since their last backup, providing the copies on the target have not changed since the last backup. For example, suppose that the C:\WP\LETTERS directory contained the files MARY.LET, ROGER.LET, and BILL.LET, and that BILL.LET already exists on the disk in drive A:. If the Archive attribute is turned on for MARY.LET and off for ROGER.LET, indicating that MARY.LET has changed since the last backup but ROGER.LET has not, then the following command will copy MARY.LET to drive A:

REPLACE C:\WP\LETTERS*.LET A: /M

This command copies MARY.LET to the A: drive because it does not already exist there, and its Archive attribute is turned on. ROGER.LET is not copied because its Archive attribute is turned off, indicating it has not changed since the last backup. BILL.LET will be copied, regardless if the following two conditions are met: its Archive attribute is turned on, and the Archive attribute for the BILL.LET file on the A: drive is turned off. The requirement that both of these conditions be met assures that files that have been changed will be copied, but only if they do not overwrite files that may have been changed themselves on the target.

/N produces a display of what the REPLACE command would do, but does not actually replace any files.

Comments: If /W is not specified the REPLACE operation will begin as soon as you press Enter.

RESTORE

Type: *External*

Purpose: Restores files that have been backed up with the BACKUP command.

Syntax: RESTORE source target filename /P /M /S /B:mm-dd-yy /A:mm-dd-yy /E:hh:mm.s / L:hh:mm:.s /N /M/R

Parameters: *source* is the drive that contains the disk that was backed up with the BACKUP command.

target is the drive to which the backed up file(s) should be restored.

filename is used to restore only certain files. A drive and path specifier, as well as wild cards, may be included. If no file name is used, the default *.* is used.

Switches: */P* causes the computer to prompt you before restoring a file that has been modified since the last backup, or has the Read-only attribute set to on. This protects against replacing a recent version of a file with an older version.

/M is used to restore files that have been modified or deleted since they were last backed up. This allows you to recover an earlier version of a file if the current version has been modified in a way that you don't like.

/S restores files in the subdirectories as well as in the current directory.

/B:mm-dd-yy restores all files modified on or before the date specified by mm-dd-yy.

/A:mm-dd-yy restores all files modified on or after the date specified by mm-dd-yy.

/E:hh:mm.s restores all files modified at or after the time specified by hh:mm.s. If /E is used with /B, then files are restored only if they were modified at or before the specified time on or before the specified date.

/L:hh:mm.s restores all files modified at or later than the time specified by hh:mm.s If /L is used with /A, then only files modified at or later than the time specified, on or after the date specified, are restored.

/N is used to restore only files that do not exist on the target. This could be because you are restoring to a disk other than the one that was backed up or because the file has been deleted from the disk.

/R displays a list of the files that would be restored, but does not actually restore them.

Comments: RESTORE only works with files created with the BACKUP command. The system files cannot be restored so RESTORE cannot be used to create a system disk. If you want to create a boot disk, you should use the SYS command to transfer the system files, or format the disk with the /S parameter, before using RESTORE. RESTORE will then transfer the rest of the files and you will have a boot disk that contains the files you want.

The file name may contain drive and path specifiers. If a path is specified a file name must also be specified.

You must RESTORE files to the same directory that they were backed up from. Attempting to restore to a different directory will result in an error message.

When you start RESTORE, you will be prompted to put the disk containing the file(s) to be restored in the source drive. If you are restoring all of the files that were backed up, this should be disk 1. RESTORE will prompt you when to insert subsequent disks. If you are restoring only one file, or a set of files, and know which disk they start with, you may immediately put that disk in the source drive. If you are not sure which disk they start with, put disk 1 in the drive. RESTORE will let you know if the file(s) requested are not there and you can then put in disk 2, and so on.

The RESTORE command sets an Exit code that can be accessed by the Batch command, IF ERRORLEVEL ... The Exit code is set according to the following table:

Exit code	*Meaning*
0	The RESTORE completed normally.
1	There were no files found to restore.
2	Some of the specified files were not restored due to file-sharing conflicts on a network.
3	The RESTORE operation was terminated by the user pressing Ctrl-Break.
4	The RESTORE operation terminated due to an error.

RETURN

Type: *Batch* and *CONFIG.SYS*

Purpose: Causes control to return from a subroutine in a batch or CONFIG.SYS file, to the command following the GOSUB or SWITCH command that called the subroutine.

Syntax: RETURN

Parameters: None.

RMDIR or **RD**

Type: *Internal*

Purpose: Removes directories from a disk. Only empty directories that contain no files can be removed.

Syntax: RMDIR drive:path

RD drive:path

Parameters: *drive* is the drive that contains the directory to be removed.

path is the path from the current directory or from the root directory to the directory being removed.

Comments: The root directory cannot be removed. A directory cannot be removed if it is the current directory.

SCRIPT

Type: *External*

Purpose: Provides PostScript support for DOS and applications.

Syntax: SCRIPT filespec filespec /O=P or L /H=nn /T=nn /R

Comments: The SCRIPT command is discussed in detail in Chapter 4.

SET

Type: *Internal*

Purpose: Creates variables that contain text strings. These variables are stored in the DOS environment and are therefore available to all programs, including batch files.

Syntax: SET variable=value

SET variable=SET

Parameters: *variable* is the variable being created.

value is the string that is assigned to the variable.

Comments: Variables defined with the SET command can be accessed by batch files in the same manner as %x parameters. For example, the command SET PW=XYZ will cause the characters XYZ to be substituted for %PW% in a batch file.

There is only a limited amount of memory reserved for the DOS environment. If there is not enough environment memory available for the variables you are defining DOS, will display an error message.

Entering SET variable= with no value will remove the variable from memory. This will free up memory for other variables.

Entering SET with no parameters will display all of the current environment variables.

SHARE

Type: *External*

Purpose: Provides support for file sharing. Must be loaded before TaskMAX can be run.

Syntax: SHARE /L:nnn /X /ML /MH /MU

Parameters: None.

Switches: /X disables SHARE, but does not reclaim the memory it occupies.

/L:nnn allocates the number of files to be locked. May be anywhere from 20 to 1,024. The default is 20.

/ML, /MH, and /MU force SHARE to load into lower, high, or upper memory, if the specified resources are available. If they are not, SHARE loads into conventional memory.

SHELL

Type: *CONFIG.SYS*

Purpose: Can be used to increase the DOS environment size, or to load a command interpreter other than COMMAND.COM.

Syntax: SHELL=filespec parameters /E:nnnn

Parameters: *filespec* is the name and location of the command interpreter to use.

parameters is any parameter and/or switch used by the specified command interpreter.

Switches: */E:nnnn* specifies the size in bytes of the environment. The range is 512 to 32,751. The default is 512.

Comments: The most common use of the SHELL command is to increase the size of the DOS environment. The following command accomplishes this, setting the environment to 1024 bytes (the default is 512):

SHELL=C:\DOS\COMMAND.COM /E:512 /P

SHIFT

Type: *Batch*

Purpose: Used in batch files to access more than 10 parameters.

Syntax: SHIFT

Parameters: None.

Comments: Each time a SHIFT command is encountered the number of each parameter in a batch file is decreased by 1, the first parameter (%0) is dropped, and an additional parameter can then be used.

The following batch file demonstrates the use of the SHIFT command:

```
DIR%0
PAUSE
DIR%1
PAUSE
DIR%2
PAUSE
DIR%3
PAUSE
DIR%4
PAUSE
DIR%5
PAUSE
DIR%6
PAUSE
DIR%7
PAUSE
DIR%8
PAUSE
DIR%9
PAUSE
SHIFT
DIR%0
PAUSE
DIR%9
```

The first DIR command, DIR %, displays the directory listing for the batch file itself. The next nine DIR commands display the directory listings for files specified in the first nine parameters passed on the command line. The SHIFT command then shifts all parameter references over one, so that the DIR %0 command on the third line from the end displays the directory listing for the first parameter, and the DIR %9 command on the last line displays the first directory listing for the tenth parameter.

The following command demonstrates the use of the batch file, where TEST is the name of the batch file being executed and parm1, parm2, etc. are the parameters being passed to the file:

```
TEST parm1 parm2 parm3 parm4 parm5
parm6 parm7 parm8 parm9 parm10
```

Within the file TEST, %0 refers to the batch file name (TEST), %1 refers to parm1, and so on. The largest parameter reference is %9 which refers to parm9. To reference parm10 the SHIFT command is used once. It will cause %0 to reference parm1, %1 to reference parm2, and so on. The new %9 will therefore reference parm10.

SHIFT can be used as many times as you like within a batch file. The only drawback to it is that each time it is used the lowest parameter is lost.

SORT

Type: *External*

Purpose: Used to sort lines in files and the output of DOS commands.

Syntax: SORT /R /+col <filename

command | SORT /R /+col

Parameters: */R* is an optional parameter that causes sorting to occur in reverse order.

/+col is an optional parameter that causes sorting to be done based on the characters starting in the column col.

<filename is the name of the file whose contents will be sorted. The name must be preceded by a less-than sign. The file name may include drive and path specifiers. The output will appear on the screen.

command is a DOS command whose output will be sorted. For example, the command DIR | SORT will create a directory listing that is sorted alphabetically.

Comments: Only ASCII text files should be sorted.

Forthe first half of the ASCII table (characters 0 through 127), all sorting is done in the order in which characters appear in the ASCII table, except that the sorting is not case sensitive—the letter *a* is equivalent to the letter *A*.

For characters greater than 127 in the ASCII table the sort order is determined by the country code currently in use.

If you want the output to go somewhere other than the screen, you may specify that with a greater-than sign and the destination following the SORT command. For example:

```
SORT /R /+col <filename >outfile
```

will create a sorted copy of filename in outfile. Outfile refers to a device or file name that will receive the output. For example, if outfile is PRN: then the output will appear on the printer. If outfile is NEWFILE.TST then the output will be placed in a file named NEWFILE.TST.

SSTOR

Type: *External*

Purpose: Used to increase the capacity of a hard disk.

Syntax: SSTOR /B

Parameters: None.

Switches: */B* specifies a monochrome monitor.

Comments: SSTOR is a menu-driven program. It should be used with caution, as it alters the structure of all the files on a disk, and renders them unreadable without the SSTOR TSR program loaded.

SSTOR is discussed in detail in Chapter 7.

SUBST

Type: *External*

Purpose: Used to substitute a drive letter for a path. It is useful for programs that do not recognize paths but do recognize drive letters.

Syntax: SUBST newdrive olddrive:path

SUBST drive /D

Parameters: *newdrive* is the drive letter that will be used to refer to the olddrive and path.

olddrive:path is the path being substituted with the newdrive letter. You may use just a path if the drive is the current drive.

	/D is used to delete the substituted drive letter specified by *drive*.
Comments:	Entering SUBST with no parameters will display all current substitutions.
	You may only specify drive letters less than or equal to the drive letter specified in CONFIG.SYS with the LASTDRIVE command. If LASTDRIVE is not included in CONFIG.SYS then the largest drive letter you may use is E. The new drive letter cannot be the current drive.
	The substituted drive letter can be used in place of the drive and path that it is replacing.
	The following commands should not be used when a substitution is in place: ASSIGN, BACKUP, DISKCOMP, DISKCOPY, FDISK, FORMAT, LABEL, and RESTORE.
	You should be very careful and test the effects before using the following commands when a substitution is in place: CHDIR, MKDIR, RMDIR, and PATH.
	If you have a very long subdirectory path that you reference frequently, using SUBST to substitute a drive letter for the path can save a lot of typing.
	If you want to replace an entire drive letter with another drive letter, you should use the ASSIGN command. SUBST is intended for substituting drive letters for subdirectory references.

SUPERPCK

Type:	*External*
Purpose:	Runs the Super PC-Kwik disk cache program.
Syntax:	SUPERPCK switches
Comments:	SUPER PC-KWIK is discussed in detail in Chapter 7.

SWITCH

Type:	Batch files and CONFIG.SYS
Purpose:	Shifts control to the specified subroutine.

Syntax: SWITCH label1, label2, ...

Parameters: *label1*, *label2*, etc. are labels of the subroutines to switch to. Up to nine labels may be specified.

Comments: Control returns to the command following SWITCH when the RETURN command is encountered in the subroutine.

SYS

Type: *External*

Purpose: Used to transfer the hidden system files to a disk.

Syntax: SYS drive

Parameters: *drive* is the drive to which the files will be transferred.

Comments: Transferring the hidden system files to a disk, as well as the COMMAND.COM file, makes the disk a bootable disk.

SYS may move files that already exist on your disk. To be safe you should back up your disk before transferring the system files.

SYS can be used on a disk that has been formatted without the /S or /B parameters, as long as the disk is blank. SYS may be used to transfer files to a disk that has been formatted with the /B parameter at any time, since /B reserves the space for the system files and does not let other files occupy that space.

TASKMAX

Type: *External*

Purpose: Runs the TaskMAX task switcher.

Comments: TaskMAX is the subject of Chapter Three.

TIME

Type: *Internal*

Purpose: Sets the time that is stored in the internal clock.

Syntax: TIME hh:mm:ss.hs

TIME

TIME /C

Parameters: *hh* stands for the hour (1-12 or 1-24).

mm stands for the minute (1-59).

ss stands for the second (1-59).

hs stands for the hundredth second (1-99).

Switches: */C* causes the time to display continuously, until you press a key.

Comments: You may specify only as much of the time as you feel is important. Entering TIME 9 will set the time to 9:00.

If you type an incorrect time, DOS will display the message:

```
Invalid time Enter new time
```

If you press Enter at this point, the time will be left unchanged.

Entering TIME with no parameters causes DOS to display the current time.

TIMEOUT

Type: *CONFIG.SYS*

Purpose: Sets a time limit to wait for the user to respond to a ? or SWITCH command in the CONFIG.SYS file.

Syntax: TIMEOUT = n

Parameters: *n* is the number of seconds to wait.

Comments: If you specify 0, or do not specify anything, then DOS will not set a time limit, but will wait until a key is pressed.

TOUCH

Type: *External*

Purpose: Resets the date and time stamps of files.

Syntax: TOUCH filespec /T:hh:mm:ss /D:date /F:E or J or U /P /R /S

Parameters: *filespec* the file specifier of the files to be touched. Wild cards may be included, or it may be a filelist.

Switches: */T:hh:mm:ss* is the time to set for the file stamp(s).

/D:date is the date to set for the file stamp(s).

/F:E or *J* or *U* specifies European, Japanese, or USA date format. This overrides the default format that is set by the Country code.

/P causes DOS to prompt you before touching each file.

/R causes DOS to touch read-only files, which otherwise are not touched.

/S causes DOS to include files in subdirectories.

Comments: TOUCH is discussed in detail in Chapter 6.

TREE

Type: *External*

Purpose: Used to display a directory, its subdirectories, and the files contained in them.

Syntax: TREE drive:path /F /B /G /P

Parameters: *drive* is the drive on which the directory exists.

path is the path to the subdirectory to be displayed.

/B is brief mode, which does not display the number of files in each directory.

/F causes the files as well as subdirectories to be displayed.

/G displays the tree in a graphical format, drawing lines to show the tree structure.

/P causes DOS to pause after each screenful, until a key is pressed.

Comments: To show the complete directory of the entire disk, specify the root directory.

TYPE

Type: *Internal*

Purpose: Prints the contents of a file on the screen.

Syntax: TYPE filename ;password /P

Parameters: *filename* is the name of the file to be typed on the screen. It may contain a drive and path specifier but may not contain wild card symbols.

;password is the password that is assigned to the file by the PASSWORD command.

Switches: */P* causes DOS to pause after each screenful, until a key is pressed.

Comments: TYPE is most useful for reviewing the contents of text files.

UNDELETE

Type: *External*

Purpose: Recovers files that have been deleted accidentally.

Comments: UNDELETE is a menu-driven program, and is discussed in detail in Chapter 6.

UNFORMAT

Type: *External*

Purpose: If a disk that has files on it is accidentally formatted, UNFORMAT may be able to undo the formatting, thereby restoring the original files.

Syntax: UNFORMAT drive

Parameters: *drive* is the drive that contains the disk to be unformatted.

Comments: This command is used to recover from an accidental reformatting. It is most successful if the format was a SAFE format, which means the /U switch was not used with the FORMAT command.

This command is discussed in detail in Chapter 7.

VER

Type: *Internal*

Purpose: Displays the version of DOS that is being used.

Syntax: VER

Parameters: None.

Comments: The version is displayed as single digit before a period and two digits after, indicating major and minor versions.

VERIFY

Type: *Internal*

Purpose: Causes DOS to verify all disk-write operations.

Syntax: VERIFY ON

VERIFY OFF

VERIFY

Parameters: *ON* causes DOS to perform a verification after every disk-write operation.

OFF causes DOS to not verify disk-write operations. The default value is OFF.

Comments: Entering VERIFY with no parameters displays the current status of VERIFY.

Disk-write errors are rare so it is not normally necessary to have VERIFY set to on. VERIFY will significantly slow down your computer's performance, since the verification is a slow process. If you have critical data being written it may be worth the extra time.

VOL

Type: *Internal*

Purpose: Displays the volume label of the specified disk.

Syntax: VOL drive

Parameters: *drive* is the drive that contains the disk whose label will be displayed.

Comments: If no drive is entered, the volume label of the current drive is shown.

XCOPY

Type: *External*

Purpose: Used to copy groups of files, including those in subdirectories.

Syntax: XCOPY source target /A /D:date /E /H /L /M /P /C /R /S /V /W

Parameters: *source* is the set of file(s) to copy. It may contain a drive and path specifier and wild cards, or it may be a filelist.

target is the path to copy to. It may contain a drive and path specifier and wild cards.

Switches:

/A is used to copy only those files that have the Archive attribute set to on. These are files that have been created or modified since the last BACKUP command or XCOPY /M command. This is useful if XCOPY is used for backing up files. When /A is specified XCOPY does not change the Archive attribute of the file.

/D:date copies files whose creation or last modification date is on or after the date specified. The date format will depend on the country code, that is shown for the U.S.

/E tells XCOPY to create subdirectories on the target, even if they are empty.

/H tells XCOPY to copy hidden and system files, which are otherwise not copied.

/L copies the disk label to the target disk, along with the specified files.

/M is used to copy only those files that have the archive attribute set to on. These are files that have been created or modified since the last BACKUP command or XCOPY /M command. This is useful if XCOPY is used for backing up files. When /M is specified XCOPY sets the Archive attribute to off after the copy is completed.

/P or */C* causes XCOPY to prompt you with a (Y/N)? before copying each file.

/R causes XCOPY to copy read-only files, which are otherwise ignored.

/S specifies that subdirectories should be copied in addition to the specified or current directory. If /S is not included, only the files in the specified or current directory are copied. If /S is included, any subdirectories that do no exist on the target will be created, as long as they are not empty subdirectories on the source.

/V turns on write verification for the XCOPY operation. This will slow down the copy process considerably due to the extra work involved in verifying that each file is written properly to the disk. This is not usually necessary, since write errors are rare. However, if your data is highly critical you may want to use it as a safeguard.

/W causes XCOPY to wait while you insert disks into the source drive.

Comments: If no drive is specified, XCOPY starts with the current directory. If no file name is specified, XCOPY assumes *.*. XCOPY does not copy hidden files.

You can rename files with the XCOPY command in the same ways you can rename them with the COPY command.

XCOPY cannot copy a file larger than the target disk. If you need to do this, you should use the BACKUP command. However, files created with XCOPY are standard DOS files so they can be used without a RESTORE operation.

XCOPY is discussed in detail in Chapter 6.

XDEL

Type: *External*

Purpose: Deletes multiple files in subdirectories, and removes subdirectories.

Syntax: XDEL filespec /D /N /O /P /R /S

Parameters: *filespec* is the specifier of the files to delete. It may contain wild cards, or it may be a file list.

Switches: */D* removes empty subdirectories.

/N does not pause to prompt before deleting files.

/O overwrites files before deleting them.

/P prompts you before deleting each file.

/R causes XDEL to include read-only files in the deletion process.

/S deletes files in subdirectories.

Comments: */O* causes the contents of the file to be replace before the file is deleted. This makes file recovery impossible, but also makes it impossible for anyone to see what the file contained.

XDIR

Type: *External*

Purpose: Provides expanded DIR functionality.

Syntax: XDIR filespec +/- ADHRS /B /C /L /N /P /R /S /T /W /X /Y /Z

Parameters: *filespec* the specifier for the filename(s) to be displayed; may include wild cards.

Switches: + or - *A,D,H,R,S* includes (+) or excludes (-) files that have the specified attribute set.

/B shows brief display, with only path and filenames.

/C computes a checksum for each file.

/L is long format, - the default.

/N does not sort the directory alphabetically; sorting is the default.

/P causes DOS to pause after each screenful.

/R reverses the sort order.

/S displays files in subdirectories.

/T sorts the files by date and time.

/W is wide format—five columns across, names only.

/X sorts by filename extension.

/Y sorts by SuperStor file compression ration. Only works if the drive is a SuperStor (SSTOR) compressed drive.

/Z sorts by file size.

Comments: XDIR is discussed in Chapters 4 and 6.

Appendix

IBM Extended ASCII Character Set

Decimal	Hex	Binary	Meaning	Control Key	Character
0	0	00000000	NUL (null)	^@	
1	1	00000001	SOH (start-of-header)	^A	☺
2	2	00000010	STX (start-of-transmission)	^B	☻
3	3	00000011	ETX (end-of-transmission)	^C	♥
4	4	00000100	EOT (end-of-text)	^D	♦
5	5	00000101	ENQ (enquiry)	^E	♣
6	6	00000110	ACK (acknowledge)	^F	♠
7	7	00000111	BEL (bell)	^G	•
8	8	00001000	BS	^H	◘
9	9	00001001	HT (horizontal tab)	^I	○
10	A	00001010	LF (line feed)	^J	◙
11	B	00001011	VT (vertical tab)	^K	♂
12	C	00001100	FF (form feed)	^L	♀
13	D	00001101	CR (carriage return)	^M	♪
14	E	00001110	SO (shift out)	^N	♫
15	F	00001111	SI (shift in)	^O	☼
16	10	00010000	DLB (data link escape)	^P	►
17	11	00010001	DC1 (X-ON)	^Q	◄
18	12	00010010	DC2 (tape)	^R	↕
19	13	00010011	DC3 (S-OFF)	^S	‼
20	14	00010100	DC4 (no tape)	^T	¶
21	15	00010101	NAK (negative acknowledge)	^U	§
22	16	00010110	SYN (synchronize)	^V	▬
23	17	00010111	EBT (end-of-transmission block)	^W	↨
24	18	00011000	CAN (cancel)	^X	↑
25	19	00011001	EM (end of medium)	^Y	↓
26	1A	00011010	SUB (substitute)	^Z	→
27	1B	00011100	ESC (escape)	^[	←
28	1C	00011101	FS (file separator)	^\	∟
29	1D	00011101	GS (group separator)	^]	↔
30	1E	00011110	RS (record separator)	^^	▲
31	1F	00011111	US (unit separator)	^_	▼

Decimal	Hexadecimal	Binary	Character
32	20	00100000	
33	21	00100001	!
34	22	00100010	"
35	23	00100011	#
36	24	00100100	$
37	25	00100101	%
38	26	00100110	&
39	27	00100111	'
40	28	00101000	(
41	29	00101001	)
42	2A	00101010	*
43	2B	00101011	+
44	2C	00101100	,
45	2D	00101101	-
46	2E	00101110	.
47	2F	00101111	/
48	30	00110000	0
49	31	00110001	1
50	32	00110010	2
51	33	00110011	3
52	34	00110100	4
53	35	00110101	5
54	36	00110110	6
55	37	00110111	7
56	38	00111000	8
57	39	00111001	9
58	3A	00111010	:
59	3B	00111011	;
60	3C	00111100	<
61	3D	00111101	=
62	3E	00111110	>
63	3F	00111111	?
64	40	01000000	@
65	41	01000001	A
66	42	01000010	B
67	43	01000011	C
68	44	01000100	D
69	45	01000101	E

continued...

...from previous page

Decimal	Hexadecimal	Binary	Character
70	46	01000110	F
71	47	01000111	G
72	48	01001000	H
73	49	01001001	I
74	4A	01001010	J
75	4B	01001011	K
76	4C	01001100	L
77	4D	01001101	M
78	4E	01001110	N
79	4F	01001111	O
80	50	01010000	P
81	51	01010001	Q
82	52	01010010	R
83	53	01010011	S
84	54	01010100	T
85	55	01010101	U
86	56	01010110	V
87	57	01010111	W
88	58	01011000	X
89	59	01011001	Y
90	5A	01011010	Z
91	5B	01011011	[
92	5C	01011100	\
93	5D	01011101	]
94	5E	01011110	^
95	5F	01011111	_
96	60	01100000	`
97	61	01100001	a
98	62	01100010	b
99	63	01100011	c
100	64	01100100	d
101	65	01100101	e
102	66	01100110	f
103	67	01100111	g
104	68	01101000	h
105	69	01101001	i

continued...

...from previous page

Decimal	Hexadecimal	Binary	Character
106	6A	01101010	j
107	6B	01101011	k
108	6C	01101100	l
109	6D	01101101	m
110	6E	01101110	n
111	6F	01101111	o
112	70	01110000	p
113	71	01110001	q
114	72	01110010	r
115	73	01110011	s
116	74	01110100	t
117	75	01110101	u
118	76	01110110	v
119	77	01110111	w
120	78	01111000	x
121	79	01111001	y
122	7A	01111010	z
123	7B	01111011	{
124	7C	01111100	|
125	7D	01111101	}
126	7E	01111110	~
127	7F	01111111	
128	80	10000000	Ç
129	81	10000001	ü
130	82	10000010	é
131	83	10000011	â
132	84	10000100	ä
133	85	10000101	à
134	86	10000110	å
135	87	10000111	ç
136	88	10001000	ê
137	89	10001001	ë
138	8A	10001010	è
139	8B	10001011	ï
140	8C	10001100	î
141	8D	10001101	ì

continued...

. . . from previous page

Decimal	Hexadecimal	Binary	Character
142	8E	10001110	Ä
143	8F	10001111	Å
144	90	10010000	É
145	91	10010001	æ
146	92	10010010	Æ
147	93	10010011	ô
148	94	10010100	ö
149	95	10010101	ò
150	96	10010110	û
151	97	10010111	ù
152	98	10011000	ÿ
153	99	10011001	Ö
154	9A	10011010	Ü
155	9B	10011011	¢
156	9C	10011100	£
157	9D	10011101	¥
158	9E	10011110	₧
159	9F	10011111	ƒ
160	A0	10100000	á
161	A1	10100001	í
162	A2	10100010	ó
163	A3	10100011	ú
164	A4	10100100	ñ
165	A5	10100101	Ñ
166	A6	10100110	ª
167	A7	10100111	º
168	A8	10101000	¿
169	A9	10101001	⌐
170	AA	10101010	¬
171	AB	10101011	½
172	AC	10101100	¼
173	AD	10101101	¡
174	AE	10101110	«
175	AF	10101111	»
176	B0	10110000	░
177	B1	10110001	▒

continued. . .

...from previous page

Decimal	Hexadecimal	Binary	Character
178	B2	10110010	▓
179	B3	10110011	│
180	B4	10110100	┤
181	B5	10110101	╡
182	B6	10110110	╢
183	B7	10110111	╖
184	B8	10111000	╕
185	B9	10111001	╣
186	BA	10111010	║
187	BB	10111011	╗
188	BC	10111100	╝
189	BD	10111101	╜
190	BE	10111110	╛
191	BF	10111111	┐
192	C0	11000000	└
193	C1	11000001	┴
194	C2	11000010	┬
195	C3	11000011	├
196	C4	11000100	─
197	C5	11000101	┼
198	C6	11000110	╞
199	C7	11000111	╟
200	C8	11001000	╚
201	C9	11001001	╔
202	CA	11001010	╩
203	CB	11001011	╦
204	CC	11001100	╠
205	CD	11001101	═
206	CE	11001110	╬
207	CF	11001111	╧
208	D0	11010000	╨
209	D1	11010001	╤
210	D2	11010010	╥
211	D3	11010011	╙
212	D4	11010100	╘
213	D5	11010101	╒

continued...

...from previous page

Decimal	Hexadecimal	Binary	Character
214	D6	11010110	╓
215	D7	11010111	╫
216	D8	11011000	╪
217	D9	11011001	┘
218	DA	11011010	┌
219	DB	11011011	█
220	DC	11011100	▄
221	DD	11011101	▌
222	DE	11011110	▐
223	DF	11011111	▀
224	E0	11100000	α
225	E1	11100001	ß
226	E2	11100010	Γ
227	E3	11100011	π
228	E4	11100100	Σ
229	E5	11100101	σ
230	E6	11100110	µ
231	E7	11100111	τ
232	E8	11101000	Φ
233	E9	11101001	Θ
234	EA	11101010	Ω
235	EB	11101011	δ
236	EC	11101100	∞
237	ED	11101101	φ
238	EE	11101110	ϵ
239	EF	11101111	∩
240	F0	11110000	≡
241	F1	11110001	±
242	F2	11110010	≥
243	F3	11110011	≤
244	F4	11110100	⌠
245	F5	11110101	⌡
246	F6	11110110	÷
247	F7	11110111	≈
248	F8	11111000	°
249	F9	11111001	∙

continued...

...from previous page

Decimal	Hexadecimal	Binary	Character
250	**FA**	**11111010**	·
251	**FB**	**11111011**	√
252	**FC**	**11111100**	^{n}
253	**FD**	**11111101**	^{2}
254	**FE**	**11111110**	■
255	**FF**	**11111111**	

Index

Symbols

Numerical

A

B

E

F

G

H

Get the Best Thing that Ever Happened to DOS for a Special Price

DR DOS ™ 6.0 ORDER FORM

YES, I've read all about DR DOS 6.0 and now I want it! Please rush me one copy of the full DR DOS 6.0 product, direct from Digital Research Inc., at the special discount price of $49*, that's a **$50 savings** off the $99 Suggested Retail Price.

I understand that DR DOS 6.0 is the most advanced, fully DOS-compatible operating system available and will help me get more out of my PC's processor, memory, and hard disk. I realize that I can return DR DOS 6.0 within 60 days of receipt for a full refund if I'm not completely satisfied. (Offer valid through June 30, 1992 - Includes Software User's Guide, and Quick Reference Guide)

DR DOS 6.0	$ 49
Shipping and handling	$ 9.95
Plus applicable sales tax in following states MA 5%, TX 7.75%, CA 7.75%, IL 6.25%, VT 5%	$ ___ . ___
Total enclosed:	________

Proof of Purchase Required

I prefer to pay as follows:

☐ Check or money order enclosed

☐ MasterCard ☐ VISA ☐ AmEx

Card No.:______________________ Exp. Date:__________

Card Holder Name ______________________________

Signature ______________________________

(all orders must be signed)

Ship to: ______________________________

Company Name: ______________________________

Street:______________________________

City______________________________ State__________ Zip__________

Daytime Phone:______________________ FAX ______________________

ORDER NOW! Complete this coupon and fax to: (408) 649-8209

Or send to: Digital Research • Box DRI • Monterey, CA 93942 • (408) 647-6675 *(orders are subject to acceptance)* ***plus shipping & handling**